Studies in Church History

14

RENAISSANCE AND RENEWAL
IN CHRISTIAN HISTORY

RENAISSANCE AND RENEWAL IN CHRISTIAN HISTORY

PAPERS READ AT
THE FIFTEENTH SUMMER MEETING AND
THE SIXTEENTH WINTER MEETING
OF THE
ECCLESIASTICAL HISTORY SOCIETY

EDITED BY

DEREK BAKER

PUBLISHED FOR
THE ECCLESIASTICAL HISTORY SOCIETY
BY
BASIL BLACKWELL · OXFORD
1977

ISBN 0 631 17780 9

Printed in Great Britain
by Crampton & Sons Ltd, Sawston, Cambridge

PREFACE

The present volume of *Studies in Church History* is the fourteenth to be produced by the Ecclesiastical History Society and the fifth to be published by the Society itself in collaboration with Basil Blackwell. 'Renaissance and Renewal in Christian History' was the theme of the fifteenth summer meeting of the Society, held at the University of Exeter, and of the sixteenth winter meeting. The twenty-seven papers included in this volume are a selection from those read at these two meetings.

The Society is grateful to the British Academy and to the Carnegie Trust for the Universities of Scotland for generous financial assistance in the production of this volume.

Derek Baker

CONTENTS

vii

CONTENTS

ILLUSTRATIONS (between pp 32-3)

Plate 1: *Fons Vitae*, the Godescalc Evangelistiary,
BN MS n.acq. Lat. 1203, fol 3^v. Photo and copyright
Bibliothèque Nationale, Paris.

Plate 2: Canon tables,
BL MS Harley 2788 fol 11^v. Reproduced by courtesy of the
British Library Board.

Plate 3: St Peter's, Rome: The seventh-century shrine with 'curly'
screen-columns. Reconstructed by J. B. Ward Perkins,
Journal of Roman Studies 42 (1952).

Plate 4: The Godescalc Evangelistiary, opening words of the gospel
for the vigil of Christmas,
BN MS n.acq. Lat. 1203, fol 4^r. Photo and copyright
Bibliothèque Nationale, Paris.

Plate 5: Lorsch Gospels,
Bucharest National Library *Codex Aureus* p 36. From *Karl
der Grosse, Werk und Wirkung: Ausstellung Katalog*.

Plate 6: BL MS Harley 2788, fol 65^v. Reproduced by courtesy of the
British Library Board.

Plate 7: Sepulchral inscription of pope Hadrian I, St Peter's, Rome.
Photo G. Chiolini, Pavia.

Plate 8: Diomedes, *Ars grammatica*,
Brussels Bibl royale MS II 2572, fol 120. Photo and copyright
Bibliothèque Royale, Brussels.

CONTRIBUTORS

J. K. CAMERON *(President)*
 Professor of Ecclesiastical History, University of St Andrews

GERALD BONNER
 Reader in Church History, University of Durham

D. A. BULLOUGH
 Professor of Medieval History, University of St Andrews

PATRICK COLLINSON
 Professor of History, University of Kent at Canterbury

A. R. VIDLER
 Honorary Fellow, King's College, Cambridge

P. G. WALSH
 Professor of Humanity, University of Glasgow

JONATHAN WRIGHT
 Student and Tutor, Christ Church, Oxford

DEREK BAKER
 Lecturer in History, University of Edinburgh

JOHN M. BARKLEY
 Professor of Church History, Presbyterian College, Belfast

BRENDA BOLTON
 Lecturer in History, University of London, Westfield College

EAMON DUFFY
 Lecturer in Ecclesiastical History, University of London, King's
 College

MARILYN DUNN
 University of Edinburgh

ROBERT DUNNING
 Editor, Victoria County History, Somerset

R. A. FLETCHER
 Senior Lecturer in History, University of Sheffield

JOAN G. GREATREX
 Associate Professor of History, Carleton University, Ottawa

CONTRIBUTORS

SHERIDAN GILLEY
Lecturer in Ecclesiastical History, University of St Andrews

BERNARD HAMILTON
Senior Lecturer in History, University of Nottingham

JOHN KENT
Reader in Church History and Doctrine, University of Bristol

F. DONALD LOGAN
Professor of History, Emmanuel College, Boston

STUART P. MEWS
Lecturer in Sociology of Religion, University of Lancaster

R. I. MOORE
Lecturer in History, University of Sheffield

JANET L. NELSON
Lecturer in History, University of London, King's College

DUNCAN NIMMO
Research Fellow in Educational Research, University of Lancaster

W. B. PATTERSON
Professor of History, Davidson College, North Carolina

DOREEN M. ROSMAN
Lecturer in History, University of Kent at Canterbury

GAVIN WHITE
Lecturer in Ecclesiastical History, University of Glasgow

MICHAEL WILKS
Professor of Medieval History, University of London, Birkbeck College

xi

INTRODUCTION

> Learning and Rome alike in Empire grew,
> And Arts still follow'd where her eagles flew;
> From the same foes, at last, both felt their doom,
> And the same age saw learning fall, and Rome.
> With tyranny, then superstition join'd,
> As that the body, this enslav'd the mind;
> Much was believ'd, but little understood,
> And to be dull was constru'd to be good;
> A second deluge learning thus o'er-run,
> And the monks finished what the Goths begun.
> At length, Erasmus, that great injur'd name,
> (The glory of the priesthood, and the shame!)
> Stemm'd the wild torrent of a barb'rous age,
> And drove those holy Vandals off the stage.[1]

Few would now concur with Pope's assessment, but in popular and general terms it remains true that renaissance and reformation are seen as marking the end of Cellarius's 'Middle Age' and the beginning of his *historia nova*: a period when, as has been remarked, it was accepted that 'the subject matter of the new faith can fill the ancient moulds',[2] revival of learning and revival of moral concern both resting on the foundation of the Christian life, and together comprising a comprehensive social reform 'within the household of the faith'. Yet it is not only in this Renaissance age that

> Rome's ancient genius, o'er its ruins spread,
> Shakes off the dust, and rears his rev'rend head!

Whatever limits or limitations the Carolingian renaissance had[3] it spoke emphatically of *renovatio*, and whether it understood it as 'a new beginning', 'the enhancement of the recent past', or 'the recovery of a more ancient past—true or false',[4] it accepted unquestioningly that its inheritance, its models, its inspiration derived from a Rome that was classical as well as Christian. It is in this sense that a 'Christian patri-

---

[1] Pope. *An Essay on Criticism*, lines 683–96, quoted [J. B.] Morrall, [*The Medieval Imprint*] (London 1967) p 8.

[2] Below p 267.

[3] *Ibid* pp 51–69.

[4] *Ibid* p 48.

mony'[5] can be indicated at the centre of twelfth-century humanist intellectual concern, that the age of Bernard was also the *aetas Boethiana*,[6] that Alan of Lille's 'new man', whatever the connection with Philip Augustus, can be seen as 'a twelfth-century *alter Christus*'.[7] Nor was the fifteenth century any different: for pre-reformation Franciscans 'the genesis of reform is confirmed as residing in the fusion of fresh vision with existing written tradition';[8] pre-reformation English Cistercians, like their Anglo-Norman predecessors four centuries earlier, found inspiration in an Anglo-Saxon past,[9] insular in spirit but shaped by Roman influences, and if the protracted turmoils of Reformation placed the status of Christian Rome in question the rival appeals to the authority, the traditions, the history, the precedents of antiquity in general served to consolidate Renaissance attitudes and aspirations into cultural and intellectual objectives which were as much the province and concern of protestant academies and universities as of catholic. In these events, as Pope pointed out, Erasmus plays a large part, but even he was 'not so much an originator as the distiller of elements of received and even perennial wisdom',[10] a cardinal figure in a continuing process. However much Milton might complain that the reformation had not been carried to its conclusion, lamenting 'our four-score years vexation of Him in this our wildernesse since Reformation began',[11] men like Sir Benjamin Rudyard speaking in 1641 were clear that they sought 'reformation not innovation, demolition not abolition'.[12] Earlier in the same year Sir Simonds D'Ewes had remonstrated against a 'brazen, leaden, yea and blockish' clergy and sought their transmutation into 'a golden and primitive condition'.[13] Thirty years later the portrayal of William Cave's 'good old Christians'[14] sprang from a similar confrontation of ideal and reality, and was founded upon patristic research, while in the mid-nineteenth century Scottish liturgists recognised that 'in the Greek and other Liturgies there are many golden sentences', but entered the caveat that 'Antiquity, the Reformation and our present

[5] *Ibid* p 121.
[6] *Ibid* p 124.
[7] *Ibid* pp 132, 137–57.
[8] *Ibid* p 172.
[9] *Ibid* pp 193–211, 213–22.
[10] *Ibid* p 225.
[11] Milton, *Animadversions upon the Remonstrants*, quoted Morrall p 6.
[12] Below p 284.
[13] *Ibid* p 281.
[14] *Ibid* p 288.

practice should be all kept in view'.[15] In the breadth of this view it is neither impertinent nor unreal to see men like G. W. Sprott as lesser figures in a succession of agents of renewal which stretches back to Mr Bonner's Augustine or Canon Mendieta's Basil.[16]

It is in this context that some justification can perhaps be found for pope Pius X's condemnation of catholic modernism as 'the synthesis of all heresies',[17] locating revelation in 'living experience, not in its intellectual and propositioned formulation'.[18] For all that, *Pascendi* has the quality of stylite unreality rather than ex cathedra wisdom: men like Tyrell, Loissy, von Hügel, Bremond—and Bishop and Duchesne if they may be included—however much they were attracted to a philosophy of action or a dynamic theology, had clearly not jettisoned the past. *Pascendi*, however, does direct attention to what Miss Bolton has termed 'the problem of individual rebirth in a renewed society',[19] and which comprises not simply individual matters of choice, interpretation and vocation but also their social impact. For F. D. Maurice, like many others before, Christianity was a corporate religion, and it was not passive resistance alone which 'was not a matter for the lone conscience and the free lance'.[20] Such problems are at their clearest when they focus upon an individual. To nickname Nikon,[21] the apostle of Crete and the Pelopponese, 'the repentance-bringer' is a double-edged compliment: the prophet is unlikely to be generally popular, and as William Cave, the advocate of practical piety discovered, it was not the objects of his strictures who saw him as 'a setter forth of new Gods'.[22] The problems are at their most profound, however, when they transcend the individual and his followers and assume sociological proportions, as in the twelfth century opposing an 'alternative orthodoxy', which located holy power in the community rather than the clerical office, to the dominant view, and responding to new social pressures by resistance to innovation and the appeal to ancient values.[23] In the twelfth century as at other times one

---

[15] *Ibid* p 341.
[16] *Ibid* pp 1–22, *SCH* 13 (1976) pp 25–49.
[17] Below p 378.
[18] *Ibid* p 381.
[19] *Ibid* p 103.
[20] *Ibid* p 368.
[21] *Ibid* pp 82–6.
[22] *Ibid* p 392.
[23] *Ibid* pp 87, 93.

man's renaissance was another man's reaction,[24] and though such movements are rarely coherent, lucid or lastingly effective they should not be ignored. This is seldom the world of culture or intellectual achievement: it is not the world for which Alan of Lille wrote. But it is the world which, in the twelfth century, recognised poverty as the badge of holiness;[25] in the seventeenth declared that 'for piety, we know the way to maintain it is to abolish whoring, swearing and drinking and to increase preaching and praying';[26] in the nineteenth sought 'good taste, decency, propriety and solemnity' in worship and protested against 'mere trimming and embellishment',[27] or in the twentieth 'either crusades for peace or treats war as a crusade'.[28] It is, too, the world of Erasmus—'To me he is truly a theologian who teaches not by skill with intricate syllogisms, but by a disposition of mind, by the very expression and eyes. . . . Life means more than debate, inspiration is preferable to erudition, transformation is a more important matter than intellectual comprehension. Only a very few can be learned, but all can be Christian, all can be devout and—I shall boldly add—all can be theologians'.[29] The unmistakeable echoes of the monk of Farne and other late medieval mystical writers only serve to emphasise the essential continuities in the Christian life across the reformation divide. When Edmund Calamy declared that 'the nature of man is more apt to be guided by *Examples* than by *Precepts*'[30] he excluded neither. Whatever the birth of the Christian tradition its rebirth and renewal are not narrowly unigenitive but richly procreative. And once more the course leads back to Erasmus, that shoal of which Professor Collinson gave warning[31]—'Moreover what else is the philosophy of Christ, which he himself calls a rebirth, than the restoration of human nature, originally well-formed?'.[32]

---

[24] *Ibid* p 361.
[25] *Ibid* pp 95, 99–100.
[26] *Ibid* p 280.
[27] *Ibid* p 348.
[28] *Ibid* p 372.
[29] *Ibid* p 223.
[30] *Ibid* p 224.
[31] *Ibid* pp 224–5.
[32] *Ibid* p 248.

VERA LUX ILLA EST QUAE ILLUMINAT: THE CHRISTIAN HUMANISM OF AUGUSTINE

by GERALD BONNER

IN 427, three years before his death, Augustine of Hippo compiled the *Retractations*, a kind of critical bibliography in which he passed in chronological review his writings as a catholic Christian, clarifying, defending and, where necessary, correcting passages which the course of events or his own theological development had called in question. In a very human way Augustine tended, in practice, to defend his previously-expressed views to a rather greater degree and to criticise them less than had been his original intention;[1] but this means that where he declares a change of opinion, this statement may fairly be regarded as his final and definitive view. Two such statements are relevant to our purposes here: in his review of his earliest Christian work, *Against the Academics*, which appeared in 386, Augustine expresses his displeasure at the praise he there bestowed on the Platonist and Academic philosophers;[2] while in his discussion of the two books *On Order*, which were written at the end of the same year, he regrets that he attributed too much to those liberal studies, of which many of the saints had been ignorant and many of their most enthusiastic disciples lacking in sanctity.[3] Such views would seem, on first reading, to be exactly what we should expect of Augustine in the last years of his life, the result of an increased rigorism brought about by many years of controversy, which had left little of the humanism which had marked his first years as a Christian.

There is, however, another piece of information, provided almost accidentally by Augustine's biographer Possidius, who records that in his last days, when the Vandal armies were over-running Africa,

---

[1] See John Burnaby, 'The *Retractationes* of Saint Augustine: Self-criticism or Apologia?' *Augustinus Magister: Congrès international augustinien* (Paris 1954) 1, pp 85–92.

[2] *Retract[ationum Liber]* I 1 12: Laus quoque ipsa, qua Platonem vel Platonicos seu Academicos philosophos tantum extuli, quantum inpios homines non oportuit, non immerito mihi displicuit. praesertim contra quorum errores magnos defendenda est Christiana doctrina.

[3] *Ibid* I 3 2: Verum et in his libris displicet mihi . . . quod multum tribui liberalibus disciplinis, quas multi sancti multum nesciunt, quidam etiam sciunt et sancti non sunt.

I

and the society which Augustine had known was falling into ruin, the saint consoled himself with the maxim of a certain wise man: 'He will not be great who thinks it a great matter that wood and stones fall and mortals die.'[4] The wise man, whose name Possidius omits—whether from ignorance, considerations of literary style, or a desire to avoid scandal we do not know—was Plotinus,[5] and thus we find Augustine, in the last months of his life, finding comfort in the words of the great pagan philosopher, whose writings had so powerfully affected his spiritual development more than forty years before.

Too much should not, of course, be made of Augustine's Plotinian citation. The thought expressed is no more than a literary commonplace and in no way characteristically Neo-Platonic; but even if this be granted, it remains significant that at the end, Augustine was prepared to cite a pagan author, when he might have turned so easily and, it might be thought, so predictably, to the scriptures. In the event, Augustine by his own words revealed how profoundly his mind had been formed by the cultural tradition which, as a Christian, he was disposed to reject on first principles. Augustine's dilemma in this matter has long been recognised by scholars. The aim of this paper is to try to discuss, inevitably in a rather superficial fashion, the degree and manner in which Augustine assimilated the classical tradition with his Christianity and transmitted the result to his fellow-Christians and to future generations, thereby bringing about in some measure reform and renewal in the church.

A warning must, however, be given at the outset against over-estimating the extent and immediacy of Augustine's influence. Because Augustinian theology has, at certain periods, played a decisive rôle in determining the development of Latin theology, it is all too easy to assume that it was already dominant in the whole Christian church within the saint's own lifetime. This is certainly an error; for in the first place, Augustine's influence throughout the middle ages was confined to the Latin west. His place in the Greek east has been examined by Bertholt Altaner in a magisterial article and need not be

---

[4] Possidius, *Vita Augustini*, ed M. Pellegrino (Cuneo 1955) 28 11: 'Et se inter haec mala cuiusdam sapientis sententia consolabatur dicentis: 'Non erit magnus magnum putans quod cadunt ligna et lapides, et moriuntur mortales' (ed M. Pellegrino, p 154 lines 77–80).

[5] Plotinus, *Enneads* I 4 7. See note by Pellegrino in his ed, p 226 and Pierre Courcelle, 'Sur les dernières paroles de Saint Augustin', *Revue des études anciennes* 46 (Bordeaux 1944) pp 205–7.

recapitulated here.[6] It is enough to say that although according to Possidius[7] Greek translations of Augustine's writings were made during his lifetime and one of them—the *De Gestis Pelagii*, not commonly reckoned among his greatest—was apparently available to the patriarch Photius in the ninth century,[8] it was only in the first half of the fourteenth century that Byzantine scholars like Maximus Planudes and Demetrius and Procheros Kydones began to produce translations of his major works. But despite their efforts, Augustine long remained for eastern orthodoxy symbolic of that element in Latin Christianity which it finds unacceptable, and this suspicion is only slowly disappearing. Vladimir Lossky, one of the most resolute exponents of an uncompromising orthodoxy, considered that a theological analysis of Augustine's *De Trinitate* by an orthodox—an exercise which he was himself admirably equipped to undertake—was a great desideratum; but this is still unprovided.[9] In short we may say that for our purposes Augustine's influence in the east was non-existent.

Secondly, if Augustine brought about reform and renewal in the western church—and few medieval historians are likely to contest the remark of Charles Homer Haskins that 'no writer had a more persistent influence on the higher ranges of mediaeval thought'[10]—this was due more to the long-term effect of his life and writings than to his immediate impact. At the time of his death Augustine was indeed regarded as the most distinguished Latin theologian of his age, as was shown by the imperial summons to attend the ecumenical council of Ephesus;[11] but the predestinarian doctrines which he was then maintaining against Julian of Eclanum had attracted strenuous opposition in southern Gaul from theologians who could not be dismissed as mere Pelagians.[12] Furthermore, the Vandal conquest of Africa destroyed the flourishing monasticism which Augustine had so powerfully influenced and hampered any immediate development of his teaching.

---

[6] [Berthold] Altaner, ['Augustinus in der griechischen Kirche bis auf Photius'], *HJch* 71 (1952) pp 37–76, repr in *Kleine patristische Schriften*, *TU* bd 83 (Berlin 1967) pp 57–98.

[7] Possidius, *Vita* 11 5 (Pellegrino p 74 lines 20–6). Altaner, pp 52–3, doubts whether many works were in fact translated.

[8] Photius, *Bibliotheca*, cod 54, ed R. Henry, *Photius: Bibliothèque*, 1 (Paris 1959) pp 42–5.

[9] V. Lossky, 'The Procession of the Holy Spirit in Orthodox Trinitarian Doctrine' in *The Image and Likeness of God* (ET London 1975) pp 95–6.

[10] C. H. Haskins, *The Renaissance of the Twelfth Century* (New York 1957) p 80.

[11] Liberatus Carthaginensis, *Breviarium*, 5, PL 68 (1866) col 977A. See G. Bonner, *St Augustine of Hippo* (London 1963) p 156.

[12] See Owen Chadwick, *John Cassian* (2 ed Cambridge 1968) pp 127–32.

Thus I would consider that Augustine's real influence began in the sixth century, through the work of theologians like Caesarius of Arles, Primasius of Hadrumetum, and Gregory the Great, and thereafter was steadily strengthened until it was modified, though certainly not superannuated, by the rise of scholasticism. Augustine did not, like Francis of Assisi or Luther, see any dramatic changes effected in the church by his influence in his own lifetime. Indeed, I am inclined to think that the influence of Augustine encouraged, rather than initiated, developments which were already latent in Latin theology. But to discuss this aspect of Augustinianism would take us outside our theme.

Augustine's attitude to secular studies, and especially to philosophy, has long been discussed in a number of works of outstanding quality. The essential problem is how we are to reconcile the influence which classical literature and Neo-Platonist philosophy undoubtedly exercised over him with his apparent rejection of both these influences in his later life as a Christian. One may mention in this connexion two well-known works: Prosper Alfaric's *L'évolution intellectuelle de saint Augustin* (Paris 1918) and H.-I. Marrou's *Saint Augustin et la fin de la culture antique* (4 ed Paris 1958). In the former Alfaric argued that Augustine's conversion at Milan in 386 was really a conversion to philosophy, and that his true Christian conversion came later; and this view, although extravagant, cannot merely be rejected out of hand, since it is apparent that Augustine's early Christianity was unquestionably deeply influenced by Neo-Platonism. Marrou, in his great study, showed how much Augustine the theologian continued to be *un lettré de la décadence*, a characteristic product of the schools of the later Roman Empire.[13] How, then, are we to reconcile the apparent contradiction between Augustine's own assertions and the testimony of his writings? We may assent to John Burnaby's trenchant observation that 'Augustine is not a compound of Plotinus and Luther, but a Father of the Catholic Church';[14] but the problem of reconciling apparently irreconcilable elements in his thought remains. The issue is not so much the question of Augustine's honesty as of the accuracy of his own understanding of his intellectual development. How did he move from his earlier philosophic humanism to the characteristic theological position of his later years?

[13] [H-I] Marrou, [*Saint Augustin et la fin de la culture antique*] (4 ed Paris 1958) cap 5: 'La bible et les lettrés de la décadence.'
[14] John Burnaby, *Amor Dei. A Study of the Religion of St Augustine* (London 1938) p 21.

The Christian humanism of Augustine

I would suggest that some of the difficulties surrounding the problem of Augustine's intellectual development can be resolved if we recognise that his conversion to Christianity was a process which was spread over many years, rather than a momentary experience dividing his life into two parts.[15] The traditional tendency to regard Augustine as having been 'converted' at Milan in 386, with the result that he becomes what William James called a 'twice-born' man, is historically misleading, in that it underestimates that other conversion, specifically recorded by Augustine as having occurred while he was composing his reply to the questions of Simplicianus of Milan in 396/7, and also makes difficult any attempt to harmonise the various influences on Augustine's thinking, on the principle that his pre-conversion experience cannot, by definition, have any real relevance to his 'converted' Christian life. But this is a theological, not an historical judgement, and a narrow one at that (Gerard Manley Hopkins, with a surer theological judgement, spoke of the 'lingering-out swéet skíll' of Augustine's conversion). I would not deny the importance of Augustine's decision to seek baptism in 386—it was undoubtedly the great decision of his life; but I would nevertheless maintain that it must be understood in the context of Augustine's religious development over many years. I therefore propose to consider briefly the intellectual and spiritual career of Augustine, in the hope of finding a key to his eventual understanding of the place of humanism in the Christian life.

Augustine, in the circumstances of his birth and education, was a characteristic product of the later Roman empire, except in one particular, that he was born into a family with a devoutly Christian mother and a father who was sympathetic to Christianity. In this respect, and in this respect only, he differed from his contemporaries, in that he took Christianity without question as the religious norm. Augustine is, indeed, an example of a type of Christian leader which becomes increasingly common in the fourth century: the product of a Christian home, who takes Christianity for granted and, in that sense, never has to make any conscious act of renunciation of paganism, which always had for him something of an academic and bookish quality. On the other hand, again like other Christian leaders of the fourth century coming from Christian homes, Augustine's education was the standard education of his day, as we find it embodied in one

[15] See Max Wundt, 'Ein Wendepunkt in Augustins Entwicklung,' *Zeitschrift für die Neutestamentliche Wissenschaft* 21 (Giessen 1922) pp 53–64.

of its most successful products, Decimus Magnus Ausonius, professor and poet, imperial tutor, pretorian prefect and consul—a paradigm of the sort of career which Augustine himself might have hoped to enjoy in other circumstances. The qualities valued by this educational system were wholly at variance with those enjoined by Christianity; yet the young Augustine was able to accept them as easily as did the majority of educated Christians; and it is worth noting that they were called into question not, so far as we can tell, by any religious considerations, but by reading Cicero's *Hortensius* in the normal course of study.[16] Augustine's assertion that it was the *Hortensius* which first turned his aspirations towards God seems, so far as we can judge from the available evidence, to be true;[17] and we may compare this initial conversion at the age of nineteen with Newman's Calvinist conversion at fifteen 'of which', he was later to write as a Catholic, 'I still am more certain than that I have hands and feet.'

The conversion experience effected by reading the *Hortensius* had certain features which apply to Augustine's later conversions and to their effect upon his attitude to humanism. First, the *Hortensius* persuaded him that the love of wisdom, which he unhesitatingly identified with Christianity, was the only true object of study. Secondly, that what was said was more important than the manner of saying it—a doctrine to which he could assent in principle, but not yet accept in practice, as was speedily shown by his revulsion from the style of the Latin bible. Thirdly, the reading of the *Hortensius* taught Augustine that philosophy was not a merely intellectual exercise but a way of life, a discipline of conduct as well as a process of thought. Accordingly, he turned to prayer and to the study of the scriptures without, it must be admitted, much result, for the style of the old Latin bible repelled him, and he continued to keep the mistress whom he had recently acquired.

The sequel to reading the *Hortensius* is notorious: Augustine became a Manichee. His motives were complex, but certain must be noted here as being relevant to his later religious development. First, he did not, in his own eyes, cease to be a Christian by becoming a Manichee—

---

[16] *Conf[essionum Liber]* III iv 7: . . . et usitato iam discendi ordine perveneram in librum cuiusdam Ciceronis . . .

[17] See the testimony in *De Beata Vita* i 4: Ego ab usque undevicesimo anno aetatis meae, postquam in schola rhetoris librum illum Ciceronis, qui Hortensius vocatur, accepi, tanto amore philosophiae succensus sum, ut statim ad eam me ferre meditarer. Compare *Solil[oquia]* I x 17. On the influence of Cicero on Augustine see [Maurice] Testard, [*Saint Augustin et Cicéron*], 2 vols (Paris 1958).

even if his mother, a woman born to believe, thought otherwise. Secondly, Augustine's adoption of Manichaeism did not impose any obligation to renounce his rhetorical studies, such as he subsequently felt as a catholic Christian. The Manichaean double standard imposed no such demands upon its catechumens. On the other hand, as a result of his conversion to philosophy, Augustine continued as a Manichee to read works of a philosophical character; and the fact that such studies had no financial motivation no doubt helped to consolidate that esteem for philosophy which he felt throughout his life. But there is another factor, which I cannot prove but of which I am fully persuaded. Manichaeism offered Augustine the inspiration of an ideal of continence in the lives of the elect, while at the same time permitting him to keep his mistress as long as he was an auditor. This situation, I suggest, satisfied a psychological need in Augustine, who experienced only too powerfully that combination of sexual attraction and revulsion which was later to cause him to pray: 'Give me chastity and continence, but not yet.'[18] In the continence of the Manichaean elect he would find a degree of devotion for which there would have been no parallel in the African church, where monasticism was unknown. Indeed by Augustine's own account it was only on the eve of his decision to seek baptism at Milan in 386 that he first heard of Saint Antony and of the great tradition of the Egyptian desert, which showed that the Manichees had no monopoly of dedicated chastity, and this discovery aroused in him the greatest enthusiasm.[19]

I would lay some stress upon the hypothesis I have just put forward, not because it is in itself either new or very original, but because it helps to explain the development of Augustine's attitude to humane studies; for his final outlook needs to be understood, in my opinion, in terms of the monastic ideal to which he became, at a later date, so enthusiastic a convert. Augustine's austerity with regard to secular culture is only part of the totality of self-denial which the monastic

---

[18] *Conf* VIII vii 17. See the discussion of marriage in the *Soliloquies*, in which Augustine declares: Prorsus nihil huiusmodi quaero, nihil desidero; etiam cum horrore atque aspernatione talia recordor (I x 17) and contrast with the later admission: Quam tibi sordidus, quam foedus, quam exsecrabilis, quam horribilis complexus femineus videbatur, quando inter nos de uxoris cupiditate quaesitum est! Certe ista nocte vigilantes, cum rursus eadem nobiscum ageremus, sensisti quam te aliter quam praesumpseras, imaginatae illae blanditiae et amara suavitas titillaverit; longe quidem longe minus quam solet, sed item longe aliter quam putaveras (I xiv 25).

[19] *Conf* VIII vi 14: Cui ego cum indicassem illis me scripturis curam maximam inpendere, ortus est sermo ipso narrante de Antonio Aegyptio monacho, cuius nomen excellenter clarebat apud servos tuos, nos autem usque in illam horam latebat.

7

state involves, a self-denial which extends not only to property and sexuality, but to the very principle of self-hood. This is why humility came to play such a part in Augustine's moral theology. He had still very far to go before he understood the need for humility; but the conversion effected by the *Hortensius* began the process within him.

The story of Augustine's eventual disillusionment with Manichaeism, though important, does not concern us here. The next episode which is essential in our discussion is the character of the conversion at Milan in 386, with the long-standing problem: to what extent was this a conversion to Christianity, as opposed to Neo-Platonism? In the past, the two professions were commonly deemed to have been mutually incompatible: if Augustine had been truly converted to catholic Christianity, then Neo-Platonist influence on him could, by definition, only have been superficial. If, on the other hand, Neo-Platonism represented a real influence, then Augustine's baptism was no more than a formality which he later, as a mature Christian, invested with a significance which it did not have at the time. Today, however, scholars are less inclined to adopt such a rigorous attitude of either-or. We can believe that a Christianised-Neo-Platonism was popular in the intellectual circles of Milan which Augustine frequented; and we can recognise the effect made upon him by the Neo-Platonic works which he read at that time, and even agree that certain Neo-Platonic doctrines, such as the characteristic view of man which sees him as a soul fallen into a body, continued to affect his thinking long after he had become a catholic.[20] At the same time, it is still possible to believe that Augustine's conversion at Milan was essentially Christian and not Neo-Platonic.

Here, I would suggest, the fact that Augustine sought and received baptism at Easter 387 is crucial, and its significance is deliberately thrown into relief in the *Confessions* by the story of Marius Victorinus, the Platonist philosopher who, before his conversion, was accustomed to declare that he was already a Christian, and when challenged to prove his claim by coming to church would ask: 'Do walls then make Christians?' Victorinus here expresses the view, held by certain pagan intellectuals, that the outward forms of religion, though necessary for the multitude of men, were of little account to the philosopher. But it was precisely this attitude which was unaccept-

[20] See Robert J. O'Connell, *St Augustine's Early Theory of Man A.D. 386–391* and *St Augustine's Confessions: the Odyssey of Soul* (Cambridge, Mass., 1968, 1969) and my review in *JTS* ns 22 (1971) pp 248–51.

able to catholic Christianity, which insisted that the one road to God was through an exclusive belief in Christ and the reception of the sacraments, which alone gave the power necessary for right living. It was precisely this power which Augustine found lacking in Manichaeism, and subsequently in Neo-Platonism: both failed to make him personally chaste, and neither was able to influence the great majority of men in the way that catholic Christianity seemed able. Augustine makes this clear in certain of the writings which followed his conversion. In what I take to be a crucial passage in the treatise *On True Religion*, written in 389 or 390, he points to the fact that Christianity, in persuading so many thousands of its followers, men and women alike, to live in chastity, had accomplished what Plato could only commend without success.[21] A year or two before the composition of *On True Religion*, in the work *On the morals of the Manichees and of the Catholic Church*, written at Rome, Augustine had, in a rather ungenerous fashion, sought to disparage the celibacy of his former co-religionists the Manichees and to contrast it with the disciplined and self-supporting lives of Christian ascetics.[22] The burden of Augustine's argument is clear: whatever may be the ideals and the claims of others, it is only within the catholic Church that these ideals are realised.

Given this view, what was Augustine's attitude towards literary and philosophical studies at the time when he determined to seek catholic baptism? He resigned his official post as the teacher of rhetoric at Milan, though without any ostentation, urging as a reason weak health, as well as the desire to devote himself to God's service;[23] but he was prepared to continue to read Virgil with private pupils.[24] Furthermore, precisely as a consequence of his conversion, he was moved to envisage the composition of a series of works on the liberal arts—of which the only certain survivor is the *De Musica*—designed 'to reach things incorporeal through things corporeal and to lead others to them!'[25]—an undertaking which indicates the influence which both traditional culture and Neo-Platonism alike exercised over his

[21] *De Vera Religione* iii 5.

[22] *De Moribus Catholicae Ecclesiae* xxx 64–xxxi 68.

[23] *De Beata Vita* i 4: . . . Itaque tantus me arripuit pectoris dolor, ut illius professionis onus sustinere non valens, qua mihi velificabam fortasse ad Sirenas, abicerem omnia et optatae tranquillitati vel quassatam navem fessamque perducerem. See also *De Ord[ine]* I ii 5; *Solil* I ix 16; *Conf* IX ii 2–4.

[24] *De Ord* I viii 26: . . . nihilque a me aliud actum est illo die, ut valetudini parcerem, nisi quod ante cenam cum ipsis dimidium volumen Vergili audire cotidie solitus eram.

[25] *Retract* I 5 [6]: . . . per corporalia cupiens ad incorporalia quibusdam quasi passibus certis vel pervenire vel ducere.

mind. Nor is this surprising, considering the part which philosophy had played in bringing Augustine to the acceptance of catholic Christianity. Through his reading of the Platonists he had come to believe—mistakenly, as it happened, but to his own satisfaction—that catholic doctrine was in accord with the most advanced, the most brilliant, and the most profoundly religious philosophy of the Greco-Roman world; and if, as seems possible, he had enjoyed some kind of mystical experience a little time before his conversion,[26] he would easily have been persuaded that the Platonist philosophers had contrived, in some degree, to see the truth from afar, even though they failed to attain to it, lacking the power which was given only by Christ in the catholic church.

The respect which Augustine, at the time of his baptism, entertained for Platonic thought, has recently been emphasised by Pierre Courcelle,[27] who draws attention to the fact that the statement by Porphyry in the De Regressu Animae[28] that there is no one way for the deliverance of the soul, not even in the verissima philosophia, is echoed by Augustine in the Soliloquies[29] (386-7); while in the Contra Academicos (386) the verissima philosophia is defined as a philosophy 'not of this world—such a philosophy our sacred mysteries most justly detest—but of the other, intelligible world.'[30] Thus it appears that in Augustine's view, Platonism is a philosophy not only recognised by, but positively acceptable to, Christianity.[31] Furthermore, in the De Ordine[32] (386)

[26] Conf VII iii 5; xx 26. See Pierre Courcelle, Les Confessions de Saint Augustin dans la tradition littéraire (Paris 1963) pp 43-58.

[27] Pierre Courcelle, 'Verissima philosophia' in Epekstasis: mélanges patristiques offerts au Cardinal Jean Daniélou (Paris 1972) pp 653-9.

[28] De Regressu Animae, Fragm 12 (preserved by Augustine, De Civ[itate] Dei X 32).

[29] Solil I xiii 23.

[30] Contra Academicos III xix 42: Non enim est ista huius mundi philosophia, quam sacra nostra meritissime detestantur, sed alterius intellegibilis, cui animas multiformibus erroris tenebris caecatas et altissimis a corpore sordibus oblitas numquam ista ratio subtilissima revocaret, nisi summus deus populari quadam clementia divini intellectus auctoritatem usque ad ipsum corpus humanum declinaret atque summitteret, cuius non solum praeceptis sed etiam factis excitatae animae redire in semet ipsas et resipiscere patriam etiam sine disputationum concertatione potuissent.

[31] Ibid III xx 43: Quod autem subtilissima ratione persequendum est—ita enim iam sum affectus, ut quid sit verum non credendo solum sed etiam intellegendo apprehendere impatienter desiderem—apud Platonicos me interim, quod sacris nostris non repugnet, reperturum esse confido.

[32] De Ord I xi 32: Unde etiam divinae scripturae, quas vehementer amplecteris, non omnino philosophos, sed philosophos huius mundi evitandos atque inridendos esse praecipiunt. Esse autem alium mundum ab istis oculis remotissimum, quem paucorum sanorum intellectus intuetur, satis ipse Christus significat, qui non dicit: 'regnum meum non est de mundo', sed: regnum meum non est de hoc mundo.

The Christian humanism of Augustine

Augustine assures his mother that scripture itself teaches that not all philosophers are to be shunned, but only the philosophers of this world, 'for that there is another world, far removed from these human eyes, which the understanding of a few, healthy souls apprehends, Christ Himself aptly indicates, who did not say: "My kingdom is not of any world" but *My kingdom is not of this world*.' Philosophy is, indeed, simply the love of wisdom, which is pursued alike by Platonists and students of the scriptures. But what is significant in Augustine's statement in the *Soliloquies* that there is no one way of deliverance for the soul, is that it is superficially in agreement with the view of pagans like Symmachus, and Augustine's African correspondent Maximus of Madaura: *Nam deus omnibus commune nomen est. Ita fit, ut, dum eius quasi quaedam membra carptim variis supplicationibus prosequimur, totum colere profecto videamur.*[33] Maximus expressed his view in a letter of 390, by which time Augustine was prepared to administer a sharp rebuff; and it is clear that even when writing in 386, he did not intend to include the pagan cults among the ways of deliverance for the soul; but, as he afterwards noted in the *Retractations*, when he echoed Porphyry in the *Soliloquies*, he had overlooked the Dominical saying: *I am the way*.[34]

Augustine's return to Africa in 388 and the three years which followed it, culminating in his ordination as presbyter of Hippo in 391, represents another stage in his conversion, for the decision to return to Africa determined Augustine's life to a degree which he could never have anticipated. In the first place, Augustine moved from the cosmopolitan intellectual atmosphere of Milan to the narrower and more puritanical atmosphere of African Christianity. Secondly, and apart from that external influence, the triennium 388–91 saw a development in Augustine himself. The academic community which he established at Thagaste appears superficially to owe more to Neo-Platonic and Stoic doctrine than to Christian monasticism; but the appeal of the cloister may be discerned under the appearance of cultured leisure.[35] Moreover, in the works composed during this period, like the *De Magistro* and the *De Vera Religione*, we can see the developing operation of Augustine's Christianity upon his thought.

---

[33] *Inter Aug, Ep* 16.

[34] *Retract* I 4 3: item quod dixi: *ad sapientiae coniunctionem non una via perveniri* non bene sonat; quasi alia via sit praeter Christum, qui dixit: *ego sum via.*

[35] See Adolar Zumkeller, *Das Mönchtum des heiligen Augustinus*, 2 ed, *Cassiciacum* bd XI (Würzburg 1968) pp 56–68.

Christ is the only true teacher. Divine authority precedes and prepares the way for the exercise of reason—a view already proposed in the *De Ordine* which will be developed in the *De Utilitate Credendi*, written soon after Augustine's ordination in 391.

This ordination, administered against Augustine's will, when he was on the point of transforming the community of Thagaste into something more formally monastic, brought about a revolution in Augustine's relationships. Up to this point he had moved largely in a world of Christian intellectuals, men for whom a knowledge of classical culture was taken for granted. From 391 onwards he was to be concerned with a different type of Christian, the *rudes ac simplices* for whom he was to compose his *Abecedarian Psalm against the Donatists* and his work on *The Christian Combat*, men for whom Christianity was, in a very real sense, an alternative way of life to that offered by the classical tradition. With a sure instinct for the requirements of the task which lay ahead, Augustine prepared himself for his priestly duties by a study of the Christian scriptures, which he recognised as providing the foundation and guide for the Christian life. For the rest of his life the bible was to be his rule and norm. Significantly, the canon of scripture was defined for Africans at the council of Hippo in 393, at which Augustine delivered his sermon on the creed, the *De Fide et Symbolo*, and again at the council of Carthage of 397—a process of definition which must have emphasised the authority of the sacred text for Augustine. From 391 onwards, then, Augustine's mind was professionally orientated towards biblical study. His concern for philosophy, except as an aid to exegesis, is abruptly cut short. As a new Christian convert, he was prepared to read Virgil with his pupils; but inquiries made to him as a bishop about Cicero received a dusty answer. A bishop has better things to do than expound Ciceronian treatises.[36]

Furthermore, although Augustine's ordination prevented him from pursuing the sort of monastic life which he had proposed for himself in 391, he still contrived to live a community-life according to rule, so that Hippo became a kind of monastic episcopal seminary. Even

---

[36] *Ep* 118 (*ad Dioscorum*, written in 410; see A. Goldbacher, *CSEL* 58 (1904) p 34): ... sed in hac re nihil esse dedecoris, non mihi videtur. Non enim dedecora facies rerum attingit sensum meum, cum cogito episcopum ecclesiasticis curis circumstrepentibus districtum atque distentum, repente quasi obsurdescentem cohibere se ab his omnibus et dialogorum Tullianorum quaestiunculas uni scholastico exponere? Nevertheless, the whole letter bears witness to the influence exercised by Cicero on Augustine's mind. See Testard 2, pp 94–106.

after becoming sole bishop of Hippo in 396 Augustine continued, so far as he could, to live like a monk, requiring his clergy to bestow their property upon the church of Hippo, and himself displaying the greatest circumspection in his relations with women, even when dealing with them as a bishop.

This background of monastic living and a growing preoccupation with biblical study as a guide to the Christian life underlies Augustine's conversion experience of 396 or 397, when he was at work on his reply to the exegetical problems raised by bishop Simplicianus of Milan, an experience which he subsequently recognised as having been one of the decisive events in his life. In a sudden flash of apprehension Augustine came to understand the wholly gratuitous character of grace, as expressed in the words of St Paul: *What have you that you did not receive? If then you received it, why do you boast as if it were not a gift?* 'In the solution of this question', Augustine was later to write, 'I indeed laboured in defence of the free choice of the human will; but the grace of God conquered.'[37]

It was about the time of his conversion–experience while replying to Simplicianus, or shortly afterwards, that Augustine composed the *Confessions*, which equally and more famously emphasise the absolute gratuity of grace, and which are regarded by a leading authority (H. Hagendahl) as exhibiting 'a deep-seated hostility to the old cultural tradition.'[38] Too much emphasis should not, perhaps, be laid upon Augustine's language in the *Confessions*, if only because that work, while avowedly hostile to rhetoric, is itself very much a product of the rhetorical tradition. Of more significance for a balanced understanding of Augustine's attitude is the evidence provided by the work on Christian culture, *De Doctrina Christiana*, begun about the same time as the *Confessions* and completed to a little way after the middle of the third book, the remainder of that book and book IV being added thirty years later, about 426 or 427; for here Augustine provides what is, in effect, a Christian alternative to the classical education of his day, with the bible replacing the pagan literary texts, and ancillary studies like history and philosophy being employed as aids to exegesis,

---

[37] *Retract* II 1 [27]. See G. Bonner, *Augustine and Modern Research on Pelagianism* (The Saint Augustine Lecture for 1970) (Villanova, Pa., 1972) pp 15–18.

[38] H. Hagendahl, *Augustine and the Latin Classics, Studia Graeca et Latina Gothoburgensia* no 20 (Gothenburg 1967) 2, p 715. See also pp 726–7: 'The *Confessions* represent the climax of an attitude of unconcern, aversion, even hostility that subsisted, though occasionally less austerely, to the end of his life.'

with the specific warning that they should not be studied to excess. The deliberate restriction of the course of studies envisaged by the *De Doctrina Christiana* is striking. It may be true, as H.-I. Marrou asserts, that Augustine was providing a course of study for intending preachers and did not mean to imply that Christians should contract out of secular life or forbid young Christian men to pursue the necessary studies to become magistrates, physicians or civil servants;[39] but the intellectual narrowness of the *De Doctrina* is striking. Augustine does not go so far as Tertullian in rejecting pagan learning; but he certainly accepts in practice his view that 'when we believe, we desire no further belief.' The only value of secular studies, according to Augustine, is that they may help us to understand the sacred text.

Yet Augustine's narrow biblicism differs from the biblicism of later protestantism. For Augustine, even the bible itself is but a means to an end: the love of God, who is to be enjoyed, and of our neighbour, who is able to enjoy God with us and the study of Scripture is but the third stage of seven, which lead to wisdom—the vision of God (*De Doctrina Christiana II*, vii 11–viii 12), to be used to the enjoyment of some other thing. Having established in his first book that God alone is the thing to be enjoyed, and all other things used to obtain that enjoyment, Augustine then proceeds in the second to discuss the nature of signs, by which truth is communicated from man to man and from one generation to another, in order to provide an epistemological basis for biblical exegesis. Now the nature of signs had already attracted Augustine's attention in 389 in the *De Magistro*, where he had come to the conclusion that the true teacher is Christ, 'Whom to love and to know is the happy life, which all men claim that they seek, though few there are who rejoice in having truly found it';[40] and it may seem surprising that he returns to the topic afresh in the context in which he was writing. The reason, I would suggest, is that Augustine wished to take into account an intellectual austerity even greater than his own, which not only rejected any study of pagan literature whatever, but even held that the bible itself was not essential for the mature Christian—a view with which Augustine

[39] Marrou p 380.
[40] *De Magistro* xiv 46: ut iam non crederemus tantum, sed etiam intelligere inciperemus quam vere scriptum sit auctoritate divina, ne nobis quemquam magistrum dicamus in terris, quod unus omnium magister in coelis sit. Quid sit autem in coelis, docebit ipse a quo etiam per homines signis admonemur et foris, ut ad eum intro conversi erudiamur; quem diligere ac nosse beata vita est, quam se omnes clamant quaerere, pauci autem sunt qui eam vere se invenisse laetentur.

agrees: '. . . The man who is supported by faith, hope and charity and maintains the same unshaken has no need of the scriptures, except to instruct others. And so by these three, many live even in solitude, without books.'[41] Augustine accepts the monastic ideal, even in the anti-intellectual form sometimes found in the Egyptian desert, where books could be regarded as the plunder of widows and orphans; yet he is prepared to offer an argued defence of the propriety both of scriptural study and of secular reading to advance that study. And from that he produces a genuine, if grudging, outline of a Christian culture; but a Christian culture designed solely to further the growth in grace of the baptised believer.

In the event, Augustine's ideal failed to transform the educational system of his age, which continued to cling to the study of the classical authors as the foundation and the norm of culture. It was the ideals of Symmachus and Ausonius, and not those of Augustine, which determined the shape of education in western Europe down to the renaissance and long afterwards. Once and once only in medieval history, to the best of my knowledge, was Augustine's ideal realised, three centuries after his lifetime, in the culture of Christian Northumbria represented by Benedict Biscop's foundation of Wearmouth-Jarrow and expressed in the writings of its brightest ornament, the venerable Bede; for Bede's work was accomplished within the framework which Augustine had envisaged, inasmuch as Bede passed from elementary grammar directly to Christian authors without any intervening study of classical models, and thereafter devoted himself to a career of teaching which found its end and fulfilment in the exposition of the scriptures to the increase of faith, hope and charity. But Bede's career remains the brilliant anomaly, made possible only because Northumbrian Christianity was a monastic culture imposed upon a Germanic society ignorant of the classical tradition. Elsewhere, outside the monasteries and sometimes within them, educational tradition proved too strong, even for the victorious Christian church, and throughout the middle ages the specious charms of the pagan classics continued to disturb the consciences of zealous churchmen.

It is however important to recognise that the *De Doctrina Christiana*, despite its deliberate limitations of outlook, does not represent a complete rejection of non-Christian culture. Secular studies which

---

[41] *De Doct[rina] Christ[iana]* I xxxix 43.

may be useful for biblical exegesis are permitted, and it is noteworthy that the writings of the philosophers, and especially the Platonists, are specifically commended, where they declare truths in agreement with the Christian faith, on the traditional Christian principle that the Children of Israel when they came out of Egypt despoiled the Egyptians.[42] This concession is, of course, hardly surprising, when we remember that in the *Confessions*, written at about the same time, Augustine had paid tribute to the part which they had played in bringing him to the Catholic church.[43]

With the *De Doctrina Christiana* and the *Confessions* we have reached the point at which Augustine's views on the value of secular studies for the Christian have become reasonably fixed and it will be convenient to recapitulate their development. The reading of Cicero's *Hortensius* at the age of nineteen, turned Augustine's thoughts to Christianity, which in turn led him to Manichaeism, partly, according to his own testimony, because his literary tastes were offended by the style of the Latin bible. Acquaintance with Neo-Platonism at Milan in 386 helped to make possible his acceptance of catholic baptism, and left him with an enthusiasm for a kind of Christian humanism, expressed in the *De Musica*. However, besides the Neo-Platonists, Augustine at Milan also discovered Christian monasticism, which seems from his own account to have played a decisive part in bringing about his conversion, and to have left him with an ideal which continued steadily to attract his allegiance over the years, and was intensified by the three years spent at Thagaste, after his return to Africa in 388. His involuntary ordination in 391 both brought him into contact with the uneducated Christian who formed the majority in the African church, and also directed him to intensive biblical study. Finally the conversion experience which occurred while he was at work on the answers to the biblical questions of Simplicianus of Milan, leaving him convinced of the absolutely gratuitous character of grace, completed the transformation of Augustine the Christian humanist to Augustine the Doctor of Grace, and explains the hostility to humanism revealed in the *Confessions* and the *De Doctrina Christiana,* while still leaving him convinced of the truth and the utility of much of the teaching of the Platonists.

This evaluation of Augustine's eventual attitude to secular studies is confirmed by the evidence provided by his treatise *On Catechizing*

[42] *Ibid* II xl 60.
[43] *Conf* VII ix 13–xxi 27.

the Uninstructed (*De Catechizandis Rudibus*), composed in 399, in which he provides a practical guide to the instruction of candidates for baptism. Here, in order to provide the most effective instruction, Augustine recognises three classes of catechumens: the ordinary uneducated; well-educated persons who have received a thorough training in liberal studies (*liberalibus doctrinis excultus*);[44] and, finally, those who have received the general literary education of the schools (*de scholis usitatissimis grammaticorum oratorumque venientes*)[45] 'who seem to surpass other men in the art of speaking.' Of these three classes, special consideration should be given to the highly-educated, who are accustomed to make diligent inquiry into matters which interest them, and who may already have discovered a good deal about Christian doctrine on their own account, in order to spare them a tedious recital of what they already know. On the other hand, Augustine shows markedly less sympathy with the third category, composed of those who have received a general literary and rhetorical education. Such persons must be warned against presuming on their literary skills and despising simpler believers who can more easily avoid faults of conduct than of grammar. They must not let themselves be deterred by the uncouth style of the scriptures or fall into the error of taking literally what is to be understood metaphorically, nor must they ridicule any bishop or minister of the church who lacks their literary training. These recommendations seem to have an autobiographical flavour. Augustine has in mind his own experience when, after reading Cicero's *Hortensius*, he turned to the scriptures, only to find their style inferior to that of Cicero; and the distaste for grammarians and rhetoricians revealed in the *Confessions* reappears in the *De Catechizandis Rudibus*. On the other hand, it is equally clear that Augustine's concern for those who come to be made Christians after prolonged inquiry conducted on a high intellectual level is based on personal experience, and constitutes a recognition of the value of secular learning as a preparation for the gospel message.

It would therefore appear that about the year 400 Augustine had come to reject the classical culture in which he had been educated, while retaining a measure of regard for non-literary studies, and especially philosophy, which he had acquired on his own account. Yet we have to take account of the regret, expressed in the *Retractations*,

---

[44] *De Catechizandis Rudibus* viii 12.
[45] *Ibid* ix 13.

that in his early writings he had over-valued the Platonists, which implies that his respect for the pagan philosophers had by this time still further diminished. Is it possible to establish to what extent there was a real change in his opinions, and if so, how this change came about?

In the *Confessions* Augustine likens the Neo-Platonists to men who see the country of peace from afar, but fail to find the way, because they do not keep to the road that leads there.[46] This recognition of the ability of the human mind, even when fallen, to see the truth, and to come to some knowledge of God from the evidences of His creation, reappears in the second tractate on St John's Gospel (perhaps to be dated 406–7): '[The philosophers] saw where they had to come; but they were ungrateful to Him who furnished what they saw, and wished to attribute what they saw to themselves, and becoming proud lost what they saw and were turned away from it to idols and images and to the cult of demons, adoring the creature and scorning the Creator.'[47] This, for Augustine, constituted the great error of the Platonists: they failed to recognise the Incarnation, and their failure was due to pride.[48] 'Oh had you but recognised the grace of God in Jesus Christ our Lord, and that very Incarnation of His, wherein He assumed a human soul and body, you might have seen it to be the brightest example of grace!'[49] It was the humility of God revealed in the Incarnation which particularly moved Augustine, and it was in this divine virtue of humility that the Platonists were deficient.

This dissatisfaction only increased in the years following the sack of Rome of 410, when Augustine was at work on the anti-pagan polemic of *The City of God*; for he now had to deal with the Platonists, no longer as the philosophers whose teaching afforded the strongest endorsement of Christian doctrine, but as the embittered defenders of later Roman paganism, who patronised the sacrificial cultus, that aspect of paganism most repulsive to Augustine. Here the tenth book of the *De Civitate Dei*, written in about 417, is particularly revealing. The Platonists are still 'the noblest of all the philosophers' (*Platonicos*

---

[46] *Conf* VII xxi 27; compare *De Civ Dei* X 29.

[47] *In Evang[elium] Ioh[annis] Tr[actatus]* 2, 4.

[48] *De Civ Dei* X 24: Eum quippe in ipsa carne contempsit, quam propter sacrificium nostrae purgationis adsumpsit, magnum scilicet sacramentum ea superbia non intellegens, quam sua ille humilitate deiecit verus benignusque Mediator.

[49] *Ibid* X 29: O si cognovisses Dei gratiam per Iesum Christum dominum nostrum ipsamque eius incarnationem, qua hominis animam corpusque suscepit, summum esse exemplum gratiae videre potuisses!

The Christian humanism of Augustine

omnium philosophorum merito nobilissimos),[50] Plotinus is 'that great Platonist' (*ille magnus Platonicus*),[51] while Porphyry is a man 'of no mean intellect' (*homo non mediocri ingenio praeditus*);[52] yet despite their wisdom, all fell alike into the popular error of polytheism, and some even maintained that divine honours might be accorded to demons. 'Porphyry was under the influence of evil powers, of which he was ashamed and yet dared not freely contradict them. He would not acknowledge Christ the Lord, by whose Incarnation we are cleansed, to be the First Principle. He even despised Him in the very flesh which he assumed for the sacrifice of our purification, failing to understand the great mystery by the very pride which the true and loving Mediator destroyed by His humility'.[53] It is not surprising that in the last twenty years of his life Augustine came to see the Platonists, not simply as more doubtful guides to Christianity than he had assumed in the enthusiasm of 386, but as the enemies of Christianity and advocates of idolatry and sorcery.

Thus his earlier enthusiasm for Neo-Platonism came (in the words of Portalié) 'to die a slow death in the heart of Augustine',[54] and this process seems to have been accomplished during the period of the composition of *The City of God*, 413–26; yet even in the last book of that work, Augustine could still quote the Platonists in defence of the Christian doctrine of the resurrection of the body, and observe that 'Plato and Porphyry each made certain statements which might have brought them both to become Christians if they had exchanged them with one another.'[55] Furthermore, we have a revealing insight into Augustine's attitude to the great pagan writers and thinkers in a letter to his friend Evodius, written in 414–5, discussing the question of Christ's descent into Hell, in which Augustine asks who would not rejoice if all the souls in Hades were set free, and especially those who have made themselves familiar by their writings—not only poets and orators who exposed the follies of polytheism, but also the philosophers.[56] This attitude is more significant, because it was about this time that Augustine was writing the fifth book of *The City of God*, in

[50] *Ibid* X 1.
[51] *Ibid* X 2.
[52] *Ibid* X 32.
[53] *Ibid* X 24.
[54] Eugène Portalié, *A Guide to the Thought of Saint Augustine*, trans R. J. Bastian (London 1960) p 95.
[55] *De Civ Dei* XXII 27.
[56] *Ep* 164 ii 4. For date, see Goldbacher, *CSEL* 58, p 42.

which he was concerned to refute the suggestion that virtuous pagans might deserve a place in Heaven for their good deeds, arguing that their virtues were made of no effect because they were practised for the sake of fame, and quoting with supreme irony the Dominical words: *They have received their reward.*[57] Writing in private, to a fellow-Christian and personal friend, Augustine did not hesitate to express his regard for the pagans whom he was obliged to disparage for the sake of controversy. Dante, when he placed the virtuous pagans in the noble castle of Limbo, was writing in the spirit of Augustine.

There would therefore seem to be some difference between what Augustine formally said about pagan literature as a Christian controversialist, and what he privately felt as an individual; and this dichotomy helps to explain his continued regard for pagan philosophy, and the fact that he continued to quote Plotinus in the last months of his life, the very time when he was engaged upon his last and most uncompromising anti-Pelagian work, the *Opus Imperfectum contra Iulianum*. The tension between Augustine the Christian humanist and Augustine the predestinarian theologian was never entirely resolved. It is expressed vividly in the twenty-fourth chapter of the last book of *The City of God* (written in 426) when Augustine, after pronouncing an enthusiastic encomium on man's achievements and the beauty of the created world, concludes that these are only the consolations of humanity under judgement, and asks rhetorically what God will give to those whom He has predestinated to life, if He has given all this to those whom he has condemned to death. The grimness of Augustine's conclusion does not altogether obscure his enthusiasm for man's abilities and achievements even in a fallen world. The divine spark of reason implanted by God in man is not wholly extinguished by Adam's sin.

If the argument which has been followed in this paper is valid, we may say that although Augustine formally rejected the literary and rhetorical training of his youth, he never wholly divested himself of its influence; and he continued to have a real regard and admiration for philosophy to his life's end, regarding the Platonic philosophy as being in large measure in agreement with the inspired teaching of Christianity. The fatal weakness of Platonism in his eyes, the deficiency which made it fundamentally insufficient to bring man to the truth, was the absence of any recognition of Christ, the true light, 'for the man

[57] *De Civ Dei* V 15.

who is enlightened is also called a light; *sed vera lux illa est quae illuminat*—but the true light is that which enlightens.'[58] For Augustine —and this is as true of him when he first read the *Hortensius* as of the mature theologian—the way to God is through Christ, 'by whom man comes, to whom man attains, in whom man abides.'[59] Philosophising is a religious activity, a form of contemplation.

It is this consideration which provides the key to Augustine's influence on Latin Christian culture in the later middle ages. He helped, more perhaps than anyone else, to bring into western monasticism that intellectual and academic element which contrasts so strongly with the traditional asceticism of the Christian east. This he did, not so much by his specific recommendations of a programme of studies, which was realised, as we have seen, only in a particular locality and for a limited time, but rather by the general influence of his life and writings. Gregory the Great's famous dictum on Saint Benedict, *scienter nescius et sapienter indoctus*, could never have been applied to Augustine who was, and always remained, a learned intellectual. Yet Augustine was also a monk, the author of a rule which was to exercise an influence in the west second only to the Benedictine. Augustine thus combined in himself the scholar's love of learning and the contemplative's desire for God, and could commend these in that moving style of which the *Confessions*—already a favourite in his own lifetime[60]—was the supreme expression. Furthermore, Augustine not only commended the Platonists as the philosophers who came closest to Christianity, but provided in his own writings a very considerable part of the knowledge of Platonism available in western Europe in the early middle ages. Augustine can therefore be seen as the ideal monastic philosophical theologian, and it is no accident that Saint Anselm, perhaps the supreme Latin Christian intellect of the pre-scholastic era, should have been soaked in the writings of Augustine, so that his works, however original they are in their matter, could well be mistaken for Augustine's own as regards style.

Yet style was precisely that element in a piece of writing which Augustine had learned, from the first reading of the *Hortensius*, to be of no account in respect to what was said; and there is a certain irony

---

[58] *In Evang Ioh Tr* 2, 6: *Erat lux vera*. Quare additum est: *vera*? quia et homo illuminatus dicitur lux; sed vera lux illa est quae illuminat.

[59] *De Doct Christ* I xxxiv 38: Sic enim ait: *Ego sum via et veritas et vita*, hoc est 'per me venitur, ad me pervenitur, in me permanetur.'

[60] *Retract* II 6 [32] 1: Quid de illis alii sentiant, ipsi viderint; multis tamen fratribus eos multum placuisse et placere scio.

in the fact that the one Christian father to have written a work which posterity has decided was a literary classic should have reacted so violently against the educational system of his day, which sought above all else to develop a moving and persuasive style. Yet the irony is more apparent than real; for although Augustine long continued— like other Christian fathers—to employ the rhetorical techniques acquired in his school education, he informed them with a personal enthusiasm and devotion, to produce a style which was both characteristic and wholly appealing. If Augustine was, in effect, the universal doctor of the early middle ages in the west, it was because his personality coloured the vast store of information which he provided. It was for this reason that Augustine became, in the words of Harnack, 'not only a paedagogue and teacher, but a Father of the Church.' Something of the charm which his biographer Possidius recognised, when he said that he thought that those gained most from Augustine who heard him preaching in church or witnessed his dealings with men, continues to haunt his pages. Sir Ernest Barker has observed that to read *The City of God* is an education, and a very liberal education. The judgement may be extended to Augustine's writings as a whole.

University of Durham

ROMAN BOOKS AND CAROLINGIAN
RENOVATIO

by D. A. BULLOUGH

J EAN Mabillon's incidental treatment in his *De re diplomatica* of
the lead *bulla* of an emperor Charles with the reverse legend
Renovatio Roman. Imp. gives no inkling of the reputation it was to
acquire in later historiography of the Carolingian empire. Mabillon
himself favoured an attribution to Charles the Fat, although between
the publication of the first and supplementary volumes of his epoch-
making work it had been correctly attributed to the first Charles by
the numismatist François Le Blanc. Without these early publications,
modern discussion of early Carolingian imperial and renaissance
ideology might have been deprived of one of its key texts: for the bull
was already in a much damaged condition in the late-nineteenth century and both sides are now almost completely illegible.[1] Its uniqueness, and the great rarity of the 'imperial bust' coins which are icono-
graphically linked with it, invite us to consider whether the slogans
and images of a 'renewed Roman empire' were known to more than
a privileged few in Charlemagne's lifetime: even so, if the *Annales
Mettenses*, completed in 805, have been rightly interpreted, someone in
the court circle had felt the need to appease critics by emphasising the
strictly-Frankish roots of his imperial authority at the same time as the
dies of the new coins were being prepared.[2]

[1] J. Mabillon, *De re Diplomatica* (Paris 1681) p 142, and Suppl (Paris 1704) p 48 with
plate; F. Le Blanc, *Dissertation historique sur quelques monnoyes de Charlemagne frappées
dans Rome* (Paris 1689, 1690) title-page and p 24. The most accessible reproductions
are now [P. E.] Schramm, *K[aiser] K[önige und] P[apste]* 1 (Stuttgart 1968) p 370;
a bibliography of other eighteenth- and nineteenth-century references is in Schramm
KKP 2 p 21 n 23 whose pp 21–5 are the most extended recent discussion of the *bulla*;
but compare my comments in *Studies [in Memory of David] Talbot Rice* (Edinburgh 1975)
ed G. Henderson and G. Robertson pp 244–5. Mabillon tells us that his design was
provided by *iam laudatus Fauvellus abbas e suo cimelio*. The abbé Fauvel does not figure
in any French biographical dictionary and Mr Robert Shackleton (Bodley's librarian)
and other students of the period whom I have asked have been unable to discover any
account of him elsewhere: he is presumably the collector of curios, two pamphlets
by whom are listed in the *Catalogue Général des livres imprimés de la Bibliothèque
Nationale* 50 (Paris 1929) col 41.

[2] I. Haselbach, *Aufstieg und Herrschaft der Karlinger in der Darstellung der sogenannten
Annales Mettenses priores*, Historische Studien 412 (Lübeck/Hamburg 1970) esp pp 184 *seq*.

Rome, however, had been presented to the Franks as an exemplar and a means of renewal of their *religio Christiana* long before learned discussion focused on the nature of their ruler's authority: and the reiteration of the notion that it was the source of what was right and good in the liturgy reached a far wider circle of educated Franks than were ever familiar with the concept of *renovatio imperii*. Eighth- and early ninth-century sacramentaries of the type conveniently described as 'Gelasian' have an introductory colophon which, with minor variations, reads: *In nomine Dei summi incipit liber sacramentorum Romanae ecclesiae ordinis per circulum anni* (or *ordinis anni circuli*). Ninth-century and some later 'Gregorian' sacramentaries have the colophon: *In nomine Domini hic sacramentorum de circulo anno exposito a sancto Gregorio papa romano editum*; to which a select few manuscripts add the words *ex authentico libro bibliothecae cubiculi scriptum.*[3]

The belief that proper liturgical practice in all the churches of the Latin west derived from the church of Rome—but also the contrary belief that local *consuetudo* had its own inherent virtue and was not lightly to be abandoned—goes back at least to the early fifth century. Answering a number of queries from bishop Decentius of Gubbio in 416, pope Innocent I declared that:

> If the priests of the Lord really wished to preserve ecclesiastical uses intact, as received from the Holy Apostles, no diversity and no variation would be found in the [eucharistic] rite and [other] ceremonial . . .; it is incumbent on [all western churches] to follow what the Roman Church observes, from which they doubtless took their own beginning, lest by favouring adventitious opinions, they overlook the real source of their own institutions.

The decretal letter of which these firm words are the prologue found a place in nearly every canon-law collection from the *Quesnelliana* and

---

[3] For the colophons of the 'Gelasians' see most conveniently B. Moreton, *The Eighth-Century Gelasian Sacramentary* (Oxford 1976) pp 176 *seq*, where also the history of the term is comprehensively reviewed on pp 2–14 (without, however, taking account of the iconographic evidence of, for example, Berlin MS Theol lat fol 192, inserted leaf; Göttingen Land–und Univ Bibl MS Theol 231, fol 1ᵛ; and Bamberg Staatl Bibl MS A II 52 fol 12ᵛ). For the colophons of 'Gregorians' see the splendid edition of [Dom J.] Deshusses, [*Le Sacramentaire Grégorien*] (Fribourg-en-Suisse 1971) p 85, which limits its apparatus to ninth-century examples: and note that according to E. Bourque, *Etude sur les Sacramentaires romains,* 2.ii (Vatican City 1958) p 37, Mainz Seminarbibl MS 1 (Deshusses's *F*) does have *editum ex authentico libro bibliothecae cubiculi.* The only listing of later examples of this phrase—which seems not to figure in any English manuscript—is L. Traube, *Textgeschichte der Regula S. Benedicti ABAW,* 3 Cl, 21 iii (1898) pp 675–6.

'Collection of Corbie' onwards. It does not follow from this, however, that copies were numerous or that it was read widely in the pre-Carolingian centuries.[4]

The attitude of *sanctus Gregorius papa Romanus* himself was very different. When the notoriously-uneasy Augustine raised with the pope the question of liturgical divergences between the Roman church and churches in Gaul and what practices he should adopt for the newly-converted English, the answer given was:

> You know the usage of the Roman Church in which you were brought up: hold it very much in affection. But as far as I am concerned, if you have found something more pleasing to Almighty God, either in the Roman or the Frankish or any other Church, make a careful choice and institute in the Church of the English —which as yet is new to the Faith—the best usages which you have gathered together from many churches . . . Choose . . . what is godly, religious and sound; and gathering all together as it were into a dish, place it on the table of the English for their customary diet.

Paul Meyvaert has shown that language and thought are characteristic of Gregory and the answer to Augustine's query a typical expression of the pope's concept of 'diversity within unity'. The same scholar's fine studies of the manuscript tradition of the *Libellus Responsionum* have also established that it was widely disseminated—primarily, apparently, from Lombard north Italy (Pavia?)—in three formally distinct versions before Bede included a variant-text of the 'question-and-answer' version in his *Ecclesiastical History*: it was a common feature of pre-Carolingian and early Carolingian canonical collections originating and circulating in Gaul and England.[5] There is nothing to

---

[4] [H.] Wurm, *Studien [und Texte zur Decretalsammlung des Dionysius Exiguus]* (Rome 1939) p 115 lists the early collections in which it figures. The most accessible text is *PL* 20 (1845) pp 551-61 (from Coustant); for other early editions see P. Kehr, *Italia Pontificia* 4 (Berlin 1909) p 82 nr 1, to be used in conjunction with Wurm, *Studien*, pp 124-8, with *Spicilegium Casinense* 1 (Monte Cassino 1888/1893) p 231 (variant readings in Novara bibl cap MS XXX), and—for c.[5]—B. Capelle 'Innocent Ier et le canon de la messe', *RTAM* 19 (1952) pp 5-16, which demonstrates that all medieval readers of the text knew only (but did not follow?) an incorrect version of the pope's ruling here! The most recent discussion of the content of the letter is by V. Monachino in *Atti del II° Convegno di Studi Umbri, Gubbio, 1964* (Perugia 1965) pp 211-34.

[5] *MGH Epp* 2, ed P. Ewald/L. M. Hartmann (1899 repr 1957) pp 332 *seq*, Bede, *HE* I, 27; [P.] Meyvaert, 'Diversity within Unity, a Gregorian theme', *The Heythrop Journal*, 4 (London 1963) esp pp 144 *seq*; Meyvaert 'Bede's text [of the *Libellus Responsionum* of Gregory the Great to Augustine of Canterbury', *England before the Conquest:*

suggest that Bede's personal experience of the liturgy and attitude to it linked him and his community with Innocent rather than Gregory; and there is indeed evidence to the contrary. The elimination of the *archicantor* John from the bibliography and history of the Roman *ordines* (magisterially edited by M. Andrieu) does not necessarily mean that his period as 'visiting professor of liturgy' in northern England was of no significance for its forms and practice of worship: but his responsibilities in Rome related to the singing of the office in the monastery of St Martin's and in St Peter's basilica, not the stational or other mass-liturgy. Apart from the office-hymns quoted in the early *De arte metrica*, surprisingly few liturgical citations or resonant echoes have been identified in Bede's writings. He quotes the 'three quite perfect petitions' introduced by Gregory into the *Hane igitur* prayer of the canon of the mass: but this extended version (with minor syntactical variations) was universal in the eighth century. He does, however, put into the mouth of Augustine and his fellow-missionaries entering Canterbury for the first time the antiphon (with *Alleluia*) *Deprecamur te* from the rogation litany, which only reached Rome from Gaul in the time of pope Leo III; and Cuthbert's account of Bede's last days reveals the community taking part in the ascensiontide rogations: northern English monastic observance in the early eighth century, therefore, included at least one specifically Gallican, non-Roman, liturgical ceremony.[6]

studies . . . presented to Dorothy Whitelock], ed P. Clemoes and K. Hughes (Cambridge 1971) pp 15–33. The dissemination from north Italy is observed but not developed by Meyvaert in 'Bede's text', p 29 n 4. A plausible context is the Rome-directed missionary activity which completed the conversion of the Lombards in the concluding decades of the seventh century, magisterially described by [G. P.] Bognetti in his 'Sta. Maria *foris portas* di Castelseprio e la storia religiosa dei Longobardi' (1948) and in a series of papers subsequently, all reprinted as *L'Éta Longobarda*, 4 vols (Milan 1966–9), even though not all his arguments and interpretations are now acceptable. The plausibility of the view that the *Libellus* was used as a convenient handbook by those working among the Lombards in this missionary period is strengthened by the fact that the (interpolated) answer permitting marriage within the fourth degree is related to rulings on marriage in the period 723–50 and a query of the bishop of Pavia to pope Zacharias: on the former see Bognetti, *L'Éta Longobarda*, 2 pp 214–17, on the latter my remarks in *Atti [del] 4° [Congr int di studi sull'Alto medioevo, Pavia,] 1967* (Spoleto 1969) p 323.

6 [M.] Andrieu, [Les] Ordines [Romani du Haut Moyen Age] 5 vols (Louvain 1931–61): for John, *Ordines*, 3, pp 6–15, 20–21 with *Hist abb anon*, cap 10 (Plummer p 391), *Hist abb Bedae*, cap 6 (Plummer p 369) and *HE* IV, 18; for his monastery see G. Ferrari, *Early Roman Monasteries* (Vatican City 1957) pp 230 *seq*, with a discussion of the evidence of the *ordines* for the monastic observance of the Vatican basilical monasteries at pp 392–9. For the hymns quoted in *De Arte metrica* see H. Gneuss, *Hymnar und Hymnen im englischchen Mittelalter* (Tübingen 1968) pp 35–6 with the

Bede's monastery, and doubtless some others which had no chronicler, could claim an alternative affiliation with Rome and its unbroken heritage—even specifically with the unique resources of the papal court—through the search for 'books to furnish a room'. Probably no texts of early medieval cultural history are better known than the passages in the *Lives of the Holy Abbots of Wearmouth and Jarrow* describing the book-collecting zeal of Benedict Biscop; and Rome is explicitly or implicitly the place where he, like Wilfrid in the same decades, made the bulk of his acquisitions. From his fourth voyage to Rome Benedict 'brought back a large number of books on sacred literature, which he had either bought at a price or received as gifts from his friends', from his fifth 'a large quantity of books of all kinds'; 'many sacred books' were among the items that he brought back from his sixth visit: and when he was near death 'he commanded that *the large and noble library which he had brought from Rome* and which was necessary for the edification of his church, was to be kept entire and neither to be damaged by neglect nor dispersed'.[7]

Where so few non-biblical manuscripts have survived that can be shown unequivocally to have been in a northern English library, it is a hopeless task to try to define the common or particular characteristics of those that Benedict took away from Rome. We must be content to recall that the *Codex Amiatinus* is a massive but no longer the only piece of evidence that among them were books—less probably, recent Roman copies of books—that had once been in the library of Cassiodorus's *Vivarium* and then for a time (as it seems) in the library of the Lateran.[8] The very different emphasis in the Wearmouth-

---

table on pp 24–5, and the new edition by C. B. Kendall, *CC* 123A (1975). The addition to the canon is recorded in *HE* II 1 (which it is not correct to say 'is borrowed from the *Liber Pontificalis*', as Colgave in the edition of [B.] Colgrave and [R. A. B.] Mynors (Oxford 1969) p 130 n 4, since the *Liber* does not quote the added petitions in full); for its presence in other eighth-century sacramentaries see the apparatus of B. Botte, *Le Canon de la Messe romaine: édition critique* (Louvain 1935) p 36. For the antiphon compare *HE* I 25 with the additions to the Compiègne and Senlis texts of the Roman *Antiphonale Missarum*, [R-J.] Hesbert [*Antiphonale Missarum Sextuplex*] (Rome 1935) 202a, p 207; for the Rogations see the *Epistola de obitu Bedae*, ed Colgrave and Mynors, pp 582–4 and L. Duchesne, *Christian Worship, its origin and evolution* (5 Engl ed, London 1927) pp 288–9.

[7] *Hist abb Bedae*, caps 4, 6, 9, 11 (Plummer, pp 367 seq).

[8] [P.] Courcelle, [*Les*] *Lettres grecques* [*en Occident de Macrobe à Cassiodore*] (2 ed, Paris 1948) pp 374–6 (but compare below n 10); R. L. S. Bruce-Mitford, 'The Art of the Codex Amiatinus', *J[ournal of the] B[ritish] A[rcheological] A[ssociation]*, 32 (London 1969) pp 1 seq, but for the text of the *Amiatinus* as an edition based on exemplars from various sources, not exclusively Cassiodoran, see B. Fischer in *La Bibbia nell'Alto Medioevo*, SS Spoleto 10 (1963) pp 559–61.

Jarrow collection, which it can hardly be doubted was much the most extensive north of the Alps c700, the deliberately chosen (but also in part probably unavoidable) limitations are, however, apparent if we look at the list of books and authors known to have been consulted by Bede in the first third of the eighth century. It is not merely that most of the books are either patristic (exegetic) or in some sense computistic: there is a conspicuous lack even of the modest minimum of non-Christian authors with whom almost all his successors of comparable learning and interests will show familiarity. In fact, apart from the late grammarians, Bede's first-hand reading in the pagan Latin authors seems to have been limited to a part only of Pliny's *Encyclopedia*—the early books, with possibly excerpts from some others.⁹ Even Virgil, it has recently been argued (and like Mr Bonner I share this view), was not available to or at least not known by Bede except through quotations in the writings of others; and if, as seems possible, Cassiodorus's *Institutions* was not among the books imported by Benedict, Bede was deprived of access to a work that could have led him to a few more of the major pagan writers.¹⁰

These conspicuous gaps in the library resources of northern England began to be filled in the four decades after Bede's death, when the cathedral church of York, under its archbishops Egbert and Aelberht,

⁹ [K.] Welzhofer, ['Beda's Citate aus der Naturalis historia des Plinius'], *Wilhelm v. Christ . . . dargebrachten Abhandlungen aus dem Gebiet der Klass.-Altertumswissenschaft* (Munich 1891) pp 25-41 thought that Bede's citations were exclusively from bks II–VI, which nicely coincides with the scope of the northern English manuscript Leiden Voss Lat F.4 (*CLA* nr 1578) and with the range of the extracts in a Leiden and a Paris manuscript published by [K.] Rück in *Sitzungsberichte München* (1898) 1 pp 257-87. [M. L. W.] Laistner, ['The library of the Venerable Bede'], *Bede, his Life, Times and Writings*, ed A. H. Thompson (Oxford 1935) pp 243-4 found evidence, however, that he also knew bks XII, XIII, XVI and XXXVII but evidently not XVIII. Since it seems likely that what Rück (the first scholar to study it) called an 'astronomisch-komputischen Sammelwerk des achten Jahrhunderts', *Programm des Ludwigsgymn. in München* (1888) containing extracts from bks II and XVIII, was produced in York or in Wearmouth-Jarrow not long after Bede's death (Rück, p 87; Welzhofer, p 37), it is reasonable to assume that the Wearmouth-Jarrow exemplar was considerably more extensive than bks II–VI.
¹⁰ Laistner, p 245 supposed that Bede used Cassiodorus's *Historia Tripartita* but [W.] Levison, *England and the Continent [in the Eighth Century]* (Oxford 1946) p 141 and note, disproved this. Laistner could, on the other hand, find no trace of the *Institutiones* in Bede's writings. Courcelle, *Lettres grecques* p 375 argues that Bede used *Inst* I. i 1-4 (ed Mynors, pp 11-12) for the dedicatory letter to his *In Genesim* (*Hexaemeron*), ed C. W. Jones, *CC* 118A, p 1. The general similarity is certainly very close but exact verbal parallels are almost entirely lacking and some other explanation than direct dependence on *Inst* I should probably be sought. Alcuin, too, shows no certain knowledge of *Inst* I although he used *Inst* II.

acquired a whole new range of pagan and Christian Latin authors, including a complete Virgil, Cicero's *De Inventione*, Statius, Vitruvius and something of Boethius; other centres may have acquired a collection of Ovid extracts as well as Virgil.[11] With them came representative examples of the distant inheritors of the antique literary tradition, tired perhaps but not dead or entirely despicable: calendar verses and Roman funerary epitaphs.[12] In the same generation, the self-styled *discipuli* of pope Gregory and his mouthpiece Augustine—now described as the *didasculus* and *paedagogus* or *praedicatores* of the English— turned their backs (probably not always for the same reason) on the pragmatism and reasonableness of their mentors and appealed instead to their supposed authoritative pronouncements. A council held at *Clofesho* for the entire southern province decreed that baptism was to be performed and the mass celebrated according to the forms received in writing from the Roman church; the *natalitia* of saints were to be commemorated in accordance with the martyrology of the same church; the canonical hours in monasteries were to include only 'what the custom of the Roman church permits'; the Roman *Laetania major* on 25 April was to be added to the customary rogations; and the *ieiuniorum tempora* (later ember-days) of the fourth, seventh and tenth months were to be observed as at Rome. There do not seem to have been any corresponding decrees in the *acta* of the Frankish synod recently communicated to the archbishop of Canterbury by its president Boniface and one of the inspirations of the *Clofesho* decrees.[13]

[11] *MGH Poet* 1, ed E. Duemmler (1880/1 repr 1964) p 204, where *rhetor quoque Tullius* implies the *De inventione*; *SS Spoleto, 20* (1973) pp 584–5; and, for Vitruvius, Bischoff, *ibid, 18* (1971) p 273. For the transmission of the *de inventione* between the late-eighth and the late-eleventh centuries see [L.] Wallach [*Alcuin and Charlemagne*] (Ithaca 1959) pp 36–7 and *EHR* 75 (1960) pp 490–1.

[12] For the latter see Wallach, pp 193–7, 263–4; but additional examples can be found both in the 'York Poem' and elsewhere in Alcuin's writings. (The epithet *iustitiae cultor* was used as late as 1225 for the epitaph of a bishop of Kotor (Yugoslavia), where it is walled into the cathedral!) The presence of calendar verses in York is a little more speculative: it can be assumed from the presence of the verses beginning *Prima dies Phoebi sacrato nomine fulget* (Riese, [*Anthologia Latina*] 1.ii p 43, nr 488) on fol 107 of London, BL Cott MS Vesp. B VI, that is, in the portion that appears to be at least in part a Mercian copy of late-eighth century York material, which may originally also have included a copy of Riese, 1 ii p 155, nr 680, beginning *Bis sena mensum vertigine volvitur annus* (so A. Wilmart in *RB* 46 (1934) p 49 n2, although his reasons are not very clear). For the later history of these verses in England see below, n 61b.

[13] [A. W.] Haddan and [W.] Stubbs, [*Councils and Ecclesiastical Documents*] (Oxford 1869–78) 3, pp 362–75, caps 13, 15, 16, 18; *Die Briefe Bonifatius und Lullus*, ed M. Tangl (Berlin 1916) nr 78. The supposed difficulty presented by the latter's reference to a letter from pope Zacharias was resolved long ago by Tangl, who saw that this was his nr 77

It was left to the author or authors of the sixteenth and last *interrogatio et responsio* in Egbert of York's *succinctus dialogus ecclesiasticae institutionis*, which I regard as post-747 and not certainly part of the original text (although the opposite case is arguable), to go one stage further and equate Roman and therefore English practice with that which Gregory had had written down.[14]

The question was whether the *ieiunia quatuor temporum*—here apparently referred to collectively by that name for the first time: one of the reasons for supposing that the *Clofesho* decrees are earlier in date—were to be celebrated at the beginning of the month or otherwise, and why they existed. The answer is far more elaborate than to any other of the *interrogationes*, beginning with a disquisition on the significance of the number four which has its closest parallels in Irish exegesis.[15] The most important point in the present context is the responder's defence of the English practice of observing the first of the *ieiuniorum tempora:*

> *indifferenter de primae epdomadae computatione, in prima epdomada quadragesimae;*

and the second:

> *in plena epdomada post Pentecosten.*

Both were prescribed *in antiphonario et missali libro* which Gregory sent to England with Augustine. For the second, however:

> *non solum nostra testantur antiphonaria sed et ipsa quae cum missalibus suis conspeximus apud apostolorum Petri et Pauli limina.*

These statements raise a whole series of problems that have hardly been considered by those who have used them to support one or other theory of the early history of the 'Gregorian Sacramentary'. The language of the *Dialogus*, including the sixteenth *interrogatio*, shows unequivocally that the responder is the (arch-) bishop. Egbert is not known ever to have journeyed to Rome—his pallium was sent to him in 735. A Roman visit by his successor Aelberht, some years before his consecration in 767, is however recorded in two separate poems by

---

(Jaffé nr 2278) of 5 January 747 and not his number 80 (Jaffé nr 2286)—clearly excluding, therefore, an ante-dating of *Clofesho* to 746, as still by Sir Frank Stenton, *Anglo-Saxon England* (3 ed Oxford 1971) p 237.

[14] Haddan and Stubbs, 3, pp 410–13, the *Dialogue* as a whole on pp 403–13, from the unique complete copy in BL Cott MS Vitellius A XII: but *interrogationes* i, ii, xii, dealing with secular legal points, are in the Wulfstan MS, Corpus Christi College Cambridge 265, p 99, which argues that a text survived at York until the eleventh century. For the question of authorship compare below pp 30–1.

[15] For example pseudo-Hieronymus, *Expositio IV evangeliorum*, PL 11 (1845) cols 549 *seq* (531 *seq*), on which see Bischoff, 'Wendepunkte in der Geschichte der lateinische Exegese im Frühmittalter', *MStn*, 1 (1966) pp 240 *seq*.

Alcuin, who accompanied the future archbishop.[16] It can be accepted
that in Rome in the eighth century, and probably long before this
time, the 'ember-days of the first month' were in fact observed in the
week after Quadragesima Sunday (the original 'first week of Lent')
and the 'ember-days of the fourth month' in the first week after
Pentecost.[17] Unlike the Leonine sacramentary and the various Gelasian
sacramentaries, which have rubrics relating to the fasts of the fourth,
seventh and tenth months at the appropriate places, neither the early
Gregorian sacramentary, in any of the forms in which it has come down
to us, nor the eighth/ninth-century *Antiphonaria missarum* refer directly
to the *ieiunii tempora:* the days on which they were observed have to
be inferred from the position of the *sabbata in xii lectiones*. It is possible
that the visiting York cleric—whose sacramentary hitherto had been,
I am sure, some variety of the Gelasian—had done just this, or had
been shown liturgical books with notable differences from those on
which modern reconstructions of the eighth-century papal liturgy are
based. In either case it must remain uncertain whether he had any
textual authority for connecting the books he saw with pope
Gregory.[18]

[16] *Continuatio Bedae, sa* 735, ed Colgrave and Mynors, p 572 and the other references
conveniently assembled by Levison, *England and the Continent*, p 243; Alcuin's 'York
poem', *MGH Poet* I pp 201–2, lines 1457 *seq*, compare 1465 *seq*, which shows clearly
that the customary dating of Alcuin's first continental journey to 767 is several years
too late; *MGH Poet I*, p 206.

[17] L. Fischer, *Die Kirchlichen Quatember* (Munich 1914) is the most comprehensive account
of 'Ember Days' but this is superseded for the period with which we are concerned
here by [G. G.] Willis [*Essays in Early Roman Liturgy*], *Alcuin Club* 46 (London 1964)
pp 49–98; for later Old English practice (interestingly conservative) see [K.] Sisam
[' "Seasons of Fasting" '], *Studies in the History of Old English Literature* (Oxford 1953)
pp 45–60 and esp pp 48–50. For the fast 'of the first month' and its early Roman
observance see esp Willis, pp 59 *seq*, although his use of the Egbert *Dialogue* to
support a Gregorian origin for observance in the 'first week of Lent' obviously does
not appeal to me: and note that the addition of *primi* in the *Liber Diurnus's* text of a
much-quoted letter of Gelasius I relating to ordinations (*form* VI: ed H. Foerster (Bern
1958) p 81)—which Willis p 61 dates, very debatably, 'c560'—would have created
a tautology after the identification of 'the first month' with 'the first week in Lent',
since *ingresso quadragesimali* is separately mentioned. (In fact Gelasius himself and
Symmachus ordained in February, Gregory I *in Quadragesima*, but no subsequent pope
in either until Sergius I ordained in March: *Lib Pont* I, pp 255, 263, 312, 376). Gregory's
introduction of the practice into England is categorically asserted in a short text that
figures among the supplementary material of the 'Leofric Missal' added at Glastonbury
c970 (ed F. E. Warren (Oxford 1883) p 53; another text from an (?) eleventh-century
continental manuscript in Haddan and Stubbs, 3, pp 52–3) and may in fact be not very
much older than this (similarly Sisam, p 49 and n 1).

[18] For the rubrics in the Vatican Gelasian sacramentary see bk I, lxxxii, lxxxiii, ed Wilson
pp 124, 125; bk II, lx, lxxxv, ed Wilson pp 200, 220. I am convinced that the type of

D. A. BULLOUGH

The earliest monastic communities in the British Isles to adapt their liturgical practice to changing Roman norms were not necessarily those of Northumbria; and Mercian and Northumbrian liturgical cismontanism or Gregorianism did not win immediate or wholehearted acceptance in the Frankish Church. A long-neglected passage in what (in the light of a forthcoming critical edition) I gladly accept as 'the First Life of St Brigid', to be dated to the second half of the seventh century, reports the saint as saying that she had heard of changes in the celebration of mass at Rome and was therefore asking for the dispatch of an *ordo* and *regula* to enable her community to celebrate properly.[19] Other saints were, liturgically speaking, more reluctant brides. The type of sacramentary used by Boniface and his circle in eastern Francia has not been finally determined, but however much the experts differ among themselves they seem to be in agreement that it was a book on which the non-Roman imprint was strong.[20] The 'difficult and doubt-

---

mass-book in most common use in the major Northumbrian centres in the early part of the eighth century was one very close to but not identical with 'the Vatican Gelasian' which in some version or versions must have included masses for south Italian as well as central Italian saints (compare [C.] Hohler in [*Tenth-Century Studies*], ed D. Parsons (London/Chichester 1975) pp 61–2 and [H.] Mayr-Harting [*The Coming of Christianity to Anglo-Saxon England*] (London 1972) pp 175–7, 273–4) as well as already commemorating saint Mark on 18 May, for which the fragmentary (Northumbrian) calendar at Munich published by R. Bauerreiss in *Studien und Mitteilungen zur Geschichte des Benediktinerordens* 51 (1933) pp 178–9 provides evidence earlier than any cited by Hohler, p 227 n 79. The rubrics *Sabbato in xii lectiones* are Deshusses pp 139, 232, 277, 299 and Hesbert nrs 7a, 46a, 111, 192. The Monza gradual and Compiègne antiphoner have almost identical prologues (Hesbert pp 2–3, nr oo) which declare that *Gregorius praesul . . . renovans* (Compiègne—*avit*) *monumenta patrum [que] priorum tum conposuit hunc libellum musicae artis scolae cantorum* (Compiègne adds *per anni circulum*) which has sometimes been attributed to pope Hadrian I. But the supposed eighth-century date of the Monza gradual is rejected by Bischoff—'nicht vor dem zweiten Drittel des 9. Jhs.'—*K[arl] d[er] G[rosse]*, ed W. Braunfels, 2 (Düsseldorf 1965) p 250 n 132; and both *renovare monumenta* (at the very least unexpected in the 770s and 780s) and the textual link with John the Deacon's *Antiphonarium centonem cantorum studiosissimus nimis utiliter compilauit; scholam quoque cantorum . . . constituit* (*Vita Gregorii* II 6, PL 75 (1864) col 90)—which has no counterpart in earlier lives—raise doubts whether it is really so early: it was, however, already in circulation in the late 830s when Agobard of Lyons challenged its validity as evidence in his *Liber de correctione antiphonarii* cap 15, PL 104 (1864) col 336. The earliest extent 'Roman' *capitularia evangeliorum* have a rubric *mense primo*—[Th.] Klauser *Das Römische Capitulare Evangeliorum*, L[iturgiegeschichte] Q[uellen und] F[orschungen] (Münster 1935) pp 19, 65, 107—which in the court-school manuscript BL Harl 2788 (a text of Klauser's type Σ) is emphasised by the use of capitals (fol 201).

[19] *Vita Prima* XV cap 89, *ASB* Febr 1 (1657/1863) p 131. For authorship and manuscript evidence see meanwhile S. Connolly in *Manuscripta* 16 (St Louis, Miss., 1972) pp 67–82.
[20] Levison, *England and the Continent*, pp 97, 283–4; H. Frank in *Sankt Bonifatius Gedenkgabe* (Fulda 1954) pp 58–88, Hohler, *ibid* pp 89–93; Mayr-Harting pp 274–5.

Plate 1: *Fons Vitae*, the Godescalc Evangelistiary,
BN MS n. acq. Lat 1203 fol 3ᵛ

Plate 2: Canon Tables
BL MS Harley 2788 fol 11ᵛ

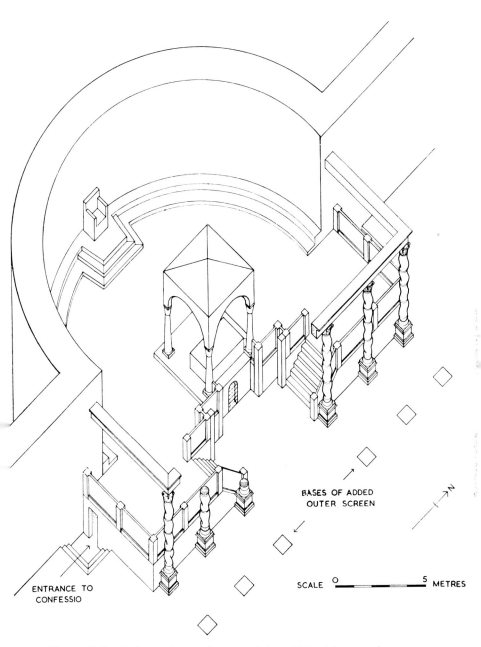

BASES OF ADDED
OUTER SCREEN

ENTRANCE TO
CONFESSIO

SCALE 0 ___ 5 METRES

Plate 3: St Peter's, Rome: the seventh-century shrine, with 'curly' screen-columns.

Plate 4: the Godescalc Evangelistiary,
BN MS n. acq. Lat 1203, fol 4^r

Plate 5: Lorsch Gospels
Bucharest National Library MS Codex Aureus p 36

DESPINIS POSUE
RUNT SUPER CAPUT
EIUS ET HARUNDINEM INDEXTERAEIUS
ET GENU FLEXOANTE EUM INLUDEBANT DICEN
TES AVE REX IUDEORUM; ET EXPUENTES
IN EUM ACCEPERUNT HARUNDINEM ET PER
CUTIEBANT CAPUT EIUS; ET POSTQUAM
INLUSERUNT EI EXUERUNT EUM
CLAMIDEM ET INDUERUNT EUM
VESTIMENTIS EIUS.

Plate 6: BL MS Harley 2788, fol 65ᵛ

Plate 7: Sepulchral inscription of pope Hadrian I, St Peter's, Rome

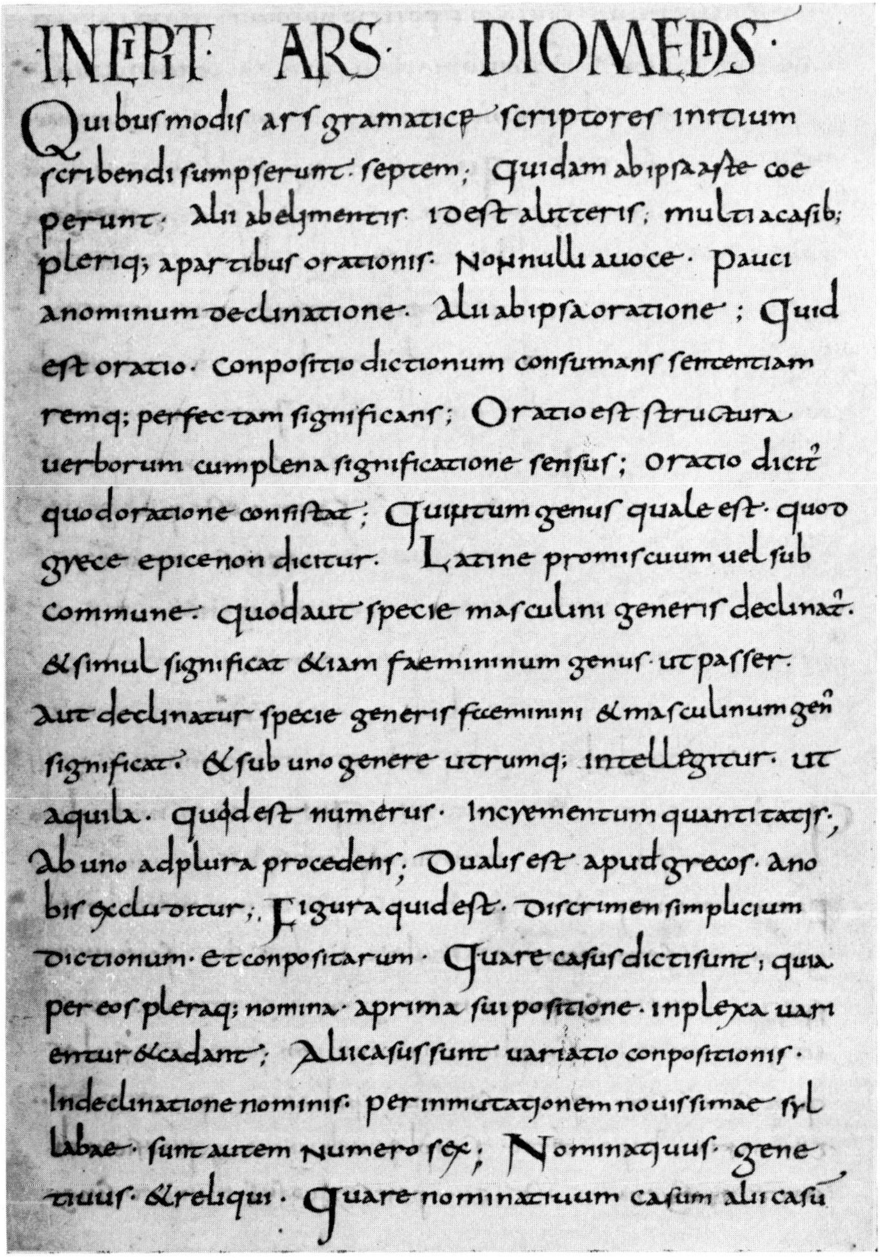

Quibusmodis ars gramaticę scriptores initium
scribendi sumpserunt septem; quidam ab ipsa arte coe-
perunt. Alii ab elementis. id est a litteris; multi a casib;
plateriq; a partibus orationis. Nonnulli a uoce. pauci
a nominum declinatione. Alii ab ipsa oratione; Quid
est oratio. Conpositio dictionum consumans sententiam
remq; perfectam significans; Oratio est structura
uerborum cumplena significatione sensus; Oratio dicit
quod oratione consistat; Quid sit genus quale est. quod
grece epicenon dicitur. Latine promiscuum uel sub
commune. quod aut specie masculini generis declinat.
& simul significat & iam faemininum genus ut passer.
Aut declinatur specie generis feminini & masculinum gen
significat. & sub uno genere utrumq; intellegitur. ut
aquila. Quid est numerus. Incrementum quantitatis;
Ab uno ad plura procedens; Qualis est apud grecos. ano-
bis excluduntur;. Figura quid est. Discrimen simplicium
dictionum. et conpositarum. Quare casus dicti sunt; quia
per eos pleraq; nomina. a prima sui positione. inplexa uari-
entur & cadant; Alii casus sunt uariatio conpositionis.
In declinatione nominis. per inmutationem nouissimae syl-
labae. sunt autem numero sex; Nominatiuus gene-
tiuus & reliqui. Quare nominatiuum casum alii casu

Plate 8: Diomedes, *Ars grammatica*,
Brussels Bibl royale MS II 2572, fol 120

ful treatise' (Levison's phrase) known as the *Ratio de cursus qui fuerunt eius auctores* asserts boldly that several forms of liturgical celebration that differ from those of Rome are equally legitimate because of their very ancient origins. It seems to have been composed in an Italian monastery with a strongly Irish element only a generation or two before the unique surviving copy, which keeps company with some equally bizarre texts, was made in an unidentified north(-east) Italian *scriptorium* during the years either side of 800.[21] The list of lenten and easter stations in Chrodegang's Metz assumes that, as in Rome, the first ember-days will be in the first week of Lent; but by the end of Charlemagne's reign the rule in the Frankish church was that the first two of the *quattuor tempora* were to be observed in the first week of March and the second week of June.[21b]

Was the author of book 1 cap 5 of the *Libri Carolini* (which on any theory of that work's composition was not the Northumbrian Alcuin) deluding himself or simply trying to deceive others when he sought to bolster the claim that the Roman church has to be consulted on all issues involving matters of faith with a 'Little Arthur's History' of the liturgy in the Frankish dominions? Gaul, he declared, from the time of its original conversion

> had always maintained a unity of holy religion with [the Roman church] and differed from it but little—not as touching the faith, that is, merely in the celebration of services: now, thanks to the care and energy of the most illustrious and excellent man (our father of blessed memory) king Pippin and in consequence of the coming to Gaul of the most reverend and most holy Stephen, bishop of Rome, it is entirely at one with it in the order of chanting.

He adds, ostensibly to clinch his argument, that God having more recently given king Charles the kingdom of Italy, he

> eager to increase the prestige of the Roman Church and glad to follow the salutary promptings of the most reverend Hadrian has

---

[21] *Corpus Consuetudinum Monasticarum* 1, ed K. Hallinger (Siegburg 1963) pp 82–91, [text], 79–82 [intro]. The manuscript, BL Cott Nero A II fols 14–45 (*CLA* 186), is the earliest source for the sermon published by Levison (*England and the Continent* pp 302–14) as 'Venus a Man' and claimed by him as Merovingian, although a neglected early-ninth-century manuscript from Reichenau, Karlsruhe *Aug* cxcvi (details in *TRHS*, 5 ser, 24 (1974) p 106 n 19) with a text that is in some respects fuller, strengthens the case for an origin in or near the Alpine regions.

[21b] Klauser, ['Ein Metzer Stationsliste des 8. Jh]' [1930], *Gesammelte Arbeiten* [*zur Liturgiegeschichte* . . .], *JAC*, Erg-Bd 3 (1974) p 28; council of Mainz, an 813, cap 34, *MGH Leg* sectio III, concilia ii, ed A. Werminghoff (Hannover/Leipzig 1906) p 269.

brought it about that many localities of that region which formerly rejected the apostolic see's teaching of chant (*traditionem in psallendo*) now are embracing it with all zeal and with him to whom they already conformed in the burden of faith are now conforming in the order of chant.[22]

Claims made with an eye on Constantinople as well as Rome may be as revealing for what they omit as for what they include; and even the latter can easily be misunderstood. *Ordo psallendi*, like *cantilena*, in the usage of the day embraces words as well as music, structure as well as content (much like our 'a good paper'). The most influential and effective instruments of even an incomplete Romanisation were, on the one hand, those who had received a musical education in a Roman *schola* and, on the other, *ordines* rather than sacramentaries. The Roman liturgical *ordo* was sometimes a quite short and strictly descriptive text, sometimes quite long and with digressions of widely-varying character but in any case designed to show how particular services and ceremonies were currently performed in the papal city or should ideally be conducted. The partial shift of focus in the ceremonial of the seventh and early-eighth-century Roman church from the altar and chancel to streets and *atria*, simultaneously with the expansion of the festal calendar—the two principal aspects of what has been called (somewhat misleadingly) the 'Byzantinisation' of the Roman liturgy—had stimulated their composition: and incidentally provided future historians with evidence of the level of Latin culture in the city at this period which they have been surprisingly slow to exploit. From mid-century copies of the *ordines Romani* were crossing the Alps; and if, as has been suggested, Rome's 'Byzantinised' liturgy made a great impression on the young Charles, it may well be that the reception of the *ordines* in Francia and the responses to them of men like Chrodegang of Metz had played their part in this some years before the king was met at the first mile-stone of the Via Cassia *sicut exarchus aut patricius* in 774.[23]

Of more immediate and measurable importance is the fact that *ordines* lent themselves to conscious propagandising in a way in which sacramentaries and other liturgical books did not. This is most clearly apparent in the shape and content of the collections of *ordines* put

[22] *Libri Carolini*, I 6, ed Bastgen, *MGH Conc* ii *suppl* (Berlin 1924) pp 21–2.
[23] E. Jammers 'Die Musik in Byzanz, im päpstlichen Rom und in Frankenreich', *Abh der Heidelberger Akademie* 1962/1, esp pp 196 *seq*; P. Llewellyn *Rome in the Dark Ages* (London 1970) cap 4, esp pp 123–6; *Lib Pont* I, p 497.

together and circulated in Francia in the second half of the eighth century such as (notably) the so-called 'Collection of St Amand' and the 'Collection of St Gallen'. The second of these, the work of an anonymous monk probably in the sixties or early seventies and certainly widely disseminated in the succeeding decade, has as its core four *ordines* in their original Roman form and a list of the 'canonical' books of the old and new testaments as a guide to liturgical reading, set, as it were, in an appropriate frame—namely, Innocent's letter to Decentius of Gubbio (changed into Capua) as the prefatory text, and an apparently original composition of the compiler as its epilogue. The latter exhorts all the faithful to adopt the practices of the Roman church as indicated in the preceding *ordines*, to identify themselves thereby with its uninterrupted liturgical tradition and save themselves from falling away from the true faith. The Latinity of this propaganda leaflet compares very unfavourably with what has gone before: it has a limited vocabulary, an uncertain orthography, a lack of concern for some of the most elementary rules of grammar. The adapted *ordines* that make up the 'Collection of St Amand' show similar deficiencies. The osmotic effect of liturgical Latin—which, as M. Andrieu remarked, 'is good Latin'—had yet to be felt in Francia in the third quarter of the eighth century by many of those who were most widely read in it. The eventual universal acceptance, if not necessarily universal application, of a 'correct' orthography and syntax had to await the wider dissemination of Christian epigraphic, patristic and pagan Latin texts and an awareness of the norms they presupposed. In the process, the language of the liturgy and of much else became fully accessible only to an educated élite.[24]

Papal Rome, however, had more to offer the Franks than liturgical texts and practices, old-fashioned Latin and a new-style kingship. Already in the seventh century the pilgrim returning home could take with him simple guides or itineraries to the Holy City. Such texts might be combined with separately-originating collections of inscriptions to make a volume like that forming the fourth part of the manuscript Einsiedeln 326; and an earlier (eighth-century) version of this collection may have included a circular map of the city.[25] Their users'

---

[24] Andrieu, *Ordines* 2, pp xlvi *seq*, 137 *seq*; 3, pp 3 *seq*. The substitution of 'Capua' for 'Gubbio' is, according to Wurm, *Studien*, p 124, a feature of the text of the letter added to the so-called *collectio Sanblasiana* in a Corbie manuscript of the second half of the eighth century, Paris BN 3836, here fol 101v.

[25] G. Meier *Catalogus codicum manu scriptorum qui in bibliotheca monasterii Einsidlensis servantur* 1 (Einsiedeln/Leipzig 1899) pp 297 *seq* (with refs to earlier literature);

interest was primarily in the martyrs and other saints associated with the named extra-mural and intra-mural Christian monuments. But the relics of saints were themselves a transportable and exportable commodity, and the Franco-papal alliance introduced a new factor. The *Liber Pontificalis* records in some detail the ceremonial transfer of the body of Petronilla (St Peter's reputed daughter) from the cemetery of Domatilla to an originally secular mausoleum at the south-west corner of St Peter's basilica by pope Paul I (757-67), in furtherance of a plan formulated by his brother and predecessor Stephen. It does not suggest any Carolingian involvement. A letter in the *Codex Carolinus*, however—written, it seems, in the early months of 758—informs Pippin that the baptismal napkin of his daughter Gisla, through whose baptism king and pope are now joined *in vinculo spiritalis foederis*, has been joyfully received into 'the chapel of St Petronilla, your helper, which commemorates your name with eternal praise'. The oldest list of relics in Aachen cathedral includes the name of Petronilla: and while the claim that the list as a whole goes back to the time of Charlemagne must be treated with some scepticism, the presence of relics of hers in association with those of St Martin and St Peter in a dependent rural church of the royal abbey of Lorsch in ?793 argues that they arrived at the palace chapel or its predecessor at an early date.[26]

Other saints made the same or similar journeys across the Alps in the same period, to enhance not only the churches and monasteries of the Carolingian dynasty and of its leading courtiers but also the *gens Francorum*. As the prologue to a new edition of *Lex Salica* expressed it in 763/4:

> This is a people strong through firmness because it was brave. They fought and threw off from their shoulders the heavy yoke of the Romans, and after the knowledge given them by baptism

---

C. Huelsen 'La pianta di Roma dell'Anonimo Einsidlense', *Atti della Pontificia Accademia Romana di Archeologia*, 2 ser, 9 (1907) pp 3 *seq*; R. Valentini, G. Zucchetti *Codice topografico della Città di Roma* 2 (Rome 1942) pp 170-207, compare pp 60 *seq.*
[26] *Lib Pont* 1, p 464, compare p 455; *MGH Epp* 3, ed W. Gundlach (1892 repr 1957) p 511; H. Schiffers *Der Relinquienschatz Karls des Grossen und die Anfänge der Aachenfahrt* (Aachen 1951) pp 81-3; *Codex Laureshamensis*, ed K. Glöckner, 3 (Darmstadt 1936) nr 2966, pp 244-5. For the cemetery-church from which the relics were taken see R. Krautheimer *Corpus Basilicarum Romanarum* 3 (Vatican City 1967) pp 128-34; for the one-time imperial mausoleum see H. Koethe in *Mitteilungen des Deutschen Archäologischen Instituts, Römische Abt* 46 (Rome 1931) pp 9-26. F. Prinz 'Stadtrömisch-italische Märtyrerreliquien und Fränkischer Reichsadel im Maas-Moselraum', *HJch* 87 (1967) pp 1-25 puts the Petronilla-translation and its political implications in a wider context.

they clothed in gold and precious stones the [rediscovered] bodies of the holy martyrs whom the Romans had put to death by fire, sword and wild beasts.[27]

When Fulrad of St Denis, some years before 775, began a new abbey-church that would be a more fitting setting for the relics of Roman martyrs as well as of its patronal saint and adopted—although not in every detail—the T-shaped (transeptal) basilican plan hitherto peculiar to the two Roman churches of St Peter's and St Paul's, Frankish *imitatio* of papal Rome was almost complete. The final stage in the process was the building of churches in which chapels and altars pro-liferated, churches otherwise as different as St Riquier, Aachen, etc., which were *perhaps* thought of as the realisation on a single site of the 'stational-church' pattern of the Holy City.[28]

This archaeological approach to the liturgy of the present—the con-stantly-renewed link between Christian past and future, between things temporal and things eternal—may throw light on some other-wise puzzling features of the manuscripts forming what used to be known as the 'Ada-group' and now universally recognised as products of the Carolingian court both before and after it acquired a stable residence at Aachen.[29] Their distinctive juxtaposition and mingling of elements drawn from Insular and different Mediterranean traditions first occur in the 'Godescalc Evangelistiary', dated on internal evidence between April 781 and mid-783, which set new standards for decorated-book production in Francia. In the context of our present theme, it is tempting but unnecessary to labour the symbolism of a book avowedly inspired by the baptism of Charles's son Pippin, 'born again in the fount' (*fonte renascentem*) and raised from the consecrated waters by

---

[27] K. A. Eckhardt, *Lex Salica: 100 Titel-Text*, Germanenrechte NF (Weimar 1953) pp 88–90.

[28] [R.] Krautheimer's epoch-making 'The Carolingian Revival of Early Christian Architecture' *Art Bulletin* 24 (Providence 1942) repr with corrections in Krautheimer, *Studies [in Early Christian, Medieval and Renaissance Art]* (New York/London 1969/1971) pp 203–54 supposed (cautiously) that the history of the single-apsed, continuous-transepted basilican church north of the Alps began with Fulrad's St.-Denis. The discovery in re-excavation of evidence for an arcade segregating the transept wings from its centre bay deprives St Denis of its priority as a 'copy' of St Peter's, which now therefore belongs to Fulda a generation later (Krautheimer, *Studies*, p 255 and private communication of 20 April 1965): but Fulrad's church still seems to me Rome-inspired. Major Frankish churches as 'Romes' is the notion of A. A. Häussling, *Mönchskonvent und Eucharistiefeier*, LQF 58 (1973) esp pp 88 *seq*, 180 *seq*.

[29] Paris BN MS n.a. lat. 1203: *CLA* nr 681; [W.] Koehler [*Die Karolingischen Miniaturen*, 2: *Die] Hofschule [Karls des Grossen]* (Berlin 1958) pp 22 *seq*, pls 1–12; D. A. Bullough *The Age of Charlemagne* (London 1973) pp 99 *seq*.

pope Hadrian. Textually, it provided the royal chapel with a strictly
Roman gospel-lectionary. The novel image of 'the Fountain of Life',
which immediately precedes the first lection, fuses a traditional motif
of Mediterranean book-art with a summary representation of the
Lateran baptistery where the ceremony took place, an image repeated
in more developed form in the later 'Soissons gospels' (plate 1).
The poem in which Godescalc explains the manuscript's commemora-
tive significance uses a number of short epigraphic formulae but also
incorporates two lines from the epitaph of pope Felix IV and a half-
line from that of pope Boniface III: the poet may have copied them
from the originals or found them in a *silloge*.[30] Two later manuscripts in
the group, the Harley and the Soissons gospels possibly of the last years
of the eighth-century and of c800 respectively, have some extraordinary
canon-tables in which the vertical dividers are not the usual straight
columns but curly figured ones (plate 2). Their identification as repre-
sentations of the columns which until the early sixteenth century
formed a screen in front of the *confessio* of St Peter (plate 3), had to
await the rediscovery of the actual columns (which Bramante had *not*
destroyed) and the reconstruction of their original disposition: although it is almost certain that the exemplar of the Carolingian
artists was an earlier, Roman, gospel-book and not the screen-columns
in situ.[31] The physical preparation, make-up and other codicological
features of these court manuscripts place them unmistakeably in the
insular tradition. Lowe (like Julian Brown more recently) supposes a
connection with Alcuin's move from York to the Frankish court, but
this is difficult to accept on chronological and perhaps other grounds.[32]
Godescalc himself, meaning by this the man who wrote the extremely
skilled Caroline minuscule on the concluding pages of the book, including the poem which tells us his name, manifestly came from the

[30] W. H. Frere, *Studies in Early Roman Liturgy*, 2: *The Roman Gospel-Lectionary*, *Alcuin Club* (Oxford 1934) pp 215–16. P. Underwood 'The Fountain of Life in manuscripts of the Gospels', *DOP* 5 (1950) pp 43–138, esp 44–67, whose interpretation of the Evangelistiary and Soisson gospels (below) picture is in my view not overthrown by Klauser's 'demonstration' (*Gesammelte Arbeiten* pp 314–27, esp 326–7) that the image is that of a ciborium over a *puteus*; *MGH Poet* 1, pp 94–5, with Wallach, p 196.
[31] BL Harleian MS 2788 fol 11v, Paris BN MS lat 8850 fol 7v, Koehler *Hofschule* pls 52, 70; J. B. Ward Perkins 'The shrine of St. Peter and its twelve spiral columns', *JRS* 42 (1952) pp 21–33; E. Rosenbaum 'The vine columns of Old St Peter's in Carolingian Canon Tables', *Journal of the Warburg and Courtauld Institutes*, 18 (London 1955) pp 1–15.
[32] E. A. Lowe, *CLA* 6 (Oxford 1953) p xxvii; T. J. Brown in *La paléographie Hébraïque Médiévale*, Colloques internationaux du CRNS nr 547 (Paris nd [?1975]) p 132.

'Austrasian' region of the *regnum Francorum*; but the minuscule hand in the Soissons gospels betrays some insular influence.[33] Was the guiding spirit, the organiser of the artists and writers responsible for the liturgical and biblical manuscripts produced at Charlemagne's court, after all an anonymous Englishman? Whoever he was, he must surely be credited with the introduction into Carolingian book-art of novel and Rome-inspired themes, which provided it with the most original if ultimately least influential of its several strands.

Godescalc's script, which intermittently betrays its native cursive ancestry by particular letter-forms and ligatures, is regarded by many palaeographers as the first fully-perfected Caroline minuscule. Others believe that that distinction more properly belongs to a minuscule created at Corbie in the time of abbot Maurdramnus (772–80/1)—by an individual, I am sure, and not by a committee—to be the fitting script for a new and unexpectedly critical edition of the old testament and doubtless, in intention, for other Christian books also.[34] Godescalc and his putative collaborators, like the scribes of the Harley and Soissons gospels, employed minuscule only for the supplementary or subordinate parts of their books; it was promoted to being the main text-script, written throughout in gold, in the psalter written by Dagulf and an assistant *c* 793–5, for presentation to pope Hadrian, who unfortunately never saw it.[35] The early Carolingian 'court minuscule', its close relatives and descendants were to be of unique significance in the history of European culture. But in the present context the other scripts used by this select group of scribes are of even greater interest and importance.

The text of the Evangelistiary is written in a stiff, slightly stylised uncial, a script with a long but by no means uninterrupted history as a vehicle of Christian writings; the display pages and some titles are in carefully-seriffed 'square' capitals; rustic capitals are used for an

[33] Bischoff in *KdG*, 2, p 234; Bischoff in [*Medieval Learning and Literature.*] *Essays* [*presented To Richard William*] *Hunt*, ed J. J. G. Alexander and M. T. Gibson (Oxford 1976) p 12.

[34] *CLA* nr 707; B. Fischer in *KdG* 2, p 186. Manuscripts written subsequently (but pre-800) in Maurdramnus minuscule are listed by Lowe *CLA* 6, p xxiv; for the identification of the grammatical texts in Amiens MS 426 fols 1–29 (*CLA* nr 712) see C. Jeudy in *Viator* 5 (Berkeley 1974) pp 78–9.

[35] Vienna Nat bibl MS lat 1861: Koehler, *Hofschule* pp 42–6, pls 31–2, but better (actual-size colour) reproductions are R. Beer, *Monumenta palaeographica Vindobonensia* 1 (1910) pls 17–26. A dating *c*793–5 is supported by the psalter's supplementary collection of creeds: see *Studies Talbot Rice* pp 242–3, 271 (n 88).

entry in the paschal table which is just possibly a later addition.[36]
Rustica is also used for some page-endings in the Harley gospels (plate 6) and for a single display-page in the Dagulf psalter (fol. 67): the calligraphic weakness of this page is the more conspicuous in comparison with the other display-pages which use an exceptionally fine capital with decorated serifs, characterised by the late Stanley Morison as 'Damasine', although the proportions of the letters are (to use his terminology again) 'Gregorian'.[37] In the Vienna coronation gospels, with which an entirely new antiquising art-style reaches the court, very delicate rustic capitals are used for the prefatory material and for the running titles; in later manuscripts of the same group (the so-called 'palace school'), the titles are in an even more accomplished *rustica.* The capitals in the Lorsch gospels, with which the court school closes, probably well on in Louis the Pious's reign, are recognisable descendants of those in the Godescalc manuscript but their proportions are squarer and the distinction between thick and thin strokes more marked (plates 4 and 5).[38]

The notion of a hierarchy of scripts, employing for titles, colophons etc. one or more varieties of capital whose earlier associations were essentially pagan, which was to reach its most perfect development in the mid-ninth-century Tours scriptorium, is adumbrated already in the Wearmouth-Jarrow *Codex Amiatinus*, to go back no further. Here, for example, a somewhat mannered and not very consistent *rustica* is used for titles and *arguments*; and the captions of the latterly much-discussed illustration of the Temple may accurately represent the

---

[36] A marginal entry on fol 125 relating to the year 781 reads, according to F. Piper, *Karls des Grossen Kalendarium und Ostertafel* (Berlin 1858) p 33: *In isto anno fuit Dominus rex Karolus ad Scm Petrum et baptizatus est filius eius Pippinus a Domino apostolico.* I have unfortunately not been able to examine the original. Doubts whether this can be a contemporary statement are raised by the *ad Scm Petrum.* The easter eve baptisms took place, of course, at the Lateran (see, in addition to the other evidence, Andrieu *Ordines,* 3, pp 471 *seq*—*ordo* XXXB, from the 'Collection of St. Amand'); and the easter day station at this period was at S. Maria Maggiore (not clear in the sacramentaries, compare Deshusses p 191, but see the gospel-lectionaries, Klauser, *Capitulare Evangeliorum,* pp 24, 70, 111 and BL Harl MS 2788 fol 202, and *Lib Pont* 1, p 498). But the *ad sanctum Petrum* could be a (hitherto ignored) reference to the Frankish Court's residence there as at Easter 774, *Lib Pont* 1, pp 497–8.

[37] S. Morison, [*Politics and Script*] (Oxford 1972) pp 138, 140, compare 93 *seq,* 126. For reproductions of all the display-pages see above, n 35.

[38] Koehler, [*Die*] *Karolingischen Miniaturen,* 3 pt 1, [*Die gruppe des Wiener Krönungs Evangeliars*], *passim* but esp pls 1, 2–17, 28 *seq; Das Lorscher Evangeliar* intro by W. Braunfels (Munich 1965); Koehler, *Hofschule* pls 99, 105, 109 etc.

capital-script used in Cassiodorus's *Vivarium.*[39] Capitals are used for display-pages and occasionally for titles in a number of continental scriptoria during the last decades of the eighth century. The court and palace manuscripts are distinguished from all other examples by the overall quality and internal consistency of the alphabets and the evidence of the scripts themselves that, as new models arrived at the court, the scribes acquired a growing understanding of their structure and the kind of penmanship required to produce them.

A very different kind of capital, monoline (that is, with a constant thickness of stroke) and with very slight serifs, was used for the epitaph of pope Hadrian sent from Aachen to Rome in 796 or shortly afterwards (plate 7). It is hardly possible that the creator of the alphabet was not familiar with imperial Roman epigraphic capitals which the mason has so closely imitated. The implications of such a gesture may not have escaped pope Leo III, whose predecessor had been guided to the 'correct' doctrine of images by the Carolingian court and who had recently received a letter from Charles giving his view (or Alcuin's) of the proper relationship between king and pope.[40] The danger of assuming that all such examples of *imitatio* were deliberate political statements is, however, indicated by the almost exactly contemporary funerary epitaph of bishop David of Benevento (d. 796), now walled upside down in the cathedral façade and unpublished, which copies the lettering of the arch on Trajan in that city: and this for a man whose documented literary activity is a sermon *in laude gloriose sancte virginis Dei genitricis Marie.*[41] The writer or writers of the capitals in the Godescalc Evangelistiary could conceivably have been influenced in the choice of letter-forms by the markedly classicising lettering of the fifth-century epistyle of the Lateran

[39] Pages with capitals are conveniently reproduced in [E.A.] Lowe, *English Uncial* (Oxford 1960) pl IXA (fol 989v), Lowe, [*Palaeographical*] *Studies* (Oxford 1972) 2, pl 97 (fol 1007v). Excellent reproductions of the Temple picture are in *JBAA*, 3 ser, 32 (1969) after p 8 and pl VII (Bruce-Mitford). For the use of Rustic capitals in eighth-century Wearmouth-Jarrow copies of Bede's *Historia Ecclesiastica* see Lowe, *Studies* 2, pp 450 *seq* and esp p 455.

[40] P. E. Schramm, F. Mütherich, *Denkmale der deutschen Könige und Kaiser* (Munich 1962) nr 12; Morison pp 143, 170–2; *MGH Epp* 4, ed E. Duemmler (1895) pp 136–8, nr 93.

[41] There is a photograph but no text of the David-epitaph in A. Silvagni, *Monumenta epigraphica Christiana saeculo XIII antiquora* (Rome 1943) 4 ii, pl 2; the inscriptions on the arch of Trajan are illustrated in, for example, A. Meomartini, *Benevento, Italia Artistica*, 44 (Bergamo 1909): the letters of the epitaph have more emphatic serifs but only the M diverges significantly from the Trajanic exemplar. For the Marian sermon in Vatican MS lat 4222 see H. Barré, 'La Fête mariale du 18 Décembre à Bénévent au VIIIe siècle,' *Ephemerides Mariologicae* 6 (Madrid 1956) pp 451–61.

baptistery, although the proportions of the latter are squarer. Nor would I exclude an occasional influence from coins, on which seriffed capitals are normal long before the 'imperial bust' coins.[42] In general, however, scribes must be assumed to have sought and found their models in scripts, particularly when they reveal a grasp of their ductus and line-balance.

When Charlemagne was in Rome at Easter 774, he was presented by the pope with a copy of a revised text of Dionysius Exiguus's canon-law collection, the so-called 'Dionysio-Hadriana'. The presentation copy is lost but a considerable number of its descendants are known.[42b] Bischoff's brilliant assembling and evaluation of the evidence for Charlemagne's court library gives proper weight to two pieces of evidence which suggest that probably in 780 the king had sent out a 'round robin' asking that manuscripts of ancient and more recent learning should be sent to the court. An early response was a text of the *ars grammatica* of Diomedes from which quotations of archaic Latin writers had first been eliminated. A later one was Wigbod (of ? Trier) on the Octateuch, a substantial piece of 'scissors-and-paste' exegesis (the best printed text of which masquerades in Migne under the name of Bede), which was to have a surprisingly long and complicated history of copying and adaptation: its mediocre verse-prologue acclaims the large number of books already assembled at the court, *sanctorum renovans patrum conscripta priorum*—apparently the earliest occurrence of *renovare* in such a context.[43] Another text

---

[42] Convenient illustrations of sections of the Lateran baptistery epistyle are in *DOP* 5 fig 24, after p 70. For the lettering of Charles's pre-imperial coinage see the plates in H. H. Völckers *Karolingische Münzfunde der Fruhzeit*, *AAWG* PhK, 3 ser, 61 (1965).

[42b] [F] Maassen, [*Geschichte der Quellen und der Literatur des canonischen Rechts*] (Graz 1870) pp 441 *seq*; Wurm, *Studien* pp 33–5, 41–5 and below, n 53.

[43] Bischoff in *KdG*, 2 pp 45–6, citing *MGH Poet* 1 pp 93–4 (from Paris BN MS lat 7494 fol 123) and pp 95–7. The latter is taken from Martène and Durand's edition of the Genesis section of Wigbod's commentary, repr *PL* 96 (1862) cols 1103–68, from a lost St. Maximin, Trier manuscript. There is, however, another text of the poem, without the *Carolus . . . scribere iussit* inscription, in Brussels Bib roy MS 3222 (seventeenth century: post–1617) where it precedes a full text of the commentary. Hervagius had previously published the whole commentary without the prefatory poem (repr *PL* 93, cols 232–430) from an unidentified manuscript in which it was apparently preceded by the (? early Carolingian) *De sex dierum creatione* (*PL* 96 cols 207–34, from Hervagius). A similar but not identical manuscript is Oxford Bodleian Laud misc 159 (Lorsch, s. IX¹/IX mid) where the text of the Wigbod commentary on fols 29–135 (now defective because of the loss of qu. 'VI'; with a title on fol 29 corresponding to that of the Martène and Durand text, not that of Hervagius) is preceded on fols 1–16ᵛ by the *De sex dierum creatione* and on fols 16ᵛ–29 by the *Exameron Bedae*, that is, Bede's *comm in Genesem* versio prima, bk I. The subsequent manuscript-history of the commentary and the other evidence for Wigbod cannot be considered here.

acquired by the Frankish court in 780/1 was Verecundus of Iunca's *adbreviatium Calcedonensis concilii*, accompanying the *pseudopittatium a Paulino pro Theodosio quondam imperatore dato*, which aroused pope Hadrian's strong disapproval when it was sent on to him.[44] The first two works will hardly have provided models for capital scripts, although the Verecundus and other unnamed patristic texts and the Dionysio-Hadriana manuscript could conceivably have done so. We might be able to see the models used by the later court scribes (although not presumably by the writers of the Evangelistiary) and particularly for their *rustica* if the actual manuscripts survived from the astonishing collection of pagan Latin writers, including Cicero, Statius, Martial and Tibullus, of which a probably partial list was made *c*790 and which after decades of uncertainty can be regarded as securely located at the court, in the period when it was still itinerant. Unhappily they do not, only some of their copies.[45]

We have to fall back on speculating whether the *Vergilius augusteus* (in square capitals) and the *Vergilius romanus* (in rustic) may not also have been in the court library and, if so, at what date; and whether the 'calendar of 354', which was almost certainly available at Louis the Pious's court in the original or in a Carolingian copy, may not already have been there in his father's time. Three purely paleographical points can, indeed, be cited in support of the latter supposition. The curling, elongated serifs of the Filocalian or Damasine letter appear from time to time in late-antique manuscript titlings but never with such consistency or elaboration as in the Dagulf psalter. Already in the Harley gospels as in the Lorsch gospels later the proportions of

---

[44] *MGH Epp* 3, p 600, *Cod Car* nr 70: for the identification of Charles's *missus* as bishop Peter II of Pavia and for the date of the letter see *Atti 4 1967* (1969) p 324. Verecundus's *adbreviatum al excerptiones* were published by J. B. Pitra, *Spicilegium Solesmense, 4 i* (Paris 1858) pp 166–79 from five manuscripts all of which he describes as twelfth-century. The identification of the *pseudopittatium* is more difficult. I am indebted to Dr J. F. Matthews for the suggestion that it is (however unexpectedly) the lost appreciation or obituary of Theodosius the Great by Paulinus of Nola which the latter is known to have sent to Jerome, who seemingly did not think much of it.

[45] Berlin MS Diez B.66 pp 218–19, ed Bischoff in *KdG* 2, pp 59–60, in his introduction to the complete facsimile *Sammelhandschrift [Diez B. Sant. 66]=Codices Selecti*, 42 (Graz 1973) pp 38–9. For the identifiable copies of court-collection manuscripts see esp Bischoff, *KdG* 2, pp 60–2; but for the Cicero Holkhamicus (ex-Cluniacensis, nr 498 in the twelfth-century catalogue), now BL Add MS 47678 see further T. S. Pattie in *The British Library Journal* 1 (London 1975) pp 15–21, with the corrections and amplifications demanded by the leaf at Geneva (Bibl publ et univ MS Lat 169), which was incompletely published by G. Vaucher in *Bulletin du Musée de Genève 1931*, pp 120–4.

the capital letters are more square and the letter-strokes more shaded. Most telling, Filocalus had introduced the practice of putting a reduced-size letter inside a preceding curved letter: the Hadrian-epitaph's most notable departure from imperial epigraphic practice is a V inside a C or a Q and an I in the angle of an L; the Harley gospels have a few examples of this practice; and on some pages of the Lorsch gospels it becomes an irritating mannerism, extended to several other letters. If the source is not the calendar, someone had supplied the court scribes with good copies of Damasine inscriptions, most of which were in Rome's underground cemeteries.[46]

Although the manuscripts it lists are frustratingly invisible, it is worth remaining a little longer with the 'court library catalogue'. It reveals that within a very few years of the arrival there of a text of Diomedes' *Ars grammatica*—which some of the court circle later read only in a much-abbreviated version (plate 8)—[47] full copies were available of a surprising number of the pagan Latin works cited in it together with others that were not: as a result, major works of Latin antiquity which might otherwise have been lost to posterity became available to interested scholars and to the trained scribes who provided them and later generations with reliable copies. Yet they played a surprisingly modest part in the intellectual preparation for the imperial coronation of 800. One of the reasons why it took scholars so long to 'place' the book-list is that most of the works named in it left no recognisable mark on the literature known to have been produced at Charlemagne's court and not much more in the works of court-trained scholars who subsequently pursued an active writing-career in bishopric or monastery. The real impact of the collection was felt one or two generations later: and some texts—the poems of Tibullus,

---

[46] The fullest account of the 'Calendar [or Chronograph] of 354', known only from sixteenth/seventeenth century copies of a lost Carolingian copy, is H. Stern [*Le Calendrier de 354. Etude sur son texte et ses illustrations*], Institut Français d'Archéologie de Beyrouth (Paris 1953): but for its availability at the Frankish court see Bischoff in *Studies Hunt*, p 16 n 3. Good examples of its capital scripts are Stern, pls 1, 4 *seq*, where, however, there are no examples of the 'embraced letter' which may therefore be proper to the inscriptions. The latter are comprehensively treated in A. Ferrua, *Epigrammata Damasiana* (Rome 1942). Court-manuscript examples of the 'embraced letter' are BL Harl MS 2788 fols 68v, 72, 109; Bucharest National Library, 'Codex Aureus' p 36 (probably the most-frequently reproduced page of the Lorsch Gospels); and Brussels Bib royale MS II 2572 fol 1 (repr *KdG* 2, p 49, fig 1), accepting this as a careful post-800 copy of a pre-800 manuscript.
[47] That is, that in Brussels Bib roy MS II 2572 fols 120–5.

for example—remained unread for centuries.[48] Someone not among
the known court scholars, whom Bischoff has recently identified as
an Italian associated with Charlemagne's grammar-teacher Peter of
Pisa,[49] was however sufficiently interested to make the list. Since he
apparently returned to Italy shortly afterwards with the book in
which he had written it, he regarded it, I suggest, as a kind of working
bibliography—a list of the texts, pagan with some Christian poets,
which he as a grammarian would recommend or hope to acquire
for the community in which he taught: although if so he was almost
certainly doomed to disappointment. Collection and list have their
place in the early Carolingian search for and acceptance of norms,
which Rome (in different senses of the word) was uniquely able to
supply.[50]

The previously-quoted colophon of the ninth-century Gregorian
sacramentaries puts this point far more forcibly. There can be no real
doubt that the scribe's *bibliotheca* is that of the popes and not that of
Charles's court, where none the less the *authenticum* became available
to Frankish copyists in the late 780s. Apart from the other arguments
in favour of the first interpretation, it seems to be demanded by the
discovery of the 'sacramentary of Trent', whose basic content is a
Roman Gregorian independent of the Hadrian-Aachen-Cambrai
copy, with an identical colophon—unless (which is unfortunately
perfectly possible) this has been introduced by the early-ninth-century
editor or copyist.[51] Subsequent copies of the colophon, very few and
perhaps none of which can have been taken directly from the palace
exemplar, make sense—of a sort—if *authenticum* had acquired a
generally-accepted new meaning. In origin it was a strictly legal term
for 'original, autograph' and not merely 'unfalsified, genuine'.

[48] Bischoff, 'Hadoard und die Klassikerhandschriften aus Corbie', *MStn*, 1 (1966) pp 49–63;
B. L. Ullman, 'A list of Classical manuscripts . . .', *Scriptorium* 8 (Antwerp 1954)
pp 24 *seq*, here esp p 31. But for knowledge of Tibullus in eleventh-century Monte
Cassino and twelfth-century Orléans (?) see F. Newton in *Transactions of the American
Philological Association* 93 (New York 1962) pp 253–86, esp pp 259 *seq* (Venice Bibl
Marciana MS Z.L. 497) and R. H. and M. A. Rouse in *Essays Hunt* pp 84–5, esp
p 85 n 1.
[49] Intro to the facsimile *Sammelhandschrift* pp 21–3, compare pp 27–30.
[50] For the use of *norma* in early Carolingian and pre-Carolingian texts, compare
Bischoff's sharp critique in *ZKG* 66 (1955) pp 176–80 of J. Fleckenstein, *Die
Bildungsreform Karls des Grossen als Verwirklichung der norma rectitudinis* (Freiburg i. Br.
1953).
[51] Deshusses pp 71–2; K. Gamber 'Der Codex Tridentinus', *Scriptorium* 24 (1970) pp
293–304: the colophon, Gamber p 295, compare Deshusses p 85.

Caesarius of Arles so used it when he placed the *authenticum* of the conciliar acts of 529 in his cathedral archive; and there are isolated examples of its use both in this sense and apparently also as 'norm' (for example, by Aldhelm) in the next two centuries. When, however, Louis the Pious commanded the archbishop of Bordeaux to see to it that all the bishops in his jurisdiction acquired a text of the Aachen decrees of 816, the *authentica* they were to follow was an 'authorised copy'.[52] It could well be that the court had derived both the term and the concept from the *Dionysio-Hadriana* given to Charles in 774 or from the sacramentary sent to him ten or fifteen years later. Three, but seemingly only three, copies of the former bear the inscription:

> *iste codex est scriptus de illo authentico quem domnus Adrianus apostolicus dedit gloriosissimo Carolo regi Francorum et Langobardorum ac patricio Romano quando fuit Romae.*

None of them is early; more important, none of them is among the manuscripts (admittedly not very numerous) which include the dedicatory verses from Hadrian I—verses which show incidentally that Rome's poetic Latinity at this time was not up to its liturgical Latin. A full study of the textual tradition of the collection may well prove me wrong but I incline to the view that in this case the *authenticus*-colophon was added north of the Alps to a manuscript that headed one branch of the later tradition, as part of the concern for authoritativeness that developed at the Frankish court in the years either side of 790.[53] One other aspect of this, which proclaims a link with the idea of 'renewal', is the comprehensive transcription of forty-five years' papal letters to the Carolingians, undertaken in 790/1, when court scribes were also engaged on the book that was to tell the pope the correct doctrine of images. The colophon of what we

---

[52] *Concilia Galliae 511–695*, ed C. de Clercq, *CC* 148A (1963) p 64; *Aldhelmi Opera*, ed R. Ehwald, *MGH AA* 15, p 566 sv; compare *Mittellateinisches Wörterbuch* 1/9 (Munich 1966) sv *authenticus* col 1282; *MGH Conc* 2, ed A. Werminghoff, 2 parts (1906/8) p 460 cap 1.

[53] The text of the colophon in Traube, *ABAW*, 3 Kl, 21 iii p 675 (copied by H. Lietzmann, *Das Sacramentarium Gregorianum* (Münster 1921) p xvi and others) omits *Carolo*: but its presence in at least one of the three manuscript sources, namely Würzburg MS M.p. th. F.72 (second third of the ninth century) is established by B. Bischoff, J. Hofmann, *Libri sancti Kyliani* (Würzburg 1952) p 119. Wurm *Studien*, pp 33–5, 41–5, does not consider the possiblity of sub-groups within the Dionysio-Hadriana group: the earliest manuscripts are apparently Paris BN lat 8921 of s.VIII ex (*CLA* 574; Corbie) and Paris BN lat 11710 of 805 ('zweifellos burgundisch': Bischoff). The latter has the oldest text of the dedicatory poem; for the origin and date of other early examples compare *EHR* 85 (1970) p 96 n 1.

are accustomed to call the *Codex Carolinus* (known only from a mid-ninth-century copy) declares that because letters had already been lost or become illegible, the king *summo cum certamine renovare ac rescribere decrevit:* so that *nullum penitus testimonium* (a powerful word as any writer of legal documents or *vitae sanctorum* knew) *sanctae ecclesiae profuturum* should be lacking to his successors.[54]

The papal response to the Frankish king's assertion of a new kind of authority was: firstly, the commissioning of *imagines regis* for Roman buildings to state another view of the hierarchy of powers; secondly, although only after prolonged exchanges with representatives of the Frankish court, the crowning and acclamation of Charles as emperor in St Peter's during the third mass of Christmas.[55] Rome and its liturgy were thus used to provide legitimation or authentication of a political and not merely a cultural renewal: and this is equally true whether the view is taken (with Schramm but with few other scholars) that the ceremony was one of recognition of a *translatio* of imperial authority that had already taken place or that it was a constitutive ceremony, the moment at which the Frankish king first acquired imperial prerogatives.[56] (In parenthesis, I note that a document that seemed to give additional and weighty support to Schramm's thesis has recently been shown to be a forgery by arguments that would have appealed to Mabillon.)[57] The use of *laudes* incorporating the predicate *augustus* gave the emperor-making ceremony and the new emperor a tenuous link with pre-Christian antiquity. But Kantorowicz's elaborate study of the way in which *laudes regiae* were composed and used in the early Carolingian period brings out the extraordinary, perhaps one can fairly say unique, character of what took place in St. Peter's: this was certainly a ceremony without a written *ordo* and perhaps without any written text.[58] It immediately

---

[54] *MGH Epp* 3, p 476.

[55] Bullough in *Studies Talbot Rice*, esp pp 243–4, 273–5 (where in n 94 'Silvester' should be substituted for 'Constantine'); [P.] Classen ['Karl der Grosse, das Papsttum und Byzanz'], *KdG* 1, pp 569–94 (also separately, with revisions, Düsseldorf 1968); compare Schramm, 'Die Anerkennung [Karls des Grossen als Kaiser]' [1951], *KKP* 1, pp 215–63, and below, n 58.

[56] Schramm, 'Die Anerkennung', last note.

[57] *Codex diplomaticus Amiatinus* 1, ed W. Kurze (Rome 1974) nr 49, ostensibly of April 800.

[58] E. Kantorowicz, *Laudes Regiae* (Berkeley/Los Angeles 1946) esp pp 13 *seq*, 76 *seq*, 101 *seq*. Kantorowicz's thesis that the acclamations were 'constitutive' and the notion of the crowning as a 'signal' to *schola* and congregation (Classen, pp 583–4) are both challenged by K. J. Benz 'Cum ab oratione surgeret. Überlegungen zur Kaiserkrönung Karls des Grossen', *DA* 31 (1975) pp 337–69: Benz's arguments for placing the

47

gave back appropriateness, however, to existing prayers in mass-books which interceded *pro imperatore* and demanded the restoration of these words where *pro rege* had latterly been substituted for them. A good example is the Holy Week prayer (not exactly in the same place in all books) which reads, in the 'Old Gallican Missal' (MS Pal. lat. 493) *pro christianissimis regibus*, in the Vatican Gelasian *pro christianissimo imperatore vel rege nostro*. The latter wording could well have been that of the Hadrianum sent to the Frankish court: but in the Cambrai copy and in almost all ninth- and early tenth-century Gregorian sacramentaries the petition is *pro christianissimo imperatore nostro*.[59]

Frankish churchmen and scholars to whom Rome had given liturgy and scripts, the relics of Christian martyrs and the works of pagan authors or who had been present at the emperor-making ceremony in St Peter's would probably have found it even more difficult than we do to say whether the *renovatio* proclaimed by the *bulla* was 'a new beginning', 'the enhancement of the recent past' or 'the recovery of a more ancient past—true or false'. The next generation of Carolingian scholars saw no contradiction in seeking out, often at the same time and from the same place, Christian and pagan texts and copying or studying them in close association. Yet the most characteristic product of their communities and scriptoria was a very different reflection of the insistence on norms and the raising of standards: it was a manuscript containing a miscellany of texts new and old, often quite short, thought essential for the proper practice of *religio Christiana*—exposi-

---

moment of crowning in the introduction to the mass at an earlier stage than the acclamations are ingenious and serious, without entirely convincing me. Classen, p 583 is rightly critical both of B. Opfermann's edition of the pre-800 *Liturgischen Herrscherakklamationen* (Weimar 1953) p 101 (Montpellier, Bibl de l'École de Méd MS 409), pp 102–3 (Paris BN MS lat 13159) and of Kantorowicz's dating of the first of these to 783–7. A particularly egregious error is (Opfermann p 102) *exercitui Romanorum* where the manuscript reading (BN lat 13159 fol 163ᵛ) is *exercitui Francorum*. The reference to *Rotruda* at the end of the litany on fol 344ᵛ of the Montpellier manuscript is even less relevant to the dating of the preceding *laudes* than Classen and others have supposed since this is clearly a later (early-ninth-century?) addition to the section of the manuscript (fols 331–46) which had been added to the original Mondsee text almost certainly *post* 788 and perhaps very shortly before the death of Fastrada (who is named in the *laudes*) in 794. This later dating of *laudes* incorporating the 'Byzantine' titulature *a Deo coronatus, magnus, pacificus* offers the possibility of a connection with the Frankish court's challenge to the emperor in the east in the *Libri Carolini*.

[59] Sacr Gel I xli (561), ed Wilson p 76; G. Tellenbach 'Römischer und christlicher Reichsgedanke in der Liturgie des frühen Mittelalters', *Sitz Heidelberg*, PhK (1934/35) I, p 52; Deshusses nr 344 and app.

tions and paraphrases of the Lord's prayer or the creed, expositions of the mass and short *ordines*, basic computistic texts, or collections of extracts from various sources on a single theme such as baptism. Surviving examples are doubtless for the most part *authentica*, from which inevitably inferior working copies were made and have long since disappeared; but their strictly practical character is shown by the inclusion in some of them of related texts in the vernacular.[60]

When the English church was faced with its own problem of renewal in the tenth century, Rome had nothing to offer; and when its leaders turned to Francia for help it was that one side of the Carolingian achievement, together with its script, which seemed particularly to meet their needs. The result is a manuscript like Royal 8.C.III, written at St Augustine's Canterbury at the very end of the tenth century: pseudo-Jerome on the musical instruments of the Bible; two *expositiones* of the mass, one certainly and one possibly incorporating material from Alcuin; Theodulf of Orleans on baptism and a text of uncertain authorship commenting on the words of the baptismal office; a confession of faith, partly from Gennadius; questions and answers on various aspects of church order and worship[61]. The major works of pagan Latin literature made a very uncertain return to England. A few lesser works entered in disguise, like the poem of Ausonius on the months which concludes a group of six calendar poems, appearing in this form for the first time, in the later-tenth-

[60] Characteristic examples are: Berlin Phillips MS 1831 (Rose nr 128) (Verona; ?an. 810) where fols 126–7ᵛ bring together (for the first time?) seven computistic or calendar poems of late-antique and more recent origin including *Prima dies Phoebi sacrato* (above n 12) and Ausonius's *Primus Romanas ordiris, Iane, Kalendas* with the non-Ausonian last line *Imbrifer ast mensis tumque December adest* (compare below, n 61b); Munich Staatsbibl MSS clm 14468 (St. Emmeram, Regensburg; an. 821); clm 14510 fols 76–186 (Bavarian; s. IX¹), combined at an early date with the St. Emmeram collection of *ordines*, fols 1–75; Merseburg Domstiftsbibl MS 136 fols 1–21 (? Fulda; c820/40); Vatican MS Pal lat 485 (Lorsch; IX², *ante* 875): for the vernacular texts in all but the first of these see now Bischoff 'Paläographische Fragen deutscher Denkmäler der Karolingerzeit', *Frühmittelalterliche Studien* 5 (Münster 1971) pp 101–34, esp pp 109 *seq*.
[61] The contents of BL Roy MS 8 C.III are adequately indicated in G. F. Warner, J. P. Gilson, *Catalogue of Western Manuscripts in the old Royal and King's Collections* I (1921) p 229. For item 1, pseudo-Jerome, *de diversis generibus musicorum*, which exists in over 60 manuscripts from the early-ninth century onwards, see R. Hammerstein 'Instrumenta Hieronymi', *Archiv für Musikwissenschaft* 16 (Hildesheim 1959) pp 117–34, H. Avenary, 'Hieronymus' Epistel über die Musikinstrumente und ihre altöstlichen Quellen', *Anuario Musical* 16 (Barcelona 1961) pp 55–80 (inclining to a fourth-century date). Item 2 is the *expositio missae* printed by D. Giorgi, *De liturgia Romani pontificis* 3 (Rome 1744) pp 371–92 from Vatican MS Pal lat 485 (above n 60) and by A. Staerk *Les manuscrits latins du Vᵉ au XIIIᵉ siècle conservés à la bibliothèque*

century Glastonbury additions to the 'Leofric missal'.[61b] Norman and more recent critics have given the Old English church too little credit for its development of the vernacular as a medium for the expression of the Christian faith.[62] But in so far as they felt that no church could continue to serve God or man well which ignored a great part of his intellectual and literary heritage, I am sure they were right.

University of St Andrews

---

imperiale de Saint-Pétersbourg 1 (St. Petersburg 1910) pp 181–90 from Leningrad MS Q.v.I. 34, fols 23v–33v (s.IX *ex* from Corbie). Item 3 is Theodulf *de ordine baptismi*, to be added to the manuscripts of this work listed in E. Dahlhaus-Berg, *Nova Antiquitas et Antiqua Novitas*, Kölner Hist Abh 23 (Cologne/Vienna 1975) pp 109–11 and to the apparatus of the prefatory letter in *MGH Epp* 4, pp 533–4.

[61b] Oxford Bodl MS Bodley 569 fols 53v–54: ed F. E. Warren, *The Leofric Missal* (Oxford 1883) pp 51–2; and identically in the prefatory material of Rouen bibl publ MS 16 ('the Missal of Robert of Jumièges'): ed H. A. Wilson, *HBS* 11 (1896) at pp 35–6, Ausonius's poem is as in Berlin Phillips MS 1831 (above n 60). The same version is found in Exeter Cath Libr MS 3507 (s.x²; ?S.W. England) fol 59v, where it occurs as the third of a group of eight calendar poems on fols 58–60v, following Hrabanus *De computo* and preceding *De septem miraculis mundi manu factis* (a copy—or a twin?— of this section is Avranches Bibl publ MS 114 of the twelfth century, the poems on fols 133–4v); and as such it forms part of a notably different Carolingian and post-Carolingian tradition, six of the eight poems occurring in the group of seven in the Berlin manuscript. Note, however, that it is also the version used for the verses terminating each monthly section of the 'metrical calendar' in BL Cott MS Galba A XVIII fols 3–14—R. T. Hampson *Medii Aevi Kalendarium* 1 (London 1841) pp 397–420; J. Hennig 'Versus de Mensibus', *Traditio* 11 (1955) pp 65–90, whose discussion fails to take account of the Berlin-Exeter group—which carries back the history of this adapted Ausonian poem in England at least to the early years of the tenth century.

[62] Bullough 'The educational tradition in England from Alfred to Aelfric: teaching *utriusque linguae*', *SS Spoleto* 19, 1971 (1972) pp 453–94; H. Gneuss 'The origin of Standard Old English and Ethelwold's school at Winchester' A[nglo] S[axon] E[ngland] ed P. Clemoes, 1 (Cambridge 1972) pp 63–83; M. Gretsch 'AEthelwold's translation of the Regula Sancti Benedicti and its Latin exemplar', *ASE* 3 (1974) pp 125–51.

An earlier version of this paper was read to the University College, Dublin, medieval studies seminar in 1975. I am grateful to members of the audience in both places for their comments and criticisms, of which I have tried to take account. The manuscript research in continental libraries on which this paper is in part based would not have been possible without the generous financial support of the British Academy and of the Leverhulme Trust during 1972–3.

ON THE LIMITS OF THE
CAROLINGIAN RENAISSANCE[1]

by JANET L. NELSON

EINHARD tells us that Charlemagne had a special liking for 'those books of St Augustine called *The City of God*'.[2] If only he had told us why. Did Charlemagne demand readings from book 5 on the happy Christian emperors?[3] Or was he, as Ladner suggests, particularly attracted by 'the idea of a society embracing earth and heaven, a society which a man could join through personal renewal'? If Ladner is right, then, he tells us, we should talk not of a Carolingian renaissance—'secondary classicising features notwithstanding'—but of a Carolingian reform 'as just one phase in the unfolding history of the realisation of the Reform idea in Christian history' and specifically 'an attempt to recreate the religious culture of the fourth and fifth centuries'.[4] But *is* Lander right about Charlemagne? I have my doubts: perhaps what he really enjoyed most was book 22's meaty chapter on the resurrection of the flesh or its rattling good miracle-story.

Of course, it is possible to insist on the primary quality of those 'classicising features', yet still deny that there was a Carolingian renaissance. Le Goff has done so precisely because of the lack of creativity in Carolingian culture: 'peut-il y avoir une renaissance avare?'[5] Schramm rejected the biological metaphor of birth and growth as, quite simply, inappropriate to what was happening in Charlemagne's time,[6] apparently discounting the metaphor's Caro-

---

[1] The wording of my title is a deliberate echo of [H.] Liebeschütz, 'Wesen und Grenzen [des karolingischen Rationalismus]', in *A[rchiv] [für] K[ultur]g[eschichte]*, 33 (Berlin 1950) pp 17 *seq*, and [H.] Löwe, 'Von den Grenzen [des Kaisergedankens in der Karolingerzeit]', in *DA*, 14 (1958) pp 345 *seq*.

[2] *V[ita] K[aroli Magni]*, ed O. Holder-Egger, *MGH SRG* (1911) cap 24, p 29.

[3] As implied by [J. M.] Wallace-Hadrill, [*Early Germanic*] *Kingship* [*in England and on the Continent*] (Oxford 1971) p 104. Compare H. X. Arquillière, *L'augustinisme politique* (2 ed Paris 1955) cap iv, esp pp 164, 196.

[4] [G.] Ladner, 'Die mittelalterliche Reform-Idee und ihr Verhältnis zur Renaissance', in *MIÖG* 60 (Vienna 1952) p 54 with n 109.

[5] [J.] Le Goff, *Les Intellectuels au Moyen Age* (Paris 1969) p 14.

[6] [P. E.] Schramm, *K[aiser], K[önige und] P[äpste]* (Stuttgart 1968) 1, pp 27 *seq* and esp 336 *seq*. E. Patzelt, *Die karolingische Renaissance* (Berlin 1923, repr Graz 1965) also rejected the notion of a renaissance under Charlemagne but on other grounds. Schramm dismisses this book too glibly: though many of her arguments must be abandoned

lingian currency and ignoring too the fact that concepts of rebirth and renewal were then, as often in Christian history, intimately linked and even interchangeable[7] (for metaphor after all need follow neither logical nor biological rules). It is not difficult to resist Schramm's appeal that we abandon this renaissance in favour of a bloodless *correctio*.[8] Far more seductive is Riché's suggestion, on the very last page of *Education et Culture* after pages of proliferating renaissances in the seventh and eighth centuries, that there were two Carolingian renaissances—one in Charlemagne's time and another 'true' one in the ninth century[9]. But we should resist any temptation thus to split up a single continuous historical process, intelligible only as such. Let us for the moment accept at least Lehmann's minimal definition of the Carolingian renaissance as 'a rebirth of studies—especially the Latin language and the writings of classical Rome'.[10] In this sense, the deliberate historiographical evocation of the fourteenth-sixteenth century renaissance seems perfectly acceptable. But the question of whether or not the Carolingian renaissance, like the later one, had broader dimensions than this cannot be evaded:[11] it is indeed implicit in the quest for limits.

Three characteristics of early medieval Christian mentality conditioned Carolingian concepts of rebirth in such a way that this renaissance amounted to more than simply 'a rebirth of studies' yet at the

---

in the light of subsequent research, Patzelt was in my view correct in emphasising continuities between the Merovingian and Carolingian periods. But she gave no consideration to law.

[7] See J. Trier, 'Zur Vorgeschichte des Renaissance-Begriffes', in *AKG*, 33 (1950) pp 45 *seq*, and 'Wiederwuchs', *AKG* 43 (1961) pp 177 *seq*. For further references and a fine analysis of the concepts involved here, see the indispensable work of Ladner, *The Idea of Reform* (rev ed New York 1967) and the same author's very useful summary in *RAC* 6 (1966) cols 240 *seq* under 'Erneuerung'. In 'Gregory the Great and Gregory VII: a comparison of their concepts of renewal', in *Viator*, 4 (Berkeley 1973) pp 1 *seq* at pp 24-5, Ladner has some interesting comments on the Carolingian renaissance, expanding the few scattered remarks in *The Idea of Reform*, and promising a full treatment of this subject in a forthcoming book, now eagerly awaited.

[8] Schramm's main reason for preferring this term was that it expressed the *actio* of Charlemagne himself. The false assumption here is that the 'biological' birth-process in the case of human beings excludes any positive exercise of the will. Could Schramm not have cast Charlemagne in the metaphorical role, if not of mother, then of midwife?

[9] [P.] Riché, *Education [et culture dans l'Occident barbare]* (3 ed Paris 1973) p 552.

[10] P. Lehmann, 'Das Problem der karolingischen Renaissance', in *SS* Spoleto 1 (1954) pp 309 *seq*.

[11] I omit any consideration of the political aspects of Carolingian imperial *renovatio*, on which see Schramm, *Kaiser, Rom und Renovatio* (Leipzig 1929) and *KKP*, 1 pp 215 *seq*, and Löwe, 'Von den Grenzen'.

same time was relatively restricted both in intention and in effect.
First, the Carolingian scholars who operated with these concepts did
so within the framework of clerical culture: *eruditio* was to be reborn
in order to serve and promote the ends of Christian *sapientia* as determined by a tiny elite of clergy and monks.[12] Lay involvement was
inevitably passive and at second hand. Second, the habit of thinking
of these same scholars—as, it seems, of their illiterate contemporaries
—was typological. Just as the old testament was fulfilled in the new,
so antiquity was reborn or renewed in christendom: *nova antiquitas et
antiqua novitas.*[13] Like Marx's *Aufhebung*, Carolingian ideas of rebirth
transcended any crude polarisation of 'conservative' and 'revolutionary'. Carolingian scholars perceived their present as fully continuous
with the Roman, and especially the Christian-Roman, past. This sense
of continuity through renewal presents, I think, a noteworthy contrast
to the renaissance ideologies of the fifteenth/sixteenth and, in some
degree, even the twelfth centuries. Historians prone to emphasising the
alleged novelties of the Carolingian age should at least consider the
implications of re-viewing it in Carolingian perspective. Third, and
perhaps especially in this period of Christian expansion, the rebirth
metaphor could have reference to baptism, the *sacramentum regenera-
tionis* through which a person is reborn into the church.[14] In this case,
the rebirth, being a personal matter, could be interpreted more directly in terms of prevailing notions of community. I shall return to
this point below.

The distinct yet related ideas of individual and social or institutional
rebirth[15] have not been neglected by Ullmann, whose great merit in
The Carolingian Renaissance and the Idea of Kingship has been to seek to
locate the rebirth of scholarship in the context of Carolingian society.

[12] Compare W. Edelstein, *Eruditio und Sapientia. Weltbild und Erziehung in der
Karolingerzeit* (Freiburg i. Breisgau 1965) *passim*, esp pp 22 and 85 n 35, some penetrating
criticisms of J. Fleckenstein, *Die Bildungsreform Karls des Grossen als Verwirklichung der
'norma rectitudinis'* (Bigge-Ruhr 1953).

[13] This phrase from the *Libri Carolini* forms the title of a remarkable book by
[E.] Dahlhaus-Berg, *Kölner Historische Abh*, 23 (Cologne 1975) with pp 35 *seq* esp
relevant in the present context.

[14] For the immediate liturgical situation, see Dahlhaus-Berg, *Nova Antiquitas*, pp 94 *seq*
and for the wider background, [W.] Ullmann, [*The*] C[*arolingian*] R[*enaissance and
the Idea of Kingship*] (London 1969) pp 6 *seq* with additional references on p 191, to which
should be added the baptismal liturgy itself, as in, for example, J. Deshusses, *Le
sacramentaire grégorien, SpicFr* 16 (1971) no 1086, p 379: 'Deus . . . qui te regeneravit . . .'
Still valuable is [K.] Burdach, *Reformation, [Renaissance, Humanismus]* (Berlin 1918)
esp pp 37 *seq*.

[15] The distinction was drawn by Ladner, 'Erneuerung', col 262.

'What I fail to understand', he writes, '. . . is how there could be a literary and cultural movement . . . floating in a vacuum, and having no links with the society surrounding it'.[16] What Ullmann argues, if I read him correctly, is that in the 'totalitarian' world of this medieval Christian society, personal renewal implies institutional renewal: those same Christian norms which applied to the baptised individual were, he suggests, applied quite naturally to society as a whole. 'The effect which this Carolingian renaissance in the social sense was to produce in the public field was a "baptism" on the largest conceivable scale'. To the question of how this was achieved, Ullmann answers: by the absorption of 'ecclesiology . . . into the governmental system itself'. For, 'just as the individual, through the juristic effects of baptism was incorporated in, or absorbed by, the Church, in the same way the component groups of Frankish society were absorbed within the corporative union of the Church'. Ullmann goes on to argue that the major instrument of his social and governmental renaissance was 'the law applicable to the whole of Frankish society'; and in subsequent parts of the book, he attempts to show how Carolingian legislation aimed at the suppression of 'Frankish or Germanic or any other naturally grown habits and usages' by 'the laws of God'. Ullmann's novel approach seems to me to focus upon a vital question, and his concern with law points to a fruitful source of answers. In what follows, however, viewing the problem from a different stand-point and Carolingian law in a different perspective, I reach some different conclusions.

I begin, I confess, with a nagging doubt as to whether in the Carolingian period individual Christian renewal was so significant an ideological theme as to imply social renewal either in theory or practice. Ullman rightly asks: 'are cultural phenomena not at all times intimately and indissolubly linked with society?'[17] Yes indeed, but the links may be complex and indirect, as, for instance, when a cultural renaissance occurs in a time of social and political disintegration: scholars have sometimes been known to inhabit ivory towers. Moreover, the institutionalisation of governmental ideas may be more or less complete, or scarcely realised at all. In any given case, we need to know what institutions are available[18] and how far these are functionally

[16] *CR*, p 5. My further quotations are from pp 8, 9, 11 and 22 of the same work.
[17] *CR* p 5.
[18] Their importance in relation to law is stressed by E. Forsthoff, 'Zur Problematik der Rechtserneuerung', in *Naturrecht oder Rechtspositivismus?*, ed W. Maihofer (Darmstadt 1966) pp 83 *seq.*

autonomous with respect to other social phenomena. In the present case, we have to ask whether Charlemagne and his church (including both clerical and monastic orders) were really in a position to seek, let alone effect, 'the transformation of contemporary society in accordance with the doctrinal and dogmatic notions of Christianity, as it was seen in patristic lore'.[19] I am enough of a traditionalist to claim that the renaissance-idea of the Carolingian period had rather severe limits. I shall now try to delineate some of them, limiting myself first to the area of law.[20]

If rebirth and renewal ideas were used fairly often by Carolingian writers in reference to learning and religious culture, they were scarcely ever applied to law.[21] What did occasionally appear were notions of emending or correcting the law.[22] Now these terms are certainly found in the vocabulary of Christian renewal ideology. But it was not from thence that they were brought to bear on Carolingian law. Rather, we have here to deal with two other sources, both legal and both of directly political relevance. First, the idea that a monarch's function was to codify and correct the law of his people stems from late Roman practice as transmitted through the sub-Roman successor-kingdoms.[23] The creation of Charlemagne's empire, in gaining direct access to the lively Roman-legal traditions of Lombard Italy and Visigothic Spain to some extent revived this influence.[24] Thus when Charlemagne stated his desire to remedy defects in the law, he followed in the footsteps of Rothari and Recceswinth.[25] Church

---

[19] Ullmann, *CR*, p 7.

[20] In arguing that law was an integral part of this renaissance, Ullmann, *CR*, though on somewhat different premises, takes the same view as [F.] Heer, 'Die "Renaissance"-Ideologie [im früheren Mittelalter]', in *MIÖG*, 57 (1949) pp 48–9.

[21] Heer, 'Die "Renaissance"-Ideologie', p 49, nn 67 and 69, cites two poetic examples. I am aware of two other references to *leges renovare*: Cathwulf, *MGH Epp* 4, p 50, and the mid-ninth century *Vita Lebuini Antiqua, MGH SS* 30, p 793, referring to the assemblies of the eighth-century Saxons: 'renovabant leges et praecipuas causas adiudicabant'. For the late classical background to this idea, see Ladner, 'Erneuerung', col 263.

[22] For example Einhard, *VK* cap 29, p 33; *MGH Cap* 1, no 33, p 92. But such expressions remained uncommon: see [G.] Köbler, [*Das*] *Recht* [*im frühen Mittelalter*] *Forschungen zur deutschen Rechtsgeschichte* 7 (Cologne 1971) p 225.

[23] [E.] Ewig, '[Zum christlichen] Königsgedanken [im Frühmittelalter]', in *Das Königtum. Vorträge und Forschungen* 3 (Konstanz 1956) pp 32 *seq*; Wallace-Hadrill, [*The*] *Long-haired Kings* (London 1962) pp 37 *seq*, and *Kingship*, pp 32 *seq*.

[24] For Italy, see below pp 57–8 with n 33; for Visigothic law in the Carolingian realms, see Ullmann, *CR*, p 81 with n 2.

[25] *Edictum Rothari*, ed F. Beyerle, *Die Gesetze der Langobarden* (Weimar 1947) prologue, p 16; Leovigild: Isidore, *Historia Gothorum*, cap 5, *MGH CM* 2, p 288;

councils of the sixth and seventh centuries had also adopted the emendation terminology of Roman law,[26] but such ecclesiastical models were, I think, of only secondary importance to a Carolingian practice representing continuity with the earlier gentile *regna*, and not something peculiar to the Carolingian renaissance.

Second, Charlemagne also inherited a specifically Frankish tradition of hegemonial imperialism enshrined in the laws issued by successive Merovingian kings for the *gentes* over whom they held sway.[27] Charlemagne was too shrewd to neglect so politically-useful a legacy: his mental sustenance included, after all, alongside Augustine's books, tales of the deeds of his predecessors.[28] Einhard seems to imply a causal link between Charlemagne's reception of the *imperiale nomen* and his concern with gentile legislation.[29] But why assume merely Roman imperial influence here?[30] Charlemagne may have been at least as strongly imbued with a *non*-Roman imperial idea. He attempted no more than had those Merovingians who 'added to the laws what had to be added . . . modified them in accordance with the *lex christianorum* . . . and gave a written law to each *gens*'. The words are those, not of any representative of the Carolingian

---

Recceswinth: *Lex Visigothorum Rec.* I, 1, 9, *MGH Leg* 1, 1, p 40, and Erwig, *ibid* 2, 1, 1, p 45. Compare Clothar II's *Edictum, MGH Cap* 1, no 9, p 20. The ultimate model was the preface to Justinian's Nov vii, referring to one law 'quae priores omnes et renovet et emendet et quod deest adiciat et quod superfluum est abscidiat'.

[26] Köbler, *Recht*, pp 215 seq.

[27] For interpretations along these lines, compare Wallace-Hadrill, *Long-haired Kings*, pp 213–14, and 'A background to St Boniface's mission', in *Early Medieval History* (Oxford 1975) p 139; and H. Wolfram, 'The shaping of the early medieval principality', in *Viator*, 2 (1971) p 45. On the 'Rome-free imperial idea', C. Erdmann, *Forschungen zur politischen Ideenwelt des Frühmittelalters* (Berlin 1951) esp pp 22 seq remains fundamental. See now also E. E. Stengel, *Abhandlungen und Untersuchungen zur Geschichte des Kaisergedankens im Mittelalter* (Cologne 1965) pp 260 seq, 289 seq, and Schramm, *KKP*, 1, pp 250 seq, both of whom, however, underestimate the significance of pre-Carolingian gentile-imperial ideas. Löwe, 'Von Theoderich dem Grossen zu Karl dem Grossen', in *DA*, 9 (1952) p 367, n 54 and 383 seq provides a valuable corrective, though he has relatively little to say on Merovingian sources. I hope to deal elsewhere with the evidence, legal, liturgical and otherwise, for a Merovingian concept of gentile, hegemonial, imperial kingship.

[28] Einhard, *VK* cap 29, p 33.

[29] *Ibid*: 'Post susceptum imperiale nomen cum adverteret multa legibus populi sui deesse . . . cogitavit quae deerant addere . . .'

[30] So, [F.] Ganshof, *Recherches [sur les Capitulaires]* (Paris 1958) pp 98 seq, and 'Charlemagne's programme of imperial government', in *The Carolingians and the Frankish Monarchy* (London 1971) pp 55 seq.

renaissance, but of the prologue to the *Lex Baiuvariorum*.[31] Charlemagne's abortive efforts at further codification of gentile laws marked no new departure, but the end of a road.

The fact that most Carolingian capitularies cannot be classed as legislation at all may be linked with the feebleness of Roman-legal traditions in this period. Previous barbarian legislation, from the fifth through to the eighth century, had been far more open than the Carolingians' to Roman-legal influence,[32] whether through the persistence within the regna of *romani*, that is, men living under, and in some cases learned in, Roman law in its late-imperial form, or through access, direct or indirect, to the surviving practice of Roman law in Italy.[33] By comparison, Carolingian Gaul was poverty-stricken: the study of Roman law was never included in Charlemagne's programme of *correctio* nor in ninth-century curricula.[34] Certainly Roman-legal texts were copied in Carolingian monasteries (though often simply by way of scholarly exercises) and sometimes used by churchmen to defend ecclesiastical privileges. But all this hardly adds up to a 'renouveau des études juridiques'.[35] And if we leave the cloister to consider the secular legal practice of the Carolingian period, we are confronted not with renewal but with a process of change continuous from the sixth and much accelerated from the early eighth century, whereby new economic and social conditions imposed legal usages very different from those envisaged even in the most 'vulgar' Roman law.[36] In those regions of the empire inhabited by *romani*, despite the

---

[31] Ed E. Schwind, *MGH Leg* 1, 1, pt 2, p 202. (The edition of K. Beyerle has unfortunately been inaccessible). For the date—probably seventh-century—see F. Beyerle, 'Die süddeutschen *Leges* [und die merowingische Gesetzgebung]', in *ZRG GAbt* 49 (1929) pp 373 *seq*, and 'Die beiden süddeutschen Stammesrechte', in *ZRG GAbt* 73 (1956) p 124.

[32] See Riché, *Education*, pp 489 *seq* (Alamannia and Bavaria), 387 *seq* and 455 *seq* (Lombard kingdom). The more 'Romanising' laws of the Burgundian and Gothic kingdoms are contrasted with those of the Franks, Lombards and Anglo-Saxons by [G.] Astuti, 'Note critiche [sul sistema delle fonti giuridiche nei regni romano-barbari dell'occidente]', in *Atti della Accademia Nazionale dei Lincei*, 377, 8 ser 25 (Rome 1970) pp 319 *seq*, at 325 *seq*. For a similar contrast on general grounds, see L. Musset, *The Germanic Invasions, 400–600* (London 1975) pp 67 *seq* and 211.

[33] See Riché, 'Enseignement [du droit en Gaule du VIe au XIe siècle', in *Ius Romanum Medii Aevi* 5b, bb (Brussels 1965), p 15, and the interesting suggestions of [D. A.] Bullough, 'Europae Pater: Charlemagne and his achievement in the light of recent research', in *EHR*, 85 (1970), pp 92 *seq*.

[34] Riché, 'Enseignement', pp 16 *seq*.

[35] *Ibid* p 16.

[36] [J.] Gaudemet, 'Survivances [romaines dans le droit de la monarchie franque du Ve au Xe siècle]', in *Tijdschrift voor Rechtsgeschiedenis*, 23 (Harlem 1955) pp 149 *seq*,

persistence of Roman-legal formulae in many documents, basic transactions of property and marriage increasingly came to be regulated —as elsewhere—by the custom of an evolving feudal society. This trend pre-dated and underlay changes in the procedures of public courts generalised under Charlemagne and his successors.

Ganshof has recently shown that not a single Roman-law text was used in its entirety in Charlemagne's capitularies, and that even in the ninth century there is very little sign of Roman law influencing the secular legislation of Louis the Pious or Charles the Bald.[37] These facts are intelligible in the light of Carolingian legislative methods: legal problems would be brought up by provincial administrators and judges to be discussed at the great assemblies and dealt with according to whatever legal expertise was available.[38] If *romani* were among those consulted, bits of Roman legal procedures and even substance might be adopted and given general currency. But this was a product of practical need and eclectic political power, and it was realised by practising law-men. There is nothing to suggest any conscious or systematic Romanising policy planned and executed by ecclesiastics for whom law, to be valid, had to be Roman and Christian. In canon law where deliberate effort towards standardisation *was* made, we now know that great diversity persisted throughout the ninth century and beyond.[39] How much more so in the realm of secular law, where legislative and administrative decisions were actually shaped very often by laymen. In 802 when Charlemagne thought to revise the gentile laws, 'he called together the dukes and counts with the rest of the

---

esp p 205: 'Si la renaissance carolingienne se traduit par des références plus fréquent plus nombreuses et plus variées . . . aud droit romain *dans les oeuvres de doctrine et dans les collections canoniques*, cette période semble au contraire correspondre à une regression due rôle effectif du droit romain *dans la pratique*'. (My stresses.)

[37] 'Droit romain [dans les capitulaires]', in *Ius Romanum Medii Aevi*, pt i, 2b, cc α–β (1969), pp 14 *seq.*

[38] The evidence is given, though not fully appraised, by Ganshof, 'Droit romain', and *Recherches*, esp pp 22 *seq*, 47 *seq*. The similarly ad hoc ways by which capitulary-texts were transmitted are indicated in W. A. Eckhardt, *Die Kapitulariensammlung Bischof Ghaerbalds von Luttich* (Göttingen 1955); reviewing this book, Wallace-Hadrill, *Tijdschrift voor Rechtsgeschiedenis*, 24 (1956) p 472, notes that texts had to be translated from the vernacular into Latin, and then back again. On the nature of the capitularies, and on other matters, I am grateful to Rosamond McKitterick (née Pierce) for valuable criticisms of an earlier version of this paper.

[39] See R. Kottje, 'Einheit und Vielfalt des kirchlichen Lebens in der Karolingerzeit', in *ZKG*, 76 (1965) pp 323 *seq*, and now H. Mordek, *Kirchenrecht und Reform im Frankenreich* (Berlin 1975) esp pp 151 *seq*.

Christian people [that is, the magnates] along with the legislators'[40]—
and these *legislatores* (the term itself seems significant) were none other
than the laymen learned and practised in the secular laws.[41] Such men
were often, no doubt, imbued with notions of Christian ethics presented
to them by priests.[42] But the church's teachings were at once too
specific and too vague to have much direct relevance to the legal life
of every day. Riché has observed a widespread anxiety on the part of
conscientious laymen—just those, one could add, who were involved
in jurisdiction—as to how far 'carnal men' could follow what looked
like clerics' rules.[43] It is hard to believe that such anxieties were dis-
pelled by the often banal prescriptions of an Alcuin or a Jonas. Lay
society continued to operate with its own values. The fundamental
ethic of *fidelitas* pre-existed the church's concern with it, and
remained despite ecclesiastical glossing a largely secular affair.[44]
Carolingian theology was in some degree laicised as it absorbed and
reproduced the features and vocabulary of the *comitatus*.[45] On the
other hand, with the obvious exception of legislation specifically
concerned with the clergy and the monks, Carolingian capitularies
show a Christian influence that, far from being attributable to the
Carolingian renaissance, is a longstanding feature of gentile law: the

[40] *Annales Laureshamenses, sa* 802, ed G. Pertz (Hanover 1826), *MGH SS* 1, p 38.

[41] The term *legislatores* here exactly reflects the character of early medieval law and
law-making: see below p 64. These men seem to be identical with those termed
iudices in other texts: see Ganshof, *Recherches*, p 22 and *Carolingians*, p 69 and p 156 n 45
for *iudices* (in southern Gaul) as '*scabini* under another name'. Compare *Lex Baiuv*,
prol, p 201: 'viri sapientes qui in regno . . . legibus antiquis eruditi erant', presumably
identical with the *judices*, ibid XVII, 5; and *Edict. Rothari*, cap 386, p 93: 'iudices et
antiqui homines' have helped to compile the code. Law-men of this type seem to me
meant by the phrase *legis doctores* in a judgement of Pippin III shortly before 751,
ed J. Tardif, *Monuments historiques* (Paris 1866) no 54, p 45. Riché, 'Enseignement',
p 14, and 'Le renouveau culturel à la cour de Pépin III', *Francia*, 2 (Munich 1975), p 64,
implies that the reference here may be to Roman law. But the passage as a whole reads:
'. . . sicut proceres nostri seu comitis palacii nostri vel *reliqui* legis doctores
judicaverunt', (my stress) which suggests a *lex*, that is *Lex Salica*, with which laymen
normally associated with Frankish judgement-finding would be familiar.

[42] On Carolingian 'Laienspiegel', with rich bibliographical data, see H. H. Anton
Fürstenspiegel und Herrscherethos in der Karolingerzeit, Bonner Historische Forschungen 32
(Bonn 1968) pp 83 *seq* and 213.

[43] *[La] Vie Quotidienne [dans l'Empire Carolingien]* (Paris 1973) pp 99 *seq*.

[44] See [W.] Schlesinger, *Beiträge [zur deutschen Verfassungsgeschichte des Mittelalters]*
(Göttingen 1963) 1, pp 33 *seq*, 316 *seq*.

[45] D. H. Green, *The Carolingian Lord* (Cambridge 1965), esp pp 115 *seq*, 288 *seq*, shows
that this process long antedates the Carolingian period, but in caps 10 and 11 argues
for major developments precisely then. See now also Wallace-Hadrill, 'War and
Peace in the early Middle Ages', in *Early Medieval History*, esp pp 31 *seq*.

JANET L. NELSON

historian impressed by the Augustinian overtones of Carolingian *pax*
and *iustitia*[46] should be no less appreciative of these same ideas on the
part of a Gundobad or a Clothar II.[47]
Did the Carolingian renaissance then have no effect on secular
legal practice or—which is something different—on ideas about
secular law? Its direct effect was significant in practical terms in
only one sense: Carolingian scholars copied and preserved the
texts of the laws, and ecclesiastical institutions in using these texts
(as, for instance, St Gall in a whole series of land cases appealed to the
Lex Alamannorum)[48] contributed to their continuing vitality. The
formal characteristics of later Carolingian capitularies owed much to
the improved latinity achieved through the renaissance of scholarship.
On the other hand, a tendency to rely on the written word in legal
procedures, though it probably increased simply through the readier
availability of scribes, was already common in the vulgar private law
of the fifth century and had shown continuous if patchy development
in the practice of the barbarian kingdoms.[49]
Turning now to ideas about law, I briefly consider three important
areas in which there seems little evidence of change occurring as a
consequence of the Carolingian renaissance. Firstly: both lay and
clerical ideas about the making of secular law continue to display that
same creative ambiguity which is embodied in the barbarian *leges*
themselves: the law is the people's but the king gives it authority.
Volksrecht oder Königsrecht[50] is a non-issue, since where the king is a
Volkskönig, law is at once gentile and royal. For Charlemagne, a

---

[46] So, Ewig, 'Königsgedanken', pp 63 *seq*, and 'La monocratie dans l'Europe occidentale',
in *Receuils Jean Bodin* 21 (Brussels 1969), p 89. That some new conception of *pax* led
Charlemagne into a frontal attack on feud is rightly questioned by Wallace-Hadrill,
Long-haired Kings, pp 145 *seq*, and *Kingship*, pp 107 *seq* (where his own immediately
following remarks imply the inaccuracy of the designation of the *Admonitio Generalis*
(789) as 'legislation against feud').
[47] *Lex Burgundionum*, ed de Salis, *MGH Leg* 1, 2, 1, pp 30–1; *Edictum Clotharii*, in *MGH
Cap* 1, no 9, pp 22–3.
[48] Köbler, *Recht*, p 99.
[49] L. Stouff, 'La formation des contrats par l'écriture dans le droit des formules du Vᵉ au
XIIᵉ siècle', in *Nouvelle Revue Historique du Droit Français et Etranger*, 11 (Paris 1887),
esp pp 259, 274 *seq*; Gaudemet, 'Survivances', pp 185 *seq*, 199 *seq*.
[50] See, with further references, [R.] Buchner, [*Die*] *Rechtsquellen* (Weimar 1953)
[*Beiheft* to W. Wattenbach and W. Levison, *Deutschlands Geschichtsquellen im Mittelalter*.
Vorzeit und Karolinger], pp 4 *seq*, suggesting *Stammesrecht* as preferable to either of
these terms. F. Beyerle, 'Die süddeutschen *Leges*', pp 388 *seq*, asserts a sharp
distinction between *Weistum* and *Satzung*, but shows that this cannot be simply aligned
with the *Volksrecht/Königsrecht* division. Compare also his 'Über Normtypen und
Erweiterungen der *Lex Salica*', in *ZRG GAbt* 44 (1924) pp 216 *seq*, where this same

60

On the limits of the Carolingian renaissance

public criminal was *infidelis noster et francorum*.[51] Where Ullmann classes the capitularies of 'the Carolingian age' all together as 'royal instruments'[52] indicative of a 'descending theme of government', Ganshof traces a shift from the 'absolute' royal legislative power of Charlemagne and (until 830) Louis the Pious to the 'conditional' power of Charles the Bald who promulgated laws with the *consensus populi*.[53] Both these views seem to me over-schematic: is not the truth of the matter that the *consensus* element in legislation was there, if in a subordinate role, all along? The shift occurred not in the realm of public law but in that of politics. Under Charlemagne, and still more clearly under Charles the Bald, the *verbum regis* was spoken only after consultation with those who were to hear and obey it. And it had to be *heard*: this was a face-to-face society organised by rules whose legitimacy depended on (amongst other things) their public oral pronouncement.[54] If Charlemagne, on one occasion at least, denied this, he was up against the conviction of his far-away Italian subjects that *capitula legibus addenda* were validly-made only when the emperor in person issued them in a formal *adnuntiatio* to the Italians themselves.[55] The sense of participation on the part of the *populus* is understandable. Were the learned cleric's views essentially different? Even Hincmar, more interested in the relation of kingship to law than any other Carolingian thinker, and himself well enough versed in canon and Roman law, had relatively little to say to kings about *leges condere* compared with his intense concern that they should *leges servare*.[56] Hincmar might have had a hand in drafting the very capitulary which mentions aristocratic *consensus* alongside royal *constitutio*;[57] and he it was, so Devisse plausibly suggests, who brought

---

non-alignment is clear. Schlesinger, *Beiträge*, p 30, observes that 'Königliche Herrschaft und adlige Herrschaft waren ursprunglich ebensowenig unterschieden wie Königsrecht und Volksrecht'. I am suggesting that the distinction remained blurred *in practice* in the Carolingian period.

[51] *MGH Cap* 1, no 67, p 156.   [52] *CR* pp 30 and 10.

[53] *Recherches* pp 29 *seq.*

[54] A. Dumas, 'La parole et l'écriture dans les capitulaires carolingiens' in *Mélanges Halphen* (Paris 1951) pp 209 *seq.*

[55] *MGH Cap* 1, no 103, p 212. The episode is discussed by Ganshof, *Recherches*, p 21.

[56] J. Devisse, *Hincmar et la Loi* (Dakar 1961). See also my forthcoming article on Hincmar's legal and political thought in *EHR*.

[57] Edict of Pîtres (864), in *MGH Cap* 2, no 273, p 313: '. . . lex consensu populi et constitutione regis fit . . .' Compare Hincmar, *De Ordine Palatii*, cap 8, ed V. Krause, *MGH Cap* 2, p 520: 'reges capitula . . . generali consensu fidelium suorum . . . promulgaverunt'. For Hincmar's presence in 864, see H. Schrörs, *Hinkmar, Erzbischof von Reims* (Freiburg-i.-Breisgau 1884) pp 232, 573.

into the vocabulary of west Frankish public law the pregnant phrase *consilium et auxilium*, already replete with feudal-governmental meaning.[58] But then Hincmar was well attuned to the sentiments of his lay fellow-*fideles*: a stickler for canon law when a Lotharingian royal divorce threatened the west Frankish realm, he practised a quite Nelsonian collusion when it came to accommodating aristocratic interests in another royal divorce affair.[59]

Secondly: the personality principle continued throughout the ninth century fundamental in secular law.[60] The laity's attachment to it can be inferred from their insistence on repeated royal assurances that the *lex unicuique competens* would be preserved.[61] Few scholar-clerics have left any record of their views, which could suggest that they simply accepted current aristocratic assumptions.[62] Such acquiescence is implicit in the fact that Hincmar assumes the personality of laws, and actually extends the principle to the canons as 'the tribal law of the priesthood',[63] even when he reminds that such laws will not apply at the final divine tribunal or insists that excessively cruel *lex saeculi* should be suppressed

---

[58] Devisse, 'Essai sur l'histoire d'une expression qui a fait fortune: Consilium et auxilium au IXe siècle', in *Moyen Age*, 23 (Paris 1968) pp 179 *seq.*

[59] See the subtle and plausible argument of C.-R. Brühl, 'Hinkmariana II. Hinkmar im Widerstreit von kanonischem Recht und Politik in Ehefragen', in *DA*, 20 (1964) pp 48 *seq.*

[60] Buchner, *Rechtsquellen* pp 4 *seq*; Astuti, 'Note critiche', pp 325 *seq*, with rich bibliography of recent literature at p 333, n 18. Gaudemet, 'Survivances', p 158, n 23, observes that in the edict of Pîtres of 864 (see above n 57) the concept of gentile law appears to have a territorial rather than a personal sense. Compare the development from gentile to regional (and pseudo-gentile) solidarities sketched by Ewig, 'Volkstum und Volksbewusstsein im Frankenreich des 7 Jhdts', in *SS Spoleto* 5 (1958) pp 587 *seq.* Such a gradual evolution of territoriality out of the personality of laws seems more plausible than the sharp break alleged by Schlesinger, *Beiträge*, p 44. But I can see no evidence of any Carolingian attempt to unify the law over the whole realm such as Devisse, 'Essai', p 181, n 11, suggests might be ascribed to Charles the Bald. This is not to deny the influence of Visigothic legislation in other respects on ninth-century clerics: see Ullmann, *CR*, p 81 with n 2.

[61] Thus, the *Pactum* of Coulaines (843), *MGH Cap* 2, no 254, p 253 *seq.* Compare also *ibid* pp 281, 296, 330, 339, and very similar expressions of the same principle in the Ostrogothic and Merovingian realms: Cassiodorus, *Variae* VII, 3, in *MGH AA* 12, p 203, and *Passio Leodegarii*, in *MGH SRM* 5, p 289 (here the *lex vel consuetudo* has become linked with the *patria*).

[62] For some evidence of this, which also suggests a 'territorialisation' of the personality principle–that is, the gentile law is attached to an estate, and only secondarily to the people who work on it—see W. Goffart, *The Le Mans Forgeries* (Cambridge, Mass., 1966) pp 144, 236; and H. Krause, 'Königtum und Rechtsordnung in der Zeit der sächsischen und salischen Herrscher', in *ZRG GAbt* 82 (1965) p 8.

[63] See [K. F.] Morrison, [*The*] *Two Kingdoms* (Princeton 1964) pp 35, 90 *seq.*

so that God's justice may prevail.[64] If Hincmar's tolerance here could be held typical of Carolingian scholars, Agobard is a well-publicised alleged exception. Others shared his concern for imperial unity, but he alone proceeded to ask if diversity of laws was not an obstacle to the unity of that *divina operatio*, the *corpus christi*.[65] Like so much else in Agobard's writings—his objections to the ordeal; his 'rational' scorn of sorcery—this is impressively modern-sounding. But its underlying assumptions prove to be far from modern, for it depends on an eschatology, probably derived from Tychonius as well as Augustine which opposed the *corpus* of God's empire to the *corpus diaboli*.[66] Agobard does not seriously challenge the personality of laws in principle: he attacks the *lex Gundobada* in particular, both because, as a southwesterner and a *romanus*, he had an outsider's aversion to the Burgundians and their interminable feuding, and because having access to the historical records of Lyons, he knew Gundobad to have been an Arian, and could not countenance the survival of a heretic's laws within a Christian empire. For various reasons, Agobard's views are *sui generis*. In general, the Carolingian renaissance made no dent in the principle of the personality of laws[67]—indeed may even have fostered it, in so far as Carolingian scribes copied and multiplied the texts in which that principle was enshrined.

Thirdly: the essential characteristic of early medieval law, so a number of German scholars have recently argued, was its lack of 'any assumption of a legal order resting either on statute or on customary law'.[68] A man could impose legal obligations on himself

---

[64] *De raptu viduarum*, in *PL* 125 (1852) col 1026; *De Ordine Palatii* pp 524 *seq*.

[65] See his letter to Louis the Pious *Adversus legem Gundobadi*, ed E. Dümmler, *MGH Epp* 5, pp 158 *seq*.

[66] E. Boshof, *Erzbischof Agobard von Lyon* (Cologne 1969) pp 41 *seq*; compare also Liebeschutz, 'Wesen und Grenzen', pp 33 *seq*. I am grateful to Ian Wood for his helpful suggestions here.

[67] The further erosion of the principle during the ninth century (the process had begun much earlier) was due, not to the Carolingian renaissance but to the growing regionalisation and feudalisation of social and political relationships. Compare n 60, above. It is worth noting the still gentile imperialism of Agobard's proposed solution to the Burgundian problem, when he requests the emperor 'ut eos [Burgundiones] transferret ad *legem Francorum*; et ipsi *nobiliores* efficerentur . . .' (My stress).

[68] [K.] Kroeschell, 'Rechtsfindung', in *Festschrift für H. Heimpel* (Göttingen 1972) 3, pp 498 *seq* at p 512. See also his '[Recht und] Rechtsbegriff', im 12 Jht', in *Vorträge und Forschungen*, 12 (1968), pp 309 *seq*; W. Ebel, *Die Willkür* (Göttingen 1953) esp pp 37 *seq*; H. Hagemann, '*Fides facta* und *wadiatio*. Vom Wesen des altdeutschen Formalvertrages', in *ZRG GAbt* 83 (1966) pp 1 *seq*, esp 28 *seq*; Köbler, *Recht*, esp pp 211 *seq*.

JANET L. NELSON

by the giving of a pledge (*fides facta*), and he was subject to the decision of a court. Studies of legal vocabulary suggest that the law (*lex*) did not condition, but was contained in, the judgement. Kroeschell has concluded that 'there prevailed a purely formal concept of law'.[69] In other words, secular law in the early middle ages was what experienced men declared to be and used as the law, whether this was written or unwritten. Kern's ritualistic and unchanging medieval law, the famous 'good old law' that could only be found, not made, is a myth. On the contrary, since law was never identified simply with what was just, it could undergo a constant process of alteration.[70] There is a Comte-ian ring about all this—sounded rather too strongly by Kroeschell. Early medieval men were no positivists: *ius* never lost its association with *iustitia*.[71] Yet the contrast stands between early medieval law on the one hand, and, on the other, classical Roman, later medieval and modern law:[72] between a law lodged in the practice of courts, palpably manmade, without system, not needing to be written, and bounded by the need to regard men's 'subjective' statuses—and a written, systematised law representing a permanent 'objective' statement of abstract justice, a law which judges merely applied and executed, a law bounded by the requirements of continuity, predictability, and conformity with explicit norms. What is significant in the present context is the fact that the Carolingian period belongs so unequivocally on the early medieval side of the line: for the *Rechtshistoriker* familiar with the jurisprudence of the gentile *Leges*, that of the Carolingian sources evidently presents no aberrant features, and any new trends discernible from the ninth

---

[69] 'Rechtsfindung', p. 513.
[70] Kern's thesis was set out in 'Recht und Verfassung im Mittelalter', in *HZ* 120 (1919), trans S. B. Chrimes in *Kingship and Law in the Middle Ages* (Oxford 1968) part 2, pp 149 seq. For penetrating revisions of Kern, see H. Krause, 'Dauer und Vergänglichkeit im mittelalterlichen Recht', *ZRB GAbt* 75 (1958) pp 206 seq, whose title epitomises 'einen anscheinend unauflöslichen Gegensatz' in medieval law (p 217): 'Ein konstituierender Faktor des Rechts ist die Länge der Zeit, das Element der Dauer—ein konstituierender Faktor des Rechts ist die Macht des gegenwärtigen Herrschers, das Element der Vergänglichkeit'. For further observations and recent literature, see also Ullmann, *Law and Politics in the Middle Ages* (London 1975) pp 30 with n 1, 48 with n 2.
[71] As noted, against Kroeschell, by Köbler, *Recht*, p 226. Kroeschell's recent reply, 'Rechtsfindung', p 510, n 66, is unconvincing. I hope to return elsewhere to this problem.
[72] I follow here Kroeschell, 'Rechtsbegriff', esp pp 325 seq. Kroeschell's book *Haus und Hauscherrschaft im frühen deutschen Recht* (Göttingen 1958) has unfortunately been inaccessible.

64

century onwards are less remarkable than the continuities.[73] I would stress the continuing absence of precisely those social and economic changes, especially urbanisation and the development of business practices, which help to explain the appearance in certain areas in the twelfth and thirteenth centuries of 'a new, objective law'.[74] This is by no means to deny that later developments were in some ways foreshadowed in the Carolingian period: the notions of equality before the law and of tutorial rulership can be found in ninth-century documents, as Ullmann has recently shown.[75] Yet foreshadowings these remained, and though of great interest as such, they appeared in the ninth century very rarely and were then much less significant, quantitatively and qualitatively, than the areas of continuity with a pre-Carolingian past.

Earlier in this paper, I mentioned the distinction between personal and institutional rebirth, and Ullmann's thesis of baptismal rebirth as the paradigm of a whole social-ecclesiological renaissance. Now, inverting that model, instead of viewing a hypostatised 'Christian rebirth idea' as the autonomous source of a legal-governmental programme, I suggest we see the interpretation of baptismal rebirth by Christians of the Carolingian age as itself heavily conditioned by prevailing legal conceptions. A man knew what it meant to be born into membership of the Frankish, or Bavarian or Burgundian *gens*; and this coloured his notion of baptism as admission to the Christian society. A Salian Frank, for instance, established his public legal identity as against the men of other *gentes* by the way he behaved in certain situations—dealt with his property, transacted a marriage, responded to an accusation. He was also a Christian, and this too

[73] Despite the innovations in Germanic legal terminology from the ninth century onwards observed by Köbler, 'Richten—Richter—Gericht', in *ZRG GAbt* 87 (1970) pp 57 *seq*, esp 108 *seq*, and assigned by him to clerical influence, Kroeschell, 'Rechtsfindung', p 513 sees no change in the assumptions inherent in persisting traditional procedures.

[74] Kroeschell, 'Rechtsbegriff', p 333, though the causal factors are here barely hinted at. Despite the qualifications of Kroeschell, p 320, and 'Rechtsfindung', pp 508 *seq*, I share the reservations of Köbler, *Recht*, p 226, as to the aptness in this context of the modern categories of 'objective' and 'subjective' law. On his own admission, Kroeschell's major contrast is in fact between two types of 'objective' law, which suggests the need for a new classification.

[75] *CR*, pp 116, 122.

was a matter of external behaviour: he did not eat meat in lent, he buried his dead in the church's cemetery, he did not go to public gatherings on Sundays.[76] Baptism had little to do with doctrinal conviction or ethical transformation, even in the case of adults:[77] private penance and remission at once compensated for and confirmed this fact.[78] When pagans were mass-baptised by force, Alcuin's was a rare voice of protest; and even Alcuin expounded baptism not in terms of rebirth but as the incurring of liability to receive and obey certain instructions, his only concession being the proposal that the new laws be imposed gradually—prohibitions first and positive commands later.[79] In practice he knew that the main effect of baptism for a Saxon or Avar was liability to pay tithes, and not even Alcuin could work a rebirth metaphor into that!

Carolingian lay piety, so far as we can reconstruct it, was dominated at aristocratic level by a barely Christianised warrior ethic[80] and at a popular level by the effort to project within each individual relations of command and subordination (between soul and body) which mirrored those of feudal society,[81] and by the need to propitiate Israel's vengeful God of Battles by certain prescribed acts. Small wonder that Mosaic law was held the model of all gentile law.[82] In the Carolingian period, sorcery flourished, external acts and

[76] For these and other similar requirements, see the *Capitulatio de partibus Saxoniae* (785), *MGH Cap* 1, no 26, pp 68–70.

[77] The normal practice of child-baptism had long since transformed the catechnmenate from 'einer Belehrungs- und Erziehungsinstitution zu einer Folge von Zeremonien rein liturgischen Charakters': so, Dahlhaus-Berg, *Nova Antiquitas*, pp 94 *seq* with further references. The candidates for adult-baptism were conquered Saxons and Avars.

[78] Compare B. S. Turner, 'Origins and traditions in Islam and Christianity', in *Religion*, 6 (1976), pp 13 *seq* at 25–6.

[79] *MGH Epp* 4, no 111, pp 159–62. The date is 796 following the victory over the Avars: Alcuin hoped to avoid a repetition of the forced conversion of the Saxons. Compare the comments of Wallace-Hadrill, *Kingship*, p 102.

[80] This aspect is stressed by A. Waas, 'Karls des Grossen Frommigkeit', in *HZ*, 203 (1966), pp 265 *seq*. See also J. Chélini, 'Les laïcs dans la société ecclésiastique carolingienne', in *I laici nella societa cristiana dei secoli XIo-XIIo*, *Acta della terza Settimana internazionale di studio Mendola*, 1965 (Milan 1968), pp 23 *seq*; [J.] Leclercq, *The Spirituality of the Middle Ages* (London 1968) pp 68 *seq*; Riché, 'Les bibliothèques de trois aristocrates laïcs carolingiens', *Moyen Age*, 69 (1963) pp 87 *seq*, *Vie Quotidienne*, pp 215 *seq*, and Introduction to Dhuoda's *Manuel pour mon fils*, *SCP* (1975), esp pp 24 *seq*. For further references, see above nn 43 and 46.

[81] This is especially clear in the short sermon, probably by Paulinus of Aquileia, ed by Leclercq in *RB*, 59 (1949) pp 159–60, esp lines 42 *seq*, where the preacher develops a series of striking oppositions: *imperium—servitium*; *erigitur—humiliatur*; *inebriatur et pascitur—fame torquetur*; *pretiosi vestes—veteres panni* . . . etc.

[82] Köbler, *Recht*, p 88.

material objects being used alike to placate a jealous deity and to manipulate other supernatural powers.[83] The gentile churches resisted such an extreme manifestation, but had long since come to terms with a religiosity of the physical. This process of acculturation[84] was now carried a significant stage further when clerics liturgified the ordeal, elaborated the symbolism of oil rituals, restructured without restraining the practice of private penance, and promoted, while not always successfully controlling, a great upsurge in the cult and social deployment of relics.[85] We should not forget that all this went on, relatively unpublicised, alongside and beneath the Romanising trend of the 'official' renaissance of the Carolingian church. I am certainly not denying that at least some Carolingian clerics sought a religious renewal that would penetrate lay society, at peasant as well as aristocratic level: sermons and *specula* directed at laymen, still more than the relevant capitularies, offer eloquent testimony to this attempted *Volksaufklärung*.[86] The case of Louis the Pious shows, perhaps, that the effort was not wholly unsuccessful. But were more than a handful of laymen—and the direct evidence is confined to rulers and aristocrats —ever really affected by it? The piety of Charles the Bald, who aspired to a divinely-blessed warrior-kingship and had clerical anointing applied to his queen as a 'fertility charm',[87] hardly seems more 'spiritualised', more 'ethically-transformed' than that of Charlemagne. Dhuoda recommended her son to read the works of the fathers, yet she herself 'n'a sans doute pas retenu de ses lectures tout ce qu'on aurait souhaité. Elle a été particulièrement séduite par la symbolique des

---

[83] Riché, 'La Magie Carolingienne', in *Comptes Rendus de l'Académie des Inscriptions et Belles-Lettres* (Paris 1973) pp 127 *seq.*

[84] Le Goff, 'Culture cléricale et traditions folkloriques dans la civilisation mérovingienne', in *Annales* 22 (1967), pp 780 *seq.*

[85] For these developments see Gaudemet, 'Les Ordalies au Moyen Age', in *Recueils Jean Bodin*, 17 (1965), pp 99 *seq*, and the evidence in *MGH Leg* 5, *Formulae* ed K. Zeumer (1886), pp 604 *seq*; my paper, 'Symbols in context: rulers' inauguration rituals in Byzantium and the west in the early Middle Ages', *SCH* 13 (1976), pp 97 *seq*; C. Vogel, *Le pécheur et la pénitence au Moyen Age* (Paris 1969) pp 43 *seq*, and R. Pierce, 'The "Frankish" penitentials', *SCH* 11 (1975) pp 31 *seq*; H. Fichtenau, 'Zum Reliquienwesen im früheren Mittelalter', *MIÖG*, 60 (1952), pp 60 *seq*, and Riché, *Vie Quotidienne*, pp 320 *seq.*

[86] So, Ullmann, *CR*, p 36, with a full appraisal of the sermon literature; compare also Bullough, *The Age of Charlemagne* (2 ed London 1973) pp 115 *seq.*

[87] So, E. H. Kantorowicz, 'The Carolingian King in the Bible of San Paolo fuori le Mura', in *Late Classical and Medieval Studies in Honour of A. M. Friend* (Princeton 1955) p 293. See also Wallace-Hadrill, *Kingship*, pp 124 *seq*, esp 135 (where, however, the reference of the capitulary of Pîtres is to confirmation-anointing, not royal consecration).

nombres . . .'[88] Without sharing Riché's value-judgement, we can agree that the significant point concerns not so much what texts Dhuoda read as how she read them, and we may well doubt whether, had Herchenfreda, mother of Desiderius of Cahors, written to her son not just letters but a whole book of exhortation, it would have been so very different from Dhuoda's.[89] I am suggesting that here again the Carolingian world can be understood only in the perspective of the Merovingian centuries and that its lay piety, if not the transmission of its learning, was fully continuous with that of the earlier *regna*.

The less frequented route seems to have led to a familiar destination. For my conclusion is that the limits of the Carolingian renaissance hardly exceeded, even in the ninth century, the dimensions of a religious culture that was largely confined to the clerical and monastic orders—what contemporaries in fact so often meant by the term *ecclesia*. At the same time, in lay society, pre-Carolingian legal and religious ideas and practices—and, I suspect, (though this has been beyond the scope of this paper) political ones too—persisted and evolved with a momentum of their own, affected but not determined by ecclesiastical *novitas*.

A cultural renaissance obviously depends on economic and political factors for its patronage and on social factors too for its personnel; but its base in society may be narrow and its unfolding relatively autonomous. This situation, which prevailed for instance in late Byzantium, was essentially that of the Carolingian renaissance, not least because the Carolingian church was, and could see itself as, in some sense *altera respublica*.[90] Within the priestly and monastic orders with their structural coherence and growing sense of identity expressed in the bid for full legal autonomy, ideas of rebirth and renewal could transcend the personal and be, at least to some degree, institutionalised, especially in the sphere of law. The third, lay, order, by contrast, with its relatively undifferentiated forms of social and legal organisation,

---

[88] Riché, Introduction to Dhuoda's *Manuel*, p 31. Riché continues: 'Mais sommes-nous ici dans le domaine de la spiritualité ou plutôt dans celui de la culture intellectuelle? Il est vrai que pour Dhuoda il n'y avait pas de frontières'. Here Riché raises, without resolving, a major problem in the methodology of historians of 'culture'.

[89] Herchenfreda's letters are preserved in the *Vita Desiderii*, ed Krusch, *MGH SRM* 4, pp 569–70. For some details of their contents, see Riché, *De l'éducation antique à l'éducation chevaleresque* (Paris 1968) pp 42–3. Riché himself suggests the comparison with Dhuoda.

[90] Paschasius Radbertus, *Epitaphium Arsenii*, ed E. Dummler, *ADAW* (1900) p 63. See also Morrison, *Two Kingdoms*, pp 36 *seq* and *passim*, where, however, the theme of 'dualism' is overstated.

On the limits of the Carolingian renaissance

its legal and religious conceptions alike embedded in the mentalities of kin-group and *comitatus*, could neither generate nor genuinely accommodate the idea of rebirth. It was not until the twelfth century, tentatively, and the fifteenth and sixteenth centuries confidently, that laymen—often lawyers—used ideas of rebirth and renewal which originated in the church or drew inspiration from Christian reform traditions to shape ideologies for radical transformations of law and politics in lay society.[91] The paradox was that these transformations depended on rapidly-accelerated processes of social differentiation: only in an increasingly secularised society could Christian laymen try to institutionalise a renaissance for themselves.

University of London
King's College.

[91] For the twelfth century, see Ullmann, *Law and Politics*, pp 83 *seq*, and Kroeschell, 'Rechtsbegriff', esp 326 *seq*; for the fifteenth and sixteenth centuries, see J. H. Franklin, *Jean Bodin and the Sixteenth-century Revolution in the Methodology of Law and History* (New York 1963), D. R. Kelley, *Foundations of Modern Historical Scholarship. Language Law and History in the French Renaissance* (New York 1970), and *The Francogallia of François Hotman*, ed R. Giesey and J. H. M. Salmon (Cambridge 1972). Burdach, *Reformation*, p 55, writes that although the idea of rebirth and reform existed throughout the middle ages, before the twelfth century 'es war verblasst und erstarrt zu einer dogmatischen Formel der Sakramentenlehre', but in the later middle ages 'verwandelt jenes Bild sich in den Ausdruck eines . . . Gefühls und Verlangens *rein menschlicher Art*' (my stress) as expressed in the ideal of the *nova vita*. Again, p 96, Burdach refers to 'die langsame Säkularisierung des Gedankens der Wiedergeburt' from the fourteenth century onwards.

EVANGELISATION OR REPENTANCE?
THE RE-CHRISTIANISATION OF THE PELOPONNESE IN THE NINTH AND TENTH CENTURIES

by MARILYN DUNN

D ESPITE its attendant manifestations of renewal, the process of the re-Christianisation of the Peloponnese during the ninth and tenth centuries has not generally been viewed in the context of a renaissance. The remarkable upsurge in church-building in the province from the end of the tenth century onwards, the approximate beginnings of which are marked by the appearance of a large church on the Spartan acropolis,[1] has had its causes ascribed to movements other than the re-vitalisation of religious life in the area. It is true that the great period of church-building in the Peloponnese occurs at a later date than the comparable flourishing in Hellas, where the famous churches of Skripou, of Gregory the Theologian at Thebes, and of John the Baptist in Athens were all built in the ninth century.[2] The late date of this architectural activity has doubtless been one factor which has led some historians to hold an unnecessarily complicated and even untenable view of the impulses which lay behind it.

The middle-Byzantine churches of the Peloponnese are often seen as the products of a deliberate drive to evangelise the pagan Slavs who first arrived in this area at the end of the sixth century and who had remained untouched by Byzantine rule until the creation of the theme of the Peloponnese in the opening years of the ninth century.[3]

[1] For the monastery and church built by Saint Nikon in Lakedaimon, see G. Soteriou's article on the excavations at old Sparta in the *Praktika tis en Athenais Arkhaiologikis Etaireias 1939* (Athens 1940) pp 107–18.

[2] A discussion of the churches of Hellas and their historical background can be found in Judith Herrin, 'Aspects of the Process of re-Hellenisation in the early Middle Ages', *Annual of the British School at Athens*, 68 (London 1973) p 124.

[3] The arrival of the Avaro-Slavs and the re-establishment of Byzantine rule over the Peloponnese is dealt with admirably by P. Charanis in a series of articles, most notably:
'The Chronicle of Monemvasia and the Question of the Slavonic Settlements in Greece', *DOP* 5 (1950) pp 141–66;
'On the Question of the Slavonic Settlements in Greece in the Middle Ages', *BS* 10 (1949) pp 254–8;

To suggest that the re-establishment of Byzantine rule over the Peloponnese was followed by an initiative to convert the Slavs to Christianity is both an attractive and a plausible theory. Its plausibility, indeed, is such that almost all religious activity in the theme has been interpreted as the manifestation of the establishment of a new church—in other words, the setting up of a mission to the Slavs. Since the publication of Fallmerayer's *Geschichte der Halbinsel Morea*,[4] the problem of the Slavs of the Peloponnese has continually upstaged many other important aspects of the region's history. They are now about to make one last appearance in a leading rôle; and their impending retirement will perhaps clear the way for an appreciation of the true nature of religious life in the Peloponnese in the ninth and tenth centuries.

The Slav penetration of the Peloponnese was effected not by invasion or conquest as these are normally understood, but rather by a process of infiltration which followed upon initial violent incursions made in association with Avar tribes. The beginnings of this movement can be dated to the reign of Tiberius II (578–82), when groups of Slavs crossed the Danube and entered the Balkans. The Avaro-Slavs entered the Peloponnese shortly after an attack on Thessalonica;[5] and Charanis draws our attention to evidence which may indicate that they captured Corinth during the reign of Maurice.[6] This would seem to disprove the statement of the *Chronicle of Monemvasia* that the eastern part of the peninsula 'from Corinth to Malea' escaped Slav influence.[7] However, Charanis also indicates the recapture of the city by the Greeks by 586.[8] Whichever view of these events the student of the period adopts, it is clear that, despite the flight of many of the native Greeks of the Peloponnese to refuges in southern Italy, Sicily, islands such as Aegina, or to the rock which was to become known as Monemvasia,[9] the gloomy statement of the *De Thematibus* that the whole country was Slavonicised during the reign of Constantine V is incorrect.[10] There

'Nikephoros I, the saviour of Greece from the Slavs, 810 AD', *Byzantina-Metabyzantina*, 1 (New York 1946) pp 75–92; and
'On the Slavic Settlement in the Peloponnesus', *BZ* 46 (1953) pp 91–103.
[4] J. Fallmerayer, *Geschichte der Halbinsel Morea*, 2 vols (Stuttgart 1830–6).
[5] *S Demetrii Martyris Acta, PG* 116 (1864) cols 1203–324.
[6] 'Slavic Settlement', pp 91–9.
[7] The text of the *Chronicle of Monemvasia* is contained in P. Lemerle, 'La Chronique improprement dite de Monemvasie', *REB* 21 (1963) pp 8–11.
[8] 'Slavic Settlement', pp 101–2.
[9] 'Chronique de Monemvasie', p 10 lines 55–7.
[10] *De Thematibus*, ed A. Pertusi, *Studi e Testi*, 160 (Vatican 1952) p 91.

is considerable evidence for the almost continual Greek settlement of the eastern part of the Peloponnese during the two hundred and eighteen years of the Slav 'occupation'.[11] Although coin finds at Corinth for this period are admittedly very scanty, they represent the reign of almost every emperor during the seventh and eighth centuries, and are comparable with those for Athens.[12] The toponymic evidence adduced by Vasmer in *Die Slaven in Griechenland* must also be considered in this context. The proportion of Slavic place-names is much smaller in the east of the Peloponnese than in the west: Corinth has a total of twenty-four, the Argolid eighteen. Against this can be set ninety-five for Achaia, ninety-four for Arkadia, eighty-one for Lakonia, forty-four for Triphylia, forty-three for Messenia, and thirty-five for Elis.[13] Areas such as Corinth and the Argolid would seem to have been repopulated by the Greeks at a comparatively early date, although it is doubtful that the central government maintained any direct administrative contacts with this part of the Peloponnese before the beginning of the ninth century.[14] Monemvasia was another Greek enclave at this period: the bishop Willibald, visiting the Holy Land between 723 and 728, describes it as being situated in 'Slav country'.[15] Ecclesiastical contacts, even if only nominal, continued to be maintained between these eastern areas and the rest of the empire. In 680, a bishop of Corinth attended the sixth ecumenical council; and in 689, the patriarch of Constantinople sent three bishops to Rome, among them the bishop of Corinth.[16] There is also a record of a bishop of Monemvasia at the seventh ecumenical council;[17] this is the first time this diocese is mentioned, and the bishop appears along with his colleague of the ancient see of Troezen which was situated in the north-east of the Peloponnese.[18]

The two hundred and eighteen years of Slav domination of the

---

[11] The figure of two hundred and eighteen years is given in the *Chronicle of Monemvasia,* See 'Chronique de Monemvasie' p 10 lines 50–5.

[12] For coin finds at Corinth see: K. M. Edwards, 'Reports on the excavations at Corinth (coins) during the years 1930–35', *Hesperia*, 6 (Athens 1937) pp 241–56; J. H. Finley, 'Corinth in the Middle Ages', *Speculum*, 7 (Cambridge, Mass. 1932) p 499; and J. M. Harris, 'Coins found at Corinth, 1', *Hesperia*, 10 (Athens 1941) pp 143–62.

[13] [M. Vasmer], *Die Slaven* [*in Griechenland*] (Berlin 1941) pp 114–20, 317.

[14] 'Chronique de Monemvasie' p 10 lines 57–8.

[15] *Vita S Willibaldi episcopi Eichstatensis*, MGH SS, 15 (1887) p 93.

[16] Mansi, 11 p 689, and Grumel, *Regestes*, 1 pt 1 p 126, no 316.

[17] Mansi, 12 pp 1099, 1110.

[18] Ibid.

Peloponnese were brought to an end with the reign of Nikephoros I. The complicated questions of chronology which surround the initial re-establishment of Byzantine rule over the province have been admirably dealt with by Charanis, and need only be summarised here.[19] The Peloponnese was elevated to the rank of theme in 805, as a preliminary to Nikephoros' invasion of Bulgaria in 807. A military campaign against the Slavs followed this elevation, and the reconstruction of the city of Patras was begun in 805.[20] Transfers of population were by no means a new instrument of imperial policy, and Nikephoros used this method to correct a potentially dangerous demographic imbalance.[21] The Slavs of Patras rose in revolt against these new conditions in 807, aided by an Arab fleet which was off the west coast at that time; but the insurgents were eventually defeated by Greeks, helped, according to Constantine Porphyrogenitus, by the personal intervention of saint Andrew![22] The fate of the rebellious Slavs themselves is particularly interesting. The emperor ordained that the Slavs themselves, 'with all their families and relations and all who belonged to them, and all their property as well should be set apart for the temple of the apostle in the metropolis of Patras . . .'.[23] The Slavs were thus reduced to the status of serfs, and were also compelled to entertain all civic guests and foreign visitors at their own expense.[24]

In order, presumably, to stabilise a still dangerous demographic position within the theme, further transfers of population were made in 810.[25] They were accompanied by the rebuilding of the city of Lakedaimon, and the establishment of the sees of Lakedaimon, Korone, and Methone.[26] Patras became the seat of a metropolitan bishop.[27] 'In this fashion,' the *Chronicle of Monemvasia* states, 'the barbarians were, with the help and grace of God, catechised, baptised, and converted to the Christian faith; glory and thanks be to the Father, Son, and Holy Ghost, now and forever, amen.'[28]

[19] For these events see 'Nikephoros I'.

[20] Ibid pp 83-4.

[21] Ibid pp 84-5.

[22] *De Administrando Imperio*, ed Gy. Moravcsik and R. J. H. Jenkins, (2 ed Washington 1967) cap 49 lines 1-38.

[23] Ibid lines 54-6.

[24] Ibid lines 65-71.

[25] 'Nikephoros I', pp 85-6.

[26] 'Chronique de Monemvasie' pp 10-11 lines 73-74.

[27] Ibid.

[28] Ibid, lines 74-76.

The re-Christianisation of the Pelopponese

The conversion of the 'barbarians' was not, as the *Chronicle* would suggest, complete. It may, indeed, be appropriate to ask to what extent Nikephoros' efforts were actually directed towards conversion: a policy which involved large-scale transfers of population must surely be classed as defensive rather than purely missionary in nature. The new sees, moreover, seem to have been established with the needs of the Greek-speaking population in mind. Patras and Lakedaimon were largely inhabited by newly-arrived Greeks, while the towns of Korone and Methone are both on the coast, and the creation of sees centring on them does not indicate any real drive into the Slavic heartland of the Peloponnese. That a substantial number of Slavs remained unconverted or at least hostile to Byzantine rule is demonstrated by chapter 50 of the *De Administrando Imperio*, which records that Slavs and other insubordinates (who unfortunately remain anonymous) rebelled 'in the days of the emperor Theophilos and his son Michael'.[29] No reason is given for this revolt, and its cause remains something of a mystery, although the sudden increase in the number of coin finds at Corinth, which eventually reaches a peak with those dating to the time of the Komnenoi, begins with coins of the emperor Theophilos.[30] The revolt may have expressed protest against a sudden tightening of the imperial administration's grip around the theme. Chapter 50 is explicit, however, in its treatment of the fortunes of the Slavs:

> . . . the *protospatharios* Theoktistos, surnamed Bryennios, was sent as military governor to the Peloponnese with a great power and force, viz., of Thracians and Macedonians, and the rest of the western provinces to war upon them and subdue them. He subdued and mastered all the Slavs and the other insubordinates of the province of the Peloponnese and only the Ezeritai and Milingoi were left towards Lakedaimonia and Helos. And since there is a great and very high mountain called Pentadaktylos which runs like a neck a long distance into the sea and because the place is difficult, they settled there, upon the flanks of this same mountain, the Milingoi in one part and the Ezeritai in the other. The aforesaid *protospatharios* Theoktistos, the military governor of the Peloponnese, having succeeded in reducing these too, fixed a tribute of 60 nomismata for the Milingoi, and 300

[29] *DAI*, cap 50 line 7.
[30] J. M. Harris, 'Coins found at Corinth, 1', p 157.

75

for the Ezeritai, and this they used to pay while he was *strategos*, as the report of it is preserved to this day by the local inhabitants.[31] The two tribes were also obliged to remain in obedience to a head man appointed by the military governor.[32] Yet they were to maintain a tradition of hostility to the imperial government and rebelled in the first half of the tenth century; and it is, perhaps, their unusual violence which has led students of the period to give undue weight to the Slav problem.[33] There are no further references to the rest of the Peloponnesian Slavs who appear to have submitted to the imperial governor after their defeat.

Because of the lack of archaeological and textual evidence for the Peloponnese in the ninth century, it is often difficult to do more than offer pointers as to what may have happened to the majority of the Slavs who had settled there. Of the civil administration, very little is known: it seems to have been distinguished only by its unremarkability.[34] The same could be said to apply to the military organisation of the theme, except for the possible stationing of Greeks as guards to watch over the Milingoi and Ezeritai in the south-east.[35]

We do, however, possess some records of the developing episcopal structure in the Peloponnese during the ninth century. The first notice of the bishoprics of the Peloponnese, dated by Gelzer to the reign of Nikephoros I, corresponds to the information given in the *Chronicle of Monemvasia*: there was a metropolitan bishop of Corinth at this stage.[36] We are not given information about any of Corinth's suffragans, but it would be reasonable to suppose that there was still a bishop of Monemvasia. It is difficult to decide whether or not the see of Troezen was still in existence as such. A second notice dating to the reign of Leo VI lists the suffragans of Corinth as the bishops of Damala, Argos, Monemvasia, Cephalonia, Zakynthos, Zemena, and Maina.[37] The former diocese of Troezen has been replaced by that

---

[31] *DAI* cap 50 lines 9–25.
[32] Ibid lines 28–9.
[33] Ibid lines 25–70.
[34] [A] Bon, [*Le Péloponnèse byzantin jusqu'en 1204*] (Paris 1951) pp 88–103.
[35] H. Ahrweiler, 'Les termes Tzakones-Tzakonai et leur évolution sémantique', *REB*, 21 (1963) pp 243–9.
[36] See G. Parthey, [*Hieroclis Synecdemus et*] notitiae [*graecæ episcopatuum*] (Berlin 1866) pp 145, 166; H. Gelzer, ['Ungedruckte und ungenügend veröffentlichte] Texte de-Notitiae [episcopatuum. Ein Beitrag zur byzantinischen Kirchen- und Verwaltungsr geschichte'] *ABAW, Ph K* 21, 3 (1901) pp 529–641.
[37] Gelzer, 'Texte der Notitiae' pt 2 pp 550–1, 556–7.

of Damala—presumably its territorial limits remained the same. Of the Peloponnesian sees mentioned in this list, all are in the east—the part of the Peloponnese which had been least affected by the Slav penetration. With the exception of Monemvasia and Damala (Troezen) none had been mentioned previously by any writer.

In the western Peloponnese, which had been extensively populated by the Slavs, only one see was founded in addition to those creations of Nikephoros I, Korone and Methone. This was the diocese of Bolaina, the precise location of which is uncertain.[38] A diocese of Helos in the south-eastern Peloponnese may also have been founded at this time, but it may, on the other hand date only to the period of the Komnenoi.[39]

The accepted view of this process is that it was directed towards the conversion of the Slavs and was initiated by the patriarch Photius and the emperor Basil I. This view may well owe its origins to the statement in the *Taktikon* attributed to Leo VI, which says that Basil I 'made Greeks of the Slavs by converting them'.[40] Bon, in his comprehensive work, *Le Péloponnèse byzantin*, applies this statement to the Peloponnese.[41] The Slavs bedevil any attempt to achieve a balanced view of the church's activities in the area. Obolensky, in *The Byzantine Commonwealth*, writes of Patras as a former bishopric promoted to metropolitan rank after 800 in order to organise and direct the conversion of the Slavs.[42] In this, Obolensky commits the initial error of ignoring the fact that Patras also possessed a newly-arrived Greek population. Referring to the Balkans in general, and including the Peloponnese in this generalisation, he maintains that: 'Although precise information is often lacking, we may assume that many of the Slavonic bishoprics were created in the reign of Basil I, who, in association with the Patriarch Photius, planned and directed the conversion of the Empire's Slav subjects'.[43] A glance at the geo-

---

[38] Ibid.

[39] The first mention of the see of Helos occurs in a very late notice (1089): see Parthey, Notitiae, pp 117, 215. The see was founded at some time before this, but because of the incomplete nature of the episcopal lists for the preceding period, it is impossible to say exactly when. It is just possible that the diocese of Helos may have been in existence at the beginning of the tenth century; but in view of the fact that it is not mentioned in the extensive list for this period, it is unlikely that it goes back so far.

[40] *PG* 107 (1863) col 969.

[41] Bon p 70.

[42] [D.] Obolensky, [*The Byzantine Commonwealth*] (London 1971 paperback ed 1974) p 111.

[43] Ibid.

graphical distribution of the new sees shows that, if Basil and Photius had any specific plans for the Peloponnese, the province's Slavs did not figure in them to any great extent. The majority of sees created in the ninth century were situated, as we have already seen, in predominantly Greek areas. Dvornik has attempted to show that the sees of Bolaina and Zemena were created for two Slav tribes, the Poliani and the Zemenliani, but we possess no other evidence of the existence of these tribes, and his attempts to form tribal names from place-names must be treated with the greatest reserve.[44] It should also be remembered that the location of Bolaina is doubtful, although attempts have been made to identify it with Olena, and that Zemena, while within the heavily-Slavicised region of Arkadia, is relatively close to Corinth. (Olena, it might be observed, is situated not far from Patras). It is not even certain that the sees of Damala, Argos, Bolaina, and Zemena were established in the reign of Basil I: our only information relating to the question comes from Constantine Porphyrogenitus who claims, perhaps with more family pride than accuracy, that his grandfather was responsible for the Christianisation of those redoubtable descendants of the ancient Greeks, the Maniots.[45] Should we attribute the foundation of the other sees to him on the basis of this scanty evidence and our knowledge of his work in the empire as a whole? Whatever the truth about the foundation-dates of the dioceses of the Peloponnese, it emerges that the conversion of the Slavs was not their primary raison d'être: indeed, the opposite could be convincingly argued. Appearances suggest that the ecclesiastical authorities were satisfied that the network of bishoprics set up by Nikephoros I—such as it was—was adequate to the needs of the areas most heavily populated by the invader. It is, in fact, unlikely that the church was the prime mover in the Hellenisation of the Slavs of the Peloponnese. Its rôle, although important, was much less conventional than historians such as Bon and Obolensky would suggest.

Before turning to the question of the date and principal means of the absorption of the Slavs, it may be appropriate to mention the figure of bishop Athanasios of Methone.[46] Like so many other famous

---

[44] F. Dvornik, *Les Slaves, Byzance et Rome au IXème Siècle*, (Paris 1926) p 141.

[45] *DAI* cap 50 lines 75–6.

[46] The encomium of Saint Athanasios of Methone by Peter of Argos can be found in PG 104 (1862) cols 1365–80.

The re-Christianisation of the Pelopponese

Peloponnesian churchmen of the medieval period, Athanasios was not a native of the theme, but came there with his parents following the siege of Syracuse in 828.[47] His career, according to the *Encomium* written after his death by Peter of Argos, was one of exemplary piety. His work, as outlined by Peter who is, unfortunately, not familiar with many of the details of his subject's life, was carried out with the greatest wisdom, and he provided a virtuous example to all.[48] It is difficult to decide whether, in a work so full of *topoi* as the *Encomium*, we should expect any mention of the Slavs of the western Peloponnese: yet Methone was one of the sees created by Nikephoros I and must have ministered to both Greek and Slav. It is not without significance that Peter never introduces any remarks about Slavs into his work: there is no account of any missionary drive towards them in the central years of the ninth century.

The activities of what it is becoming increasingly fashionable to term the 'unofficial' church also reveal a marked lack of concern for the Slavs. During the course of the ninth century, the Peloponnese was visited by a number of monks, hermits and ascetics, and our knowledge of them compensates in some slight measure for our almost total ignorance of Peloponnesian monastic establishments at this period, and even, on occasion throws some light on them. There was considerable interaction between Sicily, southern Italy, and the Peloponnese at this time: some two centuries before the prevailing modes in eastern asceticism were to flow to the west via southern Italy, southern Italy was to export ascetics to the east. Elias the Speleot, born in Reggio Calabria in 805, visited the Peloponnese and stayed for a period of eight years (880–8).[49] He settled just outside Patras in a tower haunted by devils. Another Elias (known as 'the Sicilian' or 'the younger'), a native of Castrogiovanni, visited the church of SS Cosmas and Damian in Sparta, together with his companion Daniel.[50] These two ascetics were to visit many other areas of the empire in the course of a grand tour common at the time. Whether one accepts the view of Ménager that the constant mobility of such Italian and Sicilian monks was due to Arab incursions,[51] or extends

---

[47] Ibid para 4.
[48] Ibid paras 7 *seq.*
[49] *AASS*, September, 3, pp 843–58.
[50] *AASS*, August, 3, pp 479–509.
[51] L.-R. Ménager, 'La byzantinisation réligieuse de l'Italie méridionale', *RHE*, 53 (1958) pp 747–74; 59 (1959) pp 5–40.

Judith Herrin's concept of a mobility initially caused by the iconoclast movement into the following century and beyond,[52] or simply agrees with Guillou that many monks aspired to the solitary and relatively unstable life,[53] it is evident that this movement was essentially Greek in character. These men moved in a specifically Byzantine and Orthodox milieu: it is unlikely that we should find any reference to deliberate missionary activity among the Slavs in their *Lives*, and indeed we do not. It is noticeable that these solitaries, on their visits to the Peloponnese, lived within reach of the main urban centres.[54] It would, of course, be extremely foolish to maintain that this renewal of cultural ties with other areas, together with the growth of the episcopal network within the Peloponnese itself, had no effect whatsoever on the Slavs; but any impression made on them was achieved indirectly and not as a matter of deliberate policy.

The question of the date of the absorption of the Slavs is fundamental to an understanding of the means by which they were assimilated into the Greek-speaking population. The valuable work presented by Vasmer in *Die Slaven in Griechenland*, which was published in 1941, seems to have been largely ignored in this context.[55] Vasmer associates the assimilation of the majority of the Slavs of the theme with a deliberate drive to evangelise them which never took place; but it must be emphasised that his placing of this assimilation in the second half of the ninth century is based on linguistic evidence alone.[56] His findings are corroborated by an examination of the *Chronicle of the Morea*, which with its low proportion of words of Slavic derivation, also suggests an early date for absorption.[57]

The apparent lack of initiative on the part of the church must lead us to consider the other means by which the Slav population was assimilated into the life of the Peloponnese. The forcible reduction of

---

[52] Herrin p 122.

[53] A. Guillou, 'Grecs d'Italie du sud et de Sicile au Moyen Age', *Mélanges d'Archéologie et d'Histoire*, 75 (Paris 1963) pp 79–110 esp p 84.

[54] The haunted tower inhabited by Elias the Speleot was near Patras; see his *Life*, *AASS*, September, 3 p 856 para 21. The stylites visited by Saint Luke in the early tenth century lived near Corinth and Zemena. See the Life of Luke, *AASS*, February, 2 p 90 para 36.

[55] Bon makes only one brief reference to Vasmer (p 30 n 1) and does not discuss the latter's conclusions. Obolensky refers to *Die Slaven* at p 482 only.

[56] *Die Slaven* pp 316–8.

[57] D. Zakythinos, *The Slavs in Greece*, in Greek (Athens 1945) p 71 claims to be able to find only one word of Slavic origin, together with its derivatives in the *Chronicle*. This is, perhaps, a rather extreme point of view; but it neatly illustrates the point that the language of medieval Greece was scarcely influenced at all by the Slavs.

the Slavs by the *strategos* Bryennios must have played a very important part in the process. The military defeat of the Slavs on this occasion recalls their capitulation in similar circumstances in 807, after which the Slavs of Patras became serfs of the church. The extensive landed property of the widow Danielis, the benefactress of the emperor Basil I, provides us with one indication of the growth of the rural estate in the Peloponnese.[58] The rise in numbers of holders of the rank of *protospatharios* at the beginning of the tenth century may also indicate this development: Svoronos, in his researches into the tax-rolls of eleventh-century Thebes, demonstrates the acquisition of land by persons of middling or high rank.[59] The Peloponnese was, more-over, willing to commute military service for money long before this became common practice among other themes.[60] The Slavs defeated by Bryennios may well have become serfs on rural estates—private, monastic, or even imperial.[61] The Slavs of the Peloponnese were, after all, a rustic people; and even Judith Herrin who believes that the Slavs of Hellas were eventually drawn into the towns admits that, 'While the urban centres represented a decisive factor in the final political and religious integration of the Slavs, this assimilation would not have been possible without linguistic and cultural preparation in the countryside.'[62] It seems likely that the growth of the estate ensured that the Peloponnesian countryside would provide more than 'linguistic and cultural preparation' for its Slav inhabitants. If not actual serfs, they must at least have been seen as a valuable source of cheap labour.

The transfers of population made by Nikephoros I were another important factor contributing to the Hellenisation of the Slavs. In this connection, we should also consider the return of emigré Greeks such as the family of Athanasios of Methone, although we cannot be precise about the numbers in which they arrived. We cannot say, for instance that there were more Greek-speakers than Slavs in the

[58] See Theophanes Continuatus, *Vita Basilii, PG* 119 (1864) cols 241–4.

[59] *DAI*, cap 50 lines 32–70 gives an account of political in-fighting in the theme: the main protagonists are protospatharii. Bon pp 186–94 assigns names and dates to holders of this rank on the basis of sigillographic evidence. The tax-rolls of Thebes are investigated by N. Svoronos, *Le Cadastre de Thèbes* (Paris 1971): see esp pp 19–55.

[60] *DAI*, cap 51 lines 199–204 and cap 52 lines 1–5. Also H. Ahrweiler, 'Recherches sur l'administration de l'Empire byzantin au IX–XIème siècles', *Bulletin de Correspondance Héllenique*, 84 (Athens/Paris 1960) esp pp 16–20.

[61] Bon p 191 publishes the seal of Michael, the episkeptis of the imperial domains in the Peloponnese. The seal is thought to be of the eleventh or twelfth century.

[62] Herrin p 124.

Peloponnese by the second half of the ninth century, or vice versa: it is, at present, impossible to do more than state that the number of Greek-speakers (though surely not the knowledge of Greek, as Herrin suggests) was reinforced to some extent during the ninth century.[63]

In these circumstances, the conventional missionary rôle assigned to the Peloponnesian church seems unnecessary and superfluous. After the crushing of the Slav revolt in the reign of Theophilos, the Greek inhabitants were in a position of military superiority in relation to the Slavs. Only the Milingoi and Ezeritai remained in isolation. The other tribes were now surrounded by Greek-speakers, and very probably lived in an environment dominated by Greeks. There was no need for the church do go out of its way to minister to them: the Slavs had already made their first contact with Byzantine culture through the grim media of the army and the estate. The church had only to follow where these had gone before.

Despite the researches of Vasmer, and the evidence of the episcopal lists for the ninth century, the rôle of the church and churchmen in the tenth-century Peloponnese still centres, for Obolensky, around the Slavs.[64] He sees in the most famous of Peloponnesian saints, Nikon Metanoeite, the final executor of the legacy of Basil I. This legacy is itself dubious: and Nikon, as we shall see, was the representative of a different tradition altogether.

Nikon was not a native of the theme, but was born in Pontus Polemoniacus, at some time during the first half of the tenth century.[65] He came to Greece and the Peloponnese from Crete, which he reached soon after its liberation from the Muslims in 961. The *Life* of Nikon records that, despite its liberation, the island was still a breeding-ground of impiety and superstition.[66] Nikon took it upon himself to lead the islanders back to the true faith. His first efforts consisted of calling out loudly for repentance (hence the nickname Metanoeite); but the harsh treatment which he received at the hands of the natives soon led him to change his methods and adopt a more conciliatory tone. After this, he was entirely successful: in the space of three years he had baptised the population, rebuilt or re-consecrated the churches,

[63] Ibid p 120.

[64] Obolensky pp 111-12

[65] The *Life* of Nikon, Greek version, ed S. Lampros, *Neos Ellenomnemon* 3 (Athens 1906) pp 129-223. For Nikon's early life, see pp 128-44. For other versions and editions see *BHG* 2 nos 1366-8.

[66] Ibid p 150.

and established a network of priests and deacons throughout the island.[67]

Nikon then turned his attention towards mainland Greece. After spending some time in Hellas, he returned to the Peloponnese, where he had initially landed. By this time Nikon had reverted to his old, strident, style of preaching: *tyrrhenica tuba clariorem*, as the Latin *Life* puts it.[68] His travels took him to various towns and villages which are described in the *Life* as 'Dorian': Maina, Kalamata, Korone, and Misyne.[69] It may well be around this reference that historians have based their view that Nikon was a missionary to the Slavs. However, Maina had never been penetrated by the Slavs, and had constituted a diocese since the beginning of the tenth century at least, and in all probability since the reign of Basil I.[70] Korone had been a see from the time of Nikephoros I; and it is difficult to imagine that nearby centres such as Kalamata and Misyne were inhabited by pagans.[71] The influence of Christianity may have been weaker in this area than Nikon in his zeal found desirable, but had surely not disappeared entirely. The term 'Dorian' may have been simply a reference to the Slavic past of these rustic areas, or even to their situation in, or proximity to, the Mani.

Nikon's charismatic personality and dramatic methods are demonstrated by his cleansing of the plague from Sparta by the simple if reprehensible means of expelling the Jewish population. He remained in Sparta, and built a church and a monastery there.[72] This venture into the construction industry is described not only in the *Life*, but in his own *Testament*.[73] The *Life* records that the church in Sparta was not large enough for the needs of the population, and that worship frequently took place in other public buildings. Nikon set out to build a larger church and was enthusiastically aided by the townspeople; naturally, he performed miracles during the construction.[74] The *Testament* paints an even more interesting picture. Nikon

---

[67] Ibid p 152.

[68] The Latin Life can be found in E. Martène and U. Durand *Veterum Scriptorum, Monumentarum, Historicorum, Dogmaticorum, Moralium, Amplissima Collectio*, 6 (Paris 1729) cols 837–87. For Nikon's preaching, see col 855.

[69] *Life* p 161.

[70] See p 78 above.

[71] Ibid.

[72] *Life* pp 161–2; ibid pp 166–7.

[73] The *Testament* is also edited by S. Lampros in *Neos Ellenomnemon* 3 (Athens 1906) pp 223–8. For these events see p 224.

[74] *Life* pp 166–7.

complains that he was prevented by the patricians of the town from building his church: they wanted to play *tzounganion*—translated as 'golf' by Sophocles!—on the site which he had chosen.[75] When he was finally permitted to commence work, he was allowed a considerably smaller plot of land than he would have wished. It is interesting to note that the man who brought four bushels of lime to help in the construction came from Slavochori, a village which had obviously been settled by the Slavs, but which now participated in the religious life of the area.[76] Nikon was later to build a church there.[77]

Nikon's attempts to invigorate the religious life of the Peloponnese were to bring him into conflict with authority on other occasions. The military governor of the Peloponnese played some sort of game—perhaps 'golf' again—outside Nikon's church in Sparta, disrupting the evening service. Nikon was expelled from Sparta for daring to protest, and the *strategos* only recalled him when struck down by paralysis—doubtless divinely ordained.[78] Yet the saint was able to advise the governors on political questions, and could prophesy revolts and invasions in the tradition of the Byzantine holy man.[79]

The closing chapters of the *Life* of Nikon deal not only with the last hours of the saint, but also with his posthumous miracles. Only in the latter context are Slavs mentioned, and they turn out to be the Milingoi who were evidently still leading an isolated and hostile existence.[80] Despite his willingness to confront brigands in the hills beyond Kalamata, Nikon never attempted the conversion of these people. The *Life* records that they lived by theft and murder; and they were only prevented by the miraculous apparition of the dead Nikon from carrying off a young girl from the neighbourhood of the monastery which he had built.[81]

The reasons for Nikon's success in revitalising the religious life of the Peloponnese are rooted firmly in the traditions of the domestic rather than the missionary Orthodox church. Like the travelling ascetics of the ninth century, Nikon was the typical holy man, a

[75] *Testament* p 224–6. See Sophocles *Lexicon*.
[76] Ibid p 226.
[77] Ibid p 228.
[78] *Life* pp 172–3.
[79] Ibid pp 174–8.
[80] Ibid p 194.
[81] Ibid pp 200–2.

charismatic figure untroubled by theological niceties. He was never the sophisticated Methodian missionary capable of working among pagan peoples who spoke a foreign tongue: his aggressive manner nearly cost him his life in semi-pagan Crete. The fact that he could resume his old, apocalyptic methods of preaching in the Peloponnese without danger to his life is yet another indication of the region's grounding in Christianity long before his arrival.

It is, on the other hand, evident that many of the inhabitants of the Peloponnese were, to judge by the actions of its rulers, Christians in a somewhat superficial sense. The behaviour of the governors and aristocracy towards Nikon provide one indication of this; and it is noticeable that the bishop of Lakedaimon, Theopemptos, remains a shadowy figure in the *Life*. (It is tempting to assume on this basis that the ecclesiastical hierarchy had been satisfied, in the preceding century, with a superficial Christianity on the part of the Slavs).

We may, therefore, conclude that the church in the Peloponnese was ready for renewal, and that Nikon was its instigator. The late date of this renaissance was due not to the Slavs, who had presented a problem only in a military rather than a cultural sense, but to external factors. The *Life* of another Peloponnesian saint, Peter of Argos, who flourished in the early years of the tenth century dramatically illustrates the pressures to which the Peloponnese was subject.[82] Apart from hazards such as famine, the peninsula suffered continual attacks by Arab pirates and even a fresh Slav incursion.[83] The Arab threat only finally subsided with the Byzantine recapture of Crete in 961, and it is fitting that Nikon, as the leading figure in the renaissance which was to follow arrived in Greece directly after spending some time there. The Peloponnese continued to experience difficulties for some time: there are indications of internal disturbances in the last quarter of the tenth century,[84] and the Bulgars were to invade it in 996; but it had, by the time of Nikon's ministry, almost reached the end of its days as

---

[82] The *Life* of Peter of Argos, A. Mai, *Novum Patrum Bibliotheca* ed I. Cozza-Luzzi 9, 3 (Rome 1888) pp 1–17, 17–20, XXII–XLVI.

[83] *Life* of Peter caps 13, 15, 19.

[84] J. Darrouzès, *Epistoliers byzantins du Xème siècle* (Paris 1960) cap 9 no 19 pp 356–7. Bon p 63 n 2 maintains that the name Ezeros was not preserved in the Peloponnese; however, Vasmer, *Die Slaven*, p 170, says that it did, in fact, survive as a place-name. This, taken in association with the fact that the anonymous writer sends his greetings to a 'Rendakios' a name similar to that of a Spartan who is mentioned in the *Testament* of Nikon (Rontakios p 224) would seem to justify Darrouzès' insistence in placing the revolt in the Peloponnese.

a frontier province, and was eventually combined with the theme of Hellas in the eleventh century.[85]

Nikon was, of course, a builder of churches: he constructed a church as well as a monastery at Sparta, and the remains of the church can still be seen upon the Spartan acropolis. His *Testament* also mentions that he built churches in the neighbouring villages of Parori and Slavochori.[86] Numerous small churches appeared in the Mani and other 'Dorian' areas soon after his visits and into the following century: the Asomatoi near Kitta and the church at Aläi Bey are two examples of this activity. In the south-west the churches of the Holy Apostles, St Charalambos, St Nicholas, St Demetrios and St Athanasios, all in Kalamata, date to the eleventh century.[87] The building of churches was not confined to the south and south-west, and the best-known northern example is undoubtedly St John Theologos in Corinth. These churches do not constitute the final manifestation of a mission to the Slav peoples of the Peloponnese nor the final conversion of the heathen invader. The concept of the re-Christianisation of the Peloponnese should be associated with a more dynamic religious life in the province—in other words, the resumption of Peloponnesian participation in the full range of Orthodox and Byzantine culture.

University of Edinburgh

[85] Bon p 96.
[86] *Testament* p 228.
[87] R. Traquair, 'The Churches of Western Mani', *Annual of the British School at Athens*, 15 (London 1909) p 188; G. Millet, *L'Ecole grecque dans l'architecture byzantine* (Paris 1916) pp 270–1.
[88] R. L. Scranton, *Medieval Architecture in the Central Area of Corinth*, American School of Classical Studies at Athens, Results of Excavations 16 (Princetown, New Jersey 1952) pp 50 *seq.*

SOME HERETICAL ATTITUDES TO
THE RENEWAL OF THE CHURCH

by R. I. MOORE

FOR the most part the authors of the few lurid and fragmentary accounts we have of eleventh and early twelfth-century heretics concentrated almost exclusively on their virulent denunciations of the church, its authority, its sacraments and its priests.[1] Consequently such success as they had has generally been explained in negative terms as the exploitation of anti-clerical sentiment arising from resentment of the church's corruption on the one hand and the extension of its claims on the other, or as the embrace of alien doctrines imported from outside western christendom. That the second explanation is no longer held to apply before the middle of the twelfth century makes it the more necessary to ask again whether the ability of extremely varied manifestations of religious dissent to attract support in many places did not imply the existence of some positive alternative to orthodoxy, some conception of what a church might be, or what its renewal should involve.

Our present understanding, of course, is not entirely negative. Grundmann showed us how often these preachers were animated by the same ideal of the *vita apostolica* that informed the great orthodox reforms of the period; Manselli's discovery of the record of a debate that took place between Henry of Lausanne and a monk named William makes it possible to reconstruct a theology that is both coherent and consistent; and it can be held that the charismatic power of the preacher itself constituted a positive force which enabled him to bring gifts of reconciliation, mediation and consolation to those who needed them.[2] But important as these considerations are they do

---

[1] The sources of this discussion are collected, in English translation, in R. I. Moore, *The Birth of Popular Heresy* (London 1975) pp 1–71; most of them are also in W. L. Wakefield and A. P. Evans, *Heresies of the High Middle Ages* (New York and London 1969) pp 71–150.

[2] Grundmann; [R.] Manselli, ['Il monaco Enrico e la sua eresia'], *BISMEAM* 65 (1953) pp 36–62, discussed by [R. I. Moore, The] *Origins [of European Dissent* (London forthcoming)] cap 4; Janet L. Nelson, 'Society, Theodicy and the Origins of Heresy', *SCH* 9 (1972) pp 65–77 and R. I. Moore, 'The Cult of the Heresiarch', paper presented to the fourth (Oxford 1974) conference of the Commission internationale pour l'histoire écclésiastique comparée, to appear.

not amount to the delineation of an alternative to the vision of a Gregory VII or a Bernard. Indeed to the extent that they stress what heterodoxy and orthodoxy had in common they make it more difficult to understand the ever deeper and more bitter rift between the two than if the heresies had been shown to proceed (as that of the cathars did) from a distinctive conception of man's religious needs and his proper relations with the supernatural.

Since none of the early heretics succeeded in creating the permanent institutions that would have enabled his message to survive his personal memory such a quest may seem fruitless from the outset. In one of the luminous asides that enrich *The Making of the Middle Ages* Southern remarked that satire 'implies the recognition of a certain inevitability in the thing satirized, a lack of any constructive alternative'.[3] He wrote in a different context, but satire was one of the most powerful weapons in the heretics' armoury, whether one thinks of Tanchelm's bizarre antics with his wooden statue of the Virgin, or of the knights of the Albigeois who, according to Geoffrey of Auxerre, *oderunt enim clericos, et gaudent facetiis Henrici.*[4] Douglas suggests an explanation of its ultimate impotence with the comment that 'the solution to grave problems of social organisation can rarely come from those who experience them. For they inevitably can only think according to the cosmological type in which their social life is cast.'[5] That reflection goes far to explain why the cathars could succeed where their forerunners failed. It also extends a challenge to attempt the delicate venture of tracing some of the shifting perceptions of the nature and function of sanctity which were sufficient to provoke radical dissension, though not to suggest how to give institutional form to the new ideals and values to which they pointed.

In these terms it is necessary to consider the sacraments, obviously at the core of the disagreements, from their social rather than their theological aspect. They are what anthropologists call rites of passage. In most societies the great majority of ritual acts mark the crossing of the boundary between one social role and another: the ceremonies both advertise and achieve the transition from infant to adult, maiden to wife, and so on. In principle the boundary, whether in time or space, has position but no dimension, and yet it contains the area in which the

---

[3] R. W. Southern, *The Making of the Middle Ages* (London 1953) p 154.
[4] *PL* 185 (1860) col 412.
[5] M. Douglas, *Natural Symbols* (London 2 ed 1973) p 187.

transformation—from yours to mine, from sickness to health, from guilt to absolution—takes place. This ambiguity makes it a no-man's land, an area charged with supernatural power, and therefore marked and guarded by ritual. But the boundaries themselves are drawn not by nature, but by human perception, which arbitrarily divides what in nature is continuous. As Leach puts it, 'this whole process of carving up the external world into named categories to suit our social convenience depends upon the fact that though our ability to alter the external environment is very limited, we have an unrestricted capacity for playing games with the internalised version of the environment which we carry in our heads.'[6] Hence, it must follow, changes in ritual reflect changes in the perception of social categories and the nature and importance of the boundaries between them; disagreement about ritual reflects the existence of different perceptions of the location or significance of the boundaries.

For example, until the middle of the eleventh century the prime locations of holy power and spiritual authority in the west were supposed to be the patron saints and the basilicas which enshrined their relics. They were the focus of the liturgical round which marked the rhythms of an unchanging world, and the point of appeal for protection against external menace and sanction against the malefactor.[7] In these pursuits the priests, their guardians, led and spoke for the people, and for that reason might properly be of the people, by and large, in their manners and conduct. When the guardians of Peter's see raised his claims above the rest[8] they shifted the locus of spiritual power from the shrines and relics of lesser saints and placed it in the succession from Peter itself. That succession was contained neither in buildings nor in bones, but in the priests themselves. The boundary of the holy was moved forward to embrace them. They became, far more clearly than formerly, inhabitants of the liminal region where holy power lay. The change was dramatically expressed in the withdrawal of the communion wine from the laity: part of the power which resided in the

---

[6] E. Leach, *Culture and Communication* (Cambridge 1976) pp 35–6; see also pp 33–5, 51–2, 77–9.

[7] Compare H. E. J. Cowdrey, 'The Peace and Truce of God' *PP* 46 (1970) pp 49–56; A. Vermeesch, *Essai sur les origines et la signification de la commune dans le nord de la France (XIe–XIIe siècle)* (Heule 1966) pp 25–77.

[8] This aspect of the papal reform is particularly clear in its connection with Milan; for example, H. E. J. Cowdrey, 'The Papacy, the Patarenes, and the Church of Milan' *TRHS* 5 series 18 (1968) pp 25–9.

sacrament was arrested within the boundary now drawn firmly between the priest and his congregation, and made the priest himself a liminal object. Such a change necessarily changed also the importance attached to rituals and to personal qualities. In particular, it focused attention powerfully on the validity of ordination, the rite of passage by which the priest claimed to have achieved this enhanced position, and on his celibacy which was in this as in many cultures the most universally acknowledged sign of liminal status. And it is worth remarking that on the significance of these criteria there was full agreement between those who wished to assert the new boundary and the heretics who resisted it.

In general then the conception of rites of passage is capable of describing a situation which historians are more used to think of in other terms. It may seem impertinent to labour that point, but it provides a basis for estimating the preoccupations of the heretics. Their attacks were directed most frequently at the area newly claimed for the holy, and at the rites of passage whose control the reformed church was most actively pursuing—at the authority and manner of life of the clergy themselves, and at the demands for marriage to be celebrated in church, confession to be made and penance paid to priests, burial take place in holy ground. Conversely, it was much rarer for criticism to be levelled at what had been prominent in the pre-Gregorian idea of the holy—at the mass itself, as distinct from those who celebrated it, or at saints and their relics. The last is especially worth noticing because in the classifications that are more usually adopted to characterise the concerns of the heretics (for example, as hostility to sources of ecclesiastical revenue) it is not easy to understand why they did not attack the cult of relics more frequently.

If the papal contention that holy power resided substantially in the clergy who embodied the apostolic succession was not accepted, some alternative locus must be implied. For many, it may be, the answer was a conservative one, and the great growth of pilgrimage and the veneration of relics in the years after the reform represented in part a reassertion of popular faith in the familiar repositaries of the holy which the church was wise to encourage. Our present concern, however, is with the recalcitrant minority whose preference was not so easily accommodated. Their priority in ritual could hardly be more obvious. By far the most common, almost the universal, teaching of the early heretics was the rejection of infant baptism. They stated a variety of objections, but that the child could have no faith in what he could not understand was usually among them. The corollary of that position was accepted by at least one prominent heretic, for the report reached Peter the Venerable that people were being told that they would not be saved 'unless after the baptism of Christ they are baptised with that of Henry'.[9] When he was in Le Mans in 1116 Henry was also the central figure in an episode which shows the classical characteristics of the rite of passage. He called a meeting at the church of St. Germain and St. Vincent where 'he pronounced a new doctrine, that women who had not lived chastely must, naked before everybody, burn their clothes and hair'.[10] This is a common symbol of the separation by cleansing from the status that is being abandoned. Henry accompanied it with a sermon in which he said that marriage should not be inhibited by considerations of consanguinity or the need for dowry. Then he persuaded young men to come forward and marry the reformed women, and collected money from the assembled people to replace the burned clothes and give the couples a start in their new life. Except in the case of Henry himself, who set out in his debate with William his view that marriage was a matter for those concerned, and not for the church,[11] it is not possible to say how often those accused of rejecting matrimony were in fact contesting the drive of the reformers to bring within the control of the church a ceremony which had ordinarily been conducted outside it, but the other ritual, that of public confession, is echoed in the occasional citation by heretics of saint James' 'confess your sins to one another'. The same preference for activity centred on the collective body of the faithful rather than around the priest was expressed at a less formal level by the bible study which is constantly implied by the familiarity that heretics often showed, especially with the new testament, and confirmed by Lambert le Bègue's translation of the acts of the apostles into the vernacular for the use of the women of his congregation who used to meet in their homes on Sundays to 'sing hymns and psalms, think over what they had heard in church and encourage each other to observe it.'[12]

Marriage then, as Henry conducted it, took place in the eyes of the community and untrammeled by ecclesiastical rules. The object of confession was not to gain absolution from the priest, but to make peace with the community and be received back into it, the reception

---

[9] *Tractatus contra Petrobrusianos* ed J. V. Fearns, *CC continuatio mediaevalis* 10 (1968) p 14.
[10] *Gesta pontificum cenomannensium*, Bouquet 12 p 549.
[11] Manselli, pp 55–6.
[12] Fredericq 2 p 30.

very practically symbolised at Le Mans by the provision of husbands and the collection of money. Similarly the function of adult baptism as a rite of passage is crucially different from that of infant baptism, theological considerations apart. Emphasis on it signalled that reception into membership of the community was all-important, the difference between insider and outsider exalted, while distinctions between insiders such as ordination signified were minimised or abandoned. Moreover, the transition to membership was equated with that from childhood to maturity. The orthodox view that a child was baptised in the faith of his parents and godparents was consonant with the collective structures of the early middle ages in which responsibility for a man's actions was assumed by his kin, or his lord. When the men of Arras who were questioned by bishop Gerard in 1025 objected that infant baptism provided no insurance against the sins which its subject might commit in later life[13] they expressed the loss of the confidence which a stable community might have in the ability of its customary structures to control and sanction the young. What was the good, if some migrant weaver should make trouble, of appealing to the distant kingroup which he had deserted to seek his fortune? The breakdown of collective structures had changed the relative importance of transitions, diminishing that of being born into, and accepted by, the community to enhance that of proving one's capacity to act as a responsible member of it.

The same reflection points to another change. In these times communities did not simply exist immemorially as kingroups or lordships. They had to be created afresh. In secular contexts the process is familiar, most obviously in the formation of gilds and communes which also elaborated their tests and ceremonials, their rites of passage. Adult baptism might denote in the same way that the community was deliberately and consciously created by those who would commit their loyalties to it.

In a brilliant study of trial by ordeal Brown has shown how the function of the ordeal was to provide not an arbitrary expression of 'divine' will, but a framework, a focus and a sanction for the formation of collective judgement.[14] His analysis applies exactly to the par-

---

[13] PL 142 (1853) col 1272.

[14] P. R. L. Brown, 'Society and the Supernatural: A Medieval Change', Daedalus (Cambridge, Mass., 1975) pp 133–55; see also Colin Morris, 'Judicium Dei: The Social and Political Significance of the Ordeal in the Eleventh Century', SCH 12 (1975) pp 95–111, who reflects in conclusion that the ordeal tended to assist the weak against the established order.

ticipation of the populace at large in the trials of heretics, which was always accompanied by the invocation of ritual tests, such as the ordeal of the mass or oaths sworn on relics. In this context as in others the church and the lay magnates systematically removed jurisdiction to their own courts, and the conflict set up thereby sometimes led to the execution of heretics by crowds in vindication of their traditional procedure. The clearest example is that of Clement of Bucy who was condemned by the water in 1114, and then seized from imprisonment and burned by the crowd after the bishop had gone off to Soissons to seek the advice of other prelates.[15] In the same way the condemnation of Peter Maurand, the great cathar of Toulouse who broke down when he was challenged to deny his heresy by swearing on relics in front of a large, excited and hostile crowd, or the miracles by which Bernard confirmed his victory over Henry of Lausanne in the mission of 1145, exemplify the function of the supernatural as a means of canalising collective sentiment.[16] The convictions which heretics held about the sacraments, fragmentary and incoherently presented as they usually were, expressed the same desire as the popular defence of trial by ordeal to see holy power located in the will and judgement of the community rather than in clerical office. To that extent a constructive alternative to the Gregorian vision was sensed, if not articulated, of a church which would find its spirit and its force in the needs and convictions of its members rather than in the prescriptions of its prelates. And, in the curious compound which that sense presents of response to new problems and difficulties through resistance to innovation and the appeal, partly no doubt nostalgic, to ancient values and habits, it provides in its fashion a typical example of the medieval idea of reform.

University of Sheffield

---

[15] Guibert of Nogent *De vita sua, PL* 156 (1880) col 953.
[16] Roger of Hoveden, *Chronica*, ed W. Stubbs, 4 vols, *RS* 51 (1868–71) 2, p 163; *PL* 185 cols 410–16. These points are discussed at greater length in *Origins* caps 9 and 10.

PAUPERTAS CHRISTI: OLD WEALTH AND NEW POVERTY IN THE TWELFTH CENTURY

by BRENDA M. BOLTON

T HE consequential implications for those who adopted a life of apostolic poverty in the twelfth century can in turn raise many complex questions.[1] This paper makes little attempt to resolve the questions raised. Rather it is hoped that in discussing them suggestions will be forthcoming which will help either to achieve some degree of clarification or raise further and perhaps more searching questions in the minds of others.

I would first suggest that the *vita apostolica* was adopted as a form of personal and social renewal and that poverty was considered to be a means towards *renovatio*.[2] My second and much less easily demonstrated suggestion would be that poverty became the distinguishing symbol of the 'new man' in the twelfth century. There is slight evidence for these suggestions since those who adopted the life of apostolic poverty said little about their motives. For some, no written evidence emanating from their movement exists at all[3] and there we can only rely on the reports of contemporary observers, many of whom were openly hostile to the changes taking place around them.[4] They

---

[1] Among recent works on poverty I have found especially valuable [M.] Mollat, [*Etudes sur*] *l'histoire de la pauvreté*, Publications de la Sorbonne, *Etudes,* 8, 2 vols (Paris 1974); [*Poverty in the Middle Ages*, ed D.] Flood, *FF* 27 (Werl-Westfalia 1975); *La povertà* [*del secolo XII e Francesco d'Assisi*], Atti del II Convegno Internationale (Assisi 1975).

[2] [M.-D.] Chenu, 'Monks, Canons and Laymen in search of the Apostolic Life' and 'The Evangelical Awakening' in *Nature, Man and Society* [*in the Twelfth Century: Essays on New Theological Perspectives in the Latin West*], ed and translated by J. Taylor and L. K. Little (Chicago 1968) pp 202–69; Janet L. Nelson, 'Society, theodicy and the origins of medieval heresy', *SCH* 9 (1972) p 75. Also C. Violante, 'Hérésies urbaines et rurales en Italie du 11e au 13e siècle' in [J.] Le Goff, *Hérésies et Sociétés* [*dans l'Europe pré-industrielle 11–18 siècles*], École pratique des hautes études: *Civilisations et Sociétés* 10 (Paris 1968) who offers an analysis of the movement towards the *vita apostolica*.

[3] On the lack of evidence for one such group see my article 'Sources for the early history of the *humiliati*', *SCH* 11 (1975) pp 125–33.

[4] Walter Map was expressing a widely held view when he says of the Waldensians 'they are now beginning in a very humble guise because they cannot get their foot in; but if we let them in, we shall be turned out', translated by [R. B.] Brooke, *The Coming of the Friars* (London 1975) pp 151–2; [Walter] Map, [*De Nugis Curialium*, ed M. R. James], *Anecdota Oxoniensia*, Medieval and Modern Series, 14 (Oxford 1914) pp 60–2.

BRENDA M. BOLTON

tell us that in the second half of the twelfth century, considerable numbers of people appeared to be behaving strangely: renouncing wealth and inheritance, living on alms or choosing to undertake manual work, starving themselves, wearing rags, going barefoot, inflicting personal suffering and generally harassing their own bodies.[5] Although behaving in this seemingly anti-social way, they continued to conform, accepting the established framework of the church. Of this the ecclesiastical authorities were very doubtful, regarding those who practised such poverty as socially dangerous.[6] Were they correct in this view?

This life of poverty was followed by significant numbers of lay people, mainly from the upper levels of society who chose to adopt a life style which was immediately and radically different from their previous existence. Voluntary poverty was now the basis on which they lived.[7] Groups of like-minded people came into being and amongst these we must include Valdes and the Waldensians or Poor Men of Lyon,[8] the *humiliati* of Lombardy,[9] Durand de Huesca and the Poor Catholics,[10] Bernard Prim and the converted *Vaudois*,[11] and Francis with the first friars.[12] Nor should we omit the cathar *perfecti* who behaved similarly if not for the same reasons and indeed were even more austere and extreme in their actions in regard to poverty.[13] These groups embraced the life of poverty with equal enthusiasm but with varying degrees of material deprivation and self-torture. They all seem to have originated in the new urban environment of the

5 *Ibid* p 62; *Scripta Leonis, Rufini et Angeli sociorum S. Francisci: the Writings of Leo, Rufino and Angelo, Companions of St Francis*, ed and translated by R. B. Brooke (Oxford 1970) pp 155–7, 181–7, 193–7, 240–1.
6 B. M. Bolton, 'Tradition and temerity: papal attitudes to deviants 1159–1216', SCH 9 (1972) pp 79–91 for a general discussion of these questions.
7 M. Mollat, 'Pauvres et pauvreté dans le monde médiéval', *La povertà*, pp 81–97.
8 [K.-V.] Selge, [*Die ersten Waldenser*] (Berlin 1967); [C.] Thouzellier, [*Catharisme et Valdéisme en Languedoc à la fin du xiie et au début du xiiie siècle* (2 ed Louvain 1969) and Grundmann pp 91–100.
9 On the *humiliati* see especially Zanoni; Grundmann pp 70–97, 487–538; and my articles 'Innocent III's treatment of the *humiliati*', SCH 8 (1971) pp 73–82; 'Sources for the early history of the *humiliati*', SCH 11 (1975) and 'The poverty of the *humiliati*' in Flood pp 52–9.
10 Thouzellier pp 212–32; Selge pp 104–9; *Cahiers de Fanjeaux* 2, [ed E. Privat, *Vaudois languedociens et Pauvres Catholiques*] (Toulouse 1967).
11 Thouzellier pp 232–5; *Cahiers de Fanjeaux* 2 (1967); Grundmann pp 118–27.
12 Brooke, *The Coming of the Friars*; [M. D.] Lambert, *Franciscan Poverty*: [*the doctrine of the absolute poverty of Christ and the Apostles in the Franciscan order 1210–1323*] (London 1961); *La povertà*; Grundmann pp 127–35.
13 A. Borst, *Die Katharer*, MGH SS, 12 (Stuttgart 1953); [R. I.] Moore, *The Birth of Popular Heresy* (London 1975); Le Goff, *Hérésies et Sociétés* pp 120–38; *Cahiers de Fanjeaux* 3, [ed E. Privat, *Cathares en Languedoc*] (Toulouse 1968).

period: in the towns and amongst the merchant class where, by medieval standards, they could have enjoyed a comfortable life.[14] In spite of this they deliberately chose to harass their own bodies with the infliction of indignities and hardships.

Valdes's first and personal inspiration was to go and sell all that he had acquired usuriously and live on alms.[15] The *humiliati* did not beg, but aimed to be self-supporting by working with their hands. That their life-style required considerable self-restraint and was far more austere and demanding than that of the ordinary layman we may deduce in part from their very name.[16] Durand de Huesca and the Poor Catholics stressed their determination to be poor and accepted only that which was necessary for daily existence.[17] The picture is completed by Francis who abandoned material wealth and inheritance in a dramatic and symbolic renunciation based on his literal interpretation of the gospels and who subsequently led a life of total renunciation and absolute poverty.[18]

Others as well as Francis used the gospels and epistles as lines of guidance, for the new testament was becoming more generally available in the twelfth century. Valdes for example consulted his local *schola* on theological matters as did the *humiliati*.[19] There appeared at this time bible manuscripts in small, one volume, format on thin parchment which could easily be carried among a wandering scholar's personal effects.[20] Thus through their knowledge of the gospels those

[14] On the problems posed by urban growth and money in twelfth century society see the articles by [L. K.] Little, 'Pride goes before Avarice', *AHR* 76 (1971) pp 16–49 and 'Evangelical poverty, the new money economy and violence', *Poverty in the Middle Ages* pp 11–26.

[15] *Chronicon anonymi Laudunensis*, ed G. Waitz, *MGH SS* 26 (Hanover 1882) p 447; Map pp 61–2; [C.] Thouzellier, 'Hérésie et pauvreté [à la fin du xiie et au début du xiiie siècle]', *Histoire de la Pauvreté*, pp 371–88 and especially pp 378–9. Valdes found his biblical instruction in Matt 19, 21: *si vis perfectus esses* . . .

[16] Bolton, 'The poverty of the *humiliati*'; *Poverty in the Middle Ages* p 55; Zanoni pp 261–63.

[17] *PL* 215 (1855) cols 1510–14; Potthast I nos 3571–3 p 308; Selge p 96; *Cahiers de Fanjeaux* 2 (1967) pp 173–85.

[18] Lambert, *Franciscan Poverty* pp 31–67. It is most interesting to compare this view with the chapter 'Communitas: model and process' in [V. W.] Turner, *The Ritual Process* (Harmondsworth 1969) pp 119–54 and especially pp 128–35. Celano speaks of Francis's poverty as 'the most perfect conquest of himself', J. H. Moorman, *A History of the Franciscan Order from its origins to 1517* (Oxford 1968) p 8.

[19] Chenu, *Nature, Man and Society* p 249 n 12; [C.] Morris, *Medieval Media* (University of Southampton 1972); Thouzellier pp 221–3.

[20] R. Loewe, 'The medieval history of the latin vulgate', in *The Cambridge History of the Bible* 2, ed G. W. H. Lampe, (Cambridge 1976) p 146. One extant small-format bible measures $5\frac{3}{4}$ inches by 4 inches. *Ibid* p 146 n 2.

who voluntarily chose poverty saw themselves as the successors of the apostles, attempting to live in the way of life of the first Christian community as it could best be lived in the twelfth century.[21] To them, *paupertas* represented the hardest, most intensely personal act they could perform. As with Francis, they were responding to Christ's call to the rich young ruler to give up all that he had and in so doing, hoped to achieve the salvation that was promised.[22] Poverty thus became a means whereby personal rebirth or renewal could be obtained.

To see how the *vita apostolica* could be applied, they had only to turn to the example shown them by the cult of St Alexis.[23] This example appears to have been an important catalyst in bringing about voluntary poverty and was in fact the direct impetus to conversion in the case of Valdes.[24] The values spread by the Alexis cult went back to the ascetic tradition of the *imitatio Christi* and represented a lay individualistic solution to a crisis of conscience rather than one given by the more usual monastic and institutional way. This model of aristocratic lay renunciation fitted neatly into the social and ethical phenomena of the period where a clearer image of God-made-Man was being forged. Those discontented with current social values found a vital message in the *Life of Alexis*. By changing his way of life, a man could find a personal response to the torments of the age through his spiritual renewal. Those such as Valdes and Francis were in no doubt of this.

This renunciation, when it came, was often accompanied by dramatic actions.[25] It appears that a quiet, peaceful and hidden conversion would have been inappropriate in expressing the message which they had received. Could this have been because it was at that time also that the first attempts at an intellectual, theological justification of merchants' activities were being put forward? The view, widely held in the previous century that a merchant was 'rarely or never able to

---

[21] L. Goppelt, *Apostolic and Post-Apostolic Times,* trans R. A. Guelich (London 1970) pp 25–60 for a discussion of the nature of the first community.

[22] Matt 19, 21–2; Lambert, *Franciscan Poverty* p 57.

[23] A. Gieysztor, 'La Légende de Saint Alexis en Occident: un idéal de pauvreté', *Histoire de la Pauvreté* pp 125–39.

[24] *Ibid* p 137; Morris, *Medieval Media* in which he discusses the impact of the song in transmitting new ideas and values.

[25] Lambert, *Franciscan Poverty* p 61 and Turner, *The Ritual Process* pp 133–4, both stress the immense, emotional significance which nakedness held for Francis. Such theatricality may be linked to the existential quality of *communitas* for it 'involves the whole man in his relation to other whole men' and 'is accompanied by experiences of unprecedented potency. The processes of "levelling" and "stripping" . . . often appear to flood their subjects with affect', *Ibid* pp 114–15.

please God'[26] was by the end of the twelfth century being challenged and he was coming to be regarded as the acceptable mainspring of the new commercial development. It was in the school of moral theology in Paris and among the circle of Peter the Chanter and his friends that *apologiae* appeared for the first time for the particular activities engaged in by merchants.[27] It may have been precisely the evolution of this justification which explains why the adepts of voluntary poverty often went to such lengths to renounce their possessions. They were reacting against a society which not only tolerated, but had now begun to condone, the activities of merchants.

Other possible explanations may lead us towards my second point, that poverty in the twelfth century was the distinguishing symbol of the 'new man'.

In the salvation imagery of his epistles, Paul develops the idea of the natural body and the spiritual body.[28] These are seen in terms of the old man, Adam, and the new man, Christ.[29] In order to become a new man who is fit to be part of the body of Christ the old man has to be beaten down.[30] Could therefore the flagellation of their bodies by the poor of Christ represent to them this instruction to beat down the old man in order to become the new man? The old self would be denied and the Pauline new self would be brought about. Poverty would have

---

[26] 'Mercator vix aut nunquam potest Deo placere', Chenu, *Nature, Man and Society* p 224 n 45.

[27] J. W. Baldwin, *Masters, Princes and Merchants: the social views of Peter the Chanter and his circle*, 2 vols (Princeton 1970) I pp 261–311; J. Le Goff, *Marchands et banquiers du moyen âge* (Paris 1956) pp 70–98; L. Vereecke, 'History of Moral Theology', *NCE* 9 p 1120; M.-D. Chenu, *L'éveil de la conscience dans la civilisation médiévale* (Paris 1969); T. P. McLaughlin, 'The teaching of the canonists on usury (XII, XIII and XIV centuries)', *Mediaeval Studies* 1 (1939) pp 81–147; 2 (1940) pp 1–22; J. T. Noonan, *The Scholastic Analysis of Usury* (Cambridge, Mass., 1957); R. de Roover, *La pensée économique des scolastiques, doctrines et méthodes* (Paris 1971). A recent article by [B. H.] Rosenwein and [L. K.] Little, ['Social Meaning in the] Monastic and Mendicant Spiritualities', *PP* 63 (1974) pp 4–33 especially pp 29–31 gives a useful indication of those justifications of usury which were appearing at this time.

[28] 1 Cor 15, 44. On St Paul's salvation imagery see H. Musurillo, *Symbolism and the Christian Imagination* (Baltimore 1962) pp 14–26. For evidence that Paul was widely quoted during this period by heretics and orthodox alike see C. Violante, 'La pauvreté dans les hérésies du xie siècle en occident', *Histoire de la Pauvreté* pp 347–69 and Brooke, *The Coming of the Friars* p 126. On the transmission and glosses of the Pauline epistles, B. Smalley, *The Study of the Bible in the Middle Ages* (Oxford 1952) pp 63–75.

[29] A. Richardson, 'The whole Christ' *An Introduction to the Theology of the New Testament* pp 242–65 and especially pp 242–52.

[30] 'Put away . . . the old man, which waxeth corrupt . . . be ye renewed in the spirit of your mind and put on the new man, which after God has been created in righteousness and holiness of truth' Eph 4, 22–24.

appeared to exemplify the new man whilst the old man was characterised by wealth. A careful reading of Ephesians would have encouraged them to believe that if they could create a new self they would thus be worthy members of Christ's body, the church.[31]

How far does this relate to society? Were they visiting on themselves the correction and deprivation which they really wished to apply to society itself? Were these people regarding their bodies as surrogates for society, each one being a microcosm of the social situation?[32] Could it be that by the mortification of their selves to bring about a personal rebirth, they would in some mysterious way bring about the hoped for purification and rebirth of society?[33] If we do allow that there is anything in such an interpretation, and that it was not purely the acts of individuals seeking personal salvation, then this would support the view that their harsh treatment of their own bodies represented a deliberate social act to recreate a new church in a new society.

Such suggestions are of course tentative and difficult to prove but at least they give rise to lines of enquiry. In the first place, their regard for their bodies as a substitute for society may be linked with the contemporary debate on the nature of the two bodies of Christ. The natural body, the *corpus verum* was the personal body of the eucharist in contrast with the mystical body of all believers, the church.[34] It was claimed that Christ had intended to lead men from the example of his natural body to an understanding of his mystical body.[35] Hence it was not inappropriate that those who wished to come closer to Christ should regard their own natural bodies as surrogates whereby, through suffering and purging, they could become part of the mystical body The

---

[31] Eph 2, 14–17.

[32] [M.] Douglas, *Natural Symbols* (2 ed London 1973) pp 93–112 on the use of the body as a symbol.

[33] Such ideas might possibly have stemmed from the seventh century Irish treatise *De duodecim abusivis saeculi* which stresses that the behaviour of a king affects the quality of the society over which he rules and that he must first correct himself before he can correct others, PL 4 (1865) cols 877–78; Could these ideas have filtered down through society and have led those who regarded themselves as kings and priests towards the notion of self-correction before they could become representatives of Christ? This text may have been quite widely known since it was included by Jonas of Orleans in his *De institutione Regia*, PL 106 (1864) col 288. See also J. M. Wallace-Hadrill, 'The *Via Regia* of the Carolingian Age' in *Trends in Medieval Political Thought*, ed B. Smalley (Oxford 1965) pp 22–41 and Thouzellier, 'Hérésie et pauvreté', *Histoire de la Pauvreté* p 374 for a similar suggestion.

[34] H. de Lubac, *Corpus Mysticum* (Paris 1949) pp 116–26; E. Kantorowicz, *The King's Two Bodies* (Princeton 1957) pp 193–98.

[35] J. Danielou, A. H. Couratin and John Kent, *The Pelican Guide to Modern Theology* (Harmondsworth 1971) p 134.

use of the body as a surrogate for the church was regarded as an integral part of the *vita apostolica*.

Why was it necessary to change society in this way? Many in the twelfth century shared pessimistic views of contemporary society.[36] These views were coloured by the usual problems which beset the urban dweller: problems of dislocation, overcrowding and uncertainty in the face of change. Some believed wealth to be socially divisive and commerce corrupt.[37] Their deep concern led them to reject usury and to abhor the handling of money.[38] They displayed guilt not only about their own possessions but also about the plight of the real and involuntary poor and so were concerned to set an example by distributing food and clothes to the indigent.[39]

Yet in spite of the bewildering degree of variation in social criticism from these groups, the criticism does not really develop into unorthodox relationships with the church and with society. None of this criticism led to active attempts on behalf of the Waldensians or *humiliati* to change society. Although they formed part of what was essentially a protest movement, their protest was not against the church as has already been seen in statements they made when faced with ecclesiastical authorities who regarded them as socially dangerous.[40] It may be that by the time they had taken out their hostility to society on their own bodies they had largely relieved the symptoms which had first provoked their attitudes. Additionally it could have been that the satisfaction following a feeling of individual rebirth and redemption was enough, whether they were aware of this or not.

Their professions of faith, the only written evidence, stressed their

[36] Chenu, *Nature, Man and Society* p 243 discusses those groups in society, *juvenes*, wage-earners and merchants who lived on the margins of society and who thus constituted a homogeneous milieu for the poor of Christ. Clothmakers as a group were noted above the others for a critical spirit.

[37] Lambert le Bègue appears to have believed that wealth was socially divisive, Moore, *The Birth of Popular Heresy* pp 103–11. It is paradoxical that the groups who condemned money as a source of corruption were precisely those who undertook to bring the gospels home to merchants, Chenu, *Nature, Man and Society* p 226 and Rosenwein and Little, 'Monastic and Mendicant Spiritualities', pp 22–31.

[38] Little, 'Pride goes before Avarice' p 44 figures 10 and 11 shows the revulsion which the handling of money caused. We are also told how Francis made a friar place money on a dungheap after he had accidently touched it, Thomas of Celano, *Vita Secunda*, in *Analecta Franciscana* 10 (Quaracchi 1926–41) pp 178–9.

[39] *VHM* II pp 131–2.

[40] Valdes's profession of faith states that 'we believe one catholic Church, apostolic and immaculate . . . we humbly praise and venerate all ecclesiastical orders', Brooke, *The Coming of the Friars* pp 148–50; A. Dondaine, 'Aux origines du Valdéisme—une profession de foi de Valdes', *AFP* 16 (1946) pp 191–235; Selge pp 104–9.

obedience even to the extent of receiving sacraments from priests whom they considered to be sinful. There was no hypocrisy in this since, as they were concerned with their own bodies as surrogates for the renewal of church and society, a sinful priest in an erring church and a corrupt secular society would be a matter for regret and more self-harassment and not for separation.[41] It was not until they felt the need to present their inner faith for the edification of others through preaching that any real problem of heresy arose.[42]

To all this the cathars seemed to be an exception. The *perfecti* appeared to be doing essentially the same thing as the orthodox poor of Christ only more vehemently. Contemporaries reluctantly admitted that the lives they led were more ascetic and their practice of poverty more certain.[43] Was it this more proficient exercise of poverty and suffering which made them more savagely anti-social or was there a different basis of belief? Unlike the orthodox groups the cathars did not attempt to find satisfaction in using their bodies as surrogates. The more harshly they treated themselves the more anti-social they became and this brought with it a vision of a reformed church totally removed from the real and orthodox church.[44] This was a vision which was never shared by the Waldensians and *humiliati*. The beliefs of the cathars with their need to be successful in fighting the world which to them was evil were based on those parts of the bible they recognised, notably the gospels and acts and were markedly different from orthodox Christians. Their concepts and ideas were dualistic.[45] They believed that their real selves had descended from a truly divine world and they sought in turn to remove themselves as far as possible from

[41] Brooke, *The Coming of the Friars* p 149 where Valdes professes that 'the sacraments . . . although they may be administered by a sinful priest, while the church receives him we in no way reject, nor do we withdraw from ecclesiastical services and blessings celebrated by such a one, but with a benevolent mind embrace it as we do from the most righteous'. For Durand de Huesca's *propositum conversationis* see PL 215 (1855) cols 1510–14; Potthast I, nos 3571–3 p 308. For Bernard Prim see PL 216 (1855) cols 648–50; Potthast I, no 4567 p 394. Francis too was insistent that priests be honoured and some of the first friars deliberately confessed to a priest of ill-repute because they refused to believe ill of him, Brooke, *The Coming of the Friars* p 31.

[42] For a fine discussion of this point see Thouzellier, 'Hérésie et pauvreté', *Histoire de la Pauvreté* pp 380–1 and K.-V. Selge, 'Characteristiques du premier mouvement vaudois et crises au cours de son expansion', *Cahiers de Fanjeaux* 2 (1967) pp 110–42.

[43] Peter de Vaux Cernay, *Petri Vallium Sarnau monachi Hystoria albigensis,* ed P. Guerin and E. Lyon, 3 vols (Paris 1926–39) I pp 14–17.

[44] See Moore, *The Birth of Popular Heresy* pp 122–7 for the views of cathars in Lombardy between *c*1170 and *c*1200. This extract demonstrates not only aspects of their reforming vision but also the variety of different views attributed to them.

[45] *Ibid* p 2.

those bounds of physical and historical existence found in the world in which they lived.[46] To the *perfecti*, trying to release the spirit, the excessive punishment of their bodies, including in certain cases suicide, did not matter, for as with all material things they were regarded as evil.

Thus the *perfecti* were in a very different position from the truly Christian adepts of voluntary poverty who in following the example of Christ attempted to imitate him and share some of his suffering. Coming together in groups, however, has inherent dangers. Splendid visions of new societies are created which lead to conflict with the greater entities of church and society. In understanding this we must think not only of the cathar *perfecti* of this period but also of the spiritual Franciscans of the thirteenth and fourteenth centuries with their Joachite dreams and their plans for the redemption of the whole church through the total acceptance of voluntary poverty.[47] This vision ultimately brought discredit to this reforming group within the order, and worked fundamentally and fatally against the doctrine of the absolute poverty of Christ which had been so relevant as a force for renewal in the context of the twelfth century. The church in western society had not yet found a solution to the problem of individual rebirth in a renewed society.

University of London
Westfield College

---

[46] *Cahiers de Fanjeaux* 3 (1968); Douglas, *Natural Symbols* p 17 where this attitude is discussed. 'Here the body is not primarily the vehicle of life, for life will be seen as purely spiritual and the body as irrelevant matter . . . It follows that the body tends to serve as a symbol of evil, as a structured system contrasted with pure spirit which by its nature is free and undifferentiated'.

[47] Lambert, *Franciscan Poverty* pp 184–246.

REBUILDING ZION:
THE HOLY PLACES OF JERUSALEM
IN THE TWELFTH CENTURY

by BERNARD HAMILTON

IT is unusual for a period of Christian renewal to begin with a massacre, yet that is what happened when the crusaders entered Jerusalem on 15 July 1099. Raymond of Aguilers, chaplain of the count of Toulouse, boasted that they rode through moslem corpses heaped up in the Haram al-Sharif with blood 'even to the horse bridles'.[1] This should not obscure the fact that the crusading movement was motivated partly by a growing devotion to the humanity of Christ in the western church in the late eleventh century,[2] or, as the author of the *Gesta Francorum* expressed it, a desire to 'follow in the footsteps of Christ, by whom they had been redeemed from the power of hell'.[3] It was this sentiment which led the crusaders to seek to restore the shrine churches of Jerusalem and in the eighty-eight years of their rule they filled the city with fine churches and monasteries closely resembling those which were being built in the west at the same time.

It should be emphasised that the crusaders were seldom concerned to rebuild existing churches in Frankish style: their primary interest was to restore churches which had been ruined by war and persecution in the centuries of moslem rule. The pilgrim Saewulf, who visited the east four years after the Latin conquest, reported that 'nothing has been left habitable by the Saracens, but everything has been devastated . . . in all . . . the holy places outside the walls . . . of Jerusalem'.[4]

The chief shrine was the church of the Holy Sepulchre. Constantine the Great had erected a complex of buildings there around three principal holy places and some knowledge of his work is essential in order to appreciate later developments. At the eastern end of the complex a large basilica was built over the crypt where Saint Helena had found the relic of the Cross; to the west of this was a courtyard, in the south-

[1] Raymond of Aguilers, *Historia Francorum qui ceperunt Iherusalem*, RHC Oc 3p 300.
[2] R. W. Southern, *The Making of the Middle Ages* (London 1953) pp 245-9.
[3] *Gesta Francorum et aliorum Hierosolimitanorum*, ed and transl R. Hill (London 1962) p 2.
[4] *Saewulf['s pilgrimage to Jerusalem and the Holy Land]*, transl W. R. Brownlow, PPTS 21 (1892) p 22.

eastern corner of which stood the rock of Calvary; and at the west end of the courtyard was a rotunda, enclosing a shrine built over the grotto of the Lord's sepulchre. The caliph Hakim ordered the destruction of what was left of these buildings in 1009 and the shrine which the crusaders found was that built by the Byzantine emperor Constantine IX and consecrated in 1048.

A marble canopy with a silver-gilt dome was erected above the sepulchre. This stood at the centre of the rotunda, which was rebuilt on its former site with the addition of an apse at the east end which served as a sanctuary. The rotunda was richly decorated with mosaics, and had a pillared gallery and a timber dome which was open to the sky above the shrine.[5] The former courtyard to the east was enclosed by two-storied buildings which adjoined the rotunda and the Calvary chapel was rebuilt in the south-eastern corner. The Constantinian basilica was not rebuilt and therefore the crypt-chapel of Saint Helena, which remained in use, was outside the new complex.[6]

Duke Godfrey appointed a chapter of non-resident, secular canons to serve the church,[7] but in 1114 they were forced to adopt the rule of the Austin canons and live in community.[8] A house was built for them round the ruins of Constantine's basilica, which became the new cloister-garth,[9] and a palace for the Latin patriarch was erected to the north and west of the rotunda at about the same time.[10] It was then resolved to rebuild the shrine to provide the canons with a choir and

---

[5] [The Pilgrimage of the Russian Abbot] Daniel [in the Holy Land], transl C. W. Wilson, PPTS 6 (1888) pp 11–14 describes the rotunda as it was in 1107 before the rebuilding.

[6] [C.] Couäsnon, [The Church of the Holy Sepulchre in Jerusalem] (London 1974) pp 54–7.

[7] W[illiam of]T[yre, Historia rerum in partibus transmarinis gestarum], bk 9, cap 9 RHC Occ 1, pp 376–7; [Cartulaire de l'Eglise du St.-Sépulcre de Jérusalem, ed E.] de Rozière, [Collection des documents inédits sur l'histoire de France], series 1, 5 (Paris 1849) nos 36, 37, pp 71–3.

[8] The patriarch Gibelin on his deathbed in 1112 exhorted Baldwin I to undertake this reform, de Rozière no 42, pp 79–80. It was implemented in 1114 and the canons who would not accept it were expelled, ibid no 25, pp 44–7.

[9] [A. W.] Clapham, ['The Latin monastic buildings of the Church of the Holy Sepulchre, Jerusalem'], Antiquaries Journal 1 (London 1921) pp 3–18. [C.] Enlart, [Les monuments des Croisés dans le Royaume de Jérusalem: architecture religieuse et civile], 2 vols, 2 albums (Paris 1925–8) 2 pp 173–80 argues on stylistic grounds that the monastery is, for the most part, anterior to the Latin basilica.

[10] Previously the patriarch's apartments had connected with the gallery of the rotunda and had presumably been on the second storey of the courtyard building, Daniel p 13. Arnulf is named in an inscription in the patriarch's palace, Enlart 2, p 137; Clapham p 18.

the new church was finally consecrated on 15 July 1149, the fiftieth anniversary of the capture of the city.[11]

The reconstruction was imaginative and incorporated all three shrines, the sepulchre, Calvary and Saint Helena's chapel, in a single building. The courtyard buildings were demolished and replaced by a romanesque church built in a style adapted to harmonise with that of the rotunda. It consisted of a central choir and two aisles with an apse which gave access to the canons' cloister and to the Saint Helena crypt-chapel. The Calvary chapel was rebuilt at the east end of the south aisle, but the rotunda was not altered, except that the eastern apse was demolished and a triumphal arch pierced through the wall so that the patriarch's throne behind the new high altar faced directly towards the canopy of the sepulchre.[12]

The church was lavishly decorated with frescoes[13] and mosaics: the vault of the Calvary chapel, for example, was covered with mosaics of the prophets bearing scrolls with texts foretelling the passion.[14] Work on the cathedral continued throughout the crusader period: a campanile was erected beside the great south door, probably in the 1160s,[15] and the emperor Manuel I Comnenus gave mosaics to decorate the interior of the shrine of the sepulchre.[16] Despite the damage caused by the fire of 1808 the present building is largely the work of the crusaders.

The most important of the ruined extra-mural shrines was that of mount Sion, allegedly built on the site of the house of Saint John the evangelist, and the scene, therefore, of the last supper, the descent of the Holy Spirit and the dormition of Our Lady. The crusaders at first repaired the Byzantine church and roofed it with timber.[17] It was entrusted to the Austin canons[18] who built an abbey nearby and rebuilt

[11] The guide-book known as Fetellus, compiled in c1130, speaks of the new church being built, *Fetellus* [(*circa 1130 A.D.*)], transl J. R. Macpherson, *PPTS* 19 (1892) p 2.
[12] Couäsnon pp 57–62.
[13] *Theoderich['s description of the Holy Places (circa 1172 A.D.*)], transl A. Stewart, *PPTS* 17 (1891) pp 12–13.
[14] *Ibid* pp 19, 21.
[15] The campanile was higher than it now is until 1719 when it was damaged by an earthquake. Enlart 2, pp 151–5.
[16] John Phocas, monk of Patmos, who visited Jerusalem in 1185, talks of the gold mosaics of the Sepulchre, the gift of 'my lord and master, Manuel Comnenus, Porphyrogenitus'. [*The Pilgrimage of John] Phocas [to the Holy Land. (In the year 1185 A.D.*)], transl A. Stewart, *PPTS* 11 (1889) p 19.
[17] Daniel p 36.
[18] Alexander III stated that Duke Godfrey had placed Austin canons at Sion, [E.] Rey ['Chartes de l'Abbaye du Mont-Sion'], *Mémoires de la Société des antiquaires de France*, 5 series, 8 (Paris 1887) p 39. There is no evidence for their presence there

the church, replacing the Byzantine columns with cruciform pillars to hold up the heavy stone vault.[19] They also built a chapel in the courtyard in front of the church on the site of what they believed to be the *Lithostrotos* of the Roman pretorium, and the whole complex was fortified against enemy attack.[20]

In the valley of Kidron the crusaders found a crypt-chapel containing the empty tomb of the Virgin on the supposed site of her assumption, which they called Our Lady of Josaphat.[21] The Byzantine church which had served it was in ruins and the shrine was entrusted to Benedictine monks[22] who launched a highly successful building appeal to the west.[23] They also enjoyed the patronage of the royal house of Jerusalem, two of whose queens were buried there.[24] The monks tried to make their shrine resemble that of the other empty tomb, the Lord's sepulchre, as closely as possible. An elaborate canopy was raised over the shrine,[25] the crypt was adorned with frescoes[26] and the imposing romanesque doorway and flight of broad steps which still give access to the shrine were constructed. Nearby was the abbey, which probably had its own chapel.

The monks also administered the garden of Gethsemani at the foot of the mount of olives. They built a small oratory over the cave where the apostles were said to have fallen asleep[27] and when they were richer replaced it with a larger church.[28] They also built a hospice for poor pilgrims and its chapel replaced a ruined Byzantine church on the

---

before 1112 when prior Arnald of Sion took part in the election of the patriarch Arnulf, de Rozière, no 11, pp 11–13.

[19] Enlart 2, p 248.

[20] Theoderich pp 36, 41.

[21] In 1107 the shrine was intact but the church which served it had been destroyed, Daniel pp 23–4.

[22] Saewulf p 18.

[23] This is known in a Sicilian copy of 1106, C. A. Garufi, 'Il Tabulario di S. Maria di Valle Giosafat', *Archivio storico per la Sicilia orientale*, 5 (Catania 1908) pp 337–9.

[24] Morphia, wife of Baldwin II, [Ch.] Kohler, ['Chartes de l'Abbaye de Notre-Dame de la Vallée de Josaphat en Terre-Sainte (1108–1291)—Analyses et extraits'], *R[évue de l']O[rient] L[atin]*, 7 (Paris 1899), no 18, p 128; and her daughter, queen Melisende, WT bk 18, cap 32, RHC Occ 1, p 877. The location of the mortuary chapels is discussed by [H.] Vincent, [F. M.] Abel, [*Jérusalem. Recherches de topographie, d'archéologie et d'histoire*], 2 vols in 4 parts (Paris 1912–26) 2, part 4, p 815.

[25] [*Description of the Holy Land by*] John of Würzburg [(*A.D. 1160–1170*)], transl C. W. Wilson, *PPTS* 14 (1890) p 51.

[26] Theoderich p 38.

[27] Saewulf p 18.

[28] Theoderich p 39.

alleged site of the agony in the garden.[29] This chapel was also later rebuilt and in its final form was a three-aisled basilica some seventy feet long.[30] The entire complex of Josaphat was fortified.[31]

The ruined shrine of the ascension on top of the mount of olives was immediately repaired by the crusaders, who built a small tower there round a central altar.[32] This also was given to the Austin canons[33] who built a priory there and reconstructed the shrine. This is how it appeared to the pilgrim Theoderich in about 1170: 'One ascends into the church by twenty great steps; in the midst . . . there stands a round structure, magnificently decorated with Parian marble and blue marble, with a lofty apex, in the midst whereof a holy altar is placed . . .'[34] The ruined Constantinian basilica of the Eleona which stood nearby was replaced by the crusader church of the *Pater Noster*, built before 1107.[35] This was rebuilt in grander style in 1152 as a burial place for two noble Danish pilgrims[36] and claimed to possess one of the world's most valuable documents, the autograph text of the Lord's prayer. This whole complex was fortified and a night-watch was kept there.[37]

The crusaders converted the great moslem shrine, the Dome of the Rock, into a church and called it the *Templum Domini* in honour of the presentation of Christ in the temple. It was given to the Austin canons[38]

[29] [H-F.] Delaborde. [*Chartes de la Terre Sainte provenant de l'Abbaye de Notre-Dame de Josaphat*], *Bibliothèque des Ecoles françaises d'Athènes et de Rome*, 19 (Paris 1880) no 19, pp 47–49.

[30] Enlart 2, pp 233–6; G. Orfali, *Gethsemani* (Paris 1924). There is no necessary conflict between Theoderich p 40 who speaks of 'a new church . . . being built' and John of Würzburg p 27, who seems to have been there a few years earlier, and speaks merely of 'a new church'. John's phrase is not precise and cannot be construed to mean that the church was completed when he saw it, and work on it probably continued for several years.

[31] Theoderich p 38.

[32] In 1099 there was only a hermit there, Ralph of Caen, *Gesta Tancredi in expeditione Hierosolymitana*, cap 113, RHC Occ 3, p 685. The shrine was rebuilt by 1103, Saewulf p 19.

[33] Their presence is first attested in 1112, C[artulaire] G[énérale de l']O[rdre des] H[ospitaliers de St-Jean de Jérusalem (1100–1310)], ed J. Delaville Le Roulx, 4 vols (Paris 1894–1906) no 25.

[34] Theoderich p 44.

[35] In 1103 it was a ruin, Saewulf p 19; by 1107 it had been rebuilt, Daniel p 24.

[36] Vincent, Abel, 2, part 1, pp 401–2; P. Riant, *Expéditions et pèlerinages des Scandinaves en Terre Sainte au temps des croisades* (Paris 1865) pp 226–9.

[37] Theoderich p 44.

[38] This foundation was attributed to duke Godfrey, WT bk 9, cap 9, RHC Occ 1, pp 376–7, but the earliest evidence for Austin canons there dates from 1112, CGOH no 25.

who built an abbey on the north side of the temple platform.[39] They covered the sacred rock at the centre of the shrine with a marble casing in 1114 and used it as their choir[40] and erected an octagonal iron screen about it which the moslems have preserved to this day.[41] They did not change much of the Omayyad decoration, but they added a mosaic frieze, inscribed with appropriate texts, to the upper register of the exterior walls, placed a gilded cross above the dome[42] and painted texts and a fresco of the presentation inside the church.[43] This work took time to complete and the church was not consecrated until 1142.[44]

The al-Aksar mosque at the southern end of the temple area was at first used as a palace by the Latin kings, but in 1119 Baldwin II gave part of it to the newly-founded group of knights templar.[45] Ten years later Honorius II licensed the templars as an international, sovereign order[46] and they subsequently took over the whole building, the kings moving to a new palace near the tower of David. The templars attracted large benefactions and part of their wealth was spent on extending and beautifying their headquarters. Theoderich, who visited them in about 1170, has this to say:

> No man could send an arrow from one end of their building to the other, either lengthways or crossways, at one shot with a Balearic bow . . . Those who walk upon the roof of it find an abundance of gardens, courtyards, ante-chambers, vestibules and rain-water cisterns . . . on the western side the Templars have erected a new building . . . with a roof rising with a high pitch, unlike the flat roofs of that country . . . They have built a new cloister there in addition to the old one . . . Moreover, they are laying the foundations of a new church of wonderful size and workmanship . . . by the side of the great court.[47]

Other minor shrines were set up in the temple area, among which was a crypt-chapel near the templars' garden where it was believed

[39] John of Würzburg p 16.
[40] Fulcher of Chartres, *Historia Hierosolymitana*, bk 1, cap 26, 7, ed H. Hagenmeyer (Heidelberg 1913) pp 287–8; WT bk 8, cap 3, *RHC Occ* 1, pp 326–7.
[41] Photograph in Enlart, album 1, pl 40, figs 132–3.
[42] Theoderich pp 25–6.
[43] John of Würzburg p 18; Phocas p 20; *The Autobiography of Ousama*, transl G.R.Potter (London 1929) p 177.
[44] WT bk 15, cap 18, *RHC Occ* 1, p 687.
[45] *Ibid* bk 12, cap 7, p 520.
[46] Jacques de Vitry, *Historia Orientalis* cap 65 (Paris 1597) fol 116.
[47] Theoderich pp 31–2.

that Our Lady had spent the night before her purification. This contained some unusual relics: 'the cradle of the Lord . . . stands at th easte end . . . On the south side one sees a great basin . . . of stone . . . in which . . . he was bathed . . . and on the north side is the bed of Our Lady.'[48]

To the north of the temple area was the supposed site of the birthplace of Our Lady, the house of Saint Joachim and Saint Anne. At the time of the Latin conquest it was served by a small convent, probably of eastern rite.[49] In 1104 Baldwin I's wife became a nun there and the house was more richly endowed.[50] Its prosperity was further increased when Baldwin II's daughter, Yveta, was professed there, by which time it had become a house of Benedictine nuns.[51] The nuns rebuilt the church in a fine romanesque style and it is now the best preserved example of crusader architecture in the city. The new convent stood to the south of the church, while to the north of it the nuns had charge of the pool of Bethesda and its chapel.[52]

Some fifty years before the crusaders captured the city Amalfitan merchants had founded the small monastery of Santa Maria Latina just south of the holy sepulchre, to serve the holy places and to administer an adjacent hospital for Latin pilgrims. A small convent of Saint Mary Magdalen was built nearby to look after women pilgrims.[53] After 1099 gifts poured into the hospital from grateful patients and their families[54] and in 1113 it was made independent of the abbot of Latina by Paschal II[55] and soon became the headquarters of a thriving international order, that of the knights hospitaller.[56] The small Byzantine hospital chapel of Saint John was not structurally altered[57] but the hospital was rebuilt and William of Tyre tells of the indignation of the patriarch Fulcher when in the 1150s the hospitallers began to construct

---

[48] *Ibid* pp 32–3. This shrine was established by 1130, Fetellus p 3.

[49] Saewulf p 17. There is only presumptive evidence that this house was at first of eastern rite. Queen Arda was Armenian and is therefore unlikely to have sought admission to a Latin house.

[50] WT bk 11, cap 1, *RHC Occ* 1, pp 451–2.

[51] *Ibid* bk 15, cap 26, p 699. An inscription attests that the nuns owned part of the market of Jerusalem, Enlart 2, p 191.

[52] Theoderich pp 43, 47.

[53] WT bk 18, cap 5, *RHC Occ* 1, pp 824–6.

[54] *CGOH* nos 1–29, which date from before 1113.

[55] The bull *Pie postulatio voluntatis, CGOH* no 30.

[56] For the history of the order, J. Riley-Smith, *The Knights of St. John in Jerusalem and Cyprus, 1050–1310*, (London 1967).

[57] Vincent, Abel 2, part 2, pp 642–68.

'at the very door of the holy resurrection buildings which were much more costly and lofty' than those of the cathedral.[58]

The new infirmary, which was probably the finest and certainly the largest in Christendom, excited the admiration of visitors like John of Würzburg, who saw it in the 1160s:

> When I was there I learned that the whole number of sick people amounted to two thousand, of whom sometimes in the course of one day and night more than fifty are carried out dead, while many other fresh ones keep arriving . . . This house supplies as many people outside it with victuals as it does those inside . . .[59]

The one class of people who could not be nursed in the hospital of Saint John were lepers and a separate hospital of Saint Lazarus was built to care for them, probably in about 1140. It stood outside the north-west postern of the city and was administered and defended by a small and dedicated order of knights.[60]

The abbey of Latina also prospered under crusader rule, although to a lesser extent than the hospital. To judge from drawings of its ruins, which were only demolished in 1905, it was either greatly enlarged or completely rebuilt in the twelfth century,[61] and its abbot ranked second among those in the city.[62] Nevertheless, it was not a shrine church and the community tried to gloss over this shortcoming by telling visitors how the blessed Virgin had fainted at the crucifixion and been carried to a cave on the site of their church, where she revived and tore out a handful of her hair in her grief, which they kept in a reliquary.[63] The community was also given charge of the ruined shrine of Saint Stephen, on the site of his martyrdom outside the north wall, which they rebuilt.[64]

The convent of Saint Mary Magdalen also grew in importance. In the second half of the twelfth century it was ruled by a kinswoman of king Amalric's[65] and he gave the sisters permission to extend the con-

---

[58] WT bk 18, cap 3, *RHC Occ* I, pp 820–1.

[59] John of Würzburg p 44.

[60] A de Marsy, 'Fragment d'un cartulaire de l'Ordre de St.-Lazare en Terre Sainte', *Archives de l'Orient Latin*, 2 vols (Paris 1884) 2, pp 121–57. The earliest document dates from Fulk's reign.

[61] Enlart, album 2, pl 102.

[62] [*Le Livre de*] *Jean d'Ibelin*, cap 261, *RHC, Lois, Les Assises de Jérusalem*, 2 vols (Paris 1841–3) I, p 415.

[63] Theoderich p 23.

[64] *Ibid* p 45. Saewulf p 21 reports that the Byzantine church was in ruins in 1103.

[65] Stephanie, daughter of Jocelyn I of Edessa, was abbess c1163–c1177, WT bk 19, cap 4, *RHC Occ* I, pp 898–9; Kohler no 45, pp 153–4.

vent buildings.[66] The house became known as Sainte Marie la Grande because of its size and its abbess took precedence over all others in the diocese.[67] Parts of this building have been incorporated in the modern Lutheran church.

Two other extra-mural shrines were directly under the jurisdiction of the patriarch of Jerusalem.[68] One was Bethany where in the early twelfth century there was a crypt-tomb of Lazarus and a church of Mary Magdalen a short distance away.[69] From 1114 these shrines were administered by the canons of the holy sepulchre[70] but in 1138 queen Melisende persuaded them to exchange Bethany for lands at Thecua. She then founded a Benedictine convent at Bethany in order that her youngest sister, Yveta, a nun at Saint Anne's, might become an abbess.[71] The convent was defended by walls and a large tower whose ruins may still be seen. It incorporated both shrines: the church of Saint Mary Magdalen was rebuilt and a new church of Saint Lazarus was built over his crypt, perhaps as a choir for the nuns.[72] The community was also given the church of Saint John the evangelist and adjacent property in Jerusalem as a place of refuge in time of war.[73]

The shrine of Saint Samuel, where a crypt-chapel marked the supposed place of the prophet's burial, was called Mountjoy by the Franks because pilgrims travelling from Jaffa had their first sight of Jerusalem at that point. At the request of Bernard of Clairvaux queen Melisende gave this shrine to the Praemonstratensian canons[74] who rebuilt the ruined Byzantine church above the shrine and founded an abbey adjoining it.[75] In 1180 a Spanish count founded

---

[66] *CGOH* 464.

[67] *Jean d'Ibelin* cap 261, *RHC Lois* I, p 415.

[68] *Ibid* pp 415–16.

[69] Saewulf p 22 records the shrine of Lazarus; Daniel p 22 mentions both shrines but does not name the second; Fetellus p 6 names the second as Saint Mary Magdalen.

[70] de Rozière no 25, pp 44–7.

[71] WT bk 15, cap 26, bk 21, cap 2, *RHC Occ* I, pp 699–700, 1006; de Rozière nos 33, 34, pp 60–8.

[72] S. J. Saller *Excavations at Bethany (1949–1953)*, *Publications of the Studium Biblicum Franciscanum* 12 (Jerusalem 1957).

[73] *Chronique d'Ernoul et de Bernard le Trésorier* cap 17, ed L. de Mas-Latrie (Paris 1871) p 206.

[74] *S. Bernardi . . . Claraevallensis Epistolae*, 253, 355, *PL* 182 (1879) cols 453–4, 557–8. The exact date of the foundation of this house is not known, but *L'Obituaire de l'Abbaye de Prémontré* ed R. Van Waefelghem (Louvain 1913) p 75 records the death of abbot Theoderic of Saint Samuel's in 1145.

[75] R. Savignac, F. M. Abel, 'Neby Samouil', *Révue biblique internationale*, ns 9 (Paris 1912) pp 267–79.

the military order of Mountjoy, with headquarters contiguous to the canons' house. They afforded protection to this isolated community.[76] The crusaders also built many lesser churches in and about Jerusalem. They did not have enough money to decorate all of them adequately and John of Würzburg complained that the church of Saint Peter's chains, which stood on the way to the Sion gate on the supposed site of the apostle's prison, was not 'decorated with ornaments in a manner worthy of so great a miracle.'[77] Many of these churches, some of which are still standing, were small and of no great architectural merit.[78] There were also many eastern rite churches in the city but they were not built by the Latins and do not come within the scope of this paper.

But all the great shrine churches were rebuilt on a scale commensurate with their dignity and were entrusted to monks, nuns and regular canons, who were responsible for the recitation of the day and night offices and the due observance of the cult. The cost of building, endowing and in many cases defending these shrines was considerable. The Latin kings and the Frankish baronage of Outremer gave generously to this work,[79] but almost all these foundations also received large endowments from the Christian west, specially from

---

[76] J. Delaville Le Roulx, 'L'Ordre de Montjoye', *ROL* 1 (1893) pp 42–57.

[77] John of Würzburg p 47.

[78] For example, Saint Thomas's near the tower of David, described in 1919 as 'a small church of no architectural character . . . which has been abandoned to ruin, apparently for centuries'. G. Jeffery, *A brief description of the Holy Sepulchre Jerusalem and other Christian churches in the Holy City* (Cambridge 1919) p 148.

[79] The following examples must suffice: to the Holy Sepulchre, de Rozière nos 29, 53, 144, pp 54–5, 97–101, 262–8; to Josaphat, Delaborde nos 4, 6, 18, 28, pp 26–7, 29–32, 45–7, 63–7; to Latina, J. Richard, 'Le chartrier de sainte-Marie-Latine et l'établissement de Raymond de Saint-Gilles à Mont Pèlerin', *Mélanges d'histoire du moyen âge dédiés à la mémoire de Louis Halphen* (Paris 1951) pp 605–12; to Mount Sion, Rey pp 37–53; to *Templum Domini*, F. Chalandon, 'Un diplome inédit d'Amaury I Roi de Jérusalem en faveur de l'Abbaye du Temple Notre-Seigneur', *ROL* 8, (1900–01) pp 311–17; to Mountjoy, H-E. Mayer, 'Sankt Samuel auf dem Freudenberge und sein Besitz nach einem unbekannten diplom König Balduins V', *QFIAB* 44 (1964) pp 68–71. Almost all the documents in the cartulary of Saint Lazare (see note 60 above) relate to small gifts of land and money in the crusader states. The hospital of Saint John was so richly endowed both in east and west that it would be otiose to list examples, see *CGOH* I *passim*. WT bk 15, cap 26, *RHC Occ* I, pp 699–700 gives details of the endowments of the convent of Bethany in the kingdom of Jerusalem. Little is known about the endowments of Saint Anne's, Sainte Marie la Grande, the abbey of the Mount of Olives or of the Syrian endowments of the templars in the twelfth century.

France and the Norman kingdom of Sicily.[80] Rebuilding Jerusalem as
a Christian pilgrimage centre was, like the crusades themselves, a corporate western activity in which the French in particular played a
central part.

Although there are no statistics, all the evidence suggests that there
was a great increase in the annual number of pilgrimages to Jerusalem
during the years of Latin rule. The pilgrims came from all parts of the
Christian world, the east as well as the west. John of Würzburg was
clearly astonished by the variety of peoples whom he found in
Jerusalem in king Amalric's reign:

> There are Greeks, Bulgarians, Latins, Germans, Hungarians,
> Scots, Navarrese, Bretons, English, Franks, Ruthenians, Bohe-
> mians, Georgians, Armenians, Jacobites, Syrians, Nestorians,
> Indians, Egyptians, Copts, Capheturici, Maronites and very many
> others . . .[81]

The devotion of the simple faithful is strongly conveyed by Theoderich
who relates how they brought wooden crosses with them from their
homelands which they placed on the rock of Calvary[82] and how some
of them piled up stones in the valley of Hinnom 'because they say that
on the day of judgment they will take their seats upon them.'[83] The
rebuilding of the shrines and their embellishment with vivid repre-
sentations of scenes from the gospels must have intensified the religious
experience of these pilgrims and they must have helped to diffuse that
devotion to the humanity of Christ which became an increasingly
important element in western popular piety in the twelfth century.

It was the need to care for large numbers of pilgrims which led to
the formation of new kinds of religious orders in Jerusalem, which

[80] Instances of this: to the Holy Sepulchre, de Rozière nos 16, 17, 20, 23, 166, 171, 172,
pp 18-24, 29-32, 36-41, 296-300, 309-11; to Josaphat, Delaborde, nos 3, 21, 31, pp 24-6,
50-4, 72-8; to Latina, W. Holtzmann, 'Papst-Kaiser-und Normannen-urkunden aus
Unteritalien. I. San Filippo-S. Maria Latina in Agira', *QFIAB* 35 (1955) nos 5, 7, 8,
pp 65-6, 70-2; to Mount Sion, work cited in n 79 above; to *Templum Domini*, A di
Prologo, *Le carte che si conservano nello Archivio del Capitolo Metropolitano della città di
Trani dal secolo IX fino all'anno 1266* (Barletta 1877) no 60, pp 132-3; to the hospital of
Saint John, *CGOH* 1, *passim*; to the knights templar, Marquis d'Albon, ed, *Cartulaire
générale de l'Ordre du Temple, 1119?-1150*, 1 (Paris 1913). Saint Lazare does not seem to
have had any possessions in the west, but the paucity of evidence makes it
impossible to decide whether Saint Samuel's, Saint Anne's, Sainte Marie la Grande, or
the convent of Bethany had any lands in the west or not.
[81] John of Würzburg p 69. *Capheturici* may have been Ethiopians who are otherwise
missing from the list.
[82] Theoderich p 20.
[83] *Ibid* p 51.

had a profound effect on the development of Latin Christendom in the following centuries. The templars, founded in 1119 by Hugh de Payens to protect poor pilgrims, was the prototype of a large number of military orders which spread to all parts of the western world; while the hospital of Jerusalem, which only became partially militarised, extended its charitable activities throughout much of western Europe, where its hospitals outlasted the crusader states by centuries.

In the short period of their rule the crusaders made Jerusalem a pilgrimage centre of great beauty. Its churches were equal in size, dignity and richness of decoration to the great abbeys and cathedrals of the west which were being built at the same time, and which they so closely resembled. Indeed, their mosaics could be paralleled in the west only at Venice and in the Norman kingdom of Sicily. Centuries of warfare, neglect and insensitive rebuilding have masked the crusaders' achievement, but it was recognised by some of their moslem contemporaries. This is how the cadi el-Fadel described the city when he entered it with Saladin in 1187:

> Islam received back a place which it had left almost uninhabited, but which the care of the unbelievers had transformed into a Paradise garden . . . those accursed ones defended with the lance and sword this city, which they had rebuilt with columns and slabs of marble, where they had founded churches and the palaces of the templars and the hospitallers . . . One sees on every side houses as pleasant as their gardens and bright with white marble and columns decorated with leaves, which make them look like living trees.[84]

But the crusader city was more than a work of art: it was a visual expression of the faith of the crusaders, and indeed of that of the whole Christian west, and a symbol of their deep devotion to the humanity of Christ.

University of Nottingham

[84] Quoted by Ibn Khallicân, *Extraits de la Vie du Sultan Salâh-ed-Dín, RHC Or* 3 pp 421–2.

ALAN OF LILLE AS A RENAISSANCE FIGURE

by P. G. WALSH

THE *Anticlaudianus* of Alan of Lille was composed in 1183[1] when its author was in his sixties and when the greater part of his writing must have lain behind him. That writing, as D'Alverny has most recently demonstrated,[2] overwhelmingly consists of treatises of theological and devotional learning. Whilst it would be oversimplification to suggest that these religious works offer little evidence germane to Alan as a renaissance figure, there is no doubt that the *Anticlaudianus* offers the deepest insights into the secular influences upon Alan's modes of thought. In this paper I should like to examine the essential nature and purpose of the *Anticlaudianus* against the liberating twelfth-century influences which directed the author towards its composition, against the extraordinary range of secular authors which he deploys, and finally and most importantly against the attempted synthesis between secular and sacred, between the insights of classical humanism and doctrinal Christianity, which is such a feature of the intellectual thought of the century. Alan is far from being a pioneer in this direction, but his vision of the synthesis illumines the whole intellectual tradition within which he wrote.

The *Anticlaudianus* may be described as Boethian epic, or in the spirit of the conventional definition of Boethius as the first schoolman, as scholastic epic. The main theme of the poem is Nature's creation of the perfect man, but the plot is developed in such a way as to lend prominence to a second theme, the relationship between knowledge of the world of creation and knowledge of the divine realm of God. At the beginning of the poem Nature bewails her earlier defective creation of humankind, and calls down the Virtues from heaven to help her create a perfect being. The most prominent of these virtues is Prudentia or Fronesis, human wisdom; she reminds the assembly that they can fashion only a perfect body. Her sister Ratio (reason) proposes

---

[1] See [R.] Bossuat's edition, [*Alain de Lille, Anticlaudianus*] (Paris 1955) p 13.
[2] [M-T.] D'Alverny, [*Textes Inédits*] (Paris 1965). A useful summary of Alan's writings can be found in the introduction to the translation of the *Anticlaudianus* by J. J. Sheridan (Toronto 1973).

that Prudentia should herself ascend to God to petition him to create a perfect soul; Ratio designs a spacecraft for the journey, and the Seven Liberal Arts, daughters of Prudentia, forge the sections of the chariot which Concordia then fuses together. The carriage is drawn by five horses, which symbolise the five senses, and Ratio accompanies Prudentia as her charioteer. They mount through the lower air with its demons, through the upper air and its planets to reach the firmament and the starry constellations. The charioteer Ratio and the team of horses can go no further. But a resident guide, Theologia, makes her appearance and conducts Prudentia, who is mounted on the one horse of Hearing, into the lower theological heaven. There Prudentia sees the angels and saints, the Virgin Mary and Christ, but she is blinded by the sight and rendered insensible. Fides (faith), the sister of Theologia, has to be summoned to revive her. Fides succeeds in restoring her, and then furnishes her with a mirror so that Prudentia can see in reflexion the blinding reality of heaven. She then conveys Prudentia to the upper theological heaven into the presence of God the Father. God accedes to Prudentia's plea for a perfect soul. He requests Noys, whose identity must later occupy us, to furnish an archetype and duly creates the soul in its image. Prudentia conveys the soul back to earth, where Nature creates a body from the four elements. Concordia, with the aid of Arithmetic and Music, binds body and soul together, and each of the other Virtues endows the New Man with her peculiar gift. The New Man endures an onslaught from the army of Vices led by the Fury Allecto, but Nature and the Virtues enable him to rout them. The New Man becomes ruler of the earth where the Virtues dwell and where peace and plenty flourish.

Alan thus presents two interlocking themes, each of the greatest interest to any consideration of Alan as heir and recreator of the old learning. The first is the scholastic presentation of the journey of Prudentia, human wisdom, to God. Aided by the natural virtues, reinforced by the secular learning of the Seven Liberal Arts, and advanced by the senses, human wisdom can attain knowledge of all things below the firmament. But to achieve beyond this a vision of angels and saints, of Christ and his mother, the instruction of Theology, queen of the sciences, is vital. But even Theology cannot ensure a clear and continuing vision, for which human wisdom can have recourse only to faith; so Fides must be the culminating guide. The second theme is the creation of the perfect man and the ensuing prospect of a golden age on earth, for the epic ends on a millenarist note. In the first of these two concerns, Alan shows himself the orthodox schoolman; in the second he promotes an unorthodox doctrine which fascinated the imagination of many twelfth-century intellectuals. For an appreciation of how these ideas of the *Anticlaudianus* dominate Alan's creative thinking we must turn first to the details of his career and the contemporary intellectual influences.

II

Alan is constantly cited in manuscripts and secondary sources as *Alanus Porretanus*, disciple of Gilbert de la Porrée. The designation need not mean that Alan actually studied under Gilbert, and the accepted chronology of Alan discouraged until recently the possibility of a personal encounter. In 1960, however, Alan's skeleton was exhumed at Cîteaux, and the forensic expert, with a confidence overwhelming to the layman, reported that he had died at the age of eighty-six. He was thus considerably older than has been generally assumed (though the life in the *Patrologia Latina* (210) by Chrysostom Henrique reports that he died at the age of one hundred and sixteen!). The date of death was already known as 1202–3, so this new evidence pushes back the date of birth to about 1120.[3]

Though the details of Alan's career remain speculative,[4] it is now possible to envisage an early encounter with Gilbert at Paris (or at Chartres) before Gilbert became bishop of Poitiers in 1142. The years of the 1130s and 1140s were a period of dynamic intellectual development at Paris, and as John of Salisbury informs us, grammar and rhetoric were taught as earnestly as theology. It is of the greatest importance to note that Alan's formative training, and indeed many years of his teaching, preceded the period later in the century when the study of the Latin language and literature declined before the eclipsing prestige of philosophy and theology. Alan's training was by way of the seven liberal arts, and it was from this literary base that he later turned to theology.

The evidence suggests that he spent a period at Montpellier, for he

---

[3] For the archaeological evidence, see M. Lebeau, 'Découverte du tombeau du bienheureux Alain de Lille', *COCR* 23 (1961) pp 254 *seq*, and P. Delhaye, 'Pour la fiche Alain de Lille', *Mélanges de science religieuse* 20 (Lille 1963) pp 39 *seq*. For the date of death, Aubry de Trois Fontaines in *Recueils des historiens des Gaules et de la France,* 18 (Paris 1882) p 761. For a conventional assessment of the date of birth, see J. De Ghellinck, *L'essor de la littérature latine au XIIᵉ siècle* (2 ed Brussels 1955) p 83: 'né vers 1128'.

[4] See the good survey in D'Alverny's introduction.

dedicates treatises to William VIII of Montpellier and to the abbot of Saint-Gilles, the Benedictine monastery close by; moreover Ralph of Longchamps, Alan's friend who wrote a commentary on the *Anticlaudianus*, studied at Montpellier.[5] The university there had a name for the teaching of natural philosophy, and was especially famous for its medical school which existed as early as 1137.[6] John of Salisbury, it will be recalled, waxes sarcastic about the failed philosophers of Paris who become doctors overnight at Montpellier: *et repente, quales fuerant philosophi, tales in momento medici eruperunt.*[7] Alan may have followed the same career as Adalbert, later archbishop of Mainz, did in 1137, by proceeding to Montpellier after an arts course at Paris.[8]

Alan attained fame as a teacher of liberal arts at Paris. John of Garland in a famed epitaph calls him a poet 'greater than Virgil and more consistent than Homer', and Henry of Brussels (?) claims that 'he was an expert in the liberal arts and presided over an ecclesiastical school at Paris'.[9] Such testimonies emphasise his distinction as a teacher and writer of Latin language and literature. But the list of his writings suggests that he must have transferred his teaching energies at Paris from arts to theology. This impression is confirmed by a comment in one of his sermons which condemns those who devote themselves to liberal arts or philosophy rather than to theology: 'God speaks to us wretched clerics, he speaks of the empty and frivolous studies of those of us who abandon theology and hasten to empty and transitory disciplines and to unsubstantial philosophy.'[10] These are clearly the words of a teacher condemning his own past.

Alan's status during these influential years of teaching at Paris has been a topic of speculation. His close relations with the Benedictines have been noted, as has the alternative possibility of a connexion with the canons regular at Paris. But there is no clear evidence of any such

---

[5] For the dedication of *Contra Haereticos* to William, and of *Distinctiones dictionum theologicarum* to Ermengard, see D'Alverny, p 13; for Ralph's claim to personal friendship, D'Alverny, p 12.

[6] F. M. Powicke and A. B. Emden, *Rashdall's Medieval Universities* (Oxford 1936) 2 pp 119 *seq.*

[7] *Metalogicon* 1. 4. Saint Bernard's ep 307 tells of the archbishop of Lyons attending there for a cure, spending in the medical school 'quod habebat et quod non habebat'.

[8] See the *Vita Adalberti* in P. Jaffé, *Bibliotheca rerum Germanarum* (Berlin 1873) 3 p 592.

[9] John of Garland, *De triumphis ecclesiae libri VIII*, ed T. Wright (London 1856) p 14; Henry of Brussels (?), see N. M. Häring, *RB* 80 (1970) p 82.

[10] *Sermo de clericis ad theologiam non accedentibus* (D'Alverny, pp 274 *seq*).

connexion, and it is as least as likely that he remained a secular priest like John of Salisbury. His writings certainly reveal the pastoral concerns of the ordained cleric. The *De Arte Praedicatoria*, with its forty-eight model sermons, could hardly be the work of an unordained cleric; likewise the *Liber Poenitentialis*, which offers advice on the proper hearing of confessions.

Some years before his death, Alan joined the Cistercian community at Cîteaux, where he was buried after his death in 1202–3.

III

When we speak of renaissance man in the context of the twelfth century, we must above all avoid the contamination of a fourteenth- or fifteenth-century vision. It is rare to find a humanist who allows the passion for classical writings or classical values to dislodge his Christian patrimony from the centre of his intellectual concerns. The greatest writers of the age exploit the insights of classical learning to enlarge their vision of Christian truth, or at any rate they reconcile their liberating humanism with a clear commitment to the Christian faith. A Walter of Châtillon does not deploy his knowledge of the Roman satirists Horace and Juvenal to delight in them for their own sake, but to emphasise the need for a reformation of manners in the curia and in the church at large. A Hildebert of Lavardin can praise the glories of pagan Rome in elegiacs with *Par tibi, Roma, nihil* but presents it as one side of a diptych in which the balancing poem (*Dum simulacra mihi*) describes the beneficial changes in the city following Christ's redemption.[11] Alan's Christianity is equally overt. His deep knowledge of Latin literature and Greek philosophy is placed at the service of Christian truth.

In the thousand years separating Tertullian from Alan, the attitudes of western Christians towards classical humanism varied from intransigent hostility to full-hearted acceptance. In the fourth century the spectacle of leading Christians unavailingly trying to renounce the classical authors who had formed them provides one of the more diverting episodes in the intellectual history of Europe. The ambivalence of Jerome played a leading part in subsequent controversy; his two letters espousing directly contradictory attitudes were widely quoted. On the one hand Jerome recounts his dream of the Judgement (*Ciceronianus es, non Christianus*) and vows to lay aside the

---

[11] Walter of Châtillon, *Moralisch-satirische Gedichte*, ed K. Strecker (Heidelberg 1929); Hildebert, *Carmina Minora*, ed A. B. Scott (Leipzig 1969) nos 36, 38.

seductive pleasure of favourite pagan authors. On the other hand he defends classical learning in answer to a cavilling critic, comparing it with the captive woman in the book of Deuteronomy whose head must be shaved, her eyebrows trimmed, her nails pared before she can be taken to wife. Secular learning can likewise be made fit for the true Israel by purging it of all that is idolatrous, lusting, false or pleasurable; then it can be taken in marriage clean and pure to bring forth servants for Christ.[12] When this qualified defence of classical learning, its designation as the handmaid of Christian formation, is taken over by an intellectual Christian like Cassiodorus,[13] it becomes the predominant view in the western church until the Carolingian period and after, and Alan's ideas contain clear points of connexion with it.

Such attitudes, however, are promulgated by ecclesiastical and monastic leaders, and there is one signal figure who demonstrates that the grudging attitude of qualified acceptance of classical learning is not wholly representative of the church. This is the Christian layman Boethius. Now that scholars are almost universally satisfied that he wrote the *Theological Tractates*, we must visualise him as a two-sided intellectual. On one side he devotes himself to questions of theology, and the *Tractates* reflect him at work propounding the dogmas of the church in that spirit of human reason which is so central to classical humanism. So we find him beginning his *De Trinitate* with these words: 'We must make this investigation only in so far as the insight of human reason can mount to the heights of divinity. For as in other pursuits a limit is imposed on the attainment of the journey of reason.' His avowed aim is to reconcile faith with reason (*fidem, si poterit, rationemque coniungere*) by the tool of Aristotelian logic. Throughout these theological treatises he emerges as the committed Christian applying the reason to the questions surrounding God and the world.

The other face of Boethius is that of the traditional Roman philosopher, a latter-day Cicero importing the study of Greek culture for the benefit of fellow-Italians. His publishing career began at the age of twenty with a treatise on arithmetic, and he followed with others on music, geometry and astronomy. These works are inevitably highly derivative, being inspired by the Greek writers Nicomachus of Gerasa, Euclid and Ptolemy.[14] Having thus conducted initial re-

[12] Jerome, epp 22, 70.

[13] Institutes I 27: 'utilis et non refugienda cognitio . . .'.

[14] The researches of Pierre Courcelle are fundamental here; see especially (in addition to *Les lettres grecques en occident* (2 ed Paris 1948)) 'Boèce et l'école d'Alexandrie', *Mélanges de l'Ecole française à Rome* 52 (1935) pp 183 *seq*.

searches into the four subjects of the *quadrivium*, he turned to logic and published works in this field. But his ambition to reconcile the philosophical views of Plato and Aristotle was thwarted by his arrest and early death while still in his forties.

So this Aristotelian logician with a neoplatonist vision of the world was simultaneously a Christian apologist. But when in the confinement of his library he grappled with the nature of the true *summum bonum* and true happiness, he sought his consolation not in the scriptures or in the fathers, but in secular philosophy. Likewise the artistic frame of *The Consolation of Philosophy*, Boethius's dialogue with Philosophia set in a vision or waking dream, and the Menippean texture of part prose and part verse, are both in the secular tradition of apocalyptic literature to which Martianus Capella and Fulgentius also subscribe. It is to secular philosophy that Boethius attributes first his growth in self-knowledge, then his knowledge of the universe, and finally his awareness of the laws governing man and the universe—for this is the threefold structure of the treatise.

If we ask why Boethius preferred the consolation of philosophy to the consolation of scripture or theology, the answer must be that he found it more congenial to review the problems of human existence in the customary modes of thought of the working philosopher. Courcelle has speculated that as a young man his studies were under Ammonius at Alexandria, and that his theological interests were a later development.[15] But secondly the neoplatonist philosophy which he espoused was at least half way to theology. The doctrines of Plotinus as preached by Ammonius became the philosopher's mirror for Christian beliefs. For Plotinus, all being in the world is the overflow from the immaterial and impersonal force which Plato calls the One or the Good. At the first point outward from the One is Nous (Mind), at once the Aristotelian unmoved mover and the repository of the Platonist forms. At a further point outward is Psyche, the world-soul, differing from the Stoic Pronoia in that it is a transcendent and not immanent force. Beyond these circles lies Nature and the created world. It was easy for the Christian neoplatonist to visualise the One, the Nous, the Psyche as a philosophical vision of the Blessed Trinity, with the One as Father, the Nous or Sapientia Dei as Son, and Psyche as Holy Spirit. Alan's depiction of heaven in the *Anticlaudianus* owes much to this philosophical tradition.

---

[15] See the previous note.

The twelfth-century renaissance is built on these twin facets of classical learning. On the one side is the increasing veneration accorded to Latin authors, whose role rapidly transcends that of hand-maid in the formation of Christian scholars. On the other is the liberated vision of Christianity inspired by Boethius which analyses God and the world through the spectacles of Greek philosophy. It is in this sense that the twelfth century is labelled the *aetas Boethiana*, with the commentaries on Boethius by Gilbert de la Porrée and Thierry of Chartres at the centre of this scholastic movement. But the whole attempt at imaginative synthesis of Christian faith and Greek philosophy soon withered in the schools, and moved out of the official arena of theology into the realm of creative literature.[16] We are powerfully reminded that Boethius chose to compose his *Consolation* not as a formal philosophical treatise but within the literary form of the dream-narrative; so writers like Bernard Silvester and Alan use forms of fiction to probe imaginatively the nature of God and the world without the authority of theology. The shift concedes the inadequacy of reason in the realm of the supernatural, and demands the complementary activity of the poetic imagination, just as Plato had supplemented his dialectic with the deployment of myth.

Wetherbee has reviewed some characteristic ways in which Platonism and Christianity were reconciled earlier in the century in the schools. Peter Abelard, for example, had exalted secular learning as an instrument of God's revelation comparable to the sacred scriptures. In his *Introduction to Theology* and his *Christian Theology*, he claims that God uses the scriptures and secular philosophy in harness to reveal the divine dispensation to various areas of the world: 'Divine Providence has seen fit to manifest to the Jews through their prophets, and to the Gentiles through their philosophers, such mysteries as this (that is, the Trinity).'[17] Thierry of Chartres, an enthusiastic Platonist, is also to be found aligning Greek philosophy with the Christian dispensation. His treatise *De sex dierum operibus* interprets the process of the creation of the world by harmonising the book of Genesis with Plato's *Timaeus*. God, Creator of matter, is the Platonist demiurge, the craftsman of the universe. This world of ours is a representation of the real world which is in the Mind or Wisdom of God. And the third aspect of deity is

---

[16] See [W.] Wetherbee, [*Platonism and Poetry in the Twelfth Century*] (Princeton 1972).
[17] *PL* 178 (1885) col 998. See in general D. E. Luscombe, *The School of Peter Abelard* (Cambridge 1969) cap 4.

anima mundi, so that demiurge, *nous,* world-soul are identified by Thierry with the Christian Trinity.[18]

This treatise of Thierry, *De sex dierum operibus,* is an outstanding example of the twelfth-century tendency to visualise the Greek philosophers and Roman poets as *animae naturaliter Christianae,* as authors expressing Christian truths in a hidden way. In the technical vocabulary taken over from allegorical interpretation of scripture, pagan poetry and philosophy is designated as *integumentum* or *involucrum,* a covering or wrapping beneath which is cloaked divine truth.[19] Virgil's *Aeneid* is of course the outstanding Roman book which is sacred in this sense. The story of the abandonment of Troy, the dangers of shipwreck, the descent into Hell, the eventual arrival into the *patria* of Italy are interpreted as a parable of the progress of the human soul.[20] Later in the century even a worldly poet like Ovid is reverenced as an earlier-day Aquinas of the secular sphere, the repository of pagan wisdom as *Ovidius physicus, Ovidius ethicus, Ovidius allegoricus.*[21]

From the schools of the twelfth century, then, there developed an influential and generous humanism. But the attempt to visualise the pagan authors as an alternative route of divine revelation soon withered in the schools under the lively attacks of orthodox theologians, only to re-emerge under the aegis of creative literature. By far the most influential figure in this respect is Bernard Silvester, who wrote a literary myth of creation usually called *De mundi universitate* but which is more correctly known as *Cosmographia.*[22] This imaginative account of how the universe came into being is in two books. The first, *Megacosmus* ('The Great World') treats the creation of inanimate matter and non-human life; the second, *Microcosmus* ('The Little World') describes the creation of man, who in small compass embodies all the forces in the universe. The work is set in a dramatic frame. Nature personified tearfully complains to Nous, the Mind or

---

[18] See N. M. Häring, 'The Creation and Creator of the World according to Thierry of Chartres and Clarenbaldus of Arras', *Archives d'histoire doctrinale et littéraire du moyen âge* 22 (Paris 1955) pp 137 *seq.*

[19] See Wetherbee pp 36 *seq*; [B.] Stock, [*Myth and Science in the Twelfth Century: A Study of Bernard Silvester*] (Princeton 1972) pp 49 *seq.*

[20] The earlier treatment by Fulgentius, *Expositio Virgilianae Continentiae,* is resumed by Bernard Silvester, *Commentum Bernardi Silvestris super sex libros Eneidos Virgilii,* ed G. Riedel (Griefswald 1924).

[21] See P. Demats, *Fabula* (Geneva 1973) cap 3.

[22] See Stock pp 21 *seq.*

Wisdom of God, that prime matter is shapeless and anarchic, and she begs that order and beauty be imposed on it. Nous agrees, and separates out the four elements. Then the World-soul descends to animate the dead matter. There follows a description of each feature of the ordered world—the angels, the heavens, earth and its produce, heat and light keeping the world in motion. The second book describes how Nous, Natura, Urania (goddess of the physical heavens) and Physis (goddess of the laws of physics and of medicine) together create man.

It is no coincidence that the *Cosmographia* is composed within the same Menippean texture as Boethius's *Consolation*, for it is a poetic vision of the nature and purpose of the world. Plato's *Timaeus*, the myth of the demiurge inspiring order on chaotic matter, is the main inspiration. Together with Plato, Ovid's *Metamorphoses* and a host of other writers are deployed to create this myth of the ordering of the universe by God, a universe in which man is not only the microcosm of all the elements and forces in the world, but also its crowning glory.[23] Some scholars have claimed that an anti-Christian thesis is being propounded here, but this misinterprets Bernard's purpose. His method is basically that of Boethius before him and of Alan after him; it is an attempt to interpret the world without revelation. But Christian echoes are audible at many points, including the acknowledgement of the Incarnate Christ as the appearance of true deity,[24] as if to demonstrate that the reader must regard the outer appearance as integument. Chenu's view of the *Cosmographia*, which speaks of Bernard's *christianisme du fond sous le paganisme de la forme*,[25] is relevant not only to Bernard but to others who experimented with similar poetic techniques.

Bernard's myth of creation, reflecting Chartrian preoccupations, was immensely influential, and its most immediate effect was felt by his younger contemporary Alan, whose connexion with the school of Chartres is suggested by his commentary on the *ad Herennium*; Thierry of Chartres had composed a similar commentary on Cicero's *De Inventione,* and these two treatises were the most popular sources of grammatical and rhetorical information in the twelfth century, being

---

[23] Stock pp 275 *seq*, emphasising that the idea is commonplace earlier in the century.
[24] I. 3. 53f: 'exemplar specimenque Dei virguncula Christum
        parturit et verum secula numen habent'.
[25] M-D. Chenu, *La théologie au douzième siècle* (Paris 1957).

labelled *Rhetorica Prima* and *Rhetorica Secunda*.[26] But the main thrust of Alan's writing is theological and apologetic, devotional and pastoral, in all of which he reveals himself as a zealous and orthodox Christian whose secular studies have moulded his theological approach. In this sense his religious writings do reflect Alan as a renaissance figure. For example, his *Regulae Caelestis Iuris* is remarkable for the application of techniques of proof in geometry to theology, and again the diction of *Quoniam homines* reveals his interest in natural philosophy. But like a latter-day Jerome or Cassiodorus he repeatedly stresses the subordination of such secular studies to theology: 'God does not condemn the arts and natural sciences', he says in a sermon, 'for He has instituted them in an admirable harmony. But they are useful only if they remain in their place as followers of theology and servants of the celestial philosophy. When they have played their introductory role, we must bid them farewell on the threshold' (*salutande in limine*).[27]

IV

It is in the *Anticlaudianus* that the subordinate role of the liberal arts in the search for truth about God and the world is made explicit. We must approach the poem by way of Alan's earlier work of fiction, the *De Planctu Naturae*.[28] The implicit connexion of this work with Boethius's *De Consolatione Philosophiae* should be noted. The deliberate contrast in title, the pessimism of the abstract heroine Natura lamenting that the world is out of joint (whereas Boethius's Philosophia teaches that God orders all things sweetly), the shared Menippean texture all invite us to contemplate the secular philosophising of a Boethian Christian in despair about the ordering of the world. The figure of Natura owes much to Bernard Silvester. As the *vicaria Dei*, God's vicar on earth, she is the personification of the moral law, the reflexion of God's eternal law operating on earth; her lament centres on the moral degeneration of the human race, notably in the sexual sphere. What is of interest for this paper is that Natura is depicted as a secular *Ecclesia Dei*, with her own canons and sacraments. She has her own high priest Genius, who excommunicates those whose lives are dominated by *Venus scelesta*. The lament is for the integrity of human nature as it existed before the fall. In other words, though the frame of

---

[26] W. Ziltener, *Studien zur bildungsgeschichtlichen Eigenart der höfischen Dichtung* (Bern 1972) p 25.

[27] *Sermo de clericis ad theologiam non accedentibus* (D'Alverny p 275). The threshold is that of theology.

[28] Text in T. Wright, *Anglo-Saxon Satirical Poets* 2 (London 1872) pp 429 *seq*.

the work is designedly secular, though the figures of Natura and Genius are derivative from the Graeco-Roman philosophical tradition,[29] Alan's spectacles are inevitably those of the Christian theologian. The contrast between contemporary sexual *mores* and an ideal sexuality is Christian teaching under the integument of the Menippean form.

A similar judgement must be passed on the *Anticlaudianus*. The title, the chosen medium, the initial invocation, the poetic texture all proclaim Alan's determination to visualise the world with secular eyes. The title advertises Alan's acquaintance with the work of the fourth-century poet Claudian. Alan's theme in the *Anticlaudianus*, the creation of the perfect man with the aid of the Virtues, is the exact opposite of Claudian's theme of the creation of the totally evil man, Rufinus, by the Vices. Claudian's poetry had a remarkable vogue in twelfth-century France. Geoffrey of Vitry's commentary on Claudian's *De Raptu Proserpinae* is extant and has been recently published;[30] more important for our purpose, a long fragment of a commentary on the *In Rufinum* has survived, and there is evidence of two other commentaries in manuscripts at Florence and Rome.[31] Today there is some doubt about Claudian's religious position; at the Christian court of Honorius he may have been a nominal Christian or a complaisant pagan, and perhaps there is little difference.[32] But in the eyes of the twelfth-century *litteratus*, he belonged to the great corpus of pagan epic which stretched back to Lucretius and Virgil. The implicit connexion with classical epic is suggested also by Alan's chosen medium of the heroic hexameter. In company with Walter of Châtillon's historical epic and Joseph of Exeter's mythological epic, Alan's philosophical poem proclaims itself an extension of the Roman tradition, though the allegorical presentation of the *Anticlaudianus* indicates a debt to Prudentius's *Psychomachia*, itself the most Virgilian of poems.

Alan's determination to compose in the secular mode is further underlined by the invocation in the verse-prologue. The plea to Apollo to steep the poet in his Castalian spring is a far cry from the tradition of Christian poetry which sought to excise Apollo and the Muses and

---

[29] See G. D. Economou, *The Goddess Natura in Medieval Literature* (Harvard 1972); J. C. Nitzsche, *The Genius Figure in Antiquity and the Middle Ages* (New York 1975).
[30] [A. K.] Clarke and [P. M.] Giles, [*The Commentary of Geoffrey of Vitry on Claudian, De Raptu Proserpinae*] (Leiden 1973).
[31] Clarke and Giles, pp 16 *seq*.
[32] See Alan Cameron, *Claudian* (Oxford 1970) cap 8.

to substitute Christ as patron.[33] And the texture of the poem, with its rich evocations of Virgil, Horace, Ovid, Lucan, Statius and Juvenal is a further pervasive indication of the aura of classical humanism which wreathes the poem. Alan, it should be stressed, is steeped in these classical poets much more profoundly than any modern professor of classics.

We must now turn to the absorbing question of Alan's main sources in the *Anticlaudianus*. We have stressed that Bernard Silvester's *Cosmographia* is the most important contemporary inspiration. But Boethius is the most pervasive influence; when we visualise Alan as a renaissance figure, we are constantly aware that it is Boethius above all who is given fresh birth. Prudentia, the central figure of the poem, is Boethius's Philosophia; when in the first book Alan describes the beautiful proportions of Prudentia, her elastic presence in heaven and on earth, and above all her torn garment, he wishes us to identify his heroine with Boethius's abstract teacher.[34] When he delineates the relationship between Prudentia and her sister Ratio as two identical figures differing only in age, we are reminded of the formulation of Aquinas, *prudentia proprie sit in ratione*, which goes back through Boethius to Aristotle. Ratio bears in her hand three mirrors of glass, silver and gold, connoting her three orders of knowledge; scholars have rightly pointed to the numerous twelfth-century treatments, especially that of Richard of Saint Victor, as significant parallels, but the basis is the three forms of theoretical philosophy posited by Boethius, the *naturalis*, the *mathematica*, the *theologica*.[35]

The book and a half (almost eight hundred lines) devoted to the Seven Liberal Arts draws upon a rich variety of sources with Boethius again prominent. Of course Martianus Capella's *Marriage of Philology and Mercury*, that turgid but indispensable survey of ancient educational theory, is extensively exploited in all seven sections, and Sheridan has shown that Peter of Compostella may have been an intermediate quarry. Macrobius's *Saturnalia* is to be noted as a source in the descriptions of Arithmetic and Music, and the account of Grammatica owes much to the grammarians and especially to

---

[33] See Paulinus of Nola, *Carm.* 10.19 *seq*: 'Hearts dedicated to Christ reject the Latin Muses and turn away Apollo'.

[34] Bossuat's edition does not pick up all the suggestive parallels between 1 300 *seq* and 313 *seq* and *Cons* 1.1.

[35] *De Trin* 2. For the twelfth-century background, especially Richard, see D'Alverny, pp 168 *seq*.

Priscian, who had a remarkable vogue in the eleventh and twelfth centuries.[36] But Boethius's influence is discernable in the depictions of Arithmetic, Music, Geometry and above all Logic; his translations of Aristotle's *Categories* and *De Interpretatione* had been the staple source of information on Aristotle in the west for six centuries, and his portrait stands proudly on Logic's dress in the company of Porphyry, Aristotle and Zeno the Stoic.

After describing the completion of the carriage by the Seven Liberal Arts, Alan next introduces the five horses which represent the five senses. A characteristic synthesis of Greek philosophical thought and Latin poetic adornment is observable in the description of them. Bernard Silvester has again been the chief inspiration, but behind him lies Plato's *Timaeus*, the most influential single work of Greek philosophy in the twelfth century. Then the horses are given jocose Latin literary genealogies, three of them being sired by the horses of the sun in Ovid's *Metamorphoses*.[37]

The journey upward through the lower air is described with the conventional picture of neoplatonist demons to which various writers, Christian as well as pagan, may have contributed. But once Prudentia reaches the upper air the echoes of Boethius, as Bossuat's edition shows, become predominant. The difficulty of the ensuing journey to the Christian heaven is indicated by a splendid synthesis of biblical and classical evocations. The biblical idiom expresses the idea that the way is open only to the few, but Alan delineates the qualities demanded by exploiting Roman satire. It is not nobility or beauty, wealth or strength, but virtue which is required; the echo of the final lines of Juvenal's Tenth Satire is palpable.[38]

Prudentia now meets Theology, and at this point, half way through the poem, comes a fresh beginning with a new invocation, the structural device suggesting the contrast between the realm of Natura, where reason prevails, and the realm of heaven whose interpreter is faith. Henceforth it will be the Christian God, not Apollo, who will be Alan's inspiration. This separation of prophetic spheres underlines the abandonment of secular sources in the presentation of Alan's vision of heaven. Ironically enough, however, the description of the physical world beyond the skies, the harmony of fire and water, is

[36] See R. W. Hunt and R. Klibansky, 'Priscian in the 11th and 12th Centuries' in *Medieval and Renaissance Studies* 1 (London 1941–3) pp 194 *seq*, 2 (1944) pp 1 *seq*.
[37] IV 95 *seq*; compare Bernard Silvester II 14; Ovid, *Met* II 153.
[38] V 57 *seq*; compare Juvenal X 346 *seq*.

adapted from Boethius; and though the denizens of the lower heaven —angels, saints, Mary and Christ himself—reflect the promised change from secular to sacred, the very economy of lower and upper heavens is a neoplatonist concept. So also is God's way of granting Prudentia's appeal for a perfect soul, for he summons Noys to prepare a *numinis exemplar, humane mentis ideam.* A fruitful synthesis between the Greek and the Hebraic traditions is achieved here, for the qualities of the exemplar found by Noys are those of the old testament figures Joseph, Judith, Job, Abraham and Tobias.

Prudentia duly returns to earth with the perfect soul, and Alan is able to resume his borrowings from Boethius and the secular sources. The description of Nature fashioning the body of the perfect man from the four elements may owe something to the *Commentaries on Boethius* by Thierry of Chartres,[39] who with Gilbert de la Porrée may have sharpened Alan's interest in Boethius. The list of the Virtues who present the new man with their special gifts is rather mechanically reproduced from book I; in each place they represent chiefly the antonyms of the Vices in Claudian's *In Rufinum.* But there is one addition in this second list. Fortune, who lives on a precipitous rock in mid-ocean, comes to offer her gift, only to repent of her support a little later, when the Vices congregate to attack the new man. The motif of the inconstancy of Fortune, which frequently appears in such twelfth-century contexts as the *Carmina Burana,* can be exemplified in numerous classical writers, but once again *The Consolation of Philosophy* may be the direct inspiration.[40]

Allecto now assembles the Vices for the attack. One thinks at once of the action of the second half of Virgil's *Aeneid,* where Allecto hinders Aeneas in his new foundation. But the main inspiration for the gathering of the Vices is again Claudian's *In Rufinum,* and for the ensuing battle Prudentius's *Psychomachia.*

This panoramic view of the sources enables us to specify more precisely the nature of this twelfth-century renaissance as exemplified in Alan. Knowledge of the great figures of classical poetry is taken for granted; they are constantly present in the texture of the poem, but they do not mould the ideas within it. The dynamic comes preeminently from the writers of late antiquity—Martianus Capella and Macrobius, Claudian and Prudentius, and above all from Boethius—

---

[39] See N. M. Häring, *Commentary on Boethius by Thierry of Chartres* (Toronto 1971) p 442.
[40] See the passages assembled by Bossuat at the beginning of book VIII.

and from the twelfth-century scholars, especially Thierry of Chartres and Bernard Silvester, who pave the way with earlier pioneering attempts to describe the nature of God and the world in a neoplatonist frame without recourse to Christian revelation.

V

We have noted that both Thierry and Bernard in their different ways present an account of the creation in which there is syncretism of Platonist and Christian views. In Alan's poem the Christian element is more explicit, but only because the plot demands a visit to heaven; so far as the action on earth is concerned, no explicitly Christian element obtrudes. At the same time, however, there are implicit connexions constantly made between this natural world and the theological world. The perfect man is not Christ, for Mary and Christ are in heaven when Prudentia mounts there, but he is a twelfth-century *alter Christus*. The Virtues who descend from heaven to aid Natura are not the theological or the cardinal virtues, but the natural virtues of abundance, youth, laughter, reason, generosity (a key twelfth-century concept), nobility, and so on; but in the Christian sense the Virtues are one of the nine choirs of angels, so their descent is marked by a liturgical phrase, *militie celestis honor*.[41] They meet Natura in her palace, lying in a region 'set apart from our clime'; the idea is taken over from the home of Physis in Bernard's *Cosmographia*, in which the moist matter (*hygran ousian*) permitting the luscious growth of all vegetation accounts for the name of the location Granusion. But Alan contrives to implant on this *locus amoenus* the Hebraic concept of Paradise, for the fruitful garden is described by a Hebraism, *locus locorum*.[42]

In this palace, with its murals which contrast the intellectual giants of the past (Aristotle as logician, Plato 'more divinely dreaming God's secrets', Seneca as moral philosopher, Ptolemy as astronomer, Cicero as rhetorician, Virgil as poet, and various mythological and historical characters representing different moral excellences) with the intellectual pygmies and perverted princes of the present,[43] Nature laments her defective creations and proposes the cooperative achievement of an *alter Christus*: 'Let the sinning of our creation be *redeemed* in one

[41] I 26.
[42] I 73.
[43] Ennius and Mevius (I 166 *seq*) represent Joseph of Exeter and Walter of Châtillon; see K. Francke, *Zur Geschichte der lateinischen Schulpoesie des XII und XIII Jahrhunderts* (Munich 1878) p 22.

man . . . a man not material but *divine*. Let him dwell in mind in heaven, but in body on earth. On earth he will be human, but among the stars godlike. In this way he will become both God and man; made both he will be neither . . .'[44] Ratio in her supporting speech approves the aspiration 'that a new Lucifer should be a pilgrim in the world, that in him the flaw of no fall should overshadow his rising . . . so he may be our protector, judge, athlete, advocate.'[45]

We have noted how Alan's description of heaven is a synthesis of neoplatonism and Christianity, but it must be emphasised that he explicitly confesses the Christian truths. Theologia's role—'to seek out the hidden cause of the incorporeal, to search for the beginning and end of things'—is represented as a scientific search for the Christian God, and on her garment God is depicted with a carefully orthodox description of the relationship between the three Persons.[46] When we read Theologia bidding Prudentia to proceed with the horse of Hearing alone, we recall Paul's words in *Romans* that faith comes by hearing,[47] and Fides is to be the final guide. The explicitly Christian flavour is reinforced by a litany of the Virgin and a eulogy of Christ himself. On the other hand, as we have noted, the description of God in his upper palace becomes philosophical, and the knowledge to which God is the key is exemplified by mythological and classical figures.[48]

VI

It is right therefore in the case of Alan as in that of Bernard to speak of a syncretism between Christian and neoplatonist visions of the world. Yet in one major respect—the creation of the perfect man and the optimistic vision of an era of peace and plenty under his dominion —accepted Christian orthodoxy recedes. The doctrine of millenarianism had never been officially condemned by the Church; but after being put to rout by Origen in the east and by Jerome in the west (Augustine too after earlier hesitations renounced it),[49] it had ceased to be regarded as a respectable tenet. And the notion of the perfect man regarded literally runs into difficulties with the doctrine of original sin.

Inevitably we think at once of the possible influence of Joachim of

---

[44] I 232 *seq.*
[45] II 45 *seq.*
[46] V 147 *seq.*
[47] Rom 10.17.
[48] VI 226 *seq.*
[49] See Origen, *PG* 11 (1857) col 165; Jerome, *PL Suppl* 1 (1958) cols 164 *seq* and *PL* 24 (1865) col 802; Augustine, *Civ Dei* XX 7.

Fiore. But there are two powerful arguments against this. First, though there have been brave attempts to link Joachim with Gilbert de la Porrée, there is no hard evidence that the theories of Joachim were influential outside Italy before the thirteenth century. Secondly, and more important, Joachim's notion of the third age—the age of the Father at the creation and the age of the Son at the incarnation being followed by the age of the Spirit—is that of an ideal monastic society. Alan's vision is more secular, and its roots lie in the earlier literature of the twelfth century.

The notion of the perfect man appears strongly in a curious work called *Mathematicus*, once attributed to Hildebert of Lavardin but probably to be ascribed to Bernard Silvester.[50] The work is set in classical Rome, and the hero Patricida is the perfect man who becomes king of Rome after an astrologer's prophecy that he will slay his father. He confronts that destiny, proclaims that he will commit suicide instead, and abdicates. The detail of the plot is not relevant to our concern; the character of Patricida offers one possible model for Alan. It is also reasonable to cite Walter of Châtillon's glorification of Alexander the Great in the *Alexandreis*, the more so as Walter prays for a new Alexander to lead Christendom in the context of the consolidation of Mohammedan power under Saladin. These earlier examples of the attractiveness of the theme of the perfect man suggest that the impulse comes from the idealisation of classical antiquity. One of the key points at which classical humanism, in the guise of the later Platonist philosophy, differs from Christian humanism is precisely the notion that man can attain perfection by his own efforts and without the accession of grace. But it is doubtful if Alan consciously espouses this heretical view. More probably, after his De Planctu Naturae with its pessimistic report on contemporary morals, he sought to portray a Christian optimism in which he envisages men obeying the injunction of Christ: *estote ergo perfecti, sicut et Pater vester caelestis perfectus est.*[51]

This exploitation of the *Anticlaudianus* for the study of Alan as a renaissance figure has taught us two main lessons. First, as a student and as a teacher of the liberal arts he is thoroughly versed in a wide range of classical literature, and apparently without effort he avails himself of this knowledge in fashioning the texture of his poem. But

---

[50] See Wetherbee p 153; text in *PL* 172 (1895) cols 1365 *seq.*

[51] Matt 5.48. The whole question of the perfect man is set brilliantly in historical context by the paper of Professor Wilks which follows.

as with other leading intellectuals earlier in the century, the formative authors for Alan are those figures of late antiquity—Claudian, Macrobius, Martianus Capella, Prudentius, and above all Boethius—who are so influential in the construction of the Chartrian world of ideas. But secondly for Alan the role of such secular knowledge is that of the lower rungs of the ladder which enable the human mind to ascend to theology, and by faith to gaze in a glass darkly upon God. It is this firm subordination of secular knowledge to sacred which makes the choice of medium the more piquant. But like Boethius Alan wrote his finest testament of belief in the form and presentation which he had mastered; as an arts man he wrote poetry markedly superior to his theology.

University of Glasgow

ALAN OF LILLE AND THE NEW MAN

by MICHAEL WILKS

ET them be forbidden access to this work, wrote Alan of Lille
in his *Anticlaudianus*, who would only look for the image of
sensuality and not the truth of reason . . . Do not allow those
tasteless men, who cannot take their studies beyond the bounds of the
senses, to impose their own interpretations on this book . . . lest the
majesty of its secret meanings be profaned, like pearls cast before swine,
when divulged to the unworthy.[1] But what is this majestic secret
significance which Alan wished to keep hidden from people so
lacking in good taste as to want to probe it and misunderstand it?
On the surface the *Anticlaudianus*, Alan's most famous work, is an epic
romance about a celestial journey and a great battle which is clearly
being used as a moral treatise, a *summa de virtutibus et vitiis*.[2] His long
poem tells the story of how the goddess Nature, in council with the
Virtues, seeks to make a new type of person, the *homo perfectus*.[3]
They realise that such a divine being cannot be created unless a soul
is brought from God, whereupon Phronesis, the searcher after truth
to whom the secrets of God are revealed,[4] undertakes a journey to

---

[1] [Alain de Lille (Alanus de Insulis), *Anticlaudianus, prologus*, ed R.] Bossuat (Paris 1955)
p 56, 'Ab huius igitur operis arceantur ingressu qui, solam sensualitatis insequentes
imaginem, rationis non appetunt ueritatem, ne sanctum canibus prostitutum sordescat,
ne porcorum pedibus conculcata margarita depereat, ne derogetur secretis, si eorum
magestas diuulgetur indignis. . . . infruniti homines in hoc opus sensus proprios non
impingant, qui ultra metas sensuum rationis non excedant curriculum.' All references
are to this edition. The English translation by J. J. Sheridan (Toronto 1973) now
replaces that of W. H. Cornog (Philadelphia 1935).

[2] [G. R.] de Lage, [*Alain de Lille poète du xiie siècle*] (Montreal/Paris 1951) p 52, and see
here further for an extensive comparison of the *Anticlaudianus* with the *De planctu
Naturae*; also P. Delhaye, 'La vertu et les vertus dans les oeuvres d'Alain de Lille,' *Cahiers
de civilisation médiévale*, 6 (Poitiers 1963) pp 13–25.

[3] VIII, 147–8, p 177, 'Jam perfectus erat in cunctis celicus ille et diuinus homo.' A prime
source here is the account of Nature's visit to heaven in order to complete her work by
creating man in the *De mundi universitate*, otherwise known as the *Cosmographia* or
Megacosmus et microcosmus, of Bernardus Silvestris, ed C. Barach and J. Wrobel
(Innsbruck 1876, reprinted Frankfurt 1964).

[4] II, 147, p 77, 'Fronesis, cui cuncta Dei secreta loquntur'; II, 106–7, p 76, 'quin superos
adeat, quin uisitet astra Deique imbibat archanum'; V, 166–7, p 128, 'poli regina
caduca deserit atque Dei secretum consulit'; compare V, 114, p 126, 'Hic archana Dei,
diuine mentis abyssum'. This derives from Matt. xiii.11, I Cor. ii.7.

heaven in a chariot constructed by the seven liberal arts and drawn by the five senses. With the aid of Theology and Faith, Phronesis meets the heavenly host, the Virgin Mary, and eventually God himself, who has a soul made for her. She brings this soul, carefully sealed to keep it fresh, back to the waiting body, and the *novus homo* is complete. He then has to prove himself in a great pitched battle between the virtues and the vices.

The general idea of God creating a perfect man derives from Boethius' description of the humanity of Christ, and later writers certainly understood the poem as a tract on the incarnation,[5] designed to instruct the faithful in the familiar Pauline theme that the Christian is a man reborn, who is freed from his old natural self and re-formed as a new spiritual being in Christ: the old sinful man is converted into the righteous new man, who is the *imago Christi*.[6] It follows the well-worn Augustinian principle that baptism is a contract of regeneration by which the *fidelis* gains citizenship[7] of the City of God, and through this membership of the church acquires a new identity which may enable him to escape the lethal imperfections of his natural condition.[8]

If this was all there was to it, we should be justified in regarding the *Anticlaudianus*, despite its enormous popularity in the later medieval period, as little more than another very interesting attempt by the twelfth-century renaissance to clothe traditional Christian teaching in classical garb.[9] But Alan made it clear to his readers at the beginning

---

[5] Bossuat p 35.

[6] For example Rom. vi. 3–7, I Cor. xv.44–9, II Cor. v.17, Ephes. ii.12–16, iv.13, 24; and in general see [G. B.] Ladner, [*The Idea of Reform*] (Cambridge, Mass., 1959) especially pp 39 *seq*. For an illustration of Alan's use of this principle elsewhere see his *Expositio prosae de angelis*, ed [M.-T.] d'Alverny, [*Alain de Lille: Textes inédits*] (Paris 1965) p 200.

[7] W. Ullmann, *Principles of Government and Politics in the Middle Ages* (3 ed London 1974) pp 32 *seq*, and here further references; also now 'Dante's *Monarchia* as an Illustration of a Politico-Religious *Renovatio*,' *Traditio—Krisis—Renovatio aus theologischer Sicht: Festschrift Winfried Zeller*, ed B. Jaspert and R. Mohr (Marburg 1976) pp 101–13.

[8] For a fuller discussion see my articles in *Studia Patristica* 9 (Berlin 1966) pp 477–512, and *Augustinus* 12 (Madrid 1967) pp 489–510; also 'The Idea of the Church as *Unus homo perfectus*', *Miscellanea Historiae Ecclesiasticae* 1 (Louvain 1961) pp 32–49. Alan's conception of the world as a reflection of the *civitas Dei* is also to be seen in his sermon for Palm Sunday, written in 1179 or 1184, in which he describes how the army of angels led by Christ fights to defend the *novum castrum Ecclesiae* against the army of demons: d'Alverny, pp 246–9. The similarity to the *Anticlaudianus* is noted p 141.

[9] See the valuable general assessment by M.-T. d'Alverny, 'Maître Alain—*nova et vetera*', *Entretiens sur la renaissance du xiie siècle*, ed M. de Gandillac and E. Jeauneau (Paris 1968) pp 117–35.

that this religious fable had to be treated, like the bible, on more than one level of meaning. It was not only moral and allegorical, but it also possessed a literal or true sense as an adventure story,[10] quite as suitable for schoolboys as for mature students of philosophy beating on the door of heaven,

> In hoc etenim opere litteralis sensus suauitas puerilem demulcebit auditum, moralis instructio perficientem imbuet sensum, acutior allegorie subtilitas proficientem acuet intellectum,[11]

and, we might add, for one schoolboy in particular, for one destined not only to be a man but a man born to be king. The New Man of the poem is depicted as a great prince-redeemer, a blessed being who will rule the kingdom of the world by the reins of law:[12] but greater stress is put upon his youth.

> O iuvenis cui terra fauet, cui militat ether, cui Deus arridet, celum famulatur, et omnis applaudit mundus, et totus supplicat orbis . . .[13]

The New Man, we are told repeatedly, is a young one, endowed with all the gifts poured from Nature's limitless cornucopia, a happy recipient of the grants of both favour and fame.[14] In this way he is to be contrasted, to his own considerable advantage, with his great opponent Allecto, also a king, but one oppressed by gloom and despair, on whom illness, weariness, boredom and a pervading sense of failure have brought the burdens of a weak and trembling old age, in which he constantly stirs up wars and troubles in a

---

[10] The phrase is Sheridan's, p 27. The use of literal, moral and allegorical senses is extensively applied to the bible in Alan's *Liber in distinctionibus dictionum theologicalium, PL,* 210 (1866) cols 686–1012.

[11] *Prologus*, p 56, beginning 'Hoc igitur opus fastidire non audeant qui adhuc nutricum uagientes in cunis, inferioris discipline lactantur uberibus. Huic operi derogare non temptent qui altioris scientiae militiam spondent. Huic operi abrogare non presumant qui celum philosophie uertice pulsant.'

[12] IX, 387–8, p 196, 'Nam regnum mundi legum moderatur habenis ille beatus homo.'

[13] IX, 336–8, p 195; VIII, 363–4, p 183, 'iuuenis constanter ad ista erigitur'; and for *puer* see VIII, 200 and 216, pp 178, 179.

[14] VII, 77–86, p 159, 'Dat iuueni dotes predictas Copia, pleno perfundens cornu Nature munera, nullam mensure metam retinens in munere tanto. Et cornu quod nulla prius munuscula, nullum exhausit munus, totum diffunditur, in quo se probat et quantum possit metitur in illo. Accedit Fauor in dotem, ne tanta priorum munera perfecte perdant preconia laudis. Hiis fauet ergo Fauor, donans ut dona placere possint et celeri perflat tot munera Fama'; VIII, 119–23, p 176, 'Ergo Nobilitas dotes et munera profert, Fortuna dictante modum, iuuenemque beatum Nature dono, uirtutis munere, dote electi, nulla peccati labe iacentem afflat honore suo.'

desperate attempt to regain his lost youthful vigour.[15] Theirs is a contest of youth against age[16]—as if, says Allecto, a twig can rend an oak or a young stag can turn and destroy the old bear or the tiger which pursues it.[17] Nevertheless, it is the boy, too young in years to be able to appreciate the savage nature of war,[18] but armed with all the virtues,[19] who will emerge as the victor. He is a celestial hero, who appears in triumph wearing the laurel crown, and comes to inaugurate a new golden age in the history of the world.

It comes, therefore, as something of an anticlimax when we learn that this messianic paragon has to be told to dress himself properly and not to forget to wash behind his ears. Like most schoolmasters, Alan seems to have had a horror of long hair, and the New Man is urged to keep his cut fairly short in case he gets mistaken for a girl, thereby 'robbing his sex of its honoured position'. It is to be neither too elegantly coiffured, nor allowed to hang dishevelled and matted with deep-down dirt.[20] It is an ironic admonition to offer to the heir of the Merovingians, for, as we shall see, Alan is addressing the young king Philip II of France, and the whole of this section of the poem turns into a traditional treatise *de regimine principis*.[21] The New Man has to be taught to keep his fingers to himself, to talk and write properly, and not to talk too much or start shouting. He is to hold his head up, not

---

[15] VIII, 249–54, p 180, 'Morbida, mesta, tremens, fragilis, longeua Senectus, innitens baculo nec mentis robore firma, bella mouet bellique nouo iuuenescit in estu. Debilitas, Morbi, Languores, Tedia, Lapsus illius comittantur iter, qui Martis amore succensi, pugne cupiunt impendere uitam'; IX, 149–51, p 189, 'Quamuis pigra foret, quamuis longeua Senectus, quamuis delirans, quamuis torpore fatiscens, prona tamen calet in bello, iuuenescit in armis, . . .'

[16] IX, 156–8, p 189, 'Ergo propinqua neci, morti uicina propinque, florida canicie, rugis sulcata Senectus oppositum ruit in iuuenem, . . .'

[17] VIII, 201–3, p 178, '. . . sic seuit in ursum hinnulus, in quercus armatur uirgula, uallis in montes, lepus in catulos, in tigrida damme.'

[18] VIII, 216–17, p 179, 'Qui solus, puer et belli male conscius, in nos armatur cedrosque cupit delere murica.' Compare 198–201, p 178, 'In nos maturas euo bellique potentes, in numero plures, maiores uiribus, unum expertem belli puerum, uirtute minorem armauit Natura parens'.

[19] VIII, 317–37, pp 182–3, ending 'Quelibet a simili Virtus gerit arma uiroque iurat in auxilium; que totum Martis honorem dat iuueni, cui bella mouet Natura, suamque donat ei palmam belli pugneque laborem.'

[20] VII, 148–51, p 161, 'Ne cultu nimium crinis lasciuus adequet femineos luxus sexusque recidat honorem, aut nimis incomptus iaceat, scalore profundo degener et iuuenem proprii neglectus honoris . . .'

[21] For which the alternative title *De officio viri boni et perfecti* is more appropriate. For this type of literature in general see L. K. Born, 'The Perfect Prince', *Speculum*, 3 (1928) pp 470–504; W. Berges, *Die Fürstenspiegel des hohen und späten Mittelalters* (Leipzig 1938).

leave his mouth hanging open, and should avoid making improper gestures. He must learn to walk correctly, and must not mince along with his arm akimbo on his hip.[22] With nose, ears, eyes and mouth strictly disciplined,[23] and all effeminacy banished, the young prince can then be instructed in all the virtues appropriate to a king.[24] He is to keep promises, avoid flatterers, curb avarice, and love justice. He is to be learned and literate, wise and fair, defending widows and orphans,[25] helping the poor, and seeking always the common good[26]— all the stock in trade requirements of this type of literature. In this way, Alan assures him, he will be a noble youth, strong but pious, ruling with good arms and good laws, with the sceptre in one hand and the bible in the other,[27] a true king and priest. There is no evidence that

---

[22] VII, 138–44, p 161, 'Constancia uultus scurriles prohibet gestus nimiumque seueros abdicat incessus, ne uel lasciuia scurram predicet, aut fastus nimius rigor exprimat usum. Et ne degeneres scurrili more lacertos exerat et turpi uexet sua brachia gestu, aut fastum signans ulnas exemplet in arcum, . . .'

[23] VII, 156–60, p 161, 'Ne uitanda foris oculus uenetur et auris, melliflue uocis dulci seducta canore, seducat mentem deceptaque naris odore deffluat in luxus, uisum castigat et aurem, frenat odoratum;' and see the whole section dealing with the gifts of Modestia and Constancia beginning line 117, p 160.

[24] VII, 166–396, pp 162–8.

[25] VII, 342–3, p 167, '. . . deffendat uiduas, miseros soletur, egenos sustentet, pascat inopes faueatque pupillos.' The king's obligation to defend widows and orphans features in Germanic coronation orders from at least the tenth century (although the papacy claimed the Roman church as the supreme tribunal charged with their protection) and rapidly became a standardised formula, also applied to other bishops and knights, which required them to secure their dependents' rights generally. One of the charges involved in the deposition of Adolf of Nassau in 1298 was his failure to do this. The biblical basis is Ps. lxvi. 6, Isa. i.17, 23: hence the view that widows and orphans represented all Christians.

[26] Compare II, 304–5, p 81, 'An que sola solet bona poscere, sola recidet hoc commune bonum . . .?'

[27] The principle that the function of the royal sceptre is to add the force of command where necessary to the teachings of the faith (for example V, 247–8, p 130, 'precepti robur eidem consilio miscens') is contained in the description of Theology as queen of heaven 'quam probat esse deam uultus sceptrumque fatetur reginam' (V, 181–2, p 128), who 'Librum dextra gerit, sceptrum regale sinistra gestat et ad librum plerumque recurrit ocellus; sed raro tendit ad uirgam, tandemque reuertens circuit ille manum solers, ne leua uacillet, succumbens honeri uirge, sceptrumque resignet', V, 104–8, p 126. That the figure of a king with book in one hand and sceptre or sword in the other on renaissance emblems indicates divine rulership and derives from classical descriptions of Apollo by way of Justinian's famous phrase in the prologue to the *Institutes* that the imperial majesty was 'non solum armis decoratam sed etiam legibus armatam' has been shown by E. H. Kantorowicz, 'On Transformations of Apolline Ethics', *Charites: Studien zur Altertumswissenschaft*, ed K. Schauenburg (Bonn 1957) pp 265–74. This conception of rulership is of course essentially Platonic: but note also Aristotle's account of Solon in *Const. Ath.*, XII, 4. It was rendered by Bracton, *De legibus et consuetudinibus Angliae*, I, i, 1, as 'In rege qui recte regit necessaria sunt duo haec arma

Philip Augustus, who, devoid of maternal care, was by all accounts an ill-kempt youth, who loved only hunting, and refused to do his Latin exercises,[28] paid any attention to all this.

Alan seems to have been aware that medieval boys were symbolically equated with the unrighteous,[29] and that in contemporary ecclesiastical writings the boy-king was traditionally a figure of the tyrant.[30] He was therefore at some pains to emphasise that Philip Augustus was a new type of ruler, a boy in years but with all the wisdom of age.[31] The gifts of nature and divine grace showered upon him would allow him to grow up wisely; and just as the sun, blazing in majesty, eclipses the stars and controls the movements of other planets,[32] so the French monarch, a new imperial sun-king,[33] would be a true philosopher-

---

videlicet et leges'; also Aegidius Romanus, *De regimine principum*, III, iii, 1; and frequently applied to medieval rulers before being adopted by Machiavelli: A. H. Gilbert, *Machiavelli's 'Prince' and its Forerunners: 'The Prince 'as a Typical Book 'de Regimine Principum'* (Durham, N.C., 1938) pp 64-5.

[28] C. Petit-Dutaillis, *The Feudal Monarchy in France and England* (London 1936) p 180.

[29] See further *SCH* 5 (Leiden 1969) pp 85-9.

[30] The view that child rulers were corrupt oppressors in rebellion against God follows from Isa. i.2-4, iii.12, but the text most quoted in this connection is Eccles. x.16, following its use in the *De duodecim abusivis saeculi*, 9 (ed Hellmann) p 51: for example Jonas of Orleans, *De institutione regia*, 3 (ed Reviron) p 141; Hincmar of Rheims, *De regis persona et regia ministerio*, 2, *PL* 125 (1852) col 835, and subsequently by John of Salisbury, who applied it directly to Henry II in *Entheticus*, 1463, *PL* 199 (1900) col 996. Innocent III, *Regestum super negotio Romani imperii*, 29 (ed Holtzmann) p 45 used it to dismiss the claims of Frederick II in 1200-1. Previously Gregory VII, *Reg.* I, 24, had urged Henry IV to stop being childish and imitate instead the wisdom of the *sancti reges*: on this see now G. Schneider, *Prophetisches Sacerdotium und Heilsgeschichtliches Regnum im Dialog 1073-1077* (Munich 1972) p 43.

[31] VII, 92-8, pp 159-60, 'Munera leticie largitur grata Iuuentus, et quamuis huius soleat lasciuia semper esse comes, deponit eam moresque seueros induit atque senis imitatur moribus euum: in senium transit morum grauitate Iuuentus. Sic etate uiret iuuenis, quod mente senescit, etatem superat sensus, . . . '; VII, 170-1, p 162, 'Illa monet iuuenem monitu seniore senisque largitur mores iuueni.' For a list of classical precedents see Sheridan, p. 30.

[32] IV, 376-86, p 118, 'qualiter in stellis regnans artansque planetas imperio seruire suo, nunc stare meantes cogit, nunc tumidos sectari deuia sola maiestate iubet, nunc libertate meandi concessa motus, reddit sua iura planetis; qualiter alternans uultus erroris in ortu fit puer inque die medio iuuenescit adultus, mentiturque uirum tandem totusque senescit vespere: sic uarias species etatis ad horam sol prefert unusque dies complectitur euum.'

[33] II, 48, p 74: Reason approves Nature's plan that 'sol nouus in terris oriatur'; and compare this with the description of heaven as the home of the celestial sun 'quem sol mundanus adorat, cui celum stelleque fauent et supplicat orbis . . . sol alius sed non aliud, sol unus et unum', where God rules the heavenly powers: 'qua residet rex ipse poli, qui cuncta cohercet legibus imperii, qui numine numina celi constringit, cuius nutu celestia nutant. Hec igitur uicina Deo uix sustinet eius immortale iubar, ius

statesman of Platonic calibre,[34] divinely qualified to govern his own lands and, by analogy, those of surrounding kingdoms as well.

If, as I am suggesting, the *Anticlaudianus* is really a species of court poetry,[35] combining both the form of a panegyric with a vade-mecum to aid the instruction of a Christian prince, we may reasonably ask why it was that Alan of Lille wanted to write it. In the summer of 1179 Philip Augustus was fourteen years old (he was born 21 August,

---

magestatis inundans, expectat lumen,' VI, 245–83, pp 148–9. Alan's description of the sun as *oculus mundi* (II, 121, p 76) is an expression usually applied to Christ, and for medieval sun-kingship as an *imitatio Christi* see my *Problem of Sovereignty* (Cambridge 1963) pp 276, 424. In his contemporary work the *Alexandreid* Walter of Châtillon expressed the hope that there would be a new *rex Francorum* who would 'toto radiaret in orbe', PL 209 (1855) col 518: this has been identified as a reference to Philip Augustus soon after his coronation by [C. M.] Hutchings, ['*L'Anticlaudianus* d'Alain de Lille: Étude de chronologie'], *Romania*, 50 (Paris 1924) pp 1–13, at p 6. For the prince as another sun who sees and judges all in John of Salisbury see *Policraticus*, VI, 26 (ed Webb) p 266.

[34] Alan's requirement that the New Man should not seem too much of a philosopher, but should observe the mean ('philosophum nimis esse probet, tenet inter utrumque . . . mediocriter omnia pensat', VII, 152, 155, p 161; also 119–20, p 160, 'nec in dando mensuram deserit, immo singula describit certo moderamine finis.'), although set in the context of nothing more significant than a discussion on length of hair, is curiously reminiscent of Plato's emphasis on the doctrine of the mean and his view in the *Republic* that the best ruler would prefer to be wholly a philosopher and would only become a king as well with reluctance. Alan regarded Plato as the supreme philosopher (I, 131–4, p 61; II, 345, p 83), but it still remains to be established how much of the *Republic* was known to the twelfth century. The ideal of the monarch as philosopher, later to be used by Dante, seems to have come into fashion in the latter part of the century, despite John of Salisbury's view that courts and princely households were no place for a true philosopher, *Policraticus*, v.10 (ed Webb) p 566. Rahewin's continuation of the *Gesta Friderici*, iii.1, of Otto of Freising declared that Barbarossa possessed the gift of supreme wisdom, which brought such tranquillity to Germany that men changed their nature and the land its climate and character; whilst Godfrey of Viterbo's *Speculum regum* hailed Henry VI as a philosopher king, and argued that no ruler could rule well or be happy unless he was a philosopher: 'imperator expers philosophiae . . . errare potius quam regnare videtur,' *MGH*, *SS*, 22, pp 21 *seq*; also *Pantheon, prologus*, 'Tu vero Henrice, regum omnium felicissime, sicut a pueritia curasti phylosoficis inhaerere doctrinis . . .' For the development of court literature in the empire see now W. C. McDonald, *German Literary Patronage from Charlemagne to Maximilian* (Amsterdam 1973).

[35] The poem lends itself to dramatic presentation, and a musical version by Adam de la Bassée, canon of Lille, is known from the late thirteenth century, ed P. Bayart, *Ludus Adae de Basseia canonici Insulensis super Anticlaudianum* (Lille 1930). The long description given by Alan of the *domus Nature* (I, 109 *seq*, pp 60 *seq*), its great hall (*aula*) far grander than 'palacia regum', with a series of mural paintings which are a play (*ludus*) upon fictions turning them into truth (see in particular lines 119–30, 152–64, 186) contains a number of references to contemporary figures and situations, and may also refer to an actual setting. Like John of Salisbury, Alan was later to become critical of the abuses of courtiers, especially clerics: see his *Ars praedicandi*, 36, *PL* 210 (1855) cols 180–1, which de Lage, p 28 n 52 suggests may relate to the court of Philip Augustus.

1165) and had come under the guardianship of Philip of Alsace, count of Flanders. Alan, as a native of Lille and a Fleming, may well have looked to the latter for patronage. It is well known that Philip of Alsace sought to use his position to dominate the monarchy, and to make the alliance between the crown and Flanders the cornerstone of French royal policy, thereby counteracting the influence of the family group of Blois lords supporting the prince's mother, Adela of Blois. It was a design which seemed to have every chance of succeeding, following the decision of a general assembly of French barons and clergy at Paris earlier in the year to accept Louis VII's proposal that the young prince Philip should be crowned on his fourteenth birthday as co-ruler with his father. The coronation eventually took place at Rheims on 1 November.[36] Louis VII was himself absent from the ceremony: a chill followed by a paralytic stroke, had already incapacitated him. Although Louis did not die until a year later (18 September 1180), Philip Augustus was effective ruler of France, with Flemish help, from the autumn of 1179. The alliance with Flanders was finally cemented on 28 April, 1180, with Philip Augustus' marriage to Isabella of Hainault, aged about nine, and daughter of Baldwin of Hainault, brother-in-law and dependent of Philip of Flanders. The two Philips, tutor and pupil, were to become a single monarch: there was, according to Alan of Lille, illustrating the point with a wealth of allusions to great friendships in the classical past, to be an association of true affection so strong as to make two individuals into one person. Like David and Jonathan, interchanging souls, when one became king it was as if the other had gained the kingship in his second self—and in case anybody missed the reference Alan added that he was painting here a picture with a hidden meaning and significance.[37]

> Illic arte sua vitam pictura secundam donat eis quos castus amor,
> concordia simplex, pura fides, uera pietas coniunxit et unum esse
> duos fecit purgati fedus amoris; nam David et Ionathas ibi sunt
> duo, sunt tamen unum; cum sint diuersi, non sunt duo mente
> sed unus; dimidiant animas, sibi se partitur uterque.[38]

[36] The ceremony was delayed by the prince's illness following a hunting expedition during the course of which he got lost for several days: M. Pacaut, *Louis VII et son royaume* (Paris 1964) pp 217-18; W. L. Warren, *Henry II* (London 1973) pp 147-8.

[37] II, 200-4, p 78, 'Hec pictura suis loquitur misteria signis; non res ipsa magis, non lingua fidelius unquam talia depingit talique sophismate uisum decipiens oculis, rerum concludit in umbra qui preco solet esse boni pacisque figura.'

[38] II, 181-7, p 78, following I Reg. xviii.1-3: the passage continues, 188-99, 'Vt sibi Pyrithoüs se reddat, redditus orbi Theseus inferni loca, monstra, pericula uictat, uiuere

Alan of Lille and the New Man

It was a situation which makes understandable the desperate expedient resorted to by the Blois opposition: they appealed to Henry II of England for help against the king's alliance with Flanders.

Whether the *Anticlaudianus* was specifically written for the occasion of the coronation or the king's marriage to Isabella is a secondary consideration: both would require a re-dating of the poem to a period some three years earlier than generally accepted.[39] But the image of a

---

posse negat in se, nisi uiuat in illo; Tydeus arma rapit, ut regnet Thydeus alter, in Polinice suo pugnat seseque secundum, dum regnare cupit sibi, poscere regna uidetur. Alter in Euralio comparet Nisus et alter Eurialus uiget in Niso; sic alter utrumque reddit et ex uno comitum pensatur uterque. Atride furit in furiis eiusque furorem iudicat esse suum Pilades patiturque Megeram, ne paciatur idem Pilades suus alter et idem.'

[39] A date of 1182–3 is stipulated by Hutchings, p 13, and has been accepted by de Lage, pp 20–4, and Bossuat, p 8 n 7 and p 13 n 1, although extended to 1181–4 by Sheridan, pp 24–5. The latest possible date of 1184 would seem to be determined by the use made of the *Anticlaudianus* by John of Hanville (Jean de Hauteville or Johannes de Altavilla) in his *Architrenius* of that year; but the supposed allusion to Henry II and his four sons in I, 171–83, p 62, would put the *Anticlaudianus* before June 1183, when Henry the Younger died. The mention of 'our Ennius' and his *carmen pannosum* on the fortunes of Priam in lines 165–6 is said to refer to the *De bello Troiano* of Joseph of Exeter, who was in France *c* 1180 to 1183, and completed the poem in 1184, although this does not seem to be a very firm attribution. The only substantial argument against an earlier date is the apparent reference to Walter of Châtillon's *Alexandreid* in lines 166–170: 'illic Mevius, in celos audens os ponere mutum, gesta ducis Macedum tenebrosi carminis umbra pingere dum temptat, in primo limine fessus heret et ignauam queritur torpescere musam.' The *Alexandreid* was probably started in 1176, but not finished until 1181. However Hutchings himself, p 5, makes the point that this comment sounds as if the *Alexandreid* had only been begun and that Walter was having difficulty in writing it. There is therefore no compelling reason to date the *Anticlaudianus* to 1181 or after, and serious historical objections to this later period. The Franco-Flemish alliance was relatively short-lived, and by the summer of 1180 the situation had changed dramatically. Henry II's invasion had petered out after the meeting with Philip Augustus at Gisors in June, which reaffirmed the treaty of Ivry of 1177, and the French monarchy's alliance with Flanders was finally broken when Philip of Alsace and Baldwin of Hainault joined the Blois party in rebellion against Philip Augustus in May 1181. Eventually Philip Augustus went so far as to threaten to divorce Isabella in 1184. Moreover the hostile tone of the poem towards Henry II, valid enough for the period between Henry's abortive attacks on France in 1177 and 1180, would make progressively less sense during the 1180s as Henry entered that oddly lackadaisical period of exhaustion when he seemed to be resigned to leaving the conquest of France unfinished and cultivated good relations with Philip Augustus, almost as if he was waiting for the young king to develop into a worthy opponent for Henry's sons. In medieval terms there would be nothing unusual about calling a man in his forties *senex* (Henry II was 47 in 1180), but to describe Philip Augustus as a boy or youth would be increasingly irrelevant after he was 15. At the same time the possibility must be borne in mind that the *Anticlaudianus* as we have it is a revised version of an earlier original (although Sheridan comments, p 194 n 14, on the hasty unrevised character of the last two books). The second prologue talks about rewriting an old document: p 57, 'Scribendi nouitate uetus iuuenescere carta gaudet, et antiquas cupiens exire latebras ridet'; and there are

harmonious marriage between two souls joined in the peace and concord of one body[40] would serve the poet equally well either way (although the distinctly erotic description of the Virtues as fair young maidens[41] may perhaps suggest that Alan was trying to interest Philip Augustus in his bride). The real interest attaches to the effect which this union will have. Reason, who is the oldest and wisest Virtue,[42] and who is responsible for proposing the celestial journey to find a soul for the New Man, has to overcome the doubts of Prudence, who declares that it would be better not to attempt a great enterprise rather than try and fail.[43] But Reason insists that a temporary union sealed with kisses can unite matter and form,[44] putting an end to the chaos which

---

several suggestions that the work has already been published and attacked, and returned for correction: *prologus*, p 55, 'In quo lector non latratu corrixationis insaniens, uerum lima correctionis emendans, circumcidat superfluum et compleat diminutum quatenus illimatum revertatur ad limam, impolitum reducatur ad fabricam, inartificiosum suo referatur artifici, male tortum proprie reddatur incudi'; also the conclusion, IX, 410–11, 420–6, pp 197–8, 'O mihi continuo multo sudata labore pagina, cuius ad hoc minuit detractio famam, uiue . . . ne liuor in illum seuiat aut morsus detractio figat in illo qui iam scribendi studium pondusque laboris exhausit, proprio concludens fine laborem. Si tamen ad presens fundit sua murmura liuor, et famam delere cupit laudesque poete supplantare nouas, impune post fata silebit.'

[40] Note the description of Concordia, II, 174–7, p 78, 'Forma, figura, modus, numerus, mensura decenter membris aptatur et debita munera soluit. Sic sibi respondent concordi pace ligata membra, quod in nullo discors uinctura uidetur.' Despite the reading favoured by Bossuat and Sheridan, this passage does not sound as if it is still talking about hair.

[41] Especially Phronesis, for example I, 270–97, pp 65–6; compare 476–7, p 71, 'Subiecti senio non deflorata iuuentus formarum, formas semper facit esse puellas.'

[42] I, 448–9, p 70.

[43] I, 420–7, p 69, 'Sed quia principia nullo concludere fine . . . censetur turpe, fluitans, mutabile, stultum, cedere principiis malo quam cedere fini. Sic ait et tanto dubiorum turbine tota curia concutitur turbataque turba sororum fluctuat in dubiis, . . .'; also 395–402, p 68.

[44] I, 457–60, p 70, 'subiecti formeque uidet connubia, cernit oscula, que miscet concrecio, queue propinat unio natiua, formis subiecta maritans, subiecti que forma facit, . . .' The sense of touch (represented by the fifth horse of the heavenly chariot) is a pledge of alliance binding aspirations together by a love-knot: IV, 210–12, p 113, 'Ops, superum genitrix, in signum federis isto Naturam donavit equo, quo nodus amoris firmior effectus illarum uota ligauit.' Alan makes extensive use in the poem of the *De nuptiis Philologiae et Mercurii* of Martianus Capella, ed F. Eyssenhardt (Leipzig 1866), which describes an ascent to the palace of Jupiter to arrange a heavenly marriage between Mercury and Philology. It has recently been argued by C. A. Luttrell, *The Creation of the First Arthurian Romance: A Quest* (London 1974) that the theme of love and marriage in the *Erec et Enide* of Chrétien de Troyes is adopted from the *Anticlaudianus*, although this would involve a major re-dating of Chrétien's work from c1170 to the mid-1180s. An earlier dating of the *Anticlaudianus* would narrow the gap between them.

reigns in the degenerate condition of the material world,[45] and making a heavenly ideal into a reality on earth.[46] The physical marriage of Philip Augustus and Isabella, it is implied, will represent the political marriage of the new king to the realm of France: in both senses it will make a new man of him, and permit him to recreate the French kingdom as the *civitas Dei*. In this multi-layered allegory the kingdom is itself a body,[47] the *corpus regni* awaiting the political and religious life which can only be infused into it by being taken possession of by a new prince, who, like a soul in the human body,[48] comes to unite with his kingdom like Christ to his bride the church. Together they gain a new identity and are in a sense recreated. In the same way that a man reborn through baptism acquires a new self in his political-religious character as a citizen of the divine community of the *Ecclesia*, so the king by his coronation is wedded to the realm[49] and obtains an *alter ego*,[50] a new divine political nature as the embodiment of his

[45] I, 468–71, p 70, 'Hic subiecta uidet, formis uiduata, reuerti ad Chaos antiquam propriamque requirere matrem inque statu proprio puram iuuenescere formam nec sua degeneris subiecti tedia flere.'

[46] I, 495–501, p 71, 'quomodo terrestrem formam celestis ydea gignit et in nostram sobolem transcribit abissum, . . . qualiter in mundo fantasma resultat ydee, cuius inoffensus splendor sentitur in umbra.'

[47] The principle was in use well before John of Salisbury: for example Hugh of Fleury, *De regia potestate et sacerdotali dignitate*, I, 3 (*MGH, Lib*, II, 468), 'Verumtamen rex in regni sui corpore patris omnipotentis obtinere videtur imaginem . . . ut universitas regni ad unum redigatur principium.' For the later use of this analogy in France see E. H. Kantorowicz, *The King's Two Bodies* (Princeton 1957) pp 218 *seq*; R. E. Giesey, 'The French Estates and the *corpus mysticum regni*', *Album H. M. Cam* (Louvain/Paris 1960–1) I, pp 153–71; D. M. Bell, *L'idéal éthique de la royauté en France au moyen âge* (Geneva/Paris 1962) pp 108–9, 136, 155; and in general P. S. Lewis, *Later Medieval France: The Polity* (London 1968).

[48] Compare Aquinas, *De regimine principum*, I, 12–13 (ed Parma 1865, XVI, 235), 'Hoc igitur officium rex suscepisse cognoscat, ut sit in regno sicut in corpore anima, et sicut Deus in mundo . . . ut loco Dei iudicium regno exerceat'; and note the remark, much quoted by the Roman lawyers, addressed to Nero by Seneca, *De clementia*, I, v, 1, 'tu animus rei publicae tuae es, illa corpus tuum . . .' For the ideal of the soul as a kingdom ruled by the will as king, see now E. Stadter, 'Die Seele als *minor mundus* und als *regnum*', *Miscellanea Medievalia*, 5, ed P. Wilpert (Berlin 1968) pp 56–72. With Alan the body of the New Man is to be appropriate to the soul like a hall fit for a king: 'regi respondeat aula', VI, 421, p 153.

[49] On this see further my 'Chaucer and the Mystical Marriage in Medieval Political Thought', *BJRL*, 44 (1961–2) pp 489–530; and for the theological basis of the Church as the bride of Christ, R. A. Batey, *New Testament Nuptial Imagery* (Leiden 1971).

[50] I Reg. x.6; also ix.16, x.1, 7–10: see J. Funkenstein, 'Unction of the Ruler', *Adel und Kirche: Festschrift für G. Tellenbach* (Freiburg 1968) p 10; and for an illustration of coronation as a form of political baptism making the ruler a new man, R. Deshman, 'Otto III and the Warmund Sacramentary: A Study in Political Theology', *Zeitschrift für Kunstgeschichte*, 34 (Munich 1971) pp 1–20. It was applied to Conrad II by Wipo,

kingdom. We recognise the familiar principle of the king's two bodies. He emerges as another Christ, and the fair realm of France is reborn as a *corpus Christi*, the earthly image of the heavenly church.

In Alan's description of the New Man as the divine Christ-like king, both God and man,[51] sent by God to the human race to make France into a treasury of virtue and a storehouse of heaven,[52] one can detect many of the themes which were to become commonplace during the

---

Gesta Chuonradi, 3 (*MGH, SS*, XI, 260); and compare the Anglo-Norman Anonymous, *Tractatus IV* (*MGH, Lib*, III, 664), 'quod vir unctus oleo sancto et divina benedictione sanctificatus mutetur in virum alium, id est in christum domini,' which is related (669) to Christ's baptism in Jordan as a form of coronation. For the close connection between baptism of the righteous and their enthronement in heaven in the early church see G. Widengren, 'Den himmelska intronisationen och dopet', *Religion och Bibel*, 5 (Uppsala 1946) pp 28–60; P. Beskow, *Rex Gloriae: The Kingship of Christ in the Early Church* (Stockholm/Gothenburg/Uppsala 1962) pp 147–9. A similar theory can be found in the anonymous fourteenth-century *Avis aux roys*, perhaps written for Charles V.

[51] I, 235–41, p 64, 'Non terre fecem redolens, non materialis sed diuinus homo nostro molimine terras incolat et nostris donet solacia damnis, insideat celis animo, sed corpore terris: in terris humanus erit, diuinus in astris. Sic homo sicque Deus fiet, sic factus uterque quod neuter mediaque uia tutissimus ibit'; also 363–70, pp 67–8, 'Dispar natura, dispar substancia, forma discors, esse duplex hominis concurrit ad esse; una sapit terras, celum sapit altera, celis insidet hec, illa terris, mortique tributum cogitur ista dare, mortis lex excipit illam. Hec manet, illa fluit; hec durat, deperit illa; essendi nomen gerit hec, gerit altera numen; corpus habet terras, celestia spiritus'; and compare the description of Christ in heaven, V, 443–70, pp 136–7, beginning 'Hic habitat quem uita deum uirtusque beatum fecit et in terris meruit sibi numen Olimpi, corpore terrenus, celestis mente, caducus carne, Deus uita, uiuens diuinitus, extra terrenum sapiens, intus diuina repensans . . .', although the passage is written in such a way as to make it clear that Alan is also describing the heavenly reward awaiting the man who lives a Christ-like life on earth.

[52] VI, 390–6, p 152: God says 'Hoc mihi iampridem Racio dictauit ut uno munere respicerem terras mundumque bearem numine celestis hominis, qui solus haberet tot uirtutis opes quot munera digna fauore, tot dotes anime quo saltem mundus oberrans floreret, uiciis aliorum marcidus, immo iam defloratus in flore resurgeret uno.' See also VII, 229–37, pp 163–4, 'non illas largitur opes que sepe potentum excecant animos et magestatis honorem inclinant, minuunt leges et iura retardant, sed pocius donat thesaurum mentis et omnes diuicias animi, quas qui semel accipit, ultra non eget, immo semel ditatus semper habundat, quarum rectus amor, possessio nobilis, usus utilis, utilior largicio, fructus habundans. Hec est gaza poli, celi thesaurus.' This is reminiscent of the remark attributed to Louis VII in 1179 that in contrast with the wealth of the king of England the French had nothing except bread, wine and joy: Walter Map, *De nugis curialium* (ed James) p 225; and Giraldus Cambrensis' explanation in his *De principis instructione* that the success of Philip Augustus against the tyranny of England was due to his possession of virtues symbolised by a flower, which brought such peace and justice that the two kingdoms would best be united under Capetian rule: on this see J. W. Baldwin, *Masters, Princes and Merchants: The Social Views of Peter the Chanter and his Circle* (Princeton 1970) I, p 254.

resurgence of Capetian France under St Louis and Philip the Fair.[53] But in the dark days of Louis VII and Philip II the emphasis was necessarily upon the preliminary stages of the rebirth and reformation of France as the kingdom blessed by both Nature and God, and it is of particular significance that Alan introduces the principle that the coronation creates, or rather recreates, the social contract. The crowning of a new king reaffirms or remakes the contract between God and man by which his community is reborn as a true social entity and assumes the character of a *populus Dei.* Using the language of Augustinian covenant theology, which can be compared to John of Salisbury's definition of a *respublica* as a contracted body,[54] Alan makes Phronesis, when illuminated by Faith, express her wonder that God should clothe himself in human form—'Miraturque Deum nostram uestire figuram, et nostras habitare casas flammantis Olimpi rectorem' —and ask,

> Qui gunfi, que iuncture, quis nexus et unde connectant humana Deo, divina caduco consocient hominique Deum, quis federet ordo.[55]

The New Man, we are told, is to be one who possesses what all together possess: one man who should be all men.[56] In other words, all the inhabitants of the community are bonded or stuck together to form one being: the many are contracted into the single personality of Christ himself. By their membership of a *convenientia* which unites the whole as one body, the kingdom ceases to be a mere natural gathering together of human beings, and takes on the status of a corporation whose immaterial personality is represented by the prince

---

[53] Wilks, *Problem of Sovereignty,* pp 428–30, and here further literature; also now [J. R.] Strayer, 'France: [The Holy Land, the Chosen People, and the Most Christian King', *Action and Conviction in Early Modern Europe: Essays in Memory of E. H. Harbison*], ed T. K. Rabb and J. E. Siegel (Princeton 1969) pp 3–16.

[54] See *Studia Patristica,* 9 pp 498–9, 505, for a list of passages utilising this adhesive terminology (*conglutinatio, agglutinatio, foederatio, adhaeratio, cohaerentia,* etc) deriving from the *corpus compactum* of Job, xli. 6–8, 14–17; compare the Anglo-Norman Anonymous, *Tractatus IV,* p 669, 'et sancte potestati sanctoque regimini sancti cohereant, et ministri et sanctorum decens sit copula et in glutino Dei unita conventio.'

[55] VI, 162–9, pp 145–6; also VII, 57–61, p 158, 'animam Concordia carni federat et stabili connectit dissona nexu. Iunctura tenui, gunfis subtilibus aptat composito simplex, hebeti subtile, ligatque federe complacito, carni diuina maritat.'

[56] II, 50–2, p 74, 'possideat solus quicquid possedimus omnes; omnis homo sic unus erit, sic omne quod unum: unus in esse suo, sed erit uirtutibus ominis.' Dante's *monarchia* is described as 'uno solo principato e uno principe avere, il quale, tutto possedendo e più desiderare non possendo, li re tenga contenti nelli termini delli regni, siechè pace intra loro sia . . .' *Convivio,* IV, 4 (ed Moore) p 299.

as God on earth, a Leviathan of one man who is all men. Only in this way do they become a real community, a common unity or oneness; whilst those who do not partake remain a mere amorphous mob. Thus the New Man's adversary, Allecto, is no more than the leader of a motley multitude, a dissenting assembly[57] which is no true church, but a tribal 'get-together' which has no divine unity as a proper state.[58] Being a union of Vices, it naturally fails to make a contract with God, and cannot succeed. The natural contracts of sinful man, we may say, are no true covenants, and can produce no more than an Old Man who knows nothing better than the rule of force, and keeps the world in a natural state of constant war. The contract which recreates the New Man on the other hand forms a true society dedicated to peace, justice and the rule of righteousness.[59] It is the difference, Alan is telling his audience, between England and France.

[57] VIII, 172–3, pp 177–8, 'turba furens, gens dissona, concio discors, plebs dispar, populus deformis'; compare Gregory I, *Libri moralium*, XXXIII, 14, *PL* 76 (1878) col 690, 'In pacto enim discordantium partium . . .' For *concordia* as the distinguishing feature between a *populus* and a *multitudo* in Sallust and Augustine see D. C. Earl, *The Moral and Political Tradition of Rome* (London 1967) p 123; and in general J. Y. du Q. Adams, *The Populus of Augustine and Jerome: A Study in the Patristic Sense of Community* (New Haven/London 1971).

[58] VIII, 211–13, p 179, 'Sed melius gens nostra simul collecta nouellos Nature teret insultus fastusque recentes demittet, ueteri reddens elata ruine.' For the previous history of this principle with Charlemagne see W. Ullmann, *The Carolingian Renaissance and the Idea of Kingship* (London, 1969).

[59] VIII, 176–85, 193–7, 214–15, pp 178–9, 'Allecto prorumpit in hec: Que iura, quis ordo, quis modus, unde quies, que tanta licencia pacis ut nostras Natura uelit proscribere leges et mundum seruire sibi, dampnare nocentes, et iustos seruare uelit, cum nostra potestas eius preueniat uires, nostroque senatu plebescat Natura minor, totiensque subacta legibus imperii nostri, mutare ualebit amplius et nostris subducere colla cathenis? Proh pudor! . . . Sed pudeat nos iura sequi, quas uiuere iuste non decet, aut precibus uti. Pro legibus ergo sumende uires, uis pro uirtute feratur. Nos pro iure decet assumere robur et armis res dictare noues et sanguine scribere leges . . . Ergo pari strepitu, concordi Marte, furore equali lites et bella geramus in illum . . .' At the same time Phronesis appears to be distinctly unhappy, in what I take to be a comment on the contemporary situation, at the suggestion that Philip Augustus should withdraw from the contest and accept the unnatural peace of 1177 which had left the two disparate forces existing side by side like water and flame: V, 311–24, 357–68, pp 132–4, 'Dum transit, miratur aquas, quas federat igni indiuisa loci series, nec flamma liquorem impedit, aut flamme certat liquor ille repugnans, sed pocius sua deponunt certaminis arma. Nec iam natiuos querunt memorare tumultus quos ligat assensus discors, discordia conchors, pax inimica, fides fantastica, falsus amoris nexus, amicicia fallax, umbratile fedus. Figit in hiis uisum mentemque Sophia, sagaci perquirens animo quis pacem fecit adesse, pax ubi nulla manet; quis Martem iussit abesse, Mars ubi iura tenet; quis fedus nexuit illic, fedus ubi nullum; quis pacem miscuit ire, litigio fedus, liti coniunxit amorem . . . Hoc solo magis illa stupet meliusque mouetur, qua nexus mediante fide, quo federe pacis frigida conueniunt

Despite her female sex as one of the Furies and mistress of all the Vices, notably those characterised by violence and anger,[60] Allecto is also, somewhat disconcertingly, described as a king[61] and is a thinly-veiled allusion to Henry II, who claims to rule the kingdom of France by legal title, prescriptive right and possession[62] deriving from his policy of continual conquest. Bearing in mind the extent of the Angevin empire by the end of the 1170s (as recently as 1177 Henry had added La Marche and had promptly proceeded to attack Louis VII, who was only rescued by the intervention of the papal legate), when the king of England not only surrounded but governed more of France than the French king himself, and was reputed to be seeking the imperial crown, it is not surprising that Alan accuses Henry of wanting to be *dominus mundi*. He is the earth-shaker, making the whole world tremble with his thunderbolts of war,[63] a Nero, who, like Midas or Ajax, were all turned mad by the lust for possession which their already over-great wealth had engendered.

Illic precipiti Nero fulmine concutit orbem, indulgens sceleri, cogit plus uelle furorem, quam furor ipse uelit; quicquid distillat ab illo nequicie sese totum partitur in orbem; illic diues eget, sitit aurum totus in auro Midas, nec metas animo concedit habendi.

---

calidis, fluitancia pigris. Hic ubi nullus adest pacis mediator et omne fedus abest extrema ligans, quod pace reperta deleat hostiles rixas pugnamque recidat, defficit inquirens, querendo uincitur illa; quesitu superata suo sed uicta querelis deffectus queritur proprios; sic ista querela questio fit, Fronesi suspiria sola relinquens. Nec mirum si cedit ad hec Prudencia, que sic exedunt matris Nature iura . . .'

[60] See the list of Allecto's armed supporters, VIII, 218–316, pp 179–82.

[61] VIII, 259, p 180, 'belloque calent cum rege ministri', although he figures as *domina* in lines 224 and 227, p 179. He also appears as Pluto as well as the other Furies: I, 262–5, p 65; VIII, 305–14, p 182; 339, p 183. Alan probably had difficulty with the sex of his archvillain simply on account of his use of classical sources, but it is possible that he was not averse to Allecto also being identified with Adela of Blois, in which case the four tyrants who follow Nero in I, 171–83, p 62, mentioned below, could double as Adela's four brothers: William, archbishop of Rheims, Henry, count of Champagne, Theobald, count of Blois and Chartres, Stephen, count of Sancerre. Note also the condemnation of Progne, deluded by the tyrant Tereus, as a false mother who took arms against her own son, II, 221–4, p 79.

[62] VIII, 190–2, p 178, 'Ius nostrum pax subripiet, quod tempore tanto deffendens nobis prescriptio uendicat, usus confert et iusto titulo collata tuetur?'

[63] Alan's predilection for storms is a well known characteristic: for *fulgura belli*, III, 411, p 101; and note the contrast between wars and earthquakes, thunderbolts, tempests and gales in I, 194–8, p 63. The prologue begins with a storm shaking the world, p 55.

Militis excedit legem plus milite miles Aiax milicieque modus
decurrit in iram.[64]
The classics are ransacked for suitably awful precedents. Surely I,
argues Allecto, can be another Sulla or a new Catiline, prevailing over
laws, stirring up ancient frenzies, upsetting the order of the world:
can I not be another Rufinus?[65] We may now appreciate the force of
Alan's choice of title: the work is called the *Anticlaudianus* not only
because Claudian[66] at the end of the fourth century had told a story
of the supremely wicked man, Rufinus, who undertook a great
journey (to Constantinople) to make himself lord of the world, but
also because Claudian's villain was of French stock: Rufinus was a
Gaul from Gascony, whilst Henry, born at Le Mans, came from the
old strong race[67] of Normandy and Anjou. Allecto in fact plays a
double role in the poem. On one side he is the exemplar of the tyrant,[68]
the king reigning remote from justice and law, who is therefore cast
as the *rex-diabolus*, the image of Luciferian depravity,[69] and the very
type of rulership that the New Man must reject as his antithesis. On
the other, he is an actual tyrant, the usurping Henry II, whom the
young Philip Augustus must expel from the land of France. The
internal warfare against vice within a king who is to be the perfect

---

[64] I, 171–83, p 62, continuing 'Fractus amore Paris, Veneris decoctus in igne, militat
in Venerem; dum militis exuit actus, damnose compensat in hac quod perdit in armis.
In Dauo propriam miratur noctua formam et uultus peccata sui solatur in illo.' If
Nero is Henry II, then Midas, Ajax, Paris and Davus can be seen as Henry's four sons,
Henry the Younger, Richard, Geoffrey and John respectively: see Hutchings,
pp 10–12; de Lage, p 22.

[65] VIII, 208–10, p 179, 'Numquid Silla nouus, alter Nero uincere posset leges, antiquos
rursus renouare furores Rufinus, Katelina nouus peruertere mundum?' For Atreus,
Tereus, Crassus and Pompey as examples of tyrants see II, 213–41, p 79, Concordia's
speech beginning 'Si mea iura, meas leges, mea federa mundus olim seruasset uel
adhuc seruaret amoris uincula, non tantis gemeret sub cladibus orbis.'

[66] Claudius Claudianus, *Works*, Loeb ed (London 1922) I, pp 24–97; and for further
discussion of Rufinus and the *In Rufinum* see A. Cameron, *Claudian: Poetry and
Propaganda at the Court of Honorius* (Oxford 1970) pp 63–92. Alan appears to have
thought that Claudian was the fifth-century Gallic theologian Claudianus Mamertus,
author of a treatise *De statu animae*: de Lage, p 51; Bossuat, p 34; d'Alverny, p 305
n 56.

[67] IX, 113–14, p 188, 'Gens euo, sensu, cautela, uiribus, armis pollens'.

[68] The distinction is between the tyrant who creates his own right by force and the king
who uses his power to enforce true right: VIII, 193–7, p 178 (note 59 above).

[69] The phrase is John of Salisbury's (*Policraticus*, VIII, 17): for Alan, II, 45, p 74; and note
his description of Lucifer as the divine ruler who became a slave, IV, 297–9, p 115,
'Iam seruit qui liber erat, mendicat habundans qui fuit, exilium patitur qui primus
in aula regnabat, patitur penas a rege secundus', which may be compared with Platonic
and Aristotelian views of the tyrant as a slave-ruler.

image of Christ is mirrored in the external struggle against the English ruler. The mystical war in the soul, writes Alan, merges into actual fighting, and the battle of words is replaced by the real war of weapons.[70]

The covert purpose of the *Anticlaudianus*, therefore, is to urge Philip Augustus to engage in a titanic conflict against the English domination of France which in a mystical way will reflect the great cosmic struggle between Christ and Antichrist, the giant forces of divine order and ancient chaos.[71] Alan is under no illusions about the scale of the project which he is advocating, and he recognises that it will have to savour of the miraculous if it is to succeed. Allecto-Henry's scorn at the New Man's youth and lack of experience in war is what any contemporary commentator might have felt. 'For shame,' cries one of his subordinates (Infamy) as she strikes the New Man with both arrow and sword, 'will a race with the power of age, intelligence, caution, strength and arms give way before the weak soldiery of one youth, and will yon boy triumph over our race?'[72] The New Man is saved on this occasion[73] by his helmet of right reason, just as

---

[70] VIII, 367–9, p 183, '. . . et armis cedunt uerborum pugne: iam mistica bella rem sapiunt, pugnas cum res non ipsa fatetur.' Hence the double title of the poem. The actual contest of virtues and vices is drawn from the *Psychomachia* of Prudentius: see Bossuat, p 35.

[71] Like the New Man himself (see the list of royal titles, II, 54, p 74, 'tutor, defensor, iudex, *athleta*, patronus'), Alecto appears as Athleto in the summary, p 201. Philip the Fair was hailed as 'totius christianitatis athleta' in a grant of 1294, cited Strayer, 'France', p 10. This eventually developed into the ceremony in which the new king was summoned to rise from his bed to attend his coronation in an analogy with the renewed sun rising as a bridegroom to pursue his heavenly course like a giant refreshed (Psal. xviii. 6–7, 'Exsultavit ut gigas ad currendam viam'): on which see R. A. Jackson, 'The Sleeping King', *BHR* 31 (1969) pp 525–51; also Kantorowicz, *The King's Two Bodies*, p 50 n 19, for earlier applications of the idea. Christ as *gigas* became a stock item in medieval treatises on the virtues and vices to represent zealous pursuit of duty, for example Peraldus, *Summa*, III, 5. A variant of this depicted Christ as the healer of the sick giant of mankind, who rises from his bed: R. Arbesmann, 'The Concept of *Christus-Medicus* in St. Augustine', *Traditio*, 10 (1954) pp 1–28 at 23–5. The principle of combat between two giant athletes derives from the Pauline notion of a final contest between Christ as the second Adam and the man of sin, for example II Thess. ii. 3–10, which itself owes much to the Greek belief that the rebirth of a new order would follow the appearance of Anthropos, the prime man born out of the great cosmic struggle between the forces of law and chaos. For Christ as Anthropos and the second Adam see S. Hanson, *The Unity of the Church in the New Testament* (Uppsala/Copenhagen 1946) pp 65–73, 112–17.

[72] IX, 113–16, p 188, and see above note 18.

[73] IX, 126–32, p 188. For the New Man's armour see VIII, 321–37, pp 182–3, beginning 'Armatur celestis homo superumque beata progenies, que tanta noui discrimina Martis sola subit'.

other blows are diverted by the breastplate of piety and the whole
armour of God, but from the beginning of the poem it is made
clear that the New Man will have to effect a complete reversal of the
low position to which the French monarchy had sunk under Louis,
defeated, disregarded, and generally felt to be useless: 'our decrees
are unlistened to in our lands, love for us grows cold, and our
waning reputation slumps.'

> Heu! pudeat nostra terris decreta silere, quod nostri languescit
> amor, quod fama tepescens torpet et a toto uiles proscribimur
> orbe, quod laxas mundo sceleris concedit habenas Thesiphone
> nostraque sibi de gente triumphans gaudet et a nostro luctu sibi
> gaudia suggit: uincimur et uictas pedibus summittit Herinis et
> gravibus nostra castigat colla cathenis.[74]

It is an enterprise which can only be undertaken by a messianic ruler
who can achieve a total transformation of France and secure its rebirth
as the most Christian kingdom, and whilst the traditional Christian
elements in this idea do not need underlining, it is interesting that a
poet, who so closely modelled himself on Virgil, should prefer to
render this in terms of the famous passage in the Fourth Eclogue
(iv. 6). The return of the maiden Phronesis from heaven
with the soul of the New Man is equated with the return
of the Virgin and the birth of a boy-child—later identified by Virgil

---

[74] I, 258–65, pp 64–5. For the ineffective king as himself a species of tyrant see E. Peters,
The Shadow King: Rex Inutilis in Medieval Law and Literature, 751–1327 (New
Haven/London 1970). Attention should also be paid to that section of Concordia's
speech which emphasises the disunity between the various factions and the fear of
engaging in a struggle with such daunting prospects which have led to the present
condition of the kingdom, but ends by urging all to unite in performing a great work
and service for the common good: 'acrior insultas uiciorum pugnaque maior nobis
incumbet, si nos diuiserit error; postquam cementi rumpit discordia muros, hostili
pugne muros exponit inhermes; acrius insultat seuitque profundius ensis, conserte
partes ubi nulla repagula donant nec series harum conserta recalcitrat ensi; acrius in
uolucrem Iouialis fulminat ales, cum plebem uolucrum uenientis disgregat horor;
uberius torrens effunditur, obice nullo deffendente uiam fluuioque negante meatum.
Ergo concordes uotum curramus in unum: quod Natura petit, Racio commendat,
Honestas approbat, immo cupit, Pietas deposcit et instat. Nec Fronesis sola, distans,
contraria, discors nos omnes pacis conformi lege iugatas diuidet in partes ut amoris
uincla relaxet, sed pocius constans, congaudens, consona, concors, in nostram mentem
ueniet nec uicta labore cedere credatur citra preludia lucte, vel tumido flatu perflare
superbia mentem, uel sibi liuor edax animi mordere recessus. An que sola solet bona
poscere, sola recidet hoc commune bonum, nostrum decus, utile uotum, nos omnes
que sola libens et sponte mouere in tantum deberet opus tantumque fauorem, si
flamata minus torperet nostra uoluntas nec tantum uellet animus conscendere
noster?' II, 282–309, p 81.

as Augustus[75]—under whom 'the iron brood shall first begin to fail' and the golden age of the rule of Saturn is restored: 'Iam redit et virgo, redeunt Saturnia regna.' The victory of the Christ-like New Man over Allecto-Henry will usher in an age of universal concord, in which the earth, ruled by all the virtues, becomes a reflection of heaven, and the terrestrial paradise is restored. Poverty and hunger, famine, fear and pain are banished. It is not even necessary, according to Alan, to adopt the Christian version in which swords are beaten into ploughshares,[76] since he prefers the classical tradition that ploughshares and pruning-knives are themselves superfluous: the field and the fruit-tree will be automatically fertile, and the labourer's prayer for the abolition of work and a new life of perpetual idleness will be answered.

In terris iam castra locant et regna merentur Virtutes mundumque regunt, nec iam magis illis astra placent sedesque poli quam terrenus orbis. Iam celo contendit humus, jam terra nitorem induit ethereum, jam terram uestit Olimpus. Nec iam corrigitur rastro, nec uomere campus leditur, aut curui deplorat uulnus aratri, ut tellus auido, quamuis inuita, colono pareat, et semen multo cum fenore reddat. Non arbor cultrum querit, non uinea falcem, sed fructus dat sponte nouos et uota coloni fertilitate premit.[77]

---

[75] *Aeneid*, VI, 791–5. It is probable that Philip derived his title of Augustus from this rather than the usual explanation that it was coined for him by his chaplain William the Breton because he made France grow: F. M. Powicke, *CMH* 6, p 285. Alan makes no attempt to solve the contradiction inherent in his use of the more common view of Saturn as a baneful, threatening influence (II, 115, p 76; IV, 465–83, pp 120–1; VI, 457–8, 475–81, p 154), but he may have been following Claudian's description of Theodosius as victor over the Furies, *In Rufinum*, I, 50–2, 'Heu nimis ignavae quas Iuppiter arcet Olympo, Theodosius terris. En aurea nascitur aetas. En proles antiqua redit': on this see further Ladner, *Idea of Reform*, pp 16 *seq*; N. Cohn, *The Pursuit of the Millennium* (London 1957) pp 1–21; M. E. Reeves, *The Influence of Prophecy in the Later Middle Ages* (Oxford 1969) pp 295 *seq*; and in general now F. A. Yates, *Astraea: The Imperial Theme in the Sixteenth Century* (London 1975).

[76] Isa. ii. 4, Joel iii. 10, Mic. iv. 3.

[77] IX, 391–402, pp 196–7; and compare the description of the garden of Paradise, VI, 234–72, p 148. For a convenient survey of the origins of this see J. Ferguson, *Utopias of the Classical World* (London 1975). A similar view of the terrestrial Paradise needing neither ploughshares nor ploughmen, and connected to heaven by a mountain, was transmitted to the fifteenth century via Dante: W. Oakeshott, 'Some Classical and Medieval Ideas in Renaissance Cosmology', *Essays in Commemoration of Fritz Saxl* (London 1957) pp 245–60.

Alan's claim that the reign of Philip Augustus would bring permanent universal peace was not of course to be realised, and one is never quite sure how much allowance should be made for poetic licence in this type of prophetic propaganda. Nevertheless, the history of France in the ensuing century bears adequate testimony to the serious purpose underlying the *Anticlaudianus* and Alan's skill in predicting the future renaissance of the French kingdom under a revitalised dynasty freed from the Norman yoke. And if the success story of thirteenth-century France led the French monarchs, particularly after the demise of Frederick II, to regard themselves as second Charlemagnes inaugurating a *renovatio Romani imperii*,[78] with France rapidly coming to take the place of the empire in European politics and taking on the traditional imperial capacity of being *protector Ecclesiae*, the point will bear repetition that Alan specifically foresaw the New Man appearing as a saviour for all mankind. Just as Plato had viewed his philosopher-king as not only the opposite of the tyrant but also as an alternative doing rightly what the tyrant could only do unjustly, so Alan condemned Henry for seeking to establish a universal tyranny in order to make way for the universal aspirations of his own *rex christianissimus*. The new age of reborn France would require essentially the replacement of Henry by Philip, the substitution of Capetian for Angevin imperialism, rather than a new power structure. The setting of one sun, he tells us, would be followed by the rising of another day: the tyrant might be a model of Luciferian depravity, but he would be succeeded by a new Lucifer, who would shine out over all the earth and govern an empire on which the sun never set.

> . . . utile consilium Nature iudico, uotum approbo, propositum laudo, molimen adoro ut nouus in mundo peregrinet Lucifer, in quo nullius labis occasus nubilet ortum, solis in occasu sol alter proferat ortum, sol nouus in terris oriatur, cuius in ortu sol uetus occasus proprios lugere putetur, possideat solus quicquid possedimus omnes.[79]

Alan never tried to conceal from Philip Augustus the universalistic programme which he thought the French monarchy should adopt: indeed he considered this to be an integral part of Nature's great plan

---

[78] R. Folz, *Le couronnement impérial de Charlemagne* (Paris 1964) pp 257–64; and in general *Le souvenir et la légende de Charlemagne* (Paris 1950); J. de Pange, *Le roi très chrétien* (Paris 1949).
[79] II, 45–9, p 74.

which he was unfolding, and for which he claimed his laurels as a poet. As he said, his muse may well have been Clio, and even if one thinks that Calliope or Erato might be equally appropriate, he was surely right to add that he was also the poet of Apollo.[80]

University of London
Birkbeck College

---

[80] *Prologus*, p 57, 'Autoris mendico stilum falerasque poete, ne mea segnicie Clio directa senescat, . . . Fonte tuo sic, Phebe, tuum perfunde poetam, ut compluta tuo mens arida flumine, germen donet, et in fructus concludat germinis usum.' It would be interesting to know exactly what is meant by his 'laudes poete nouas', IX, 425–6, p 198.

REFORM AT THE COUNCIL OF
CONSTANCE: THE FRANCISCAN CASE

by DUNCAN NIMMO

IN the history of Christian renewal, the council of Constance
(1414–18) holds an important, and on the whole unhappy,
position.[1] It embodied the highest aspirations: as is well known,
its aim was the regeneration of the Roman church at every level—the
familiar 'reform in head and members'; this cause was the council's
chief preoccupation from mid-1415 until its close; yet by common
consent its achievement was, if not null, then negligible, in relation
both to the task it had set itself, and to the real requirements of the day;
and thus—it is tempting to conclude—in failing to reform itself, the
medieval church made necessary the different and in many respects
regrettable reform of the sixteenth century.

For all that, there were instances of effective renewal at the
council; this paper presents one which, though doubtless modest in
terms of the overall destiny of western Christendom, was nevertheless
deep and enduring, and perhaps for that very reason has been generally
overlooked: that of the Franciscans. More precisely, two Franciscan
reform movements, mutually independent and quite different in
character, received formal sanction at Constance, one in 1415, the
other in 1418. Both went on to survive strenuous opposition within
the order. More important, they laid the foundations for the
definitive division of the Franciscans into three separate families
which was accomplished in the first half of the sixteenth century, and
which in essence has survived down to the present day; and in so doing
they may be said, taken together, to have embodied the first
satisfactory solution to fundamental problems of Franciscan observance
which had been pending since the thirteenth century—perhaps since
the lifetime of Francis himself.[2] In this sense the transactions at
Constance may quite correctly be called the most influential in the

---

[1] For a detailed account of the council's quest for reform see FM 14, 1 (1962)
pp 188–215.

[2] This conclusion is advanced in the writer's PhD thesis for the university of Edinburgh,
The Franciscan Regular Observance 1368–1447 and the divisions of the Order 1294–1528
(1974), which, subject to revision, has been accepted for publication by the Capuchin
Historical Institute, Rome. The present paper is based on part of this study.

entire history of Franciscan reform, medieval and modern. It is, evidently, a large claim, modifying at least in one field the accepted judgment on the council. In elaborating the claim, the rest of this paper will concentrate on its internal Franciscan dimension, rather than on events at Constance itself; but in conclusion we shall return to the nature of the general renewal which the council delegates sought so anxiously, if ultimately to little avail.

The reform which received decisive impetus from the council of Constance in 1415 was the so-called regular observance movement of northern France.[3] The most illuminating way to approach it is to compare it with an earlier and more famous reform movement, that of the Franciscan spirituals in the late thirteenth and early fourteenth century; for at many points the resemblance between the two is indeed uncanny. The story of the spirituals is familiar enough,[4] and only a few points need be recalled here. Whereas the majority of the friars, the so-called community, adhered—more or less—to an observance of the rule laid down in a series of papal interpretations and in the order's own legislation, the spirituals, inspired partly by the writings and stories of their founder, campaigned for a more austere and, as they held, more authentic observance, that of the rule as it stood, together with the testament of Saint Francis, and without the papal interpretations—the 'literal observance'. Tension between the two groups escalated into a bitter and sometimes violent campaign of repression against the spiritual minority, and eventually the conflict

---

[3] Basic accounts: P. Gratien, 'Les débuts de la réforme des cordeliers en France et Guillaume Josseaume', *Etudes Franciscaines* 31 (Paris 1914) pp 415–39; [H.] Holzapfel, *Handbuch [der Geschichte des Franziskanerordens]* (Freiburg 1909) pp 101–6; [J. R. H.] Moorman, [A] *History [of the Franciscan Order from its origins to the year 1517]* (Oxford 1968) pp 380–3. The narrative which follows will not again cite these accounts, but only the relevant primary sources, or more specific secondary studies. The one important contemporary narrative is that of the observants themselves, given in their 'Quaerimoniae [propositae in concilio Constantiense]', in *Speculum Minorum* (Rouen 1509) fols 175^r–84^r.

[4] The literature on the spirituals is extensive. Introductions in J. Poulenc, 'Spirituali', *Enciclopedia delle Religioni*, 5 (Florence 1970) cols 1313–17; L. Oliger, 'Spirituels', *DTC* 14 (1941) cols 2522–49. A substantial account in English is M. D. Lambert, *Franciscan Poverty* (London 1961). Fundamental historically are the studies and documents published by F. Ehrle in F. Ehrle and H. Denifle, *A[rchiv für] L[iteratur- und] K[irchen] G[eschichte des Mittelalters]*, 7 vols (Berlin/Freiburg 1885–1900), in particular: 'Die Spiritualen, ihr Verhältniss zum Franciscanerorden und zu den Fraticellen', 1 (1885) pp 509–69, 2 (1886) pp 106–64, 249–336, 3 (1887) pp 553–623, 4 (1888) pp 1–190; 'Zur Vorgeschichte des Concils von Vienne', 2 pp 353–416, 3 pp 1–195; 'Petrus Iohannis Olivi, sein Leben und seine Schriften', 3 pp 409–552.

claimed the attention of the council of Vienne (1311–12), to which representatives of both sides were summoned. The foremost spiritual spokesman was Ubertino of Casale, who in one treatise, the *Sanctitas vestra*,[5] argued that the only solution to the problem was to make the spirituals an autonomous body, independent of the community, and thus to divide the order; a policy which had been briefly followed by pope Celestine V in 1294, only to be revoked by his successor Boniface VIII. In the event neither Ubertino's plan, nor the pacification attempted by Clement V, came to anything; conflict broke out again, more violent than before; and, in sanguinary fashion, the whole grievous affair was brought to some sort of a conclusion by John XXII's condemnation of the spirituals between 1317 and 1318.

The spirituals' raison d'etre had been the aspiration for an observance, or way of life, more austere, and in some sense more Franciscan, than that pursued by the majority. The same was true of the French regular observance; and it is this identity of purpose that accounts for the often striking parallels between the two movements. Thus the new reform was born in the moment when, around 1390, three friars of the province of Touraine, despairing of the collapsed state of discipline they saw around them, approached their general and provincial minister for permission to withdraw to a secluded friary where they might live 'according to the purity of their rule'.[6] Their experience then insofar diverged from the spirituals' that they encountered, not hostility, but approval and support; and so, with a small increase in numbers the position remained for about fifteen years. Perhaps the reform's low profile had something to do with the unwonted quiet; for as soon as it entered on a phase of expansion, from about 1404 onwards, a more familiar pattern of hostility asserted itself. The strict friars were subjected to various forms of harassment by their laxer brothers, under whose authority they stood at provincial level, until they concluded that the future of the reform was in jeopardy. Their response to the situation was a replica of that of certain Italian spirituals in 1294: they took their plight to the general minister, and he in turn directed them to the pope. The Avignonese pontiff of the day, Benedict XIII, was no Celestine, but his judgment of the issue was the same, and in characteristically decisive bulls of 1407 and 1408 he exempted the strict brothers from the whole existing

[5] Printed in *ALKG* 3 (1887) 51–89.
[6] 'Quaerimoniae' fol 177^v.

apparatus of provincial authority, and gave them instead a hierarchy of their own, including not only provincial superiors, but even a superior general, to act as representative of the minister general himself.[7] Benedict, in short, turned the French regular observance into a virtually independent and sovereign body within the Franciscan family. Not even Celestine V had acted so boldly on behalf of the cause of Franciscan reform.

The sense of injury felt by the unreformed friars was commensurate, and, not unexpectedly, they moved heaven and earth to have the position reversed. Very much as in 1294, fortune came to their aid; not, this time, in the shape of a papal resignation—events were to prove Pedro de Luna the last man on earth to step down from Peter's throne —but through French national policy regarding the great schism. In 1408 allegiance to the Clementist papacy was finally withdrawn, and disfavour fell on all its works, the regular observance being one. Immediately the existence of the reformed friars became extremely precarious; and in the following year their discomfiture was completed. As luck would have it, the pope—Alexander V—who emerged from the council of Pisa, and was promptly recognised in France, was a Franciscan of the unreformed school. His sympathies could hardly be in doubt, and in September 1409 he put an end to the separate existence of the observance.[8]

That made it, so to speak, one-all, with everything left to fight for; and in fact from then until the conciliar decision of 1415 there existed something like a state of undeclared war between the two groups of friars, strikingly reminiscent of the relations between spirituals and community in the two-year papal vacancy between Clement V and John XXII. Both sides appealed for support to whatever authority, lay or ecclesiastical, they thought might lend it, and met decisions in favour of the rival with non-compliance and counter-appeal.[9] The uncertainty of the situation, as always in the middle ages, bred violence

---

[7] B[ullarium] F[ranciscanum], 7 (Rome 1904) pp 350–1, 361.

[8] Ibid pp 417–18.

[9] For particular cases see 'Quaerimoniae' fols 177v–9v; [L.] Oliger, 'De relatione [inter Observantium quaerimonias Constantienses (1415) et Ubertini Casalensis quoddam scriptum]', Archivum Franciscanum Historicum 9 (Quaracchi 1916) pp 3–41, at pp 39–41; C. Schmitz, 'Der Anteil der suddeutschen Observantenvikarie an der Durchführung der Reform', F[ranziskanische] S[tudien] 2 (Münster 1915) pp 359–76, esp 360–4; P. Gratien, 'Le grand schisme et la réforme des cordeliers à St. Omer (1408–9)' Franciscana 5 (Iseghem 1922) pp 5–15, 142–80; BF 7 p 483.

and lawlessness, and in at least one known case the possession of a friary was decided by armed force.[10]

Such was the state of affairs that the council of Constance was called upon to resolve. The analogy with the council of Vienne is obvious; and, when we consider the course of the proceedings, it becomes uncanny. The matter was, in July 1415, handed over to a commission, on which spokesmen of both sides were represented. The members had before them, in addition, a written deposition from the strict friars, the *Quaerimoniae*. This argued that the observance should again be made autonomous, with its own superiors. And most striking of all, it was little more than an edited version of the *Sanctitas vestra* of Ubertino of Casale—the very document which had put the same case on behalf of the spirituals before the council of Vienne, one hundred and four years earlier.[11]

With this fact, the parallel between the two Franciscan reform movements becomes apparent identity. Does this make the regular observance the heir of the spirituals? The answer is no; and for a simple reason. Despite all the similarities between their respective situations, the actual observance of the two movements was different. The spirituals, we know, strove for the 'literal observance'—that is, to do without the papal declarations on the rule. By contrast, the regular observance bent all its effort to the faithful implementation of the declarations. In this decisive point, therefore, it was the heir, not of the spirituals, but of the thirteenth century community.

The fact is made particularly clear by the French friars' handling—not to say manipulation—of Ubertino's *Sanctitas vestra*. At one point the spiritual wrote: '[Saint Francis] commanded the rule to be observed purely and simply as it sounds, and rejected every gloss and privilege . . .'[12] The later reformers made this passage give a quite different directive as to how the rule should be observed: '. . . simply, as was declared and done by Saint Francis, without any privileges . . . according to the papal declarations.'[13] The addition of the last three words stood the meaning of the original passage on its head, and amounted to a betrayal of all that the author and his party had fought

---

[10] That of St. Jean d'Angély, in the province of Touraine: 'Quaerimoniae' fol 179^r/^{v}.

[11] This is established by Oliger, 'De relatione'; see particularly the printing of extracts from the two documents side by side, pp 27–34. The article includes an account of the procedure followed.

[12] *ALKG* 3 (1887) 87.

[13] 'Quaerimoniae' fols 182^v–3^r.

and suffered for; but, as we know, medieval conventions with regard to literary borrowing were not ours.

If, then, the regular observance reform took the position, not of the spirituals, but of the thirteenth century community, why was it needed? The answer is obvious enough: the rest of the friars no longer fulfilled the obligations which their rule and the papal declarations theoretically laid upon them; they were, in short, relaxed; and the aim of the reformers was to restore discipline to the state in which it should have been.

The aim was unexceptionable, and could hardly be regarded otherwise by a body committed to the regeneration of every branch of the church. Accordingly, against the overwhelming weight of opinion within the order, the deliberations of the conciliar committee culminated in the total vindication of the regular observance.[14] The arrangements set up in 1407 and 1408 by Benedict XIII were restored, with several improvements in points of detail; and thus the French reform obtained at Constance what at Vienne the spirituals—and it was the one crucial difference in the experience of the two movements—had sought in vain: a position of effective independence within the larger Franciscan body, and therewith, a formal division of the order.

Nor, despite occasional temporary reverses, was that position ever again seriously threatened. In France and elsewhere, the regular observance went on from strength to strength, so that by the beginning of the sixteenth century the unreformed friars, or conventuals, had dwindled to hardly more than a rump; and in 1517[15] pope Leo X declared the brothers observing their rule according to the papal declarations the true, central family of Franciscans—the order of friars minor *tout court*; and so they have remained till the present. If we think this the right and proper outcome, we should remember that it was the often maligned fathers of Constance who played a decisive part in bringing it about.

It was another story with the second Franciscan reform to surface at Constance. This matter, we know, was not dealt with until 1418, by which time the holy see again had an unchallenged occupant, Martin V, and national delegations, anxious to be homeward bound, were negotiating their individual reform concordats with him;[16]

---

[14] Contained in the decree 'Supplicationibus personarum' of 23 September: *BF* 7 pp 493–5.
[15] See Moorman, *History*, pp 582–5.
[16] See FM 14, 1 (1962) pp 211–15.

accordingly it seems to have devolved primarily upon the Franciscan general minister (a staunch enemy of the regular observance) and the new pope himself. It concerned two Castilian friars, Peter of Villacreces and his disciple Lope of Salazar, and the future of their small reformed family of two friaries, the so-called *Recollectio Villacreciana*; and its implications were quite different from those of the observance. For there can be little doubt that the *Recollectio* was that which the French reform, as we saw, was not: the true heir of the spirituals.[17]

As we know, the spirituals aimed to do without the papal declarations on the rule; Villacreces taught his followers to repudiate them utterly. As Lope of Salazar later put it:

> . . . their friars should never adopt or hear those relaxations, and lax opinions, and declarations, and constitutions, but only the strict ones, and pure, and to the letter . . . he would rather burn his books than consent that his friars should study those constitutions and declarations departing from the sincere wishes of Saint Francis . . .[18]

And it was on this explicit basis that a recruit joined the reform:

> If he decides to join us, they declare the rule to him simply, *au pied de la lettre*, without the subtlety of any distinctions, as the rule itself requires . . . disregarding the sophistry of its division into precepts, and counsels, and exhortations, and admonitions . . . so that he shall keep the greater and the less with equal devotion . . .[19]

This is a classic statement of Franciscan literal observance, and, in terms of the order's previous history, represents an extremely radical standpoint. Something yet more striking followed. Declarations and constitutions were in effect but a corpus of interpretation of the order's rule. Having done away with them, Villacreces replaced them by another body of interpretation, with a different and in one sense greater claim to authenticity: the written traditions about the earliest days of the order, contained in the writings of Saint Francis himself, and the recollections of his particular companions. This was to work out

---

[17] The indispensable work for the *Recollectio* is [*Las*] *Reformas* [*en los siglos XIV y XV*], special issue of *A[rchivo] I[bero-]A[mericano]* ns 17 (Madrid 1957). This contains studies of contemporary reform movements, including the Spanish regular observance (pp 17–173); studies on the *Recollectio*, covering the sources, the four main leaders, and its spiritual and other characteristics (pp 175–660); and all the important primary sources (nearly all in Spanish) (pp 661–945).

[18] *Reformas* p 855.

[19] *Ibid* p 856.

in full an approach already adumbrated by the spirituals;[20] its upshot was the attempt to recreate from scratch, in early fifteenth century Castile, the lifestyle of the first Franciscan generation in Umbria.

Thus the fundamental character of Villacreces' two friaries was not conventual, but eremitical.[21] Their numbers were not to exceed twelve,[22] and were to include both priests and lay brothers; the function of the latter was to attend to all practical and active duties, so that the former might pursue in unbroken seclusion a life of 'due prayer and contemplation and holy meditations'.[23] Even for the lay brothers, claustration was strongly emphasised: there was to be a minimum of going out into the outside world, and equally, a minimum of strangers coming in; and, to underline the break with the world, claustration was reinforced by a severe discipline of silence.[24]

These characteristics are probably not what we, and undoubtedly not what the middle ages, would tend to think of as typically Franciscan; so are they authentic? The answer is supremely yes; for they reflect in one case the certain, in another case the probable directives of the founder of the order. Their sources are the short *Regula pro eremitoriis data*, an accepted *opusculum* of Saint Francis,[25] and instructions given for the Portiuncula, Francis' cherished settlement outside Assisi, recorded in three chapters of the *Speculum Perfectionis* and its analogues.[26] As is well known, the reliability of these sources is debatable, and very much debated; Peter of Villacreces at lease regarded them as genuine, and it must seem probable that, basically, he was right to do so. In any event, as the briefest comparison would show, his congregation was modelled with an almost slavish literalness upon his two chosen sources.

And what is true of its central characteristic, eremiticism, is as

---

[20] For example, by Ubertino of Casale in the *Sanctitas vestra*: *ALKG* 3 (1887) pp 53–4, 56, 76, 85.

[21] This is best shown by reading through Villacreces' *Memoriale religionis* in *Reformas* pp 687–713 (in Spanish).

[22] *Ibid* p 784 line 193, p 656.

[23] *Ibid* p 713 lines 4–5.

[24] See particularly *ibid* p 694 lines 5–16.

[25] See K. Esser, 'Die "Regula pro eremitoriis data" des hl. Franziskus von Assisi', *FS* 44 (1960) 383–417.

[26] [P.] Sabatier, *Spec[ulum] Perf[ectionis seu S. Francisci Assisiensis legenda antiquissima]* (Paris 1898) caps 55, 82, 112. The most convenient guide to the analogous collections are the tables in R. B. Brooke, *Scripta Leonis, Rufini et Angeli sociorum S. Francisci* (Oxford 1970) pp 73–8. This is also the major recent English work on a much vexed question.

true of its other features. Prominent among these were, as we might expect, poverty, physical austerity, and a mistrust of study and learning; and prominent among the sources by which Villacreces justified them were the writings of Saint Francis, and records deriving from his companions and the spirituals, above all the *Speculum Perfectionis*.[27]

Of the two, it was probably the *Speculum* which was decisive for Villacreces, rather than any of his founder's own writings—certainly not the rule, not even the *Regula pro eremitoriis*. The Castilian reformer's aim was to reproduce the lifestyle of Saint Francis and his earliest followers, particularly on its eremitical side. Can it be a coincidence that many chapters of the *Speculum* show Francis pointing both to the Portiuncula, and to himself, as the 'form and example' for every true friar minor to imitate?[28]

In adopting this message, apparently, at face value, Peter of Villacreces and his followers may be said to have taken a stance more radical than that of the spirituals. The latter's recompense had been hostility and violent repression; and, in the laxer conditions of the early fifteenth century, the same lot befell the far less radical reform of the French regular observance, the contemporary of Villacreces' own movement. What else, then, could possibly be in store for the small group of Castilian friars?

They did meet with hostility and attempted suppression; but these took a perhaps unexpected form. Their instigators were none other than Spanish adherents of the regular observance; and, to complete the irony, the stoutest defenders of the austere Villacreces were those who otherwise rejected and obstructed reform, namely the conventuals. If heads begin to spin at this conjuncture, they may be steadied by a political analogy: what have we here but an alliance of right and left against the centre?

Obscurity surrounds the initial relations between the *Recollectio Villacreciana* and the Spanish wing of the regular observance, which emerged and grew up side by side in the first two decades of the fifteenth century. An intriguing but unexplained feature is that, at some point, Villacreces' very first adherent, Peter of Santoyo, deserted

27 The features are evident throughout Villacreces' *Memoriale Religionis*, and the sources in the footnotes to it: *Reformas*, pp 687–713. On the question of studies, see also *ibid* pp 862–3.
28 For the Portiuncula: Sabatier, *Spec Perf*, pp 17, 19, 27, 101, 160; for Francis, *ibid* pp 34, 47, 56, 110, 118, 130, 159.

him and went over to the other side; and it was he who led the observant assault on his former master.[29] The thrust of the attack is contained in two bulls which Santoyo obtained from the still surviving Benedict XIII in June 1417: he was empowered to take charge of one of Villacreces' two existing friaries, and to introduce into it the observance which he himself followed, namely that of the papal declarations.[30]

It was this simple enactment which brought Peter of Villacreces to Constance, for it spelt the end of his congregation's autonomy, and of the literal observance which was its most prized possession. Approaching his seventieth year, taking the young Lope de Salazar with him, he set out, barefoot, to walk to the council.

As previously mentioned, the major responsibility for deciding his case seems to have lain with the Franciscan general and the pope. This was, one would have thought, hardly propitious: on previous form the highest authority in the order and the church were not likely to be sympathetic to outright Franciscan radicalism. Yet in the event they gave Villacreces everything he could have dreamed of; and thus in 1418 the two prelates showed themselves as favourable to the literal observance as the conciliar assembly had been in 1415 to the regular observance.

The authority over Villacreces' friary accorded to Peter of Santoyo by Benedict XIII was revoked; indeed the tables were turned, for now it was Santoyo who was asked to accept the Villacrecian observance (one must hope that this provision reflected something more than an old man's vindictiveness).[31] Thus the immediate threat to the *Recollectio* was exorcised; but that was only a beginning; and a series of further decisions confirmed the reform's aspirations in every particular. Both its rules of claustration and its discipline of silence received explicit and detailed recognition; and, moreover, formal approval was given to the two sources from which, as we have seen, these features of its life were derived, namely the *Regula pro eremitoriis* and *Speculum Perfectionis*, here respectively named *ordinacio antiqua beati Francisci de*

---

[29] On the early years of the *Recollectio*, the observance in Castile, and the career of Santoyo, see respectively *Reformas* 299–334, 119–65, 335–71. There are enigmatic glimpses of the relations between Villacreces, Santoyo and the observants in the later reminiscences of Lope de Salazar: *ibid* p 784 lines 170–91, p 785 line 228–p 786 line 246, p 803 lines 100–12, p 809 line 191–p 810 line 199, p 840 lines 11–13.

[30] *BF* 7 pp 402–3.

[31] *Reformas* p 658.

Sancta Maria de Porciuncula, and—something to catch the imagination of all students of the Franciscan sources—*legenda antiqua*.[32]

The document enshrining these concessions bears the *placet* of Martin V himself, and this may prompt us to reflect on the significance of his action. Papal approval of the Franciscan literal observance as such, although certainly atypical, was not quite unprecedented: there had been the somewhat exceptional case of Celestine V in 1294, and in 1350 Clement VI had shown similar favour—shortlived in the event—to a group of Italian Franciscans.[33] But if Martin's attitude was not in itself new, certain of the terms in which it issued were: namely the formal acceptance of texts other than the order's rule as the basis of the reformed friars' life. This might be thought to alter the canonical foundation of their profession; it should also be seen as a response to a question which bedevilled Franciscans from the first—what status to give to the many documents besides the rule (the most prominent being the testament) which contained more or less reliable indications of the ideal and intentions of their founder.[34]

If the pope's action thus bears remark, even more so does that of the Franciscan general. Antony of Pireto was the long-standing opponent of reform, when it took the unexceptionable shape of the French regular observance; yet he appears to have lent unqualified support to the much more drastic reform embodied in the *Recollectio Villacreciana*. We may explain the paradox as the alliance of right and left; and there is little doubt as to the bond by which it was cemented: in fighting off a take-over by the regular observance, Villacreces also repudiated the observant claim for independence of the conventuals. In other words, at Constance, as throughout his life, he proclaimed untrammelled obedience to the order's existing hierarchy.[35] We may be certain that it was the perfect way to his general minister's heart.

Villacreces' protestations were without doubt sincere, and yet they contain the final twist in the story. The truth is that, despite what both sides believed, the *Recollectio* was in practice entirely free of conventual authority—not one whit less so than the regular observance itself. The very document ratified at Constance, while declaring Villacreces

[32] *Ibid* pp 656–7. On the use of 'legenda antiqua' by medieval Franciscans, see [S.] Clasen, *Legenda antiqua [des heiligen Franziskus]* (Leiden 1967) 214–25.

[33] See Moorman, *History*, 369–71.

[34] For an interesting contemporary view of the problem, with a historical basis, see O. de Veghel, 'La réforme des frères mineurs capucins dans l'Ordre Franciscain et dans l'église', *Collectanea Franciscana* 35 (Rome 1965) pp 73–108.

[35] See *Reformas* 583–6.

subject to both the general and the Castilian provincial, gave him such extensive powers within his own friaries as to make him almost the general of an indpendent religious congregation;[36] and thus Antony of Pireto assumed the bizarre role of creating with one hand, and trying to suppress with the other, two reform movements which, although different in point of observance, were at one in their practical independence of himself. It is convincing illustration of the truth that to take the cowl is no guarantee against the normal inconsistencies of human nature.

And this dispensation too, like that struck in 1415, was to have a considerable future. Thanks to the support of the unreformed conventuals, purchased by protestations of an unreal subjection, the Villacrecian reform held out against unremitting pressure from the observant reform.[37] Thus Peter of Villacreces' conception of the literal observance survived into the sixteenth century; and in 1528 it was taken up in the foundation of yet one more reformed branch of the Franciscan family, which still exists today, namely the capuchins.[38] With their appearance the ideal of the literal observance, which had been the inspiration of individual groups of Franciscans since the thirteenth century, may finally be said to have achieved lasting recognition; it was during the closing phase of the council of Constance, and by the agency of the pope whom the council created, that the way was pointed and the ground prepared.

This conclusion puts us in a position to make a brief assessment of the historical importance of the council in the story of Franciscan renewal. In a word, by confirming the French regular observance in 1415 and the *Recollectio Villacreciana* in 1418, the council first recognised a truth which men in the middle ages, and Franciscans perhaps in all ages, have found extraordinarily difficult to grasp: the truth that there is room within the one fraternity of Saint Francis for three different and distinct levels of observance, that of the rule as it stands, that of the rule as interpreted in the papal declarations, and that of the rule modified by dispensation on particular points; and furthermore, that the brothers would always be at loggerheads until the validity of all

---

[36] *Ibid* 656–9. The powers included control over admissions to and expulsions from the two friaries concerned, general powers of discipline, and extensive spiritual authority.

[37] See *Reformas* 494–504; L. Carrion, 'Origenes de la Custodia de "Domus Dei" y "Scala Coeli" ', *AIA* 4 (Madrid 1915) pp 161–77.

[38] See Holzapfel, *Handbuch*, pp 609–14; O. de Veghel, 'Le fonds franciscain de la réforme capucine' in *Miscellanea Melchor de Pobladura*, 2 (Rome 1964) pp 11–59, esp pp 39–41.

three positions was recognised. It may be commented that the council's merit in giving practical recognition to this truth should not be placed too high, since in its unco-ordinated way it can hardly have been aware of what it was doing. It is a fair comment; and yet is it not also the case that some of the most vital historical developments take place thus unawares, as it were by stealth, rather than by design?

Having thus characterised the importance of the council of Constance to Franciscan renewal, we may in conclusion reverse the perspective, and, through the regular observance and the *Recollectio*, attempt to illuminate the general issue of religious renewal, both at the time of the council, and at other times. For the two movements we have considered are anything but an isolated phenomenon. The first years of the fifteenth century witnessed analogous reforms in the sister mendicant order, the preachers, and in some communities of white and black monks, as well as the perhaps more distinctive new devotion;[39] and behind these contemporary developments there is the whole pattern of alternate decline and renewal which, as is well known, is almost the leitmotif of the medieval history of the regulars.[40]

From the account which has been given we may already conclude that the regular observance and the *Recollectio Villacreciana* in essence conform to the general pattern. In a word, their common aim was to restore, in the face of prevailing laxity and neglect, a strict and faithful observance of the order's rule, statutes and other primitive traditions.

Insofar as this aim is entirely typical, it has nothing new to tell us about the general process of renewal. On the other hand, there are one or two peculiarities about the Franciscan case which enable us to pin-point features of the process with particular clarity.

First, the new reforms of the schism epoch for the Franciscans represented a new birth, a completely fresh beginning. That is, the order had always had its groups of friars dedicated to a life more austere than that of the majority, reaching back into the thirteenth century, even to the lifetime of Saint Francis himself. However in each case, so it seems, an unbroken tradition of personal contacts led from one group to the next; thus the spirituals claimed the inspiration of companions of Saint Francis,[41] and later fourteenth century Italian groups, both orthodox

---

[39] See FM 14, 2 (1964) pp 911–41, 1031–63.
[40] See M. D. Knowles, *The Monastic Order in England* (Cambridge 1963) pp 219–20, 692.
[41] See above n 20.

and heterodox, in turn were connected with the spirituals.[42] It was otherwise with both the French regular observance and the *Recollectio Villacreciana*: each was the first known Franciscan reform in its area, not the outcome of a living tradition of reform. That being so, we can only understand their inspiration as a spontaneous awakening to the order's authentic vocation, enshrined for the one in the rule and papal declarations, and for the other in the writings of Saint Francis and his companions.

Thus the genesis of reform is confirmed as residing in the fusion of fresh vision with existing written tradition. Common sense suggests that, of these two factors, the active, creative one is freshness of vision; a second peculiarity of the Franciscan case underwrites this assumption.

It concerns the traditions at the heart of the *Recollectio*, the writings of Saint Francis and his companions; for these may be said to have a history of their own. Surprisingly enough, for the first century of the order's existence they went almost unknown, or at least unacknowledged, by the great majority of Franciscans.[43] Then, in an equally surprising reversal, they seem together to have become the focus of a well-nigh frantic outburst of copying, which by the end of the fourteenth century had made them familiar throughout the length and breadth of Europe.[44] The cause of this dramatic change has yet to be explained. Its best known result is the celebrated conundrum of the primitive Franciscan sources, the so-called *question franciscaine*, since almost all the important pieces in that most complex jigsaw puzzle belong to this period. For our purposes, however, the important point lies elsewhere. We can say that all the vital literary sources of the *Recollectio Villacreciana* were known to, indeed prized by, many friars for over fifty years, without any visible effect on the conduct of their lives. It must, then, have been through a new vision of the same texts that Peter of Villacreces and his like derived from them an existential implication, and so made them the basis of a deep and lasting reform.

---

[42] First shown by Ehrle, 'Spiritualen', *ALKG* 4 (1888) pp 160–7, 181–5.

[43] J. R. H. Moorman, *Sources for the life of Saint Francis of Assisi* (Manchester 1940) pp 152–3; Sabatier, *Spec Perf* p lx. The exiguous number of references to Francis' testament in the sources covering the order's first hundred years is displayed in K. Esser, *Das Testament des heiligen Franziskus von Assisi* (Münster 1949) pp 55–7.

[44] This is most clearly seen from the lists of manuscripts in Clasen, *Legenda antiqua* pp 43–166, and K. Esser and R. Oliger, *La tradition manuscrite des opuscules de Saint Francois d'Assise* (Rome 1972). Particularly striking is the very high degree of overlap between the two lists; in other words, most manuscripts contain both the writings of Francis and those deriving from his companions.

This conclusion on the Franciscan case prompts a reflection on the fate of the wider movement for renewal from which it received decisive support. If the council of Constance ultimately bore little fruit, was it because it failed to generate a fresh vision of the church's literary foundation, the gospels and her own accumulated tradition; and likewise, was it the achieving of just such a new appraisal that accounts for the enduring reform of the sixteenth century, catholic no less than protestant?

Cartmel College
University of Lancaster

THE IDEA OF RENEWAL IN GIROLAMO
ALEANDER'S CONCILIAR THOUGHT

by W. B. PATTERSON

THE climax of the Italian renaissance in the early sixteenth century merges almost imperceptibly and rather surprisingly with the beginnings of the catholic reformation. Within a single generation, it seems, religious and moral interests came to rival, or even to supplant, that interest in pagan antiquity which had long been the inspiration of Italian culture. The stages by which this transformation occurred have not been clearly defined, but the process can be seen at work in the case of one prominent humanist who decided to devote his career to the defence and then to the renewal of the church of Rome.

Girolamo Aleander's place in the world of humanism is now well known as the result of researches conducted over the past century, particularly in France and Italy.[1] Equally well known is the part he played at the diet of Worms, where, as German scholars have related in detail, he laboured strenuously and with some success to give effect to the papal excommunication of Martin Luther.[2] In recent years the publication of papal diplomatic papers has also focused attention on the significant part played by Aleander in the attempt by the curia to contain the spread of protestantism, especially in the Empire.[3] But little

---

[1] For Aleander's life, see [Jules] Paquier, [*L'humanisme et la réforme:*] *Jérôme Aléandre* [*de sa naissance à la fin de son séjour à Brindes (1480–1529)*] (Paris 1900); *Lettres familières* [*de Jérôme Aléandre (1510–1540)*], ed J. Paquier (Paris 1909); and Aleander's 'Journal autobiographique', ed H. Omont, in *Notices et extraits des manuscrits de la Bibliothèque Nationale*, 35 (Paris 1895) pp 1–116. Also, for a shorter account with good bibliographies, the article on Aleander by G. Alberigo in the *Dizionario biografico degli italiani*, 2 (Rome 1960), pp 128–35. His place in the development of humanism is described in A. Renaudet, *Préréforme et humanisme à Paris pendant les premières guerres d'Italie (1494–1517)* (Paris 1953) esp pp 509–13, 610–20, 647.

[2] See T. Brieger, *Aleander und Luther* (Gotha 1884); *Die Depeschen des Nuntius Aleander vom Wormser Reichstag 1521*, ed P. Kalkoff, 2 vols (Halle 1897), and 'Nachtrag zur Korrespondenz Aleanders während seiner ersten Nuntiatur in Deutschland 1520–1522', *ZKG* 28 (1907) pp 201–34. Also A. Renaudet, *Erasme: sa pensée religieuse et son action, d'après sa correspondance (1518–1521)* (Paris 1926) pp 87–129.

[3] For narrative accounts, see [Franco] Gaeta, *Un nunzio pontificio a Venezia* [*nel Cinquecento (Girolamo Aleandro)*] (Venice/Rome 1960) and [Gerhard] Müller, 'Die drei Nuntiaturen Aleanders in Deutschland, [1520/21, 1531/32, 1538/39]', *QFIAB* 39

attention has been paid to the collection of conciliar writings attributed to Aleander which emanated from the discussions within the curia in the 1530s and early '40s about the pressing need to reform the church.[4] In these writings Aleander links the project of reform with the convocation of a general council.

Aleander's advocacy of a council comes as an unexpected development in light of his frequently expressed opposition to conciliar proposals earlier in his career. While serving as rector of the university of Paris he refused, in 1512, to attend the council of Pisa as his university's elected representative, explaining to Erasmus that the council, which a modern writer calls 'the last anti-papal Council in the history of the Church', was a risky undertaking.[5] Later, in 1535, writing to pope Paul III, Aleander explained his attitude in more decisive terms: 'I was serving the apostolic see when—having been made rector of the university of Paris and the task having been assigned to me by the most Christian king Louis of dealing with the authority of the council of Pisa—I was the chief instigator and helper in its extermination and dissolution.'[6] Later, when Aleander was sent from Rome, where he served as vatican librarian, to Germany, to oppose Luther and to prevent the dissemination of Lutheran ideas, he found himself confronted on all sides by the demand for a council to deal with the Lutheran problem. 'All Germany is in commotion', he wrote from the diet of Worms, 'and everyone demands and shrieks "Council! Council!"

(1959) pp 222–76. Documents for his missions are provided in *Nunziature di Venezia*, 1 (*12 marzo 1533–14 agosto 1535*), ed F. Gaeta (Rome 1958); *Nuntiaturberichte aus Deutschland* [*1533–1559*], pt 1, 1–2 (*Legation Lorenzo Campeggios 1530–1531 und Nuntiatur Girolamo Aleandros 1531; Legation Lorenzo Campeggios 1532 und Nuntiatur Girolamo Aleandros 1532*), ed G. Müller (Tübingen 1963–69), and pt 1, vols 3–4 (*Legation Aleanders 1538–1539*), ed W. Friedensburg (Gotha 1893).

[4] Aleander's papers on the reform of the church, a project he associated with a future council, are described by J. Pasquier in *DTC* 1 (1930) pp 694–95; several have been published, with critical comments by V. Schweitzer, in *Concilium Tridentinum*: [*diariorum, actorum, epistolarum, tractatuum nova collectio*], ed Societas Goerresiana, 12 (Freiburg 1930). The links between Aleander and other members of the reform group at Rome are described in [Hubert] Jedin, [*A History of the*] *Council of Trent*, transl E. Graf, 1 (St. Louis 1957) pp 198, 311, 328, 338, 345, 423–36.

[5] *Opus epistolarum* [*Des.*] *Erasmi* [*Roterodami*], ed P. S. Allen, 1 (Oxford 1906) p 504. The description of the council by Jedin, *Council of Trent*, 1, p 112. See also *HL*, 8, pt 1, pp 314–39; A. Renaudet, *Le concile gallican de Pise-Milan: documents florentins* (*1510–1512*) (Paris 1922) *passim*; and Walter Ullmann, 'Julius II and the Schismatic Cardinals', *SCH* 9 (1972) pp 177–93.

[6] Aleander, *Lettres familières*, pp 165–6.

and will have it in Germany.'[7] In spite of the widespread agitation in the 1520s for what was called a 'free Christian council in German lands', Aleander refused to recommend such a project. It seems likely that pope Clement VII's policy on the question of a council was based at least in part on Aleander's advice: 'Never offer a council, never refuse it directly; on the contrary, show a readiness to comply with the request but at the same time stress the difficulties that stand in the way; by this means you will be able to ward it off.'[8] By such means a council was indeed averted during the eleven crucial years of Clement's pontificate, while in northern Europe the protestant movement assumed institutional form.

This policy changed abruptly when, on 13 October 1534, cardinal Alessandro Farnese assumed the papal throne as Paul III, and Aleander was soon identified with the conciliar initiatives of the new pope. Within three months of pope Paul's accession, nuncios were starting out for the principal countries of Europe to win support for a general council. A little over a year later a commission was appointed to draw up a bull of convocation. Finally, in the last days of April, 1536 a draft of this bull, prepared by Aleander, was submitted to the emperor's chief counsellors.[9] It soon became apparent, however, that what had seemed so difficult for Clement VII to avoid was at least as difficult for Paul III to bring successfully into being. The rivalry between king Francis I and the emperor Charles V, and the unsettled political conditions within Italy itself, were major obstacles to any immediate realisation of the pope's conciliar plans.

In the same year in which the bull for a council was issued, however, Paul III took the equally forthright and courageous step of appointing a committee of nine to make proposals for the reform of the church, thereby beginning the process of setting the church's house in order even before a council could be convened. The committee, which was to produce the celebrated *Consilium de emendanda ecclesia* in March,

---

[7] *Monumenta reformationis Lutheranae*, ed P. Balan (Ratisbon 1881) p 98; *Documents Illustrative of the Continental Reformation*, ed B. J. Kidd (Oxford 1911) p 82. For Aleander's anti-Lutheran activities see, in addition to works on the Diet of Worms, [A.] Renaudet, *Erasme et l'Italie* (Geneva 1954) pp 87, 96, 146–56.

[8] Jedin, *Council of Trent*, 1, pp 224; see also, for the agitation for a council, pp 197–219, 246, 250. For the discussions in Germany in 1531–2, in which Aleander participated, see Müller, 'Die drei Nuntiaturen Aleanders in Deutschland', pp 243–54.

[9] Jedin, *Council of Trent*, 1, pp 291–2, 310–11. See also, for the new pope's policies, [L.] Pastor, *History of the Popes*, transl R. F. Kerr, 11 (London 1911) pp 14–28; and [R. M.] Douglas, *Jacopo Sadoleto, [1477–1547: Humanist and Reformer]* (Cambridge, Mass., 1959) pp 89, 266.

1537,[10] included Contarini, taken only recently from the service of Venice, Carafa and Giberti, known as supporters of a new piety and discipline in the church, and Sadoleto, a former papal secretary who now far preferred his diocese to residence in the papal city. Reginald Pole was included, though he was still a layman, as Contarini had been until the year before. The other members were Fregoso, well known as a humanist, Cortese, a Benedictine, and Badia, a Dominican, both of the latter products of monastic reform.[11] Aleander completed their number. Though Aleander was perhaps more closely associated with the curial administration at the time of his appointment than any of the other members of the committee, the events of the next few years were to show that he was among those most committed to reform. When, for example, the proposals of the committee, read aloud before the pope and cardinals, provoked bitter dissension within the curia, Aleander was one of the signers of the *Consilium quattuor delectorum*, the major defence of the projected reform of the Dataria, which had engaged in many profitable but dubious financial transactions.[12] The authors argued that to reform an institution which the protestants had attacked would not play into the hands of the attackers but would undercut their position by restoring the good name of the papacy. 'The Lutherans', they asserted, 'will be ruined when this reformation is heard; and Christendom, which is wavering, will most ardently embrace its ancient piety towards the holy see.'[13]

---

[10] For the text of the *Consilium delectorum cardinalium et aliorum prelatorum de emendanda ecclesia*, see *Concilium Tridentinum*, 12, pp 131–45. Aleander's account of the presentation of the report may be found in [W.] Friedensburg, 'Zwei Aktenstücke [zur Geschichte der Kirchlichen Reformbestrebungen an der Römischen Kurie (1536–1538)]', *QFIAB* 7 (1904) pp 251–67.

[11] For the members of the committee, see F. Dittrich, *Gasparo Contarini, 1483–1542* (Braunsberg 1885); P. Paschini, *S. Gaetano Thiene, Gian Pietro Carafa, e le origini dei chierici regolari teatini* (Rome 1926); [A.] Prosperi, *Tra evangelismo e controriformo: [G. M. Giberti (1495–1543)]* (Rome 1969); Douglas, *Jacopo Sadoleto*; Dermot Fenlon, *Heresy and Obedience in Tridentine Italy: Cardinal Pole and the Counter Reformation* (Cambridge 1972). Also J. B. Ross, 'Gasparo Contarini and His Friends', *Studies in the Renaissance*, 17 (Austin/New York 1970) pp 192–232, and 'The Emergence of Gasparo Contarini: A Bibliographical Essay', *CH* 41 (1972) pp 22–45; and Marvin A. Anderson, 'Gregorio Cortese and Roman Catholic Reform', *Sixteenth Century Essays and Studies*, 1, (St Louis 1970) pp 75–106.

[12] The *Consilium quattuor delectorum a Paulo III super reformatione S. R. ecclesiae* is found in *Concilium Tridentinum*, 12, pp 208–15. The other signers were Contarini, Carafa, and Badia. For the course of the disputes over the *Consilium de emendanda ecclesia*, see Jedin, *Council of Trent*, 1, pp 427–32; *Concilium Tridentinum*, 12, pp 155–8, 215–56; and Friedensburg, 'Zwei Aktenstücke', pp 263–7.

[13] *Concilium Tridentinum*, 12, p 214.

Aleander's concern for the reform of the church was also expressed in a document from approximately the same period as the *Consilium de emendanda ecclesia* in which reform is firmly linked to the project for a general council. The *De convocando concilio sententia*,[14] perhaps requested by Paul III in anticipation of the council planned for Mantua in May, described in vivid terms not only the lamentable state of Christendom but the means by which the church could be restored to its former unity and glory. Though all of Christendom was threatened by the Turks from without and by religious divisions from within, Germany was in the worst state of all. Formerly as devoted to Christ as any nation she had fallen prey to the false teachings of such pernicious innovators as Luther, Zwingli, and Oecolampadius.[15] Yet there was reason to think that those who had recently departed from the church might be successfully recalled, if the appropriate steps were taken. An encouraging sign was the more moderate tone adopted by the protestant princes, who had become aware of the momentous upheaval which the new movement was causing.[16]

Aleander's account of this religious upheaval is of particular interest because of the place he assigned to the humanists of the renaissance in the developing crisis of the church. He acknowledged that a 'vast and foolish superstition' had been widespread in the church before Luther's time. This superstition had been opposed by certain writers who were understood as representing a 'reflowering in the minds of men.' When, however, their quite legitimate criticism had been extended to matters which should have been respected—worship, the 'doctrine of Christ', the 'practices of the past'—it had incited the most violent rebellions against the church.[17] Church buildings had been thrown down, clerics had been mocked, monks and nuns had broken their vows and married. Thus, the 'originators' of this revolution had accomplished little of what they had hoped to do. The sacraments had been ridiculed and, in Germany especially, there was now a dearth of true religion. Worst of all, the revolution had given rise to a new theology which robbed man of free-will and made God the author of evil.[18] In such a

[14] This document, assigned by Schweitzer to Aleander, is printed in *Concilium Tridentinum*, 12, pp 119–31. Douglas mentions it in a footnote, *Jacopo Sadoleto*, p 271; Pastor and Jedin not at all.

[15] *Concilium Tridentinum*, vol 12, pp 120–1.

[16] *Ibid* p 121.

[17] *Ibid* pp 121–2.

[18] *Ibid* pp 123–4.

climate of thought it was not to be wondered that many had been led to the mad notion that there was no God at all. These were of all men the ones whose plight was most hopeless, as they had not the capacity even to ask for God's grace and pardon and thus could not be healed through the act of penitence. Aleander's view of the literary figures who had criticised the church and helped to bring it into disrepute helps to explain the hostility which sprang up between himself and Erasmus in the period of the diet of Worms.[19] Nevertheless, it was a curious argument for one whose analysis of the ills and abuses of the church echoed the analyses which had issued from a succession of Italian humanists reaching back to the beginning of the fifteenth century.[20]

The sources of evil in the church, Aleander contended, were not only the wolves but, to an even greater extent, the wicked shepherds of the flock. Aleander observed that there had often been wolves— Arius, Nestorius, Pelagius, Mohammed—yet the church had survived their attacks.[21] In the present crisis good shepherds were the church's most pressing need. Not that wicked priests were any the less priests— it was their office rather than their lives which should be regarded. And if Saint Paul could command that wicked rulers should be obeyed, how much more should the popes be obeyed, even those who had abused their office. Nevertheless, it was now more important than ever before that the pious should not be offended by the scandalous behaviour of the clergy. The main cause of the continuing tempests within the church was the wickedness of far too many bishops and priests.[22]

The church's situation was now, Aleander felt, full of hope and promise. Paul III, the kind of pope Christian people had long desired, had begun the restoration of the church which he had found nearly in ruins. Knowing, moreover, that he could not carry out this work single-handedly, the pope had enlisted the aid of well-qualified assistants. 'You, therefore', wrote Aleander to the pope, 'chose great and holy men to be your associates and assistants, who were together with

---

[19] See Renaudet, *Erasme et l'Italie*, pp 87, 96, 146–56; Aleander, *Lettres familières*, p 224; *Opus epistolarum Erasmi*, 9, p 165.

[20] For references to reform proposals from Salutati to Pico, see Eugenio Gain,r 'Desideri di riforma nell'oratoria del Quattrocento', in *Contributi alla storia del Concilio di Trento e della Controriforma*, ed Luigi Russo (Florence 1948) pp 1–11.

[21] *Concilium Tridentinum*, 12, p 125.

[22] *Ibid* pp 125–6.

you to prune thoroughly and cultivate carefully the Master's vineyard, now overgrown and deformed with briars and brambles.'[23] Chief among these associates were Contarini, Sadoleto, Pole, and Schönberg, whom Aleander praised for their virtue, learning, and piety. If an earlier age had had popes and cardinals of this sort, he contended, the conspiracies and contentions of the present time would never have arisen. In any case, now that the church had been provided with such leadership, there was a way, 'by which those who have left the Church can be called back as quickly and easily as possible.'[24]

The way was by the convocation of a council. From the earliest days, Aleander reminded the pope, this had been the method by which peace and concord had been restored to the church. He recalled the council of the apostles at Jerusalem, which dealt with the question of circumcision, the council of Nicaea, which vanquished the Arian heresy, and others which had overcome the heresies of later times. The God who had promised to be with his people to the end of the world had not deserted them. And who could doubt that when His people asked Him to show men the truth of religion—what they ought to do and believe—he would hear their prayers?[25] A most dangerous state of affairs now existed in which each man proclaimed that his own church was holy and the others were in error. If, however, a council were held, there the Holy Spirit would show which the true church was, whose head and leader was Christ. Moreover, those would be refuted who said that the ancients believed differently about many things from the church of the present day. 'Wherefore, in order that we may all think alike and that there not be schisms and dissensions among us', Aleander argued, 'a public council seems indispensable. . .'[26]

The council planned for Mantua in May had, however, to be post-poned, though several of the pope's advisers, including Aleander, were apprehensive lest such a postponement should do irreparable harm to the pope's prestige.[27] In the autumn of 1537 the idea of a council at Mantua was finally abandoned and new plans were laid for a convoca-tion in May, 1538. Before the end of the year it was decided that the new site would be Vicenza. It was a mark of the pope's confidence in Aleander that when the papal legates were appointed for Vicenza,

[23] *Ibid* p 127.
[24] *Ibid* p 128.
[25] *Ibid* p 129.
[26] *Ibid* p 130.
[27] Jedin, *Council of Trent* I, p 328.

Aleander, now raised to the cardinalate, was included in their number.[28] He left at once to gather his books and papers in Venice, and then to await, in Vicenza, the arrival of the delegates and the two other papal legates. But this council, too, failed to materialise. On the twenty-fifth of April, 1538, Paul III directed that the opening of the council be put off for an unspecified period because of the non-arrival of delegates.[29] What proved to have been Aleander's major opportunity to participate in a general council had quickly passed. When plans for a council at Vicenza were revived, in 1539, Aleander was, indeed, again named legate. This time, however, prospects for a council were even less favourable than in 1538. The plans had, in fact, largely foundered even before the legates were appointed.[30]

The last years of Aleander's life were interrupted by sieges of illness. He took no part in the religious conferences at Worms and Ratisbon though he had been sent to Germany in 1538 to watch over the development of plans for a religious concord there and was asked, in 1540, to undertake another mission to that country.[31] He declined, on the grounds of health, and nominated Contarini in his stead, praising him in the highest terms.[32] The embarrassment caused in Rome by the attempted, though abortive, compromises of these conferences did not diminish Aleander's ardour for a general council. In 1541, the year before his death, he noted that the Germans had 'greatly relented' and were much milder than before; he also felt that it was more imperative than ever that a council be held.[33]

In his *De habendo christianorum concilio* of 1541, addressed to Paul III, Aleander reiterated many of the arguments he had used in 1537 about

[28] *Ibid* p 333; Gaeta, *Un nunzio pontificio a Venezia*, pp 149–50. Aleander had apparently been made a cardinal *in pectore* by Paul III in December 1536, but his appointment was not announced until 13 March 1538, seven days before he was named legate to Vicenza.

[29] For Aleander's legatine correspondence, in which he speaks poignantly of the missed opportunities resulting from delays in the convening of a council, see *Concilium Tridentinum*, 4 (Freiburg 1904) pp 157–71.

[30] Jedin, *Council of Trent*, 1, pp 340–5.

[31] Aleander, *Lettres familières*, pp 174–5. For Aleander's misgivings over the idea of making concessions to the Lutherans, see his memorial *In tractanda concordia cum Lutheranis haec maxime consideranda et perpendenda videntur*, in *Nuntiaturberichte aus Deutschland*, pt 1, 3, pp 135–6.

[32] Aleander, *Lettres familières*, p 175. For Contarini's mission and its results, see Heinz Mackensen, 'The Diplomatic Role of Gasparo Contarini at the Colloquy of Ratisbon of 1541', *CH* 27 (1958) pp 312–37; and Peter Matheson, *Cardinal Contarini at Regensburg* (Oxford 1972) passim.

[33] *Concilium Tridentinum*, 12, p 355.

the need for reconciling the German nation to the church.[34] Now, however, political considerations seemed to him of critical importance. He was especially apprehensive lest the Turks advance not only into Germany but into Italy as well. After pointing out what a short distance it was from the nearest Turkish bases in 'Illyria' to the Italian coast, he speculated about possible allies in the event of an attack from the east. Ferdinand was already fully occupied with the Turks. Francis I was likely to be unreliable, distracted by jealousies and enmities. Henry VIII might even side with Suleiman. Italy's hope, Aleander concluded, lay with Charles V and Germany.[35] If Italy were to depend upon Germany as her potential ally, however, it was all the more essential that the Germans be won back to the church. Otherwise, said Aleander, perhaps recalling the events of 1527, if they were called in to defend Italy they might well remain to oppress the church after they had driven out the enemy.[36]

Aleander's main theme, however, as before, was the need to reform abuses in the church, especially among the clergy. Too often the higher clergy were ignorant of sacred letters and had been chosen for their positions because of their family connections rather than because of their own abilities.[37] There could be little wonder that Germany felt herself unable to tolerate any longer the dissolute men set over her people in positions of spiritual authority. Pluralities were an especially pernicious device, for while they increased the incomes of the higher clergy they intensified also the clerical taste for luxuries; meanwhile, the flocks languished for lack of care.[38] Aleander felt that under existing conditions the clergy of the church were almost universally hated, and that it was this hatred which had led to such violent storms in Christendom. 'If our forefathers', he said to the pope, 'often thought they had a most important and well-grounded reason for calling a council of Christians, when a few individuals—not peoples—deserted the church . . . , how much greater a necessity there is for your holding a council, O most holy father, when, as at this time, all Christian peoples incline towards defection, so that, by abolishing wicked practices and extinguishing the bad repute and hatred of the clergy, you

---

[34] For text and brief introduction see *Concilium Tridentinum*, 12, pp 342–62; Schweitzer assigns the document to Aleander on the basis of internal evidence.
[35] *Concilium Tridentinum*, 12, p 357.
[36] *Ibid* p 360.
[37] *Ibid* pp 348–50.
[38] *Ibid* p 351.

may hold all together in loyalty and allegiance to you and in sincere piety towards God.'[39]

There remains the intriguing problem of how a man who had been most remarkable in the 1520s as an intransigent and rather bombastic defender of Roman orthodoxy and authority became, in the '30s, an outspoken advocate of catholic reform and a general council. No doubt much of this is to be explained by Aleander's association with Paul III and the circle around Contarini. It was the genius of the elderly Farnese pope, a legacy from the Borgia era, that he was able to bring a new intellectual and moral atmosphere into the Rome of his day. Yet by no means all, or even a majority, of the members of the curia were affected by the new reign in the way Aleander was. We must ask ourselves, therefore, if there are any indications before Paul III's pontificate began that Aleander's interests were moving in a new direction. There are, and they fall in the years 1524-9.

Though he entered minor orders as early as 1509, Aleander was not ordained to the priesthood until 1524, the year in which he was named archbishop of Brindisi.[40] His ordination seems to have marked the beginning of a new stage in his spiritual life which his biographer does not hesitate to call his conversion. The evidence for this new stage includes the fact that he turned at this time from classical to sacred studies, that he became associated with the oratory of Divine Love, and, probably most important of all, that he became an intimate friend of Gian Pietro Carafa, whom Aleander called 'father' and 'preceptor'.[41] It seems to have been Carafa, his predecessor at Brindisi and the man who consecrated him bishop, who filled Aleander with the desire to begin to carry out his pastoral duties within his diocese. In December, 1526, he wrote to Giberti, a friend of a good many years' standing, to ask if he or Carafa or someone else could obtain for him the permission he needed to approach his *Ecclesia*.[42] No place was so loathesome as Rome, where ambition and avarice abounded. He lamented especially the corruption of the ministry evident in Rome, where bishops wore out the pavement on frivolous errands, rather than resid-

[39] *Ibid* p 354.
[40] Paquier, *Jérôme Aléandre*, pp 300, 349-50; Aleander, 'Journal autobiographique', *Notices et extraits des manuscrits de la Bibliothèque Nationale,* 35 (Paris 1895) p 43.
[41] Paquier, *Jérôme Aléandre*, pp 349-54; Letter to Carafa, 1526, in Aleander, *Lettres familières*, p 127.
[42] Aleander, *Lettres familières*, p 124. For the friendship between Aleander and Giberti, which went back to the last years of Leo X's pontificate, see Prosperi, *Tra evangelismo e controriforma*, pp 17-23, 28, 52, 92.

ing in their dioceses, where they should be diligently exercising their office—'a thing now unheard of for many centuries.'[43] In the same month Aleander was given permission to reside in Brindisi, where he remained until recalled for a papal mission in 1529.[44] It would be foolish to deny the possibility of there being, in the months immediately preceding the sack of Rome of 1527, other than purely spiritual and pastoral motives for Aleander's ardent desire to begin his episcopal duties within his own diocese. Yet at the same time there is evident in his state of mind in this period a new awareness of the abuses of the Roman church and a new ideal of the pastoral ministry which strikingly suggest the emphases of the reform commission of 1536, and which make it extremely unlikely that, when Contarini asked Paul III to include Aleander in the committee of nine,[45] he was suggesting a man untouched by a longing for reform. It might also be noted that Aleander had begun to take something of a new approach to the question of a council even before the end of Clement VII's pontificate. In early 1533 he wrote to the pope a memorial entitled *An expediat hoc tempore celebrare concilium an non*, in which he developed the idea that a general council was certainly preferable to a purely national (that is, German) council for the resolution of the church's problems. Pending its decrees, no religious innovations should be permitted in Germany.[46]

Aleander has not, on the whole, been treated kindly by the historians of his era, whether catholic or protestant. In particular, his commitment to reform has been viewed as half-hearted.[47] It is true that he was not one of the original members of the catholic reform movement of his time and was not, perhaps, moved by the same impulses which moved Contarini, Carafa, Pole, Sadoleto, Giberti and others—though the major figures in the movement were themselves hardly of a single mind.[48] Aleander seems to have been, ecclesiastically

---

[43] Aleander, *Lettres familières*, p 124.
[44] Paquier, *Jérôme Aléandre*, p 357.
[45] Pastor, *History of the Popes*, 11, p 155.
[46] *Concilium Tridentinum*, 12, pp 77–82.
[47] See Paul Kalkoff, 'Zur Charakteristik Aleanders', ZKG 43 (1924) pp 209–19; Jedin, *Council of Trent*, 1, p 423; Douglas, *Jacopo Sadoleto*, pp 113, 271. For a more recent and balanced assessment—though one which still contains echoes of the traditional view—see G. Müller, 'Zum Verständnis Aleanders', *Theologische Literaturzeitung*, 89 (Leipzig 1964) cols 526–36.
[48] See the useful distinctions made by Gaeta, *Un nunzio pontificio a Venezia*, pp 87–90, 101–5, 115. The diversity of interests and points of view in the reform movement was very definitely reflected in the Italian delegation at Trent. See G. Alberigo, *I vescovi italiani al Concilio di Trento (1545–1547)* (Florence 1959) pp 382–94 and *passim*.

and theologically, a conservative. His initial response to Lutheranism was to come aggressively to the defence of the church he served. In time, however, he became acutely aware of the Roman church's weaknesses, and became convinced that it could only meet the challenge of protestantism by being freed from corruption and strengthened by a new discipline and sense of purpose. It is this conviction, firmly and courageously held to by Aleander, which appears to lie behind his conciliar activities and writings during the last years of his life. His vision of what might be accomplished by a council proved, in some ways, to be remarkably accurate. The council of Trent, successfully convened in 1545, did eventually set in motion the kind of disciplinary reform of the Roman church, directed and controlled by the papacy, which Aleander seems to have had in mind.[49] And it made clear, as Aleander had wished to do from as early as his first papal mission to Germany, that many key Lutheran ideas were incompatible with the theology of Roman catholicism. But like so many of his contemporaries, Aleander erred in his assumption that such actions would suffice to heal the rifts in western Christendom.

Davidson College
North Carolina

[49] H. O. Evennett, *The Spirit of the Counter-Reformation*, ed John Bossy (Cambridge 1968), pp 89–125, 135–40.

HUMANISTIC SCRIPT IN A
MONASTIC REGISTER:
AN OUTWARD AND VISIBLE SIGN?

by JOAN G. GREATREX

'LEARNING to write the new humanistic script can surely be taken as a sign of humanistic interests'[1] in the fifteenth century. This is the conclusion of the compilers of a catalogue entitled *Duke Humfrey and English Humanism in the Fifteenth Century* which was produced in conjunction with an exhibition held in the Bodleian library, Oxford in 1970. As long as our interests are confined to the small circle of English humanists in this period who are known by name this statement may not lead us on to reflection or comment since its truth is self-evident. The situation is altered, however, and the words quoted above assume a new meaning and suggest a new line of approach in the light of an unexpected encounter with anonymous attempts to imitate the script in the unusual setting of a monastic letter-book or register.

Among the fifteenth century registers of English bishops and cathedral priories which I have examined over the past few years, I can recall only two occasions on which my attention has been drawn to examples of handwriting which are clearly recognisable imitations of the script that first came into vogue in renaissance Italy among the humanists in the early part of the century and was taken up by English writers and copyists several decades later. John Farley, to name one of those whose work was displayed in the Bodleian exhibition,[2] was registrar of the university of Oxford from about 1458 until his death in 1464[3], and he 'introduced a humanistic script into the records of the University . . . though it should be noted that he did not always use it'.[4] My examples occur in the earliest register of Winchester cathedral

---

[1] R. W. Hunt and A. C. de la Mare in the catalogue of which the title and date are given in the text immediately below, p 66.

[2] *Ibid* p 16.

[3] For further details about Farley and other Oxford humanists referred to below see the appropriate entries in Emden (O).

[4] [R. W.] Hunt and [A. C.] de la Mare, [*Duke Humfrey and English Humanism in the Fifteenth Century*] (Oxford 1970) p 16.

priory which has come to be known as the register of the common seal. From the point of view of its contents, which cover a wide range of subjects, it is an interesting volume,[5] since it contains a miscellaneous collection of more than five hundred documents copied for the sake of record and future reference, the earliest entry bearing the date 1345 and the final entry 1497. Those who are familiar with this type of register will find the usual assortment of deeds relating to land, appointments to office and manumissions, many of which pertain to the episcopal administration because of the necessity of obtaining ratification from the prior and convent for all episcopal actions concerned with land; in addition there are interesting details of several episcopal elections and other items bearing on monastic and ecclesiastical affairs.

On folio 93 of this volume, four[6] of the six items have been written in a humanistic hand, two of these being appointments of proctors by the convent, one an episcopal appointment to the office of apparitor-general and one a manumission. The date of all four documents, which are probably the work of one scribe, is 1470. The writing is irregular and uneven in comparison with the humanistic script of an accomplished copyist but it is nonetheless striking and contrasts sharply with the other more usual contemporary hands in the register.

The reason for the outward and visible sign of renaissance influence and interests in the unlikely context of this Winchester priory register can only be suggested; but this and other evidence should lead us to consider the possibility that the cathedral monastery may have contained a small group of scholars with humanistic interests of which this handwriting is the one manifest example. The other evidence referred to begins with the fact of the presence of the Italian humanist Poggio Bracciolini in cardinal Beaufort's household in the early 1420s; and the continuing connexions of Winchester with humanist activities, if these connexions did exist, must have been fostered by a group of Englishmen who are known to have been associated both with the humanist movement and with the episcopal households of Beaufort and his immediate successors, William Waynflete and Peter Courtenay.

[5] It is described by Pantin, 'English Monastic Letter-books' in *Historical Essays in Honour of James Tait*, ed J. G. Edwards, V. H. Galbraith and E. F. Jacob (Manchester 1933).

[6] These items are numbered 361, 363, 364, and 365 in the edition which the present writer is completing under the sponsorship of the Hampshire record office. It is worth noting that in these legal and administrative documents the wording follows the customary formulae, and there is therefore no trace of humanistic influence on the style or language.

Further evidence can be found in the connexion between Winchester College and New College, Oxford, the two foundations of William of Wykeham, bishop of Winchester and predecessor of Beaufort. Among the scholars who 'proceeded from Winchester [College] to New College are several of the first Englishmen to make contact with Italian humanism',[7] for example Thomas Bekynton, and Andrew Holes.[8]

The names of five of these occur in the common seal register in twelve places between the years 1414 and 1492. The two best known are Nicholas Bildeston and Richard Petworth, both of whom were attached to Beaufort's household as secretaries, and were friends of Poggio. The register which covers the last thirty years (1417–47) of Beaufort's episcopate at Winchester has been lost, but the priory register records three gifts of annual pensions granted to Bildeston by his employer in 1429[9] while he held the offices of archdeacon of Winchester and chancellor to the cardinal. Emden notes that he was also in Rome in the middle of this decade as king's proctor in the curia,[10] so that he would have had an opportunity through Poggio to make contact with Italian humanists there. There are six entries which refer to Petworth[11] between the years 1414 and 1447. In 1432[12] the prior and convent felt sufficiently indebted to him for his good help and advice to award him an annual pension of four marks a year for life. In 1447 he was the scribe for the proceedings of the election by which Waynflete succeeded Beaufort,[13] and the previous year he performed the same office in the proceedings by which several churches in Winchester diocese were appropriated to the new royal foundation of King's College, Cambridge.[14] Bildeston was described by Poggio as *homo perhumanus* and some of Poggio's correspondence with Petworth[15] survives as evidence of their continuing friendship; the

---

[7] Hunt and de la Mare p 15. Another example is Thomas Chaundler, who was warden of Winchester College from 1450 to 1454 and of New College from 1454 to 1475. For these and other English humanists, see R. Weiss, *Humanism in England during the Fifteenth Century* (3 ed Oxford 1967).

[8] The careers of these men have been summarised by Emden.

[9] These are numbered 208, 209 and 210 in the register.

[10] See note 8 above.

[11] Items numbered 172, 220, 244, 257, 316 and 355.

[12] No 220.

[13] No 316.

[14] No 355.

[15] The quotation is from a letter of Poggio to Niccolo Niccoli and is referred to in Hunt and de la Mare p 9; some of Poggio's letters to Petworth are printed by T. Tonelli in *Poggii Epistolae* (Florence 1832).

influence of these two men who were employed at Wolvesey palace in close proximity to the cathedral priory, must surely have extended to the inhabitants of the close.

A third figure who belongs to this circle is Vincent Clement, Aragonese by birth, who obtained letters of denisation in 1439 and who like Bildeston held the archdeaconry of Winchester. Between the years 1440 and 1442 he was orator of both king Henry VI and duke Humfrey. His relationship with Thomas Bekynton is clear from a number of letters in the Bekynton correspondence which are printed in the *Rolls Series*;[16] Bekynton was duke Humfrey's chancellor in 1423 and bishop of Bath and Wells from 1443 to 1465.

John Neele, a Hampshire man by birth who held livings of several churches in the diocese, was chaplain to bishop Waynflete in 1460, and the deed of his appointment to the office of treasurer of the bishop's hospice in 1466 is in the priory register.[17] The exhibition to which I referred displayed one of his books (all of which he bequeathed to Magdalen College, Oxford), a copy of the *De Consolatione Philosophiae* of Boethius which was written by the English humanistic scribe known only as 'Thomas S.'[18]

These four men were all Oxford graduates and thus they must have been familiar with the promoters of humanism there; to what extent is of course unknown. The single Cambridge humanist who appears in the register is Lincoln-born Simon Aylward,[19] a fellow of King's College from 1453 to c1459. His handwriting was shown in the duke Humfrey exhibition and is described in the catalogue as 'a stiff but quite skilful humanistic hand';[20] the book, the *De ludo scacchorum* of Jacobus de Cessolis, is signed on folio 71[v], 'Simon Aylward scripsit hunc librum' and the date is 1456. On the front flyleaf is a fifteenth century note *Wynton. Episcopi*;[21] to which bishop this refers remains uncertain but it may possibly have been Courtenay for the priory register records the latter's appointment of Aylward as receiver of Farnham castle in 1492 at a salary of threepence a day.[22]

---

[16] *Memorials of the Reign of King Henry VI. Official Correspondence of Thomas Bekynton . . ,.* ed G. Williams, 2 vols (London 1872) *passim*.
[17] Item no 360.
[18] Hunt and de la Mare p 33.
[19] For Aylward's career see the entry in Emden (C).
[20] Hunt and de la Mare p 54.
[21] *Ibid* p 55.
[22] Item no 471.

In presenting these five men and providing a few of the biographical details relevant to my theme, I am sure that I have not exhausted all the humanistic connections with the priory and bishopric of Winchester in this period. However, the evidence already uncovered clearly points to the existence of a small circle of humanist enthusiasts in Winchester, although it is disappointing that their activities do not seem to have borne any significant or lasting fruit. In these few lines of an unknown scribe we have an indication that renaissance humanism attracted adherents within the monastic community at Winchester.[23]

Carleton University
Ottawa

[23] Because of the rarity of examples of the humanistic script in England at this early date they are being reproduced in a forthcoming collection of facsimiles compiled by Hunt and de la Mare and published by the Oxford Bibliographical Society.

OLD WINE IN NEW BOTTLES:
ATTITUDES TO REFORM IN
FIFTEENTH-CENTURY ENGLAND

by DEREK BAKER

W HEREVER one turns in the pages of those who have
written about the later medieval church there are
reminiscences of Eliot's 'Hollow Men':
Shape without form, shade without colour
Paralysed force, gesture without motion[1]
As Knowles put it, 'by and large the whole body ecclesiastic was
lukewarm', adding of monasticism in particular that 'it had little
warmth to spare for others'.[2] It was, he commented elsewhere, 'an
age of waning fervour' – 'the rhythm of life becomes universally
slower, and scarcely any new feature appears until the abrupt end'.[3]
To other less compelling and considered writers it has been all too easy
to characterise these waning medieval years simply as ones of 'inevitable decline', the retreat of the spiritual tide proceeding unchecked by
the vain efforts of even the most able and dedicated men of the period
to halt its recession – 'it was his misfortune', it has been said of
Marmaduke Huby, one of the major English monastic figures of the
period, 'to be born at a time when ideals were at a low ebb, when the
spirit of monasticism had grown languid and when material preoccupations demanded far too much attention'.[4] There is little to be
gained from such generalised speculation, which, if the subject of the
passage was not known, could readily be ascribed, with equal non-
validity, to almost any period in monastic history. Nonetheless, it
remains true that the particular circumstances of church and society
in the fifteenth century placed massive obstacles in the way of men
like Huby, and there is ample evidence of the difficulties with which
they had to contend. The attractive and admirable recent study of the
cathedral priory of Durham in the first half of the fifteenth century[5]

---

[1] T. S. Eliot, 'The Hollow Men', lines 11–12, *Collected Poems 1909–35* (London 1936) p 87.
[2] *RO* 3 (1959) p 466.   [3] *MRHS* p xiii.
[4] C. H. Talbot, 'Marmaduke Huby, abbot of Fountains (1495–1526)', *ASOC* 20, fasc 3/4
(1964) pp 165–84 at p 165.
[5] [R. B.] Dobson, [*Durham Priory 1400–1450*], *Cambridge Studies in Medieval Life and
Thought*, 3 series, 6 (Cambridge 1973).

gives a selective insight into the period through the workings of a major black monk house. Built around the sympathetic, perhaps over-sympathetic, portrayal of prior John Wessington (1416–46) it exemplifies in microcosm the problems which faced the institutional church at all levels, aggravated in the age of schism and council, but not entirely contingent upon them—the tensions and crises produced by the clash of competing jurisdictions, even when in apparent partnership; the tendency, and necessity, for the ablest men to be submerged in details of administration and litigation, to be preoccupied with the problems of maintaining status and privilege against erosion by churchmen and laity alike; the constant need to compromise with forces, families and interests which could not otherwise be resisted or gainsaid, legitimising unsatisfactory de facto solutions in order to preserve appearances. It is certainly true of Wessington, as his biographer concludes, that he did a great deal for his house, and presided over a policy of 'comparatively successful conservatism',[6] but he seldom appears upon any larger national or ecclesiastical stage. Whatever his inclinations, the demands of his priorate and community confined him with rare exceptions, willy-nilly within a localised context. In such circumstances, and even amongst those most concerned to sustain the flagging spirit and ageing members of the most substantial component of the medieval church, there is already a whiff of that après moi atmosphere which was to become so pronounced as the century wore on.

If the patient was geriatric, however, this was no tranquil senescence. A later scholar-monk like Robert Joseph of Evesham might dilate upon the delights of Oxford, and relish his literary friendships—'how pleasant, how delightful, how sweet a time we had together' he wrote to one parochial correspondent[7]—but he was scarcely typical, and his letterbook reflects the man rather than the circumstances of his community. At all events, more disturbed conditions prevailed elsewhere. On St George's day 1517 the abbot of Fountains wrote to the abbot of Cîteaux on behalf of Thomas Fassington, a Scot, who sought permission to return to Cîteaux from his onerous and futile labours in his native land.[8] Fassington had been sent to Scotland 'to reconstruct our

[6] *Ibid* p 10.
[7] [*The Letter-Book of Robert] Joseph*, [ed H. Aveling and W. A. Pantin], *OHS*, ns 19 (1967) no 63, pp 89–90.
[8] *Letters [from the English abbots to the chapter at Cîteaux 1442–1521*, ed C. H. Talbot], *CSer*, 4 series 4 (1967) no 127, pp 246–7, =D[ijon, Archives départmentales de la Côte d'Or, Fonds 11 H 19], 8. For the Cistercian archives in general see *Repertoire Numerique des Archives Départmentales antérieurs à 1790, Côte d'Or, Archives Ecclésiastiques, Série*

order, which had virtually disappeared as a result of destruction, and of secular encroachment by savage wolves who covet milk and wool, and seek their own interests rather than those of Jesus Christ: mercenaries, nay much worse, who ravage the flock like ravening wolves, the allies of evil. He has suffered much—oppression, injury, even imprisonment—at the hands of these invaders of our monasteries, and now being convinced that he can achieve nothing amongst this depraved and perverse nation he would rather lead a more holy and useful life at Cîteaux than to live amongst such ostriches.'[9] At first sight Huby's letter may seem extreme and exaggerated, overemphatic in support of the plea that was being made, but Fassington's report is in accord with what is known of the fate of Scottish regular communities, and there is ample evidence that monasteries south of the border could be as turbulent as their Scottish counterparts.

Later in the same year Huby wrote to Cîteaux to complain of the conduct of the new commissary in Wales,[10] the abbot of Neath, who visited the houses in his charge with a military escort of some three hundred. At Margam 'he despoiled the abbot of his office, compelling him from fear of death, and terror at such a force, to resign, and intruded one of his monks, who was virtually illiterate, into his place'.[11] The Welsh houses had long been a notorious problem, but similar conditions could be found outside the principality. In the same letter another commissary, the abbot of Ford, was indicted by Huby for deposing the abbot of Kingswood, and replacing him with a monk of his own choice in circumstances analogous to those at Margam.[12] Twenty years earlier, in 1497, Huby himself had become involved in a disputed abbatial election which resulted in his citation before the

---

H, clergé régulier, 11 H, Abbaye de Cîteaux, ed J. Richard (Dijon 1950), pp 48. Earlier lists and catalogues are still of some use and value, given the disordered and dilapidated nature of the collection, upon which Talbot and earlier commentators have remarked. Talbot's edition is not altogether satisfactory, nor always wholly accurate. A new edition, with translation and commentary is in progress.

[9] . . . pro redintegracione ordinis nostri, ibidem pene lapsi per destructores, per invasores seculares, lupos graves, qui lac et lanam querunt, qui sua colligunt et non Jhesu Christi, qui vere mercenarii, ymmo multo peiores sunt, raptores gregis sicut lupi graves, socii furum, multas valde sustinuit oppressiones et iniurias, ymmo quodammodo carceres ab huiusmodi monasteriorum invasoribus. Et iam considerans se nichill posse in medio huius nacionis prave et perverse proficere . . . arbitratur fore sanctius et utilius in domo habitare quam cum strucionibus in eorum medio conversari.

[10] *Letters* no 129, pp 249–53, dated 8 August 1517, =D 6.

[11] Abbatem de Morgan [Margam] suo officio spoliavit, et timore mortis et terrore tantorum armatorum cedere compulit, et monachum suum pene illiteratum loco alterius intrusit, p 251.

[12] *Ibid* p 252.

king, and placed at risk the privileges and status of the order itself in England.[13] It is, however, Huby's extensive account of the local aspects of the case which are of significance here. The abbot of Furness had died on 12 July 1497, and his death at once produced dissension within the house. Two candidates emerged—the cellarer and 'a certain scholar, bachelor of theology'—who 'contended simoniacally and ambitiously, the one against the other, for the abbacy'. In these circumstances the subprior and community appealed to Huby in his capacity as commissary, to intervene in order to avert serious trouble and a great scandal. It was clear that their fears were well-founded, for the two rivals 'by all kinds of promises and commitments had sought, and gained, the support of the whole isle [of Furness] for their candidacy: one had won over the princes, the other the magnates; one the nobles, the other the knights, one the clergy, the other the people'.[14] When Huby arrived at Furness at the end of the month, on the day he had fixed for the election, he found 'the whole monastery filled with knights and esquires, and a great mass of people, there to support their candidates. I, however, made a regal progress into the heart of the multitude, greeting them all favourably and with kindly words, and promising to act in good faith and without any bias, according to our statutes. I asked them, therefore, to disperse quietly so that they should neither disturb our consultations nor be a burden on the community, adding that they could return after two days, if they wished, to see whom Christ, the prince of shepherds, should have seen fit to choose as abbot and shepherd. And so', Huby added, 'I managed to get this great and formidable gathering to disperse, not without extreme difficulty and great trouble.'[15] The ensuing election was deadlocked, and both

[13] See *Letters* no 101, pp 204–9, dated 21 August 1497, =D 15.

[14] Duo quoque fratres erant eiusdem monasterii, videlicet, cellerarius et alter scolaris quidam sacre theologie bachalarius, qui adeo symoniace et ambiciose alter adversus alterum pro abbaciatu illius monasterii optinendo contendebant, ut quidem nec preci nec precio parcere decreverunt, ut baculum illius lucrifacerent. Contraxerant namque et illexerant plerisque sponsionibus et promissis totam insulam ad sui favorem, ille principes, alter magnates, ille nobiles, alter milites, ille clerum, alter vulgum, in sue cause defensionem suscitabat, pp 205–6.

[15] . . . invenimus totum monasterium militibus et armigeris ac numerosa wulgi multitudine, qui pro partibus advenerant supradictis, constipatum. Nos vero inter medias turbarum acies regiam viam incedentes, omnes favorabiliter cum lenitate verborum salutantes promisimus nos fide bona et indifferenti animo secundum statuta religionis in actu futuro processuros, ita tamen ut quiete discederent nec nos inquietarent neque monasterium superfluis sumptibus aggraverent, sed post biduum, si qui vellent, revenirent et qualem suum abbatem et pastorem princeps pastorum Christus dignaretur providere aspicerent. Sicque tandem gravem et formidabilem multitudinem abire fecimus, non absque maxima difficultate et instancia, p 206.

candidates proved intransigent, preferring exile to being ruled by the other. Huby thereupon quashed both elections, and using his commissary powers appointed 'an excellent and remarkable young man, though thirty years of age, endowed with great gifts, wisdom, letters, experience, modesty and many notable virtues, Alexander [Banke] by name'.[16] With his nominee's general acceptance, and the community and its neighbours once more at peace Huby returned home. It was an impressive and masterly resolution of a dangerous problem, and is instructive for the state of English monasticism in relation to its social environment—so too is its aftermath. Within three years Banke was in trouble,[17] and twenty years later was faced with deposition *pro suis sceleratis ac nephariis criminibus*,[18] but far from accepting his impending deposition he fortified Furness; garrisoned it with three hundred men; despoiled it of its treasures, and fled to the royal court. The secular arm was called in by the visitors to clear the monastery; Banke was deposed, and a successor—whose piteous letter records these events—elected. Banke, however, appealed to York and, it was alleged, bought influential support at the royal court. In consequence his successor and four senior members of the community were lodged in the Fleet prison. Banke then seized the abbey by force, consigned another four monks to prison in Lancaster, where the subprior died, and appropriated the revenues of the house to his own purposes. It is difficult to see Huby's gifted and virtuous nominee for the abbey in

---

[16] . . . optimum et spectabilem iuvenem, etatis tamen triginta annorum, preclaro ingenio imbutum, sciencia, litteratura, experiencia, pudicicia ac multis virtutibus insignitum, Alexandrum nomine, eiusdem monasterii sacerdotem et commonachum denominavimus, providimus et prefecimus in abbacialem dignitatem illius monasterii, p 207. The most recent, and extended, account of Banke's career is to be found in [Christopher] Haigh, [*The Last Days of the Lancashire Monasteries and the Pilgrimage of Grace*], Chetham Society, 3 series 17 (Manchester 1969) pp 14–20. There is, however, little about his origins and background, though it would appear that he had relatives within the community, and was well-connected: see, for example, the prohibition of any member of the abbot's 'fee, kin or allied' from service on the jury when Banke was cited to the duchy court in 1516 (Haigh p 58), and *Letters* no 128, pp 247–9, dated 29 April 1517, =D 81, at p 249 for a reference to Banke's relative John Clapham.

[17] Banke's election was not, however, entirely unopposed. John Dalton, probably one of discarded candidates in 1497, and Banke's successor in 1514 (below n 18), intrigued unsuccessfully against him, and at the general chapter of the order in 1500 Banke was absolved from 'incontinence, irregularity, simony and other proven crimes'. See Canivez 6, p 237, no 23; 6, p 238 no 25; Haigh pp 14–15.

[18] See *RO* 3 (1959) p 33; *Letters* no 128, pp 247–9, dated 29 April 1517, =D 81. The letter was addressed to the abbot of Cîteaux by Banke's unfortunate successor, John Dalton, and sent from the Fleet prison, where Banke had had Dalton consigned. For Furness and the Lancastrian houses generally see Haigh and my '*Scienter nescius*, [*sapienter indoctus*: English scholar-monks and the monastic life]', forthcoming.

this man, and though 1517, the year of this complaint, was one of
great activity for the abbot of Fountains the situation at Furness seems
to have provoked neither response nor comment from him.[19]

It might be argued that Furness, placed at the tip of its 'island', and
closely integrated into a society strongly conscious of its own local
interests, was sufficiently isolated to be atypical:[20] but for Huby in
1497 it had been only a day's journey from Fountains.[21] Nor can it be
suggested that Furness was one of those underpopulated houses whose
decline had long since negated any real attempt to live a regular life outside the world. In the election of 1497 twenty-six monks had voted:
a total which may be compared to the community of twenty-two at
Fountains to which Huby had succeeded only two years earlier. It is
true that Furness did not subsequently double its numbers, as Fountains did under Huby,[22] but it must nonetheless be regarded as one of
the greater houses of the time, and, as events elsewhere indicated, could
fairly be taken to characterise the problems and attitudes affecting contemporary English cistercianism. At Meaux and Fountains itself, for
example, there were major disturbances at abbatial elections;[23] at
Wardon and Fountains serious allegations of poisoning.[24] Charges of
misconduct, arbitrary action and peculation abounded, commissaries
and abbots regarding each other with suspicion, and often antagonism.
The scholar monks, of whom Huby and others expected so much were
frequently the cause of trouble, not only in the communities to which
they returned, but more widely within the English provinces of the

[19] It should, however, be noted that this dispute appears to have begun in 1514, and it is
possible that Huby was involved in it in the years before 1517, for which no correspondence survives, though the tone of Dalton's letter (above n 17) does not seem to suggest
such an involvement. No letters from English abbots to Cîteaux now survive at Dijon
for the years between 1500 and 1517. The texts included by Talbot for this period (nos
111–20, 122–4) are not letters from England, and, for the most part, not letters at all,
nor from the same liasse as the bulk of the correspondence.

[20] See, for example, *RO* 3 (1959) p 34—'in a class by itself'.

[21] See *Letters* no 101, p 205.

[22] For Huby's own account of the growth of Fountains under his rule see *Letters* no 131,
pp 258–9, dated 1520, =D 10.

[23] See Baker, 'Scienter nescius'; A. E. Goodman, *The Loyal Conspiracy* (London 1971)
pp 75–7.

[24] See *Letters* no 2, pp 22–39, =D 27. This is in fact a dossier of letters and depositions
concerned with the protracted and notorious case of William Downam, former monk
of Fountains. Though the final compilation may be dated, as by Talbot, to 28 December
1449 the constituent documents are variously dated between 11 June 1447 and the term-
inal date. It must be said that of all the items in Talbot's collection the transcription
of this important dossier is the least satisfactory: indeed, in some respects it is difficult to
accept that it can have been made directly from the manuscript. For Wardon see *Letters*
nos 78–82, pp 154–66, dated 19 June 1492–10 May 1493, =D 33, 54, 94, 97.

order.[25] As with Alexander Banke, appeals to external tribunals streng-

[25] See Baker, 'Scienter nescius', and below. In a letter written on 19 April 1517 (no 126, pp 242–6, = D 7, at pp 244–5) Huby complained of the intrusion of an unworthy provisor for the Oxford house of studies by the abbot of Ford, but his comments in this particular instance are more widely significant of attitudes with regard to Cistercian scholar monks—Aliud eciam restat pro utilitate scolarium et ibidem studencium providendum, quia provisor eiusdem collegii, contra voluntatem maioris et sanioris partis studencium per Venerabilem patrem dominum Abbatem de fforda institutus, proprie voluntatis et affeccionis arbitrio, nullo alio commissariorum secum coassistente, pocius quam discreta racione, monachus sibi professus, necdum in sacerdotali ordine constitutus, iuvenis tam moribus quam sciencia, spretis multis aliis maturioribus tam moribus quam sciencia, non tam assumptus quam intrusus esse videbatur. Sigillum commune illius collegii substractum aut perditum fore publice declaratur, et ob has consideraciones maior pars patrum Anglie, has videntes enormitates, scolares suos ad dictum collegium Oxonie dedignantur transmittere, sed pocius ad parisiense studium intendunt eos dirigere. Plures utique Anglie patres, presertim borealium parcium, ubi religio et ordinis ceremonie conservantur, cum nutrierunt iuniores fratres in croceis studii claustralis et regularis observancie, ac sic direxerunt hiis diebus suos scolares ad studium, qui debent esse electi ex milibus, necgligencia ac torpore provisoris incumbentis, viri utique pertinacis animi, ut plane et vere fateamur, ineffrenata libertate vagantur foras, et neclecto studio amplexantur vanitates et unusquisque agit pro libitu absque debite cohercionis remedio. Cumque defectu bone provisionis patres viderint filios suos ire per abruta talium semitarum obliquarum retrahunt desidiose studentes et nequaquam proficientes ad monasteria sua multo deteriores quam prius fuerant in virtutibus. Talia sunt ibidem iam infelicia tempora nostra. Adest, ut dicunt, in presenti aut nuper affuit vobiscum, dictus provisor, et si hec ex nostra relacione eidem pro sua correccione dixeritis, uti nichil in occulto agamus, contenti erimus. Bonus utique et religiosus provisor multa bona ac utilia conferre poterit, non solum studentibus, sed eciam omnibus Anglie patribus et eorum monasteriis, si bene et religiose scolares sui educati et eruditi fuerint in studio. Sic econverso malus et negligens ac improvidus provisor plura dampna procurare poterit.

Compare the complaint of the abbots of Fountains and St Mary Graces seventeen years earlier (*Letters* no 109, dated 20 August 1500, p 222): . . . Sed non solum hec et huiusmodi illi facere conantur contra sacrum ordinem qui in claustris conversantur, sed et illi de quorum mentibus presumere videbamur, qui scolasticis deputantur disciplinis, mox cum ad bachalariatus gradum, licet non ad condignum, sciencia salutari que edificat, sed illa que inflat, debreati fuerint, immediate spiritu extollencie et elacionis contra suos superiores eriguntur, vendicantes sibi iura et quedam insignia abbacialia non ex gracia sed ex debito, videlicet proximum stallum post abbatem, publicum birreti usum, impudenter se dicentes secundos post abbates esse, non humillia, sed alta sapientes, ambulantesque in mirabilibus supra se, putantes se scire omnia, cum nichil noverint, presertim cum ipsum non noverint, qui omnia novit. Pro premissis quoque privilegiis defensandis iuraque ordinis protegendis curialibusque monachis et contra patres suos abbates pervalidas conspiraciones suscitantibus, freno correccionis reprimendis aliisque insolenciis, ac novarum rerum molitoribus et inventoribus cohercendis et corrigendis, si nequaquam consultissime fuissent Reformatores, cum habundantissima superiorum potestate ordinati et suffulti tanquam coadiutores dei, qui predictis pestiferis malis et incommodis viriliter resistendo obviarent, profecto ut magistra omnium rerum experiencia cognoscimus, ordo ipse totus cum suis legibus et privilegiis verteretur in citissimum ac profundissimum precipicii laberinthum . . . See also *Letters* no 95, pp 191–3, dated 28 August 1496, = D 5, at p 193; no 137, pp 265–6, dated 1521, = D 124.

thened the hand of those who sought to break the control of Cîteaux,
and subject the English houses nominally to the papacy, but in practice to the local bishop and patron. Even within the ranks of the
English cistercian abbots there were those who favoured such a
development: when the abbot of Cîteaux failed to get royal assent for
his projected visitation of the English houses in 1490 the chief agent
of the refusal was alleged to be the abbot of Conway—'why', he said
to Huby, 'do you get into such a sweat trying to arrange the abbot of
Cîteaux's entry into England? If he comes he will be concerned only
with his own affairs, and there will be nothing to our profit. He will
cause division and dissension amongst the abbots, and leave the order
here in a worse state than he found it in. It was for these reasons that I
blocked his road with thorns, and prevented him coming here'.[26] All
these disruptive elements make their appearance in a lengthy letter,
written to the abbot of Cîteaux in August 1500 by the two commissaries, the abbots of Fountains and St Mary Graces, reporting on the
recent chapter of the English houses, held at Leicester,[27] but perhaps
the most telling indication is to be found in one of Huby's last surviving
letters.[28] Written, apparently in 1520, and now incomplete, it relates
briefly the growth of Fountains under Huby before revealing that a
group within the community had formed around one Edward Tyrry
with a view to securing his election as abbot should Huby die or resign,
a not unlikely event in view of his age. Tyrry's canvassing had involved *crebras commessaciones, illicitas potaciones, et multa miranda . . . que
longum esset stilo committere*,[29] and though he and six others were disciplined, being dispersed to other houses, other members of the community seem to have been implicated. Huby's particular concern in
writing was to ensure that there should be no rehabilitation for Tyrry
or his accomplices, whatever pressures were brought to bear, and no
opportunity for their 'pernicious example' to lead others astray.
Discussion of a successor to Huby was natural enough as he neared the

---

[26] *Letters* no 64, pp 128–30, dated November/December 1490, = D 18: 'Ut quid', inquit, 'pro introitu domini Cisterciensis tanto tempore desudatis? Hic, si venerit, nichill nobis proficiet sed sua queret, brigas et dissensiones inter patres faciet, et in peiori statu ordinem dimittet quam reperiet. Propter hoc obstruxi vias eius spinis ne veniret', p 129.
[27] *Letters* no 109, pp 220–5, dated 20 August 1500, = D 9, and see above n 24.
[28] Letters no 131, pp 258–60, dated 1520, = D 10. The final paragraph is in Huby's own hand.
[29] *Ibid* p 259. For a hint that Huby's advancing years had already, in 1517, become a matter for comment see *Letters* no 125, pp 239–41, dated 17 April 1517, = D 80, at p 241.

inevitable end of his long reign, but as Huby's letter makes clear there was more to it than that, and if the Marmaduke who was acting as bursar of Fountains in 1517[30] can be identified with Marmaduke Bradley, who was rehabilitated by the abbot of Cîteaux by 1521,[31] and who later, in 1535, bought the abbacy from the royal commissioners, then the extent of the trouble can be envisaged, while the danger of rehabilitation of men like Tyrry was clearly not remote. Huby's successor was the much-maligned William Thirsk,[32] and at his deposition ten years later it was remarked that 'ther is never a monke in that howse mete for that rowme',[33] though 'ther is a monke of that howse called Marmaduke [Bradley], to whom Mr. Times lefft a prebende in Repon churche, now abydying upon the same prebende, the wysyst monke within Inglonde of that cote and well lernede, XX[ti] yeires officer and rewler of all that howse, a welthie felowe, wiche will gyve yowe syx hundreth markes to make hym abbot ther, and pay yowe immediatly afftter the election withoute delay or respite, at one payment, and as I suppos wythoute muche borowyng . . . I am sure all th'abbotes of his religion will thynke him a ryghte apte man hereunto, and the most mete of any other'.[34]

Whatever assessment may be made of Bradley in the succession of Huby, it is clear that he and his predecessor, William Thirsk—who seems for a time at any rate to have succeeded to Huby's commissary powers, and acted as visitor-general of the English cistercian houses[35]— were more representative of their time and their kind than Huby. It may be true, as Knowles remarked of Scotland in this period, that 'development and deterioration continue side by side,'[36] pointing in particular to the arrival of the Franciscan observants half a century

---

[30] See *ibid* no 127, dated 23 April 1517, = D 8, . . . per fratri nostri Marmaduci bursarii nostri . . ., p 246. This is possibly the same man as the Marmaduke referred to as an emissary of the abbot of Fountains in 1510/11, . . . per manus fratri Marmaduci . . .: see *ibid* no 117, p 232. The report of Layton and Legh to Thomas Cromwell on the resignation of William Thirsk, abbot of Fountains, referred to Marmaduke Bradley as 'xx[ti] yeires officer and rewler of all that howse', see [*The Memorials of*] *Fountains* [*Abbey*], 1, [ed J. R. Walbran], *SS* 42 (1863) p 266.

[31] *Ibid* no 139, pp 267–8, dated by Talbot 1517–21. A dating of 1520/1 might be preferable in the light of the trouble at Fountains reported by Huby (above n 28) and the possible involvement of Bradley in it.

[32] See *Fountains* 1 pp 250–76. The episcopal commission for Thirsk's benediction as abbot was issued on 22 October 1526, *ibid* p 268 n 2. For further comment about Thirsk see Baker, '*Scienter nescius*'.

[33] *Fountains* 1 p 266, Layton and Legh to Thomas Cromwell 20 January 1536.

[34] *Ibid* pp 266–7.

[35] *Ibid* pp 260–4; Haigh p 19.

[36] *MRHS* p xiii.

before they appeared in England, while in that kingdom, as he stressed, the disappearance at the dissolution of Carthusians, Bridgettines and the best of the nunneries removed 'an ideal and a practice of life that had always attracted a spiritual *élite* and, in things of the spirit, as in works of art, the best has a value and a price which no quantity, however great, of the mediocre can supply'.[37] But however measured the judgement, whatever the caveats, it is plain that the leaven was scanty, the lump excessively large. If Bradley really was 'the most mete of any other' then the careful and confined conservatism of men like Wessington is bound to seem unreal, the laborious and incessant activity of men like Huby essentially futile. Vitality and purpose was to be found in new devotions, and in individual creeds and responses—in Kemp and à Kempis. The immediacy of Margery Kemp's boisterous suffering with a suffering Jesus; the surprising popularity of a book— if such it may be termed—like *The Imitation of Christ* supply a perspective in which it is legitimate to speak of 'bare ruined choirs, where late the sweet birds sung' long before any formal dissolution. And yet this is our perspective, not theirs. In all Huby's extensive correspondence, and whatever the difficulties which confronted him, there is no hint of self-deception, no touch of desperation or despair, no stoic confrontation with destiny. Rather, it is a busy correspondence, instinct with optimism and a sense of achievement, and with an eye to the future. If he and his confreres insisted continually on the need for reform, they were equally insistent that they could accomplish it.

In the problems which faced them, and in the pressures to which they were subjected, the white monk houses differed little from contemporary black monk communities, though their continuing status as components in the structure of an international order added dimensions which were absent in the case of a house like Durham. The same is true of the instruments of reform. What was required was sound local government within the community itself, supplemented by visitation, oversight and policy-making effected and expressed through the agency of provincial chapters. With the cistercians there was the additional tier provided by the annual general chapter of the order, held at Cîteaux, and the occasional visitation by the abbot of Cîteaux himself, his emissaries, or by the continental heads of extensive filiations. The fragmentary records of the general chapters, however, reveal

[37] *RO* 3 (1959) p 466.

how inadequate attendance had become, and how seldom capitular decrees were decisive in resolving problems. Visitation by the abbot of Cîteaux, or by other continental heads, in like manner, did little to improve matters. There was some substance in the abbot of Conway's cynical comments to Huby,[38] and for a time a clash between the abbot Cîteaux and the abbot of Clairvaux, with his extensive English filiations, created a virtual schism in the order.

There is little here—in the problems, and in the structures, decrees and activities for dealing with them—which is other than entirely commonplace or traditional, but as a context it has some significance for the career of a man like Huby, for his assessment of his role, and for his attitude towards reform. Huby seems to have entered Fountains in the early 1460s, during the abbacy of John Greenwell (1442–71),[39] and twenty years later can be found active as bursar, intimate and representative of his predecessor as abbot of Fountains, John Darnton—and, according to his own account, at an even earlier date under Darnton's predecessor, Thomas Swinton.[40] It is plain that Huby was a great

---

[38] Above n 26. See also Rose Graham, 'The Great Schism and the English Monasteries of the Cistercian Order', *EHR* 44 (1929) pp 373–87. For attempts to undermine the exemption of the English houses of the order, and the authority of the abbot of Cîteaux and his commissaries, see *Letters* no 59, pp 120–2, dated 8 August 1489, =D 42; nos 65–6, pp 130–7, dated 20 November 1490, = D 46; no 129, pp 249–53, dated 8 August 1517, = D 6. For a comment on the isolation of the English houses see Huby's letter regretting the death of the abbot of Cîteaux, James of Pontaille, in 1516 (*Letters* no 126, pp 242–6, dated 19 April 1517, = D 7, at p 242): Ante vero relacionem suam [Thomas Fassington] huius rei nullam habuimus cognicionem utpote in remotioribus huius regni Anglie partibus constituti.

[39] In the course of a letter to Lord Dacre, dated 18 July 1523/4, Huby remarked 'I have beyn professyd in this Monastery of Fontaynes by the spaice of iiixx yeres', *Fountains* 1 p 241.

[40] On 19 April 1517, after the departure of James of Pontaille, abbot of Cîteaux (20 November 1501–25 October 1516, resigned, 1–2 November 1516, died) Huby wrote to his short-lived successor Blaise Larget (1516–10 September 1517), asking for the renewal of his powers as commissary, and emphasising his long period of service— Nam per triginta sex annos in negociis ordinis, viz. viginti et tres in abbaciali regimine, et residuum annorum eorumdem sub duobus predecessoribus nostris [Thomas Swinton, abbot of Fountains 1471–8, John Darnton, 1478–95] et Reverendissimis patribus et dominis Hymberto, Johanne et Jacobo, predecessoribus vestris, utcumque militavimus, eorum fulsiti [sic] auctoritate, et nunc in vestro obsequio diem claudere extremum cupimus. *Letters* no 126, pp 242–3, =D 7. If Huby's claim to have served Swinton (1471–8) and Humbert de Losne (abbot of Cîteaux 1462–76) *in negociis ordinis* is accepted then his thirty-six years of service cannot have been continuous. His claim implies that he was active in the interests of the order before 1476. For further testimony to the trust placed in Huby before he became abbot see the letter of John Haryngton (no 66, pp 131–7, dated 20 November 1490, = D 46, at pp 132, 136). For Huby as bursar of Fountains see no 64, pp 128–30, dated November/ December 1490, = D 18.

organiser and administrator, with a grasp of financial and business detail, and a passion for order.[41] He was responsible, amongst much else, for the massive five volume fifteenth-century cartulary of Fountains,[42] which parallels the contemporary nine volume cartulary of Cîteaux, produced under the aegis of Jean de Cirey, the great reforming abbot who ruled the order for twenty-five years (1476–1501).[43] Outside his own house Huby was active in the affairs of the order long before he succeeded to the abbacy of Fountains, receiving high praise for his part in the long drawn out dispute over the church of Scarborough, and in the development of the Oxford house of studies, quite apart from playing a more general role as representative and visitor. It is clear that he came into increasing prominence as Darnton became incapacitated by old age: he was, said the provisor of the Oxford studium in 1495 'the staff of his old age',[44] and his election to succeed Darnton was inevitable. It has been usual to regard Huby as a product of the Oxford studium with whose completion he was so much concerned. The evidence for this is, however, slight and equivocal: the provisor of the Oxford house might remark that Huby 'had been thoroughly grounded in letters since his earliest years, and had no small learning in the scriptures, nay rather I should say he was very learned',[45] but neither here nor anywhere else is there any attempt to claim him for the Oxford studium, and I am inclined to regard him as a man of intelligence and perception who had received a good education at York before he entered religion, and then at Fountains: in some respects his devotion to, and concern for, the Oxford studium, his high regard for the purposes and possibilities of monastic university studies, might seem to indicate a man who revered the ideal, rather than having experienced the reality.[46] However that may be, there can be no ques-

---

[41] See Talbot p 167; *Letters* no 86, pp 172–4, dated 12 August 1495, = D 92.

[42] See G. R. C. Davis, *Medieval Cartularies of Great Britain* (London 1958) pp 47–8, nos 414–19.

[43] Resigned 1501, died 27 December 1503.

[44] *Letters* no 86, p 173, dated 12 August 1495

[45] *Ibid*: ab ineunte aetate in litteris assidue educatus, nutritus, in sacraque scriptura non mediocriter edoctus, immo ut ita dixerim doctissimus. Compare the descriptions of the abbot of Stratford Langthorne, *qui eiusdem studii* [Oxford] *alumpnus erat* (*ibid* no 95, dated 28 August 1496, = D 5, p 193), and the abbot of Rievaulx in Huby's letter of 19 April 1517 (no 126, pp 242–6, = D 7): . . . venerabilem et religiosissimum virum dominum Willelmum abbatem Rievallensem, virum vestre Reverencie cognitum, litteris, sciencia et multis virtutibus insignitum, qui primo apud Oxonie studium et eciam postea una vobiscum in Collegio Sancti Bernardi religiosam et honestam vitam ducere studuit, p 243.

[46] See, for example, Huby's memoranda of 1495 (*Letters* no 89, pp 181–3, = D 19) and August 1496 (*ibid* no 94, pp 189–91, = D 106) and above n 25.

tion of his intellectual capacity, and he combined considerable practical experience with a clear overall view both of the problems, and of the possibilities open to him.

Having said this, his attitudes and activities are likely to seem disappointingly conventional. He found *novitates et presumpciones*[47] of any sort abhorrent, and seems to have been content to work within the established procedures, however frustrating they might be. It never, for example, seems to have occurred to him that, however suspect their motives might have been, the attempts by English prelates to break the direct links with Cîteaux might have led to more efficient government of the English cistercian communities, or accelerated reform, particularly at the hands of a man like himself, persona grata with Henry VII and his mother, close to Wolsey, and of high reputation in his own order.[48] 'I am certain', wrote the abbot of

[47] *Letters* no 129, pp 249–53, dated 8 August 1517, =D 6, at p 252.
[48] For brief accounts see *RO* 3 (1959) pp 35–6; Talbot p 167. Knowles' references to the letters in Talbot's edition are unfortunately consistently inaccurate, and probably reflect the prepublication order and numeration of the transcripts supplied by Talbot, see *RO* 3 p 28 n 1. Writing in the context of the complaint lodged against Huby by the abbot of Stratford Langthorne, as a result of Huby's intervention at Furness in 1497 (see above nn 13–15), the abbot of St Mary Graces recorded—Habet insuper idem dominus abbas de ffontibus (non obstante predicta querimonia omnibus iustis causis suis) cum omni gracia dominum regem faventissimum (*Letters* no 100, pp 202–4, dated 16 August 1497, = D 50, at p 204). For Huby's ensuing discussion with the king see below. For his experiences at the royal court while still bursar of Fountains see *Letters* no 64, pp 128–30, dated November/December 1490, = D 18. For his relationships with the king's mother see *Letters* no 66, p 137: Placeat Reverendissime paternitati vestre harum latori litteras vestras cum graciarum accionibus pro amore suo ostenso et ostendendo venerabili viro magistro Thome Burwel, in decretis Bacallario, secretario nobilissime principisse Margarete comitisse Richemundie et Derbie, ac domini nostri Regis Henrici septimi matris, . . . una cum litteris suffragia ordinis nimirum coenobiorum vestrorum continentibus, tam dicte principisse, mulieri devotissime, cuius ope in Wallia Marmaducus suffultus est, quam eidem secretario concedendum. For Huby's relationship with Wolsey see an addition to a letter of 8 August 1517 (no 129, pp 249–54, = D 6, at p 254) in which Huby advised the abbot of Cîteaux: Consulimus, si sic placuerit, ut littera suffragialis de confraternitate sapienter, pulchro dictamine ornata ac formosa manu scripta, fiat . . . The object, as Huby said, was to secure especially favourable treatment for the order from Wolsey. Huby's praise of Wolsey might seem fulsome—. . . virum sapientissimum regni, post regiam maiestatem moderatorem maximum, insignem iusticie cultorem, pauperum et oppressorum relevatorem precipuum—but it is clear that he was well-acquainted with the cardinal: the archbishop of York was, as Huby recalled, *huius monasterii de ffontibus fundatorem et defensorem egregium*, and he promised, if such a letter of confraternity was sent from Cîteaux, *eandem litteram manibus nostris propriis sue Reverencie offerre*, and, at the same time, to seek all possible benefit for the order from the legate. Earlier in the same year (17 April 1517) the abbot of Rievaulx had stressed Huby's influence over Wolsey—dominus cardinalis dominum abbatem eiusdem loci [Fountains] singulari favore prosequitur, qui, ut a pluribus estimatur,

Rievaulx of him in 1517, 'that there is no one in the kingdom so experienced as he is, so friendly with the magnates of our kingdom, and so well-known to them.'[49] Yet Huby seems to have accepted without question the procedures of chapter and visitation, and the complications and delays attendant upon the need to consult Cîteaux. Equally, his energetic attention to reform produced no new initiatives: this may be the inhibiting result of the sheer weight of tradition upon an antiquated and ossified structure, but it seems more likely that Huby's actions indicated not merely what was possible, but what he desired, and that the concern of the visitors of Wardon in 1492, that 'the whole uniformity of the order should be observed . . . in chant, action, habit and tonsure, in reading, prayer and the other ceremonies of the order, according to the forms bequeathed to us by our holy fathers',[50] coincided with Huby's. In this connection there is the record of a remarkable conversation between Huby and the king in 1497, and if it is of particular interest for the unusual light it throws upon Henry VII it is also of interest for the abbot of Fountains. The account occurs in the long letter about the disputed election at Furness which Huby sent to Cîteaux in August 1497,[51] but the occasion was a series of discussions which had taken place some months earlier, and which had been concerned with the reform of the cistercian houses in Wales, on which Huby had been actively engaged; with the condition of the Irish cistercian communities, and with the disputed church at Scarborough. He had found the king, said Huby, *tam in causis istis quam in nostris nobis semper faventissimum*, and prepared to take an active interest. 'Amongst other things', he continued, 'the most famous prince wondered greatly that we had in England no conversi like those who, in the early years of the order, had been of such use and profit, serving as the pious draught oxen of Christ. In the days to come he said that he himself would issue letters and obtain six or eight honest conversi of this sort, trained in different crafts, for whom he would make provision in our greater monasteries, and by whose

---

per influenciam ipsius abbatis non sinistra sed pocius prospera procurabit, *Letters* no 125, pp 239–41, = D 80, at p 241.

[49] *Ibid*: Certi enim sumus, quod nullus in regno nostro Anglie tantam experienciam habet, neque cum magnatibus regni nostri tam familiaris et notus.

[50] *Ibid* no 80, pp 159–62, dated 26 September 1492, = D 33, at p 159: Et quia summa uniformitas in ordine debet observari, statuimus et ordinamus ut in canta, gestu, habitu et tonsura, in leccione, oracione, ceterisque ceremoniis ordinis secundum formam a sanctis patribus nobis relictam, omnes huius domus professi vivere et se conformare studeant, . . .

[51] *Ibid* no 101, dated 21 August 1497, pp 204–9, = D 15, at p 208.

example other devout laymen, fired by pious fervour, might be led to put on the habit of religion without any sense of shame.' Nothing came of the proposal, and it would be easy to dismiss it as airy theorising, but that would be to disregard its context. It formed part of a discussion of real and pressing problems, and Huby's own concluding remark showed that it was no mere frivolity to him, or to some of his contemporaries—'for not one single conversus is to be found amongst us at present, at which everyone is amazed.'[52]

The age and the society has been characterised as one of 'institutional resistance to social and intellectual change',[53] and the implication is that men, even men like Huby, hung on to traditional forms, procedures and values until their institutions inevitably disintegrated under the pressures to which they were increasingly subject. Every revolution, it has been said, is essentially an unfulfilled reform, and the processes of history are littered with the misdirected good intentions of men like Huby, struggling to redecorate when it was the foundations which had been undermined and needed attention. But there are signs that the men of the time were not afraid to innovate— the complex involvement of Huby, or of his collaborator Richard Grene, in the affairs of the order long before he became abbot was hardly in accord with traditional cistercian practices,[54] and if, both at

[52] Fuimus namque cum Regia celsitudine circa finem aprilis, et tribus vicibus de plerisque rebus coram sua maiestate conferentes, de statu ordinis reformando viisque et mediis sue assistencie, presertim partium Walliarum, qui multum digressi sunt a semitis sancte religionis, tam in habitu et tonsura quam in ceteris ceremoniis. Similiter et de Hibernensibus et de ecclesia de Scardeburgh, et invenimus suam magestatem tam in causis istis quam in nostris nobis semper faventissimum, sicut adhuc in presenti graciose perseverat, et ex mera mente sua asseruit sub proprio signeto suo in nostrum favorem suas Regales litteras vestre dirigere reverencie, quas per fratrem nostrum presencium baiulum recipietis: cui, si placet, fidem indubiam adhibere diginimini [*sic*] in multis aliis que scribere non valui. Inter alia multum admiratur princeps clarissimus quod conversos fratres in Anglia non habemus, qui solent ordini antiquitus esse tanquam ad utilitatem et profectum, tanquam christi pia iumenta. Pro sex vel octo huiusmodi conversis honestis et in diversis artibus practicatis dixit se suas graciosas litteras directurum in futurum, quibus et honestam provisionem procuraret in potioribus nostri ordinis monasteriis, ut horum exemplo alii devoti laici ad fervorem religionis excitati religionis habitum assumere nullatenus erubescerent. Namque nullus hic conversus apud nos reperitur in presenti, qui faceret ut omnes mirarentur.

[53] See Dobson p 10.

[54] For the association of Huby and Grene, and the high opinion in which they were held, see *Letters* no 59, pp 120-2, dated 8 August 1489, = D 42, at p 121, . . . quibus similes in hac re non visurum me spero unquam, doleo, . . .; no 66, pp 131-7, dated 20 November 1490, = D 46, at pp 132, 134, 136—Meliores aut certe (pensata locorum et personarum qualitate) illis pares vel consimiles saltem duos dumtaxat in Regno invenietis hac etate nullos; no 77, pp 152-4, dated 7 December 1491, = D 66, at p 153. For separate references to Grene see *ibid* pp 66, 196, 198.

Oxford and in the north, Huby was a great builder the fine tower at Fountains shows that he was not entirely subservient to the statutes of his order, and may typify a more independent attitude than is generally allowed.[55] It is, in fact, worth considering whether change was needed, and how far contemporary regard for traditional forms could be regarded as positive rather than negative, as constituting as fertile a ground for regeneration as the better publicised, more individual and exuberant manifestations of the piety of the age.

There is, of course, little evidence to go on,[56] but if Galbraith can assert sweepingly of later medieval English historical writing 'by this time we are well into the fifteenth century and the best days are past',[57] he is later led to qualify his judgement—'when we turn from national and international history to historical collections relating to particular abbeys and cathedrals, the case is rather different. We are at once conscious of a livelier interest in the remote past, and a truer grasp of the contemporary world'.[58] With a slightly different emphasis this gets to the heart of the matter. Wessington of Durham, Kidderminster, can easily be characterised as 'antiquarian', but Huby's career makes it clear that such interests can have a more positive and contemporary significance. In a letter written in 1517 he had referred to the northern parts of England 'where religion and the ceremonies of the order are particularly preserved',[59] and it is clear that he felt and inculcated a lively patriotism,[60] with a pride and interest in the traditions, achievements and personalities of the past, as focal and growth points in the piety and religious observance of laity and religious alike—if the avaricious pressures of secular lords on monastic wealth and privileges is one aspect of the relations between regulars and society, another is to be found in flourishing late medieval fraternities associated with houses like Fountains. For a man like Wessington, and his community at Durham, the traditions of Cuthbert were obviously

[55] See Canivez 1, p 61, no 16, referring to the statute of 1157. Fountains was not alone in acquiring a tower: 'in the years before the Reformation a new West Tower of magnificent proportions was added at Furness', Haigh p 56, and n 3.

[56] See the comments of Knowles, *RO* 3 (1959) p 28.

[57] V. H. Galbraith, *Historical Research in Medieval England* (London 1951) p 30.

[58] *Ibid* p 36.

[59] *Letters* no 126, pp 242–6, dated 19 April 1517, = D 7, at p 244.

[60] For an insight into Huby's attitude see his last recorded letter, to Lord Dacre on 16 July 1523/4 (*Fountains* 1, pp 239–42). For the renewed interest in the history of Fountains in the later fifteenth century see Derek Baker, 'The Genesis of English Cistercian Chronicles: the Foundation History of Fountains Abbey', *Analecta Cisterciensia*, 25 1 (1969) pp 14–41; 31, 2 (1975) pp 179–212, and forthcoming.

of pre-eminent interest. With Huby the emphasis is similar. In 1495, in a memorandum to the general chapter,[61] he sought, and obtained, permission for an enhanced observance, at Fountains and her daughter houses, of the feast of Oswald, king and martyr, of whom Fountains possessed notable relics and memorials. At the chapel of Wynkesley, built by Huby, Cuthbert joins Oswald in the dedication,[62] while in Ripon Huby obtained the site of Wilfrid's old abbey from the archbishop of York and prebendaries of Ripon, and erected a new chapel to the honour of our lady, including in it, as Leland records, inscriptions relating to the Saxon saints associated with the place.[63] This chapel was itself the first stage in the creation of new white monk cell, dependent on Fountains, at Ripon, and though never apparently completed the project is further testimony to the vigour and vitality of Huby's work: there was ample justification for his claim in 1520 that under him Fountains had flourished internally, in its religious observance, and in external prosperity.[64]

The principles of Huby's policies, applied throughout the English provinces during his long years as commissary and visitor, can be exemplified in his own community at Fountains, though to limit them simply to his own period as abbot would be to undervalue the achievements of his able predecessors. The foundation of Huby's reforms lay in the vigorous, prosperous monastic community, well-governed at every level, growing in numbers, and giving its recruits a thorough training, both within the house and at the schools: all this within the framework of established and reinvigorated tradition and statute. Within local society such a community could, and should, focus and embody local piety by its nurturing of local cults, and its commemoration of the saints. The close relationships which, at an individual level, existed between Huby and king, cardinal, prelates and magnates could be achieved by communities at a local level,[65]

---

[61] *Letters* no 89, pp 181–3, = D 19, at pp 181–2. A later memorandum (*ibid* no 94, pp 189–91, dated August 1496, = D 106, at p 190) requested permission for a further enhanced observance, on the pattern of that accorded to St Edmund, claiming: nullus ordo, nulla religio, nullusve sexus videtur diem nathalicii sui debitis preterire laudibus et exequiis, excepto nostro dumtaxat ordine Cisterciensi, qui quamquam plures eiusdem gloriosi martiris habet, ut predicitur, exuvias, . . . Both letters refer to the relics at Fountains, but there is no mention of them at the dissolution. See *Fountains* I, p 150 for a reference to devotion to St Wilfrid.

[62] See *Fountains* I p 152 for the archiepiscopal indulgence, dated 13 February 1502–3.

[63] *Ibid*, quoting Leland's *Itinerary*.

[64] *Letters* no 131, pp 258–60, = D 10.

[65] See, for example, the involvement of John Greenwell (abbot of Fountains 1442–71) in the settlement of local disputes, *Fountains* I p 148 n, and the making of Thomas Swinton

provided they could be seen to have a function and purpose, and to inspire respect. Nor was it simply the Bedan past which could profitably be cultivated anew in the fifteenth—'enter, I beg, the house of Simon the Pharisee, watch closely how loving, how sweet, how joyous and merciful a face He shows to the prostrate sinner, with what compassion He allows those most holy feet to be washed with the tears of repentance, dried with the hair which had formerly served pride and wantonness, and gently kissed by lips so often defiled. Kiss, kiss, kiss, O happy sinner, kiss those dearest, sweetest, most beautiful of feet . . . kiss them, clasp them, hold them fast, those feet venerated by angels and men alike . . . and what are you doing, O my soul, O my wretched, O my sinful soul? . . . Why do you hold back? Break forth sweet tears, break forth, let nothing impede your course . . . I will cling to your feet my Jesus, I will hold them fast with my hands, press my lips to them, and I will not stop weeping and kissing them . . .' The intense directly-involved piety, the individual expression and commitment are those of the age of Margery Kemp: the voice is that of Ailred, speaking directly and clearly to the age of Huby.[66]

It must, of course, be allowed that Huby was an exceptional man, and even at Fountains his successors were inadequate. Major developments, however, seldom depend solely upon great men, and many of those who shaped and implemented the reformation were men of mediocre talents and uncertain resolve. It is not, I think, altogether fanciful to suggest that the English cistercian community had within itself the possibilities and potential for decisive change and growth based upon a rediscovery and reapplication of past glories and standards, and a renewed expression of earlier spiritual values and teaching, once

---

(Abbot 1471–8) and the abbot of Jervaulx brothers of the York Corpus Christi guild in 1471, *ibid* p 150 n. For a passing reference to local opinion of Cistercians, at Scarborough, see *Letters* no 103, pp 210–13, dated 10 August 1498, = D 17, at p 212. More generally see the newly-published *Borthwick Paper* no 50—M. G. A. Vale, *Piety, Charity and Literacy among the Yorkshire Gentry, 1370–1480* (York 1976).

[66] Expositio venerabilis Aelredi abbatis de Rievalle de evangelica lectione cum factus esset Jesus annorum duodecim, edited with critical introduction and French translation by A. Hoste, '*Quand Jesus eut douze ans . . .*', SCR 60 (1958); English translation in *The Works of Aelred of Rievaulx* 1, *Treatises, The Pastoral Prayer*, Cistercian Fathers Series, 2 (Spencer, Mass., 1971), translation by Theodore Berkeley. Brief extracts from the treatise also occur in translation in Squire's study (below). Hoste's introduction to his edition provides an excellent sketch of the literary and spiritual context of the treatise. See also Giles Constable, 'Twelfth-century spirituality and the later Middle Ages', in *Medieval and Renaissance Studies*, ed O. B. Hardison, Jr. (Chapel Hill, N. Carolina, 1971); Aelred Squire, *Aelred of Rievaulx, a Study* (London 1973) particularly pp 67–70.

again in vogue.[67] How such a policy could have been fully implemented in the English provinces can only be a matter of speculation, but it is likely that it could only have been realised in communities like Fountains, Rievaulx or a disciplined Furness, and that houses whose numbers no longer matched the requirements of the life and the cistercian statutes would have been dissolved in any case. At a higher level, Huby's own career hints at an adjustment of traditional relationships towards a greater degree of independence from Cîteaux, and a closer association with national authorities in church and state. His position on occasion seems vice-regal, and though he always defers his letters to Cîteaux are now and then reminiscent of those of Boniface to the popes of his later career.[68] That such adjustments would have preserved the white monks from the general politico-ecclesiastical cataclysm which overtook English regular life is unlikely, but the course of events, and the decisive intervention of other non-ecclesiastical factors should not be allowed to pre-empt possibilities. If it was indeed a monastic winter

> When yellow leaves, or none, or few do hang
> Upon those boughs which shake against the cold[69]

it is as well to recall that the tree was not yet dead: bare boughs are the prerequisite of a new spring, and an old tree refreshed from deep sources is likely to produce sound fruit.

University of Edinburgh

---

[67] For another monastic revival of interest in the past outside the ranks of the white monks see the comments of Robert Dunning, 'Revival at Glastonbury 1530-9', below pp 213-22.

[68] See, for example, M. Tangl, *Die Briefe des heiligen Bonifatius und Lullus, MGH Epp Sel* 1 (1916) no 50.

[69] Shakespeare, sonnet 73.

REVIVAL AT GLASTONBURY 1530-9

by ROBERT W. DUNNING

IT is curious that Glastonbury abbey should have attracted more attention for its beginnings than for its ending. The no-man's-land between history, archaeology and legend, as misty and mysterious as the climate so often makes the abbey and its surroundings, has produced theory and counter-theory in abundance. In contrast, though the tragic deaths of abbot Whiting and his two companions have been described in minute detail a thousand times, little enough attention has been paid to the community which the king's visitors found so much difficulty in bringing to an end. This community, well enough documented to permit the identification of all its members over the last fifteen years of its life, reveals characteristics which stand in marked contrast to the general level of religious life in the years immediately before the dissolution.

The essential sources are six lists of members of the community: the first at the election of Richard Whiting as abbot in January 1524-5,[1] the second an episcopal visitation in 1526,[2] the third the cash allowances made to each monk according to his seniority by one of the departments of the abbey for the year 1532-3.[3] These are followed in chronological order by the names, if not the signatures, to the acknowledgement of royal supremacy in 1534,[4] and then by cash liveries from two other abbey departments for the years 1537-8 and 1538-9.[5] In addition there is the record of a second episcopal visitation in 1538.[6] This material is supplemented by ordination lists, though these only survive to 1526.[7] There is no surviving document of

---

[1] [*The Registers of Thomas*] *Wolsey,* [*John*] *Clerke,* [*William*] *Knyght and* [*Gilbert*] *Bourne,* ed H. Maxwell-Lyte, S[omerset] R[ecord] S[ociety] 55 (Taunton 1940) pp 84-8.

[2] 'Visitations [of Religious Houses and Hospitals,] 1526', ed H. Maxwell-Lyte in *Collectanea 1, SRS* 39 (1924) pp 211-13.

[3] PRO SC 6/Henry VIII/3115.

[4] [R.] Warner, [*An History of the Abbey of Glaston: and of the Town of Glastonbury*] (Bath 1826) pp lxx-lxxi.

[5] PRO SC 6/Henry VIII/3117-18. The second list is printed in A. Watkin, 'Glastonbury 1538-9 as shown by its account rolls', *DR* 67, no 210 (1949) pp 449-50.

[6] [*Dean Cosyn and*] *W*[*ells*] *C*[*athedral*] *M*[*iscellanea*], ed A. Watkin, *SRS* 56 (1941) pp 159-64.

[7] S[omerset] R[ecord] O[ffice] D/D/B reg 7-12.

surrender, if indeed such a formal act was ever made, and the pension list of cardinal Pole is limited to twenty-five monks, of whom six were recently dead.[8] Little can be found about the fate of most of the Glastonbury monks, but enough can be pieced together of the years before the fall to suggest that renaissance and renewal are words not too strong to characterise some aspects of that great community.

> The whole world knows by what noble and shining acts of munificence this ancient abbey was formerly endowed, and so flourished under a succession of wise and holy abbots. But it would not be at all right to omit from the number of our benefactors him who still in full splendour before all men's eyes most deservedly holds the high office of abbot of Glastonbury: I mean of course Richard Bere, a man of strict monastic obedience, much given to the godly virtue of abstinence, and a most saintly benefactor of the poor . . . so that one may truly say he does not hide his light under a bushel, but rather in the words of Our Saviour, shines forth before all that are in the house of the Lord. . . .

With this and more, brother Thomas Sutton, reading rather as the puff of a modern estate agent than the foreign cellarer or steward of the abbey, began the monastic terrier which bears the abbot's name.[9] Leland bears witness to Bere's building enterprises: a new lodging by the great chamber called the king's lodging, with a gallery; new quarters for secular priests and clerks of Our Lady; the Edgar chapel at the east end of the abbey church and two chapels elsewhere, as well as essential repairs to the fabric; an almshouse for poor women within the monastic precinct, and improvements to manor-houses and churches far and wide.[10]

The magnificence which this represents, serving as in so many similar houses to emphasise the gulf between abbot and community, is given further weight by the evidence of the disparity between senior and junior monks revealed in the visitation of 1538, and by a picture of abbot Whiting given in a later lawsuit. The seniors had the best food, the juniors the worst; the juniors had no charity towards the seniors; the prior had favourites; the abbot 'is very weak in his doing and by his means the convent seal goeth largely out to such

[8] [W. A. J.] Archbold, [*Somerset Religious Houses*], *Cambridge Historical Essays* 6 (1892) pp 151–2; *MA* 1 p 9.
[9] *Abbot Bere's Terrier and Perambulation*, ed H. F. Scott Stokes (Glastonbury 1940) pp 3–4.
[10] J. Leland, *Itinerary*, ed L. Toulmin Smith (London 1906–8) 1 p 289.

persons as cannot help the house nor further a good word'.[11] Abbot Whiting's household was like that of any great secular lord: he had gentlemen and servants in his hall at dinner, and collected personal debts discreetly in an arbour in his garden on a Sunday while the community sang high mass in the abbey church a few yards away.[12] Renaissance and renewal seem to be confined to outward magnificence.

Those angels of death Richard Pollard, Thomas Moyle and Richard Layton informed Cromwell in September 1539 that there was 'never a doctor within that house, but three bachelors of divinity, meanly learned.'[13] A year earlier a monk had complained to the visiting bishop that 'the brethren hath no library nor books to resort unto', though whether the great collection which so impressed Leland had already been taken by the king's visitors or was simply out of bounds to juniors will never be known.[14] Several monks at that same visitation claimed that study of scripture was impossible because they lacked books and because the services were 'so tedious' that there was no time left; one said they lacked 'learned men' to instruct them in both scripture and grammar, and another claimed that lectures were only given when a visitation was imminent 'and when the visitation is done then the lectures doth cease'—with the consequence that they spent their time playing dice and cards instead.[15]

The novices, too, it was said, found themselves paying up to twenty shillings a quarter for their own instruction, though the abbot should have paid, and perhaps for the same reason the schoolmaster employed to teach the chapel boys had to exist on a pittance.[16] It was, according to three monks, the fault of the prior who was 'but meanly learned in good scripture' and 'divers times' altered the abbot's mind 'touching learning'; and he and his crony the abbey cook were 'ever against that; that young men shall have any learning'. Yet in contrast John Neot was the object of general envy: he had been absent at Oxford for anything between seven and twelve years, and in the eyes of his fellows was thereby little improved. The cause of this envy is not far to seek. Roger Wilfred, he who was to suffer with his abbot on the Tor, pointed out that John Pantalion was 'well learned if he

[11] SRO D/D/Ca 10a p 29. The version in *WCM* is inaccurate.
[12] *RO* 3 p 348.
[13] *LP* 14 (2) pp 60–1.
[14] *WCM* p 162 and n.
[15] *Ibid* pp 159–64; *RO* 3 p 347.
[16] *WCM* pp 159–64. The deposition of John Pantalion is inaccurate and incomplete.

might go to Oxford' and Pantalion's own statement includes the sentence, quickly erased, that 'this deponent hath been kept from his school this five years'.[17] Others made it clear that Neot stayed at Oxford so long only with the support of the prior and of John Verney, successively master of the novices, third prior and *medarius*.[18]

The complaints against Neot came from eight monks. Simon Edgar, Richard Ultan and Roger Wilfred had been in the community for at least twenty years but never achieved senior status nor held office. They may well have felt a sense of frustration, for there was obvious favouritism in the house, and they were not favoured. A fourth objector, William Joseph, had been a monk a little longer, though at least he had been a senior for some five years. For three others the grounds for complaint may well have been different. John Ambrose, made subdeacon in March 1523, was one of those mentioned in letters of Robert Joseph, the humanist monk of Evesham.[19] He was a scholar at Gloucester college, Oxford, by March 1528 and may well have continued his studies until 1536-7.[20] What caused his withdrawal without a degree can only be conjectured, but Robert Joseph found him such a poor correspondent that he sent him paper and arranged that the messenger would lend him pen and ink.[21]

Another critic was Geoffrey Bennyng, a little younger than Ambrose and a senior by 1533,[22] who like Ambrose was receiving a cash allowance from the *medarius*, John Verney, in 1536-7 for study outside Glastonbury.[23] There seems to be no trace of him at Gloucester college, and his scholastic career may also have come to a disappointing end. The third man to have hard words for Neot was John Pantalion himself. He was much younger than the other two, but had been in the community for at least four years, and though a priest was still a junior at the dissolution. His complaints bore him some fruit, for from

[17] Taken from the original, SRO D/D/Ca 10a p 23.
[18] PRO SC 6/Henry VIII/3116.
[19] [*The Letter Book of*] *Robert Joseph*, [ed Dom H. Aveling and W. A. Pantin], OHS ns 19 (Oxford 1967) p 270.
[20] Emden (O) 1501-40 says he was there until 1530, but he received cash because of absence from Glastonbury in 1536-7: PRO SC 6/Henry VIII/3116.
[21] *Robert Joseph* pp 13, 48, 270.
[22] Made deacon in December 1525: SRO D/D/B reg 12 (register of bishop Clerk) fol 117v; PRO SC 6/Henry VIII/3115.
[23] PRO SC 6/Henry VIII/3116.

Michaelmas 1538 he found himself one of the last students at Gloucester college.[24]

Judging by the visitation complaints there seem to be no grounds for claiming anything like academic renaissance and renewal at Glastonbury, but frustrated scholars are not the best sources of balanced opinion. Certainly abbot Whiting himself was without a university education,[25] and though later claims have been made for him that he supported young men at the university,[26] there is no direct evidence that any of these were members of his own community. Perhaps the agreement drawn up between himself and a new organist in 1534 reflects his interests more closely, when he insisted on the instruction of choir boys in prick-song, descant and organ playing.[27]

Yet in face of the supposed opposition from senior monks, a number of juniors did attend Gloucester college from 1530, an obvious reversal of a trend which had produced only six students since 1513.[28] There were still no outstanding scholars in the 1530s, and only Thomas Athelstan and John Neot took degrees, both in theology, in 1535.[29] But to them must be added six or seven others who went to Oxford for the first time in the 1530s.[30] Glastonbury thus progressed from six monks there in two decades to ten in the last nine years, one fifth of the whole community.

For all the snide remarks made about John Neot, he was the closest friend of Robert Joseph of Evesham. He spent some nine years at Oxford before graduating in 1535, and returned to Glastonbury to promotion as guestmaster and third prior in 1539.[31] His friends knew well that the bowling green and the river bank were quite as congenial as his books, but whatever they thought at Glastonbury he was something of a preacher, he produced some special prayers for St Leonard's day, and astonished Joseph by writing a letter more polished than

---

[24] Emden (O) 1501–40.

[25] *RO* 3 p 379n. Whiting was made acolyte in September 1498, subdeacon in the following December, deacon in September 1499 and priest in March 1501: SRO D/D/B reg 9 (register of bishop King) fols 119^r, 119^v, 120^v, 123^r.

[26] *MA* 1 p 7.

[27] [A.] Watkin, 'Last Glimpses [of Glastonbury]', *DR* 67 no 207 (1948) pp 76–9.

[28] Nicholas London, Nicholas Andrew, John Dunstan, John Ambrose, John Neot and Thomas Athelstan: Emden (O) 1501–40.

[29] With Nicholas Andrew making the three graduates referred to by the king's visitors.

[30] Geoffrey Bennyng, Thomas Brent, John Marke, John Pantalion, John Phagan, Thomas Weston and possibly John Aldhelm: Emden (O) 1501–40; *Robert Joseph* pp 270, 274, 280–1; PRO SC 6/Henry VIII/3116.

[31] Emden (O) 1501–40.

anyone else at Oxford could compose.[32] Thomas Athelstan was an exact contemporary, and like Neot later joined the restored community at Westminster. He too was a correspondent of Joseph, and was linked in letters with two other Glastonbury friends, John Phagan and John Aldhelm. Between them these monks brought something of the new humanism of Oxford to Glastonbury; and if religion finds little place in their communications,[33] it is surely not without significance that of the four Westminster monks who petitioned queen Mary to restore Glastonbury, three of them should have been Thomas Athelstan, John Phagan and John Neot.[34]

Glastonbury was not always circumspect in its choice of founders, saints and sepulchres. If it may perhaps be allowed St Patrick and the martyred Irish pilgrim St Indracht, who rested on either side of the altar of the 'old church', Joseph of Arimathea, St Phagan and St Deruvian are misty figures of a less reliable tradition. Ine and Edgar, Dunstan and Aldhelm and Britwald were genuinely part of its history, and Edgar, Edmund and Edmund Ironside were buried within her walls. They were witness to Glastonbury's key role in the life of Wessex in the tenth and eleventh centuries.[35] The 'discovery' of the remains of king Arthur, so fortunately coinciding with a crisis in the economy of the house at the end of the twelfth century, for ever identified Glastonbury with the isle of Avalon, and made the community the focus of popular interest without the political overtones of Becket, but providing a curious mixture of nationalism, chivalry and religion, a mixture which continues to make both Arthur and Glastonbury so popular in the twentieth century.

Such a combination of nationalism, chivalry and religion was not unacceptable in the early sixteenth century, and abbot Bere seems to have been instrumental in the revival of Glastonbury's traditions. For him both the cult of Joseph of Arimathea and the Saxon past were points of emphasis, and as he began the building of the chapel later to house the copper-gilt tomb of king Edgar, so he laid claim to exclusive ownership of the relics of St Dunstan, a claim quite evidently refuted by the monks of Canterbury.[36] At the same time his monks

---

[32] *Robert Joseph* p 280.

[33] *RO* 3 p 105.

[34] *MA* 1 pp 9–10.

[35] *VCH Somerset* 2 (1914) p 85; C. A. Ralegh Radford, 'The Church in Somerset down to 1100' in *Proceedings of the Somersetshire Archaeological Society* 106 (Taunton 1967) p 31; R. F. Treharne, *The Glastonbury Legends* (London 1967, 1975).

[36] *MA* 1 pp 7–8; *VCH* Somerset 2 pp 93–4.

began a tradition which continued until the dissolution by taking names in religion from the great names of the past. Patronymics and places of origin gave way to kings and holy men.

Probably the earliest example of this practice was Thomas Dunstan, who took the name by the time he was made a subdeacon in December 1499.[37] A few after him like John Selwood, John Exeter and Richard Besyll held to the old ways, and indeed Dunstan may possibly have been a surname at the time.[38] From 1505 onwards, however, the tradition was established with the appearance of Robert Arimathey or Abaramathia, Richard Bede, John Benet, John Bennyng (Benignus) and John Ceolfryde.[39] Their names are a roll-call of the history of the church, from Ambrose and Urban of the church universal, Alban the protomartyr, Aidan, Oswald and Wilfrid from the Age of Saints, and Athelstan, Edgar, Ine and Kentwine from the history of Wessex. From Glastonbury's own traditions came Deruvian and Indracht, Neot and Phagan and Patrick, Joseph and Arimathey, Arthur, and above all Dunstan. All represented an intense desire to remind themselves and the world of the antiquity of their house, and perhaps also of its links with the crown and with the reforming movements of the past. Edgar and Dunstan might find parallels in the 1520s if not later. It was a roll-call of the great without peer, revived and reborn.[40]

Perhaps the strongest argument of all for revival and renaissance at Glastonbury was the fact that its religious life was still attractive. Almost alone among the large houses of black monks, its numbers were increasing.[41] When Richard Whiting was elected abbot in January 1524–5 there were forty-six monks present;[42] at a visitation in July 1526 there were fifty-one.[43] Neither figure is necessarily complete, though John Neot, the perpetual student, was the only known absentee on the first occasion.[44] Fifty-two monks received cash liveries from the keeper of the obit of abbot Monyngton for the year

---

[37] SRO D/D/B reg 9 (register of bishop King) fol 121ʳ.

[38] SRO D/D/B reg 9 (register of bishop King), fol 123ᵛ; reg 10 (register of bishop Hadrian) fol 150ʳ. But Besyll first appears as Basill.

[39] SRO D/D/B reg 10 (register of bishop Hadrian) fols 139ʳ, 140ᵛ, 141ʳ.

[40] Other founders cited in *Valor Ecclesiasticus* (Record Commission, London 1810–34) I p 147 included king Lucius, queen Guinevre and king Henry VII. Athelney attempted a similar policy in the 1520s: SRO D/D/B reg 11 (register of Wolsey) fol 29ᵛ.

[41] Knowles and Hadcock.

[42] *Wolsey, Clerke, Knyght and Bourne* pp 84–8.

[43] 'Visitation 1526' pp 211–13.

[44] *Wolsey, Clerke, Knyght and Bourne* p 86 gives the total as 47.

1532–3,[45] and the same number subscribed to the declaration of royal supremacy in September 1534.[46] Fifty-five monks had cash liveries from the keeper of abbot Selwood's anniversary in 1537–8, and the chamberlain paid allowances to fifty-four brethren in 1538–9.[47]

This increase of eight monks between 1526 and 1539 must be viewed against a background of general decline, and also in a context in which death caused regular vacancies in the community. Between 1525 and 1538, in fact, at least twenty-two men joined the house, eight of them after 1534. In face of these new vocations one may well echo Emden's remark that the 'imminence of the catastrophe of suppression was not suspected' at Glastonbury.[48] Certainly the agreement between abbot Whiting and the new organist, drawn up in August 1534 when the abbot had full knowledge of the oath of succession which he and his monks were soon to acknowledge,[49] suggests that the new relationship between church and state might be the beginning of years of friendly co-operation. So the organist agreed to serve 'the abbot and his successors' for life, and if he should by royal authority be 'taken up' to serve the king, he should be able to return to his post within a year and a day without financial loss.[50] This agreement survives because the organist successfully claimed payment of his annuity and arrears, a claim approved as late as 1568.

The persistence of the organist suggests a final line of enquiry, to establish how members of the dispersed community retained the elements of religious life which some had only just assumed, and which others had followed for many years. Of the community of fifty-four monks in 1538–9, Richard Whiting, Roger Wilfred alias James and John Arthur alias Thorne were hanged on the Tor. Twenty-five names appear in cardinal Pole's pension list in 1553, although six men were recently dead;[51] but these are secular names, not the names the monks took in religion, so it is often not possible to identify them.[52] So Thomas Dovell, who was working as a curate at St John's,

[45] PRO SC 6/Henry VIII/3115.
[46] Warner p lxxi.
[47] PRO SC 6/Henry VIII/3117–18.
[48] Emden (O) 1501–40, p xxii.
[49] *RO* 3 p 177.
[50] Watkin, 'Last Glimpses' pp 76–9.
[51] Archbold pp 151–2; *MA* 1 p 9.
[52] Four rare cases are Robert Touker or Ider, John Shepard or Deruvian, John Pydesley or Phagan and William Godson or Dunstan: SRO D/D/B reg 10 (register of bishop Hadrian) fols 157ʳ, 160ʳ.

Glastonbury, in 1555 was known by the diocesan authorities as a former monk, though in 1539 there were six Thomases in the community.[53] Nicholas Andrew, whose patronymic was evidently religious enough and was not changed, and who held high office as archdeacon of Glastonbury and chamberlain, probably held the living of Huish Episcopi from 1551 until his death early in 1554.[54] John Benet went to the same parish as chantry priest at Langport by 1548,[55] and John Waye was rector of Seaborough at his death in 1573. The parish register of Crewkerne records him as 'the parson of Seaborough and parson of Gosham, sometimes a monk of the abbey of Glastonbury'.[56]

Two other men took up work in parishes and, taking advantage of relaxed rules, took wives in Edward VI's reign. When Mary came to the throne William Bishop, aged 50, curate of Doulting, a former Glastonbury living, and John Pallye, aged 43, curate of Babcary, found themselves arraigned and suspended for so doing.[57] And there were, of course, the four men who went to join Feckenham at Westminster and who petitioned queen Mary for Glastonbury's restoration—John Neot, John Phagan, William Athelwold and William Kentwine.[58]

Other former members of the community appear in less usual circumstances. Thomas Waye, formerly Whiting's chaplain and then aged 68, was still living in 1544 when he gave evidence about buildings at Mells erected by the husband of Whiting's niece.[59] And can there be more than one Aristotle Webb, in religion Aristotle Alwyn or Alvernon, a junior monk in 1538–9, whose young daughter survived for only a few days early in 1572, and who himself was buried in 1577?[60] He lived and died within the jurisdiction of the mother church of Crewkerne, the same parish as his brother in religion, John Waye. The parish clerk certainly did not record him as a former monk, and but for his name he would have passed for a layman.

Ten men remaining in religion or finding work in the secular ministry, a fifth of the suppressed community in 1539, is not at first

---

[53] SRO D/D/Ca 21.
[54] Emden (O) 1501–40.
[55] *VCH Somerset* 3 (1974) p 34.
[56] SRO D/P/crew 2/1/1.
[57] SRO D/D/Vc 66.
[58] *MA* 1 p 9.
[59] Watkin, 'Last Glimpses' pp 80–1. Probably the same as John Wattes referred to in F. A. Gasquet, *The Last Abbot of Glastonbury* (London 1895) p 75.
[60] SRO D/P/crew 2/1/1.

compelling evidence for that community's spiritual vigour and religious enthusiasm. At the same time there was a significant element of men who could hardly have survived for many years. The oldest monk at Glastonbury was probably Edmund Coker, who was there by March 1487, and had thus been in religion for half a century.[61] Not much younger were prior Robert Clerk, Nicholas Wedmore and William Newport, who entered the house before 1495, and Thomas Dunstan, John Glastonbury and John Taunton, who came before 1500.[62] By the standards of the time they were old men in 1539, too old to find fresh employment, in the church or outside. And for others of whom no trace has been discovered, whose private activities are totally unknown, there still remained the opportunity for the private practice of at least some elements of their religious life. That would be no less valid a continuation of tradition than a change to a secular, priestly ministry, though in an arid and often solitary context, with hope of renaissance and renewal only in the life to come.

Victoria County History of Somerset

[61] SRO D/D/B reg 7 (register of bishop Stillington) fol 218v.
[62] SRO D/D/B reg 8 (register of bishop Fox) fols 43r, 43v, 44r; reg 9 (register of bishop King) fols 117r, 119r, 121r.

'A MAGAZINE OF RELIGIOUS PATTERNS': AN ERASMIAN TOPIC TRANSPOSED IN ENGLISH PROTESTANTISM

by PATRICK COLLINSON

IN his *Paraclesis* or *Adhortatio ad christianae philosophiae studium* Erasmus of Rotterdam proposed a famous anti-scholastic definition of the theologian:

To me he is truly a theologian who teaches not by skill with intricate syllogisms but by a disposition of mind, by the very expression and eyes . . .

In this kind of philosophy, located as it is more truly in the disposition of the mind than in syllogisms, life means more than debate, inspiration is preferable to erudition, transformation is a more important matter than intellectual comprehension. Only a very few can be learned, but all can be Christian, all can be devout, and—I shall boldly add—all can be theologians.[1]

In the context of this preface to the new testament the model was the supremely Christian life, 'the speaking, healing, dying, rising Christ himself'. Elsewhere, Erasmus sketched a portrait of exemplary Christian character as he had witnessed it at first hand, among his contemporaries. In response to a correspondent whom he judged to be in search of 'some eminent pattern of religion' he described the obscure Jehan Vitrier, 'a man unknown to the world but famous and renowned in the kingdom of Christ', as a foil, in the manner of Plutarch, for the more celebrated John Colet. Of Vitrier Erasmus said that 'in truth his whole life was nothing else than one continual sermon'; of Colet that 'nothing could divert him from the pursuit of a gospel life.'[2]

---

[1] [Desiderius Erasmus, *Christian Humanism and the Reformation: Selected Writings*, ed John C.] Olin (New York 1965) pp 92–106. The Latin text of the *Paraclesis* has been reproduced in facsimile in Desiderius Erasmus, *Prefaces to the Fathers, the New Testament, on Study*, ed Robert Peters (Menston 1970) pp 116–21.

[2] Letter to Jodocus Jonas on Vitrier and Colet, 13 June 1521, *Opus Epistolarum Des. Erasmi Roterodami*, 4 ed, P. S. Allen and H. M. Allen (Oxford 1922) pp 507–27; English translation by J. H. Lupton in *The Lives of Jehan Vitrier and John Colet* (London 1883), reprinted, Olin, pp 164–91. See Peter G. Bietenholz, *History and Biography in the Work of Erasmus of Rotterdam*, *Travaux d'humanisme et renaissance* 87 (Geneva 1966).

Erasmus's 'practical divinity' was transposed in English religious life after and well beyond the protestant reformation. The most distinct echoes were returned from as far away as the third quarter of the seventeenth century when the appetite for exemplary Christian biography was not to be satisfied with a mere couple of lives such as Erasmus had composed for his friend Jodocus Jonas (although the sketch of Colet was put into print at that time[3]) but called forth 'living effigies' by the score, published in voluminous folios of many hundreds of pages, not to mention at least as many (well over two hundred) spiritual autobiographies.[4] 'The nature of man is more apt to be guided by *Examples* than by *Precepts*.' That is not Erasmus but the puritan divine Edmund Calamy, commending Samuel Clarke's *Marrow of ecclesiastical historie*. 'These. . . did not reason but run.' That is Clarke himself, introducing the second part of the *Marrow, The lives of many eminent christians*. 'A Magazeen of religious patterns' is Thomas Fuller's typically spicy term for the celebrated collection of the lives and deaths of modern divines known as *Abel redivivus*.[5] Fuller and Clarke, opposites in churchmanship and literary style, found the field of ecclesiastical biography (and the market for it) expansive enough to contain them both.[6] It is the 'magazeens' published over the name of Clarke, actor-manager in a considerable collaborative enterprise, which provide the centrepiece for this paper.[7]

It would be rash to claim a distinctly Erasmian parentage for this literature. Others have struck that reef and there are now warning buoys

[3] As an appendix to the edition by Thomas Smith of *A sermon . . . made to the convocation at S. Pauls church in London by John Colet D.D. . . . . writ an hundred and fiftie years since* (Cambridge 1661); doubtless the source of the *Life* of Colet in *The lives of thirty-two English divines*, appended to Samuel Clarke, *A generall martyrologie* (London 1677).

[4] [Owen C.] Watkins, [*The Puritan Experience*] (London 1972).

[5] *Abel redivivus. Or, the dead yet speaking. The Lives and deaths of the modern divines. Written by severall able and learned men* (London 1651).

[6] Fuller wrote of 'Master Samuel Clarke, with whose pen mine never did, nor never shall interfere.' Like the flocks of Jacob and Laban their styles were 'set more than a Months journey asunder.' Quoted [William] Haller, [*The Rise of Puritanism*] (ed New York 1957) p 107.

[7] *The marrow [of ecclesiastical historie]* (London 1650, 2 ed 1654, 3 ed in 2 pts 1675); [*The*] *second part of the marrow* (bk 1 1650, bk 2 1652); *A generall martyrologie* (London 1651, 2 ed 1660, 3 ed 1677); *The lives of two and twenty English divines* (London 1660); [*A collection of the lives of*] *ten eminent divines* [. . . *and of some other eminent christians*] (London 1662); *The lives and deaths of such worthies* (London 1665); [*The lives of the*] *thirty-two English divines* (London 1667, another ed 1677); [*The*] *lives and deaths of most of those eminent persons* (London 1675); [*The*] *lives of sundry eminent persons* (London 1683). On the collaborative aspect, see the *Life* of Thomas Hill, who died in 1653: 'He was a great friend to the publication of the lives of godly and eminent ministers and christians.' *Thirty-two English divines* (1677 ed) p 234.

in position—'beware "influence studies"'[8] 'avoid "Erasmianism"'[9]
—which only a clumsy navigator could fail to notice. Since Erasmus
was not so much an originator as the distiller of elements of received
and even perennial wisdom, his influence cannot be isolated. In 1561 a
London preacher published an abridgement of a celebrated Erasmian
text, the *Enchiridion*, without knowing what it was: 'And as I know
not the author thereof, no more found I any title or name given unto
the book.'[10] This scarcely credible episode can serve as a symbol of the
insidious rather than overt means whereby Erasmian values may have
continued to colour the religion of English protestants.

The argument will rather be that in English protestantism, and even
in the unlikely setting of puritanism, the notion that Christian truth
was more persuasive mirrored in the particularities of human
existence than argued in dogmatic abstractions, which is an Erasmian
but not a peculiarly Erasmian idea, was persistent; and that when this
principle was applied to the recorded observation of particular lives it
carried with it at least some taste for those classical virtues which were
at a premium in Erasmus's 'philosophy of Christ', if only through
the continued reception of a rhetorical tradition which furnished the
models, categories and vocabulary for any large-scale undertaking in
biography.

But first it is necessary to state a paradox. Erasmus was a man of
letters. Yet the *Paraclesis* seems to say that life is more than learning,
and perhaps more to be valued even than literature. The only con-
crete examples it provides of a true theologian are a weaver or common
labourer. It is character which counts, expressed as much in the
disposition of a man's face and eyes as in words. But the *Paraclesis*
is the preface to a book, the new testament. The notion that life and not
literature is the best of schools is itself a literary and pedagogical
conceit. It is eloquence which can catch the life and convey its value

---

[8] Quentin Skinner, 'The Limits of Historical Explanations', *Philosophy* 41 (London 1966)
pp 199–215; Quentin Skinner, 'Meaning and Understanding in the History of Ideas',
History and Theory 8 (Middletown, Conn., 1969) pp 3–53.

[9] Reviewing J. K. McConica, *English Humanists and Reformation Politics under Henry VIII
and Edward VI* (Oxford 1965), which somewhat overstates the influence of
'Erasmianism', A. G. Dickens wrote in *History* 52 (1967) pp 77–8: 'After all, what
educated man did not know at least some of the writings of Erasmus? Who had not
breathed atmospheres subtly perfumed by his ubiquitous presence?' G. R. Elton wrote in
HJ 10 (1967) pp 137–8: 'People did not read Erasmus . . . and say with a sudden
inspiration: indeed, indeed, this is what we will do.'

[10] *Elizabethan Puritanism*, ed L. J. Trinterud, Library of Protestant Thought (Oxford 1971)
pp 19–39.

more transparently than the life itself. We cannot improve on the hyperbole which the *Paraclesis* itself contains: the new testament renders Christ 'so fully present that you would see less if you gazed upon Him with your very eyes.'[11]

As historians we must take these words on trust and apply them to the lives of English protestants in the century after the reformation. For if these lives had not been turned into a literature—*Lives* in another sense—we should not be able to see them at all. What we see is what the writers permit us to see, and perhaps more than was originally there. The full ambiguity inherent in the very word 'life' appears to have been missed by one of the greatest of literary historians, the late William Haller. The question may be asked whether in his book *The Rise of Puritanism*[12] Haller was recording the rise of puritanism or the rise of a puritan literature, including puritan biography. Between 1570 and 1643, while their plans to reorganise the church were checked, the puritans are said by Haller to have 'devoted themselves to the production of a literature'. It is only as they appear in that literature that they begin, as it were, to exist. Haller's account of the 'physicians of the soul' and 'the spiritual brotherhood', celebrated chapter headings in *The Rise of Puritanism*,[13] describes those puritan divines who achieved 'full expression in writing' and draws heavily on Clarke's *Lives*. The earliest of these biographies belong to men born in Elizabeth's reign who came to maturity in the time of James I. This was not the first generation of puritanism, still less of the protestantism with which it was in so many ways continuous. But Haller, while not fully satisfying our curiosity as to why such a literature came into existence when it did, seems to be incurious himself about puritanism before it received 'full expression in writing'. The consequence is to make an unnatural separation between puritanism and its protestant roots. And there is no mention of John Foxe, to whom Haller later devoted years of study.[14]

The Erasmian ambiguity suggests that there are two themes to be

---

[11] Olin p 106.

[12] First published 1938; Harper Torchbooks, New York 1957.

[13] Haller, caps 1 and 2.

[14] Haller told me in conversation in 1953 that he supposed that he was the only person who had seen every page of every edition of Foxe's *Acts and Monuments*. In *Foxe's Book of Martyrs and the Elect Nation* (London 1963) he identified (p 207) the Marian martyr John Bradford as 'a prototype of all the physicians of the soul who would presently be undertaking the spiritual direction of more and more of Elizabeth's subjects', and developed the point.

pursued within the scope of this paper. There is first the possibility that in the English reformation life itself in the sense of character was more persuasive than doctrine, or than anything put into writing, except for the English bible. There is then the theme of the persuasiveness of the recorded life, published biography, chronologically secondary to and dependent upon the first.

There is not very much than can or needs to be said about the first and more elusive of these topics. Paradoxically, the evidence that the wisdom of the *Paraclesis* was received and applied in the English reformation would have to be looked for in the absence of positive documentary record. It hardly needs to be argued that protestant Christianity in its original propagation was preached as much or more by example as by doctrine, in the old cliché caught rather than taught. It was not theological expertise or originality which made Thomas Bilney, in Foxe's phrase, 'the first framer of [Cambridge] university in the knowledge of Christ.'[15] But the documentary and literary bias of historians tends to let this almost self-evident fact go by default. There are some leads in the career of the Alsatian reformer Martin Bucer which can serve to develop this point. When Peter Martyr Vermigli first shared Bucer's household in Strasbourg he described it to his old friends in Lucca in a letter which was later well enough known to readers of his correspondence in English:

> Beholde, welbeloved brethren, in our age, Bishopes upon the earth, or rather in the Church of Christ, which be trulie holie. This is the office of a pastor, this is that bishoplike dignitie described by Paul in the Epistles unto Timothie and Titus. It delighteth me much to read this kinde of description in those Epistles, but it pleaseth me a great deale more to see with the eyes the patternes themselves.[16]

In Edwardian Cambridge Bucer maintained another model establishment which must have impressed in much the same way the future

---

[15] E. G. Rupp, *Studies in the Making of the English Protestant Tradition* (Cambridge 1966 ed) p 22.

[16] *Martyrs divine epistles*, bound with *The common places of Peter Martyr*, tr Anthonie Marten (London 1583) pp 62–3; whence printed in G. C. Gorham, *Gleanings of a Few Scattered Ears During the Reformation in England* (London 1857) pp 19–27; original Latin text in *Petri Martyri epistolae theologicae*, appended to *Loci communes* (London 1583) p 1071. Reference was made to the letter by S.T. (Samuel Torshell of Bunbury, Cheshire) in a funeral sermon of 1639, 'Gods esteeme of the death of his saints', in *The house of mourning* (1640). (See p 246 below.)

leaders of the English church who were his friends.[17] The influence of Bucer on the English reformation has been learnedly discussed,[18] but with difficulty once the discussion moves beyond his death and the matter of his proven contribution to prayer book revision. For very few of Bucer's writings were ever published in England, and even the great volume of *Scripta Anglicana* printed at Basle in 1577 does not appear to have been widely read. Bucer's prolixity was notorious. It is not unlikely that the more profound influence was of a personal character, exerted on the lives of English churchmen such as John Bradford and Edmund Grindal with whom the great reformer had been intimate. Both Bradford and Grindal would later appeal to the memory of Bucer's living impact on their generation, not to anything in print.[19]

The Elizabethan puritan vision of a church rightly reformed was a reflection not only of abstract ecclesiology but also of much human and social experience, mediated in 'the meetings of the godly' and in ministerial confraternity and conference. A frequent observation in the seventeenth-century biographies that many lit their lamps from this or that celebrated divine was to turn this into a cliché. But we can meet it fresh and at first hand in such Elizabethan sources as the minutes and other papers of the so-called Dedham *classis*[20] or the diary of the Essex minister Richard Rogers.[21] Rogers's sense of inadequacy was both aroused and in some measure allayed by the compelling example of the brethren whom he had cause to admire. 'No smalle helpe herto was our whetting on one the other who being 4 daies togither communicated many things togither.'[22]

We turn from real life to the mirror held up to life by religious

---

[17] 'Formula vivendi praescripta familiae suae a M. Bucero et propria manu revisa', Corpus Christi College Cambridge MS 418 pp 627-33; printed and discussed, François Wendel, 'Un document inédit sur le sejour de Bucer en Angleterre', *Revue d'histoire et de philosophie réligieuses* 34 (Strasbourg 1954) pp 223-33.

[18] A. E. Harvey, *Martin Bucer in England* (Marburg 1906); Constantin Hopf (Hope), *Martin Bucer in England* (Oxford 1946); Herbert Vogt, *Martin Bucer und die Kirche von England* (Inaugural dissertation, Westfälischen Wilhelm-Universität zu Münster 1966).

[19] Patrick Collinson, 'The Reformer and the Archbishop; Martin Bucer and an English Bucerian', *JRH* 6 (1971) pp 305-30.

[20] John Rylands Library, Rylands English MS 874; partially and imperfectly published in R. G. Usher, *The Presbyterian Movement in the Reign of Queen Elizabeth*, *CSer*, 3 ser 8 (1905).

[21] Original in Dr Williams's Library; partially printed in *Two Elizabethan Puritan Diaries*, ed M. M. Knappen, American Society of Church History (Chicago 1933).

[22] Knappen p 64. Compare the passage (p 95) in which Rogers takes to heart the exemplary life of John Knewstub, rector of Cockfield, Suffolk, headed: 'The example of Mr Knew[stubs]'.

biography. In the whole sweep of English religious history from the beginnings of the reformation to the Glorious Revolution there were two major episodes of edifying protestant biography, the one represented by the *Acts and Monuments* of John Foxe, a massive undertaking begun in 1554 and substantially complete by 1570, the other dominated by the biographical tomes published by Clarke and Fuller between 1650 and 1683. To identify Foxe as a biographer is to defy the convention which separates martyrology from the experimental vein of autobiography, and even biography. But Foxe, and more especially some of the independent sources which Foxe, like Clarke, ingested, was no less a biographer for being a martyrologist, both in respect paid to certain ethical conventions in the biographical tradition and in the attention paid to individuality and even idiosyncracy of character. As for Clarke, he was as much martyrologist as biographer, author of a *General martyrologie* which incorporated a potted version of Foxe and brought it up to date. But if we can distinguish between martyrology and biography with Clarke it is biography (or hagiography) which predominates. He was at pains to insist that the divines of the seventeenth century were in some sense themselves martyrs, but this served as little more than a polite fiction to bring these moderns within the scope of ecclesiastical history in the Eusebian tradition. So between Foxe and Clarke there was continuity, acknowledged in the congratulatory messages which accompanied Clarke's ambitious ventures: 'On our English Martyrs and Martyrologers, Master FOX and Master CLARKE'.[23]

But between Foxe and Clarke there also lies a chasm of eighty years, separating the definitive edition of *Acts and Monuments* from the earliest of Clarke's compilations, and a narrower gap of some forty years between the last events chronicled by Foxe and the first of Clarke's lives. Clarke's attempt to bridge the gap with sketchy accounts[23a] of the Elizabethans only draws attention to it. So far as their careers and reputations can be reconstructed from a variety of scattered sources, such Elizabethan divines as John More of Norwich, Percival Wiburn of Northampton, Eusebius Paget, Dudley Fenner, Thomas Wilcox the Londoner were as famous in their generation, at least locally, as Gouge or Sibbes or Preston in the next.[24] It is by no

---

[23] [A] *general martyrologie* (London 1677 ed) Sigs C2 –4 .
[23a] These resemble in length the mini-biographies of modern authors found in successive editions of Bale's *Catalogus* which I distinguish from 'edifying' biography.
[24] Patrick Collinson, *The Elizabethan Puritan Movement* (London 1967).

means clear that they were deficient in 'practical divinity' or untried as 'physicians of the soul'. Foxe himself was no mean practitioner.[25] But they were not the authors of books devoted to these matters, nor did they provide the subjects for biographies exemplifying their personal and pastoral attainments. We should not forget the memoir of Foxe himself, written in 1611 by his son Simeon, who deplored the recent neglect of biography which had robbed 'of their future memory these great men whose labours have won for us the blessings we enjoy.' But this did not see the light of day until 1641, when it was appended to the edition of *Acts and Monuments* of that year.[26]

Why was the biographical genre so slow to revive and mature? The keen interest in living examples which Foxe both expressed and aroused had not expired. In 1576 a letter-writer could easily turn his hand to a Foxeian character sketch: 'But now I will tell yow of a good byshope indeed. There is not far from Asheby a pore town called Mesham; the most parte there are colliers. They have had one Peter Eglesall, a grave and godly man, to their minister . . .' And so we proceed with the colourful detail of 'two auncient old men above three-score years a pece', riding with their preacher to the bishop to assure him that they would still have been ignorant and obstinate papists if it had not been for his ministrations and example.[27] The more militant and organised of the Elizabethan puritans continued and extended Foxe's history through the 'registering' of the troubles of their party, including biographical and autobiographical narratives. But these materials were assembled for a narrowly polemical, even political purpose. They remained for the most part in manuscript and were without literary impact.[28] Throughout the Elizabethan period and its immediate sequel the only steps taken to perpetuate the memory of a deceased divine of note, and that somewhat rarely, was to promote the posthumous publication of his writings.[29] And even then, when the

[25] J. F. Mozley, *John Foxe and his Book* (London 1940) pp 105-7.
[26] *Ibid*, pp 1-11. The Latin version of the *Life* is in BL MS Lansdowne 388.
[27] *Letters of Thomas Wood, Puritan, 1566-1577*, ed Patrick Collinson, *BIHR* Special Supplement 5 (1960) pp 20-1.
[28] Partially published in *A parte of a register* (n.p. 1593?); the remainder, comprising part of the Morrice MSS in Dr Williams's Library, calendared in Albert Peel (ed) *The Seconde Parte of a Register* 2 vols (Cambridge 1915). See my 'John Field and Elizabethan Puritanism', in *Elizabethan Government and Society*, ed S. T. Bindoff, J. Hurstfield, C. H. Williams (London 1961) pp 127-62.
[29] The prototype was perhaps John Day's publication *The worckes of T. Becon, whiche he hath hytherto made and published*, 3 pts (London 1560-4). The *Works* of William Perkins were published posthumously in eds of 1597, 1600, 1603, 1605, 1609 and 1613, this

collected *Works* of such a model Christian and divine as Edward Dering were printed (in 1590, 1597 and 1614) no information about his life was included. It was left to Holland in his *Herωologia anglica* of 1620 to publish (alongside a portrait of Foxe) a sensitive engraving of Dering which would presumably have been available to his editors if there had been sufficient interest in the personality of the original to have employed it. This was forty-four years after Dering's premature death.[30]

Literary historians will tell us that biography is more of a seventeenth-century than a sixteenth-century phenomenon.[31] This is a reminder that the question is broader than the scope of this occasion but the statement is too circular to provide an explanation. A more satisfactory if partial answer to our problem may be that for the three generations which intervened between the Elizabethan settlement and the puritan commonwealth the bible and Foxe between them entirely satisfied the demand for edifying biographical history. Foxe was their Plutarch. He was read not once but repeatedly, and devotionally. Ignatius Jourdain, mayor of Exeter in the 1620s (and we know this from Clarke) read Foxe seven times over, and the bible above twenty times.[32] Clarke's *Lives* contain examples of references to episodes in Foxe so cryptic as to suggest that a knowledge of the context could be assumed, as with scripture itself.[33] So the missing generation was hidden in the long shadow cast by the *Book of Martyrs*. Although for the Elizabethans this was nearly contemporary history, the new dispensation had a distancing effect, and this sense of distance could not be experienced with respect to the Elizabethan and Jacobean saints

---

last the definitive three volume edition, several times reissued. Richard Greenham's *Works* were published in 1599 and were in their fifth edition by 1612. *The works of that late divine Mr T. Wilcocks* were published in 1624. Wilcox had died in 1608.

[30] [Patrick] Collinson, *A Mirror of Elizabethan Puritanism: [the Life and Letters of 'Godly Master Dering']*, Friends of Dr Williams's Library 17th Lecture 1963 (London 1964).

[31] 'Even biography was an undeveloped art during the reign of the first Elizabeth.': Margaret Bottrall, *Every Man a Phoenix: Studies in Seventeenth-Century Autobiography* (London 1958) p 1.

[32] *Ten eminent divines* p 453.

[33] 'If the Word will not prevaile, the Cross will come, and make a *Hooper*, and a *Ridley* imbrace one another.' (*Ten eminent divines* p 260.) The reference is to the letter from bishop Ridley to bishop Hooper, written from prison in 1555, John Foxe, *Acts and Monuments*, ed S. R. Cattley, 6 (London 1838) pp 642–3. In a codicil to his will made in 1636 Robert Harris told his wife: 'You shall find the substance of that I would say to you printed in the Book of *Martyrs* vol. 2 p. 1744, to wit in John Careless his letter to his wife: keep the Book and often read the letter.' (*Ten eminent divines* p 322.)

themselves until after the 1640s, another watershed. Then again in substantial tomes which physically matched the *Book of Martyrs* the reader would encounter the 'ancients', 'the good old puritans of England'. Of the Suffolk preacher John Carter and his wife it was said that their clothing was 'of the old fashion', so that visitors came away saying that they had seen 'Adam and Eve, or some of the old Patriarchs'. Of William Gouge it was noted that 'towards his latter end' he did 'much resemble the Picture that is usually made for *Moses*. Certainly he was the exact *Effiges* of *Moses* his spirit.' Robert Harris, master of Trinity College Oxford in the interregnum, 'much bewayled the vast difference both in garb and practice betwixt new and old professors' and Richard Blackerby's biographer thought that he would have been amazed if he could have lived beyond the restoration to see 'the professors' garbs' in the wealthier congregations.[34] To be canonised the old puritan way had to be historicised, and to historicise it was to canonise it.

Further reasons for the late flowering of puritan biography will suggest themselves if we dismember the *Lives* into their component sources.[35] The most material were funeral sermons. Others included prefaces to books containing biographical information, spiritual letters, diaries, and collections of sayings on matters of conscience, preserved in the conventional form of 'To one who asked him . . . he said . . .'[36] The sayings were readily converted into improving and diverting anecdotes which influence the somewhat episodic rhythm of many of the lives. Here is an example from the life of John Carter:

> There dwelled in that Parish a Tanner, that was a very godly man, and one that had much familiar society with Mr *Carter*. This man as he was very busie in Tawing of a Hide with all his might, not so much as turning his head aside any way: Mr *Carter* coming by accidentally, came softly behinde him, and merrily gave him a

[34] *Ibid* pp 7–8, 114–15, 316; *Lives of sundry eminent persons* p 64.
[35] Haller, pp 100–6.
[36] The sayings of Richard Greenham were celebrated. *Godly instructions for the due examination and direction of all men* was printed in 1598 and *Short rules sent to a gentlewoman* in 1621. John Rylands Library, Rylands English MS 524 contains a large collection of Greenham's sayings, apparently recorded by Arthur Hildersham. Ignatius Jourdain's biographer records: 'There is a somewhat like saying of Mr Greenhams, and possibly Mr Jurdaine might borrow it thence, it suiting so well the temper of his spirit.' (*Ten eminent divines* p 481.) In 1659 Samuel Clarke published *Golden apples. Or, seasonable and serious counsel from the sanctuary to the rulers of the earth, held forth in the resolution of sundry questions, and cases of conscience about divisions, schisms, heresies, and the tolleration of them, gathered from the writings of twenty divines.*

little clap on the back: the man started, and looking behinde him suddenly, blushed, and said, Sir, I am ashamed that you should find me thus: To whom Mr *Carter* replied, *Let Christ when he comes finde me so doing:* What (said the man) doing thus? *Yes* (said Mr *Carter* to him) *faithfully performing the Duties of my Calling.*[37]

All these were available to Clarke either as raw materials or, more commonly, in the form of finished biographies, some of them written or even published somewhat earlier in the century by such polished hagiographers as Thomas Gataker, others prompted by the advertisements which Clarke inserted in successive volumes: 'I intend not . . . to sit downe here, but to make some further progress in writing the lives of others of Gods Worthies: Wherefore my request is to all such as can furnish me with materials for the continuance of the blessed Memorials of their deceased friends, and for the publick good, and utility of the Church, to send them in to me . . .'[38]

Of these sources only the spiritual letters seem to have been deliberately preserved from as early as the middle years of Elizabeth.[39] Biographical prefaces were a novelty of the early seventeenth century and themselves reflective of heightened biographical interest. The clue to the problem must lie in the funeral sermons on the one hand and in the collected sayings of notable 'physicians of the soul' and diaries on the other. The sayings were a by-product of the pastoral art of resolving cases of conscience, and although this art was practised from the earliest years of the reformation it was only with the turn of the century that the theology of conscience, puritan casuistry, became systematised as a pastoral science and in the literature which began with Perkins's pioneering *Cases of conscience* and culminated in Baxter's *Christian directory.*[40] The recording of case-book morality was but one

[37] *Ten eminent divines* pp 11–12.

[38] *Second part of the marrow* (1675 ed) Sig A2v.

[39] Examples are Edward Dering's *Certaine godly and comfortable letters*, printed in 1590 and also extant in manuscript in Kent Archive Office, MSS Dering U 350 C/1 and 2; and Thomas Wilcox's *A profitable, and comfortable letter for afflicted consciences: written and sent . . . 1582* (London 1584?) and *Large letters. Three in number, for the instruction of such, as are distressed in conscience* (London 1589). A large collection of Wilcox's spiritual letters was still extant in manuscript in the late seventeenth century and is described in Dr Williams's Library MS Morrice I pp 617(2), (4).

[40] [I.] Breward, ['William Perkins and the Origins of Puritan Casuistry'], in *Faith and a Good Conscience: (Papers Read at the Puritan and Reformed Studies Conference, 18th–19th December 1962)]* (London 1963) pp 5–17; *The Work of William Perkins*, ed I. Breward, *Courtenay Library of Reformation Classics* 3 (Appleford, Abingdon 1970).

manifestation of the growth of a system of practical divinity in which the developed tradition of biography eventually took its own place: a programme to satisfy the desire expressed by Francis Bacon 'that a man may be warranted in his particular actions, whether they be lawful or not.'[41] It was the discipline of self-warranting by means of regular self-examination which produced the puritan diary. But while these sources sometimes yielded invaluable information, directly or indirectly, they were not determinative of the structure or intention of the biographies.

Published funeral sermons, which connected more directly with the biographies, made their appearance at about the same time as the earliest literature of puritan casuistry, and only became a staple of the book trade in the second and third decades of the seventeenth century. The funeral sermon was another sign of a quickened interest in individual conduct and in exemplary models. But as something of a cuckoo in the protestant nest it had a delayed domestication in the puritan tradition: a matter to be explored in the second part of this paper.

II

Protestant and puritan biography served two major as well as any number of subsidiary purposes. The merits of the exemplary life were a recommendation of the faith in which the life was pursued and triumphantly concluded. This was a theological purpose and, often, more crudely a partisan purpose, butressing protestantism against catholicism, as in Foxe, or puritan orthodoxy against sectarianism, as in Clarke. But there was also a practical and ethical purpose, within the economy of casuistry: the conscience of the dead available for the instruction of the living. 'We must eye them for imitation. We must look upon the best, and the best in the best.'[42] Either way the emphasis was on character, active in rational moral choice. Of the divine Samuel Crook we learn that his entire life was 'but one continued commentary upon his doctrine, and an exemplary sermon consisting of living words, or of words translated into works.'[43] Of Robert Harris: 'He lived religion, while many only make it the subject of their discourses.'[44] Of Julines Herring: 'His sermons, preched in the congre-

[41] Quoted, Breward, *The Work of William Perkins*, p 61.
[42] *Ten eminent divines* Sig A3r.
[43] *Ibid* p 30.
[44] *Ibid* p 303.

gation, were printed in his conversation.'[45] It must have been an assumption of this as of any protestant discourse that (to quote Perkins) 'all actions that please God must be done in faith' and have their ground in the word of God.[46] But there was often no occasion or means to spell this out, so that the stress appears in practice to fall the other way, life validating faith.

Since its descriptive content is more ethical than theological it is not surprising that this literature contains many reminders of the Erasmian 'philosophy of Christ', or rather of older voices underlying Erasmus. Somewhere not far away is the moral framework of Plutarch and the general currency of classical ethics in their Aristotelian formulation, so essential to Plutarch. The remainder of this paper will advance the thesis that the ethics of protestant and puritan biography were the ethics of Aristotle transposed, a surprising discovery if we regard Aristotelian man and Pauline man as opposites; by no means startling if we remind ourselves of the classical education which was still a necessary acquisition for divines as for any other educated persons, and of the diffusion of classical literature in translation.[47] Since Sir George Paule in writing his *Life of Whitgift* of 1611 chose Plutarch, Suetonius and Tacitus for his models, it was natural that he should make moderation and restraint the leading motifs of Whitgift's character and of his conduct of ecclesiastical affairs. The fact that Whitgift was 'choleric' and quick-tempered was too notorious to be concealed, but had somehow or other to be squared with the general reputation of a 'grave and prudent' archbishop.[48]

These influences were not absent even from the character studies in Foxe's *Book of Martyrs*.[49] At first sight this looks unlikely. What more certain to smother the Aristotelian mean than the smoky fires of Smithfield? What could be more extreme and in an inverted sense violent than to offer one's body to be burned, rather than to recant and reach a reasonable accommodation with the authorities? But whereas the issue of conscience which took the martyrs to the stake was a moral absolute and according to Aristotle's own reasoning no occasion

---

[45] *Thirty-two English divines* p 164.
[46] Quoted, Breward, *Faith and a Good Conscience,* p 11.
[47] H. S. Bennett, *English Books and Readers 1558 to 1603* (Cambridge 1965) cap 4.
[48] George Paule, *The life of John Whitgift* (London 1699 ed) pp 82, 90, 108–9. Compare [D. A.] Stauffer, [*English Biography before 1700*] (Cambridge, Mass., 1930) p 67.
[49] I follow the Townsend-Cattley ed of [*The Acts and Monuments of John*] Foxe, 8 vols (London 1837–41).

for applying the ethics of mediocrity,[50] on their long way to the fire these confessors had many opportunities to pursue the golden mean. According to the Foxeian narratives they were men and women of dispassionate moderation, temperate in speech, given to no extremes of behaviour, even in their utter extremity. Even Julius Palmer,[51] a prototypal Angry Young Man, always espousing the minority opinion, is said to have been 'of manners courteous without curiosity, of countenance cheerful without high looks, of speech pleasant without affectation.'[52] It is always the persecutors who fall into passions and furies: 'in the midst of his rage'—'the prolocutor in his ruff . . . how stoutly he stood'; and of the deaths of the persecutors: 'he desperately died'—'and so most miserably died'—'his horrible end'.[53] The martyrs are even physically appealing, thanks no doubt to a sensibly moderate diet. Hugh Latimer in his worn-out clothes and with halting gait is affectionately drawn as a decent old man who knows how to take care of himself.[54] In the gruesome appendix which relates the miserable fates of the persecutors in the manner of Lactantius there is a tale of how years later divine judgement fell upon a certain ploughman for gossiping about Latimer, whom he had seen burned, and for saying 'in despite' that he had teeth like a horse. In the same hour his son hanged himself, not far away.[55]

Some of the martyrs are 'merry' and jest all the way to the stake. (We may recall that Sir Thomas More, who had been that way before, could 'see the humorous side of martyrdom', Chambers's comment[55a] on the famous 'mocks' with which he mounted the scaffold.) Thomas Rogers, woken betimes to 'break the ice' as the first of the martyrs says: 'Then if it be so I need not tie my points.'[56] In similar circumstances the portly Rowland Taylor hugs the pillar in his chamber and tells his cell-mate: 'O master Bradford, what a notable sway I should give if I were hanged!' And then on the way to burn in Suffolk he cracks his grisly joke about cheating the worms in Hadleigh churchyard of their expected 'jolly feeding' upon his 'great carcase'.[57]

[50] W. F. R. Hardie, *Aristotle's Ethical Theory* (Oxford 1968) cap 7.
[51] This narrative was reproduced as a discrete biography, 'The Life of Mr Julines Palmer', in Clarke's *General martyrologie* pp 475–81.
[52] Foxe, 8 p 202.
[53] *Ibid* pp 629, 633, 635, 637.
[54] See many passages in the account of Ridley and Latimer, *Ibid*, 7 pp 406–583.
[55] *Ibid*, 8 p 641.
[55a] R. W. Chambers, *Thomas More* (London 1938) p 347.
[56] Foxe, 6 p 609.
[57] *Ibid* pp 700, 696.

The fisherman Rawlins White of Cardiff, a kind of Grandpa Moses of the persecution, settles himself down at the stake to listen to the sermon to be preached before the faggots are lit, makes two stays for his elbows with a little straw, leans forward and gives 'good ear and attention'.[58] There is room for a little book on 'The Wit and Wisdom of the Marian Martyrs'.

These were all aspects of classical *apatheia*. Once in the flames there were further opportunities for the display of a kind of heroic indifference. Bishop Hooper washed his hands in the fire as though it had been in cold water.[59] Rogers was 'nothing moved' by the sorrowful sight of his wife and eleven children: that is to say, nothing moved from his purpose.[60] Bishop Ferrar said that if he were seen once to stir in the pains of burning no more credit should be given to his doctrine. 'And as he said, so he right well performed the same; for so patiently he stood, that he never moved.'[61] But this was not the unnatural *apatheia* of stoicism for which Plutarch found that he had no use.[62] The Marian martyrs felt pain but were not overcome or deterred by it. Theirs was a true Aristotelian courage, midway between cowardice and temerity. The point of it all, no doubt, was to vindicate the protestant religion. Seven thousand people were present not just to see Hooper die but to observe 'his behaviour towards death', and the question for them was the question which Foxe intended to resolve for his readers: did he die in true faith?[63] Nevertheless, the manner of recording these transactions has the power to suggest, for this reader at least, that these were also victories of character and for humanity.

In the world of Samuel Clarke, a century later, we are still in the thick of the Aristotelian virtues. And since Clarke wrote hack biographies of the likes of Alexander the Great, Pompey and Tamburlaine, it is a Plutarchan world too. 'Plutarcha cede', suggested one of his well-wishers in congratulatory verses prefacing one of his collections.[64] The qualities most often admired in the spiritual biographies are humility, modesty, and, once again, a sure instinct for the safe sure middle way, expressed in a wide variety of clichés.

[58] *Ibid* 7 p 32.
[59] *Ibid*, 6 p 611.
[60] *Ibid* p 612.
[61] *Ibid*, 7 p 26.
[62] D. A. Russell, *Plutarch* (London 1973) pp 84–5; Alan Wardman, *Plutarch's Lives* (London 1974) pp 107–8.
[63] Foxe, 7 p 656.
[64] *Second part of the marrow*, Sig B.

Samuel Crook was 'grave without austerity, pleasant without levity, courteous without dissembling . . . seldome the first speaker although he was best able to speak'.[65] John Carter 'never made Feasts, yet always had wholsome full and liberal Diet in his house.' 'He had a sharp wit, and was sweet, milde, affable, and pleasant in his conversation; yet were there not any of his most facetious passages, that did not savour of holiness.'[66] Thomas Gataker was commended for 'that low esteem he had of his own gifts', 'his freedome from ambition of outward advantages', 'his meek conversation with, and condescention to the meanest christians.'[67] Richard Capel was a 'constant and stable man . . . set up a sure Sea-mark.'[68] Robert Harris was 'grave without affectation, pleasant without levity';[69] Herbert Palmer 'neither wastfull nor covetous'.[70] Mrs Jane Ratcliff was 'a woman of a well composed spirit, discreetly advised'. As for humility, she had 'got it so by heart that there was no need of Art to make profession or ostentation of it.'[71]

A particular aspect of the restraint described in the *Lives* suggests a close parallel with the Erasmian evaluation of academic learning. As in the late medieval devotionist tradition to which Erasmus had given fresh expression, a consistent polemic was trained against the vanity of useless knowledge. Typically the divines of the biographies showed outstanding promise in their university careers. They were the ablest disputants, the best linguists, the 'choicest ornaments' of their colleges. But learning was never a source of pride. The model divine was 'one that did not vainly encrease his Liberary for ostentation but chose books for use.'[72] Knowledge of ancient languages was applied 'only upon necessary occasions, not for ostentation, to amuse . . . but for the more full, and clear opening of the Text.'[73] By a kind of 'holy Alchimy'[74] learning, having been acquired, had in a sense to be lost again, or at least lost to view, in the plain preaching of 'solid and savoury truths' to 'poor simple people that never knew what Religion meant.'[75] Of Robert Harris it was said that 'his chiefest Learning lay where he made

[65] *Ten eminent divines* p 44.
[66] *Ibid* p 8.
[67] *Ibid* pp 148–9.
[68] *Ibid* p 258.
[69] *Ibid* p 305.
[70] *Thirty-two English divines* p 200.
[71] *Ten eminent divines* pp 419, 443.
[72] *Ibid* p 156.
[73] *Ibid* p 27.
[74] *Ibid.*
[75] *Thirty-two English divines* p 177.

least shew of it in publick', and that he had 'learned to cancel his Art'.[76] If these reports are placed alongside the published output of some earlier writers in the puritan tradition they illuminate a situation which might otherwise appear problematical. The Elizabethan Edward Dering was reported to be the best Greek scholar of his time in Cambridge, but little enough of this learning obtrudes in his sermons and biblical commentaries, although they contain a denunciation of others who 'use the pulpit like a philosopher's chaire.'[77] Perkins in his *Art of prophesy* recalled the proverb: 'Artis etiam est celare artem.'[78]

Among the many saints enshrined in Clarke there appears but one extremist, the only life to resemble Malvolio or to approximate to the popular stereotype of later nonconformity. This was Ignatius Jourdain, a substantial merchant of Exeter, mayor and MP. Jourdain is described as 'for his temper . . . a man of a raised zeal, and *heroicall* spirit, one of those rare examples which the Lord giveth the world now, and then, and therefore his actions are not to be measured by an ordinary standard.' He was a man of exceptional and humourless severity, a relentless punisher of sin with the whip and the stocks, and the unsuccessful promoter of a law to punish adultery with death. When he moved this bill on the floor of the house of commons the members cried: 'Commit it, Mr Jourdain, commit it; upon which a great laughter was occasioned; whereupon he presently said unto them (in a zealous manner like himself) *Do you laugh when a man speaks for God's honor, and glory?* Upon which there was a more than ordinary silence in the House.'[79] Admittedly a 'private Christian' needed some exceptional, even 'heroical' quality to achieve canonisation, having none of the professional advantages of the divine. But even in this company Mr Jourdain, 'the wonder and *Phoenix* of his age', was the exception to prove the rule of 'mediocrity'.

There were historical and polemical reasons for the stress on moderation in Clarke. His divines all without exception espoused what may be called orthodox puritan opinions, in terms still a shade anachronistic for the times in which they lived, presbyterians or moderate episcopal men, rarely independents and certainly never

[76] *Ten eminent divines* pp 310–11.

[77] Collinson, *A Mirror of Elizabethan Puritanism*, pp 4–6.

[78] Quoted, Watkins p 7. I am indebted to Mr John Morgan of Cambridge University for alerting me to this theme.

[79] *Ten eminent divines* pp 480–1, 464, 477.

sectaries. When Simeon Ashe and John Wall wrote a commendatory epistle for one of Clarke's earliest ventures, in December 1649, they expressed interest in the further publication of the 'characters' of such as Preston, Sibbes, Dod and Hildersham who all their lives had 'kept a due distance from *Brownistical* separatism and were zealously affected towards the *Presbyterial* Government of the Church.'[80] Clarke himself might well complain of the odium cast upon some of the subjects of his *Lives*, 'as though they were Fanaticks, Anabaptists, . . . enemies to the State, Traytors, etc.'[81] In the circumstances of the 1650s, and even more after 1662, it became all the more desirable to insist on the general moderation of these worthies and on their detestation of schism. The life of Hildersham disclosed that he had been called 'the *Hammer* of Schismatickes'.[82] Clarke's own father, a minister in Warwickshire, was said to have 'mightily confuted' and 'reclaimed' Brownists, as far back as the 1580s.[83] Edmund Staunton called separatism 'England's incurable wound', but would always converse and communicate with those that 'were sound in the vitals of christian religion'.[84] 'Moderation' therefore was a keynote struck for a purpose, but the conventions of biography made it a particularly suitable polemical medium.

These discoveries may appear commonplace. The admirable qualities displayed by the puritan saints were not very distinct from those associated with Christian perfection in almost any age. That the biographies should make much of the 'catholic' moderation of the presbyterians is no more than we should expect. But the most striking feature of this literature has still to be mentioned. It is the fact that the conventional virtues of the godly life were represented as indeed virtues, not so noticeably the work of grace as inherent properties and achievements of human character, a suitable subject for admiration and even for eulogy. To recognise this is to see seventeenth-century religious biography in a new light and to link it very closely to the classical biographical tradition.

This will sound like heresy to anyone who supposes that the inevitable centrepiece of puritan biography was a story of the conversion of a naturally vicious and abandoned sinner, and to readers of Haller's *Rise of Puritanism* in particular. According to Haller, the

---

[80] *Lives and deaths of most of those eminent persons*, Sig d^v.
[81] *Ten eminent divines*, Sig A4^r.
[82] *Thirty-two English divines* p 120.
[83] *Ibid* p 129.
[84] *Lives of sundry eminent persons* p 170.

pattern to which the life of the elect was supposed to conform required an account of a sinful state 'from which the soul destined to be saved was called and after terrific struggle converted'; followed by the chronicle of a lifelong struggle against temptation, especially the temptation to despair: and culminating in a deathbed scene, 'one last terrific bout with Satan and then triumph and glory forever after.' Summaries follow of three of the *Lives* which conform more or less to this model and Haller concludes his analysis: 'We need not further multiply illustrations.'[85]

What the reader will not suspect is that in the majority of the lives chronicled by Clarke there is no mention of conversion at all, only casual references to a calling by grace, and little enough about a lifelong struggle to prove that calling. Although too much should not be made of this, it may be significant that two out of Haller's three conversion narratives, as well as other accounts of conversion which he did not mention, had their origins in Lancashire and neighbouring Cheshire.[86] For the north-west was a region polarised between the old and new faiths, where the pilgrimage of a puritan saint was more than likely to begin with conversion of, so to speak, a primary order, from one religion to the other. It is also from Lancashire that one of the most remarkable stories comes of the last 'terrific bout' with Satan, on the deathbed. The story was told because the Lancashire catholics had spread a tale of the failure of protestant faith *in extremis*.[87] These were special cases and the framework of reference was not that of interior spirituality. Narratives of conversion and of the dealings of God and Satan with the Christian, seen as it were from the inside, derive from the personal testimonies made by the members of gathered congregations as the condition of their admission, a procedure alien to the ecclesiology and practice of more 'orthodox' puritans.[88] Clarke's

[85] Haller pp 108–11.

[86] Conversion is a significant element in the following Lancashire and Cheshire lives: Robert Bolton (*Lives and deaths of most of those eminent persons*), Richard Rothwell (*Thirty-two English divines*), these two included by Haller among his examples, John Ball (*Lives of thirty-two English divines*), Richard Mather (*Lives of sundry eminent persons*) and John Bruen Esq of Bruen Stapleford, Cheshire (William Hinde, *A faithfull remonstrance of the holy life and happy death of John Bruen* (London 1641) and in *Second part of the marrow*). Haller's third example, Samuel Fairclough, born at Haverhill in Suffolk, provides the most elaborate conversion narrative outside of the north-west.

[87] The story comes from *A brief discourse of the christian life and death of Mistris Katherine Brettargh*. (See p 245 below.)

[88] Watkins pp 29–30. But non-sectarian puritans sometimes required a form of public renewal of baptismal vows as a condition of admission to the Lord's Supper. (See the *Life* of Samuel Fairclough in *Lives of sundry eminent persons* p 169.) Mrs Elizabeth

Lives have little to do with this interior world, known to us from the puritan diary and the spiritual autobiography into which it fed. The world of Bunyan is not the world of Samuel Clarke.

It would be foolish to suggest that Clarke's *Lives* indicate any theological divergence from the fundamentals of puritan religion, that they were not in some sense governed by the doctrines of covenanted grace, assurance and sanctification which were so incessantly expounded from the pulpit and in countless publications. But the doctrines were not explicitly taught in the biographies. If the godly were twice-born their biographers often neglect to mention the fact and proceed for much of their space to delineate the admirable intellectual and moral qualities with which the saints would appear to have been endowed from birth. The account of the early life of Herbert Palmer, a moderate presbyterian member of the Westminster Assembly, may be cited, not because its features are necessarily typical, but because it offsets the impression left by Haller. Palmer, we are told, 'had excellent natural parts, both intellectual and moral', and enjoyed 'the happiness of a prudent and pious eduction'. From his infancy he was 'addicted to the study both of religion and learning'. 'The *Symptomes* of Grace and Piety began betimes to put themselves forth to the view and observation of others, as soon almost as the exercise and use of reason; so that we may not without good ground esteem him sanctified from the Womb.' When little more than five years old he read the story of Joseph and wept. From a child he intended himself for the ministry and would not be deterred. In a lengthy biography of twelve thousand words, Palmer proves to be faultless, and in ways which could hardly be more puritanical. All this was presumptively the work of grace, but the emphasis is wholly on Palmer's faithfulness to God, not on what God may have wrought in him. He was 'subservient to the glory of God', maintained 'an even walking with God', 'wholly laid himself out for God', 'zealous and tenacious in things that concerned God's glory.'[89]

To sum up the impression gained from our survey of the world of Samuel Clarke: It was an encomiastic world, and this is not surprising, since the proper origins of this literature lay not in the internalised

---

Wilkinson, no separatist, composed a lengthy 'narrative' of 'God's gracious dealing with her soul' and sent it to Dr Robert Harris in order to give account of herself before admission to the Lord's Supper. But this was in the unusual circumstance of her regular parochial ministry being interrupted. (*Ten eminent divines* pp 515-24.)

[89] *Thirty-two English divines* pp 183-201.

A Magazine of Religious Patterns

doubts and fears of the tender conscience but in the public encomium. The most fruitful and influential source for the puritan biography was the funeral sermon, which I have already dubbed the cuckoo in the protestant nest. This specimen had hatched from the dubious egg of the classical panegyric, which was not laid by Luther or Calvin, nor yet by St Paul. So to the funeral sermon, as the heart of the matter, we finally come.

Originally not only funeral sermons but even the barest forms of prayers at burial were rejected, at least by the more extreme and austere of the early puritans. It was said that burial of the dead was an office belonging to every Christian and a 'surcharge' on the ministry. The *Admonition to the parliament* of 1572 compared funeral sermons to popish trentals 'whereout spring many abuses, and therfore in the best reformed churches, are removed.'[90] Since there was evidence even in the liturgy of the English congregation which had worshipped in Geneva in Mary's reign that this was not so,[91] a discussion followed between John Whitgift and Thomas Cartwright in the course of the mammoth engagement known nowadays as 'the Admonition Controversy'.[92] Under pressure, Cartwright shifted from an absolute objection to funeral sermons as superstitious in implication and socially discriminatory to the concession that it was desirable that notable men should have their public commendation, but that this should take the form of a civil oration and should not be confused with the office of preaching. Both Cartwright and the separatist Henry Barrow plausibly derived the funeral sermon from the burial orations of heathen orators, Cartwright remarking that the Christian oratory of Gregory Nazianzus 'savoured of the manner of Athens, where he was brought up.'[93]

But the godly laity, while deploring such popish funeral customs

[90] *An admonition of the Parliament* (London 1572), in *Puritan Manifestoes*, ed W. H. Frere and C. E. Douglas (London 1954 ed) p 28; *Seconde Parte of a Register*, 1 pp 132, 259, 2 p 45; *The Writings of Henry Barrow 1587–1590*, ed Leland H. Carlson, E[lizabethan] N[onconformist] T[exts] 3 (London 1962) pp 459–62; *The Writings of Henry Barrow 1590–1591*, ed Leland H. Carlson, ENT 5 (1966) p 83.

[91] W. D. Maxwell, *John Knox's Genevan Service Book* (London 1931) pp 56–7, 161–4. Variations in the Genevan tradition with respect to the burial service can be traced through *The Book of Common Order of the Church of Scotland*, ed G. W. Sprott (London 1901) p 80, *The Middelburgh Prayer-Book* (Middelburgh 1586) in *Reliquiae Liturgicae* 1, ed Peter Hall (Bath 1847) p 69, and *A directory for the publique worship of God* (London 1644) pp 73–4.

[92] *The Works of John Whitgift*, ed J. Ayre, PS (1851) 1 pp 250–1, 3 pp 361–80.

[93] *Works of Whitgift*, 3 p 375.

as the giving of blacks and the ringing of bells, commonly provided in their wills for a sermon to be preached at their burial.[94] Such sermons were doubtless a nearly universal institution in the Elizabethan church and social pressure soon made a general stand against them a peculiarity of some separatists. As for the funerals of notable preachers, these became occasions for triumphalism, with six brethren of the ministry to carry the bier, a memorable sermon, a large congregation, and lavish entertainment.[95] Nevertheless, individuals retained serious reservations, not on account of any inference of superstition, but for fear of flattery. Alas! Those who revealed that scruple ran the risk of having it added to their other virtues in the panegyric which was certain to follow their demise whether they desired it or not. Samuel Ward, 'the glory of Ipswich', came to John Carter's funeral with his mourning gown, ready to preach to the large congregation assembled, only to be told by Carter's children that their father had charged them 'and that upon his blessing' that there should be no sermon. 'For it may give occasion to speak some good of me that I deserve not and so false things may be uttered in the pulpit.' Ward went away disappointed, but preached his funeral sermon on the next lecture day at Ipswich 'to the great satisfaction of the whole Auditory. *Gloria fugentes sequitur.*'[96] The wealthy and munificent Richard Fishburne towards his end 'did divers times . . . grate upon the abuse of this custome of over-spicing the dead in large commendation' and begged his minister, Nathaniel Shute, to include nothing personal in his funeral sermon. He might have saved his breath. Shute could not disappoint 'the common expectation', and having told this story which only served to prove Fishburne's modesty, he then proceeded to speak of him to the length of twenty-one pages of text, specifying the large amounts bestowed on various charities, to the last penny.[97]

Once again life, or, in this case, death, anticipated the appearance of

[94] See, for example, the will of Basil Fielding, a Warwickshire gentleman (ob. 1584) which required that 'at the daie of my burriall a godly sermon be made by some godly learned man, moving the people to prayse God for his mercies bestowed on me in my lyfe and the contynuance thereof to my deathe, and for his comforte and victorye of faythe in a christian lief, and he to have for his paynes six shillings eight pence.' (PRO P.C.C. Will Registers Brudenell 5.)
[95] See accounts of the Suffolk funeral of Robert Walsh of Little Waldingfield in 1605 in *Winthrop Papers* 1 *1498–1628*, Massachusetts Historical Society (1929) pp 89, 153; and of the Chelsea funeral of William Bradshaw, in *Thirty-two English divines* p 51.
[96] *Ten eminent divines* p 20.
[97] [Nathaniel] Shute, *Corona charitatis.* [*The crowne of charitie*] (London 1626) pp 25–46.

a literature. Up to the end of Elizabeth's reign almost the only funeral sermons thought suitable for publication commemorated members of the nobility and notable gentry, and they appeared with plain and formal titles. All others were allowed to waste their sweetness on the desert air. But in 1602 a little book was published which pointed to a new literary fashion and perhaps even initiated it. This was *Deaths advantage little regarded*, containing the two funeral sermons preached at the burial near Liverpool of a lady remarkable only for her religion, Mrs Katherine Brettergh, together with an account of her life.[98] Mrs Brettergh was a young person of twenty-two at the time of her death, married but two years, and she was the sister of John Bruen, a Cheshire squire who would later provide the subject for one of the earliest and most elaborate of puritan biographies.[99] *Deaths advantage* proved to be a best-seller and went into its fifth edition by 1617. From the beginning of James's reign there was a steady flow of published funeral sermons honouring the memories of divines and notable 'private Christians'. A peak was reached in 1619 with at least eleven such publications,[100] and some preachers, such as Thomas Gataker, began to acquire a special reputation not only as funeral preachers but as the authors of funeral sermons. The floodgates were not yet opened as they would be with the general torrent of publication in the forties and fifties. By a rough count there were some seventy separate funeral sermons printed between 1600 and 1640 which survive,[101] a tally which must surely have

---

[98] *Deaths advantage little regarded, and the soules solace against sorrow. Preched in two funerall sermons at Childwal in Lancashire at the buriall of Mistris Katherine Brettargh the third of Iune 1601*. The preachers were William Harrison and William Leigh. The institution of two sermons, separated by dinner, seems to have been a north-country custom— see my article 'Lectures by Combination: Structures and Characteristics of Church Life in the 17th-Century England', *BIHR* 48 (1975) pp 201–2. The second sermon is followed by a separate title: *A brief discourse of the christian life and death of Mistris Katherine Brettargh*. There is also an engraved portrait of the lady.

[99] William Hinde, *A faithful remonstrance of the holy life and happy death of John Bruen of Bruen-Stapleford in the county of Chester, Esquire* (London 1641); reprinted in *Second part of the marrow* pp 80–104.

[100] John Barlow, *The joy of the upright man*; John Barlow, *The true guide to glory*; Samuel Crooke, *Death subdued. Or, the death of death* (for Queen Anne); Stephen Denison, *The monument, or tombe-stone* (for Mrs Elizabeth Juxon); Thomas Gataker, *The benefit of a good name and a good end*; Thomas Gataker, *Pauls desire of dissolution and deaths advantage* (for Mrs Rebekka Crisp); Timothy Oldmayne, *Gods rebuke in taking from us Sir E. Lewkenor* (of Denham, Suffolk); John Preston, *The patriarchs portion* (for Sir T. Reynell); John Preston, *A sermon preached at the funeral of Mr Arthur Upton Esquire in Devon*; William Sclater, *Three sermons* (including a funeral sermon).

[101] This figure has been arrived at after a cursory perusal of *STC* and investigations in the British Library, Dr Williams's Library and the library of New College, London (shortly before its dispersion). I am particularly grateful to the librarian of New

been exceeded in the following twenty years. But in 1640 itself there was a kind of apotheosis with the publication of an ambitious folio volume containing no less than forty-seven funeral sermons, *The house of mourning*.[102] By this time the convention of curious titles was formalised: *Deliverance from the king of feares. Or, Freedom from the feare of death; The destruction of the destroyer. Or, The overthrowe of the last enemie; Sinnes stipend and gods munificence.*

But the preachers still assumed a defensive tone and sometimes paraded ancient authorities to justify their enterprise: not so much the epistle to the Hebrews ('and these all having obtained a good report through faith') as Cicero, Seneca, Pliny, Basil and Gregory Nazianzus, a great standby.[103] Moreover among the puritans a strict convention required that what was termed the 'testimony' or 'commendation' should be detached from the sermon proper, so partly meeting Cartwright's requirement that epideictic oratory should not impersonate preaching.[104] There were habitual ways of marking the transition from the sermon to what was no doubt often regarded as the major business: 'And now brethren beloved and longed for (I say now) that I have finished my course, ended the text, and closed up the booke, give me leave a little to turne me to the dead . . .'[105] 'Thus much of my text. Give mee leave to adde a fewe words about the particular occasion of this our meeting.'[106] 'And so I fall downe from the text to the occasion.'[107] The change of gear was sometimes a further occasion

College, the Reverend Dr G. F. Nuttall, for his kindness in enabling me to look into the remarkable collection of some 1900 funeral sermons amassed in the last century by Mr Charles Godwin of Bath and among the holdings of that Library.

[102] *Threnoikos. The house of mourning. Delivered in XLVII sermons, preached at funeralls of divers faithfull servants of Christ. By Daniel Featly Richard Sibbs Martin Day Thomas Taylor and other reverend divines* (London 1640). However the subject of this collection is mortality. Few of the preachers and fewer still of the deceased are identified and the motive of 'memorial' or 'testimonial' is largely absent.

[103] See especially the epistles to two of Thomas Gataker's publications: *Two funeral sermons much of one and the same subiect: to wit, the benefit of death* (London 1620); *The decease of Lazarus Christs friend* (for Mr John Parker) (London 1640). There are quotations from Nazianzus in I.F., *A sermon preched at Ashby de la Zouch* (for Elizabeth, countess of Huntingdon) (London 1635).

[104] See, for example, [Robert] Harris, in his funeral sermon for Sir Anthony Cope of Hanwell, *Samuels funeral* (London 1618) Sig A4: 'Onely I could wish that our age would distinguish betwixt funerall orations and funeral sermons, as former ages have done, and not confound so different things.'

[105] William Leigh, *The soules solace against sorrow*, with *Deaths advantage*, p 69.

[106] Nicolas Guy, *Pieties pillar. Or, a sermon preched at the funerall of Mistresse Elizabeth Gouge* (London 1626) p 37.

[107] Shute, *Corona charitatis*, p 24.

for critical reflection on the common abuse of flattery: 'I professe first to you, that I have often greved at the licentiousnesse of my brethren in this kind.'[108] Alternatively the 'testimony' could be wholly separated from the sermon and published as a separate item, or as a preface.[109] With Mrs Brettergh it appears as a freestanding biography with separate title page: *A brief discourse of the christian life and death of Mistris Brettargh*. Such a 'relation' or 'true narration' was sometimes contributed by a husband or other relative of the deceased,[110] reminding us of how close we are to the 'testimony' of the funerary inscription, still with us in an attenuated form. Puritan funerary monuments were sometimes expressive of a triumphalism strangely out of keeping with the humility with which the godly dead had been credited in life.[111]

Haller knew that the funeral sermon and more especially its testimonial 'lean-to' fed into puritan biography,[112] but he was insensitive to the implications of this parentage when he represented the *Lives* as typically stories of conversion and spiritual struggle. Detached from the sermon, or only loosely associated with it as a kind of 'use' or application of the text, the testimony was not only free to become in essence an encomium in the classical manner: it was almost obliged to assume this shape for want of any other model to follow. Reformed theology was an accidental, not a substantial element in these orations. Consequently the preachers were sometimes conscious of stepping well outside their proper role into unfamiliar and uncongenial territory. Robert Harris began his testimony to his patron, Sir Anthony Cope of Hanwell, by explaining that 'as I never flattered him living, so I will not deifie him (as the Heathens did their Patrons) being dead. He had his wants, his faults, nor did wee concurre in all opinions.' But

---

[108] Richard Stock, *The churches lamentation for the losse of the godly* (for Lord John Harrington) (London 1614) p 61.

[109] See, for example, [Thomas] Wilson, *Christs farewell [to Jerusalem and last prophesie]* (for Dr Colfe, sub-dean of Canterbury) (London 1614) Sig A4.

[110] See, for example, the 'short relation' added by the husband of Mrs Mary Gunter to the funeral sermon preached by Thomas Taylor, *The pilgrims profession* (London 1633). From a much earlier date one may recall a similar office performed for his wife by the moralist Philip Stubbs: *A chrystal glass for christian women. Containing a most excellent discourse of the godly life and death of Mrs Katherine Stubs, who departed this life in Burton upon Trent in Staffordshire the 14th December* (London 1591). The fame of Stubbs suggests that he may have set the fashion followed a decade later with the elaborate commemoration of Mrs BretterGh.

[111] I may refer to my remarks on the tomb of Sir Edward Lewkenor of Denham, Suffolk (ob. 1605) in my essay 'Magistracy and Ministry: a Suffolk Miniature', to be published in 1977 as part of a *Festschrift* for Geoffrey Nuttall.

[112] Haller pp 101–2.

this was no way out of a classic *circulus vitiosus*. Harris had achieved only a subtler brand of flattery. In life when he had preached sharply against his patron's sins Cope would say: 'Goe on, spare us not . . .' What could be worthier of praise and imitation than that?[113]

Most funeral preachers were not over-subtle in their eulogies. In the words of Donald Stauffer, who was not appreciative of this grossly repetitious, heavily stylised rhetoric, 'they damned with great praise.'[114] 'An anniversary to his fame' is a phrase which appears in one title.[115] A wealthy London merchant is 'a man of a thousand'.[116] Of a twelve-year old girl it is said: 'She hath deserved praise, having not onely done vertuously, but exceeded all others of her sexe and age.'[117] Goodness is the sovereign word. 'I say but this, God's Church in him hath lost a good Minister, this Parish a good Pastor, his Wife a good Husband, Schollers a good Patron, the poore a good friend, and we all a good neighbour.'[118] 'He was first bonus vir, secondly bonus Christianus, thirdly bonus Theologus, fourthly bonus Pastor,'[119] The question asked of old 'Why callest thou me good?' seems for the purpose of these occasions to have been forgotten; and with it that other question 'What has Athens to do with Jerusalem?'

Allow me to admit that when this paper was first proposed the inclusion of 'Erasmian' in the title was little more than a ploy, a wedding garment to preserve the puritans of the seventeenth century from being cast into outer darkness from a feast dedicated to 'Renaissance and Renewal'. But after all there has turned out to be something in it. In his *Paraclesis* Erasmus put his own rhetorical question which has always been at hand throughout this discussion: 'Moreover what else is the philosophy of Christ, which He himself calls a rebirth [*renascentia*], than the restoration of human nature, originally well formed?'[120] But knowing Erasmus, as we must all feel that we do, a little, he would surely have been disconcerted by the volume of the response which has been measured in this paper: too indigestible to be a truly 'godly feast'. In a sense only one pattern for living was needed. And if living

[113] Harris, *Samuells funerall*, Sig A4v.
[114] Stauffer p 89.
[115] Shute, *Corona charitatis*.
[116] Gataker, *The decease of Lazarus*, p 33.
[117] John Bryan, *The vertuous daughter* (Mistress Cicely Puckering, ob. 1636) (London 1640) p 10.
[118] Richard Pecke, *Christs watch word. Occasioned on the funerall of the truly reverend M. Laurence Bodley* (London 1635) p 1.
[119] Wilson, *Christs farewell*, Sig A5.
[120] Olin p 100.

examples were called for, two or three were sufficient: not a whole 'magazeen of religious patterns'. Erasmus would probably wish to be exempted from parentage of what has turned out to be a chapter in *The Rise of Moralism*,[121] a somewhat depressing foretaste of the routinisation of the puritan spirit which lay in the future. It was, after all, in the future that the literature reviewed in my paper was to do its work. My copy of Clarke's *Marrow of ecclesiastical history*, picked up in the Charing Cross Road in 1961, carries the inscription: 'Mary Estwicks book given her by old Mr Williams of Peldon which she give to Elizabeth Estwick after her Death'; and in a nineteenth-century hand 'M. Hudson's Book'.[122]

University of Kent

[121] I quote from the title of the book by C. F. Allison, *The Rise of Moralism. The Proclamation of the Gospel from Hooker to Baxter* (New York 1966).
[122] I am indebted to my colleague Miss Marion O'Connor for a number of helpful comments on this paper.

THE RENAISSANCE TRADITION IN THE REFORMED CHURCH OF SCOTLAND[1] (PRESIDENTIAL ADDRESS)

by JAMES K. CAMERON

IN the sixteenth century Scotland was in close conscious relation with the continent. In international politics she had through the dynastic connections of her royal house acquired a crucial importance, and in ecclesiastical, academic, and literary spheres that relationship had never before and perhaps has never since been quite so intimate or so fully developed. The end of the Auld Alliance in 1560 did not weaken although it may have changed these ties. Indeed they were in many ways strengthened. In ever increasing numbers the sons of Scottish nobility went abroad in the furtherance of their general education and experience of the world. Almost every university in Europe was at some time visited by Scottish scholars and almost every educated Scot who in this century achieved distinction in religion, education or politics had spent some time at one or more of the great centres of learning. Nor was this traffic one way. Scotland had its modest share of travellers from overseas in the early days of the grand tour, and although only a few itineraries have so far come to light there is ample evidence in surviving *alba amicorum* and in the university rector's books that a visit to the northern kingdom and an extended period of residence at one of its universities was unexceptional.[2]

Through such long established channels humanist influence first began to make itself felt in the early decades of the century, but it was not until plans were set out for the foundation of St Mary's College in St Andrews in the 1530s that 'the most notable attempt to introduce

[1] I am grateful to several colleagues for help in the preparation of this paper, in particular to Dr J. S. Alexander and Dr S. W. Gilley.
[2] [T.] McCrie, [*Life of Andrew*] *Melville* (Edinburgh 1856) pp 467–71, provides a list of foreign students at Scottish universities which could now be considerably enlarged. See also [J. K.] Cameron, *Letters of [John] Johnston [c. 1565–1611] and [Robert] Howie [c. 1565–1645]* (Edinburgh 1963) pp xiii–xv; [M.] Sieber, 'Die Universität Basel [im 16 Jahrhundert und ihre englischen Besucher]' *Basler Zeitschrift*, 55 (Basel 1956) pp 75–112.

humanism in Scotland was made'.[3] With the appointment of Archibald Hay as provost in 1546 it seemed for a brief moment that the humanist dream to have established in St Andrews a trilingual college primarily concerned with the renewal of the church might come to fruition. A close relative of the powerful Beaton family,[4] Hay was intimately connected with humanist circles in France and had there published elaborate plans for the cardinal's college, but died within fifteen months of taking up office.[5] His programme was not to be realised until much later in a much altered form and in a radically different ecclesiastical climate. Likewise a decade or so later the efforts to lay the foundations of humanist education in Edinburgh by bishop Reid of Orkney were halted by his death and had to await fulfilment for thirty years.[6] That there was in fact 'no little sympathy' for humanism in influential circles in the pre-reformation period despite an unfavourable political situation has been well illustrated by Durkan in a series of periodical articles.[7] The renaissance in Scotland was in its origin 'not merely a revival of learning but also a revival of moral concern'. What really interested Hay and Reid and many others 'was reform within the household of the faith'.[8] In this way they show themselves heirs to one of the central themes of much continental humanism—educational reform as the foundation of the Christian life—which received its finest literary exposition in the works of Erasmus. The twin ideals of renaissance and renewal in the church formed the legacy of the pre-reformation humanist reformers to the reformed church in Scotland in the second half of the century.

Renaissance and renewal are recurring themes in the history of the church from the days of the apologists in the second and third centuries down to the challenges of modernism and liberalism in the nineteenth and twentieth centuries, and in this paper I propose to examine the revival of learning in the sixteenth century as it affected one section of the reformed church.

---

[3] [J.] Durkan, 'The Beginnings of Humanism [in Scotland]', *IR* 4 (1953) p 14; [A. I.] Dunlop, *Acta* [*Facultatis Artium Universitatis Sanctiandree*] (Edinburgh 1964) p lv.

[4] See further J. Herkless and R. K. Hannay, *The Archbishops of St. Andrews*, 3 and 4 (Edinburgh 1910 and 1913).

[5] Durkan, 'Beginnings of Humanism' p 14; Dunlop, *Acta*, p lxii.

[6] Durkan, 'Beginnings of Humanism', pp 16-17; [D.] Horn 'The Origins [of the University of Edinburgh'], *University of Edinburgh Journal*, 22 (Edinburgh 1965-6) pp 213-25, 297-312.

[7] *IR* 4 pp 5-23; 'Education [in the Century of the Reformation]', *IR* 10 (1959) pp 67-90; 'The Cultural Background [in Sixteenth Century Scotland]' *IR* 10, pp 382-439.

[8] Durkan 'Beginnings of Humanism', p 17.

The renaissance tradition in Scotland

That the renaissance had a profound effect in bringing into existence the reformed or Calvinist churches hardly needs to be mentioned. Zwingli, Bucer, Farel, Calvin, Beza, Knox, were all in their youth inspired by the ideals of humanism and all in the development of their religious ideas owed much to the study of the scriptures in the original languages and of the Greek and Latin fathers, facilitated by the editions of Erasmus and others that were issuing from the presses of Paris and Basel, Antwerp and Geneva, and in conjunction with the great wealth of classical literature which rejuvenated and enriched so much contemporary thinking. These studies in their turn did much to foster the ideals of sound learning based on the appeal *ad fontes*, and of moral integrity based on the understanding of man as a responsible being created in the image of God. It should not be forgotten in these days of political and economic emphasis that the reformation in Scotland was humanist and that to a considerable part humanism in Scotland was Calvinist. The role of the renaissance in that reformation has received scant attention from leading historians in this century though not by such worthy pioneers of modern Scottish ecclesiastical historiography as Thomas McCrie, David Laing and A. F. Mitchell.

Reform of education throughout the country is rightly recognised as one of the essential features of the reformation programme. In the *First Book of Discipline* the sections on the schools and universities exceed in length and in detail those devoted to any other topic.[9] Provision was to be made for a school in every parish, an arts college in every notable town and a radical reorganisation of all three mediaeval universities. Of the success of this scheme at the parish level Donaldson rightly remarks that although much work remains to be done 'on the whole the indications are that . . . great progress was made' and that by 1633 the proportion of parishes with schools was 'very high'.[10] The arts college may have had its native predecessor in the older grammar schools where 'in some of the more notable towns some familiarity with Greek and to a lesser extent with Hebrew was already a fact'.[11] Nevertheless the proposed colleges were not intrinsically a home product. An arts college or *schola publica* or

[9] [J. K.] Cameron, [*The First*] *Book of Discipline* (Edinburgh 1972) pp 54–61, 129–55.
[10] G. Donaldson, *The Scottish Reformation* (Cambridge 1960) pp 95–6.
[11] Durkan, 'Education' p 75. See also J. Grant, *History of the burgh schools of Scotland* (Glasgow 1876) pp 1–75; J. Edgar, *History of Early Scottish Education* (Edinburgh 1893) pp 107–24.

schola illustris which provided an intermediate programme for those between the ages of fifteen and twenty and preliminary to study in one of the higher faculties formed an essential part of the humanist education inaugurated by Zwingli in Zurich in 1525, followed by Bern in 1533, advocated by Gouvea for the Collège de Guyenne at Bordeaux in 1534, by Sturm for Strasbourg in 1538, by Baduel for Nîmes in 1542 and was followed by Basel in 1544, by Heidelberg in 1546, by Cordier in Lausanne in 1547 and by Calvin in Geneva in 1559.[12] A more obvious humanist lineage could scarcely be found, a fact which is borne out in the ordering of the graded Scottish course with its emphasis on Greek as the foundation of the study of rhetoric and ethics. It is worth remembering that Knox was in Geneva along with the retired Baduel when similar plans were being laid for Calvin's academy, and that John Row,[13] another of the authors of the *Book of Discipline*, had recently returned from many years on the continent and was skilled in the languages of the bible.

Like so much else this part of the reformers' 'devout imaginings' is often written off as nothing more than 'a paper scheme'. That, however, is too hasty a judgment. The first decades of the reformation were unsettled times hardly conducive to implementing far-sighted programmes, but before the century was out two such new colleges were in existence and several had been planned but failed to develop. The church did not intend that Scotland should lag behind the reformed churches in France[14] or the Low Countries[15] and if in the end Scotland did not have the number of colleges envisaged her sons played a prominent part in the life of the academies of Sedan, Saumur, Montauban, Leiden and Middelburg to name but a few.

A second and elaborately detailed part of the educational scheme dealt with the mediaeval universities and reflects both traditional and contemporary humanist ideas.[16] The plans were specifically laid out in relation to St Andrews and provided that one of the three colleges was to be devoted wholly to Hebrew, Greek and the exposition of

[12] Cameron, *Book of Discipline*, p 131; [P. D.] Bourchenin [*Etude sur les*]*Académies protestantes* [*en France au XVIe et au XVIIe siècle*] (Paris 1882); [H.] Meylan, *D'Erasme à Theodore de Bèze* (Geneva 1976) pp 191–9.

[13] Durkan, 'The cultural background' p 387.

[14] For details see Bourchenin, *Académies protestantes;* Meylan, *D'Erasme à Theodore de Bèze*, pp 191–9.

[15] J. J. Woltjer, in the introduction to *Leiden University in the Seventeenth Century*, ed Th. H. Lunsingh Scheurleer and G. H. Posthumus Meyjes (Leiden 1975) pp 1–19.

[16] Cameron, *Book of Discipline*, pp 137–43.

the scriptures. The philological basis of exegesis was stressed and the study of Greek was to include the reading of Plato as well as the new testament. The parallel with contemporary developments on the continent is unmistakable, but it is possible that the authors of this part of the *Book of Discipline* were also influenced by earlier plans for St Mary's College. John Douglas,[17] one of them, had studied in Paris, had a reputation for his knowledge of languages and as Hay's successor in the provostship had an unbroken connection with the college since 1547.

The projected university reforms had little immediate effect. The contemporary revision of both the arts and divinity statutes at St Andrews is markedly traditional,[18] yet the reformers' ideals were not abandoned or forgotten and were in time to come to maturity. In their programme for the renewal of the church education was to play a major role, education in accordance with the highest and finest aims of Christian humanism, education ordered according to a graded progression of studies especially in languages, rhetoric and moral philosophy, education freely available to all able to benefit from it for the service of the church and the nation. That was the legacy of 1560.

In the disturbed period that followed—the troublesome reign of Mary and the minority of James VI—the church continually sought to advance the cause of education at all levels and in conjunction with the privy council aimed to reform the universities. Conspicuous among those who took part was the celebrated George Buchanan. Prior to his return to Scotland soon after the reformation, Buchanan spent his life in humanist circles and in the teaching of the young. And although there may be some doubt as to the degree to which he accepted the theological doctrines of Calvin, Beza and Knox, there can be no doubt about his participation in the life of the church—he was moderator of the general assembly in 1566—or of his desire to further educational reform.[19]

Buchanan's outlook owed virtually everything to his experience in France, in particular Paris and Bordeaux, and to settings in which the principles of the *First Book of Discipline* took their rise. It is not

[17] Dunlop, *Acta* pp lxviii, clviii.
[18] R. K. Hannay, *The Statutes of the Faculty of Arts and the Faculty of Theology at the period of the Reformation* (St Andrews 1910) pp 56–66, 81–5.
[19] A new and authoritative biography of George Buchanan by professor I. D. McFarlane is in the press. I am grateful to professor McFarlane for permitting me to read his manuscript.

surprising that Buchanan and leading churchmen should be appointed in 1563 to serve on a commission set up by parliament to investigate the state of the university of St Andrews and to report on how best 'the tongues and humanity'[20] should be taught. All that has survived of the commission's work is Buchanan's *Opinion*,[21] and as one might have suspected it embodies principles that can be traced to Ste Barbe, the Collège de Guyenne and Strasbourg. The authors to be read, for example, are those beloved by the humanists: Terence, Cicero, Virgil, Horace, Ovid, Homer. His programme for theology, which he considers primarily as exegesis, is not nearly as ambitious as that of the *Book of Discipline*, but he does stress the study of Hebrew. With greater realism than his predecessors Buchanan was seeking to impart the outlook that had been formed on the continent and in his friendship with André de Gouvea, Nicolas de Grouchy, Elie Vinet and other men of letters. The commission had no effect on the university, nevertheless Buchanan's report is significant evidence that church leaders continued to see education along humanist lines as the essential foundation for the renewal of the church. His close association for the next fifteen years with churchmen and academics continued while he was tutor to the young James VI and, as his writings continued to circulate among his friends and to appear in print, his influence among the younger generation of Scottish scholars began to bear fruit.

A slight improvement in the general educational picture resulted from the statesman-like settlement reached between the government and the church in 1572 which in certain of its provisions reflected the principles of progressive education.[22] But it was not until the return of Andrew Melville from Geneva in 1575 that a decidedly marked interest in education for the ministry is seen in the activities of the general assemblies. In recent studies Andrew Melville's influence on the development of the church's polity and her relation with the state have been stressed and subjected to criticism almost to the total neglect of his contribution to education, yet it should not be forgotten that he was throughout his life an academic. For some thirty five years

---

[20] *Acts of the Parliaments of Scotland*, 2 (Edinburgh 1814) p 544.

[21] *Vernacular Writings of George Buchanan*, ed P. H. Brown, *Scottish Text Society*, 26 (Edinburgh 1892) pp 1–17; [R. G.] Cant, [*The University of*] *St. Andrews* (new ed Edinburgh 1970) pp 48–9.

[22] See for example the regulated periods in the education course for which financial support was to be given. *Acts and Proceedings of the General Assemblies of the Kirk of Scotland* (Edinburgh 1839) pp 214–15.

until deprived by king James, he was intimately connected with the universities of Glasgow and St Andrews and was the one person primarily responsible for the revitalisation of education in the service of church and state.[23]

For this long-delayed task Melville had undergone a remarkable apprenticeship. In ten years on the continent he had studied under royal lecturers and other eminent humanists at Paris and Poitiers, and at Geneva where he had also taught in Calvin's academy he had deepened his knowledge and understanding of classical and oriental languages and literatures, had enjoyed the friendship of Henri Estienne, Joseph Scaliger, Francis Hotman, Edmund Bonnefoy, Isaac Casaubon and Henry Scrimger, a fellow Scot and at one time Fugger librarian. All in all Melville was an ardent humanist as well as a devoted churchman.

Between 1575 and 1593 he instigated the complete restoration of the university of Glasgow,[24] the radical reorganisation of St Andrews, crowned with the establishment of St Mary's College as the nation's theological seminary,[25] and the reform of King's College, Aberdeen,[26] at the hands of his close friend and fellow humanist Alexander Arbuthnot, which, if we have regard to the scholars it nurtured in the 1580s must have been far more successful than has been generally admitted. Further Melville directly and through his colleagues and pupils was intimately associated with the foundation of the College of Edinburgh in 1582[27] and Marischal College in Aberdeen in 1593.[28]

Much has been made of Melville's advocacy of Ramism, which has possibly an earlier if somewhat elusive history in Scotland,[29] but equally if not more important is the impetus which he gave to the study of Greek and Hebrew, more especially Hebrew and the allied oriental languages of the bible. The basis of all theology was to be in the original texts in Hebrew, Aramaic, Syriac and the septuagint for the old testament, and Greek and Syriac for the new—a programme

---

[23] McCrie, *Melville*, caps 2, 4.

[24] Dr James Kirk has written a detailed account of Melville's tenure of the principalship of the university of Glasgow for a forthcoming history of that university of which Dr Durkan is a co-author. I am grateful to Dr Kirk for allowing me to read his section of this work in manuscript.

[25] Cant, *St. Andrews*, pp 50–8.

[26] [G. D.] Henderson, [*The Founding of*] *Marischal College* [*Aberdeen*] (Aberdeen 1947) p 11–15.

[27] Horn, 'The Origins' pp 302–8.

[28] Henderson, *Marischal College*, pp 21, 56–62.

[29] See further W. S. Howell, *Logic and Rhetoric in England 1500–1700* (New York 1961) pp 179–89.

which obtained uniformly in Scotland until little over a decade ago—and all instruction was to be in the hands of specialist teachers.[30] The expressed aim was not, of course, scholarship for its own sake, but that of the Christian humanists, the renewal of Christian life brought about by raising a highly qualified ministry learned in the scriptures. This feature was expressly written into the St Andrews *Nova Fundatio* of 1579. This is a university charter and yet it stated that four years after the introduction of the reforms no one was to be admitted a minister of word and sacraments or have cure of souls unless he had completed the course and had 'by rigorous examination' been found worthy.[31]

It is difficult to judge the level of Melville's success in St Andrews. But one must give full weight to the facts that the university drew its students from every part of the continent,[32] among them the son of Franciscus Junius[33] and that among Melville's contemporaries and pupils were scholars of such repute as Robert Rollock, the first principal of the university of Edinburgh.

It might well be argued that with three ancient universities undergoing radical reform Scotland should have been content. Yet the proposal for arts colleges was an essential part of the reformed scheme. Protestants in France, Switzerland, and the Low Countries, who shared the same tradition had already embarked on similar developments.[34] Had the *Book of Discipline* been implemented, Edinburgh would have had its college in 1562 and not twenty years later. The foundation of what is now the university of Edinburgh was due to the combined efforts of the church and the city, but especially the ministers and arose out of a desire to 'create a reservoir of learned and godly men . . . who could make the educational blueprints of the *Book of Discipline* a reality'.[35] Within the same decade plans were laid for the establishment of a college and university of Fraserburgh[36] and for Marischal College in Aberdeen.

---

[30] Cant, *St. Andrews*, pp 54–5.

[31] *Evidence . . . taken and received by the commissioners . . . for visiting the Universities of Scotland*, 3, *St. Andrews* (London 1837) p 184.

[32] See the incomplete lists given by McCrie, *Melville*, pp 467–9.

[33] Cameron, *Letters of Johnston and Howie*, p lix.

[34] Bourchenin, *Académies Protestantes;* Meylan, *D'Erasme à Theodore de Bèze*, pp 191–9; C. Borgeaud, *L'Académie de Calvin 1559–1798* (Geneva 1900);P. A. G. Dibon, *L'enseignement philosophique dansles universités néerlandaises à l'époque pré-cartésienne (1575–1650)* (Leiden 1954).

[35] Horn, 'The Origins' p 297.

[36] R. G. Cant, 'Scottish Paper Universities', *The Scots Magazine* (Dundee September–October 1945) pp 11–14; Henderson, *Marischal College*, pp 32–3.

We need not go into details. In his notable study on the foundation of Marischal College, the late G. D. Henderson offered ample proof that it was designed as a centre of humanistic influence and drew attention to passages in the foundation charter that do more than echo Erasmus.[37] By the end of the century an epoch-making transformation had taken place in higher education at a critical period. It was primarily through the efforts of the reformed church that native institutions were being established as channels of humanism. As Henderson remarked,[38] protestantism like humanism was individualistic and demanded that one should think for oneself, and it stressed the value of the individual. The intellectual demand of Calvinism on its followers is reflected in the educational programme of its churches and that educational programme is fundamentally the humanist one.

Important as it may be to look at the progress of the plans for educational reform and their implementing, it is equally necessary to discover to what extent the humanist tradition and outlook was embodied in the theological writings of the period. The material from which to draw is markedly extensive although little of a theological nature from Melville's pen has survived. We select for particular attention two of his contemporaries, Robert Rollock,[39] one of his earliest students at St Andrews, and John Forbes of Corse[40] one of his students at Sedan towards the close of his life.

Rollock appears to have been entirely a home product yet in his lifetime he published several theological writings which quickly won for him a European reputation and the highest praise from Theodoer Beza. In a letter to one of Melville's colleagues in St Andrews Beza praises Rollock's commentaries that had just come to his notice.

> I chanced of late to meet a great treasure, which I know not by what mishap, being frequent in other men's hands, hath hitherto missed my fingers. For why should not I esteem as a treasure, and that most precious, the commentaries of my honourable brother, Maister Rollocke upon the epistles to the Romans and Ephesians, both of them being of special note among the writings apostolical? For so I judge them. And I pray you that it be spoken

[37] *Ibid* p 13.
[38] *Ibid* p 4.
[39] *DNB* 49, pp 171–3; [*Select Works of Robert*] *Rollock*, [ed W. G. Gunn], *The Wodrow Society* (Edinburgh 1849) 1, pp lix–lxxxvii.
[40] *DNB* 19, pp 402–4.

without all flattery or partiallity, that I never read or met with anything in this kind of interpretation more pithily, elegantly and judiciously written.[41]

In his commentaries Rollock had employed to advantage his philological knowledge and this approach to the sacred text had undoubtedly greatly impressed that Greek new testament scholar, Beza. It was Rollock's purpose that doctrine should rise clearly from the text. In one of his sermons we find this sentence. 'Learne the wordis for all doctrine rysis of the wordis.'[42] The philological approach was not confined to learned commentaries. In a sermon on 2 Cor 5 v9, 'wherefoir also we covet that baith dwelling at hame and removing fra hame we may be acceptable to him' Rollock set forth the Christian aspiration to heavenly bliss and explained that the word translated 'we covet' imported in 'the first language' not only a common desire but an ambition, so that by choosing this word Saint Paul was saying that he was greedy of honour and ambition.[43] The Greek is φιλοτιμέομαι, 'to love or seek after honour . . . hence to be ambitious, emulous, jealous'.[44] And the preacher seeks to show that there is a type of ambition, a holy ambition, necessary to every Christian. Again in a sermon on 2 Cor 5 v5, 'And he that hath created us for this thing is God', he points out that the English version could be misleading. Paul was referring to regeneration, to the second creation in Christ and not to the first in Adam. The Greek words κατεργασάμενος ἡμᾶς together with the context make it clear that the reference is to the new creation in Christ.[45]

With his precise, accurate, linguistic knowledge Rollock sought to convey in simple terms to his congregation the full meaning and force of the text. Scripture philologically understood was the doorway to biblical truth. This emphasis so integral a part of Christian humanism was long to continue a feature of the Scottish pulpit.

John Forbes of Corse (1593–1648) was amongst the most widely known of Scottish theologians in the first half of the seventeenth century. Educated at King's College, Aberdeen, Heidelberg, Middelburg and Sedan, Forbes was appointed first professor of divinity at King's College in 1620 and was to become an outstanding

[41] *Rollock*, I, p 10. See also Cameron, *Letters of Johnston and Howie*, pp 331–4.
[42] *Rollock*, I, p 318.
[43] *Ibid* I, p 331.
[44] H. G. Liddell and R. Scott, *A Greek-English Lexicon* (new, ninth, ed Oxford 1966) p 1941.
[45] *Rollock*, I, pp 316–17.

member of that group of northern scholars, the Aberdeen doctors.[46] Forbes undoubtedly considered himself in the reformed tradition and is probably best remembered today for his *Irenicum*,[47] in which in line with the ecumenical ideals of David Paraeus and Franciscus Junius he sought to reconcile presbyterian and episcopalian. His most significant contribution to ecclesiastical history and theology, the *Instructiones Historico-Theologicae*,[48] and his *Theologia moralis*[49] won for him wide acclaim, particularly in the Low Countries. As a testimony to the continuing humanist tradition, which was already beginning to give way to a new form of scholasticism, these works are outstanding. Forbes had in ample measure the qualities of the humanist, an extensive knowledge of classical authors, of patristic theology both Greek and Latin and of early Christian writers, Lactantius, Prudentius, Paulinus of Nola, of mediaeval theologians and canonists, of fifteenth and sixteenth century humanists.

In the *Instructiones*, which we may translate as 'Studies in Historical Theology', Forbes brings to the discussion of theological topics an historical outlook and treatment that is both extensive and illuminating. For example in the chapters on the doctrine of purgatory, he devotes much attention to ideas found in Plato, Cicero, Virgil as well as the fathers.[50] Of his use of historical documents as a critical tool we may cite his discussion of early British Christianity in which he employs his sources to reject the jurisdictional claims of Boniface VIII.[51] In his interpretation of scripture his knowledge of languages is fully employed. On almost every page his debt to classical and oriental learning unmistakably appears. In examining the nature of worship he inquires into the meaning of *religio, similacrum,* and *imago* with the help of Cicero, Varro, Virgil, Minutius Felix, Suetonius, Pliny the Younger, Lactantius, and of course Laurentius Valla and Ludovicus Vives and others.[52] He employs not only his knowledge of the languages of the bible but draws extensively upon the rabbinical

---

[46] D. MacMillan, *The Aberdeen Doctors* (London 1909) pp 227–34

[47] *Irenicum amatoribus veritatis et pacis in ecclesia Scoticana* (Aberdeen 1629). The first book was translated and edited by E. G. Selwyn (Cambridge 1923).

[48] *Instructiones Historico-Theologicae de Doctrina Christiana* (Amsterdam 1645 and Geneva 1680); this work was republished as the second volume of his *Opera omnia* (Amsterdam 1702). References are to this edition.

[49] *Theologiae moralis libri decem* was published in the first volume of Forbes's *Opera omnia* in 1703.

[50] *Ibid* 2, pp 625–7.

[51] *Ibid* 2, p 158.

[52] *Ibid* 2, pp 313–24.

commentaries, the various Targums, and he may well have known Arabic as he devotes an interesting if not original section to the rise and early development of Islam.[53]

Not surprisingly the humanists' moral emphasis clearly appears in the *Theologia moralis* in which he discusses the decalogue. He stresses the importance of understanding the law spiritually and sees love as the basis of the law—the love of God and the love of man that are essentially linked.[54] Forbes is anxious to stress the basic morality in all men and hence in his discussion of conscience he writes of the law inscribed in the hearts of men, as Paul says in Rom 2 v 15, and asserts that from this same source arise those *insignes sententiae* about worshipping God, honouring parents, upholding justice, abhorring evil and cultivating a good conscience, which are found in the best classical authors. Having cited Cicero, whom he held to have been taught by nature or by God *per lumen iudicii naturalis et inditae homini conscientiae*, he continues, *Concordant ista cum doctrina in sacris scripturis nobis tradita.* He does, however, stress that according to scripture we must have faith to have and to preserve a good conscience.[55]

Probably the least known of Forbes' writings is his book on pastoral care[56] in which he exhibits all the qualities already mentioned and in particular the humanist reformers' emphasis on clerical and pastoral responsibility. He attacks contemporary pluralists, titulars, non-residents, clergy employed in civil or military affairs and does so by quoting extensively from church history. Perhaps worth noting in the passing is his quotation from the *Fasti* of Baptista Mantuanus[57] who appears to have been popular amongst Aberdeen neo-Latin poets.

Further illustration of the humanist tradition can be found in the works of other theologians whose writings still await modern critical study, among them Robert Boyd of Trochrig (1579–1627),[58] one of Rollock's students at Edinburgh and probably the most distinguished of a remarkable company. On completion of his course at Edinburgh

[53] *Ibid* 2, pp 161–205.
[54] *Ibid* 1, *Theologia Moralis*, cap 13, pp 26–9.
[55] *Ibid* cap 16, p 38.
[56] *Ibid* pp 531–619.
[57] In his discussion of clerical celibacy, he quotes pp 580–92, from his lines on Hilary of Poitiers and approves of the contemporary description of Mantuanus as *insignis theologus et poeta vere pius.*
[58] *DNB* 6, pp 98–9; J. Walker, *The Theology and Theologians of Scotland* (Edinburgh 1872) pp 3–5; [R.] Wodrow, *Collections [upon the lives of the Reformers]*, Maitland Club (Glasgow 1845) 2, pt 1.

Boyd studied abroad, mainly in France, and became a minister of the French protestant church and subsequently a professor at the academy of Saumur. In 1615 he returned to Scotland to become principal of the university of Glasgow where following in the path laid down by Andrew Melville he taught Hebrew and Syriac. An excellent lecturer in Latin Boyd maintained that had he been free to select a language for his public lectures he would have chosen Greek as being 'the most appropriate to express his thoughts'. An extensive commentary on the epistle to the Ephesians[59] forms his main contribution to theological literature. The wide range of his classical scholarship and his patristic knowledge is evident throughout but particularly in his *apparatus criticus* which fully illustrates the thoroughness of his early education at Rollock's hand and the depth of influence he had upon his pupil's textual method. We will again encounter Boyd along with some of the theologians whom we have been unable to mention when we speak of their contribution to Scottish neo-Latin verse.

Undoubtedly Scottish theology in the sixteenth and early seventeenth centuries was both enriched and coloured by its basis in the humanist tradition in reformed education. For a brief period that tradition with its critical approach was to be eclipsed by a new scholasticism only to reappear in much of the writings of theologians and preachers affected by the enlightenment. That the enlightenment produced no serious challenge to the church in Scotland is probably in large measure due to the church's intellectual heritage. Principal George Hill at the beginning of the nineteenth century was more than echoing that tradition when he spoke of the advantages to religion of

> A more rational criticism . . . a more enlightened philosophy
> . . . a sounder logic . . . and a language less technical. It was, he
> said, by the 'patient exercise of criticism that a student of divinity
> is emancipated from all subjection to the opinions of men and
> led most certainly to the truth as it is in Jesus Christ.'[60]

Scottish humanists as participants in a cosmopolitan movement wrote quite naturally in Latin, the universal language of the day, and sought for their works a European audience. Hence Latin rather than the vernacular was cultivated as the primary form of literary

---

[59] *In Epistola Pauli Apostoli ad Ephesios* (London 1652). An edition was also printed at Geneva in 1661. A short *vita* by A. Rivet is prefixed to both editions.
[60] G. Hill, *Lectures in Divinity* (Edinburgh 1825) 1 pp 439, 443; see further J. K. Cameron, 'The Church of Scotland in the age of reason', *Studies on Voltaire and the eighteenth century* 18 (Geneva 1967) pp 1939–51 at p 1951.

expression, 'the elegant evidence of humanistic learning'.[61] To all aspirants the example of George Buchanan (1506–82) Scotland's greatest sixteenth-century poet, dramatist, political philosopher and national historian, was a constant source of encouragement and an inspiration to write verses as the credentials of their learning. The extensive output of Latin verse by Scotsmen from almost every walk of life amply illustrates the atmosphere in which education was being conducted and more importantly the extent to which the humanist literary tradition had permeated the cultural and religious life of the nation.[62]

In his *Musae Anglicanae* Leicester Bradner included the poetical writings of all the prominent Scottish poets[63] of whom the most significant ecclesiastical writers for the late sixteenth and early seventeenth centuries were Patrick Adamson, Andrew Melville and John Johnston. To what Bradner has written[64] I have little to add apart from the facts that he unfortunately knew nothing of Melville's unfinished manuscript paraphrases of the psalms and only a little about Johnston's Περὶ στεφάνων *sive de coronis martyrum*, but not in their finished state and prepared for the press. Many of Melville's psalm paraphrases were written in the Tower of London and still await critical study and publication.[65] As they belong to a literary genre that was in general vogue they need only be mentioned. Adamson's main contribution also lay in the area of scriptural paraphrase, in particular a Latin verse paraphrase of the book of Job; although after his death a volume entitled *Poemata sacra*, was published in London in 1619 and contains a variety of verses, some of which are not strictly either sacred or biblical.

John Johnston (*c*1565–1611), MA of Aberdeen, King's College, and subsequently one of Melville's colleagues in St Mary's College, St Andrews undoubtedly gave the best completed poetical treatment to historical and religious subjects in the Scottish renaissance. Subsequent to his education in Aberdeen, where classical instruction must have been of a very high order both in the grammar school and in the

[61] [L.] Bradner, *Musae [Anglicanae]* (London 1940) p 19.
[62] See for example the chronological list of publications of Anglo-Latin poetry given by Bradner, *Musae*, pp 346–60; *Musa Latina Aberdonensis, New Spalding Club*, 1, 2, ed W. D. Geddes (Aberdeen 1892, 1895) 3, ed W. K. Leask (1910); *Delitiae Poetarum Scotorum huius aevi illustrium*, ed A. Johnston, 2 vols (Amsterdam 1637).
[63] Caps 5 and 6, pp 123–200, are devoted to Scottish neo-Latin poets.
[64] On pp 155–7.
[65] These are contained in the Edinburgh University Library MS, *Melvini Epistolae*.

university Johnston studied at such celebrated centres of northern humanism as Rostock, Helmstedt and Heidelberg, before paying extended visits to Zurich, Bern, Basel and Geneva. His considerable correspondence, particularly after he returned to Scotland, with scholars of distinction such as Isaac Casaubon, J. J. Grynaeus, Abraham Ortellius, Caspar Waser and William Camden amply illustrates that he was held by his contemporaries at home and abroad to be a figure of considerable academic and literary importance.[66]

In his writing of neo-Latin verse Johnston took as his principal models the works of Ausonius and Prudentius who in the fourth century sought to recreate the style of the classical period of Latin literature, writers who were especially popular among reformed churchmen and scholars on the continent. In four of his published works Johnston executed a series of parallel compositions on biblical and Scottish history which are clearly inspired by Ausonius's *De Caesaribus* and *Epitaphia heroum, qui bello Troiano interfuerunt et aliquot aliorum.* Johnston fully acknowledges his debt in the dedicatory preface of his *Inscriptiones historicae regum Scotorum* published at Amsterdam in 1602:

> *Incitavit me huc cum studium historiae nostrae, tum exemplum illustrium Poetarum, Ausonii, Mycilli, Velii, Sabini, qui simili modo descriptos Caesares Romanos et Germanicos invulgarunt.*[67]

At the same time he indicated the didactic and moral aim of his verses by asking king James VI to whom the book was dedicated that it be put into the hands of prince Henry, the young heir to the throne, that from it *discat mature discernere inter imperium et tyrannidem, et inde capere (ut est apud Romanum scriptorem) sibi reique publicae utile ac frugiferum, quod imitetur.*[68] In his *Heroes ex omni historia Scotica lectissimi*, Leiden, 1603, there is also acknowledgement that he has drawn inspiration from classical writers and a similar emphasis on the moral qualities of the men of valour of whom he sings, men who had excelled in the defence of liberty, above all he stresses the example of those *quos una cum beata purae religionis luce excitavit Deus, qui Spiritu fortitudinis et zelo pietatis divinitus afflati, vitam, fortunam et amicos pro libertate religionis et patriae omnibus periculis obiecerunt constantissime.*[69]

Johnson's religious interest is given more explicit expression in the

---

[66] See further, Cameron, *Letters of Johnston and Howie.*
[67] p 2; see also Cameron, *Letters of Johnston and Howie*, p 166.
[68] p 2; Cameron, *Letters of Johnston and Howie*, p 167.
[69] p A3v.

parallel series on biblical subjects, entitled *Icones regum Iudae et Israelis*, Leiden 1612, and *Sidera veteris aevi, sive heroes fide et factis illustres in veteri testamento,* Saumur 1611. These two works, together with a collection of scriptural paraphrases, also published at Saumur, were the product of his latter years when he was suffering from repeated periods of ill health and show that he was employing his talents to more specifically religious ends, nevertheless the practical value of moral instruction to be gained from the bible for prince Henry to whom the *Icones* was dedicated is given prominence in the dedication.[70] The literary inspiration is still of course in large part classical and humanist. The religious interest is also in evidence in his only prose writing *Consolatio piorum sub cruce ex vivifico Dei verbo* which forms an extended commentary on a passage from 2 Corinthians and to which were added several poems expressing his faith in time of distress.[71]

In addition to the works mentioned the influence and inspiration of Ausonius's *Ordo nobilium urbium* led to the writing of a collection of poems on Scottish towns which Camden included in the 1607 edition of the *Britannia.*[72] Towards the end of his life the more distinctly Christian poet Prudentius inspired him to turn his attention to the famous men of Christian history. From Prudentius he took the title of his last completed work, Περὶ στεφάνων *sive de coronis martyrum in Britannia,* in which in two books he brought together verses in honour of the martyrs and men of faith in English and Scottish History. Until comparatively recently this work had been known only from Johnston's working manuscript notebook, preserved in the national library of Scotland,[73] but a completed and bound manuscript prepared for printing had in fact been in the university library, St Andrews, since 1919.[74] Again Johnston acknowledged his debt to his classical source although it must be conceded that he did not seek to emulate Prudentius in his choice of metrical forms. What was written by H. J. Thomson of this fourth century Christian poet could with truth and only slight alteration have been written of John Johnston:

> He is steeped in the work of the classical Latin poets . . . He regards the pagan literature and art not as things to be rejected but

---

[70] Cameron, *Letters of Johnston and Howie,* pp 246–8.
[71] *Ibid,* pp lxxii, 235–7.
[72] Ibid pp lxiii, lxxv, 227–8, 230–1, 244; *Musa Latina Aberdonensis,* 3, pp 147–58.
[73] *Musa Latina Aberdonensis,* 3, pp 102–37.
[74] J. K. Cameron, 'A St. Andrews Manuscript of Poems by John Johnston (c. 1565–1611)', *Aberdeen University Review,* 39 (Aberdeen 1962) pp 230–2.

as part of the inheritance into which Christian Rome enters; and in appropriating Latin poetic forms, lyric, epic, didactic, he is willing to show the world that the subject matter of the new faith can fill the ancient moulds.[75]

Something of Johnston's debt to the revived classical literature has been illustrated by W. K. Leask in the third volume of the monumental *Musa Latina Aberdonensis*, published by the New Spalding Club in 1910 in which he edited selections from a wide range of Scottish neo-Latin poets, many of them ministers in the reformed church. In editing his selection from Johnston's Muse Leask noted many of the classical echoes and allusions that would have delighted his readers. Two lines from his tribute to John Spottiswoode, superintendent of Lothian, with their allusion to the famous passage on the golden bough in Aeneid VI, 136–44 and the word play, which must indeed have pleased and amused his readers, must here suffice by way of illustration

Aureus hic Ramus maculoso in tegmine silvae;
Silvae ubi nunc Ramos que ferat aureolos?[76]

In the publication of his religious verse at Saumur in 1611 Johnston had been indebted to his friend Robert Boyd of Trochrig to whom he had sent his manuscript[77] and who was subsequently, as we have seen, to return to Scotland as principal of the university of Glasgow. As well as their devotion to the protestant and Melvillian cause Johnston and Boyd had a common bond in their attachment to the humanist tradition in reformed theology and in the writing of neo-Latin verse. His finest verse composition, *Hecatombe ad Christum Salvatorem* was included in *Delitiae Poetarum Scotorum*[78] by Sir John Scot of Scotstarvet and was highly praised by contemporaries. Unfortunately his *Philotheca* which according to Wodrow 'consists of 1070 beautiful hexameter verses containing a short view in a way of thanksgiving to God of his own birth, education, settlement in France and marriage'[79] has not been published and the whereabouts of the manuscript has not been traced. The inclusion of the *Hecatombe* in the *Delitiae* has, however, preserved for him an honourable place among the nation's neo-Latin poets.

---

[75] H. J. Thomson, *Prudentius* (Cambridge, Mass., 1949) I, p viii.
[76] *Musa Latina Aberdonensis*, 3, p 125.
[77] Cameron, *Letters of Johnston and Howie*, pp lxxv, 259–61; Bradner, *Musae*, pp 156–7.
[78] Vol I, pp 209–18; see also Wodrow, *Collections*, 2 pt I, pp 251–2, and appendix 6 pp vi–xvii.
[79] *Ibid* p 257.

It has sometimes been a matter of regret that the leading figures of the Scottish renaissance confined themselves almost enclusively to writing in Latin to the neglect of their native tongue as a vehicle of literary expression.[80] The relation between Scottish literature in the vernacular and the neo-Latin poetry of the late sixteenth and early seventeenth centuries still awaits much detailed critical study, and it would be misleading to give the impression that those who were so strongly under the spell of classical humanism did not venture to write in the language of the day as did Dunbar and that great advocate of reform, Sir David Lyndesay of the Mount, who by his *Ane plesant satyre of the thrie estatis* and other literary attacks upon the failings of the king, the court and the clergy did much to prepare the way for the success of the reformation.[81] Of those few who did write in their mother tongue John Davidson, minister at Prestonpans may be briefly mentioned.[82]

A professor in St Leonard's College, St Andrews, Davidson was offended by the ecclesiastical policy of the regent who, in order to direct much of the revenue to which the reformed church laid claim into the coffers of the state, planned to unite several parishes under one minister. This attempt to impose upon the reformed church one of the evils which had so crippled the mediaeval church called forth in true humanist style from Davidson's pen a skilful attack in a long satyrical poem entitled *Ane dialog or mutuall talking betuix a clerk and ane courteour, concerning foure parische kirks till ane minister*, which calls to mind Erasmus's *Colloquies*. The *Dialog* although not a work of high poetic order is nevertheless interesting in that it uses the humanistic weapon of satire in the interests of ecclesiastical reform and reflects the moral earnestness of its employers and their desire to provide the church with the educated clergy that true religion deserved.

Printed without Davidson's knowledge, the satire raised a considerable furore which eventually compelled the author to leave the country for England and the continent. Shortly thereafter he matriculated at the university of Basel for the session 1575–6 in the company of Laurence Bodley, the younger brother of Sir Thomas who subsequently visited Basel and signed the matriculation register for

---

[80] See for example P. H. Brown, *George Buchanan* (Edinburgh 1890) pp 3–5, and Bradner, *Musae*, p 123.

[81] *The Poetical Works of Sir David Lyndsay*, ed David Laing (Edinburgh 1879) pp xxxix–li.

[82] *DNB* 14, pp 125–7; [C.] Roger, [*Three Scottish*] *Reformers* (London 1874) pp 31–53; *Ane dialog* is printed on pp 53–80.

1578–9.[83] Davidson was in all probability acting as tutor to Laurence who later became a canon of Exeter and who, according to the *Dictionary of National Biography*, was probably responsible for the donation by the dean and chapter of Exeter, in 1602, of 'eighty-one early and valuable manuscripts from the library of their cathedral to the new library at Oxford, including . . . the well-known Leofric Missal'.[84] When he returned to Scotland and was settled in the parish ministry Davidson became a zealous promoter of education, was responsible for the erection of a school at Prestonpans in which instruction was to be given in Latin, Greek, and Hebrew, provided it with a substantial endowment, and secured as its first teacher Alexander Hume, a scholar of repute.[85]

The renaissance tradition in the reformed church of Scotland has been briefly reviewed in three aspects: its programme for educational reform throughout the country, its stress upon biblical study and exposition based on an understanding of the sacred text in its original tongues both for theology and preaching, and its encouragement and praise of Christian faith, morality, and piety set out in the revived forms of classical literary expression. In all these pursuits the marks of Christian humanism as it worked for the renewal of the church are clearly discernible. It has been said of Erasmus that what he envisaged was 'a reform in the sense of a union of the Scriptures, the church fathers, *humanitas* and *bonae literae* within the Church'.[86] To this heritage the reformed church owed much and in this tradition along with her sister churches on the continent the church in Scotland must be seen to stand.

St Mary's College
University of St Andrews

[83] *Die Matrikel der Universität Basel,* ed H. G. Wackernagel (Basel 1956) 2, pp 236–7; Sieber, 'Die Universität Basel', pp 102, 110.
[84] *DNB* 5, p 294.
[85] Roger, *Reformers*, pp 51–2.
[86] L. W. Spitz, *The Religious Renaissance of the German Humanists* (Cambridge, Mass., 1963) p 204.

THE ORIGINS OF THE SO-CALLED REGIUS PROFESSORSHIPS: AN ASPECT OF THE RENAISSANCE IN OXFORD AND CAMBRIDGE

by F. DONALD LOGAN

THE universities at Oxford and Cambridge constituted two of the principal *foci* for the forces favouring renewal in sixteenth-century England.[1] The towering personalities of John Fisher and Erasmus of Rotterdam set the goal of loosening the bonds of the traditional pedagogy and curriculum. The establishment of new foundations such as, at Cambridge, Christ College and, even more immediately, St John's College and, at Oxford, Corpus Christi College and Cardinal College provided an institutional framework for the new learning. So, too, did the provisions for new 'professorships'—the term will be used for the moment.

The Lady Margaret established her 'professorships' in divinity at Oxford and Cambridge by 1503. Corpus Christi College, Oxford, in its statutes provided for 'professors' in Greek and Latin. At Cambridge, chancellor Fisher appointed Richard Croke as 'professor' in Greek for the whole university in 1518, and in 1524 Thomas Linacre established two 'professorships' in medicine, although actual appointments were not made until 1558. Undoubtedly the best known of the 'professorships' established in sixteenth-century England were the so-called regius professorships (divinity, Greek, Hebrew, law, and medicine) created, according to the accepted chronology, in 1540 for Cambridge and in 1546 for Oxford. Although, indeed, these regius appointments were parallelled in a way by similar royal appointments in Paris, there is no evidence suggesting any direct connection, and firmer ground is to be had in seeing ample precedent in England for the so-called regius professorships.[2] This paper will treat these Henrician creations by

---

[1] The author would like to record here his gratitude to Dr A. B. Emden for his generous help at various stages in the preparation of this paper.

[2] See generally [H. C.] Porter, [*Reformation and Reaction in Tudor Cambridge*] (Cambridge 1958) caps 1–3; J. K. McConica, *English Humanism and Reformation Politics under Henry VIII and Edward VI* (Oxford 1965) cap 4; also, [S.] Gibson, ['The University of Oxford',] *VCH Oxon* 3 (1954) pp 18–19. For the Lady Margaret's provisions see George Dyer, *The Privileges of the University of Cambridge*, 2 vols (London 1824) 1, p 103.

correcting the accepted chronology, explaining their purpose, and, finally, commenting on the appropriateness of their designation as *regius*.

To begin with terms. In the sixteenth century the term 'professor' did not have the precise meaning that it has today—and even today it has different connotations on the opposite shores of the Atlantic. There were undoubtedly scores of 'professors' in the English universities in Tudor times, when the term was used descriptively in some of the higher faculties as a synonym for 'doctor' (that is, an authorised teacher). Contemporary accounts in English which refer to the so-called regius professor invariably call him a 'reader', whereas the contemporary Latin references call him a *praelector*. In view of the danger of confusion and anachronism associated with both the terms 'professor' and 'reader' this paper will make use of the term *praelector*. The question of the appropriateness of the term 'regius' will be discussed at a later point.[3]

The obvious question to ask—when were these praelectorships established by Henry VIII?—has been the question posed by the classical historians of the universities. The Cambridge historians, following Cooper, accept that five praelectorships—in divinity, Greek, Hebrew, law, and medicine—were established by the king in 1540[4] and the Oxford historians, following Wood, set the date for the establishment of praelectorships in these same subjects at 1546 for their university.[5] These dates are inaccurate and, in a sense, have emerged because the wrong question has been asked: it is more productive for the historian to ask not *when* but rather *how* these praelectorships originated. An analysis of this question reveals three stages in the early history of these praelectorships.

The first stage belongs neither to 1546 nor to 1540, but, rather, begins in 1535-6 and extends to 1540: at this stage a single praelectorship was established by royal mandate at each university. In 1534 parliament had subjected the universities, much to their irritation, to the payment of

---

[3] For the use of these terms see H. Rashdall, *The Universities of Europe in the Middle Ages,* new ed F. M. Powicke and A. B. Emden, 3 vols (Oxford 1936) 1, pp 19–20.

[4] C. H. Cooper, *Annals of Cambridge,* 5 vols (Cambridge 1842–1908) 1, p 397; [J. B.] Mullinger, [*The University of Cambridge from the Royal Injunctions of 1535 to the Accession of Charles the First*] (Cambridge 1884) p 52; J. P. C. Roach, 'The University of Cambridge,' *VCH Cambs* 3 (1959) p 177; Porter p 51.

[5] [Anthony à] Wood, [*The History and Antiquities of the University of Oxford*], ed J. Gutch, 2 vols (Oxford 1792–6) 2, pp 840–61; W. E. Mallet, *A History of the University of Oxford,* 3 vols (London 1924–7) 2, p 71; Gibson, p 19.

first fruits and tenths.[6] As a consequence, letters passed from Oxford and Cambridge to those in and near the seats of national power as the universities pleaded for the remission of these exactions.[7] While this question remained unsettled, the visitation of the universities took place. During the autumn of 1535 visitors were sent by Cromwell to Oxford and Cambridge for the first visitation of the universities undertaken by the state. Their injunctions amounted to an endorsement of the new learning and effected the banishment of canon law, the abolition of use of commentaries on the *Sentences* of Peter Lombard, and the dethronement of Duns Scotus. The visitors gave victory to the humanistic party, although in so doing they presided gleefully over the destruction of a large quantity of medieval manuscripts. What is often overlooked is that the visitors, in addition to accomplishing these things, ordered Cambridge and, perhaps, Oxford to establish a public lecture in either Greek or Hebrew at the university's expense.[8]

This injunction of the visitors, with some modifications, was to receive parliamentary sanction the following year. The last session of the reformation parliament, meeting in the late winter and early spring of 1536, resolved the question of the exaction of first fruits and tenths by absolving the universities of any obligation on the condition, *inter alia*, that they establish a public lecture, the king Henry the VIII, his lecture:

> In consideration of which his most gracious pardon and release of the said first fruits and tenths and for increase of learning in the said universities, his grace's pleasure is that it be enacted by author-

---

[6] 26 Hen VIII c 3, *Statutes [of the Realm]*, ed A. Luders *et al.*, 10 vols (London 1810–28) 3, pp 493–9.

[7] For Oxford see BL Cotton MS Faust C VIII, fols 196ʳ/ᵛ, 202ʳ; for Cambridge see *ibid*, fols 492ʳ/ᵛ, Cambridge University Archives Lett. 1, fols 71ʳ/ᵛ, 72ᵛ–74ʳ, and *Grace Book B*, [ed Mary Bateson], 2 pts (Cambridge 1903–5) 2, pp 194, 208.

[8] 'Praeterea volumus et praecipimus quod haec universitas unam publicam lectionem sive graecam sive hebraicam ex libera optione eorum qui de gremio eiusdem universitatis sunt utram earum maluerint et conducere arbitrati fuerint suis impensis continue sustentet et suppediet quodque tam in illius lecturae quam in aliarum lecturarum ubicunque infra hanc universitatem praelectoribus diligentissime suam operam adhibeant ut eos ad praelectiones huiusmodi delegant qui literarum scientia et morum integritate maxime florere noscantur ac qui pure, sincere, et pie legere velint omni affectu carnali aut quocumque alio respectu iniquo penitus se moto et postposito: Cambridge, Peterhouse Archives Register, fol 169ʳ, imperfectly printed in *Statuta Academiae Cantabrigiensis* (Cambridge 1785) p 140. This is found in Dr Thomas Leigh's additional injunctions of 22 October 1535. The Oxford injunctions have not survived, although it is generally presumed that they were substantially the same as those to Cambridge. Whether a similar addition was made by the visitors to Oxford is not known.

ity of this present parliament that all the colleges, houses, and halls corporate in either of the said universities shall perpetually from henceforth at their own proper costs and charges find in every of the said universities one discreet and learned personage to read one open and public lecture in every of the said universities in any such science or tongue as the king's majesty shall assign or appoint to be most profitable for the students in either of the said universities, every which lecture shall be called perpetually King Henry the eighth his lecture.[9]

Thus, a perpetual praelectorship was to be established both at Oxford and at Cambridge, royal in name, held by a praelector chosen and paid by the university, and concerning a subject selected by the king.

The two universities implemented this parliamentary statute in quite different ways. Oxford simply assessed the wealthier colleges an annual amount scaled according to their wealth. Thirteen colleges were assessed (Magdalen and New College the most—£3 1s. 10d. and £2 11s. 4d. respectively—and University and Balliol the least—3s. 1d. each), and the praelector was to receive twenty marks (£13 6s. 8d.)[10] Richard Smith, fellow of Merton College, was appointed praelector in divinity at Oxford by May 1536.[11] The Cambridge picture is not quite so clear, but it appears that the university shuffled its accounts and took the amount of money normally expended on the mathematical lecture and applied it to the new lecture. A grace of 1536 permitted such a transfer as did graces in the next two years.[12] The vice-chancellor and proctor at Cambridge were allowed to raise the salary for this praelector, if they saw fit, from the £4 normally given to the mathematical lecturer. The praelector selected for the Hebrew lecture at Cambridge was probably Thomas Wakefield.[13] Thus, praelectorships at Oxford in divinity and at Cambridge in Hebrew were established in 1536. 'The King Henry the VIII his lecture', although designed to be perpetual, lasted only four years.

---

[9] 27 Hen VIII c 42, 4 (*Statutes III*, p 600). Spelling and punctuation have been modernised.

[10] *Statuta Antiqua Universitatis Oxoniensis*, ed S. Gibson (Oxford 1931) pp 339–40.

[11] Oxford University Archives Reg. I, 8, fol 14ᵛ, where he is described as 'praelector theologicae lectionis nuper a regia maiestate institutae.' For Smith see [A. B.] Emden, [*A Biographical Register of the University of Oxford A.D. 1501 to 1540* (Oxford 1974)] pp 524–6.

[12] *Grace Book* Γ [ed W. G. Searle] (Cambridge 1908) pp 310, 315, 327.

[13] He was the most distinguished hebraist at Cambridge; his name with Smith's led the list of the 1540 appointments (see below). See also [J. Venn and J. A. Venn,] *Alumni Cantabrigienses* I (1922–6) 4, p 312.

That brings us to the second stage: 1540–6. What undoubtedly pleased the universities about the arrangement which ushered in the second stage in 1540 was the shifting of the financial burden from their shoulders. This stage can be called, in a shorthand way, the Westminster stage, for it was to the newly created cathedral church of Westminster that the financial responsibilities were transferred.[14] But much more than that happened. The number of praelectorships was increased at each university to five, although at one point an increase to only four was considered.

Three schemes were drawn up in 1540 for the financial arrangements of the new bishopric. In the first of these, from very early in that year, no mention was made of supporting any praelectorships at the universities.[15] The second scheme, probably drawn up by Stephen Gardiner, bishop of Winchester and now chancellor of Cambridge, provided for the support of *eight* praelectors, *four* at each university (divinity, Greek, Hebrew, and civil law) at an annual stipend of £40 each.[16] In the final scheme of the establishment of the cathedral church the number was extended to *five* at each university by the addition of a praelectorship in medicine ('physic'). Also in this final scheme were added some specific names: for Cambridge, in Hebrew Thomas Wakefield, in civil law Geoffrey Glynne, and in Greek William Bill; for Oxford, in divinity Richard Smith and in medicine John Warner.[17] Thus in 1540 the cathedral church of Westminster was required to support, at a total cost of £400 per annum, five praelectorships at each university. These praelectorships were not collectively named; they were known merely as the praelectorship in divinity, the praelectorship in Greek, etc.

14 There is no obvious reason why Westminster was drawn into this arrangement save, perhaps, for the fact that the abbey was experienced in such matters for in 1503 it had been endowed by the Lady Margaret with estates from whose income the abbey was to pay the Lady Margaret praelectors in divinity.

15 *King Henry the Eighth's Scheme of Bishopricks*, ed H. Cole (London 1838) pp 4–6. It did contain arrangements, however, for the support of ten students in divinity at both Oxford and Cambridge.

16 *Ibid* p 34. For the Gardiner connection see *ibid* p 73. A similar draft providing for eight praelectorships is to be found in BL Add MS 40061, fol 2ʳ.

17 PRO MS E. 315/24/81; also Westminster Abbey Muniments no 6478, fol 2ʳ and *A Supplementary Volume to the Record of old Westminsters*, comp J. B. Whitmore and G.R.Y. Radcliffe (London 1938) p 9; it is calendared in *CalLP* 16 (1898) no 333. For Bill and Glynne see *Alumni Cantabrigienses* I, i, p 151 and I, iv, p 312. In 1537–8 Glynne had received £1. 6s. 8d. and in 1538–9 an unspecified sum *pro cathedra iuris civilis* (*Grace Book B II*, pp 213, 220). Gardiner described Bill as one of the most learned men he knew, [*The*] *Letters* [*of Stephen*] *Gardiner*, [ed J. A. Muller] (Cambridge 1933) p 431.

Appointments were made during this Westminster stage, presumably in each of the subjects at both universities, although it is admittedly difficult to supply a full roster of the names. Those scholars mentioned in the final scheme might well have been appointed in 1540. At Cambridge on 9 November of that year Thomas Wakefield was appointed by a royal letter patent the praelector of Hebrew for life[18]—no other appointments by royal letter are extant for the period covered in this paper. Roger Ascham, writing in 1542 to a friend and relating the recent news and gossip from Cambridge, indicated that Edward Wiggin had been appointed in divinity, Thomas Smith in civil law, John Cheke in Greek, Thomas Wakefield in Hebrew, and John Blythe (who married Cheke's sister, he added) in medicine.[19] Only Wakefield's name appeared for Cambridge both on the final Westminster list and on Ascham's list; Smith and Cheke, at least by 1542, have replaced Glynne and Bill, if indeed these latter two had ever been officially appointed. Does a saga in academic politics hide behind these discrepancies? The Oxford evidence is not very clear. The names of two Oxford men appeared on the Westminster list, and indeed Richard Smith and John Warner might very well have been appointed in divinity and medicine. The names of other Oxford appointees have not survived.

The founding of Christ Church, Oxford, and Trinity College, Cambridge, in 1546 occasioned the beginning of the third stage. The cathedral church of Westminster by granting to the crown manors, lands, and testaments valued at £400 was relieved of the burden of supporting these ten praelectors.[20] At the same time the diocese of Oxford with Christ Church as its cathedral was established and given an endowment, and from this endowment was to come the funds necessary to support three of these praelectors (divinity, Greek and Hebrew) at £40 per annum each.[21] Similarly, at Cambridge there was established a new foundation, Trinity College, out of a number of dissolved societies, most significantly King's Hall and Michaelhouse; the new college was likewise to support three praelectors in the same sub-

[18] The royal letter patent can be found in *Foedera*, 6, iii, p 61, and also in *Endowments of the University of Cambridge*, ed J. W. Clark (Cambridge 1904) p 153.

[19] Roger Ascham, *The Whole Works*, ed J. Giles, 3 vols (London 1864–5) 1, i *Letters* no 12. For Blythe, Cheke, and Wiggin see *Alumni Cantabrigienses* 1, i, pp 171, 328, and 1, iv, p 402.

[20] Westminster Abbey Muniments nos 12960, 18400, 32337.

[21] Gibson p 19.

jects at £40 each per annum.[22] The other two praelectorships—civil law and medicine, for which Christ Church and Trinity College bore no responsibility—now began to receive their support from the court of augmentations (and later from the office of augmentation in the exchequer).[23]

The pattern was now set: three praelectors supported by the colleges and two by the state. An unsuccessful attempt was made in 1549 to found civil law colleges at Oxford at All Souls College and at Cambridge by uniting Clare Hall and Trinity Hall. The praelectors in civil law would surely have been supported by these law colleges, but the plan came to naught, principally, it seems, because of the opposition of Stephen Gardiner and the members of Clare Hall.[24] The pattern of 1546 remained in force until Hanoverian times.

These praelectorships as public lectures were established (as the Lady Margaret praelectorship had been) for the free 'reading' by their holders. By the mid-1530s the term 'public' had received precise meaning. It did not mean that the praelector was free to teach anything he liked: quite often as, for instance, in the cases of the Lady Margaret and Corpus Christi College praelectorships, the authors whom the praelectors should teach were specifically prescribed. Rather, they were free in the sense that the students were admitted to them without any payment: the praelector was supported by the funds from the endowment. These perpetual endowments assured permanence to these chairs. What the foundation of these five praelectorships at Oxford and Cambridge accomplished was the setting of direction, particularly in underlining the significance of the study of divinity, Greek, and Hebrew. Civil law was included quite probably to buttress the law school, which had suffered from the elimination of canon law as a university subject. Medicine was included only in the last scheme at Westminster in 1540. And, when the final arrangements were made in 1546, civil law and medicine were to be supported not by Christ Church and Trinity College but from elsewhere. These three subjects —divinity, Greek and Hebrew—were three pillars in the edifice of the new learning. Their place was special.

[22] In early April 1546 a scheme was drawn up under the title *Distribucio collegii*, see W. W. Rouse Ball, *Cambridge Notes* 2 ed (Cambridge 1921) p 14. The earliest statutes date from 1552, see P. A. Bezodis, 'Trinity College,' *VCH Cambs* 3 (1959) p 463.

[23] PRO MSS E. 315/256 fols 69[r], 70[r], 71[r]; E. 315/257 fols 59[v], 60[r], 61[v], 62[r]; E. 315/258 fols 48[r], 53[v], 55[v].

[24] See for Cambridge, Mullinger pp 133–7, and for Oxford, Wood p 98. For Gardiner's view and Somerset's reply see *Letters Gardiner* pp 493–6.

To return, finally, to the term 'regius'. Contemporary sources fail to use this adjective in describing these praelectorships, and the *Oxford English Dictionary* does not record its use in this connection before 1622.[25] Yet it would be mean-spirited to question the modern application of this term, now long-hallowed by use, to a sixteenth-century context. But one should certainly ask: in what sense can these praelectorships be considered regius in the years of their origins? The evidence suggests that they were regius only insofar as they were established by the crown and that perhaps some of the appointments were royal appointments. There is no evidence which links the king personally to these events. Only indirectly was the crown involved in their funding.

The single praelectorships of stage one were supported by the universities themselves; the five praelectorships, at each university, of stage two were supported from confiscated monastic estates through a cathedral church, and after 1546 three of these same five were supported by a college at each university and the other two from augmentations No small achievement, however, that there came into existence under royal initiative praelectorships which have been occupied in the last four hundred years and more by some of the most distinguished scholars of their day. Now, with the more recent addition of chairs in other disciplines, they have an almost unshakeable place in the established firmament of the academy.

Emmanuel College
Boston, Massachusetts

[25] *OED*, ed J. A. H. Murray, 12 vols (Oxford 1933) 7, p 1429.

CONCERN FOR RENEWAL IN THE ROOT AND BRANCH DEBATES OF 1641

by ANTHONY FLETCHER

THE root and branch bill was debated in the house of commons between 27 May and 27 July 1641. The original bill introduced by Sir Edward Dering was short, simply abolishing bishops, deans and chapters with all their dependents. But after the house had wrestled for two months with the business of replacing episcopacy with a new form of church government the bill had grown to more than forty pages.[1] No complete copy of it, as it stood when it was dropped in August, has survived, but its main provisions can be reconstructed from the commons journals and parliamentary diaries. A new system of government was to be set up in two stages: its final form would be determined by a synod of divines, which it was intended should meet in the autumn of 1641 and work fast enough for the new jurisdiction to be established by 1 March 1642;[2] in the meanwhile parliament would take all ecclesiastical jurisdiction into its own hands and proceed with the redistribution of the church's financial resources. This paper is concerned with the first of these two stages, the commons's interim programme of action to fill the vacuum left by root and branch. The speeches of MPs on three topics that dominated the June and July debates—church courts, ordination and deans and chapters— strikingly reveal their concern to use a period of temporary control over the church for reform and renewal.

Much has been written about the decline in the effective power of the church courts between the reformation and the civil war. Their revival for narrow and partisan ends by the Arminians undoubtedly increased their unpopularity.[3] Yet the MPs of 1641 believed that the courts still

---

[1] The fullest account of the progress of the bill is in [W. A.] Shaw, [*A History of the*] *English Church* [*during the Civil Wars and under the Commonwealth*], 2 vols (London 1900) 2, pp 78–102. See also P. Zagorin, *The Court and the Country* (London 1969) pp 238–41; E. Dering, *A Collection of Speeches* (London 1642) p 119.

[2] [HMC], Cowper MSS, 2, p 288.

[3] C. Hill, *Economic Problems of the Church* (Oxford 1956); R. A. Marchant, *The Church under the Law* (Cambridge 1969); *Continuity and Change* [*: Personnel and Administration of the Church in England 1500–1642*], ed [R.] O'Day and [F.] Heal (Leicester 1976) pp 18–29, 239–57.

had a role to play in the propagation and enforcement of their conception of piety. Sir Simonds D'Ewes defined this conception in terms
which the house as a whole found acceptable in an exchange with
Sir John Hotham on 27 July: 'for piety, we know the way to maintain
it is to abolish whoring, swearing and drinking and to increase preaching and praying'.[4] Members regarded moral reform as urgent, so they
planned to name in the act nine lay commissioners for each shire who
would exercise the old ecclesiastical jurisdiction. The parts of
Lincolnshire and the ridings of Yorkshire were to have separate commissions, and there were to be two further commissions to execute the
archiepiscopal jurisdictions of Canterbury and York. The practical
difficulties of suddenly adapting the existing highly complex system
of diocesan and archdeaconry courts to a county basis are obvious. It
is not clear that the house tackled these difficulties. A subcommittee
on the bill in July simply recommended that all writs would be
directed to the commissioners; 'all ecclesiastical courts devolved to
them and to meet monthly'.[5] A remark by the Derbyshire MP Sir
John Coke to his father on 14 July suggests that there was no intention
to change the procedure of the courts: the commissioners would
govern, he wrote, 'in such manner as the bishops should have done'.[6]

But was it proper for laymen to exercise ecclesiastical jurisdiction?
Susceptible though the commons was to the anti-clericalism inherent
in the whole scheme, some members doubted this. William Pleydell,
the Wiltshire lawyer, who was the only man to fight the bill stage
by stage during July, denied that laymen could act. John Selden, on
the other hand, argued forcefully that laymen might exercise
ecclesiastical jurisdiction. The decision, despite his advocacy, to give
commissioners authority to appoint clerical deputies to deal with
certain 'particulars' reflected the unease that was felt.[7] These 'particulars', it seems, were never clarified. Nor was the role of the two archiepiscopal commissions. The house rejected Sir Edward Hyde's proposal
that appeals from county to metropolitan commissioners should be
allowed,[8] a predictable reaction which reflected the gentry's strong
prejudice in favour of county independence. The memory of Laud was
too fresh for any tolerance of central busybodies.

[4] [BL], Harley MS 163, fol 798ʳ.
[5] *Verney Notes on Proceedings in the Long Parliament*, ed J. Bruce, CSer, 1 series, 31 (1845)
p 104.
[6] Cowper MSS, 2, p 288.
[7] Harley MS 163, fol 777ᵛ.
[8] *Ibid* fol 789ᵛ. **Shaw** misread D'Ewes on this point, *English Church*, 1, p 96.

Every member of the long parliament recognised that the achievement of an informed and zealous protestant society depended on the qualifications and pastoral care of the clergy. The reformation of the ministry had been a principal concern of puritan gentry since the 1570s.[9] By the 1630s stress by the church's hierarchy on the importance of formal higher education had produced a largely graduate clergy. Attempts had been made by the more conscientious Elizabethan and Jacobean bishops to impose a rigorous examination before ordination.[10] Yet the petitions which flowed in to Westminster in November and December 1640 from the localities complaining about non-preaching and scandalous clergy amply justified the preoccupation of MPs with clerical inadequacy.[11] D'Ewes spoke for many, on 13 January 1641, when he declared that 'it would much conduce to the glory of his majesty's reign that we could change the greater part of the clergy from brazen, leaden, yea and blockish persons to a golden and primitive condition, that their authority might be warranted by their godly example.'[12]

The committee established by the commons on 19 December 1640 to consider petitions against scandalous ministers was several times discontinued and revived between then and July 1641. Little was being achieved in individual cases and in March the committee was directed to formulate a general bill on the subject. This at last received a first reading on 23 June.[13] The delay was a tacit recognition that the matter could not easily be tackled in isolation. The root and branch bill, however, forced the house to face the whole question of the suitability of men for the ministry and control of entry into it. Again diverging views emerged about the exercise of authority. Pleydell was out on his own in the debate of 17 July in objecting on principle to non-episcopal ordination; at the other extreme some MPs, well tutored by the presbyterian Scots commissioners, argued that 'all the ministers in the county had right of ordination *iure divino*'. A proposal by D'Ewes, occupying the middle ground, commended itself because it was both

[9] P. Collinson, *The Elizabethan Puritan Movement* (London 1967) particularly pp 280–2.
[10] R. O'Day, 'The Reformation of the Ministry 1558–1642' in *Continuity and Change,* ed O'Day and Heal, pp 55–75.
[11] For example see *Proceedings in Kent*, ed L. B. Larking, CSer, 1 series, 80 (1861) pp 101–240.
[12] *The Journal of Sir Simonds D'Ewes*, ed W. Notestein (Yale 1923) pp 249–50.
[13] C[ommons] J[ournals], 2, pp 54, 109, 183–4; *The Suffolk Committees for Scandalous Ministers*, ed C. Holmes, *Suffolk Records Society* 13 (Ipswich 1970) pp 9–11; Shaw *English Church*, 2, pp 176–9.

practical and likely to bring about higher standards. Allowing all the clergy to ordain, he insisted, would involve such a multitude in some counties that it would be 'as impossible as inconvenient'. Moreover those who were themselves scandalous and ignorant would let 'wicked men creep in' as the bishops had done. Five outstanding clergy, he suggested of 'known learning, piety and integrity' should be trusted with nomination and ordination in each shire.[14] The attraction of this proposal, which the commons adopted, was that it neatly fitted the provincial pattern of social relationships between puritan gentry and divines,[15] the patronage system and the tradition of local recruitment into livings. MPs and their friends, acting as commissioners, would nominate ordination committees in their own counties, appointing local clergy whom they knew well, who depended on their patronage and who served in their home parishes or even their households.

Cross has shown how the cathedral foundations were seen, in a tradition of protestant protest between 1540 and 1640, as 'dens of loitering lubbers'. The cathedrals were regarded as anachronisms; their clergy were charged with idleness and luxurious living; they did little to answer the expectations of pastoral involvement held by puritan gentry.[16] There were exceptions to this dismal picture. The new foundation of the dean and chapter at Durham, for example, became active in preaching: bishop Barnes, who was at Durham from 1577 to 1587, insisted that the cathedral clergy should help him 'in his great cure and parish'.[17] A few isolated initiatives of this kind were not enough though to win the deans and chapters firm friends. By 1641 many MPs believed the cathedrals were ripe for reform. Thomas Pury, an alderman and lawyer of Gloucester, was one of them. He was particularly concerned about the lack of preaching in his native city. An assertive man, he had backed puritan lecturers and schoolmasters against royal pressure in the 1630s.[18] On 14 June he asked the commons to insist that the dean and chapter should allow Sunday afternoon sermons in Gloucester cathedral, since none were given in any of the

[14] Harley MS 163, fol 790r.
[15] For this pattern see [A. J.] Fletcher, *A County Community [in Peace and War]* (London 1975) pp 72–3; [R. C.] Richardson, *Puritanism in North-West England* (Manchester 1972) pp 115–52.
[16] C. Cross, 'Dens of Loitering Lubbers: Protestant Protest against Cathedral Foundations, 1540–1640', *SCH* 9 (1972) pp 231–7.
[17] D. Marcombe, 'The Durham Dean and Chapter: Old Abbey Writ Large?', in *Continuity and Change*, ed O'Day and Heal, pp 125–44.
[18] M. F. Keeler, *The Long Parliament*, (Philadelphia 1954) pp 316–17.

city's churches and some churches did not even have a regular sermon in the morning.[19]

Pury's bold and imaginative proposals, in a speech the following day, formed the basis of the scheme adopted for the reallocation of the resources of cathedrals to the support of a preaching ministry. He reminded members of the role envisaged for the Henrician foundations by their founder. Indeed he quoted the king's grant to Gloucester: instead of monastic ignorance and superstition, 'the sincere worship of God should flourish and the holy Gospel of Jesus Christ be daily and purely preached. And further that the increase of the Christian faith and piety, the instruction of youth in good learning and the sustentation of the poor should be for ever there kept, maintained and continued.' It was notoriously known, declared Pury, that not one of the statutes of Gloucester was or had been kept: no common table was available for canons, scholars and choristers; the local poor were not relieved; most important of all preaching, which was enjoined 'in season and out of season', was wholly neglected by the canons, who also prevented outsiders from occupying the cathedral pulpit. 'Infinite are the pressures that many cities near unto deans and chapters have endured by them and their procurement'.[20] MPs from counties such as Sussex, Wiltshire and Worcestershire, which had experienced similar clashes during the 1630s between corporations and the clergy of the close, knew exactly what Pury was talking about.[21]

The commons voted on 15 June that dean and chapter lands should be confiscated and employed by feoffees 'to the advancement of learning and piety'. By applying the model Pury proposed for Gloucester—preachers based on the cathedral living off its rectories, vicarages, tithes and manors—to the nation as a whole the house sought to achieve a crucial advance. England might enjoy the fruits of a 'rich and flourishing clergy'. The sub-committee which met in July wanted to go further and put the bishops' lands as well into the hands of feoffees, but a compromise was eventually reached on this point: their lands would go to the crown but their impropriations and advowsons to the feoffees for dean and chapter lands.[22]

[19] Harley MS 163, fol 696ʳ.
[20] [J.] Rushworth, *Historical Collections* (London 1692) part 3, vol 1, pp 288–300.
[21] Fletcher, *A County Community*, pp 235–7; P. Slack, 'Poverty and Politics in Salisbury 1597–1666' in *Crisis and Order in English Towns*, ed P. Clark and P. Slack (London 1972) pp 187–8; A. Dyer, *The City of Worcester in the Sixteenth Century* (Leicester 1973) pp 195, 233–5.
[22] Shaw, *English Church*, I, pp 90, 94.

The root and branch bill was thus a more radical measure than has been appreciated. In the first months of the long parliament there were only a few men, such as Nathaniel Fiennes and Sir Henry Vane the younger, who were prepared to contemplate a drastic solution to the religious question.[23] But during June and July 1641 moderate opinion was brought into line. Men like Sir Benjamin Rudyard were convinced by the positive and constructive clauses tacked onto the bill during the summer debates. On 11 June Rudyard called for 'reformation not innovation, demolition not abolition'. The preaching ministry which MPs yearned for, he urged, implied a well paid ministry. He referred to current rumours that the root and branch men merely wished to grasp church lands for secular uses: 'it will be a shameful approach to so flourishing a kingdom as this to have a poor beggarly clergy . . . burning and shining lights do well deserve to be set in good candlesticks'.[24] Pury's scheme answered Rudyard's lament. The use of dean and chapter lands for the payment of preaching ministers satisfied the hopes and expectations of many like him.

If there was solid support for the root and branch bill, why then was it abortive? Not because it was seen as too divisive, as has been commonly supposed, nor because it was obvious that the lords would never agree to it. The attainder of Strafford provided a precedent for overawing the lords. August 1641 simply proved too hectic a month. As plague and smallpox raged in the capital, reaching Westminster itself, members sat late night after night over pressing political affairs. Disbandment of the two armies, the collection of the poll tax, the repercussions of the army plot and the instruction of the members sent north with the king left no time for religion. On 13 August there was a resolution to return to the bill the following Monday, but this proved impossible.[25] In the final debate of 9 September, just before the house adjourned until 20 October, Sir Simonds D'Ewes noted sorrowfully that, despite the political achievements of the previous nine months, the session had done nothing to restore the liberty of men's consciences. 'Some good bills', he reminded the house, had languished in committees while they had discussed root and branch: 'for our falling upon one great bill (I meant the bill of episcopacy) which had yet

[23] Rushworth, *Historical Collections*, part 3, vol 1, pp 174–83; *Clarendon's History of the Rebellion*, ed W. D. Macray (Oxford 1888) 1, p 309.
[24] J. Nalson, *Collection of the Affairs of State* (London 1683) 2, pp 298–300.
[25] *CJ*, 2, p 255.

proved too great to pass out at these doors made us unhappily to neglect and lay aside all the rest'.[26]

Root and branch was a 'great bill'. The solutions it offered were administratively highly complex. It seems clear that at the end of July debate was becoming bogged down in detail. There were demands for full surveys of cathedral revenues and the number of inadequately supported livings, so that a detailed scheme for the disposal of the revenues could be included in the act.[27] The energy to accomplish such surveys was lacking; the distractions were too overwhelming. Many must have shared D'Ewes's disappointment that religious reform by statute had not been achieved. Members knew that when they arrived home for their vacation friends and neighbours would question them earnestly about progress in reforming the church.[28] D'Ewes himself was sufficiently apprehensive about his reception in Suffolk to suggest that the commons should issue a declaration excusing them, on the grounds that the 'great business of disbanding had kept them from reform', and promising that religion would be the first item on the new agenda for October.[29]

Abortive plans and programmes have their significance no less than successful ones; this one is particularly important for the shaft of light that it throws on men's ideas about the church just before the civil war. The presuppositions of the interim scheme for a church which was to be suddenly shorn of episcopacy were parliamentary control and lay initiative. Some members of the Lancashire delegation were so eager to go into action that as early as 15 July they had decided upon their nominations for the county's commissioners. A lead was probably given by Ralph Assheton, a patron of puritan ministers who had presented the county's root and branch petition on 21 April,[30] or the diarist John Moore, another committed root and branch man.[31] Five of the nine nominations were MPs for the county or boroughs within it. The assumption that men who managed the politics and administration of their own shires could properly extend their jurisdiction into

[26] Harley MS 164, fols 913^r/^{v}.

[27] Harley MS 163, fols 787^v–8^r.

[28] For accountability see D. Hirst, *The Representative of the People* (Cambridge 1975) pp 178–88.

[29] Harley MS 164, fol 913^v.

[30] Harley MS 163, fol 80^r; Richardson, *Puritanism in North-West England*, p 127.

[31] Harley MS 479, fols 60^r/^{v}, cited but misunderstood by S. R. Gardiner *History of England from the Accession of James I to the Outbreak of the Civil War*, 10 vols (London 1884) 9, p 408; Shaw, *English Church*, 1, p 82.

the religious and moral spheres was implicit in the bill. The interregnum scheme took erastianism to its logical conclusion.

In the debates of February 1641 on the root and branch petition fear of the social and religious disorder which might follow the removal of the bishops was a prominent theme.[32] The group who drove the bill forward in June and July skilfully allayed this fear. Members were persuaded to put confidence in their own ability to handle such disorder as might occur in the interval before a new form of church government was settled. D'Ewes proposed dealing with mechanic preachers, for example, by a short bill against tradesmen and 'other ignorant persons' who dared to invade the pulpits.[33] Common social prejudices were assumed, but so were common reforming ideals. The purpose of the scheme that has been discussed was spiritual renewal by preaching and moral discipline. If it was a bid for power by country gentlemen, it was also a sincere attempt to realise at last the authentic puritan programme of evangelical revival, which had preoccupied gentry in many parts of England since the 1570s and 80s.[34]

University of Sheffield

[32] Rushworth, *Historical Collections*, part 3, vol 1, pp 170–3, 184–7.
[33] Harley MS 164, fol 1015v.
[34] I am grateful to my wife and to Lynn Beats for their comments on a draft of this paper.

PRIMITIVE CHRISTIANITY REVIVED;
RELIGIOUS RENEWAL IN
AUGUSTAN ENGLAND

by EAMON DUFFY

THE restoration of Charles II seemed to the men of the church of England the miraculous inauguration of a golden age— 'When the Lord turned again the captivity of Sion: then were we like unto them that dream. Then was our mouth filled with laughter: and our tongue with joy.'[1] The clerical beneficiaries of the settlement of 1662 had much to rejoice them; the act of uniformity symbolised the secure replanting of the Laudian ideal, an ideal which, as R. S. Bosher has shown,[2] had stiffened and intensified in the years of adversity. The restored church was more certain of itself, more intransigent in its *jure divino* episcopal claims, than the church of the 1630s. This new assurance was nourished by the flowering of anglican patristic learning which is so striking a feature of the later seventeenth century.[3] The magisterial works of Ussher and Pearson on the Ignatian epistles, of Pearson and Fell on Cyprian, and of Bull on the ante-Nicene fathers, each contributed to a deepening sense of the continuity of the church of England with the catholic church of the first centuries. More and more the appeal to antiquity became the criterion of orthodoxy, and in that antiquity anglicanism found not merely its origins, but, occasionally and increasingly, a mirror image of itself. William Beveridge told his hearers at St Peter's Cornhill.

> there are [some] who blame our Reformation as defective, as if the Church were not reformed, not purged enough from the errors it had before contracted; but if such would but lay aside all preju- dices and impartially consider the constitution of our church, as it is now reformed, they might clearly see that as there is nothing defective so neither is there anything superfluous in it, but that it exactly answers the pattern of the Primitive and Apostolical Church itself, as near as it is possible for a national church to do it.[4]

---

[1] [Norman] Sykes, *From Sheldon to Secker* (Cambridge 1959) p 1.
[2] R. S. Bosher, *The Making of the Restoration Settlement* (London 1951).
[3] Sykes, *From Sheldon to Secker*, pp 105–42.
[4] William Beveridge, *Works*, 12 vols, Library of Anglo-Catholic Theology (Oxford 1843–8) 2 p 444; G. V. Bennet, 'Patristic Tradition in Anglican Thought 1660–1900', *Oecumenica* 1971/2 (Strasburg/Minneapolis/Paris/Neuchatel 1972) pp 63–76.

Despite the complacency of such utterances, there was at the heart of the restored church an uncomfortable sense of contradiction. The parliament which was so uncompromisingly anglican, and which forced Charles II to a humiliating capitulation over his attempts at toleration in 1672, harboured men whose lives were anything but an ornament to the church they championed. Restoration society was not godly. Henry More, even in the euphoric year of restoration, had found the 'face of Christendom' an uncomely prospect 'What a *Den* of *Thieves* and *Murderers* it is become; what a *Region* of *Robbers* and *Oppressors*; what a *Stye* of *Epicures*; what a *Wilderness* of *Atheism* and *Profaneness*, in a manner wholly inhabited by *Satyers* and *Savage Beasts* . . .'[5] John Milton found matters no better in 1673. 'It is a general complaint that this nation of late years is grown more numerously and excessively vitious than heretofore; Pride, Luxury, Drunkeness, Whoredom, Cursing, Swearing, bold and open atheism every where Abounding.'[6] The church possessed in its courts a weapon against vice, and in the years after 1661 those courts boomed, yet they could make no real headway against the tide of immorality, and churchmen puzzled over the discrepancy between the excellency of the national religion, and the baseness of the lives of so many of its professors. It was this contradiction which prompted William Cave in the same year as Milton's gloomy utterance to seek a remedy in Christian antiquity. *Primitive Christianity: or, the Religion of the Ancient Christians In the first Ages of the Gospel*[7] was his attempt to harness patristic research to the service not of doctrinal purity but of practical piety. It was, he claimed, no part of his design 'to enquire, what was the judgement of the Fathers in . . . abstruse and intricate speculations of Theology, but what was their practice, and by what rules and measures they did govern and conduct their lives.'[8] He offered 'a Specimen of Primitive Christianity', the 'divine and holy Precepts of the Christian Religion drawn down into action . . . breathing in the hearts and lives of these good old Christians.'[9] Cave's work presented a lucid and highly idealised picture of the life of the Christians in the first three or four centuries; after which he believed 'the life and spirit of Christianity

---

[5] Richard Ward, *The Life of the Learned and Pious Dr Henry More* (London 1710) p 178.

[6] John Milton, quoted in John Redwood, *Reason, Ridicule and Religion* (London 1976) p 173.

[7] [William] Cave, *Primitive Christianity* [*or, the Religion of the Ancient Christians In the first ages of the Gospel*] (London 1673).

[8] Cave, *Primitive Christianity*, preface (no pagination).

[9] *Ibid* Sig A²v.

did . . . visibly decline apace'.[10] He described every aspect of the early church's life—their church order, modes of worship, attitudes to the state and the magistrate, their peculiar virtues, their exemplary sufferings. Many of the descriptive portions of the book were clearly intended for information and edification, rather than imitation, but the overwhelming effect is that of an idealised portrait of *anglican* devotion as it might and should be, and Cave never moved far away from the pastoral concerns of the 1670s. There is a whole chapter on the 'passive obedience' of the Christians to their rulers, and an account, with a glance at the puritans, of the use of the sign of the cross in those early times, and of the primitive emphasis on church buildings: there is even an excursus on the evils of 'patching' and 'painting' for fashion's sake. His description of the primitive eucharist owed as much to the pattern of prayer-book worship as to the sources he cites, while occasionally the contemporary application is direct, as when he turned aside to lament the neglect of confirmation in England, or to administer a drubbing to the papists.[11] The book concluded with an exhortation to his readers 'to *admire* and *imitate* their piety and integrity, their infinite hatred of sin, their care and zeal to keep up that strictness and purity of manners that had rendered their Religion so renowned and triumphant in the world'.[12]

Cave was convinced that his enterprise was a new departure, that there were no satisfactory models to save him 'the labour of this search'.[13] Yet the search for a distinctively anglican devotional and moral ethos was being pursued by others—Walton's *Life* of George Herbert is the most enduring literary expression of that search, though its method differs from Cave's. The nation, after so many years of anarchy and disruption, had to be trained in the religious norms of the church. The alliance of mitre and crown could do much here, and there is evidence to suggest that in the 1670s and 80s church attendance and numbers of communicants were extremely high.[14] Yet if the law could take men to church, it could not make them holy; more was required than the coercion of the constable or the social pressure of conformist neighbours. Above all in the towns there was need of a

[10] *Ibid* Sig Ar.
[11] *Ibid* pt 2 pp 318–402; pt 1 pp 124–50, 156, 330, 339.
[12] *Ibid* pt 2 p 439.
[13] *Ibid* Sig Av.
[14] [G. V.] Bennet, 'Conflict in the Church', in *Britain After the Glorious Revolution*, ed Geoffrey Holmes (London 1969) p 157.

pastoral device which would capture the religious vitality of the people for the church. In the London of 1678 one such device was created. The religious societies which began in that year at the Savoy chapel, and at St Peter and St Michael, Cornhill, were an attempt to translate the ideal of 'primitive Christianity' into a practical, above all an anglican, reality.[15] Their moving spirit, oddly enough, was a German, Anthony Horneck, minister of the Savoy. Horneck, who had settled in England in 1661, was a high-churchman whose Lutheran upbringing had produced a fervent devotion to 'the crucified Jesus'. For Horneck Christianity was cruciform, the Christian way a way of renunciation; 'we are not to regulate our Religion by the sickly Fancies of half Christians, but by the standing Laws of that Jesus . . . whom the Primitive Believers thought themselves obliged to follow in external, as well as internal simplicity.[16] In the 'heavenly lives of the Primitive Christians' Horneck found a model for the Christian life; in the patristic orientation of restoration anglicanism he found an encouragement to revive that 'strictness of the Primitive Church'. The societies were the result. Drawn up at a time 'not over favourable to any kind of Religious Meetings' the rules of the societies bear the marks both of Horneck's high-church convictions, and of dread of the conventicle act. The societies were under the iron hand of the church—each group had a priest as director, no prayers might be used but those taken from the prayer-book, there was to be no discussion of 'controverted points of divinity' or 'the government of Church or State'. Membership was confined to confirmed anglicans. Their activities were all directed towards growth in holiness—meetings for spiritual reading and discussion, fasting, prayer, more frequent communion, charitable works.[17] The ascetic and sacramental emphases of the societies brought charges of popery, but they were central to the whole enterprise. 'I never expect to see our church settled, primitive antiquity revived, and true piety and virtue flourish again among us', wrote William Beveridge, 'till the holy communion be oftener celebrated . . .'[18] Horneck himself provided a rationale for the movement in his *Happy Ascetick* with its annexed *Letter . . . concerning the Heavenly Lives of the Primitive*

[15] [G. V.] Portus, *Caritas Anglicana* (London 1912) pp 1–27; [F. W. B.] Bullock, *Voluntary Religious Societies [1520–1799]* (St Leonards on Sea 1963) pp 125–49.

[16] [Anthony] Horneck, *The Sirenes; or, Delight and Judgment* (2 ed London 1690) preface sig A³–A³v.

[17] Bullock, *Voluntary Religious Societies*, pp 128–9.

[18] [C. F.] Secretan, *[Memoirs of the Life and Times of the] Pious Robert Nelson* (London 1860) p 175.

Christians. Here, in language more rhapsodic than Cave had permitted himself, Horneck derived from the lives of the primitive Christians not only condemnations of the follies and vices of his own age, and endorsements of the concerns of the contemporary church of England in such matters as non-resistance to rulers and obedience to all forms of authority, particularly clerical. He found also the charter for his societies—'In the Cities and Towns where they liv'd, none was unknown to the other; for they Pray'd together, heard the word together . . . and were continually helpful to each other . . . This is one of us, saith such a Saint, for we have seen him in our Oratories, we have pray'd with him, we have kneel'd together, we have been instructed together. O happy Kindred! which comes by Prayer and Communion . . .'[19] Horneck's 'happy kindred' faced considerable opposition, but the pastoral usefulness of the societies in attaching devoted and charitable groups of communicants to parish churches was soon evident. In the reign of James II the societies provided a convincing alternative to the devotional splendours of court catholicism, and were adopted by clergy who were far from being high-churchmen. In the period after the revolution they came into their own, spreading outside London to provincial towns, while in the city itself by 1714 twenty-seven percent of the anglican places of worship were receiving support of some sort from the societies.[20]

Yet if the societies did much to deepen and encourage anglican piety, the concept of primitive Christianity had less comfortable undertones. As applied to doctrine, 'primitive' meant pure, unspoiled, the original and best, and here church of England men, of whatever school, felt themselves on firm ground. Simon Patrick's uncompromising assertion in 1687 that 'The Religion of the Church of England, by Law established, *is* the true Primitive Christianity' is representative.[21] 'Primitive Christianity' in Cave's and Horneck's sense, however, the sense which the societies were making almost universal, implied something rather different. Behind the search for primitive Christianity lay the notion of corruption, falling away.

---

[19] Horneck, *The Happy Ascetick [: or The Best Exercise, Together with . . . a Letter to a Person of Quality, concerning the Holy Lives of the Primitive Christians]* (5 ed London 1711, first published 1681) p 488.

[20] Portus, *Caritas Anglicana*, p 19.

[21] Quoted in P. E. More and F. L. Cross, *Anglicanism* (London 1935) p 141, my emphasis. Compare *The Diary of John Evelyn*, ed W. Bray (Everyman edition London 1907) 2 p 242 (October 2, 1685).

Christianity, declared Horneck, 'is decay'd in the Glory and Brightness of its Life'; zeal in these latter ages 'is grown cold, and the lukewarmness of the present times is such, that he seems to be a setter forth of new Gods, that preaches up this kind of Exercise'.[22] His aim was not to confirm men in the conviction that they lived in the 'best reformed church', to 'prove' the truth of anglicanism by the appeal to the past; primitive Christianity was *essentially* something which had to be revived. And here the quest for primitive Christianity touched anglicanism on a vulnerable spot, for the insistence on an ascetic, penitential, and sacramentally orientated life-style, in an age so lax as that of later Stuart England, raised the whole vexed issue of 'discipline'. The legislation of the cavalier parliament had restored the diocesan courts, but it had left the church still without any effective means of chastising sinners, of correction by means of canonical penance, or of fencing the lord's table from the hardened and unrepentant. This lack of 'discipline' was a weapon for the church's enemies; it was a continual source of embarrassment and regret to churchmen themselves.[23] Year by year they were reminded in the commination service that 'in the Primitive Church, there was a godly discipline, that, at the beginning of Lent, such persons as stood convicted of notorious sin were put to open penance, and punished in this world, that their souls might be saved in the day of the Lord'; it was 'much to be wished' that 'the said discipline may be restored again'. Powerful as the church courts could be, they were no substitute, for they left 'discipline' in the hands of lawyers, laymen with no spiritual commission. 'Excommunication is become a kind of Secular Sentence,' complained Gilbert Burnet in 1681, 'and is hardly now considered as a Spiritual Censure, being judged and given out by Laymen, and often upon grounds, which, to speak moderately, do not merit so severe and dreadful a Sentence'. It was one of the glories of the primitive church, he went on 'that they were so governed, that none of their number could sin openly without publick censure, and a long separation from the Holy Communion.' The lack of 'publick Penance, and penitentiary canons' in the church of England was 'a very great defect.'[24] Burnet's concern was pastoral, he deplored the

---

[22] Horneck, *The Happy Ascetick* p 409; for a similar, though more radical, use of antiquity as a criticism of 17/18th century Christianity, see M. Schmidt in *Oecumenica* 1971/2 pp 88–98.

[23] [George] Every, [*The*] *High Church Party* [*1688–1718*] (London 1956) pp 7–10.

[24] Gilbert Burnet, *The History of the Reformation of the Church of England. The Second Part* (2 ed London 1683) preface (no pagination).

lack of a discipline which would help the clergy set a 'yoke or restraint' on the conscience and 'manners' of the people. Many churchmen saw in the ascetic discipline, pastoral exhortation, and brotherly rebukes employed by the religious societies 'a Preparation of the Minds of the Laity for the Reception of that Discipline which is wanted in the Church'.[25] Yet they were voluntary organisations, and those who submitted to them were already numbered among the saints; what was needed if primitive Christianity was to flourish was some method of reaching the sinner in his sins, to bring him to a 'Sense of [his] Sin and Folly', that he might be 'reclaimed'.[26] This was one of the functions which the societies for the reformation of manners aimed to fulfil.

These societies, the first of which was formed in 1691, were an attempt by private individuals to put into effect the laws against profanity, prostitution, Sunday trading and other moral offences. Groups of citizens, mostly lay-people and, from about 1694, including many dissenters, formed societies whose business it was to inform or procure informations against public sinners of one sort or another, to secure warrants against the culprits from friendly magistrates, and to assist constables in their arrests. They also distributed edifying and monitory literature, and, through the SPCK, information, legal advice and even blank warrants for the aid of like-minded groups in the provinces. It has become customary to draw a sharp distinction between these groups and the religious societies, and D. W. R. Bahlman in the most authoritative modern account declares uncompromisingly that 'they were essentially and fundamentally different from the religious societies; any similarities were superficial.'[27] The reasons for this judgement are, on the face of it, cogent enough. The religious societies were anglican, the reformation societies were not. The religious societies worked for the improvement of their members, the reformation societies for the 'punishment of wickedness and vice'. The religious societies were approved by all the clergy, the reformation societies were disliked by high-churchmen as 'mongrel combinations'. In fact, few if any of these differences are so clear cut as Bahlman supposes, at least in the early years of the reformation

[25] [Robert] Nelson, *A Companion for the Festival and Fasts of the Church of England* (24 ed London 1782, first published 1704) p vi; [*An*] *Address* [*to Persons of Quality and Estate*] (London 1715) pp 138–9.
[26] Nelson, *Address* p 153.
[27] Dudley W. R. Bahlman, *The Moral Revolution of 1688* (Yale 1957) pp 67–70.

societies' existence. Many high-churchmen approved of, and even joined, reformation societies. Anthony Horneck 'was for Reformation of *Manners*', and agreed with Josiah Woodward that the two movements were complementary.[28] 'Pious Robert Nelson', one of the chief pillars of the religious societies, was equally zealous in his support of reformation societies, and included them in a list of projects for devout attendance at church, the better observation of the church's fasts and festivals, and 'the more exact Conformity to the Rules of the Catholick Church, and of the Church of England in particular', with no sense of incongruity or even distinction.[29] Edward Stephens, a churchman whose pursuit of primitive Christianity we will have cause to note later, founded, in succession, the first reformation society, a religious society which had as its object the daily celebration of the eucharist, and a convent.[30]

Above all, however, there is a mass of evidence to show that contemporaries saw an intimate connection between the religious and reformation societies, as complementary expressions of the search for primitive Christianity, and remedies for the lack of primitive discipline. The sermons preached before the societies for the reformation of manners at St Mary-le-Bow between 1696 and 1701 may be taken as representative. For John Russell the reformation societies were 'Religious Associations' of awakened Christians who had 'felt the warmings of the Divine Spirit in [their] hearts', and who were 'engag'd' to 'own the Cause of a Crucified Jesus', by declaring war on 'Vice and Ungodliness'.[31] For Lilly Butler the zeal required of those who would reform society was that 'of the Primitive Christians' which 'prevailed with them, even to *sell their possessions, and to lay the price at the Apostles feet*'.[32] For Josiah Woodward the need for reformation societies sprang from the fact that this 'Nation of professed Christians' had become 'unlike to those Primitive Christians, whose holy fervency . . . scattered the gross Fogs of Profaness and

---

[28] [Richard] Kidder, [The] Life of [the Reverend Anthony] Horneck [D.D. Late Preacher at the Savoy] (London 1698) pp 45–7: Horneck read and approved Josiah Woodward's An Account of the Rise and Progress of the Religious Societies (London 1701) in which this claim was made.

[29] Nelson, Address p 139.

[30] [Edward] Stephens [The Apology of] Socrates Christianus (London 1700) passim; A True Account of the Unaccountable Dealings of some Roman Catholick Missioners (London 1703) pp 14–52; Cane—Wood: OR, a Dialogue (no place or date) pp 4–10.

[31] John Russell, A Sermon Preach'd . . . June 28 1697 (London 1697) pp 441–2, 46–8.

[32] Lilly Butler, A Sermon Preach'd . . . April 5 1697 p 15.

Superstitions'; if ever the nation's 'Holy Religion' were to regain its 'primitive Reputation and Renown', it must be by the 'exemplary Purity Zeal and Fervor of its Professors; even by a general, vigorous, and resolute opposition to Vice.'[33] Preacher after preacher linked the religious and reformation societies as 'two hopeful Prognosticks' and signs that *'our dry bones could live'*.[34] The anonymous author of one of the most influential accounts of the reformation societies made the same link, and rendered explicit the service which the reformation societies could offer the church. He rehearsed the usual account of the admirable discipline of the primitive church, 'when such offenders, which now make too great a part of the visible Church, were looked on as a kind of Monsters, and, like putrefy'd Members were cut off' till they gave some signs of their repentance. This lack the church now laments yearly, but till 'the Ecclesiastical Power is recovered to its Primitive Design', the reformation societies must stand in the gap. This view of the societies as in some sense exercising 'discipline' was acceptable enough to low-churchmen committed to the voluntary principle. White Kennet, preaching for the reformation societies in 1701 saw the members as 'Fellow Labourers in converting of Sinners, and Savers of Souls', though he thought that the 'discipline' might be yet more satisfactory if 'every Parish-Priest might by Law be made a Magistrate in *things pertaining unto God*, i.e. in being made capable to inflict all the legal Penalties, for cursing and Swearing, and Profanation of the Lord's day, and other open notorious breach of conscience and good Manners'.[35] Such an erastian expedient, however, was unlikely to appeal to high-churchmen, particularly after the accession of queen Anne, when hopes for a greater authority for the church ran high. The convocation controversy, and the Bangorian controversy which destroyed convocation itself, were expressions of the same issues of

---

[33] Josiah Woodward, *The Duty of Compassion to the Souls of Others, in endeavouring their Reformation* (2 ed London 1698, preached December 28 1696) pp 53–5.

[34] Gilbert Burnet, *Charitable Reproof. A Sermon Preached . . . 25 March 1700* (London 1700) pp 26–7; Samuel Bradford, *A Sermon Preach'd . . . Oct 4th 1697* (London 1697) dedication, no pagination. Bradford was rector of St Mary's where the reformation society sermons were preached. He was noted for his exercise of 'discipline' in excluding notorious sinners from communion—see William Whiston, *Memoirs of the Life and Writings of Mr William Whiston* (London 1749) pp 183–6; see also Whiston's *Primitive Christianity Reviv'd*, 4 volumes (London 1712) I, p I xxiii. St Mary-le-Bow was also one of the two churches at which weekly communions were held for the religious societies.

An Account of the Societies for Reformation of Manners in London and Westminster, and other Parts of the Kingdom (London 1719, I ed 1699) p 113; Portus, *Caritas Anglicana* pp 223–8.

church authority and independence which were raised by the question of 'discipline'. The influx of dissenters into the societies after 1694 made them even less attractive as wielders of the power of the keys. High-churchmen set to work for a restoration of the church's authority in society by more direct methods. William Reeves, in a notable essay on the 'right use of the Fathers', published in the summer of 1709, on the eve of the Sacheverell affair, turned aside to consider this issue of 'Church-Discipline'. 'I acknowledge freely', he wrote, '. . . that the Spirit of Reformation now moving upon the Hearts of many excellent Lay Christians, and quickening the Execution of the Laws of the Land . . . is a mighty check upon disorderely Walkers, and has given a new Life and Resurrection to Piety and good manners, and in some measure made amends for the lamentable Relaxation and Decay of Discipline; but then I must freely own likewise, that the Laws of the State are not the Discipline of the Church; the Things of Caesar and the Things of God, are not under the same Predicament, but of quite a different Nature.' High-churchmen were as alert to the church's part in the task of social control as Kennet, with his talk of clerical magistrates, but Reeves's understanding of that function is relentlessly ecclesiastical, though by no means exclusively spiritual.

> The Noise of the Seas, and the madness of the People go together in Scripture and Experience, and we may as well preach stilness to the one without a Sea-Wall, as Obedience to the other without Discipline . . . when the Ancient Fences are broken down, and the Reins of Discipline let loose upon the Necks of the People . . . they seldom stop short of the . . . Pitch of Religious Frenzy. We have felt something like it at home and what has been, may be.

His programme for reformation, therefore, consisted of an examination of the scriptures and 'Primitive Fathers' to discover 'what particulars in Discipline are appointed by God'; the church should then strive 'to have them restored to Life again'.[36] The Sacheverell affair and its euphoric aftermath gave grounds for hope that something might indeed be done along these lines; Nathaniel Marshall's *Penitential Discipline of the Primitive Church*, prepared as a programme for legislation for the convocation of 1714, is the most enduring monu-

---

[35] White Kennett, *A Sermon Preach'd . . . 29 December 1701* (London 1702) pp 45–6.
[36] William Reeves, *The Apologies of Justin Martyr . . . with a Prefatory Dissertation about the Right Use of the Fathers* (2 ed London 1716) dedication dated 22 June 1709, pp lxxv–lxxviii.

ment of that hope.[37] The death of queen Anne, and the Bangorian controversy, put an end to all this, however. The restoration of primitive discipline remained a thing, in the words of the commination service 'much to be wished' for.

It was not only the aspect of primitive Christianity to run into the sand. The trauma of revolution damaged many ideals and many idols, and primitive Christianity was among them. Both Cave and Horneck had 'proved' from antiquity that the early Christians hated rebellion against their rulers 'as Witchcraft, and ever thought it safer to suffer, than to resist'.[38] This 'primitive' principle was abandoned by both in 1689, and Horneck lost some of his support by his conformity to the new regime.[39] The high-church was divided; Robert Nelson, that 'fair Image of *Primitive Christianity*' joined the non-juring schism,[40] and in its communion were to be found many of the most fervent 'primitives'; the ideal moved further away from the centre of the nation's religious life. The process can be seen in an extreme form in the career of Edward Stephens. This Gloucestershire squire who practised as a solicitor, a high-churchman deeply committed to the programme of asceticism and frequent communion advocated by the religious societies, had welcomed the revolution as a providential intervention by God to save the nation from 'Popery and Arbitrary Government'. King William had been raised up by God to cleanse the nation from its sins. As part of this process of cleansing Stephens founded the first of the reformation societies, in the Strand in 1691, pressing his legal expertise into the service of godliness. Pursuing the same programme of national reformation he founded in the following year a small religious society intended to restore the 'primitive' practice of daily communion.[41] The hoped-for renewal of England's morals and her church did not materialise, however, and Stephens grew increasingly disillusioned with the revolution, the king, and the episcopal bench; he became convinced that 'primitive discipline' could never be restored by the means of the societies. 'Had we Bishops of true Christian Spirits, we should need no societies for Reformation of

---

[37] (Nathaniel Marshall), *The Penitential Discipline of the Primitive Church*, Library of Anglo Catholic Theology (Oxford 1844, first published London 1714) pp 161–84.

[38] Horneck, *The Happy Ascetick* p 515; Cave, *Primitive Christianity* pt 2 pp 318–402.

[39] Kidder, *Life of Horneck* p 19.

[40] Secretan, *Pious Robert Nelson* pp 46–80.

[41] [Edward] Stephens, *Reflections upon the occurences of the last Year* (London 1689) pp 4–5, 13–15, 20, 29; *Socrates Christianus* pt 2, pp 4–5; [*A Seasonable and Necessary*] *Admonition* [*to the Gentlemen of the First Society for Reformation of Manners*] (no place or date) p 4.

Manners among the Laity.' He also became convinced that the church of England 'hath been in Bondage under the Civil Power' ever since the reformation, that her 'primitive Liturgy' had been maliciously defaced by 'a Cranmerian faction', who hypocritically mourned the 'Christian Discipline' in the commination, but 'never had the courage to attempt to restore'.[42] Stephens eventually declared himself out of communion with everyone but a small handful of disciples, forming what he believed to be the only truly catholic church in the world, and began a tireless series of letters and memorials to the king, the bishops, the judges, the commons and the societies for reformation, designed to bring about the return of England to primitive Christianity.[43]

Stephens was a crank, but his oddities are significant. Dr Grabe, the Prussian pietist who had come to England and anglicanism in search of a truly primitive church, and whose *Spicelegium* was to provide generations of high-churchmen with their first direct contact with primitive antiquity, held communion with Stephens. Grabe too, at the time of his death, had been planning a work designed to reform the church of England nearer to 'the most Primitive model'.[44] Primitive Christianity had become eccentric.

Indeed, even the orthodox study of Christian antiquity was becoming so. The publication of Toland's *Amyntor* in 1699 turned the whole fabric of 'Primitive Christianity' on its head—the *Primitive* times were not ages of purity and truth, but rather, ages when 'commerce was not near so general as now, and the whole Earth entirely overspread with the Darkness of Superstition.' The Ignatian letters, the *Apostolic Constitutions*, the epistle of Polycarp, the Shepherd of Hermas, those pillars on which primitive Christianity was raised, were monuments of ignorance and superstition, 'the silliest Book(s) in the World'. The age of Reason had arrived.[45]

All these trends may be seen in three friends associated with Cambridge at the turn of the seventeenth and eighteenth centuries—

[42] Stephens, *Admonition* p 6; *An Apology for . . . the People call'd Quakers* (London 1697) p 22.
[43] These are to be found in Stephens, [*A Collection of*] *Tracts and Papers* [*Lately Written for the Service of the Church and Kingdom of England*] (London 1702)
[44] Stephens, *Tracts and Papers*, general preface p 9; Johannes Ernst Grabe, *Spicelegium SS Patrum ut et haereticorum seculi post Christum natum I, II et III*, 2 vols (London 1698-9); [V. H. H.] Green, [*The Young Mr*] *Wesley* (London 1967) pp 273-4; (J. Knight) *Primitive Christianity Vindicated, in a Second Letter to the Author of the History of Montanism* (London 1712) p i.
[45] John Toland, *Amyntor; or a Defence of Milton's Life* (London 1699) pp 12-45.

William Whiston, Samuel Clarke and Benjamin Hoadly. All three men were initially committed to primitive Christianity. Clarke wrote a reply to *Amyntor* in 1699, and in the same year a series of essays commending the 'strict Piety' and 'severity of Discipline' of the primitive Christians.[46] Hoadly was a high-churchman, who believed that the disciplinary canons of the *Apostolic Constitutions* should be introduced into the church of England.[47] Whiston even as an undergraduate was deeply involved with the aims of the religious societies and the recovery of the 'Golden Age' of the early church.[48] Of these men, only Whiston retained his commitment to primitive Christianity. In his hands it became as eccentric as Stephens' enterprise, and rather less orthodox, a paranoid conviction that primitive Christianity had been smothered in a vast conspiracy of which the villain was not Cranmer but Athanasius; Christian antiquity and rationalism come together and bring forth Arianism.[49] Clarke decisively repudiated his patristic learning; his most significant work was a massive demonstration that between the Christological orthodoxy of the primitive church, and God's revelation in scripture, there was an unbridgeable gap.[50] Hoadly became, in *his* rejection of the primitive ideal, the means by which the whole concept of independent church authority, the power of the keys, and the exercise of discipline, were overthrown, in the eclipse of convocation.[51] The ideal would linger still, high-churchmen even after the advent of the bishop of Bangor would assure themselves that by divine grace the church of England held still 'almost to the Purity of the Primitive Standard', but the vitality was gone. Its last great eighteenth-century anglican exponent was the young John Wesley, 'Mr. Primitive Christianity', and in 1738 he was

---

[46] Samuel Clarke, *Some Reflections on that part of a book called Amyntor . . . which relates to the Writings of the Primitive Fathers and the Canon of the New Testament* (London) 1699); *Three practical Essays on Baptism, Confirmation and Repentance . . . with Earnest Exhortations . . . drawn from the Consideration of the Severity of the Discipline of the Primitive Church,* in *The Works of Revd Samuel Clarke,* 4 vols (London 1738) 3 pp 569, 920; [William] Whiston, [*Historical Memoirs of the Life and Writings of Dr Samuel*] *Clarke* (3 ed London 1748) p 6.

[47] Every, *High Church Party* p 72n: Whiston, *Clarke* p 20–1.

[48] [E.] Duffy. 'Whiston's Affair; [the trials of a Primitive Christian 1709–1714'], *JEH* 27, 2 (April 1976) pp 129–50, esp 131–2.

[49] Duffy, 'Whiston's Affair' pp 134–6; compare Frank E. Manuel, *The Religion of Isaac Newton* (Oxford 1974) pp 53–75.

[50] Samuel Clarke, *The Scripture Doctrine of the Trinity* (London 1712).

[51] For Hoadley's later views on the use of the Fathers see Sykes, *From Sheldon to Secker* p 168.

to abandon the ideal of 'primitive' for that of 'real' Christianity.[52] The tradition however, was not entirely forgotten, for Wesley was to include both Cave's *Primitive Christianity* and Horneck's *Happy Ascetick* in his *Christian Library*. Perhaps, after all, the river had found its way to the sea.

King's College
University of London

[52] Green, *Wesley* pp 271-6; Frank Baker, *John Wesley and the Church of England* (London 1970) pp 30-4, 42-57.

'WHAT HAS CHRIST TO DO WITH APOLLO?': EVANGELICALISM AND THE NOVEL, 1800–30

by DOREEN M. ROSMAN

IN December 1800 the *Evangelical Magazine* published a 'Spiritual barometer; or, a scale of the progress of sin and of grace'. Towards the positive pole it was calibrated with the attributes and practices thought to characterise those destined for 'glory' and 'dismission from the body'; at the other extreme, graded in degrees of depravity, were the activities of those assumed to be heading heedlessly to 'death' and 'perdition'. Among the most heinous of sins, even more damning than attendance at the theatre, was 'love of novels'.[1]

Novel-reading was condemned as a hallmark of worldliness. Evangelicals believed that church and world were diametrically opposed and that the safest route to sanctity lay in separation from the world, its contaminating company and perverting practices: 'If we are not to think, to feel, to act, and to perish with the world, let a deep and wide interval yet exist between the habits of pleasure of the two parties.'[2] Ignorance of evil was deemed bliss: to read novels was to become familiar with just such beliefs and behaviour as were avoided in everyday life. Moreover, it was argued that novelists rarely upheld Christian values: they depicted wickedness sympathetically and effectively denied that sin, an affront to God, had dire consequences. They therefore misled their readers in matters of ultimate importance. Evangelicals maintained that the worthiness of characters should be evaluated according to criteria which God might be assumed to adopt. Failure to reflect a biblical outlook on life was a culpable mis-representation of reality.

A further criticism was that novels aroused false expectations in young girls, who imagined that their lives would correspond to the heroines'; filled with distaste for the comparative dullness of daily living, they were likely to be deterred and distracted from more

---

[1] E[vangelical] M[agazine], 1 series, 8 (London 1800) p 526.
[2] C[hristian] O[bserver], 16 (London 1817) p 301.

serious and demanding studies and from the disciplines of spirituality. These involved the exercise of the intellect and the will, facets of the personality which evangelicals valued far more than the imagination and the passions, to which the novel appealed. The novel-reader, immersed in an imaginary world, was believed to suffer 'injurious excitement' caused by an 'intoxicating stimulant'; the novelist aroused emotions but did not usefully channel them into active benevolence. Novels were therefore 'enervating' and 'dissipating'. Even the least objectionable were criticised for engrossing more time than could legitimately be devoted to relaxation, for evangelicals believed that they were accountable to God for the proper use of every moment. Hannah More, one of their best known spokesmen, commented on the works of Sir Walter Scott: 'Had he written before the flood . . . all would have been well . . . A life of eight hundred years might have allowed of the perusal of the whole of his volumes; a proportionate quantity in each century would have been delightful: but for our poor scanty threescore years and ten, it is too much . . .'[3]

Evangelicals were not alone in objecting to the novel: arguments similar to some of theirs were commonly put forward by eighteenth-century critics.[4] But by the third decade of the nineteenth century the more general distrust of the genre had been largely effaced. The *Quarterly Review* of January 1821 introduced its essay on *Northanger Abbey* and *Persuasion* with the affirmation: 'The times seem to be past when an apology was requisite from reviewers for condescending to notice a novel'. The writer was not surprised that novels had been indiscriminately condemned at a time when most were highly improbable, engaged the passions, and portrayed vice favourably. He believed, however, that the novel had since changed to become a vehicle of morality.[5]

Evangelical reviewers disagreed. When Sir Walter Scott died the *Methodist Magazine* wrote of his novels, the popularity of which had done much to make the genre respectable, 'Their capital defect is,

[3] W. Roberts, *Memoirs of the Life and Correspondence of Mrs Hannah More*, 4 vols (London 1834) 4 pp 204-5. For detailed evangelical criticism of novel-reading see, for example, H. More, *Moral Sketches* (London 1819) pp 238-49; CO 14 (1815) pp 512-17; 16 (1817) pp 298-301, 371-5, 425-9; 22 (1822) pp 157-72, 237-50; E[clectic] R[eview], 2 series, 7 (London 1817) pp 309-36; M[ethodist] M[agazine], 2 series, 16 (London 1819) pp 606-9.
[4] See for example I. Richards, *Novel and Romance 1700-1800 A Documentary Record* (London 1970) pp 1-24; J. T. Taylor, *Early Opposition to the English Novel; the popular reaction from 1760-1830* (New York 1943); W. F. Gallaway, *Publications of the Modern Language Association of America*, 55 (Menasha, Wisconsin 1940) pp 1041-59.
[5] *Quarterley Review*, 24 (London 1821) pp 352-7.

that they appear to have been written without any moral aim'.[6] Similarly the editor of the evangelical newspaper, *The Record*, found himself unable to give the Waverley novels the approbation which they were generally accorded. He did not deny their genius and charm, nor that they were less coarse and hence superior to eighteenth-century productions. But this increased their insidious danger for readers were less on their guard: Scott was condemned for sporting with that which was holy, for bringing his readers into familiar contact with immorality, for leading their minds away from God, and for setting their attention on the things of the earth.[7] *The Record* was the mouthpiece of the increasingly strident anglican evangelicalism of the 1830s, but similar sentiments about Scott were expressed at the time of his death in the more cultured and liberal *Christian Observer*, organ of the Clapham sect. Contributors protested that Scott misrepresented religion, and that his novels, while not licentious, were far from positively moral.[8]

Nevertheless not even evangelicals were proof against the power of Walter Scott. In 1817 the *Christian Observer* noted that novel-reading prevailed to a considerable extent even in the religious world and on more than one occasion it blamed Scott for this: 'The habit of novel-reading introduced into many families where it did not formerly prevail, by means of Sir Walter Scott's publications, has always appeared to us so pernicious and alarming that we have never ceased to remonstrate against it'.[9] Such virtuous indignation was not altogether justified, for not all *Christian Observer* contributors categorically condemned the novel. While some were hostile, some, including the editor's son, Tom Macaulay, justified the reading of certain classes of fiction.[10] Admittedly the periodical refrained from reviewing any of Scott's novels until the thirty-ninth was published in 1822, when it determined to make its views known on an author who wrote so prolifically and had so extensive an influence: much of the review was devoted to a reasoned condemnation of novel-reading.[11] But the reviewer admitted that Scott's were the best of 'mere novels'. Moreover, Scott's poetry had received regular attention

---

[6] *MM*, 3 series, 12 (1833) pp 17–18.
[7] *The Record*, 27 September 1832, 4 October 1832.
[8] *CO*, 32 (1832) p 814; 33 (1833) pp 478–82.
[9] *Ibid* 16 (1817) p 64; 22 (1822) p 158; 32 (1832) p 819.
[10] *Ibid* 15 (1816) pp 784–87; compare 16 (1817) pp 230–1.
[11] *Ibid* 22 (1822) pp 157–72, 237–50.

from the *Christian Observer*, which spoke, with qualifications, favourably of much of it.[12] Readers permitted to sample Scott's stories when he wrote in the genre sanctioned by Milton and Cowper could hardly be blamed if they then turned to his prose fiction.

Further evidence of growing permissiveness comes from the dissenting *Eclectic Review*. Unlike the *Christian Observer* which contained primarily although not exclusively religious matter, this regarded itself as a counterpart of contemporary literary reviews, differing from them in that its values and criteria of judgement were specifically Christian: it aimed 'to blend with impartial criticism an invariable regard to moral and religious principle'.[13] Its contributors reviewed a number of novels, and while some spoke derogatively of the genre, 'a species of literature which, with rare exceptions, we have not submitted to the drudgery of reading', 'a class of works which has but doubtful claims on our notice', it was by no means condemned out of hand.[14] On the contrary reviewers admitted that 'To the authors of fictitious Narratives the literary world is certainly indebted, for some of the most sublime and useful works in poetry or prose', and suggested that the skill needed to write prose narrative was such that 'the performance, though it be but a tale, will appear to deserve no mean rank among the efforts of genius'.[15] In particular reviewers, including those most uneasy about the novel, were convinced of Scott's genius, although some voiced regret that he did not put his undoubted talents to better use.[16] If not positively moral, Scott at least eschewed the libertinism of his predecessors, while he was regarded as a far greater writer than his contemporaries:

> . . . seeing that the constant demand for such works necessitates a supply of some kind . . . we will not dispute that a service is rendered to the lovers of light reading, by writers of superior talent . . . who furnish the public with amusement more deserving of the name of intellectual, than the generality of novels.[17]

More positively, several reviewers spoke very highly of Scott's achievements, acclaiming his talents and whetting their readers' appetites by quoting at length from his works. His plots were criticised,

[12] See for example *CO*, 9 (1810) pp 366–89; 11 (1812) pp 29–33; 14 (1815) pp 750–60.
[13] *ER*, 1 series, 1 (1805) prospectus p 2.
[14] *Ibid* 2 series, 15 (1821) p 280; 13 (1820) p 526.
[15] *Ibid* 1 series, 2 (1806) p 140; 2 series, 12 (1819) pp 429–30.
[16] *Ibid* 2 series, 14 (1820) p 268.
[17] *Ibid* 12 (1819) p 423.

but such is his faculty of identification, so perfectly to the life are his characters drawn, coloured, grouped, and put into action, and with such veritable circumstance does he surround them, that we are insensible to deficiencies in his fable, that would be fatal to any less powerful spell than that by which he contrives to enthrall us . . .[18]

Comments like this make plain the problems such evangelicals faced. Eclectic reviewers were in varying degrees convinced by the traditional arguments against novel-reading. There was, moreover, much in Scott's works of which they disapproved. Yet they acknowledged his moral and aesthetic superiority over other novelists past and present, and, so lured, succumbed to his spell. Their difficulty was explicitly stated in an 1833 review of a novel by Mrs Hall: 'In perusing works of this class, we too often find ourselves forced to admire what we cannot approve; pleased, interested, fascinated by the perusal, and dissatisfied with ourselves on reflecting what has so much pleased us'.[19]

The dilemma found typical expression in William Wilberforce who in later life delighted in Scott's novels. Nevertheless he felt that he had sat up too late reading *Old Mortality*, and wrote of *Peveril of the Peak* 'I am glad we have finished the work; this class of writings is too interesting; it makes other studies insipid, or rather other light reading; but yet much to be learned from this class of writings . . .'[20] The last statement represents Wilberforce's attempt, conscious or subconscious, to justify and account for his interest. In 1822 he read *The Fortunes of Nigel* and commented:

It is strange how much Nigel has haunted me while reading it. In spite of all my resistance and correction of the illusion by suggesting to myself that the author may order events as he pleases, I am extremely interested by it. But I think it is partly because I consider it all as substantially true, giving the account of the manners and incidents of the day.[21]

But the books appealed to more than a purely academic interest in the past and Wilberforce was not wholly convinced by his own explanation. In the last resort he was unable to justify the reading he

[18] *Ibid* 18 (1822) p 163.
[19] *Ibid* 3 series, 9 (1833) p 41.
[20] [R. I. and S.] Wilberforce, [*The Life of William Wilberforce*], 5 vols (London 1838) 5 pp 268–70.
[21] *Ibid* p 133.

enjoyed so much. As an evangelical he believed that 'one thing is needful', and that all—or nearly all—activity should be directed to that end.[22] He continued to delight in Scott's writings and noted with satisfaction any Christian emphases, but he was forced to lament the general absence of 'moral or religious object. They remind me of a giant spending his strength in cracking nuts. I would rather go to render up my account at the last day, carrying up with me *The Shepherd of Salisbury Plain*, than bearing the load of all those volumes, full as they are of genius'.[23]

Hannah More's tract, *The Shepherd of Salisbury Plain*, was one of many religious tales which flooded the market in the first thirty years of the nineteenth century, a period which saw the effective birth of the religious novel. Indeed if some evangelicals were seduced into novel-reading by Sir Walter Scott, far more were led onto the downward track by Mrs More and her successors. Unlike the Waverley novels, religious fiction was reviewed in all the evangelical periodicals, and, particularly in its infancy, received considerable approbation. The *Evangelical Magazine* was exuberant that the tables were now being turned on the devil: 'because the enemy of mankind hath dressed Vice and Licentiousness in these engaging forms, must we therefore wholly surrender them to his service? By no means. Rather let us restore them to the cause of Virtue and Religion'.[24] 'With great pleasure we announce and recommend this publication', wrote the *Eclectic Review* of a widely acclaimed novel by Harriet Corp; 'She . . . embodies her instructions in a form which must attract attention'.[25] The *Christian Observer* quoted several pages from another work by the same author to encourage young people to read it: they would do so with pleasure and profit.[26]

But religious novels also provoked criticism which became increasingly marked as their production escalated in the years after the Napoleonic wars. The term 'novel' was one of such disapprobation that evangelicals were initially loath to apply it to a Christian work: in 1806 the *Evangelical Magazine* wrote of John Satchell's *Thornton Abbey* 'Were this work written on any other subject than religion, we should not hesitate to call it a *Novel*, in the form of Letters: but that

---

[22] Luke 10: 42, a favourite evangelical text.
[23] Wilberforce, 5 p 254.
[24] *EM*, 1 series, 13 (1805) p 515.
[25] *ER*, 1 series, 5 (1809) pp 972–3.
[26] *CO*, 6 (1807) pp 522–26.

name has been too much degraded to be admitted into religious literature'.[27] There was considerable unease about mixing sacred and secular. Momentous religious truths should surely not be presented in so gaudy a garb: in 1823 the *Baptist Magazine* protested 'we cannot help calling in question the propriety of stating . . . divine principles, or sacred influence, through the plot of a romance . . .'[28] Also questioned was the propriety of producing fiction for adults. Stories were for children; the *Eclectic Review* was therefore 'unwilling to believe, what seems indeed implied in the practice of many useful writers, that in addressing *men* and *women*, of any class, it is really necessary, or really desirable, to tickle their ears, and lure their eyes with tales and pictures'.[29]

The underlying assumption was that 'tales and pictures' were merely sugar to the pill. Evangelicals believed that religious truth was conceptual, a matter of doctrine and precept. And so they communicated it not on the whole through narrative, but within the framework of narrative—through long and sermonic comments and conversations. Too much narrative was regarded as not only inappropriate but also counterproductive. The *Christian Observer* feared that some might read religious fiction for the plot and the incidents, vicariously sharing the experiences and emotions described, but skipping the moral lessons and religious observations.[30] Thus, it praised one novel because it was '*not* novelish in its character: its incidents being few and simple, and only as pegs for the moral'.[31] Similarly it stated of Mrs More's *Coelebs in search of a wife* 'It may be very true that novels are mischievous; but we cannot allow this work to be called a novel . . . the preceptive parts are not choked with incidents'; 'Mrs More, with her lively imagination, must have felt some difficulty in *preventing* her *Coelebs* from degenerating too much into matters of plot and incident, of which she has admitted only so much as seemed necessary for her higher purpose'.[32] Paradoxically the *Christian Observer* was giving highest praise to those novels that made least use of the genre's potentiality.

That the novel was not factually true was a further cause of concern to some evangelicals and gave rise to casuistry such as that described

---

[27] *EM*, 1 series, 14 (1806) pp 514–15.
[28] B[aptist] M[agazine], 15 (London 1823) p 111.
[29] *ER*, 2 series, 9 (1818) pp 61–2.
[30] *CO*, 11 (1812) pp 713–14.
[31] *Ibid* 30 (1830) p 432.
[32] *Ibid* 8 (1809) pp 109, 111; 23 (1823) p 648.

in the *Evangelical Magazine* of 1805: 'to avoid the offence some well-meaning Christians have taken at fictitious narrative, the Author, like the celebrated Bunyan, hath told his pleasing story as a dream'.[33] A few evangelicals clearly had very rigid ideas about what was 'true': a reviewer of Mrs Sherwood's *Stories explanatory of the catechism* complained that events illustrative of catechetical teaching were unlikely to occur in the right order.[34] Such bizarre objections were rare, but concern for authenticity was sufficiently widespread to provoke the multiplication of tales 'founded on fact'. These were praised more highly than mere fiction, but were not free from censure: in 1825 the *Baptist Magazine* pronounced 'We are jealous of these little tales *founded on fact*—not knowing how far they are so—and we think an intelligent child should be encouraged, in every instance, to ask, "is it true?" '[35] The *Eclectic Review*, catering for the more educated, recognised that even reputable histories were but 'fictions founded upon fact', suggested that verisimilitude was more important to a story than factual truth, and argued that a work could be both fictional and true.[36] Nevertheless it was generally accepted that fact was more potent and edifying than fiction. Virtuous characters in fiction, the *Christian Observer* pointed out, might or might not be imitable; certainly there was no obligation on the reader to emulate them as there was in the case of lives of real people.[37] Moreover testimonies and memoirs were believed to provide authoritative evidence of the activity of God, which fiction by definition could not supply. 'The God of truth' the *Baptist Magazine* argued 'cannot be so fully expected to use the creations of fancy, as he may be the correct relations of his own righteous acts and gracious operations'.[38] It was a mystery to some evangelicals why people should want to read the inventions of fiction when real life accounts were just as exciting. In 1827 the *Evangelical Magazine* hailed a set of biographies with the comment 'There would be little occasion for works of fiction, were a due attention paid to the narratives of those who have actually figured on the stage of life'.[39]

Underlying all such criticisms of fiction and attempts to woo

---

[33] *EM*, 1 series, 13 (1805) p 270.
[34] *Ibid* 26 (1818) p 477.
[35] *BM*, 17 (1825) p 124.
[36] *ER*, 2 series, 13 (1820) pp 276–7, 349.
[37] *CO*, 25 (1825) p 162.
[38] *BM*, 15 (1823) p 385; see also *ER*, 2 series, 7 (1817) p 313.
[39] *EM*, 2 series, 5 (1827) p 342.

evangelicals from the novel was the nagging fear that religious novel-reading might be accompanied by the same ill effects as ordinary novel-reading, over-excitement, an unwillingness to read more serious matter, and an insatiable thirst for fiction. The *Christian Observer* maintained that 'though occasional stimulants may be salutary, they cannot with impunity become our daily food'.[40] From the beginning there was concern lest religious fiction proliferated: thus the *Eclectic Review* of 1806 praised *Thornton Abbey* but feared 'a serious calamity, if the success of the present work should let loose a pack of religious novels upon the public.'[41] By the 1820s its fears were realised and protests against a continuing inundation of religious fiction became increasingly common in all evangelical periodicals. An *Evangelical Magazine* reviewer would have given one book unqualified praise had he not been afraid that the increase in religious fiction would prevent the study of real history and would imperceptibly encourage the young to read dangerously worldly novels.[42] The same prevalent fear that people would progress from religious novels to secular novels, and hence become more worldly and less religious, was voiced by the *Methodist Magazine* when it spoke disparagingly of

> . . . those religious novels which abound in the present day, and which threaten very extensively to pervert the taste of our youth. In the books to which we refer, evangelical sentiment is mixed up with flippant and fictitious narrative, which is only calculated to induce a habit of novel-reading, and to render the mind indifferent to sober truth and fact.[43]

But despite all their unease and antagonism the reviewers felt unable totally to condemn such novels. Christ had taught in parables. The need to provide wholesome reading matter for the evangelical young remained, as did the initial evangelistic incentive:

> . . . it seems pretty clear that, while the rage for that kind of reading, which gratifies an irregular appetite and a distempered fancy, continues so inordinate, the only choice left to the friends of wisdom, is, to encounter folly on its own ground, and to make their way to the understanding by addressing themselves to the imagination.[44]

[40] *CO*, 30 (1830) p 432.
[41] *ER*, 1 series, 2 (1806) p 1030.
[42] *EM*, 1 series, 26 (1818) p 208–9.
[43] *MM*, 3 series, 3 (1824) p 693.
[44] *ER*, 1 series, 8 (1812) p 924.

When the aim was laudable, critics could not but approve.[45] In any case they often enjoyed the books themselves. Although he disapproved of tales, a *Baptist Magazine* reviewer confessed that he had derived considerable pleasure from *Procrastination; or the Vicar's daughter*.[46] The ambivalence of the reviewers' position over religious as over secular novels was reflected even within individual reviews. Many started by condemning the genre and then proceeded to exempt from censure the particular novel under review. The *Eclectic Review*'s analysis of *Dunallan; or Know what you judge: a story* commenced 'We still think the light viands now so much in request, a bad substitute for the more healthy, spiritual food of our forefathers . . .' But the reviewer acknowledged that it was a novel-reading age and if fictions were to be read 'their being made subservient to moral or religious lessons cannot be held criminal'. He admitted that tales could have good effects upon their readers and 'when religious truths are recommended by the charms of graceful fiction, and kept, at the same time, in their genuine purity, we should not know exactly in what terms to express our disapprobation'.[47]

Ultimately the reviewers had no option but to accept the religious novel because the evangelical public for which they wrote liked it and made profitable its increasing production. This state of affairs was regretfully acknowledged by the *Eclectic Review* of 1832 when it lamented that whatever it said would be disregarded: 'Our recommendation they scarcely need, nor would the public wait for it. Our interdict would not be respected. Tales the public will have . . .'[48]

It is clear from the periodicals that between 1800 and 1830 evangelical novel-reading, partly secular, but largely religious, increased significantly. The reactions of the reviewers reveal that, while they were at least partially responsible, they were far from sanguine about a change in practice that looked like a concession to worldliness. Fears that the revival had lost its impetus and that Christians were becoming worldly were widespread in the 1820s: many evangelicals looked for a further revival, held prayer meetings to this end and followed eagerly the reports of contemporary American awakenings.[49] In his 1816 defence of the novel Tom Macaulay had

---

[45] See for example *ER*, 3 series, 3 (1830) p 565.
[46] *BM*, 17 (1825) p 173.
[47] *ER*, 2 series, 23 (1825) p 462.
[48] *ER*, 3 series, 7 (1832) p 346.
[49] See for example *EM*, 2 series, 6 (1828) pp iii–iv.

suggested that the way for the reformation had been paved by the renaissance of romances.[50] His argument merely reflects the extent of his divergence from mainstream evangelicalism. In the 1820s the renaissance of the novel was regarded as symptomatic of a prevalent worldliness: far from foreshadowing, it attested to the need for religious renewal.

University of Kent at Canterbury

[50] *CO*, 15 (1816) pp 784–5.

JOHN LINGARD AND THE CATHOLIC REVIVAL

by SHERIDAN GILLEY

HE nineteenth-century histories of England were inspired by and reflect the political and religious ideologies of the era; the liberal anglican school described by Duncan Forbes,[1] the varieties of high church scholarship from Christopher Wordsworth to canon Dixon,[2] the optimistic whiggery of Hallam and Macaulay, the protestant high toryism of Southey, the political protestantism of Froude and the teutomania of Freeman[3]. Most of these writers had two ideas in common; a strong sense of the importance of national history as a reinforcement of the English sense of self identity, and the oneness of English history. This was a view given classic expression in John Richard Green's *Short History of the English People*,[4] and has been perpetuated by Trevelyan and Churchill into the twentieth century. Far better than most of his predecessors, Green's history was more than just a history of the nation written from a partisan point of view, and owed its popularity as much to its breadth of sympathy as to the author's gift for quicksilver generalisation and narration which move the reader on at the pace of a hare. In this last quality, it was most unlike the most popular nineteenth-century history of England before its publication,[5] the work of a Roman catholic priest John Lingard,[6] though Lingard also professed to rise above the turmoil of parties to write an impartial history.[7]

---

[1] [Duncan] Forbes, [*The Liberal Anglican Idea of History*] (Cambridge 1952).

[2] E. G. Rupp, 'The Victorian Churchman as Historian: a Reconsideration of R. W. Dixon's History of the Church of England', *Essays in Modern Church History in Memory of Norman Sykes*, ed G. V. Bennett and J. D. Walsh (London 1966) pp 206–16.

[3] On this historiography see H. Walker, *The Literature of the Victorian Era* (Cambridge 1910) pp 818–931; [G. P.] Gooch, [*History and Historians in the Nineteenth Century*] (London 1913); [T. P.] Peardon, [*The Transition in English Historical Writing 1760–1830*] (New York 1933). See also notes 11, 17 below.

[4] (London 1874).

[5] [John] Lingard, [*The*] *History* [*of England from the First Invasion by the Romans to the Accession of William and Mary in 1688*], 10 vols (edition cited unless otherwise stated Dublin 1888). For earlier editions see note 28 below.

[6] [Martin] Haile and [Edwin] Bonney, [*Life and Letters of John Lingard 1771–1851*] (London 1912).

[7] On Lingard as historian, Forbes p 8; Walker pp 829–30; Gooch pp 284, 290–2;

Lingard had both advantages and defects for becoming a dispassionate historian. He was a well matured product of the very English anglo-gallican catholicism, recently treated to such close and sympathetic analyses by John Bossy and Eamon Duffy.[8] His unassertive self confidence, his solidity of judgment, his unassuming Englishness, reflected the dominant mood of his English catholic contemporaries. They were men secure in the vigorous native tradition of their own spirituality. Before 1830 their church enjoyed both the modest revival subsequently submerged by the Irish and tractarians, and the minor scholarly renaissance in which Lingard is the principal figure.[9]

Their moderation of tone was encouraged by the logic of the catholic predicament, as a minority demanding political and religious freedom. The catholics were allied to whigs, radicals and rational dissenters, the 'enlightened' wing of British politics, who urged religious toleration on the grounds of reason and utility and encouraged catholics to make their case for emancipation as essentially liberal and reasonable men. Thus the past intolerance and persecutions of the Roman catholic church were a grave embarrassment to her champions, while the more spectacular aspects of Roman catholic folk religion and hagiography, if given publicity, might undermine the claims of catholics to be as 'rational' and 'enlightened' as their friends. Thus the tendency in catholic apologetic to understate the difference between protestant and catholic was appropriate to catholic political needs. A whig like earl Grey or lord Holland, a liberal anglican like bishop Bathurst of Norwich, strengthened their case for catholic emancipation with the theological point that catholics and protestants were not in essential disagreement over fundamentals, as indeed had been shown by past ecumenical contact: as between archbishop Wake and the gallicans. This woolly if kindly ecumenism rested upon the sort of scholarly distortions of past positions so dear to ecumenists today, and enabled

---

Peardon pp 277–83; D. F. Shea, *The English Ranke: John Lingard* (New York 1969). Shea is a good guide to Lingard's own opinions, but my interpretation of Lingard differs from his, inasmuch as Lingard's 'impartiality' was in part the product of political need, which greatly modified it. I do not know what to make of the depth of background knowledge of a writer who thinks that Strype and Burnet were chroniclers contemporary with Mary Tudor, George Oliver a bishop and Joseph Priestley a tory: Shea pp 3, 65, 94–5.

8 John Bossy, *The English Catholic Community 1570–1850* (London 1975); Eamon Duffy, 'Ecclesiastical Democracy Detected: i, 1779–87 ii, 1787–96,' *Recusant History* (January and October 1970) pp 193–209, 309–31; 'Doctor Douglass and Mister Berington—an eighteenth century retraction,' *DR* 88 (July 1970) pp 246–69.

9 Bernard Ward, [*The Eve of Catholic Emancipation*], 2 vols (London 1911) 2, pp 270–87.

catholics to put their opponents at the disadvantage of appearing to be bigoted and illiberal, for resurrecting an ancient prejudice. On this basis catholics sought acceptance and integration into English society. They did not want social separation into a wholly distinct community standing four square on Peter's rock against the protestant world.

Thus by circumstance, Lingard was a mild progressivist, a very moderate whig; his friends included that arch whig and heresiarch Henry Brougham. As a mission priest in Hornby in Lancashire, he was on the best of whist-playing terms with the local gentry and with the local anglican parson. In this setting, catholic emancipation was no divisive measure; it would set its seal on a harmony already in good part achieved. Lingard's gallican theology suited his surroundings, and naturally impelled him to oppose the ultramontane bishop Milner, whose stress on the exclusive claims of Rome implied a more socially exclusive catholicism. Both as a whig and as a catholic Lingard's moderate positions inclined him to moderation as a scholar. Indeed moderation was the key note of his calm and undivided personality and his long and uneventful life within a stable and circumscribed set of institutions, and a daily round of duties which were both undemanding and fulfilling. Moreover Lingard's medium perfectly fitted his message. He wrote in a formal, slightly stiff and stilted eighteenth-century prose, with epigrammatic overtones of Hume and Gibbon, and with the rounded periods and stylised elegance of a polished writer of the Georgian era: characteristic products of a mind and temper always under perfect self control.

Thus Lingard's desire to be an impartial historian was itself a re-flection of catholic polemical needs; and his own writings divide into the polemical and historical. His first book, about the antiquities of the anglo-saxon church,[10] belongs to the renaissance of anglo-saxon studies pioneered by Sharon Turner.[11] Still Lingard's eulogy of monasticism and early medieval Christianity gave offence to protestants, and set him on his career as a controversialist. His earliest opponents were the high church and high tory protestant apologists for corrupt establishments in church and state; and from the range of Lingard's anti-anglican pamphlets, he might be called the hammer of the anglican hierarchy. In 1807, he rebuked the no-popery pastoral charge of Shute

---

[10] 2 vols (Newcastle 1806; second edition, 1810).
[11] A. L. Sanders, *Some Aspects of the Use of Anglo-Saxon Material in Nineteenth Century Literature* (Cambridge MLitt 1975) pp 26–59 on anglo-saxon historiography.

Barrington bishop of Durham; in 1808 there appeared the first of his polemics with Henry Phillpotts, later bishop of Exeter. These exchanges were followed in 1813 and 1815 by his attacks on the bishops of Gloucester, Lincoln and St David's and the future bishop of Peterborough.[12] Though ostensibly theological in part, Lingard's writings were political in intent, and belonged to the debate over catholic emancipation, as the anti-catholic polemicists turned the charge of illiberality back upon its makers, and tried to show that catholicism was an irrational superstition which no reasonable man could approve, and that there was an essential connexion between intolerance and disloyalty and a bigoted catholic theology. From that point, it was an easy step to the conclusion that catholics were insufficiently 'liberal' and 'enlightened' to enjoy the freedoms of free-born Englishmen, so that catholic emancipation ought to be denied them.

As a controversialist, Lingard always preserved the excellent good temper necessary to refuting this kind of charge, but the increasing self-confidence of catholic political demands and the strength of the vested interest opposed to them indicated a heating of the religious atmosphere,[13] and the passing of that eighteenth century spirit of tolerance to which English catholics had appealed. In 1829 catholic emancipation was conceded not to the English catholic accommodating temper but to Irish catholic intransigence; catholicism became more aggressive and ultramontane as it became more successful, and Lingard himself helped begin a new age of religious controversy. Thus his *History of England* is a relic of the catholic struggle for emancipation. It was begun as early as 1809. The first three volumes, from Roman times to the death of Henry VII, appeared in 1819. In 1820, Lingard published a fourth volume about the reigns of Henry VIII and Edward VI and four subsequent volumes issued between 1820 and 1830 covered the remaining Tudors and Stuarts. Thus the *History* was written over two decades of no popery controversy, and was itself the subject of no popery attacks in *Blackwood's* and the *Quarterly*.[14] It appeared within seven months of Milner's most famous catholic polemic *The End of*

---

[12] See these and other polemical works in the list in Haile and Bonney pp 383–4.

[13] On the parallel development of dissenting sectarianism see W. R. Ward, *Religion and Society in England* (London 1972) pp 177–205.

[14] George Croly, 'Dr. Lingard', *Blackwoods* 19 (Edinburgh March 1826) pp 313–6; Henry Hart Milman, 'The Reformation in England', [*The*] Q[*uarterly*] R[*eview*] 33 (Edinburgh December 1825) pp 1–37. These span the range of anti-catholic attitudes: Croly rants, Milman is a serious critic.

John Lingard and the catholic revival

Controversy,[15] and gave William Cobbett materials for his violently anti-Anglican *History of the Protestant Reformation* published in instalments between 1824 and 1826.[16] Lingard believed that the poet laureate Robert Southey had written in reply his *Book of the Church*, an apologetic history of the Church of England which appeared in 1824. The direct dependence of Southey's work on Lingard's which has been alleged by modern scholars rests on mistaken evidence.[17] But Lingard himself contributed to the second of Charles Butler's two book length replies to Southey,[18] and otherwise shared in the controversy embracing Milner[19] and Butler on the catholic side, and more than a score of protestant writings which included another book and further articles by Southey himself.[20] Nor does Lingard's later vogue among catholics suggest that he was in any sense impartial, or that he deserves the title, the 'English Ranke', recently bestowed upon him.[21] The *History* was highly acceptable to combative Irish catholics, and was abridged for the use of catholic schools during the following century of dominant ultramontanism.[22] It had the blessings of cardinal Wiseman, Gibbons and

---

[15] For the context see Bernard Ward 2, pp 283–7.

[16] James Sambrook, *William Cobbett* (London 1973) pp 135–41.

[17] Gooch p 291, probably based on Lingard's own opinion. Sir Adolphus Ward says that Southey's criticisms of the reformation volumes in *QR* 33 (December 1825) 'were expanded in his popular *Book of the Church*': but the *Book of the Church* had already been published in 1824, and the article cited is by Henry Hart Milman. Sir A. W. Ward, 'Historians, Biographers and Political Orators', *The Cambridge History of English Literature*, 14 vols (Cambridge 1907-16) 14, p 55; *The Wellesley Index of Victorian Periodicals 1824–1900*, ed Walter E. Houghton, 2 vols (Toronto 1966) 1, p 704.

[18] Charles Butler, *Vindication of 'The Book of the Roman Catholic Church'* . . . *With copies of Doctor Phillpotts' Fourth Letter to Mr. Butler containing a charge against Dr. Lingard; and of a letter of Doctor Lingard to Mr. Butler in reply to the charge* (London 1825).

[19] John Merlin (anagram for Milner), *Strictures on the Poet Laureate's Book of the Church* (London 1824).

[20] Robert Southey, *The Book of the Church* (London 1824); *Vindiciae Ecclesiae Anglicanae* (London 1826); 'The Apocalypse of the Sister Nativité', *QR* 33 (March 1826) pp 375–410.

[21] See note 7 above. Shea (p 101) limits the strict comparison between Lingard and Ranke to their common recourse to primary sources; yet as his title *The English Ranke* shows, he seeks to give the phrase a vaguer and wider sense. Lingard had a more complex commitment than Ranke, both to truth and to an avowedly sectarian history.

[22] James Burke, *Abridgement of the History of England by John Lingard, D.D. with continuation from 1688 to the reign of Queen Victoria. Adapted for the use of schools* (London 1854). Burke pronounces the work as a contribution to 'the glorious progress of Catholic truth' (p 5); Townsend Young, *Introduction to English History from the text of Rev. John Lingard, D.D. arranged for the use of schools; with continuation to the reign of Queen Victoria* (Dublin 1867); Dom Henry Norbert, OSB, *Lingard's History of England. Newly abridged and brought down to the accession of King Edward VII* (London 1903).

Gasquet,[23] while Hilaire Belloc's continuation in a supplementary volume carried it down to the twentieth century.[24] Given its origins and subsequent career, there would at first sight seem to be no doubt that Lingard's *History* was itself polemic, the national past interpreted from a narrowly popish point of view.

Indeed Lingard had set himself a two fold task: to tell the truth and to serve the catholic faith by persuading protestants without offending them. Thus he wanted protestant readers, and was contracted to a protestant publisher: so that while he wrote as an apologist, his methods were the very opposite of Milner's. In fact he saw his double aim as one, for he could only influence protestants by telling the truth, and he did not care that by doing so he might offend the ultra-montanes. 'Through the work I made it a rule to tell the truth, whether it made for us or against us', he wrote; 'to avoid all appearance of controversy, that I might not repel protestant readers; and yet to furnish every necessary proof in our favour in the notes; so that if you compare my narrative to Hume's, for example, you will find that, with the aid of the notes, it is a complete refutation of him without appearing to be so. This I thought preferable. In my account of the reformation I must say much to shock protestant prejudices; and my only chance of being read by them depends upon my having the reputation of a temperate writer. The good to be done is by writing a book which protestants will read ... This, however, I can say, that I have not enfeebled a single proof in our favour, nor omitted a single fact or useful observation through fear of giving offence to Mawman, as bishop M[ilner] asserts. Such a thing never entered my mind. Whatever I have said or purposely omitted has been through a motive of serving religion.'[25]

This might be caricatured as a balancing act between truth and catholic truth, and in the best tradition of English catholic circumspection Lingard tried to hide his apologetic purpose as far as possible. No one looking at his title page would know he was a catholic priest, while as he declares, his refutations of Hume and of protestant scholars are consigned to footnotes to lessen the appearance of controversy.[26]

[23] On Wiseman, Lingard's pupil and friend, Haile and Bonney p 370. On Gasquet and Gibbons see notes 22, 24.
[24] Published as the eleventh volume of the *History of England ... by John Lingard With an introduction by His Eminence James Cardinal Gibbons*, 11 vols (London 1915).
[25] Lingard to Kirke, 18 December 1819, Haile and Bonney pp 166-7.
[26] The gulf between Hume and Lingard is shown in David Hume, [*The*] *History [of England from the Invasion of Julius Caesar to the Revolution of 1688. With notes ... exhibiting the most important differences between this author and Dr. Lingard*], 2 vols (Philadelphia 1856).

On the other hand, his deep desire for truth and for the reputation of an impartial writer with a protestant audience had a wholly desirable effect on his working methods. It gave him a passion for accuracy and attention to detail and to fullness of chronological information which placed him far above his rivals. It also inclined him to a critical severity which Macaulay in praising him thought excessive: his 'fundamental rule of judging seems to be that the popular opinion on historical questions cannot possibly be correct'.[27] The popular opinion was more often protestant than catholic; and that circumstance sharpened Lingard's weapons for dissecting protestant prejudice. Above all his critical sense determined him to state no fact for which he lacked a good first hand authority, and that carried him into manuscript research. He was the first British historian to make worthwhile use of the vatican archives and other Italian libraries, and of the dispatches of the French and imperial ambassadors. Friends tried with more limited success to secure materials for him from the Spanish collections at Valladolid and Simancas, and Sir Robert Peel allowed him to transcribe the gunpowder plot documents in the state paper office. The *History* went through five editions in England in Lingard's life time,[28] and was also published in the United States, and translated into French, German and Italian. In successive editions, he rigorously corrected all errors of fact, and incorporated matter from new and important collections of source materials—Kemble's *Codex Diplomaticus* of Saxon charters, Palgrave's *Parliamentary Writs*—as soon as these became available.[29]

But Lingard's ideal of impartial rigour also narrowed his conception of what history was. He desired no higher praise than that which Southey gave him, for 'true earnestness and a desire to state the facts',[30] so that he increasingly saw the true historian as a mere passive recorder of evidence. This imposed upon him a desirable reticence in matters of political passion and moral value, but its tendency was to turn him into a technician, and reduce his *History* to chronicle. This role was forced on him by a more fundamental failing, his lack of the intellectual resources with which to overturn the rationalism dominant in

---

[27] [T. B.] Macaulay, [*Critical and Historical*] *Essays*, 2 vols (London 1946) 1, p 222; Haile and Bonney p 342.

[28] First edition 1819–30; second 1823–30; third 1825–30; fourth 1837–49; fifth 1849. A sixth edition with Mark Tierney's memoir of Lingard appeared in 1854–5.

[29] Lingard, *History* 1, preface pp vi–xiii.

[30] C. C. Southey, *The Life and Correspondence of Robert Southey*, 6 vols (London 1850) 5, p 302.

English historical studies. When Lingard began his work, the histories by Gibbon, Hume and Robertson still dominated British historiography; and though Robertson was a Christian clergyman, he shared the general rationalist scorn for Rome. The minor historians who followed this triumvirate rejected some of their attitudes and methods, but did not speak with the same authority.[31] Indeed the rationalist antithesis of medieval barbarism and modern civilisation and the rationalist interpretation of motive in terms of an unchanging human nature[32] recur in Lingard's contemporary Henry Hallam, and in Macaulay, who called rationalist historiography 'philosophical history'.[33] Lingard loathed their contempt for catholicism; above all he wanted to replace Hume's history with his own; but he had something of Hume's own rational temper despite his popish theology.

The resemblances between Lingard and Hume are more than matters of content or prose style, though Lingard wrote in a similar idiom, and his history like Hume's covers the period from the Roman conquest to the glorious revolution. His least creditable borrowing from the rationalists is his tendency to write about heretics and protestants with the kind of affectation of superiority—the famous Gibbonian 'covert sneer'—with which Gibbon had treated all religion.[34] Thus Lingard calls Cromwell's faith insanity, and like Hume makes 'fanatic', 'zealot', and 'enthusiast' interchangeable with puritan. In rationalist manner, he despised chivalry,[35] and had none of the strong love of gothic and of the medievalism which so revivified Victorian catholicism.[36] Rationalism oddly mingles with English catholic circumspection in his description of the 'romantic and credulous' character of Joan of Arc, the victim of an 'enthusiasm which, while it deluded, yet nerved and elevated the mind of this young and interesting female'.[37] Lingard also suppresses exotic miracles like the scourging of Laurentius by Saint Peter, and the spectacular exploits of Dunstan,[38] so that his medieval people behave rather like the modern Englishmen to whom he is recommending them.

[31] See Peardon pp 214–52 (cap 'Romanticist History').
[32] On this theme in Hume, see J. B. Black, *The Art of History* (New York 1965) pp 95–103.
[33] Macaulay, *Essays* 1, pp 1–2; *Miscellaneous Essays* (London 1932) pp 1–39.
[34] As Henry Hallam noted. Review of Lingard's *History*, [*The*] E[*dinburgh*] R[*eview*] 53 (March 1831) p 40; compare Forbes p 2.
[35] Lingard, *History* 3, pp 196–7, on the Black Prince's courtesy to knights and carnage of commoners.
[36] Haile and Bonney pp 300–3.
[37] Lingard, *History* 4, p 26.
[38] Compare Hume, *History* 1, pp 26, 53.

Yet despite his low opinion of deluded enthusiasm, even that of a catholic heroine, Lingard was in fact in revolt against rationalism, which threatened both his faith and his impartial ideal by explaining religious motivation in terms of a rational self interest manifested in cunning, ambition and hypocrisy. This superimposition of a discreditable motive on scanty evidence was his chief complaint against the philosophical historians. 'It is long since I disclaimed any pretensions', he wrote, 'to that which has been termed the philosophy of history, but might with more propriety be called the philosophy of romance . . . no writers have proved more successful in the perversion of historic truth than speculative and philosophical historians'.[39] He compared them to novelists who invent freely from their own fancy. In difficult cases of interpreting motive he preferred to reserve his judgment, and his departure in this from the philosophical school can be seen from comparing his treatments of Dunstan and Thomas Becket with Hume's.[40]

But Lingard equally disliked philosophical history for imposing on the past too simple a theory of progress from barbarism to civilisation,[41] and a partisan enthusiasm for the movements and parties which had helped this progress along. Lingard was a modern whig; he genuinely despised religious bigotry and blessed the tolerance of England under George IV, but the growth of religious toleration did not satisfy him that English history was the history of progress. A catholic might have many criteria for progress, including that of morals and of true religion, and history saw no sustained advance in either. More important, Lingard and the mass of Englishmen had different ideas about true religion, and his reticence forbade him to identify true religion with the catholic faith. The same consideration excluded God from his history as the ally of protestant or catholic, and that makes Lingard appear as agnostic as Hume—indeed rather old fashioned in the midst of the new religious fervour of the early nineteenth century.[42] There was nothing in Lingard of the overpowering nineteenth-century sense that England had been especially guided by providence with its irresistible corollary that providence had guided England into protestantism.

---

[39] Lingard, *History* I, preface pp xvii–xviii.
[40] Hume, *History* I, pp 53–4, 157.
[41] In the advertisement to his first edition, Lingard shows vestiges of rationalism in referring to 'the silent progress of nations from barbarism to refinement', *History*, 3 vols (London 1819) I, p iii. Yet the idea hardly appears in the *History*.
[42] See Peardon p 276, on the providentialist shift in English historical writing.

Because of his catholicism, Lingard was equally remote from some of the broader currents of national feeling, so that his dislike of the glories of Elizabethan England makes his account of them carping and niggling. Even his style was staccato and abrupt, 'better adapted,' as a contemporary wrote, 'to short essays than to the solemn march of history'.[43] For all these reasons, he was inclined to purge his works of philosophical judgments offered as a systematisation of history or as an explanation of human behaviour; instead he would leave the documented facts to speak with their own authority. History had for him no set laws or underlying structure; it was just one damned thing after another, a kind of fancy dress pageant of passion and intrigue through which move the catholics who have the saving truth, though Lingard is too polite to say so.

This historicist purism is a receipt for a bare bones Gradgrind history, without form or criteria of historic significance, apart from the interest in catholicism. Later romantic historians from Green to Churchill were to define the unity of the national past as arising from continuities of race, law, language, culture and tradition; but Lingard's divisions are simply dynastic, like those of Hume and the chroniclers. Dynastic divisions might seem to have the advantages of being undisputed facts and not interpretation, except that sort of interpretation which sees an ultimate importance in kings. But Lingard's method in this had the inevitable dryness immortalised by Alice at the pool of tears, and barely disguised the fact that like Hume he lacked any synthesising principle for writing a national history.[44]

In other matters Lingard's mind was formed too early to oppose Hume with a wholly new set of assumptions based on romantic historicism. As Macaulay noted in 1828, the delight in the particular and non-recurring in the past was still largely confined to romantic novels. The different manners and mores of the past, its architecture and art, dialect and dress had their place in philosophical history; but the philosophical historians like Hume had written about them with enlightened contempt, and without placing them in organic relation to the history of religion and politics. Macaulay was to try to combine the rationalist historical mode with the social detail exploited by Scott and his copyists; moreover from the 1830s, liberal anglicans and tractarians wrote about the past without eighteenth-century prejudice. Lingard

[43] Joseph Berington to Thomas Berington, 13 July 1819. Berington family papers, Worcester County Record Office.

[44] On Hume's lack of 'synthesising principle', Peardon p 22.

was aware of the wider view, and in his account of the anglo-saxons promised a study of the 'genius and manners of that people',[45] while in the preface to his fourth edition, he attacked Carte's rigid separation of social and political history. 'It is easy for a skilful hand', he declared, 'to interweave into a continuing narrative . . . the manners and habits of thinking, the arts, the literature, and the legislative principles of the age'.[46] But his practice did not fulfil his theory. Indeed he falls below Carte and even Hume in confining his *History* to political, constitutional and religious themes, so that despite brief excurses on the black death, the great fire and plague, English silk stockings and Jacobean drunkenness, he ends by lacking Hume's breadth as a philosophical historian and the strength of the romantics as well. Yet he tried to make this failure seem a virtue. 'The historian, the genealogist, the typographer, the biographer, the antiquary, the architect, the ecclesiologist, the lecturer . . . have all their peculiar spheres of action': he wrote 'but if the historian encroach on their domain, if he take upon himself their respective duties, he will probably desert the stately and dignified march of the historic muse, to bewilder himself in a labyrinth of dry details and tedious computations; or perhaps substitute, in the place of pure history, an incoherent medly of fragmentary and elementary essays . . .'[47] In the 1820s, Coleridge and Macaulay had repudiated this idea of the dignity and purity of history, unsullied by details of everyday life; Lingard wrote his words twenty years later, and they sum up his mature conviction.

Yet that very idea of the dignity of history might lend itself to the romantic doctrine that historical study existed to exalt the spirit of a nation, to edify and enlighten them: so that Lingard saw the English past as 'fraught with animating scenes of national glory, with bright examples of piety, honour, and resolution, and with the most impressive and instructive lessons to princes, statesmen, and people.'[48] He can convey this excitement in his narrative, which gains its significance from this ideal; and he has passages which in colour and inspiring quality belong to the realm of romantic historiography, for all his remoteness from its theory. For the most part, however, he is content to practise an austere emotional self-denial. This has its rewards in his medieval volumes, in which he writes without uncritical tractarian

[45] Lingard, *History,* first edition, 3 vols (London 1819) 1, advertisement p iv.
[46] Lingard, *History*, fourth edition, 13 vols (London 1837–39) 1, preface p vii.
[47] Lingard, *History* 1, preface p xix.
[48] *Ibid* pp xix–xx.

adulation and without littering his pages with rationalist abuse of barbarism, folly and superstition. His sober rehabilitation of the monastic reformers represented an advance in the study of figures whom protestants and rationalists had agreed to condemn, while romantics obscured them in clouds of incense. Unlike Hume, Lingard believed that the entire British past was worth studying; and his judgment is most fair where it reflects the breadth and even balance of his political and religious opinions. On the other hand, his indifference to the parties to a dispute sometimes tempts him to judge both with harshness. Thus in the English civil war, his sympathies and antipathies were divided; as a whig, his dislike of tyranny pushed him to one side, his dislike of puritans to the other. He was also strongly conscious of the general catholic alignment with the Stuart cause, and that it had done very little for catholics; so that where Hume had praised Charles I, Lingard applauds his private character and queries his public policies. Laud and his foes he condemns as 'equally obstinate, equally infallible, equally intolerant'.[49] Again, as an anglo-gallican, Lingard had no special brief for the popes or the Jesuits or James II.[50] So he shows that medieval catholics carefully distinguished between the papacy's temporal and spiritual power,[51] and stresses catholic loyalty to the crown, while as a catholic noted, he had 'indelibly fixed on [the Jesuit] Father Garnett the crime of Equivocation'.[52] His cautious and not wholly generous treatment of Thomas Becket outraged the ultramontane Milner, who denounced him to Rome and to the Irish bishops,[53] and it might seem in his favour that he was so roundly condemned by both the catholic and protestant extremes.

The worst of his partiality lies in his presentation of the reformers. Having no understanding of the reformers, he could hardly explain

---

[49] *Ibid* 4, p 85.
[50] He wrote privately that 'the zealous in the time of James knew no more how to accommodate themselves to the public feeling than the ultras lately in the reign of Charles X ... There were things which I could have wished to suppress: but I dared not.' Lingard's foe John Allen also had access to Barillon's despatches, and 'if he can find any pretence for a charge of partiality, will not suffer it to escape him. I have therefore mentioned the follies or madness of James and the Jesuits, but at the same time omitted nothing which I could discover in their favour.' Lingard to Gradwell, 27 November 1830, A[rchdiocesan] A[rchives of] W[estminster].
[51] Lingard, *History* 3, pp 251–65, 343–4, on limitations on papal power in England in the later middle ages, especially p 265: 'In the obstinacy with which the court of Rome urged . . . these obnoxious claims, it is difficult to discover any traces of that political wisdom for which it has been celebrated.'
[52] Charles Butler to John Kirk, 6 August 1825, AAW.
[53] Haile and Bonney pp 167–72.

them. The force of his criticism rests in part on his concentration on political history to the neglect of theology; and it is difficult to believe that as his biographers assert,[54] the first reformation volume was read in proof and approved by C. J. Blomfield, who in 1828 became bishop of London. Lingard as always spoke with circumspection; but his implicit moral is that the English reformation was conceived in adultery, born in bigamy and baptised in catholic blood. His method of saying so is indirect, and he disguises his wider historical judgments as judgments of character, which are cunningly compacted from a seemingly factual narrative. His unfavourable portraits of Henry and Elizabeth gradually emerge from their story, without undue recourse to expressions like 'heretic' or 'tyrant'. Lingard also condemns Mary unsparingly, but he does not linger over her persecutions, which are insensibly softened by his exposition of the sins of her father, brother and sister. There is an exhaustive amount of now discredited polemic, notably on the Machiavellian personality of Thomas Cromwell,[55] while Lingard searched the Roman archives for proofs that Anne Boleyn was pregnant before her wedding.[56] Elsewhere he blackens her character by rehearsing with apparent indifference the charges of adultery against her, and then refusing to acquit or condemn her. The hesitations and subtleties of Thomas Cranmer also lent themselves to unfavourable treatment, and archdeacon Todd's attack on Lingard's sketch of the archbishop[57] left the catholic scholar unconvinced that he had underestimated Cranmer's sincerity or courage.[58] As Jasper Ridley has pointed out, Lingard's charges merely reproduced those of Cranmer's contemporary accusers.[59] Todd convincingly corrected Lingard on only minor points, but ought to have shown him that impartiality is more than a matter of fundamentalist fidelity to ascertainable fact, and that an historian is not a prosecuting counsel in a court of law.

[54] *Ibid* p 178.
[55] Lingard, *History* 4, p 556.
[56] And found them. Lingard's Roman correspondent Gradwell noted that the historian 'wants proofs of Anne Boleyn's crim. con. with Henry, and that Rome inculcated Loyalty to Eng. Catholics.' Gradwell's Diary, 28 June 1819. AAW.
[57] John Todd, *A defence of the true and Catholick doctrine of the Sacrament . . . By the Most Reverend Thomas Cranmer . . . against . . . the Reverend Doctor Lingard, the Reverend Doctor Milner, and Charles Butler, Esq* (London 1825); *The Second Edition, with notices of Dr. Lingard's and Mr. Butler's remarks . . .* (London 1826); *A Reply to Dr. Lingard's Vindication . . .* (London 1827).
[58] John Lingard, *A Vindication of certain passages in the fourth and fifth volumes of the History of England* (London 1826).
[59] Jaspar Ridley, *Thomas Cranmer* (Oxford 1962) pp 1, 7.

Lingard was happier in another confrontation, with lord Holland's librarian John Allen, an atheist of the kind who believes that all the world's woes are caused by religion. In the *Edinburgh Review* Allen resumed with Coultonesque rigour an earlier assault on Lingard's eulogy of the Saxon clergy.[60] In another article, Allen tried to prove that the massacre of St Bartholomew had been premeditated from the first, against Lingard's argument that it arose from the attempt to assassinate Coligny.[61] Like Macaulay's opinions on catholic history, Allen's writings show the anti-catholic prejudice common among the whig supporters of catholic emancipation, though the very same whigs also tended to accept Lingard's unfavourable portrayal of anglicans.[62] Thus another whig historian Henry Hallam in his *Constitutional History of England*, published in 1828, rejected Lingard's apologetic for Mary Tudor and Mary Stuart, while reproducing his strictures on Cranmer and Elizabeth.[63] Lingard's reply to Todd and Allen went through five editions, Allen's further reply into two, and there were more polemics as Lingard, Todd, Hallam and the *Edinburgh Review* all fell foul of Christopher Wordsworth for denying the favourite high church belief that Charles I had written the *Eikon Basilike*.[64] The susceptibility of scholarship to party politics was mirrored in the great quarterly journals, which each judged these disputes according to its distinctive prejudice, and proved the subservience of English historical writing to partisan points of view.

Yet if judged by these partisan contemporaries, Lingard stands as a marvel of dispassionate enquiry. His quiet strength of conviction and want of passion must appear a merit to an age in which the best lack all conviction and the worst are full of passionate intensity. His vision of the world is formal, sober and exact, and rather bloodless, as he distances himself from events to survey them from the heights; but his very lack of theory has dated his work less than the confident generalities of nationalist and progressive and protestant historians, for whom the past had been a preparation for imperial greatness, or for the

---

[60] [John] Allen, ['Lingard's History of England'], *ER* 42 (April 1825) pp 1–31.
[61] John Allen, 'Lingard's History of England: Massacre of St Bartholomew', *ER* 44 (June 1826) pp 94–155.
[62] Allen, p 8.
[63] Henry Hallam, *The Constitutional History of England from the accession of Henry VII to the death of George II*, 3 vols (first edition 1828; London 1855) 1, notes on pp 62, 98, 105, and, on Elizabeth's treatment of catholics, see p 164.
[64] Christopher Wordsworth, *King Charles the First the author of Icon Basilike further proved, . . . in reply to the objections of Dr. Lingard etc* (London 1828).

triumphs of protestantism and liberty. Lingard wrote as an apologist for a losing side which in reduced and modest circumstances is prospering again, though it makes little noise in the world. Yet Lingard was also the authentic spokesman of a Christian community undergoing renaissance and renewal, proud of its traditions and place in the nation's life, and determined to reclaim for its members the freedoms of other Englishmen. Its very successes in Lingard's lifetime were to carry it away from his own ideals; had he been born a generation later, he would have written more stridently, but probably less well. His theory of history was imperfect, and his practice was less perfect than his theory required; and yet there are still historians who have to learn his guiding principles, to keep one's temper and look to the facts.

University of St Andrews

NEW NAMES FOR OLD THINGS: SCOTTISH REACTION TO EARLY TRACTARIANISM

by GAVIN WHITE

STORMS are more easily studied in tea-cups than in oceans. Early tractarianism was clearly a storm and the Scottish episcopal church was equally clearly a tea-cup. It is assumed for this study that tractarianism was only one aspect of a wider movement which affected the church of England and Roman catholicism in similar ways, though it affected the church of Scotland in dissimilar ways.[1] Its basic tenet was that God is holy and cannot be approached directly, or known directly, but only through a cultural screen. This screen, which was also a lens, would extend throughout the world as did Christianity. Its specific form might be gothic architecture or language or any other purely ecclesiastical form of expression. Such forms were essentially a matter of style, and style mattered.

The Scottish episcopal church embraced two traditions. The former Jacobites of the north-east had survived the penal times until toleration was granted to them in 1792, and they had a distinctive Scottish liturgy almost unknown in the south. The qualified chapels of the south had long existed without episcopal supervision, but after 1792 they gradually united with the Scottish episcopal church, maintaining their right to use the English prayer book. Although the laity of the south were described as 'Church of England men' many were actually Scottish by name at the beginning of the century, though by 1856 it was estimated that three-quarters were English by descent. The growth of the whole body was greatest between 1839 and 1854 when the seventy-six congregations doubled their number, as did the clergy. Thereafter the rate of growth tapered off, though episcopalians continued to increase until the close of the century and only began to decline about 1921. In 1849 thirty-three out of one hundred clergy were in English or Irish orders, but eight years later there were sixty-five out of one hundred and forty in English orders, including thirty-

---

[1] Emmet Larkin, 'The Devotional Revolution in Ireland, 1850–75', *AHR* 77 (June 1972) pp 625–52; [A. L.] Drummond and [James] Bulloch, [*The Church in Victorian Scotland, 1843–74*] (Edinburgh 1975) pp 199–207.

four of the fifty-two clergy in the south. In that year fifty out of one
hundred and forty chapels used the Scottish liturgy, and only nineteen
of those fifty were in the diocese of Aberdeen.[2]

These figures suggest that the spread of the Scottish liturgy south-
wards from Aberdeenshire coincided with the influx of clergy from
England. Prior to this period it had been the 'policy of the south to
preach a somewhat harmless gospel and to win cultured people through
the quiet beauty of the prayer book services', and even the old episcopalians of the north-east regarded their freedom from the strict
Calvinism of the church of Scotland to be their distinctive characteristic.[3] The arrival of tractarian ideas can best be seen in minor dis-
ruptions which occurred at Aberdeen, Edinburgh, and Glasgow, and
in the objections there raised to the new style and language.

Saint Paul's chapel in Aberdeen had existed for well over a century
before joining the Scottish episcopal church in 1841, with a deed of
union which would dissolve that union if anything but the
English prayer book was used. They then brought in Sir William
Dunbar as minister but in 1843 Dunbar withdrew both himself and the
chapel from the episcopal church. There had always been some in
Saint Paul's who opposed the union, and Dunbar seems to have been
caught between them and William Skinner, bishop of Aberdeen, who
had administered confirmation at Saint Paul's and used some collects
not in the English prayer book. Skinner was the son of the former
bishop and grandson of a saintly priest-poet, but he had been sent to
Oxford and ordained in England. He was charitably described as
having 'a good heart and a fairly good head',[4] but he was sufficiently
tractarian to feel it his duty to surround his pronouncements with
gothic bombast. He was obliged to inform his clergy that Dunbar was
no longer of their number; he informed not only his clergy but bishops
throughout Britain and even America that 'all his ministerial acts are
without authority, as being performed apart from Christ's mystical

[2] [William] Walker, *Three Churchmen; [Sketches and Reminiscences]* (Edinburgh 1893)
p 125; Anon. *Considerations of an Englishman in Scotland* (Edinburgh 1856) p 12;
[William] Blatch, *[A Memoir of the Right Reverend David Low]* (Edinburgh 1855)
pp 206–7; [F] Goldie, *[A Short History of the Episcopal Church in Scotland]* (London 1951)
p 88; *Revised Report of the Debate in the House of Lords, May 22 1849* (London 1849)
p 27; Charles Popham Miles, *The Scottish Episcopal Church antagonistic to The Church
of England in Scotland* (Glasgow 1857) pp 28, 39.
[3] [William] Perry, [*The Oxford Movement in Scotland*] (London 1933) p 39; Drummond
and Bulloch p 230.
[4] William Walker, *The Life and Times of John Skinner, Bishop of Aberdeen,* (Aberdeen
1887) p 318.

body, wherein the one spirit is', while Christians were to 'avoid all communion 'with him, 'lest they be partakers with him in his sin'.[5] An Aberdeenshire priest named Taylor demurred at reading such words in his chapel, holding that Dunbar was 'still a minister of Christ'. By declining to recognise a precise limit to the church, or perhaps by recognising that his bishop was indulging in a game of make-believe, Taylor incurred Skinner's wrath. The language of the latter became plain and contemporary. 'Your mulish obstinacy in so simple a matter is extremely silly and vexatious', 'Your letters are all most confused and unsatisfactory', and, more prelatical, 'my episcopal authority must be upheld and obeyed'. Skinner then concentrated on the last point and accused Taylor of having set limits to episcopal authority, which he elevated into even more of a principle when he deprived Taylor of his license for having denied apostolic succession by questioning his bishop.[6]

All this made wonderful copy in London, and evangelicals such as Bickersteth endured the rigours of the Scottish roads in order to preach at Saint Paul's and show their support for Dunbar. As for the reverend baronet himself, he behaved as a Victorian gentleman should and sued Skinner for libel in the civil courts. The case dragged on and on, Skinner being judged to have used 'an excess of language quite unpardonable' by the court of session, but Skinner appealed to the house of lords. What finally settled the matter was Dunbar's desire to return to England so that he submitted on honourable terms to the Scottish bishops and the sentence against him was withdrawn.[7] But even when Skinner was succeeded by Thomas Suther in 1857 this did not bring peace and harmony. For his part Suther suspended Patrick Cheyne, an Aberdeenshire priest who had asserted that the Dunbar sentence had force in 'the unseen world' and who was later held to teach unsound doctrine concerning the eucharist.[8]

In Edinburgh Dunbar's case was taken up by D. T. K. Drummond who had removed himself from the episcopal fold in 1842. Drummond had been incumbent of Trinity chapel but had also held prayer-meetings in a hired room. More ominously, he had also held such a meeting 'on the north-eastern coast of Scotland', that is, in Skinner's

[5] [D. T. K.] Drummond, [*Historical Sketch of Episcopacy in Scotland*] (Edinburgh 1845) p 88.
[6] *Ibid* pp 17–30.
[7] George Grub, *An Ecclesiastical History of Scotland*, 4 (Edinburgh 1861) p 250.
[8] Goldie p 103; [Charles Popham] Miles, *An Address* [*to the Members of St Jude's Congregation, Glasgow*] (Glasgow 1844) p 49.

diocese. Until 1838 the canons only required the use of the liturgy on formal occasions in church buildings; thereafter the prayer book liturgy was required on every occasion and the new climate of opinion did not recognise that any prayer could be informal. Bishop Terrot of Edinburgh was an old-fashioned mathematical parson and no zealot who only intervened at the request of 'influential churchmen of the straighter sect', perhaps including Skinner. Most churchmen probably agreed with the historian William Walker that Drummond's meetings should not have been forbidden, but that he should have obeyed the canon anyway.[9] But this he could not do, and instead he resigned his charge, sought legal advice, and then opened Saint Thomas's as an English episcopal chapel. Saint Thomas's exists to this day, though in a new location, and after a process of gradual reconciliation it has found its place as a private chapel within the Scottish episcopal church.

In retrospect the Drummond case seems even less substantial than that of Sir William Dunbar. Yet there was an issue at stake. What seems to have mattered to both sides was Drummond preaching in his hired room to 'large mixed audiences';[10] mixtures of churchmen and non-churchmen were anathema to the tractarian view. Like Taylor, Drummond had blurred the edges of the visible church.

The story of Saint Jude's chapel in Glasgow began with a dispute in Saint Mary's, then one of the two episcopal congregations in that city. By the intervention of bishop Russell, the dissidents were enabled to found Saint Jude's in 1839 as an integral part of the Scottish episcopal church. The second incumbent of this chapel was C. P. Miles, a volatile and quarrelsome cleric newly arrived from England, who only overcame his doubts about subscribing to the canons at the last moment, and that because he had concluded that the Scottish liturgy was obsolete and would soon disappear. When he had had time to read about the Dunbar case he rushed off to Aberdeen to support Dunbar against the tyranny of bishop Skinner. Miles then demanded that bishop Russell should either identify himself with Skinner or disown him, which Russell refused to do. In fact Russell was sympathetic to some tractarian ideas, and he admired the Scottish liturgy though he had never used it himself, being incumbent of Leith near Edinburgh throughout his episcopate, but his primary concern was keeping the peace.[11]

[9] Walker, *Three Churchmen* pp 190–189; Drummond pp 69–78.
[10] Blatch p 266.
[11] Miles, *An Address* pp 39, 7, 40; [Charles Popham] Miles, [*Reply to Bishop Russell*;] *A Second Address* [*to the Members of St Jude's Congregation, Glasgow*] (Glasgow 1844) p 43; Walker, *Three Churchmen* p 74.

That his bishop was not only an older man but a distinguished biblical scholar did not prevent Miles lecturing Russell as if he were a schoolboy. He several times compared Scottish bishops with English presbyters to the advantage of the latter, and he took a special joy in repeatedly mentioning in the most casual way that Russell had formerly been a dissenter, by which he meant that he had been a minister of the established church of Scotland. When Russell mildly urged Miles to keep the peace with his fellow-clergy, Miles replied that he would do so 'provided that they do not offend God'. In one respect Miles did have his bishop at a disadvantage. Russell had no sooner asserted that Skinner's acts were his own and not the responsibility of the other bishops than Skinner claimed that other bishops had given him support, though in private discussions which Russell, no doubt quite truthfully, said he had not remembered. However Miles had been urged to change his ground during his visit to Dunbar in Aberdeen and he therefore opened a new campaign against the Scottish liturgy. He claimed Russell had falsely told him this would soon be discontinued even in the north. This claim Russell convincingly rejected.[12] Miles then attacked the consecration of a new chapel in Jedburgh, where the congregation had requested the Scottish liturgy to the astonishment of Russell who wrote, 'I did not expect an application for it from the edge of the Cheviot hills and backed by natives of England'.[13] As for the consecration, Russell said it was normal save for 'the giving of new names to old things, and thereby exciting the fears of the ignorant. This I regret'.[14] That there were present several bishops and a large contingent of English clergy, of whom Miles claimed four were 'avowedly the supporters of a particular school', Russell said was not his doing. He had not invited them and had never met most of them before, though he felt bound to write that when he spoke with them he was favourably impressed. That style was the matter at stake in the Jedburgh affair may be seen by Miles' contention that the service was not protestant since clergy went to the chapel in procession. Russell countered this charge by arguing that it could not have been a procession since it was raining and they carried umbrellas.[15]

Late in 1844 Miles formally withdrew from the Scottish episcopal

[12] Miles, *An Address* pp 34, 41, 43; Miles, *A Second Address* p 13; Charles Popham Miles, *A Third Address to the Members of St Jude's Congregation, Glasgow* (Glasgow 1844) pp 7–14.
[13] Walker, *Three Churchmen* p 75.
[14] Miles, *An Address* p 44.
[15] *Ibid* pp 53, 58.

church and Russell warned his flock to 'avoid professional communion' with him 'in public prayer and sacraments'. The contrast between this restrained language and that used by Skinner against Dunbar greatly impressed Drummond who was not sure whether to damn Russell for his tyranny, or to use his linguistic restraint as evidence that Skinner had been unnecessarily harsh.[16] But Miles was not finished in Glasgow for his chapel managers asked him to continue and in due course followed him out of the Scottish episcopal church. Under a succession of English clergy the chapel maintained an independent existence for nearly forty years. But these adherents of the united church of England and Ireland in Scotland, as they formally described themselves, were financially dependent upon the sale of bonds to evangelicals in England. Furthermore, their numbers must have been divided by the establishment of a new English episcopal chapel on a better site, Saint Silas's, which still exists in a state of total independence, though its relations with the Scottish episcopal church are good. In due course those who remained at Saint Jude's failed to meet the interest charges on the bonds, and the building was left to the bond-holders. These last tried to sell it at ever-reduced prices from 1884 until 1909 when it was allowed to go to the free presbyterians who not only kept the name Saint Jude's but in 1975 transferred it to a larger building.[17]

There can be no doubt that Miles was primarily warring against tractarianism, and he warned that he might even be obliged to renounce his connections with the church of England for the same reasons which had caused him to renounce his connections with Scottish episcopacy. Yet he was also representative of a certain type of Englishman in Scotland, the carpet-bagger. He intended to replace the local leaders and to be a new Wilfrid who would benefit northerners by bringing them into conformity with the customs of the south. And yet he was a failed Wilfrid, for the particular form of anglicanism which he hoped to propagate was dying behind him, and dying around him. A new anglicanism largely carried the day in England, and it also carried the southern episcopalians in Scotland, giving them an attraction they had not known before.

Yet this leads to new questions. It has been said that southern episcopalians accepted the aesthetic element of the Oxford movement,

---

[16] *Drummond* p 110.
[17] Saint Jude's chapel title deeds (Bishop and company, solicitors, Glasgow).

while their northern brethren accepted the doctrine but not the ritual.[18] But Scottish presbyterians also accepted the doctrine but not the ritual. There may therefore have been some factor amongst Scots, whether presbyterian or Aberdeenshire episcopalian, which caused them to accept the doctrine immediately, but the ritual consequences only later and to a limited degree. The southern episcopalians, who were either English or anglicised Scots, accepted the ritual element first, along with the new names and the new language. This then allowed them to welcome lowland Scots who were going through a process of domestic anglicisation, and perhaps southern episcopalianism was itself an anglicising agency; it has constantly met this accusation at the hands of patriot presbyterians. Yet insofar as it was an anglicising agency, it was also conscious of being Scottish and it did provide a Scottish home for those who were only willing to be anglicised on their own terms. And towards the end of the nineteenth century the episcopal church may well have exerted a contrary influence on the vast numbers of English immigrants, eventually even surpassing the Irish in number, who were so rapidly and painlessly assimilated to Scottish ways that historians now wonder where they have gone.[19]

That factor which caused Scots to reject the ritual but embrace the doctrine of the new movement cannot be easily identified; no attempt will be made to identify it here. But there is another factor which must be identified, and that is the English consciousness of the type most clearly seen in Miles. The three separated chapels, with a few other small congregations in which English clergy functioned from time to time, called themselves English episcopal. Yet they claimed a legal basis in a parliamentary act of 1792 which gave toleration to episcopal chapels and clergy in Scotland.[20] On the face of it this act referred to Scottish episcopalians who were no longer Jacobite, but the English episcopalians insisted that it only referred to the qualified chapels with which they now identified themselves. Historically only Saint Paul's in Aberdeen could claim any such identity, but the English episcopalians were right to claim that charges of schism were over-dramatic in an age which had been recently accustomed to many episcopal chapels which did not recognise the Scottish bishops. What is significant is this identification with the qualified chapels rather than with the church south of the border. It was only on a comparatively minor key that some

---

[18] Perry p 40.
[19] Drummond and Bulloch p. 70.
[20] *Revised Report of the Debate in the House of Lords, May 22 1849* (London 1849) pp 9–10.

English episcopalians claimed that as Englishmen they should never be expected to conform to alien ways. If English consciousness did not play a major part in these chapels, it may have been because many of their adherents, like Miles, recognised that few in England supported them anyway. But it may also have been because what lists survive of office-bearers in these chapels suggest that a good many of them were not English but Scottish.

This leaves one major question. The storm in a tea-cup was surrounded by another aspect of the same storm in a real sea. It was in 1843 that a third of the church of Scotland broke off to form the free church on principles parallel to those of the tractarians. Yet the English episcopalians seemed totally unaware of all that. Some, like Miles, would not have stooped to consider the affairs of the church of Scotland; he probably regarded it as so Scottish that its days were numbered, and he even observed that, 'It is natural that the British government, itself episcopalian, should look with favour upon episcopalians northward of the Tweed'.[21]

But there is a revealing phrase in an open letter to the primus written by Alexander Ewing, bishop of Argyll, in 1858. Ewing described himself as the only bishop born, ordained, and consecrated in Scotland, and he claimed that the twenty years of his ministry had been disturbed by eucharistic controversies which had crippled the church. Had it not been for this, 'at the time of the great presbyterian disruption', he argued, 'we should have absorbed within our pale the bulk of the sober-minded and educated of Scotland'. So much for the past, but Ewing feared that continuing controversy within a small body would lead to 'a set of independent chapels' with 'some colonial bishop (at home disabled) engaged to confirm and consecrate at intervals'.[22] This may have referred to bishop Gobat of Jerusalem, who had confirmed in Saint Jude's at Glasgow.[23]

Ewing's answer to all this was to convene a general synod in order to determine 'if uniformity, and if possible incorporation with the church of England may be effected'. This would contain the violence of controversy within wider bounds. Ewing made it clear that he was not unsympathetic to tractarian ideals, though he went against the basic

[21] Miles, *A Second Address* (Glasgow 1844) p 27.

[22] [Alexander] Ewing, [*A Letter to the Rt Rev the Primus of the Scottish Episcopal Church from the Bishop of Argyll*] (Edinburgh 1858) pp 3–10.

[23] W. J. Trower, *A Remonstrance addressed to Archibald Campbell, Esq, of Blythswood, on certain resolutions* . . . (Glasgow 1856) pp 5–7.

themes of tractarianism in writing, 'Let us hear less of the apparatus, and more of that for which it exists . . .'[24] A real tractarian would have retorted that it was only by hearing of the apparatus that one did hear of that for which it existed.

But Ewing's significance is his identification of the Scots with a policy of anglicisation, and of the English with a policy of romantic gothicism. History has treated him as a poetic eccentric, unfaithful to Scottish interests. He was more probably typical of the truly Scottish reaction to tractarianism which was deeper and ultimately more successful in using that movement than was the reaction of the English in Scotland.

University of Glasgow

[24] Ewing pp 16–17.

THE RENAISSANCE OF PUBLIC WORSHIP
IN THE CHURCH OF SCOTLAND, 1865–1905

by JOHN M. BARKLEY

O N his way to one of the early meetings of the church service society, Story met Charteris on the street, who asked what were their aims. He replied, 'To restore the ring in marriage, the cross in baptism, and the denial of the cup to the laity'. Charteris fled in horror.[1]

Before discussing the renaissance of public worship in the church of Scotland it is necessary to look at the background. The lineage of reformed worship can be traced from Diebold Schwarz's translation of the *Hagenau Missal* into German in 1524[2] through Bucer and Calvin, both of whom desired weekly communion,[3] to the Scottish *Book of Common Order* (1564). When the civil authorities forbade weekly communion, Bucer and Calvin did not prepare an order of service for Sunday morning, but rubricated the order for communion as to how it should end when there was no celebration of the supper: that is, the eucharist was the norm for public worship.

Three other features are relevant: (i) the *Book of Common Order* was bound with the *Psalter*, and so was a book in the hands of the people; (ii) the structure of the service, the substance of each of its parts, and, even though provision was made for 'free prayer', some of the prayers were intended to be invariable, for in 1563 the privy council defined public worship as 'the preaching of the Word of God, ministration of the Sacraments, and the *reading* of common prayers';[4] and (iii) the book contains some set forms, for example, the Lord's prayer and the apostles' creed.

In 1645, the *Book of Common Order* was replaced by the Westminster *Directory for the Public Worship of God*, which in form was really 'an extended rubric' in the hands of the minister, not a book of the

---

[1] J. Cameron Lees to John Kerr 31 January 1907.
[2] J. Smend, *Die evangelischen deutschen Messen* (Göttingen 1896) p 146. [F]. Hubert, [*Die straszburger liturgischen Ordnungen im Zeitalter der Reformation*] (Göttingen 1900) pp 57–75.
[3] M. Bucer, *Psalter mit aller Kirchenuebig* (Strasburg 1539). See Hubert p 99. J. Calvin *Opera* 10 i 7, 25, 213; 2 1047–8; 4 xvii 46; 15 538.
[4] italics mine.

people. It was a compromise between the English presbyterians, the Scottish presbyterians and the independents,[5] and the vagueness of some of its directions resulted in every man doing 'that which was right in his own eyes'.[6] In this way the connection of the church of Scotland with the church catholic was loosened and English independency became dominant. The result was a veritable dark age 'which lasted for full two hundred years'.[7] So true was this that Sprott could write in 1905,

> Till within the memory of many still living the order of Public Worship was—Praise . . . Prayer, [Praise], Lecture or Sermon, Prayer, Psalm or Paraphrase, Benediction . . . The mutilated form of the Protestors had come to be regarded as embodying that purity of worship which the Reformers restored . . . The defense of old Reformed usages, such as the reading of Scripture and of prayers, the reciting of the Creed and the Lord's Prayer, and the singing of the Gloria, by the Covenanting Assemblies and their leaders . . . against 'sectarian conceits' borrowed from England, was entirely forgotten. The educated opinion of the country was at one with the belief of the common people.[8]

At the same time, this worship had a realism at which one must not sneer. Its defect was that it had lost its catholic roots and become unbalanced, the didactic element being so prominent that the devotional and sacramental was all but excluded. A reaction against the stress of seventeenth-century Calvinism on instruction was bound to come. Writing on the origins of the church service society, Kerr says, 'There seemed to be at the time a *wave* of revival in the way of ritual in the Church, due no doubt to the fact that worship had reached such a degraded and deplorable condition that something must be done to end matters.[9]

There can be no revival without advocates of reform. Limitation of space forbids more than a reference to these. The more important publications were Robertson's *Scotch Minister's Assistant* (1802), reissued in 1822 with the title *Forms of Prayer for use in the Church of Scotland*; Cumming's edition of *Knox's Liturgy* (1840) in which he argued the case for reading prayers; Brunton's *Forms for Presbyterian Worship*

[5] H. R. Davies *Worship of the English Puritans* (London 1948) p 157.
[6] T. Leishman *Westminster Directory* (Edinburgh 1901) p xxxi.
[7] C[hurch] of S[cotland *Manual of*] *Church Praise* (Edinburgh 1932) p 37.
[8] G. W. Sprott *Euchologion* (Edinburgh 1905) pp vii-viii.
[9] [J]. Kerr *Renascence [of Worship]* (Edinburgh 1909) p 8.

(1848); Lee's *Order of Public Worship* (1857), and Bonar's *Presbyterian Liturgies* (1858).[10] Within the church of Scotland itself an aids to devotion committee had been set up in 1859, and *Prayers for Social and Family Worship* had been issued in 1858 and revised in 1863. There was also the charge against Marshall Lang in the presbytery of Aberdeen for introducing standing for singing and sitting for prayer in East St Nicholas, and one against Robert Lee in the general assembly for his 'innovations' in old Greyfriars, Edinburgh, both of which attracted much attention.[11] To this has to be added the musical revival begun under Channon in Monymusk and Aberdeen in 1753.[12] There was also the deposing of Edward Irving for heresy in 1833 which led to the formation of the holy catholic apostolic church, whose *Liturgy* exercised a tremendous influence.[13] In addition, the work of Schaff and Niven in the German reformed church in America was widely known, as well as Baird's *Eutaxia* (1855) and *Chapter on Liturgies* (1856).[14]

Lee published his *Reform of the Church of Scotland, Part I* in 1864, but he had a facility for creating 'distrust where none need have existed'.[15] Much more influential was Sprott's pamphlet, *The Worship, Rites, and Ceremonies of the Church of Scotland* (1863), in which he said,

> There should be a self-constituted society of the liturgical scholars in the Church, who would, after due time and full consideration of the whole subject, draw up a Book of Prayers for Public Worship, and of forms for the Administration of the Sacraments and other special subjects, as a guide to the clergy. Antiquity, the Reformation, and our present practice should be all kept in view by the compilers... The basis of this book should be the old Reformed Liturgy, but in the Greek and other Liturgies there are many golden sentences . . . which should also be incorporated with it . . . This book when compiled I would leave to work its own way. It would be prized by the laity, be a guide to the clergy and correct their taste, and as respects the sacraments would I have no doubt, in the main be followed.[16]

---

[10] Other important works were—Mason's *Letters on Frequent Communion* (1803), Carstair's *Services for Holy Communion* (1829), Brichan's *Communion Service* (1842) and Liston's *Services of the House of God* (1843).

[11] Marshall Lang to John Kerr 7 April 1905.

[12] C of S *Church Praise* p 45.

[13] *Euchologion* (1867) p 43; (1869) p 151.

[14] G. W. Sprott *Euchologion* (1905) pp xiv–xv.

[15] [A. K.] Robertson 'The place of Dr Robert Lee [in the Developments in the Public Worship of the Church of Scotland]', *Church Service Society Annual*, no 28, ed D. A. Hodges (Cupar-Fife 1958) p 32.

[16] G. W. Sprott *Euchologion* (1905) pp xvii–xviii.

This 'wave' led to the founding in the religious institution rooms, Glasgow, on 31 January, 1865, of the church service society, which throughout its history, broadly speaking, has followed the procedure set out by Sprott. Its object is set out in article five of the constitution, 'the study of the liturgies—ancient and modern—of the Christian Church, with a view to the preparation and publication of forms of Prayer for Public Worship, and services for the Administration of the Sacraments, the Celebration of Marriage, the Burial of the Dead, etc.' At its first meeting a sub-committee was appointed with Story as convener 'to consider what steps it is advisable to take in order best to carry out the intention of the Society'. Its report on 21 March firmly rejected any 'design of *introducing a Liturgy into the Church of Scotland*' and continued,

> The work of the Society may be appropriately divided into two main branches: the one of which may be called the *Constructive*, the other the *Eclectic*. The first of these would embrace the compilation or composition of *forms for special services*. And the special services which ought first to be attended to, seem to be those for the administration of the two Sacraments—for the celebration of marriage, and for the burial of the dead . . .
>
> The Members of the Society value highly the privilege of what is called *free prayer* and . . . would be unwilling to submit themselves to the yoke . . . of a liturgy so rigid . . . as that of the Anglican Church. But the privilege of free prayer is not to be taken to mean simply each clergyman's liberty to lead the devotions of his congregation according to his own idea or fancy . . . It most legitimately may have the higher meaning, that each clergyman . . . is at liberty as a minister of the Church Catholic to use whatever in the recorded devotions of that Church he finds most suitable to his congregation's need . . . The *eclectic* branch of the Society's work would proceed on the recognition of this principle. Its aim would be to search for . . . the prayers of the Faithful in all divisions of the Catholic Church, and to gather these, not into a formal *Manual* of Devotion, but into a great *Magazine* of prayers, to which every minister might have access, and from which each might draw, even as from a Living Fountain.[17]

In revised form this report formed the preface in the early editions of the Society's *Euchologion*. Before proceeding to discuss this work

---

[17] Kerr, *Renascence* pp 53–60.

reference must be made to the paper issued on public prayer as a result of the editorial committee's report in 1866. It was addressed not 'to the clergy . . . but to the people'. Having pointed out that 'individual worship is offered in private—in the congregation the individual is merged in the general body of worshippers', and that 'the idea of public prayer is that it is *common*' prayers of the congregation, it asks what are the ideas which 'ought to direct true and appropriate worship as far, at least, as the prayers of the congregation are concerned' and continues,

> This seems to need to be first of all considered:— Who is the object of the worship: to whom are the prayers offered? To God, and not to a god unknown, but to One who has revealed Himself to us through a Saviour—who bids us go to the Father, and ask whatsoever things we have need of in His name. He is a God, too, against whom we have sinned, and of whose kindness we are not worthy.
>
> Then by whom is the worship rendered: who offer or make these prayers? The congregation; not the minister. He is but the representative and spokesman of the body of faithful people 'over whom the Holy Ghost has made him overseer'. They are not his own prayers which he offers. These he offers at home. It is the prayers of the congregation—their united supplications, confessions, and giving of thanks. For these it is his office to provide a fitting vehicle that shall convey them to the throne of grace.

On the basis of these two facts it is held that public prayer should be *simple, reverent*, marked with a certain *uniformity of expression,* and 'not merely by a certain *uniformity or catholicity of language*', but, 'moreover, by a certain *uniformity of plan* in its subjects—each part following in its right place or order'.[18]

Needless to say, the founding of such a society caused considerable controversy. There was much misrepresentation and distortion. Members were accused of subverting the church of Scotland, romanising, aping episcopacy, sacerdotalism and sacramentarianism (as if these two were identical), abrogating the sermon and introducing a liturgy into the church. On grounds of age they were described as 'a set of beardless youths'. With true 'evangelical' fervour they were denounced as Romanists, ritualists, prelatists, Jesuits, conspirators and traitors.

Nevertheless the work of the society went quietly forward and

---

[18] *Ibid* pp 74–83.

won its way as Sprott had suggested it would. Its achievements can be grouped into several areas, but central was the publication of the *Euchologion*, the first edition of which appeared in 1867. It contained forms for baptism, holy communion, marriage and burial in that order, a lectionary and 'materials for the construction of a service for public worship on the Lord's day'. Introductory articles were provided on baptism, holy communion, burial and 'the use of holy scripture in the service of God', to which others on the admission of catechumens and ordination were added in the second edition in 1869.

Relevant to our subject here are the article and form for holy communion, the lectionary and materials.

The introductory article on holy communion discusses Justin Martyr, the *Apostolic Constitutions*, the eastern liturgies, the Roman mass, seven reformed rites—Calvin, present Genevan, Neufchatel, Dutch, *Book of Common Order, Book of Common Prayer* and Westminster *Directory*—and two modern services—the catholic apostolic and the German reformed in America. Knowledge of liturgical forms was much more limited than it is today, for example, Hubert's work on the Strasbourg rites was not published until 1901, and Maxwell's *John Knox's Genevan Service Book* not until 1931. Consequently this article contains a few errors of fact. It, however, sums up,

> There are no exhortations in ancient forms . . . but in all the Reformed Services there is at least one . . . 'Table Addresses' are alike unknown to the old forms, and to the Reformed Services . . . Omitting everything objectionable, it appears from the analysis made that the following material may be considered as common to all Christendom, and should have a place in every Communion Service:— The Offertory; Bringing in of the Elements; Salutation; Creed; Confession and Prayer of Approach; Eucharistic Prayer, with Versicles and Seraphic Hymn; Words of Institution; Invocation and Lord's Prayer; Intercession for the Church Militant, and Thanksgiving for the Righteous Departed; Communion; Prayer of Thanks for the Sacrament, and of Self-Dedication, Praise and Benediction.[19]

Then the compilers set out an order. While, no doubt, because of the use of the term 'action sermon' for the sermon on communion Sunday the liturgy of the word and the liturgy of the faithful was a unity in their

---

[19] *Euchologion* (1867) pp 42–3.

thinking, no liturgy of the word is provided. The first rubric reads, 'The Prayer after Sermon being ended, the Minister may give this Exhortation.'[20] Here there is a departure (as in the Westminster *Directory*) from the eucharistic norm of reformed worship. This is further aggravated by the fact that the 'Exhortation before the Communion' is followed by the dismissal of all 'who do not intend to be present at this solemn service with the benediction', thus pointing to the concept of a 'preaching service' followed by a 'communion office'. The order is

> Great entrance
> The grace . . . as in *Clementine Liturgy*
> Scriptural warrant (I Cor.11.23–26) . . . as in *Directory*
> Address . . . as in *Directory*, based on Lee, catholic apostolic and
>   German reformed
> Apostles' Creed (We believe . . .) as in some reformed liturgies
> Prayer of access, based on catholic apostolic and Syrian
> Eucharistic prayer: based on catholic apostolic
>   Thanksgiving for creation
>   Anamnesis
>   *Sanctus* and *Benedictus*
>   Epiclesis based on *St James* and *Directory*
>   Lord's prayer
> Manual actions
> Communion at table in aisle
> Pax
> Exhortation to thankfulness . . . based on Dutch
> Prayer: Thanksgiving
>   Self-dedication
>   Intercessions
>   Thanksgiving for church triumphant
> *Nunc dimittis* (Metrical)
> Benediction: 'Now the God of peace . . .'.

This remained substantially the form in all editions of the *Euchologion* except that in the fifth edition (1884) the *Sursum corda* was introduced and the Nicene creed was placed as the first alternative; from the sixth edition (1890) the Nicene creed alone is given and the *Agnus Dei* is introduced before the prayer of access, and from the seventh edition (1896) the self-oblation is moved from its Zwinglian position to the

[20] *Ibid* p 45.

345

catholic, that is, in the eucharistic prayer. While this rite is open to many criticisms, at the same time it did prepare the way for the restoration of the eucharistic norm in *Prayers for Divine Service* (1923) issued 'by authority of the General Assembly of the Church of Scotland'.

The introductory article to the lectionary points out that the Westminster *Directory* required 'that all the canonical books should be read over in order'. Two tables are provided, in which the Sundays are numbered 1–53 and the readings set out 'in course'. At the same time, selected readings are provided for Christ's nativity, crucifixion, resurrection, and ascension, for pentecost, and for occasions of humiliation and thanksgiving. This remained the practice in all ten editions of the *Euchologion* and also in the first edition of *Prayers for Divine Service* (1923), but it sowed the seed for a lectionary based on the Christian year in the second (1929) edition, and for the publication of *Prayers for the Christian Year* (1935, revised 1952). The first edition of the *Euchologion* had rejected proper prefaces to the eucharistic prayer as 'complicated' and 'objectionable',[21] but these are provided in the *Book of Common Order* (1940), where the lectionary gives an old testament reading, epistle and gospel.

'The materials for the construction of a Service for Public Worship on the Lord's Day' consist of scripture sentences, twelve groups of prayers, canticles and benedictions. The prayers are drawn from the eastern and western rites and reformed, anglican, and modern sources. Anglicanism is represented by the *Book of Common Prayer*, Jeremy Taylor and Laud. As well as Bucer, Calvin and Knox use is made of the Neufchatel and Waldensian rites. The modern rites are represented by *Prayers for Social and Family Worship*, Lee's *Order of Public Worship*, and the Dutch, German, and catholic apostolic rites.

In the second edition (1869) the lectionary and materials are placed at the beginning of the book and are followed by two 'specimens of complete services for the morning and evening of a Lord's Day' (the prayers in the first being drawn from Jeremy Taylor and in the second from the catholic apostolic liturgy),[22] and forms for baptism, admission of catechumens, holy communion, marriage, burial, and ordination.

It is recommended that the first prayer should consist of introductory collect, confession and pardon, supplications and

[21] *Ibid* p 31.
[22] *Ibid* (1869) p 151.

concluding collect; the second (before sermon) of thanksgiving and illumination; the third (after sermon) of intercession; and the Lord's prayer 'may conclude either the First or Second Prayer'.[23] To use the Lord's prayer in either of these positions was contrary to Scottish usage both before and after the reformation. The position recommended here derives from the influence of anglican morning and evening prayer.[24]

It is not until the third edition (1874) that forms are provided for morning and evening worship on each Sunday of the month. These were compiled by G. W. Sprott, J. Cameron Lees, George Campbell, R. H. Story, and an unknown member respectively. In them the above order is followed, with the Lord's prayer ending the second prayer and the intercessions following the sermon.

In the fifth edition (1884) the apostles' creed was added after the new testament reading,[25] and in the sixth (1890) the intercessions were moved to follow the saying of the creed.[26] Both these changes were departures from the eucharistic norm of reformed worship[27] owing to anglican influence. Writing on this Robertson says, 'The seventh edition . . . was quite bare-faced in its copying of the *Book of Common Prayer*; the order of public worship was altered from the traditional Scottish Order, putting the Intercessions and Thanksgiving before the sermon, and adding the Lord's Prayer to the first prayer. Sprott, who went so far as to say that "deference to Anglicanism is a crime", along with Leishman and others protested at this departure from the order of the Eucharist; but the damage was done.'[28] While it did not appear in the sixth, the old order was printed as an alternative in editions seven to ten.[29] This departure from the eucharistic norm remains uncorrected in the *Book of Common Order* (1940). This was not done until the publication of *Divine Service* in 1973.[30] All editions also contain a wide selection of prayers 'for daily and other services'.

Reference has been made to the abuse hurled at the society and its members. Sometimes, on the other hand, the criticism aimed at being

[23] *Ibid* p 20.
[24] [W. D.] Maxwell, *History of Worship [in the Church of Scotland]* (Oxford 1955) p 178.
[25] *Euchologion* (1884) p 40.
[26] *Ibid* (1890) p 49.
[27] W. D. Maxwell, *John Knox's Genevan Service Book* (Edinburgh 1931) pp 85–104.
[28] Robertson 'The place of Dr Robert Lee', p 40. See also Maxwell *History of Worship* pp 180–1. This is equally applicable to the sixth edition.
[29] *Euchologion* (1896, 1905, 1913, 1919) p 176.
[30] *Book of Common Order* (Oxford 1940, repr 1962) pp 13, 19, 25, 32, 38, 46, 114, 135. *Divine Service* (Oxford 1973) pp 5, 18, 33.

constructive, for example, prior to the publication of the sixth edition the broad church party presented a representation to the editorial committee. Its aim was to achieve a 'more general adoption by ministers' of the *Euchologion*. The criticisms were:—

1. The morning and evening services are in general too doctrinal in tone and expression . . .

2. Many of the confessions of sin are of an unreal character, and not likely to attain the end in view at this part of worship . . .

3. We do not object to the occasional use in worship of the 'Apostles' Creed' but deprecate its inclusion in every service . . .

4. We feel that the prayers of the Church ought to tend practically not only to form but to all the duties of men . . . It appears to us to be the noble function of Christian worship to infuse a Christian spirit into all the occupations of society, and not only to save the members of the Church out of the world, but to save the world by making it increasingly Christian . . .

5. The benefits of Christianity are connected too directly, and in too mechanical a way, with Baptism and the Lord's Supper.

6. We respectfully ask that at least one new morning and one new evening service be included in the forthcoming edition . . .

7. We suggest that the general order of service is capable of improvement, and that extempore prayer should be more clearly recognised.[31]

As a result the society made this party responsible for the services on the fifth Sunday of the month in the sixth edition.[32] Beyond omitting the creed, how far they met their own criticisms it is difficult to say.

More serious, however, was the founding of the Scottish church society in 1892, that is, two years after the publication of the sixth edition of the *Euchologion*. From the beginning men like Sprott, Leishman, Cameron Lees and Story aimed at restoring the worship of the early Scottish reformed church. But there were others whose liturgical theology was to put it mildly indeterminate and similar to Lee's desire for 'good taste, decency, propriety, and solemnity'.[33] Part of the Scottish church society's aim was a protest against 'mere trimming and embellishment' in the interests of doctrine. So not

---

[31] This is a summary so not always verbatim. For actual text see Kerr *Renascence* pp 95–7.
[32] *Euchologion* (1890) pp 148–72.
[33] R. Lee *Reform of the Church of Scotland*, part i (Edinburgh 1864) pp 47–8.

only its own members, but also those of the church service society, were led to seek a reason for the form of public worship in the church's doctrine.[34]

The main defects of the movement were, first that it regarded the *Book of Common Order* (1564) and the Westminster *Directory* as in some measure a sort of 'golden age' of reformed worship, and this was accepted historically rather than because of its theological basis, and, secondly, a failure to recognise that, to use Archibald Scott's phrase, 'scissors and paste prayers'[35] alone can never adequately express devotional aspirations. This is an easy criticism to make, but there is no doubt that the society should have given more emphasis to 'free prayer'.

It is from these weaknesses that the main liturgical error of the movement springs, namely, the failure to provide a liturgy of the word in the eucharistic rite instead of seeing it as an office following a preaching service. Consequent on this was the failure to recognise that the eucharist, not anglican matins, is the source of the reformed rite.

Two other activities of the movement require mention. First, in the first edition of the *Euchologion* an appendix was included listing the liturgical works in the libraries of the Scottish universities.[36] In 1881 the society started 'a collection of liturgies, ancient and modern, for the use of members'. This in 1884 was presented to the library of the general assembly.

Secondly, as well as issuing suggested services for special occasions the society published a series of *Liturgies and Orders of Divine Service used or prepared for use in the Church of Scotland since the Reformation.* Sprott edited the *Book of Common Order (Knox's Liturgy)* (1868, revised 1901), *Book of Common Order (Euchologion)* (1905), *Scottish Liturgies of the Reign of James VI* (1901), and the *Liturgy of Compromise* (1905). Leishman edited the *Westminster Directory* (1868, revised 1901). Cooper edited the *Liturgy of 1637 (Laud's Liturgy)* (1904). Wotherspoon edited the *Second Prayer Book of King Edward the Sixth* (1905).[37]

The works of Sprott and Leishman in 1868 were written partially as a corrective to Lee's mistaken ideas and arguments,[38] and the whole

---

[34] W. Milligan *The Scottish Church Society: Some account of its aims* (Edinburgh 1892) pp 15–18.
[35] *Scotsman* 27 May 1902.
[36] *Euchologion* (1867) pp 216–20.
[37] These were all published by William Blackwood and Sons, Edinburgh.
[38] Robertson 'The place of Dr Robert Lee', p 32.

series together with the society's *Annual*, which commenced in May 1928 have made a significant and useful contribution to liturgical studies in Scotland.

In its early years, 1865–84, the movement was reformed in perspective, though on historical rather than theological grounds. By 1890 it had become anglican-dominated in outlook. This called forth a re-assessment of the basis of the movement and by 1905 the quest was well under way for a liturgical theology the fruits of which are evident in the current service-books of the aids to devotion committee of the church of Scotland.

What were the achievements of this renaissance? It built up a library of liturgical books, stimulated liturgical studies, and sought a larger place for such studies in theological faculties. It led to a transformation in the conducting of public worship and stimulated a devotional attitude in congregations. It led to public worship being centred on the mighty acts of God in creation, redemption and pentecost by its emphasis upon the significance of the Christian year. It led to a fresh interest in church lay-out and furnishings. It enabled the church of Scotland to recover the roots of its public worship in the church catholic. It worked a reformation without revolution.

At the same time, those who have entered into and reaped the harvest of this renaissance must remember that no form of public worship can ever be considered final in detail. History and experience of the God of history do not stand still.

The Presbyterian College
Belfast

A LATE NINETEENTH CENTURY
NONCONFORMIST RENAISSANCE

by JOHN KENT

ET us start from the propositions that we need a new model of late nineteenth-century English nonconformist history, and that one might be found by making some use of the idea of 'renaissance', especially if one uses 'renaissance' to point to the emergence at a particular time of humanist attitudes. This new model needs to be both less anglican and less nonconformist than its predecessors. The anglican model of nineteenth-century nonconformity is obsessed with anglicanism, and the nonconformist model is equally obsessed with the behaviour of an earlier, largely unrelated evangelical protestantism in the seventeenth and eighteenth centuries. Both, in other words, are affected by shallow ideas of historical continuity. The individual nineteenth-century anglican often thought of nonconformity as the shadow cast by anglicanism; individual nonconformists believed that seventeenth-century independency had founded English political freedom, or that eighteenth-century non-anglicans had saved evangelical protestant truth from total disappearance. These were myths, however.

It was part of the nature of the nonconformist myth that it was socially enveloped within the anglican myth, so that the former cannot be properly understood without the latter. How the anglican mind worked in relation to the non-anglican (including Roman catholic) at the turn of the century may be seen in two quotations from Mandell Creighton, when he was bishop of London. The first comes from a private letter written in 1898:

> The English people are committed to the care of the English Church. From time to time they express their opinion about the mode of teaching which is applied to them. The Church of Rome is a small body in England, which stands in no relation to the life of the nation. It is quite impossible that any considerable number of Englishmen should be Roman Catholics. To join yourself to that Church is simply to stand on one side and cut yourself off from your part in striving to do your duty for the religious future of your country.[1]

[1] L. Creighton, *Life and Letters of Mandell Creighton*, 2 (London 1904) p 349.

The same argument, from size to significance, applied to the free churches as far as Creighton was concerned. He was perfectly serious; he had a reputation for being sensible, even worldly-wise; but one should not take him seriously except as evidence for the state of an individual anglican consciousness. There was no question of a late nineteenth-century English Roman catholic believing that Roman catholicism stood in no relation to the life of the nation. Creighton's knowledge of history, his sense of historical continuity, his passionate conviction that the church of England must be 'the religious organ of the English people' and 'the religious consciousness of the nation'[2] had almost cut him off from his own historic present.

The second quotation is from an official statement which Creighton made in 1899:

> It is quite natural that the nonconformists should wish to separate the Church from the State, that they should wish, that is, that there should be no religious body which is supposed in any way to express the sentiments of the English more than any other. That is the point at issue . . . A national church means a national recognition of the supreme law of God. Without a national church there cannot be that.[3]

From the nonconformist point of view, however, it was not so obvious that 'a national church' existed, or that without one there could be no national recognition of the supreme law of God.

I have emphasised the anglican position because in the case of nineteenth-century protestant nonconformity the problem is how to find a self-understanding which is not either made irrelevant by appeals to the seventeenth or eighteenth centuries, or made inadequate by a tacit acceptance of the anglican view. One reason for this has been a twentieth-century nonconformist fascination with images of institutional and religious decline, images which are not very useful for explaining the expansion of the past. It is agreed, that is, that the non-anglican religious institutions expanded between 1860 and 1906, but the significance of this is then over-shadowed by an interpretation in terms of the decline of the free churches which followed between 1906 and 1939, so that the earlier growth and influence are treated as almost meaningless, as a process which needs little analysis. This approach seems to underlie, for example, D. M. Thompson's distinction between a free church 'golden age' stretching from 1863 to 1886, and an 'ebb

[2] *Ibid* pp 301, 373.
[3] *Ibid* p 384.

tide' running from the home rule split to the first world war.[4] The perspective seems wrong: if there was a 'golden age' it was surely between 1886 and 1906, when nonconformity committed itself to wresting complete social equality from the church of England. The effort was symbolised in political figures like Asquith, Campbell-Bannerman, Lloyd George and Keir Hardie, and in the liberal election victories of 1906, 1910 and 1911. One has to allow for the exuberance with which Hugh Price Hughes, the Wesleyan leader, could declare:

> We represent at this moment a majority of the English people who attend places of worship and take a real interest in Christianity . . . the number of our sanctuaries registered and licensed for public worship largely exceeds that of the Anglican Church. It may perhaps be replied that our sanctuaries are small, if numerous, and do not accommodate as many worshippers as the Anglican sanctuaries. But that is a complete mistake . . . the Congregationalists, the Baptists and the Methodists—leaving out all other denominations of Evangelical Dissenters—provide in this country accommodation for 7,000,000 of people. But the total provision of the Anglican denomination in all her cathedrals, churches and mission halls is much less than that. Again, the Anglican Church provides in her Sunday-Schools for 2,700,000 children. But the three Evangelical Churches I have just named provide for 3,100,000. Even in this country, therefore, we provide more religious accommodation for adults and have more children in our Sunday Schools than the Anglican Catholics . . . Representing a majority of the Christian people at home, we represent an immense majority in the British Empire, and an overwhelming majority in the English-speaking world. If the failures and humiliations of the past, as well as the bright hopes of the present, have at last taught us their Divinely-appointed lessons, the future of British Christianity and of the British Empire is in our hands.[5]

It is so obvious to us that the future of British Christianity and of the British empire was in very different hands that we pass too lightly over the point in history at which free church leaders could talk in this way.

[4] D. M. Thompson, *Nonconformity in the Nineteenth Century* (London 1972) pp 177–80, 226–30.
[5] *Proceedings of the First National Council of the Evangelical Free Churches, held at Nottingham, March 10 to 12, 1896* (London 1896) p 37.

To escape the numbing effect of this perspective of decline, one has to remember that what was formative in this period was the growth in numbers, wealth, social stability and culture of new urban middle-classes, one of whose characteristics was the generation of the powerful religious sub-culture in its later Victorian and Edwardian form. This socio-economic development underlay the recovery of anglicanism as well as the advances of nonconformity,[6] but the religious sub-culture was wider than the traditional ecclesiastical structures dear to the heart of the church historian. This wider grouping is important, because one needs a model of the religious sub-culture in which Arnold Bennett, for example, becomes a logical, integral part of Wesleyan methodist history in the midlands, and D. H. Lawrence, though marked out by the genius which Bennett lacked, a logical, integral part of the history of the story of mining congregationalism. Bennett's recent biographer, Margaret Drabble, hurries over his Wesleyan years to the real life in London; her image of nonconformity, all 'puritanism' and 'work ethic', is negative: she has no idea that one might talk about the sub-culture from which Bennett came in terms of 'renaissance' or revival (though not as Wesleyans revive), or in terms of a humanism which, however strange in such quarters, had its roots there nonetheless.[7]

But of course there is an orthodox obstacle at this point. Matthew Arnold, as much as anyone, set the tone of the ancient but durable model which historians still use to describe the late Victorian middle-class and its religious sub-culture:

> It has been jokingly said of this class, that all which the best of it cared for was summed up in the alliterative phrase—Business and Bethels: and that all which the rest of it cared for was the business without the Bethels. No such jocose and slighting words can convey any true sense of what the religion of the English middle-class has really been to it; what a source of vitality, energy and persistent vigour . . . But the puritanism of the English middle-class, which has been so great an element of strength to them, has by no means brought them to perfection. The most that can be

---

[6] For the anglican increase see A. D. Gilbert, *Religion and Society in Industrial England, Church, Chapel and Social Change 1740–1914* (London 1976) pp 27–9. Easter day communicants increased from 995,000 in 1861 to 2,226,000 in 1914. Over the same period the total methodist figure grew from 513,628 to a peak of 800,234 in 1906.

[7] Bennett lived 1867–1931; Lawrence 1885–1930. Ivy Compton-Burnett (b. 1892) and Malcolm Lowry (b. 1909) both had Wesleyan backgrounds; so had Herbert Palmer, the poet (1880–1961).

said of it is, that it has supplied a stable basis on which to build perfection; it has given them character, though it has not given them culture . . . In this sphere of religion, where feeling and beauty are so all-important, we shrink from giving to the middle-class spirit, limited as we see it, with its sectarianism, its under-culture, its intolerance, its bitterness, its unloveliness, too much its own way[8] . . . The Dissenters have been very angry with us for saying that they are an obstacle to civilisation. They are indeed, our greatest.[9]

The negative classes, in fact: uncultured, uncreative, unattractive; unable to appreciate the beauty of morality touched by emotion; naturally wallowing in Moody and Sankey.

This is a familiar picture, but if one turns to the congregationalist, Daniel Jenkins, whose *The British, Their Identity and Religion* (1975) was a genuine attempt to make a case for the social usefulness of a surviving nonconformity, one finds that he tamely accepts Arnold's judgement:

When Matthew Arnold in *Culture and Anarchy* sneered at the Philistinism which was displayed pre-eminently by nonconformists (mark that pre-eminently—does he really know? did Arnold really know?) he was speaking about something that was real enough. What made his superior person's sarcasm so offensive was his failure to see, even though he was his father's son and an inspector of schools to boot, how much people like himself carried responsibility for their being like that. Nonconformist worship was impoverished, Nonconformist education was limited and utilitarian, Non-conformist social habits and styles were made either insecure or complacently provincial because the custodians of high culture in England, the clerisy, of whom Matthew Arnold was one of the chief, snubbed them at every turn and refused to have anything to do with them except at the price of the surrender of their convictions and their loyalties.[10]

This is a good example of the influence of images of institutional decline. Jenkins knows that between 1860 and 1914 the free churches aimed at mastering the whole religious sub-culture; he knows that they failed, and he imagines that he knows why. Nonconformity cannot argue with Arnold, he says in effect, it can only blame him. Of course

---

[8] This description of the 'middle-class spirit' would apply very well to anglo-catholicism.
[9] M. Arnold, *A French Eton* (London 1892) p 116.
[10] D. Jenkins, *The British: Their Identity and Religion* (London 1975) p 100.

dissent became aesthetically impoverished, produced no literature, dried up religiously, but it was not the nonconformists who wanted it that way, but the custodians of the high culture.

Once one has combined the images of decline and under-culture there remains no further reason to analyse nineteenth-century nonconformity. This is why, for example, E. R. Norman's *Church and Society in England 1770–1970* (1976)[11] is actually about the political theology of the church of England alone, the political theology of non-anglican institutions being treated as either imitative or uninteresting; in the index the references to nonconformity are divided between 'legal position of' and 'opposition to claims of the Establishment'. And even Valentine Cunningham, dissent's revenge on the Victorian novelist, could make little of the period after 1900 except to say that 'there had been decline, but not the fall anticipated by the Victorian novelists and confirmed by their successors like D. H. Lawrence',[12] a judgement which fails to reflect any sense of Lawrence as himself a writer from the nonconformist sub-culture. Cunningham argued that Charles Dickens, George Eliot, Elizabeth Gaskell, Margaret Oliphant and 'Mark Rutherford' had given an unfair (and in our terms, Arnoldian) portrait of the dissenting minister, but he allowed the novelists to dictate the terms of his subject, so that for him also dissent became essentially Victorian, protestant and evangelical, and therefore inevitably the subject of adverse criticism by novelists. At odds with George Eliot, for whom religion seemed doomed, he suggests that the appropriate model for sectarian and dissenting history is not linear but cyclical, but this is surely misleading: what matters is whether institutions can adapt, not whether they can go round in circles.

It was all the more unfortunate that Cunningham chose to end with William Hale White (Mark Rutherford) for although his novels were issued in the 1880s and 1890s they referred emotionally to White's early life and should not be taken as evidence for the state of dissent outside White's consciousness in the later nineteenth century. His bitter, grievance-ridden criticism of nonconformity had a political rather than a literary vogue precisely because his jaundiced images confirmed the Arnoldian tradition and served the anglican cause in the full-blooded inter-denominational conflict which can be traced in Hughes' speech quoted above. If there was any kind of renaissance in the late

---

[11] E. R. Norman, *Church and Society in England 1770–1970* (London 1976) p 503.
[12] V. Cunningham, *Everywhere Spoken Against, Dissent in the Victorian Novel* (London 1975) p 284.

A late nineteenth-century nonconformist renaissance

Victorian nonconformist religious sub-culture White would not have been the man to know that it was taking place. By giving White more space than he deserved Cunningham committed himself to Arnold's company. And by ignoring Arnold Bennett, whose *Anna of the Five Towns* (1901) was very much a Victorian novel, he robbed himself of a standard of comparison, for Bennett wrote, painfully, from inside.

Yet Arnold's amateur sociological generalisations need not be a stumbling-block. One has to put out of one's mind the anglican shadow, 'the philistines', and the Oliver Cromwell myth, and look instead at what was happening at the end of the nineteenth century, not simply in religious institutions, but in nonconformity as a religious sub-culture which had been changing and developing since 1860. Then one may see going on a renaissance in the English under-culture —to transform Arnold's derisive phrase—one may see a return of the human as the subject of value, a humanism which might employ some Christian imagery, but might equally resist the cramping effects of some religious systems and institutions on the human personality. This nonconformist renaissance was not parasitic on anglicanism, nor itself particularly anti-anglican; its existence did not necessitate images of decline.

Three different elements have to be distinguished here. The first is the wealth and position which the growth of Victorian capitalism gave to some nonconformist families, such as the Colmans of Norwich, the Palmers of Reading and the Wills of Bristol. The second is the parallel and largely consequent extension of nonconformist religious institutions, which reached a peak of social and political influence in the Edwardian period. The third is a renaissance *within the nonconformist milieu* of values often opposed to the official: art, liberal Christianity and many kinds of socialism. As Moore has recently shown in the case of Durham, there was a ready welcome c1900 among some young Wesleyan and primitive methodists for the ideas of Tolstoy, William Morris, Thoreau, Robert Blatchford and the suffragettes;[13] hints of the same pattern can be found in Stella Davies' *North Country Bred* (1963),[14] an autobiography from the Manchester region. A group of religious writers, C. J. Cadoux, R. J. Campbell, John Oman and

---

[13] R. Moore, *Pit-Men, Preachers and Politics, The Effects of Methodism in a Durham Mining Community* (London 1974) pp 169–90. Moore believes that methodism prevented the labour party in Durham from becoming thoroughly socialist; nevertheless, much of its radical thought came from the same methodist sub-culture.

[14] C. S. Davies, *North Country Bred, A Working-Class Family Chronicle* (London 1963). Her family was methodist.

A. S. Peake, for example, mediated between orthodox protestant evangelicalism and a new, more liberal Christianity.[15] As for literature, Arnold Bennett's almost marxist vision of the corrosive effect of money on the religious sub-culture; D. H. Lawrence's recognition that the same sub-culture had nothing positive to say about sex—these judgements were signs of a further rebirth of the human as the standard of value within the existing religious world of the sub-culture. Nor should one take it for granted that such men slough off their origins completely: Lawrence's late story, *The Man Who Died* (1929), a brief, pantheistic myth, may be interpreted as in part a return to ideas current in congregationalism years before.

There is space here to consider only one of the products of this renaissance. Arnold Bennett's *Anna of the Five Towns* may be called the missing Wesleyan novel, an account of the Wesleyan society as it was about 1900: Bennett's own statement, made when he was starting the novel in 1896, that it was 'a study in paternal authority',[16] is misleading as an interpretation of the finished work. *Anna* is an elaborate analysis of the value of 'Wesleyanism', set against the background of the Staffordshire pottery trade, itself a characteristic methodist milieu. Anna's father, Ephraim Tellwright, the miser, represents the extreme form of the acquisitiveness of the developing capitalist system; Anna herself, living in her father's wilful external poverty, symbolises the poorer Wesleyanism of the early movement, now submitted to the strains of the market society. In her heart she does not like a religion which has decayed into a revivalism which demands an act of will ('only believe'), but cannot give a clear description of what the act is to contain. Mynors, the successful pottery manufacturer who finally marries her for her money, tells her that she has expected too much: 'we cannot promise you any sudden change of feeling, any sudden relief and certainty, such as some people experience; at least, I never had it'. It is in her struggle against money, for it is money and not her father that she is really fighting, that Anna finds protestant evangelicalism useless, because it always subtly combines with the enemy. She is driven to invent for herself a protective humanism of a limited kind. In revolt against her father's exploitation of the Prices (the unsuccessful pottery manufacturers), she tears up Willy Price's forged note, and this denial of profit and obliteration of debt (whose

---

[15] Cadoux lived 1883–1947, Campbell 1867–1956, Oman 1860–1939; Peake 1865–1929.
[16] A. Bennett, *The Journals*, ed F. Swinnerton (London 1971) p 22.

religious symbolism Bennett makes no crude attempt to impose)
are the sins which her father will not forgive her. Anna becomes
aesthetic in her attitude to money at times: she is distressed because
Mynors makes his profits from poor-quality china.

This aestheticism is more thoroughly exhibited in the family of
alderman Sutton, who has made a fortune as a potter's valuer and
commission agent, and whose daughter, Beatrice, befriends Anna.
Beatrice's emotional life works on the aesthetic, not the religious,
level, her revolts are a matter of style, over food or dress, or over her
family's rampant delight in the coming mayoral title of her father. She
asserts her personality to the degree that Anna fails to assert hers.
Anna, after all, had ['sucked in with her mother's milk the profound
truth that a woman's life is always a renunciation, greater or less': she
survives by her own strength, but within other people's parameters.
At the Sunday school treat Beatrice gives the opposite example:

A carriage rolled by, raising the dust in places where the strong
sun had already dried the road. It was Mr. Sutton's landau, driven
by Barrett. Beatrice, in white, sat solitary amid cushions, while
two large hampers occupied most of the coachman's box. The
carriage seemed to move with lordly ease and rapidity, and the
teachers, already weary and fretted by the endless pranks of the
children, bitterly envied the enthroned maiden who nodded and
smiled to them with such charming condescension. It was a social
triumph for Beatrice. She disappeared ahead like a goddess in a
cloud, and scarcely a woman who saw her from the humble
level of the roadway but would have married a satyr to be able
to do as Beatrice did. Later, when the field was reached, and the
children bursting through the gate had spread like a flood over
the daisied grass, the landau was to be seen drawn up near the
refreshment tent; Barrett was unpacking the hampers, which
contained delicate creamy confectionery for the teachers' tea;
Beatrice explained that these were her mother's gift, and that
she had driven down in order to preserve the fragile pasties from
the risks of the railway journey. Gratitude became vocal, and
Beatrice's success was complete.[17]

The Lawrentian criticism of Bennett: 'I hate Bennett's resignation;
tragedy ought to be a great kick at misery', seems irrelevant to *Anna*.

[17] A. Bennett, *Anna of the Five Towns* (London 1913) p 147. Mynors's remark to Anna
(see above) is on p 84, and the description of Anna on pp 253-4.

JOHN KENT

The kick is there: in Beatrice's self-display, in Anna's hopeful attempts to make money serve affection, in young Willy Price's suicide; and its being there is Bennett's indirect witness to the renaissance in (not of) nonconformity. The novel itself is part of the evidence that the nonconformist sub-culture was capable of creativity. Of course, *Anna* is not a simple historical document; one cannot just read off from it the decline and fall of evangelical protestantism. The Wesleyans at the time said that Bennett had left out the religion, but that charge looks unconvincing now. Perhaps he also paid his tribute to Arnoldianism. *Anna* is not as bleak as *Riceyman Steps* (1923), an essay in the same plain style, where a second-hand bookshop symbolises western culture, its guardians now utterly secularised by the market society. *Anna* is only one useful source of information about the circumstances in which the late nineteenth-century non-conformist sub-culture became, all over England, a place where young men and women sickened for the time being of the new industrial society which was forming, and turned for inspiration to Blatchford, Campbell, Morris, Tolstoy and many others. The brotherhood movement, the *Clarion* and its cycling clubs, the independent labour party were some of the organisations in which one may find the traces of a stifled revolution; and in that stifling, which explains something of what is shallow and cold in present-day British culture, orthodox nonconformity no doubt played a part. The creative elements in the nonconformist sub-culture had chosen the radical path and did not return.[18]

University of Bristol

[18] For a recent discussion of the relationship between religion and politics in the Edwardian period, see S. Yeo, *Religion and Voluntary Organisations in Crisis* (London 1976) pp 253–89.

NEO-ORTHODOXY, LIBERALISM AND WAR: KARL BARTH, P. T. FORSYTH AND JOHN OMAN 1914-18

by STUART MEWS

'THERE is a theological renaissance today', proclaimed the American theologian Daniel Day Williams in 1952. 'The rebirth of theology means a renewal of the effort to discover the foundations of the Christian life'. He maintained that following the publication of Karl Barth's commentary on *Romans* in 1918 'there has been a deepening consciousness that there is a radical settlement to be made between Christianity and the thought and values of the modern world'.[1] Williams' assertion is better read as an indication of the mood of 'pessimistic optimism'[2] manifested by many American theologians in the post world war two era than as an accurate description of the development of American theology from 1918. Moreover one man's 'renaissance' is another man's 'reaction', and there is something distinctly bizarre in the use of the former term in connection with a thinker like Karl Barth who devoted the most productive period of his life to total opposition to those intellectual assumptions which were characteristic of the sixteenth-century renaissance and were further developed in the European enlightenment. Nevertheless the historian of religion would be the last to deny the importance of investigating the factual basis of mythical beliefs, especially when they were as widely held as those put forward by Williams.

Fourteen years later a British critic of Barth could nevertheless maintain that he 'initiated a theological renaissance which is of truly world-wide importance',[3] while Heinz Zahrnt, perhaps the best popular exponent of modern German theology, argued that what he calls 'the renewal of protestant theology in the twentieth century'

---

[1] Daniel Day Williams, *Interpreting Theology 1918-1952* (London 1953) pp 11 *seq.*
[2] The phrase was coined by Robert N. Bellah, *Beyond Belief. Essays on Religion in a Post-Traditional World* (New York 1970) p xvi. On post-war religious optimism and pessimism in the USA: Stuart Mews, 'Paul Tillich and the Religious Situation of American Intellectuals', *Religion* 2/2 (Newcastle-on-Tyne 1972) pp 122-40.
[3] James Richmond, *Faith and Philosophy* (London 1966) p 142.

361

was the direct consequence of the events of August 1914. Zahrnt contrasted the heady optimism of Adolf von Harnack's famous lecture series of 1899–1900 on *Das Wesen des Christentums* with his behaviour in 1914 when he drafted the German emperor's appeal to his people, and signed the so-called 'manifesto of the intellectuals'. 'The manifesto of the ninety-three intellectuals' wrote Zahrnt, 'signified the collapse of [the] bourgeois idealist thought of the nineteenth century'.[4] In this contention he was following Karl Barth who recalled in 1957 that the publication of the manifesto 'stands out in my personal memory as a black day':

> Among these intellectuals I discover to my horror almost all of my theological teachers whom I had greatly venerated. In despair over what this indicated about the signs of the time, I suddenly realised that I could not any longer follow either their ethics and dogmatics or their understanding of the bible and of history. For me at least, nineteenth-century theology no longer held any future.[5]

The 1957 account gains dramatic power through its concentration on the 'sudden' shock impact of a single event, and the picture it evokes of the collapse of idols. There have since been suggestions, however, that Barth in his old-age over-dramatised this particular event and ascribed to it a personal significance which it could not have possessed.[6]

It can easily be demonstrated that Barth's alienation from the bourgeois idealist thought of the nineteenth century predated the publication of the manifesto of the intellectuals and that his disenchantment with the theological giants of his generation, had begun even before the outbreak of the war. In 1920 he recalled having listened to Ernst Troeltsch in 1910 'with the dark foreboding that it had become impossible to advance any further in the dead-end street where we were strolling'.[7] This 'dark foreboding' might perhaps have become

---

[4] Heinz Zahrnt, *The Question of God. Protestant Theology in the Twentieth Century* (ET London 1969) pp 15–17.

[5] [Karl] Barth, [*The Humanity of God*] (Fontana ed London 1967) pp 12 *seq*.

[6] Wilfried Härle, 'Der Aufruf der 95 Intellektuellen und Karl Barths Bruch mit der Liberalen Theologie', *Zeitschrift für Theologie und Kirche* (Tübingen 1975) pp 207–24. My understanding of Barth's early theological development has been greatly clarified in conversation with my colleague Dr John Powell Clayton, which I would like to acknowledge.

[7] Karl Barth, *Theology and Church. Shorter Writings 1920–1928* (ET London 1962) pp 60 *seq*. See also K. Barth, 'On Systematic Theology', *Scottish Journal of Theology* 14, 3 (Edinburgh 1961) pp 225 *seq*. The conference at which Troeltsch read the paper

a settled conviction through the shock of the manifesto, but it is significant that Barth does not even refer to it in his wartime correspondence with Eduard Thurneysen. Instead, on 4 September 1914, he told his friend that he found 'symptomatic significance' in the fact that 'such a man as' Martin Rade editor of the influential liberal religious paper *Die Christliche Welt* 'can lose his head so completely in this situation'. Barth was disappointed that Rade 'seems to be so naive as to think that we must without question be pro-German (and not neutral) in our attitude':

> The unconditional truths of the gospel are simply suspended for the time being and in the meantime a German war-theology is put to work, its Christian trimming consisting of a lot of talk about sacrifice and the like . . . It is truly sad! Marburg and German civilisation [*die deutsche Kultur*] have lost something in my eyes by this breakdown, and indeed forever.[8]

This declaration of a final disenchantment with Marburg the chief centre of liberal protestant theology, and *die deutsche Kultur* occurred a full month before the publication of the manifesto of the intellectuals which appeared in the *Frankfurter Zeitung* on 4 October 1914. In his lecture of 1957 Barth had mistakenly backdated its publication to 'early August' but this is immaterial in the face of the contemporary evidence of his reaction to Rade's editorials which demonstrates that the Rubicon had been crossed some time before the dawn of the 'black day'.

Yet whether or not Barth had been confused about the manifesto, there seems no good reason to doubt his claim in a lecture in 1956 that it was 'precisely the failure of the ethics of the modern theology of the time with the outbreak of the First World War', which 'played a decisive role for me personally'.[9] But we might ask if it need necessarily have done? Was there some inner logic in that theological tradition against which Barth was rebelling which inevitably led its proponents to endorse the action of the state and beat the religious war-drum? Conversely, is it equally certain that adoption of a

---

to which Barth alluded in 1920 was actually held 13–15 March 1911 and not in 1910 as Barth recalled. Troeltsch's paper was 'Die Bedeutung der Geschichtlichkeit Jesu für den Glauben': Wilfried Groll, *Ernst Troeltsch und Karl Barth—Kontinuität im Widerspruch* (Munich 1976) pp 14 *seq.*

[8] Karl Barth, *Gesamtausgabe* 5 (Zurich 1973) p 10. I have reproduced here the English translation by J. D. Smart from *Revolutionary Theology in the Making. Barth-Thurneysen Correspondence 1914–1925* (London 1964) p 26.

[9] Barth p 37.

theology of transcendence would lead naturally, as Barth seemed to think in 1914, to a position of religious detachment or even neutrality? The consideration of these questions involves entering the debate most provocatively opened up by the followers of Max Weber when they suggest that differences in behaviour must be sought in the permanent intrinsic character of religious beliefs, and not only in temporary external historico-political situations.[10]

One of the impressive features of Weber's work was his eagerness to test his hypotheses in different historical and cultural situations. Following his example, it might be profitable in understanding Barth's position to consider the relationship between the attitudes taken to the first world war by those holding both similar and different views in other countries. The remainder of this paper is an attempt to provide another perspective by examining the response of British theologians to the issuing of manifestos and support for the national cause and in particular to the war-time views of the two leading free church theologians of the period from 1900 to 1940, P. T. Forsyth and John Oman,[11] both men who stood with Karl Barth in the reformed tradition.

Before considering their reactions, the wider religious context in which they were working should be considered.[12] Even before the appearance of the manifesto of the intellectuals, an 'Appeal to Evangelical Christians abroad' had been issued by a group of German theologians, who included Harnack, Eucken, Deissmann, Richter, Spieker and Kaftan—all men who had been involved in the Anglo-German friendship movement and the Edinburgh missionary conference of 1910. This testament to German innocence and indictment of the 'web of conspiracy' which the allies had 'long secretly and cunningly been spinning', could not in the opinion of the archbishop of Canterbury, Scott Lidgett, Sir Willoughby Dickinson and Sir Claud Schuster (who was responsible for organising British reactions to German propaganda) be left unanswered. 'It is staggering', wrote Scott Holland, 'to find that Christian theologians think so lightly

---

[10] This view has frequently been adopted as a hypothesis and empirically tested by modern sociologists, for example Günter Golde, *Catholics and Protestants. Agricultural Modernization in Two German Villages* (New York 1975). It is an over-simplification of Weber's view: Michael Hill, *A Sociology of Religion* (London 1973) cap 5.

[11] In the opinion of W. M. Horton, *Contemporary English Theology. An American Interpretation* (London nd) p 126.

[12] See also: [Stuart] Mews, ['Spiritual Mobilization in the First World War'], *Theology* (London June 1971) pp 258–64.

of violating neutrality'.[13] But what was the correct response? F. C. Burkitt, Norrisian professor of divinity at Cambridge, at first thought that silence was the best reply.

> Before the war broke out, when it seemed only to be a question of another Balkan trouble, I joined a certain number of scholars in deprecating a war with Germany. I still think we should not have been justified in going to war with Germany except in such circumstances that it would be better to be beaten and crushed than to keep out of it. Such circumstances did arrive with dramatic suddenness almost before the letter appeared. It was a warning to me to hold my tongue for the future till peace returns.[14]

Charles Gore, the high church bishop of Oxford, was another who at first refused to associate himself with the archbishop's reply. In his case the refusal was based on an objection to the slant of the reply which in his view shared too much ground with that of the Germans in being an appeal from protestants to protestants. Eventually both Gore and Burkitt added their signatures.[15]

The first response to the German theologians had come from William Sanday, Oriel professor at Oxford. Sanday had always been interested in military tactics and absorption in the war came as a welcome relief from the wordy and wearying battles in which he had been engaged following his public rejection of the new testament miracles in the early part of 1914 with old friends like Gore in Oxford.[16] Yet even in his patriotic endeavours he was not free from the pestering of old friends interested in scoring a theological point. T. B. Strong, dean of Christchurch, agreed to sign the archbishop's reply, but had refused to sign one drafted by Sanday:

> It seemed to me when I saw the draft to be rather twittering and indecisive, but as you know, Dr. Sanday shies at anything like a definite adjective. I wanted to get the word 'stupid' in if I could, because I think the theologians have displayed exactly the same stupidity in interpreting the situation as they have displayed in interpreting history, and I am afraid it is difficult to persuade Sanday of the value of this parallel.[17]

[13] [Lambeth Palace Library,] Davidson MSS: H. S. Holland–R. T. Davidson 17 September 1914.
[14] *Ibid*, F. C. Burkitt–R. T. Davidson 17 September 1914.
[15] *Ibid*, C. Gore–R. T. Davidson 18 September 1914.
[16] W. Sanday, *Bishop Gore's Challenge to Criticism* (London 1914). For a detailed account of this debate: Stuart Mews, 'Liberalism and Liberality in the Church of England 1911–22' (university library, Cambridge: Hulsean prize essay for 1968) cap 4.
[17] Davidson MSS: T. B. Strong–R. T. Davidson 18 September 1914.

The extension of the animosity aroused by German war tactics to German *Kultur* and German theology, was a danger which liberal theologians soon came to appreciate. The British reply was distributed to allied and neutral countries by the government's propaganda organisation at Wellington House.[18] The declaration organised by the archbishop of Canterbury was not however the first manifesto produced by British theologians. Even before they knew about the German appeal, a group of congregationalist and presbyterian scholars had signed a letter to Harnack. On 27 August 1914 they expressed their deep distress at the Berlin professor's description in a public speech, of the conduct of Great Britain 'as that of a traitor to civilisation'. They felt sure that 'you could never have been betrayed into such a statement if you had been acquainted with the real motives which actuate the British nation in the present crisis'. Unfortunately their efforts to persuade Harnack that Britain had gone to war because of her government's belief 'in the sanctity of treaty obligations' fell on deaf ears. Whilst the free churchmen might insist that 'we sincerely believe that Great Britain in this conflict is fighting for conscience, justice, Europe, Humanity and lasting peace', Harnack simply pointed to the brute fact of the alliance with Russia and panslavism, the hereditary enemies in German eyes of all that European civilisation stood for. This British letter had been signed amongst others by W. B. Selbie of Mansfield college, Oxford, and Richard Roberts, a young presbyterian minister who was shortly to change his mind. The first signature at the very head of the list, was that of P. T. Forsyth.[19]

---

[18] M. L. Sanders, 'Wellington House and British Propaganda during the First World War', *HJ* 18, 1 (1975) pp 119–46.

[19] Adolf von Harnack, *Aus Der Friedens-Und Kriegsarbeit* (Giessen 1916) pp 290–9. Church leaders in neutral countries were much impressed by Harnack's view. On 31 August 1914 Hensley Henson received a letter from Nathan Söderblom, archbishop of Uppsala: 'he is evidently much impressed by the German view of England's attitude as implying a treason against "culture". This view has seemed to receive confirmation by the announcement that Indian troops are to be employed in Europe. The Scandinavians are petrified by dread of Russia, and they cannot see beyond the single fact that England is Russia's ally'. Even Henson's formidable apologia failed to convince. On 7 January 1915 he received a reply from Söderblom 'evidently filled with an irremovable suspicion of Russia, and his liking for England only just succeeds in holding him back from accepting the German version of the war'. (Durham cathedral chapter library, Henson Diary). See also: Nils Karlström, *Kristna Samför-standssträvanden Under Världskriget 1914–1918. Med Särskild Hänsyn Till Nathan Söderbloms Insats* (Stockholm 1947) pp 250 seq.

Forsyth has frequently been described as 'a Barthian before Barth'.[20] According to Allan Galloway the distinctive emphases in their writings were identical—'the social and political realism of human sinfulness, the primacy of objective grace over subjective illumination, the intrinsic authority of the person of Christ, the power and finality of the Cross'.[21] Barth is once said to have remarked, 'If Forsyth had not said what he said when he said it, I would have said he was quoting me'.[22]

Given the similarity of their basic theological position, it might be expected that Forsyth's reaction to the first world war would have been similar to that of Barth. The very opposite was in fact the case. For a Christian even to consider the possibility of rising above the conflict or taking a neutral position was in Forsyth's eyes to 'shirk the issue', to become 'accessories of unrighteousness', to 'fall from being moral persons to mere animate things'. 'It is throwing on God the dirty work you are called to do. It is to step out of the category of moral beings.'[23] Forsyth might have differed from Barth on the possibility of Christian detachment but he shared, both in anger and in sorrow, Barth's assessment of the tragic consequences of the liberal protestant tradition. 'One of the banes of modern religion', wrote Forsyth, 'is its Idealism. And for Germany the one has ruined the other':

> For we are faced in Germany with the extinction of the old Idealism (which has become its chief religion) and the growth of an idealism which is but materialism glorified to a megalomania, a combined worship of Mammon, Mars and Mercury (thief and liar), a compound of militarism, commercialism, and a rationalism based on these, rooted in force and reckless of morals.[24]

In Forsyth's view, Germany had declared war on the kingdom of God,[25] and for that she must be judged and punished. A real, objective atonement involved judgement, and Britain was being used as the rod of God's anger. He insisted that:

> There is now, indeed, no chosen nation as nation, no nation with divine reversion of the world. God does not thus prefer one people to another. But still a nation is elect to service and sacrifice

---

[20] [Harry] Escott, [*P. T. Forsyth and the Cure of Souls*] (London 1970) p 22; [A. M.] Hunter, [*P. T. Forsyth. Per Crucem ad Lucem*] (London 1974) p 12.

[21] Review in *Expository Times* (London November 1972) p 58, quoted in Hunter p 13.

[22] Escott p 22.

[23] [P. T.] Forsyth, [*The Christian Ethic of War*] (London 1916) pp 20 *seq.*

[24] *Ibid* pp 121, 123.

[25] *Ibid* p 43.

for the righteousness of the kingdom of God. It owes to that
service its real and final right to exist. And the present issue has
long ceased to be—ever since Belgium has ceased to be—a struggle
between people equally egoist and ambitious to whom the
Christian moralist could say 'A plague on both your houses'. It
has become a contest for the righteousness of the New Humanity
in the Kingdom of God now by one side openly disavowed.[26]
Forsyth was equally, indeed obsessively, vehement against what he
regarded as one of the most ugly manifestations of the idealist tradition
in Britain, pacifism. For over twenty years he had championed what
A. M. Hunter has called 'a neo-orthodoxy of a very vital and evangelical kind' against that 'type of religion, part humanist, part mystic, and
all too unhistoric, [which] has engaged the interest of large numbers
of people, especially among the young, and such as are by nature as
yet more in love with man than with righteousness'.[27] Throughout
this period he was often regarded as a hangover from Victorian
orthodoxy. 'Theological liberalism', wrote J. K. Mozley, 'and popular
sympathies found themselves in close alliance, the same fire cheered
them, with its pleasant warmth: and Forsyth was out in the cold'; 'his
mind and the Zeitgeist have never marched in sympathy'.[28]

Pacifism, in Forsyth's view provided a devastating exposure of the
inadequacy of the vague, undogmatic idealism which had been so
popular in the Edwardian era. 'It is the climax of a generation of genial
and gentle religion with the nerve of the Cross cut; which, therefore,
breaks in our hands at a great historic crisis for lack of the moral note'.
Pacifism, he maintained, was subjective and individualist. 'The inner
light deepens the darkness without, and loses the signals lighted for the
conscience there'.[29] F. D. Maurice had taught that Christianity was a
corporate religion. Only the church had the right to sanction passive
resistance: 'it was not a matter for the lone conscience and the free
lance'.[30] This was the answer he could give to those who argued that
the free churches were guilty of double standards in condemning conscientious objection to military service in 1916 when they had sanctioned it in opposition to the education act of 1902.[31] Forsyth argued

[26] Ibid p 34.
[27] Hunter p 15; Forsyth p 112.
[28] [J. K.] Mozley, [The Heart of the Gospel] (London 1925) pp 68 seq, 66.
[29] Forsyth pp 39, 83.
[30] Ibid p 69.
[31] In later years the view was expressed that passive resistance in 1902 cheapened the
concept of conscientious objection and made it more difficult for those who took

that in 1902 conscientious objection and passive resistance had been the corporate response of the nonconformist churches as a whole. Indeed he had himself described it at the time as 'expressing the collective conscience of the Free Churches'.[32]

Forsyth's views on these matters were powerfully set out in his book on *The Christian Ethic of War* which he completed in June 1916. His close friend A. E. Garvie, principal of New College, London, recalled that Forsyth was 'extremely disturbed and distressed by the war' and that the book 'bears the mark of abnormal strain':

> The worst said about Germany is echoed here, although there is a kindly reference to pre-war Germany: the cause of Britain and her allies is alligned with the divine judgement on human sin on the cross. Like Assyria of old we were the rod of God's anger, and our victory would be the triumph of God's holiness over sin. Pacifism is unreservedly condemned: the right of the individual to disobey the obligation of citizenship even is challenged. The doctrine of the Atonement is restated even with vehemence of language.[33]

This time the *Zeitgeist* and Forsyth walked hand in hand. Earlier in the year, his fulminations against the fellowship of reconciliation and pacifism had been rejected as articles by the *British Weekly*. 'Perhaps the time for it hasn't come', he admitted to the editor, Robertson Nicoll.[33a] But the book's publication in the autumn coincided with the new mood of public anxiety and hysteria which followed the gigantic loss of life in the battle of the Somme. 'In that book', claimed Mozley, 'his mind did move in agreement with the general opinion of the time'.[34]

The congregational union had shown amazing sympathy for the plight of the conscientious objector in its May meetings in 1916. When Morgan Gibbon had declared that the conscientious objector 'stands precisely today where the majority of us stood yesterday, and where

---

that position in 1916: A. H. Dodd, 'The Nonconformist Conscience in Public Life', *Hibbert Journal* 26 (London 1938) p 233.

[32] Sir James Marchant, *Dr John Clifford* (London 1924) p 141.

[33] New College, London MS 537/1, A. E. Garvie, 'Placarding Jesus Christ the Crucified. The Theology of the late Dr Peter Taylor Forsyth' (manuscript of unpublished book) nd p 90. For Garvie's relationship with Forsyth: A. E. Garvie, *Memories and Meanings of My Life* (London 1938) pp 186 seq.

[33a] Nicoll MS (courtesy of Mrs M. Kirkaldy) P. T. Forsyth–W. Robertson Nicoll, 12 April 1916.

[34] Mozley p 67.

we shall be standing again tomorrow or the day after', he was interrupted by a great outburst of applause.[35] But in October, the atmosphere had totally changed. On that occasion the union had invited younger men to give the main addresses, but it was Forsyth whose teaching dominated the gathering. 'Dr Forsyth was obviously—and naturally—gratified to find himself quoted by both Mr. Brook and Mr. Pringle in their weighty address on the ethical impact of Christian teaching, as a standard authority on the subject', wrote the *British Weekly*.

A sense of outrage, exasperation, and indignation against those who had saved their skins by refusing to fight surged to the surface. Attacks on conscientious objectors by Arthur Pringle and Herbert Brook were received with 'a great crash of approving cheers.'[36] It was one thing to speak out for COs in the first few months of the military service act's operation; it had seemed a strange and alien measure, and many free churchmen who could not agree with those who refused to be enlisted nevertheless championed their right to dissent. But though many continued to be perturbed by the treatment of conscientious objectors, they could not hide their scorn of the false grounds on which conscientious objection was based. For Forsyth it must have been a moment of supreme irony. For Arthur Pringle had been one of the earliest followers of his theological arch-enemy, the R. J. Campbell of the new theology. 'It is odd', Forsyth had mused, 'that some of the most "tender" exponents of a sentimental religion are among the most belligerent critics of the pacifists they have been making for many years.'[37]

Forsyth's views now carried weight not only in crowded assemblies but also in the minds of those trying to decide on the practical implications of their sense of duty and Christian convictions. Ronald Rees was a young Wesleyan minister and a member of the fellowship of reconciliation. In 1914 he had signed a manifesto with other free church pacifists in opposition to Robertson Nicoll's rabble-rousing recruiting leaflet. By the summer of 1916 his mind was beginning to change and in June he resigned from the fellowship.[38] In April 1917 he told his

[35] B[ritish] W[eekly] 18 May 1916. A misleading account of this meeting appears in R. T. Jones, *Congregationalism in England 1662–1962* (London 1962) p 359. See also the letters in *Manchester Guardian* 18 May 1916.

[36] *BW* 5 October 1916.

[37] Forsyth p 140.

[38] Imperial War Museum, R. D. Rees MS: R. Roberts–R. D. Rees 9 June 1916.

father that he was thinking of joining the army. In June he rejected an approach from the Wesleyan army chaplains committee and enlisted for combatant service in the Royal Field Artillery.[39] Friends wondered what had led him to change his mind, a question which cannot be answered with any certainty. What is certain, however, is that amongst the bundle of letters which he kept from this period is a careful summary, chapter by chapter, of P. T. Forsyth's *The Christian Ethic of War*.[40]

But was Forsyth right in his contention that the theology of immanence had inevitably issued in pacifism? It was not true of the former leader of the new theology movement, R. J. Campbell, who was almost as bellicose as Forsyth himself,[41] nor of men in the second rank like Arthur Pringle and Bernard Snell. On the other hand W. E. Orchard and Stanley B. James both took up the pacifist cause, and one of Campbell's pioneer preachers, Fenner Brockway, was a leading light in the no conscription fellowship.

Those who combined moderate support for the war with a liberal outlook in theology were greatly disturbed by Forsyth's volume. John Day Thompson, the only president of the primitive methodist church to have been tried for heresy, totally rejected this slur on the patriotism of those holding liberal religious views. He asserted that on the contrary many pacifists shared Forsyth's theological position. The tribunals had had before them, he claimed, 'Plymouth Brethren, Christadelphians, and others of that ilk, besides many members of the regular churches, who associate with their misconception of the Sermon on the Mount this very same view of penal substitution and expiation'.[42]

Despite the very considerable research into the pacifism of the first world war, insufficient attention has been paid to its sources.[43] Keith Robbins, who has probed more deeply than anyone else, suggests that there was no single ethic behind the peace movement. He does, however, associate the basic postulates of the fellowship of reconciliation with the prevailing theological climate of liberalism.[44] But it is one

[39] *Ibid:* R. D. Rees–R. M. Rees 28 April 1916; J. H. Bateson–R. D. Rees 28 June 1917, 2 July 1917.
[40] *Ibid:* Tommy–R. D. Rees 8 May 1918.
[41] R. J. Campbell, *The War and the Soul* (London 1916).
[42] Review in *Holborn Review* (London October 1916) p 593.
[43] John Rae, *Conscience and Politics. The British Government and the Conscientious Objector to Military Service 1916–1919* (London 1970) p 72.
[44] K. G. Robbins, 'The Abolition of War: A Study in the Organisation and Ideology of the Peace Movement 1914–1919' (Oxford D.Phil thesis 1964) p 451.

thing to say that much religiously-based pacifism was held alongside liberal religious views, and another to see pacifism as the inevitable consequence of liberalism. Indeed Barth's critique of his German professors, as well as the stand of Campbell and Pringle in Britain, might point to the need for alternative explanations. 'Liberal idealism'. argued David Martin, 'either crusades for peace or treats war as a crusade'.[45]

Tempting though it is to settle for Martin's dichotomy, there remains the problem of explaining the position of those like John Oman, who came closer to liberal idealism than to the neo-orthodoxies of either Barth or Forsyth. When Barth was writing on *Romans*, Oman was finishing *Grace and Personality* which was published in 1917 and went through two editions in two years. With his Calvinistic background, Oman understood the force of what came to be the neo-orthodox stress on man's utter dependence upon the sovereign will of God, but he was much more impressed by the liberal faith in the moral independence of the individual. In *Grace and Personality* he presents an interpretation of the divine-human encounter which is fundamentally different from that to be taken by Barth.[46]

In his attitude to the outbreak of war, however, Oman was able to maintain precisely that degree of detachment which Barth found lacking in his theological teachers. When the manifestos has been flying backwards and forwards, Oman in England shared Barth's sense of horror at the ease with which religious leaders had adopted their nation's cause. 'If one were to judge by such outward manifestations as the tone of the religious press', he wrote, 'resolutions at ecclesiastical gatherings, sermons on the war . . . and of the frequency with which in private gatherings the religious official is the most belligerent person present, no kind of problem exists for the religious of mind to solve.' Indeed Oman had noted that 'the sounder the orthodoxy the less the sense of any possibility of conflict between war and Christianity.' The sheer complacency of the Christian mind in the presence of a European conflagration seemed to him to be the most staggering fact of all:

That our whole conventional Christianity may be going up in flames with other results of man's labour is so little feared, that part of this warlike zeal is derived from the hope that, among other results, we are to build again Zion after the old external traditional

---

[45] David A. Martin. *Pacifism. An Historical and Sociological Study* (London 1965) p 77.
[46] See F. G. Healey, *Religion and Reality. The Theology of John Oman* (London 1965).

outwardly visible and prosperous institutional form, and the liveliest hope of all is to see German theology perish in the flames with German Imperialism.

He could only wonder that so many preachers seemed to think that defending 'the political justice of our cause, not without satisfaction that a good thousand years of Christianity have passed over our enemies in vain, would appear to be the sole religious task'.[47]

In January 1915 Oman signed a letter with a group of fellow presbyterians, who included John Skinner, William Paton and Richard Roberts (who had now changed his mind on the question of the rightness of the war), setting out 'the reasons why we believe the Church ought to refrain from official declarations which may be regarded as sanctioning war':

1. The Church of Christ is bound by allegiance to her Lord to declare to the world only those things which are in accord with the teaching, the example and the spirit in Jesus, whose life is the light of men.

2. The central truth of Christ's teaching is the Gospel of the Kingdom, which is a Kingdom not of this world, whose weapons of warfare are spiritual, which transcends the division of race and nationality, uniting men of all peoples and tongues in a common brotherhood in the bond of peace and under the law of love.

3. The catholicity of the ideal Church forbids us to identify the cause of Christianity or the interests of the Kingdom of God with the cause of a particular nation, or, indeed, with any side of a quarrel which is to be settled by the sword . . . it is not the concern of the Church to advocate the redressing of wrong by violence or the establishment of righteousness in the earth by other than moral and spiritual agencies.

4. . . . the great lesson of the Cross is that God Himself can only remove the evil of the world through patient, self-sacrificing love. And it is only in this aspect of His self-revelation that we may seek to be like God.

There followed two final points which dealt with the positive role of the church, which was to 'bear witness to the truths of the Eternal Order', and this in turn was held to involve an assertion of the blessings of peace and goodwill between nations, the sacredness of human life, love, forgiveness and conciliation. Healing and reconstruction

[47] [John] Oman, [*The War and Its Issues*] (Cambridge 1915) pp 8 *seq.*

would be required after the war, and if it was to contribute, the church must avoid the possibility of the damaging charge that it had taken a purely national view.[48]

Elsewhere Oman insisted that the churches' judgment of the war must be both individual and catholic. God's love 'is fundamentally an estimate of man as an individual spiritual being whose own choice determines his destiny'. The church must always possess 'an unwavering respect for the individual's judgments of his own duty, with the one requirement that it be wholly sincere, and never detached but sensitive to the movements around him, though never submerged in them'.

> Wherefore, any church which takes up a mere sergeant's relation to recruiting and which simply tells men their duty without manifesting to them the sources of guidance by which they may discover it for themselves, is manifestly denying the supremacy of its own order and subjecting it to the temporal necessities of the state.[49]

But Oman spoke for a minority and in the first two years of the war the association between the Christian community and the nation became increasingly close. For some religious leaders, the identification was so complete that the two became merged. The barriers became entirely obliterated. The nation at war became the church militant. The war became in the bishop of London's words, 'the greatest fight for the Christian religion'.[50]

We might conclude from this brief examination of the reaction of two British theologians to the first world war, that Barth would have been unfair if he had renounced the liberal protestant tradition solely because of the failure of its ethical teaching in 1914. Despite his later reminiscences, he does not seem to have done so. It seems to have marked the final break in a process of gradual disenchantment.

Viewed in a larger context, the evidence suggest that there was little connexion between belief and behaviour in the first world war, or

---

[48] *The Presbyterian Messenger* (London) January 1915 p 9. Although Richard Roberts had signed Forsyth's letter to Harnack in August 1914, it was probably the British reply to the German theologians which was the decisive factor in his decision to join the fellowship of reconciliation: 'I was even ready to admit that the term "just" and "righteous" might be used concerning it [the war]. But to have it spoken of as being a Christian enterprise seemed to me to be going beyond fact and reason. That settled the matter for me'. H. G. Wood, *Henry T. Hodgkin. A Memoir* (London 1937) pp 152 *seq.*

[49] Oman pp 51 *seq.*

[50] For the bishop of London's attitude, see Mews.

rather, that any theological tradition could be used to validate whatever position its adherents might choose to take on other grounds.[51] It is not possible here to do more than hint at other factors which might, consciously or subconsciously, have swayed men's minds. The most obvious is, of course, nationality. If Karl Barth had been German instead of Swiss, he might have reacted differently. At a more subtle level it would be valuable to attempt to assess the possible effects of the structural position of theologians within their respective societies. The fact that German Lutheranism was established inevitably imposed its own expectations and limitations. These were compounded for those who also held university chairs at a time when it was becoming gradually more difficult to integrate the increasing differentiation of knowledge within the German idealist tradition.[52] A manifesto of the intellectuals could provide a gratifying expression of unity in the service of German *Kultur* for an academic elite becoming increasingly conscious of its fragmentation and diversification. If we want to understand the position which religious leaders took in the first world war it is necessary to look not just at their pre-war ideas (though these are important) but also at the total context in which they were operating. As Edith Cavell might have said, 'Theology is not enough'.

University of Lancaster

[51] The evidence presented here could be supplemented by widening the perspective to include the USA. It appears that the majority of American liberal theologians remained very critical of the war and religious jingoism even after America's entry in 1917: William R. Hutchinson, *The Modernist Impulse in American Protestantism* (Harvard 1976) cap 7.

[52] Fritz K. Ringer, *The Decline of the German Mandarins: The German Academic Community 1890–1933* (Cambridge, Mass., 1969).

AN ABORTIVE RENAISSANCE:
CATHOLIC MODERNISTS IN SUSSEX

by A. R. VIDLER

STORRINGTON in Sussex, at the beginning of this century, was described as 'a quiet, peaceful village.'[1] Although in the intervening period its population has more than doubled, it is still known as a village and has retained much of that agreeable character. In 1909 it suddenly became the centre of an ecclesiastical *cause célèbre* that attracted international attention. Anyone who was in Storrington on 21 July in that year could have witnessed an extraordinary funeral.

It was the burial of a Roman catholic priest. The mourners, who numbered about forty, assembled in the garden of the house in the middle of the village where the priest had died and walked from there in silence to a grave that had been prepared in the anglican or parish churchyard. There was no requiem or formal funeral service, but prayers were said and an address was given by an unrobed priest who was in fact a Frenchman, though that might not have been evident since he was fluent in English. He said that he spoke in the name of many French, Italian and German friends, for father George Tyrrell, whose funeral it was, had become well-known in those countries and in others too. He was one of the most conspicuous representatives of what is known to historians as the modernist movement in the Roman catholic church and of what may be described as an abortive renaissance.

The mourners at his funeral included some of the principal participants in the movement and also sympathisers with it in other churches. On no other occasion was there such a gathering in England of catholic modernists and their friends. It took place, as I have said, at Storrington in Sussex and it happens that several of the small but varied company of catholic modernists were domiciled in Sussex. Storrington, more than any other place, was their focal centre. It is these coincidental circumstances that make it appropriate for me to take 'catholic modernists *in Sussex*' as my subject. No other English county would afford similar material.

[1] See F. M. Greefield, *Round About Old Storrington* (Storrington 1973) p 1.

A gathering like that at Storrington in 1909 might have taken place many years later—in June 1940—when the other most conspicuous catholic modernist, Alfred Loisy, was buried at Ambrières in France; but that was at the time of the fall of France and many, among them I myself, who in more favourable conditions would have been present were prevented.

I am going to begin with a few general remarks about the modernist movement and then propose to show how those modernists who in one way or another had Sussex connexions, if only by reason of their presence in Storrington on this memorable occasion, embodied or illustrated different characteristics of the movement, different degrees of association with it, and different aspects of its abortiveness.

The word 'modernist' is now-a-days used in so many disparate contexts, both theological and non-theological, and with so many shades of meaning, that it cannot be said to have any definite meaning in itself. On 27 October 1958 a London newspaper[2] described an incident in Islington when two gangs of youths were knifing one another, and it concluded with the report that 'one youth declared: "Don't call them Teddy boys, guv. They was modernists".' Please forget that and all other uses of the word that are extraneous to our present subject.

By modernists I mean here those members of the Roman catholic church who from about 1890 to 1910 were looking for an intellectual and spiritual renaissance in their church. They were hoping for, and variously working for, such a revision or reinterpretation of its teaching and stance as would take account of new developments in human knowledge and ways of thinking—philosophical, scientific and sociological as well as theological and ecclesiastical. They had no formal organisation or agreed policy, but they had enough in common to constitute a movement in the church which had its sympathisers and collaborators elsewhere and which was deemed by the Vatican to have sufficient menacing substance to merit solemn acts of papal condemnation and drastic measures of espionage and suppression.

Pope Pius X, in his encyclical *Pascendi* of September 1907, purported to provide a systematic and elaborate account of the doctrines of the movement which he called 'modernism' and denominated 'the synthesis of all heresies'. But none of the supposed modernists allowed that the papal representation of what they stood for corresponded to the facts of the case, so that a distinction should be drawn between

[2] *News Chronicle.*

modernism as an abstract system which the papacy condemned and which certainly has an interest of its own, and *modernists*, that is the body or loose collection of people in the church who wanted change or reforms, varying in kind and in degree, but all of them obnoxious to the papacy which at that time was able to exercise a rigid control over the church.

My concern here is not with modernism but with modernists and, to be precise, with those who had Sussex connexions such as I have indicated. They happened to be a good, though incomplete, sample of the modernists as a whole and to illustrate their differences of background, outlook and experience.

First, I will mention one who may be described as a pre-modernist, that eminent lay historian of liturgy, Edmund Bishop.[3] His connexion with Sussex is that he lived with his sister at Castlegate in Lewes from 1901 to 1903 when the modernist movement was in full flow. I call him a 'pre-modernist' because his sympathy with the movement derived from the profound influence that had been exercised upon him as a young man by Acton and Simpson and *The Home and Foreign Review*. As he privately confessed to his friends in 1908: 'I am an irredeemable modernist from long before the days when modernism was thought of . . . a modernist of before modernism'.[4] He was a rigorous historical positivist or historicist and consequently a severe critic of the scholastic theologians of his time who were determined to subordinate history to theology. Thus on many points he was in agreement with the modernists and would like to have seen such an intellectual renaissance in the church as they were bent upon. On the other hand, I call Bishop a pre-modernist for the further reason that, before the movement started moving, he had come to the conclusion that the cause was hopeless. In no future that he could foresee would the papacy allow a radical revision of doctrine, in particular with regard to the bible.

His position was in fact similar to that of another eminent historian, Louis Duchesne. Duchesne was indeed described, after the condemnation of the movement, as a modernist and even as the chief of the modernists,[5] but although he had a good deal to do with the initiation of the movement he did not participate in it, because at an early stage he had come to the same pessimistic conclusion as Edmund Bishop

---

[3] See cap 6 in my book *A Variety of Catholic Modernists* (Cambridge 1970).
[4] See *ibid* p 135.
[5] See *Monseigneur Duchesne et son temps* (École Française de Rome 1975) p 315.

A. R. VIDLER

about its prospects.[6] Were it not that I cannot claim for Duchesne any
connexion with Sussex, it would be tempting to say more about him.
Although there is as yet no biography, much more information about
him is accessible since the colloquy about him that was held at the
Ecole Française de Rome in 1973, the proceedings of which have since
been published.[7]

If we turn now to those who were indisputably modernists, it is
natural to begin with George Tyrrell. He was an Irishman, and that is
a fact that should be noted. He once wrote to père Laberthonnière, the
French philosophical modernist, about himself and his friend, abbé
Bremond, who was a native of Provence:

> You take us . . . much too seriously. You are neither provençal
> nor Irish, who are both incurable jokers and wags. In conversa-
> tion, we love to try out hypotheses, to propound paradoxes, to
> blaspheme our idols, to mock our most cherished convictions.[8]

I shall have more to say about Bremond later on. Tyrrell would sometimes in fun sign his letters: '+Georgius Storringtonensis'.[9]

He was born in 1861 and brought up in Dublin and in the church of
Ireland, but while still in his 'teens he was attracted to catholicism and
after a brief passage through high anglicanism he became a Roman
catholic and almost at once prepared to become a Jesuit. He formally
entered the novitiate in 1880. Thus began the first phase of his career
in the church during which he was ardently orthodox, a Thomist in
theology, and much valued as a conductor of retreats and as a spiritual
director and confessor. He also began to show his gifts as a writer and
in 1896 joined the staff of the English Jesuit review, *The Month*, which
was edited from Farm Street in London.

His first book, *Nova et Vetera* (1897), a book of meditations and
spiritual reflections, caught the attention of baron Friedrich von Hügel,
a catholic scholar and sage with ecumenical contacts. He had a zest for
discovering promising catholic thinkers who were disposed to work
for an intellectual and spiritual revival in the church, of the kind that
had unsuccessfully been sought by various liberal catholic groups and
individuals during the nineteenth century.[10] Already von Hügel had
become a close friend of abbé Loisy, the biblical scholar, of Maurice

[6] On Duchesne's relation to the modernist movement, see *ibid* pp 348, 353–73.
[7] See n 5 above.
[8] See *Laberthonnière et ses amis*, ed Marie-Thérèse Perrin (Paris 1975) p 205.
[9] See A. L. David, [*Lettres de George Tyrrell à Henri Bremond*] (Paris 1971) p 280.
[10] See *Les catholiques libéraux au xixe siècle* (Grenoble 1974).

Blondel, the non-scholastic philosopher, and of bishop Mignot, the most liberal and cultivated French prelate of his time. The baron made it his business to introduce such men to one another's work and, when possible, to establish personal relations between them. In this way he did more than anyone else to generate the incipient modernist movement.

It was von Hügel who acquainted Tyrrell with the work of the French philosophical modernists (the philosophy of action, as it was called), and also brought home to him the importance of the critical study of the bible and its effects upon traditional orthodoxy. He encouraged Tyrrell to proceed with essays in doctrinal restatement. Tyrrell first got into trouble with the church authorities because of an article in which he questioned the conventional Roman catholic teaching about everlasting punishment in hell. This was in 1899, and from then on, with some fluctuations, his relations with church authority and with the society of Jesus became increasingly strained, and at the same time his writings, some of which were anonymous or pseudonymous, became increasingly radical.

Broadly speaking, Tyrrell's stance came to be that, while he was convinced that the life of the catholic church mediated the fullest experience of God and of Christ and of the spiritual life, the church's theological system should not be regarded as an adequate, logically watertight or immutable statement of absolute truth. Theology was the inevitably inadequate expression or formulation of the living experience of the church. Revelation consisted in this living experience, not in its intellectual and propositional formulation. This dynamic, somewhat pragmatic, view of revelation and dogma contrasted sharply with the static and deductive rationalism of the official theologians. It also obviated the discord between dogma and scientific and historical knowledge, since dogma was always reformable. But in the conditions that then prevailed in the Roman church it was considered to be extremely dangerous and subversive, all the more so as Tyrrell was an eloquent writer with a seductive charm of style. It would be near the mark to say that he found himself struggling to fufil a prophetic mission in what was then in effect a police church, a church in which, as was said, there was a 'reign of terror',[11] so that a break was inevitable.

[11] 'It is a real "reign of terror" in the R. Catholic body.' M. D. Petre to A. L. Lilley, 24 December 1907 (Saint Andrews university library); 'C'est une *terreur blanche* qui s'organise.' E. I. Mignot to F. von Hügel, 7 January 1908 (*ibid*).

In February 1906 Tyrrell was dismissed from the society of Jesus: he preached his last sermon and said his last mass when staying with modernist friends at Eastbourne in Sussex. Attempts to regularise his position as a secular priest all proved abortive and, when in 1907 he attacked the encyclical *Pascendi* in two articles in *The Times* newspaper, he was deprived of the sacraments.

He first stayed at Storrington in the spring of 1906 as a boarder in the Premonstratensian priory there. (Hilaire Belloc and Francis Thompson had stayed there before him.) Tyrrell said of the Storrington monks that not only had they never heard of liberal catholicism but their conversation was all about receipts for cooking![12] It was in August of that year that his friend, Miss Maude Petre (to whom I shall be turning presently), bought Mulberry House in the centre of the village and made a small cottage in the garden in which two rooms were set apart for father Tyrrell. Von Hügel called it a *modeste maisonnette*.[13] It was here that Tyrrell spent much of the last years of his life and here that on 15 July 1909 he died of Bright's disease, which had not been diagnosed till the last. He had just completed his most characteristic and prophetic book, which was published posthumously, *Christianity at the Cross Roads*.[14]

Mulberry House is still there in the centre of Storrington and is still so called although regrettably the name is nowhere displayed. It has been turned into offices. The cottage, in which Tyrrell died, may still be seen behind the house. It has been somewhat enlarged and is now called 'Malt Cottage'.

On his deathbed Tyrrell received the last sacraments in so far as his paralysed and semi-conscious condition permitted him to do so. His friends Dr Dessoulavy and abbé Bremond ministered to him. He was in no state to make any retractation of his alleged errors even if he had wanted to do so. It was because Miss Petre, with the advice of von Hügel, at once publicly stated that he had not made a retractation that catholic burial was forbidden by the bishop of Southwark, in whose diocese Storrington was situated, and the funeral took place as I have described. The tombstone over Tyrrell's grave is a good example of the early work of Eric Gill who, I may remark, was born and brought up in Sussex, the son of a minister in the countess of

[12] See A. L. David p 221.
[13] See *Laberthonnière et ses amis*, p 192.
[14] New edition, Allen and Unwin (London 1963).

Huntingdon's connexion. He did not however become a Roman catholic till after the condemnation of the modernist movement and apparently did not interest himself in it.

I come now to Miss Maude Petre who was chiefly responsible for the connexion of the catholic modernists with Storrington. She was born in 1863 and was a grand-daughter of the eleventh Lord Petre, an old catholic family. The ninth Lord Petre, whose life she wrote, had been a leading cisalpine (or anti-ultramontane) in the eighteenth century and a pioneer of catholic emancipation. She herself was a woman of great courage, independence and intellectual ability, though some found her a bit of a bore![15]

She got to know father Tyrrell through a retreat he conducted in 1900 for a religious society of which she was for ten years the superior. Their friendship ripened rapidly, and her diaries, which are now in the British Museum and were at one time in my keeping, show clearly that she was deeply in love with him. He did not feel for her like that although he owed a great deal to her friendship both in his life time and as his literary executor, biographer and faithful disciple and champion till the end of her life in 1942. It has never been suggested that there was anything improper in their relationship. She was a devout catholic who respected his vocation to celibacy. Tyrrell himself, while he was much indebted to his women friends, seems to have been something of a misogynist[16], and he certainly said some extremely harsh and unpleasant things about Miss Petre behind her back, notably in his letters to Henri Bremond, but these may be partly put to the account of the unrecognised effects of Bright's disease upon his mentality.

Miss Petre was a woman of letters who wrote perceptive books and articles, most of which bore on the modernist movement. Professor Claude Jenkins said that she had 'an almost uncanny gift of description and analysis at the same time'.[17] The church authorities tried to browbeat her as they did the other modernists, but with singularly little success, although she was forbidden to receive the sacraments in the diocese of Southwark. (She continued to make her home at Storrington until 1938.) As a lay woman she was not so easily disciplined as those who were priests, and it was thought prudent

[15] See A. L. David pp 257-9.
[16] Compare *ibid* p 28.
[17] In *Theology* 34 (London 1937) p 252.

to treat an aristocratic 'cradle catholic' with a certain respect. However, she had a series of encounters with church authority in which she firmly held her ground.

For instance, in December 1909 she returned to Storrington after ten days' absence and next morning went as usual to mass at the priory church intending to receive communion. But just at communion time the prior rushed into the church and told her she could not receive the sacrament. 'Did the bishop say so?' she asked. 'No, but you cannot,' he said. 'You have no right to stop me,' she answered, and it was only to avoid scandalising the congregation that she desisted, and afterwards wrote to the bishop to ask for his ruling. The bishop side-stepped the question and countered by saying that it would help him to reach a decision if she would send him in writing her submission to the papal acts condemning modernism. That she declined to do in these characteristic terms:

> I only read the 'Pascendi' and 'Lamentabili' once and that was a long time ago. They made on me a very painful impression which I found was shared by a great many Catholics; for they seemed to condemn writers like Cardinal Newman and Fr Tyrrell who had been our greatest Catholic apologists; they seemed to hamper the mind in the acceptance of scientific and historical fact; and the Pascendi seemed to advocate a line of conduct contrary to general notions of charity. If I am wrong in this, I shall be very glad to be convinced of my error; but your Lordship will understand why I do not want to read them again.[18]

Whenever subsequently the authorities tried to get her to submit to the condemnation of modernism, she replied by asking them questions that they deemed it impolitic to attempt to answer.[19] Miss Petre's persistent and public adherence to the modernist cause was unique. Her last book, about which incidentally she consulted me, was an extremely sympathetic appreciation of the work of M. Loisy with whom she had always maintained cordial relations.

Nearly all other declared modernists, after the condemnation of the movement and the imposition of the anti-modernist oath in 1910, either broke with the church and so secured their freedom, or decided to submit and become silent in the hope that better times would come in the future.

[18] M. D. Petre to A. L. Lilley, 10 December 1909 (St Andrews).
[19] See my book, *The Modernist Movement in the Roman Church* (Cambridge 1934) pp 211–12.

An abortive renaissance: catholic modernists in Sussex

Baron von Hügel was a partial exception to this rule. Although he had been a prime, if not the principal, instigator of the movement and after its condemnation encouraged others to stick to their guns, he himself was cautious and escaped condemnation. On 29 December 1907 Tyrrell told Bremond that the baron was preaching passive and active resistance on all sides, and then added sarcastically that he might himself be practising it before long.[20] If he had been called upon to make a public act of submission, it is uncertain how he would have responded. It would undoubtedly have caused him agonised grief to have been deprived of the sacraments. Probably the authorities had regard for his personal prestige. It should be added that, while he never disowned his modernist convictions in the field, for instance, of biblical criticism, he did avoid the provocative utterances of a Tyrrell or a Loisy and also dissociated himself from the 'immanentism' or rejection of the transcendent which he claimed to detect in the thought of many of his erstwhile modernist friends. In consequence the assertion was even made that he had never been a modernist! But that was absurd, as has been conclusively shown in Dr L. F. Barmann's *Baron von Hügel and the Modernist Crisis in England* (1972).

I will now say something about other modernists or sympathisers with the movement who were present at father Tyrrell's funeral or were domiciled in Sussex. Alfred Fawkes and H. C. Corrance, who during the first decade of this century resided respectively at Brighton and Hove, were both clerical converts from high anglicanism. I have written about them elsewhere.[21] Whereas Fawkes was reordained in the Roman church, Corrance as a married man, though separated from his wife, became a layman. He was much more active than Fawkes in the modernist cause. Fawkes was a friend of Tyrrell and Miss Petre and is buried beside them in Storrington churchyard, but he seems never to have had much in the way of modernist hopes, though he wrote admirably about the movement in his book *Studies in Modernism* (1913), which was a collection of his articles. When the movement was condemned he quietly returned to minister in the church of England as an erastian broad churchman, while Corrance appears eventually to have drifted away from any definite profession of Christian faith. It has been said[22] that Fawkes, Loisy and Tyrrell exemplified three typical attitudes to the condemnation of the

[20] See A. L. David p 105.
[21] See *A Variety of Catholic Modernists* pp 155–65.
[22] See A. Fawkes, *The Church a Necessary Evil* (Oxford 1932) p 16.

modernist movement. 'Fawkes said: "I am not wanted, I will go"; Loisy said, "I will go when I am put out"; Tyrrell said: "You cannot put me out, I stay".'

There is another English modernist who lived in Sussex about whom I will say more. He has received little attention in the literature of the subject and should certainly be noticed here. William John Williams was known to his friends as 'Little Willie' because of his small stature. There are somewhat inconsistent testimonies to the impression he made on people. In 1897 von Hügel described him as 'shy, sensitive, thoughtful and original'.[23] Earlier in that year he had had the enterprise to visit Loisy in France together with an anglican friend who acted as interpreter.[24] At Eastbourne he struck up a friendship with John Cowper Powys, who always speaks of him as 'The Catholic'[25], and in his *Autobiography* describes his 'soft black-brown hair . . . his nobly rounded forehead, . . . his deep hazel eyes, eyes that had the peculiarity of turning black, yes! of shooting forth *black fire* when he got excited . . . his thin classical nose, his frail body.' 'The Catholic,' he says, 'had been trained to be a priest and though he had never taken the final orders, it was an instinct with him to wear the dark clothes and assume many of the external manifestations of a man set apart to ponder day and night upon God and immortality.'[26]

Both Tyrrell and Miss Petre thought highly of Williams' book, *Newman, Pascal, Loisy and the Catholic Church* (1906). On 14 July 1904 Tyrrell wrote to A. L. Lilley: 'Williams' "Pascal-Newman-Loisy" which I have just read in M.S. is really *quite* excellent and he is perfectly willing to be excommunicated for it . . . it is a stand for a sane Catholic Christianity such as we all want.'[27] On 12 December 1906 Miss Petre wrote in her journal: 'W. Williams' book "Newman Pascal etc." is splendid, and a grand apologia for Newman.' J. C. Powys recalled Williams at work on this book: 'that convoluted piece of sophisticated argument . . . How it all comes back to me, his meticulous small handwriting . . . and the intense passionate eloquence of his complicated reasoning! His favourite word . . . was

[23] See [M. de la] Bedoyère, [*The Life of Baron von Hügel*] (London 1951) p 90.
[24] A. Loisy to F. von Hügel, 10 February 1897 (BN, naf 15644).
[25] See Powys, *Letters to Louis Wilkinson* (London 1957) p 71.
[26] *Ibid* pp 280–1.
[27] G. Tyrrell to A. L. Lilley, 14 July 1904 (St Andrews). On p 300 of his book, Williams wrote: 'As theologians . . . and not only as critics and historians we may conceive that Christ was speaking of the coming of the Kingdom in the immediate future in a literal sense.'

the word "Relative". By the help of this magic word he would evoke a body of rich and subtle thought that served as a sort of covered bridge between conservative orthodoxy and the most rebellious modernism.'[28]

Maisie Ward says that Williams was so absent-minded that father Tyrrell once said of him: 'Willie W. is here in my armchair, smoking and swooning. He does not know where he is; or who I am; or what century he is living in.'[29] Perhaps absent-mindedness accounts for his reputation for indiscretion. Apparently, he could not be depended on to hold his tongue. When in 1905 a group of modernists was hoping to produce a set of 'New Tracts for New Times' (a project that did not materialise) we find von Hügel writing in his own inimitable way to A. L. Lilley as follows:

> I am a bit worried by one detail or consequence of our proposed set of writers . . . It is that, as Miss Petre reminds me (but this is, of course, quite confidential), W. J. Williams though, by his ideas, training and powers, *quite* a man, and a rarely appropriate man, for the work is a *hopelessly unreticent* person,—we know this from much experience . . . I have been thinking whether W. could not be, somehow, got to join as a writer, without his being informed of all his fellow-writers' names . . . But this wd evidently be most difficult,—practically impossible, I expect, if he came to the constitutive, deliberating meeting, and he would almost or quite have a right to be hurt (and he is very sensitive) if he were not invited, and found out that the other writers had thus met. You may see some way out of the *impasse:* I look about for one, in vain.[30]

This is a typical piece of von Hügel's scheming. In this case he wanted to prevent Tyrrell's association with the project from coming to the ears of his Jesuit superiors.

It was with Williams, and his sister Miss Dora Williams, that Tyrrell was staying at Eastbourne in February 1906 when he said his last mass. After the condemnation of modernism Williams boldly supported Tyrrell's attack on the *Pascendi* and asserted that the teaching of cardinal Newman was disowned by the encyclical.[31] Tyrrell wrote to A. L. Lilley: 'I learn that little Williams' letter (to *The Times*)

[28] Powys, *Autobiography* (London 1934) p 282.
[29] M. Ward, *The Wilfrid Wards and the Transition* (London 1934) I, p 360.
[30] F. von Hügel to A. L. Lilley, 27 January 1905 (St Andrews).
[31] See his letter to *The Times*, 2 November 1907.

frightened the Vatican more than anything—more than . . . my antics. If they only *saw* Williams! "They feared where there was no fear" and conversely. They are a pack of silly old women governed by scares and panics and dreams and gossip. We do ill to take them so seriously.'[32] No doubt it was at this time that the *Catholic Times* referred to 'the revolting Mr Williams'![33]

Williams accompanied Tyrrell when he visited Oxford in June 1909 (the month before his death) to read a paper to the university philosophical society on 'The Divine Fecundity'[34], and after Tyrrell's death he wrote to G. W. Young, who was the modernists' unofficial liaison officer in Oxford:

> I am glad to say the sense of a dead man's being really alive was never stronger in my mind than after his burial: all his friends seemed to feel the same and even a certain settled triumph. Indeed, the monstrous behaviour of the authorities (which would have made Fr Tyrrell himself laugh till he screamed) made it impossible to feel the dismal sensations of ordinary funerals. What a humour he had! . . . We could not think of him without remembering the delicate shafts of wit he would have discharged had he known that the authorities continued to demand recantation after he was speechless and even after he was dead![35]

Williams himself died in 1930.

If there were time, I should like to speak of other interesting associates of father Tyrrell who were present at his funeral, such as his close anglican friends C. E. Osborne and A. L. Lilley (both of whom I knew personally), who like him were Irish by origin. They were modernists *extra ecclesiam romanam*, so to speak. Then there were those active lay modernists Mr Robert Dell and the Hon. William Gibson (afterwards Lord Ashbourne).[36] I should also like to know more, and to be able to say more, about Dr Dessoulavy, who cycled over from Mayfield, where he was chaplain to a catholic school, to minister to Tyrrell on his deathbed. He is referred to as 'Father D.' in Miss Petre's *Life of George Tyrrell* (ii, p 429). He did not attend the funeral as she thought it inadvisable for him to do so.[37] I suppose I might also

[32] G. Tyrrell to A. L. Lilley, 28 November 1907 (St Andrews); compare A. L. David p 282.
[33] See Bedoyère, p 90.
[34] See G. W. Young to A. Loisy, 18 June 1909 (BN, naf 15662).
[35] W. J. Williams to G. W. Young, nd (St Andrews). Concerning Williams' articles in the French paper *Demain*, see A. L. David pp 206–7.
[36] See *A Variety of Catholic Modernists*, pp 167–8, 176–7.
[37] See also *ibid* p 175.

have brought Teilhard de Chardin into the picture since he certainly had Sussex connexions. He spent two years of his Jesuit novitiate at Hastings and was one of the palaeontologists who was hoaxed by the Piltdown skull! But although he was a friend of the French modernist, Edouard Le Roy, and if his theological views had been published during the modernist crisis he would certainly have been condemned, he really belongs to a later generation and is in a class by himself.

I want to devote what time remains to Henri Bremond who was the central figure at Tyrrell's funeral. The extent of his involvement with the modernists was carefully concealed during his life time and indeed after his death, which took place in 1933. It has been plainly revealed only in recent years.

Bremond was not a new-comer to Sussex when he hurried to Storrington as soon as he was apprised of Tyrrell's grave illness. He too had spent two years of his Jesuit novitiate at Hastings (1883–5) and had visited Storrington before. He was in fact thoroughly at home in England. His was a fascinating and enigmatic personality. A friend of mine who had met him told me that someone once said to him, 'There are two men in me', to which Bremond replied, 'There are twelve men in me'.[38] He and Tyrrell were kindred spirits though they differed in their origins, interests and attitude to the church.

Bremond was born and bred in a conservative, indeed royalist, catholic family at Aix-en-Provence. Two of his brothers became Jesuits, and Henri was pressed into the society by powerful influences rather than by his independent choice. Tyrrell on the other hand, as we have seen, started as an Irish protestant and it was of his own free volition that he became a Jesuit. Both however fell foul of the society about the same time and in slightly different circumstances, but fundamentally because both felt the need to be free and independent and found intolerable the discipline and ethos of an institution which seemed to represent those elements in the catholicism of the time that they had come to deplore. There was some doubt whether Bremond would continue as a priest at all, but in the event he became a secular priest attached to the diocese of Aix. He was as free from ecclesiastical responsibilities and involvements as it was possible for a priest in good standing to be.[39] He devoted his life to scholarship and

---

[38] Compare [J. Dagens and M. Nédoncelle], *Entretiens sur Henri Bremond* (Paris 1967) p 47.

[39] On 20 June 1904 Loisy wrote to von Hügel: 'J'ai vue hier M. *l'abbé* Bremond. Il est toujours dans la joie de sa liberté reconquise.' (BN, naf 15645). As a Jesuit Bremond had been '*Père* Bremond'.

literature. His magnum opus was the many volumed *A Literary History of Religious Thought in France*, and in 1923 he was elected a member of the Académie Française.

In these respects he was unlike Tyrrell who, when his break with the society of Jesus became inevitable, had so far committed himself as a church reformer and a rocker of the barque of Peter that he was unable to get his position as a priest regularised. He differed from Bremond too in that he conceived himself to the last to be called to exercise a prophetic, not to say revolutionary, role in the church.

We are concerned here only with Bremond's relation to the modernist movement. Miss Petre who had a close friendship with him, especially at the time when he was breaking with the Jesuits, declared that he 'had nothing to do with Modernism itself'.[40] While that statement is not untrue, it can be very misleading. It is true that Bremond took no interest in modernism as defined by Pius X and never publicly involved himself in the modernist movement. He was reluctant even to read the encyclical *Pascendi* which appalled him by its style as well as by its content.[41] His intellectual interests and expertise lay elsewhere.

But while he was a detached spectator of modernism, he was warmly attached to many of the principal modernists—Tyrrell, Loisy, von Hügel, Miss Petre, Blondel, Laberthonnière, etc. He was interested in, and devoted to, persons, not to ideas or causes. As he said to Laberthonnière, *Les hommes sont tout, les idées rien*.[42] He strongly objected to being regarded as a representative of modernism, and with good cause.[43] The best summing up of his relation to the modernist movement is Loisy's: 'Bremond was not intimately involved in the modernist struggle. But he enlisted in the service of the Red Cross. He brought in the dead and tended the wounded.'[44]

But Bremond himself was more of a modernist than Miss Petre's words suggested and than she probably realised. She certainly was not aware of the extent to which he was attached to Loisy, shared his opinions, and privately, or rather pseudonymously, championed him. She may indeed have known that in 1901 Bremond, when attending Loisy's lectures on the new testament, had enthused about them as

---

[40] [M. D.] Petre, *My Way of Faith* (London 1937) p 261.
[41] See [Henri] Bremond [et Maurice] Blondel, *Corr[espondance]*, ed. A. Blanchet (Paris 1971) 2, p 105; *Laberthonnière et ses amis*, p 156.
[42] See *ibid* p 204.
[43] See *Bremond-Blondel, Corr*, 2, pp 150, 180-1.
[44] See *Entretiens sur H. Bremond* p 238.

strengthening, not undermining, faith in Christ, his own in particular.[45] But she will not have known how after Loisy's excommunication Bremond maintained his close friendship with him, though to his regret he felt bound to preserve secrecy about it. In particular, she will not have known about Bremond's pseudonymous defence of Loisy's part in the modernist movement and of his integrity as a priest.[46] This was published in Miss Petre's life time, but she no more than anyone else knew that it was Bremond's work. He and Loisy and a few other people directly concerned with the publication kept the secret to themselves and it did not become known till about 1960.

Bremond's position was, as he put it to Miss Petre in September 1909, 'Whatever I may believe I have made up my mind, long ago, to remain in the church, of which resolution it seems I must bear the consequences'.[47] He would not have been able to remain as a priest in good standing if he had let it be known how much he was at one with Loisy in his religious opinions. As it was, he had anxious times, notably when his book *Sainte Chantal* was put on the index,[48] and still more when he was suspended for what he had done at Tyrrell's deathbed and funeral. After July 1909 there were several months of negotiation before Bremond was compelled to make a pretty abject act of submission in order to be allowed to exercise his ministry again. It is now known that he could have cleared himself if he had been willing to inculpate the Premonstratensian prior at Storrington, but he was too chivalrous to do that.[49]

In short, Bremond may fairly be described as a crypto-modernist. The line he took involved him not only in deceiving the church authorities but in deceiving some of his friends. For example, though to the end of his life he kept up an extensive correspondence with Maurice Blondel, he never let him know that he continued to be in very friendly communication with Loisy, which would have been quite shocking to Blondel. It is difficult to justify Bremond's duplicity with regard to Loisy's book *La Religion*, published in 1917. He told

[45] See H. Bremond to F. von Hügel, 14 November 1901 and December 1901(?) (St Andrews).

[46] Sylvain Leblanc (=H. Bremond), *Un clerc qui n'a pas trahi: Alfred Loisy d'après ses Mémoires* (Paris 1931). For the autograph of this brochure and correspondence relating to it, see BN, naf 15667. See also *A Variety of Catholic Modernists*, pp 41–3; E. Poulat, *Une oeuvre clandestine d'Henri Bremond* (Rome 1972).

[47] See Petre, *My Way of Faith*, pp 267–8.

[48] See A. Blanchet, *Histoire d'une mise à l'index* (Paris 1967).

[49] See *Bremond-Blondel, Corr*, 2, pp 152–6.

Loisy that he would need more than forty pages to thank him for it. He would class Loisy with Bossuet. *La Religion* was a *chef-d'oeuvre* in the full sense of the word. Its one great fault was that it came fifty years too soon.[50] To Blondel, on the other hand, Bremond wrote two or three weeks later: 'Have you seen Loisy's *La Religion?* Very subtle and dangerous.'[51]

Miss Petre said that she had never 'met a more fascinating personality than that of Bremond . . . His very faults were part of his attractiveness; his whimsicality, his *gaminerie*, his *esprit Gaulois*, his mocking spirit.'[52] On another occasion she justly remarked that Bremond was subtle and prudent, while Tyrrell was without regard for his personal safety.[53] For the present we must leave it at that, but more light will no doubt be thrown on Bremond's extraordinary personality when the second volume of his biography appears.[54]

Dr Owen Chadwick in his Gifford lectures[55] speaks of 'the suppression of the modernists in 1907 and after' as the rejection of 'the most promising and courageous ways by which Catholics of that generation might aim to meet the intellectual challenges of the age'. Many Roman catholics who would not have cared or dared to say that twenty years ago would do so now. To write about the modernists, whether in Sussex or elsewhere, is an attractive but saddening task: attractive, because they were a gifted and very interesting set of people; saddening, because, if their efforts towards a renaissance had not been cut short and rendered impotent by ecclesiastical authority, the history of Roman catholicism in this century might have been more spring-like than autumnal.

Rye, Sussex

[50] See *Bulletin de littérature ecclésiastique* (Toulouse 1968) pp 180–1.
[51] See *Bremond-Blondel, Corr,* 2, p 327.
[52] See Petre, *My Way of Faith,* p 261.
[53] See M. D. Petre to A. Loisy, 4 September 1936 (BN, naf 15660).
[54] Vol I by the late A. Blanchet, *Henri Bremond 1865–1904,* appeared in 1975.
[55] O. Chadwick, *The Secularization of the European Mind in the Nineteenth Century* (Cambridge 1975) p 251.

THE GERMAN PROTESTANT CHURCH
AND THE NAZI PARTY IN THE PERIOD
OF THE SEIZURE OF POWER 1932-3

by JONATHAN R. C. WRIGHT

IT was clear to the German people who lived through the Nazi
seizure of power that they were witnessing a process of profound
political and social change. It seemed natural to those who were
active Christians to ask what was the spiritual nature of this change?
Did it offer hope of Christian renaissance and renewal? In retrospect
it seems obvious that it did not and even surprising that Christians
should have entertained hopes that it might. But, at the time, this was
not at all obvious to millions of German protestants.[1] The very
volume of their publications centred on the year 1933 is eloquent testimony to the urgent need they felt to understand, explain and interpret
what was going on around them.[2] This paper is about the questions
they asked and the reasons why the answers were not clear to them.

National socialism was in the first place a political movement.
Church members reacted to it according to their political traditions.
It was nationalistic, anti-democratic and anti-semitic. So in large numbers were they: this fact is uncomfortable but unsurprising. Church
members shared the attitudes of their society, class and generation:
authoritarian political traditions, inability to come to terms with the
defeat of 1918, and from 1930 the polarising influence of the world
economic depression, a deadlocked democracy, the grip of reparations,
and a slide to civil war—a situation that has no parallel in British history since the seventeenth century except in terms of that polarisation
prevailing in Northern Ireland. For many church members in the final
phase of the republic, the Nazi party simply answered to their despair.
Even more in the first months of the Third Reich saw in Nazi victory
the welcome alternative to total collapse or a communist take-over.
In the words of the leading official of the protestant church, president

---

[1] For a discriminating account of German catholicism at this time, see Konrad Repgen,
Hitlers Machtergreifung und der deutsche Katholizismus (Saarbrücken 1967), reprinted in
Konrad Repgen, *Historische Klopfsignale für die Gegenwart* (Münster 1974) pp 128–52.

[2] See, for instance, Günther van Norden, *Kirche in der Krise. Die Stellung der evangelischen
Kirche zum nationalsozialistischen Staat im Jahre 1933* (Düsseldorf 1963) pp 200–11.

Kapler, in April 1933 'the political uprising has preserved us from either becoming totally bogged down or going Russian-Bolshevik'.[3]

Although the importance of the political background to the protestant reaction to Nazism can hardly be overemphasised, most protestants felt that questions of religious belief were also involved. Indeed as Hans Asmussen recorded even those who looked to Karl Barth for leadership were surprised at his initial reserve and sobered, when they finally moved Barth to comment, to find that his message consisted essentially in saying (I paraphrase) 'The business of the gospel as usual'.[4] What part did their faith play in the decision of that large proportion of active church members who felt drawn to the Nazi party in or before 1932 and who identified themselves with its success in 1933? Did it re-enforce their political inclinations or act as a brake upon them? The answer has many sides and variations. I shall attempt to identify some of the commoner ways in which religious and political belief inter-acted.

A simple and widespread reaction in 1933 was the feeling that God should be thanked for the change of political fortunes which I have already described. To many parish members, clergy and theologians it seemed as though the downward spiral of the German nation had been halted and reversed. Was this not an occasion for thanksgiving, as victories in the first world war had been and, conversely, as the tenth anniversary of the treaty of Versailles had been an occasion for corporate mourning? In various statements in the spring of 1933, the protestant leadership responded to this mood. A committee formed to prepare a new church constitution, consisting of president Kapler, the Lutheran bishop Marahrens of Hanover and the reformed (calvinist) church representative, pastor Hesse, issued a joint declaration in May saying: 'A mighty national movement has gripped and raised up our German people. A comprehensive reshaping of the Reich is taking place in the awakened German nation. To this turn of history we say a thankful yes. God has given it to us. To him be the glory!'[5]

[3] [Johannes] Kübel, *Erinnerungen* (Villingen nd preface 1973) p 89. Kapler was from 1925 until 1933 president of the *Oberkirchenrat* of the Old Prussian Union, the largest and most important of the protestant *Landeskirchen* and simultaneously president of the executive committee of the *Kirchenbund*, the federal organisation of the *Landeskirchen*. For the background to protestant anti-semitism see Richard Gutteridge, *Open thy mouth for the dumb! The German Evangelical church and the Jews 1879–1950* (Oxford 1976) pp 1–68.

[4] Hans Asmussen, *Begegnungen* (Wuppertal-Barmen nd (1936)) pp 6–7.

[5] [J. R. C.] Wright, *'Above Parties [: The political attitudes of the German Protestant church leadership 1918–1933]* (Oxford 1974) p 124.

When Barth criticised such statements because they were a 'political judgement', the Erlangen theologian Paul Althaus defended them on the grounds that '. . . what has happened lies in its essence beyond what could humanly be considered by those who love their nation'. Barth would have agreed to a simple recognition of the state's *Obrigkeit* in the sense of Romans 13, but in answer Althaus argued from the experience—significant in the formation of nationalist opinion in Germany in the 1920s—of Germans under foreign rule as a result of the treaty of Versailles.[6] Did the church not have the right, which individuals had, to express its special feelings for its own national state as compared with its acceptance of any state?

Is it not a gift of God, when He presents a nation with the task of creating its own state—and here are there not again great differences between a type of state in which a nation's helplessness, exhaustion, and loss of identity is expressed [the Weimar republic] and another, in which a nation comes to find itself again? Does not the transition from one to the other belong just as much to the religious experience of a nation as does illness and recovery in the life of an individual?[7]

It was not only in their view of the Third Reich as having saved Germany from imminent disaster that many protestants saw religious significance. They had also for the most part been out of sympathy with the values of democracy during the whole course of the republic—indeed the lack of support for it from the non-catholic lower middle class upwards is a major explanation for the republic's failure. Again those protestants who were active church members—some eleven million or eighteen per cent of the total population were communicants —often felt their anti-republican views and their religious beliefs were related. They could look for support to eminent professors of theology. Friedrich Gogarten, for instance, argued that the state should not (as under the Weimar republic) be the expression of a man-centred

---

[6] Of the leaders of the pro-Nazi German Christian movement (see below, p 403) Hossenfelder had fought with the volunteer *Freikorps* against the Poles in Silesia and Kuptsch had been minister of culture in Latvia. An example on the other side is Asmussen who records that the combination of Danish nationalism and pietism in his north Schleswig homeland had early made him suspicious of nationalist religion; Hans Asmussen, *Zur jüngsten Kirchengeschichte. Anmerkungen und Folgerungen* (Stuttgart 1961) pp 9–11.

[7] [Paul] Althaus, [*Die*] *Deutsche Stunde* [*der Kirche*] (Göttingen 1933, 3 ed 1934) pp 5–7. Compare [Karl] Barth, *Theologische Existenz heute!, Zwischen den Zeiten*, Beiheft 2 (Munich 1933) pp 10–12.

liberalism but on the contrary was necessary to counteract the innate evil of human nature.[8] He held that no *Ordnung* such as marriage, family or the state could be derived from the concept of individualism.[9] Emanuel Hirsch, with Paul Althaus the leading exponent of a theology of 'creation' which prized the value of the 'nation', criticised democracy because the masses had no interest in safeguarding the heritage of future generations. He argued that the state should be the highest good of the nation allowing it life, freedom and development but Germany did not have such a state because it had been forced to assume a democratic, parliamentary system which did not suit it. This he said had been Germany's fault because it had had two souls in the first world war— the spirit of August 1914 and that which believed in a peaceful humanity and which had caused the revolution of 1918. It was he affirmed Germany's duty to regain its lost position.[10]

Views such as these were common among church members. Liberals and socialists within the church felt keenly that they were minority groups isolated from the main stream of opinion.[11] Of course schools of nationalist and conservative political theology cannot be held responsible for these attitudes. They gave expression to them and reenforced them. But most often the association of religious and political beliefs was instinctive and automatic, not derived from the study of theology. Martin Rade, a liberal, gives one telling example from the election of field marshal von Hindenburg as president of the Reich in 1925. In the Berlin church he attended on polling day, the pastor announced 'Today is a day of decision for the German people. Today it must show whether it will return to its old faith' and with the church notices 'Today is election day. Every protestant Christian knows whom he must vote for'.[12] Pastor Johannes Jänicke, a member

---

[8] Friedrich Gogarten, *Politische Ethik* (Jena 1932); compare Theodor Strohm, *Theologie im Schatten politischer Romantik. Eine wissenschafts-soziologische Anfrage an die Theologie Friedrich Gogartens* (Munich 1970).

[9] Friedrich Gogarten, *Wider die Ächtung der Autorität* (Jena nd (1930)).

[10] Emanuel Hirsch, *Deutschlands Schicksal* (Göttingen 1921, 3 ed 1925) pp 83, 141–6; compare Wolfgang Tilgner, *Volksnomostheologie und Schöpfungsglaube, A[rbeiten zur] G[eschichte des] K[irchenkampfes]* 16 (Göttingen 1966).

[11] For instance Johannes Rathje, *Die Welt des freien Protestantismus. Ein Beitrag zur deutschevangelischen Geistesgeschichte dargestellt an Leben und Werk von Martin Rade* (Stuttgart 1952) pp 265–82.

[12] 'Das konfessionelle Motiv bei der Reichspräsidentenwahl' *[Die] C[hristliche] W[elt]*, 39, nos 22/23 (Gotha 1925) col 505. Compare Karl Holl, 'Konfessionalität, Konfessionalismus und demokratische Republik—Zu einigen Aspekten der Reichspräsidentenwahl von 1925' *Vierteljahrshefte für Zeitgeschichte* 17 (Stuttgart 1969) pp 254–75.

of the religious socialist group, gives another illustration. Having succeeded in gaining his church council's agreement to the inclusion of social democratic representatives, he found that the day of their induction coincided with the anniversary of the kaiser's birthday. The *Superintendent* who was to conduct the service would not forego a word of thanks to the former royal *Summus Episcopus* but the new councillors threatened to walk out. The service had to be postponed.[13] These examples illustrate a problem for the historian of protestant attitudes in 1932–3. It is not enough to listen to the theological debate, important though that is.[14] An explanation also requires attention to the grass roots; what were the instinctive reactions of ordinary church members to the phenomenon of Nazism? How was that mixture of faith and politics which characterised their attitudes to the Weimar republic affected by it?

It is clear from what we have said already that rank and file church members were predisposed to welcome the Third Reich and that this attitude was seen to be quite consistent with their religious beliefs. However, there were at least three questions which even many of those willing to endorse Nazism recognised were proper questions for Christians to address to the movement. There was first the question of race. Was race in effect the goad of national socialism as it appeared clearly to be the dominant principle of Alfred Rosenberg? Secondly, were the manners and methods of the Nazi party so radical, violent and primitive that Christians could not support it even where they approved of its goals? Thirdly, did it threaten the independence of the church? It was on these questions that the debate within the main body of protestant opinion on the religious nature of Nazism turned.

The Nazi party differed from the many other small racialist groups of the Weimar republic in one crucial respect. Hitler was determined to make it a party with mass appeal for the conquest of power. While its rivals debated the fine points of a racialist *Weltanschauung*, the Nazi party was intended to win votes.[15] As part of an electoral strategy it

[13] Johannes Jänicke, Lebenserinnerungen (unpublished manuscript, nd (1974) in A[rchive of the] E[vangelische] A[rbeitsgemeinschaft für] k[irchliche] Z[eitgeschichte, Munich]) pp 7–8.
[14] It is usefully summarised by O. G. Rees, 'The Barmen Declaration (May 1934)' *SCH* 12 (1975) pp 405–17. There is as yet no general history of protestant theology during the Weimar republic, only studies of individual figures and schools. The perspective of the *Kirchenkampf* tends to simplify the subject into a struggle between Barthianism and nationalist theology. The variety of Weimar theology is indicated by Wolfgang Huber, 'Evangelische Theologie und Kirche beim Ausbruch des Ersten Weltkriegs' in Wolfgang Huber, *Kirche und Öffentlichkeit* (Stuttgart 1973) pp 135–219.
[15] [Albrecht] Tyrell[, *Vom* ']*Trommler*[' *zum* '*Führer*'] (Munich 1975) pp 87–9.

sought to show that it posed no threat to the Christian churches and was indeed their ally against the anti-clerical left. To be convincing Hitler had to resist two types of ideological fanatics who naturally resorted to racialist circles. The first were anti-catholics typified by general Ludendorff's campaign against Jesuits and ultramontanism. The second were neo-pagan crackpots with theories of a new Germanic religion. Hitler roundly condemned both these attitudes in *Mein Kampf* because they introduced division where none was necessary and diverted the party from its primary struggle against the Jews.[16] The Nazi party programme's commitment to 'positive Christianity' was much vaguer than that of its early rival, the German socialist party, which declared itself in favour of Christianity 'on an Aryan-Germanic foundation'.[17] Another, the German racialist freedom party, in 1928 like the Nazis affirmed only a 'true Christianity' but went on to attack in the spirit of Ludendorff 'all counter-reformation attempts and all ultramontane encroachments'.[18] Hitler on the other hand enforced a policy of neutrality in matters of religious belief. When this was challenged by gauleiter Artur Dinter who wished to make his own brand of *Geistchristentum* party policy, he was expelled.[19] Rosenberg had to be content with publishing his *Myth of the 20th century* as his private work. Nothing was to get in the way of the most advantageous propaganda which combined friendship for the Christian churches with neutrality as between different denominational or religious persuasions.

This created an interesting situation for protestants trying to make a judgement about the party in 1932–3. They were faced with a racialist group which had within a very short time become the largest single party in the country. Like all racialist groups it contained theorists who were clearly anti-Christian. But they had not been allowed to make the party the instrument of their views. At the same time there were other prominent Nazis who were prepared to welcome the advice of Christians. Hitler himself had written that 'The religious teaching and institutions of a nation must always be sacrosanct to the political leader . . .'[20] In these circumstances, how were church members to decide?

---

[16] [Adolf] Hitler, [*Mein Kampf*] (Munich 1925–7) 1, pp 381–3, 2, pp 209–14.
[17] Tyrell, *Trommler* p 241.
[18] Reimer Wulff, *Die Deutschvölkische Freiheitspartei 1922–1928* (Diss Phil Marburg 1968) p 309.
[19] [Albrecht] Tyrell, *Führer befiehl* (Düsseldorf 1969) pp 149, 202–5, 210–11.
[20] Hitler, 1, p 121.

The German protestant church and Nazi party

From the religious socialists came fierce and uncompromising criticism. Paul Tillich in 1932 (then a professor at Frankfurt-am-Main) answered those who would build theological bridges to Nazism with the crushing thesis:

In so far as it [protestantism] justifies nationalism and the ideology of blood and race by a doctrine of the divine order of creation, it is surrendering its prophetic basis for the benefit of a new, open or concealed, paganism and betraying its commission to bear witness to the one God and single humanity.[21]

From the same standpoint pastor Emil Fuchs asked:

Is it not frightful evidence that the church itself no longer knows what protestant Christianity is that it takes this confession of 'positive Christianity' seriously? What is left of 'Christianity' if it can be combined with this agitation to war, to violence against others . . .? What is 'Christianity' if it no longer recognises the dignity of man in foreigners, the Jews, the weak . . .?

He predicted that if the church fell to the Nazis it would be a force for doom in the following years and then 'finished'.[22]

From the other side of the political spectrum, Ewald von Kleist-Schmenzin voiced the scepticism of a Prussian Junker. The basis of conservative thought is obedience to God, he wrote in 1932, whereas Hitler's highest law was in fact the race and its demands. He exposed the unscrupulous disregard for truth of the party's press and election literature which was only concerned with popular appeal, following the precepts of *Mein Kampf*. He was scathing about the willingness of the political right to excuse Hitler's 'slips'. If Hitler were to say that theft would be permissible in the Third Reich, they would explain that this was necessary because there were so many thieves in Germany and it was the only way they could be taught to be good Germans and Christians.[23]

Others based their criticism on concern for the sovereignty of the gospel and the independence of the church. In 1932 the new editor of the church year-book, Hermann Sasse, a convinced Lutheran, condemned the Nazi party programme because its promise of freedom to

---

[21] [Die] Kirche und das dritte Reich. [Fragen und Forderungen deutscher Theologen], ed [Leopold] Klotz, 2 vols (Gotha 1932) 1, p 126.

[22] 'Kreuz und Hakenkreuz', Vorwärts (Berlin 15 May 1932). See also Emil Fuchs, Mein Leben, 2 vols (Leipzig 1957–9).

[23] Der Nationalsozialismus eine Gefahr (Berlin 1932). This is reprinted in Bodo Scheurig, Ewald von Kleist-Schmenzin. Ein Konservativer gegen Hitler (Oldenburg/Hamburg 1968) pp 255–64.

all creeds was qualified by the clause 'in so far as they do not endanger the existence of the state or offend the ethical and moral feelings of the German race'. Sasse commented that protestant teaching was in principle a permanent insult to the moral feelings of the German race.[24] Otto Piper, who belonged to the opposed camp of theological 'liberals', but who believed equally in the gospel's independence of all political programmes, also warned that in the Third Reich the churches would only have rights 'in so far as they are willing to place themselves at the service of the government'.[25]

Most protestant comment, however, reflected the view that the evidence about the Nazi party was conflicting and its future uncertain. There was certainly room for doubt about the religious goals of the movement but the time was not ripe for a final judgement. The confusion within the party was described by Helmut Schreiner in a widely circulated pamphlet entitled *National Socialism before the question of God:*

> What opinion is not represented in National Socialism? Woden worshippers and Lutheran Christians, patriotic agnostics and believing catholics, conservatives and liberals, aristocracy and proletariat. It is working out its spiritual base. But it is still ambiguous. Nobody knows where it will go.

Schreiner's analysis of the literature and character of Nazism led him nevertheless to the conclusion that it was essentially a religion of blood in opposition to the gospel. Schreiner distinguished between Hitler whose language in *Mein Kampf* showed that he had a concept of obedience to the will of God, and Rosenberg for whom race was the measure of all things. But the whole character of the movement was ruthless, brutal and dictatorial in the service of its racialist ideology. For this reason, although the movement pointed to a divine purpose, it would be betrayed. Christians should say a clear 'No' to 'those streams within the movement which will deliver up its political construction to the demons of racial belief'.[26]

---

[24] 'Kirchliche Zeitlage', K[irchliches] J[ahrbuch], 59 (Gütersloh 1932) pp 65–6.
[25] 'Die Stunde des Protestantismus' *Vossische Zeitung*, no 517 (Berlin 28 October 1932). In 1933, Piper found kinder words for the Third Reich but continued to warn against political exploitation of the church; Otto Piper, *Kirche und Politik* (Calw 1933).
[26] [Der] Nationalsozialismus [vor der Gottesfrage. Illusion oder Evangelium?] (Berlin 1931). Schreiner was professor of practical theology at Rostock. Similar criticisms were made by Walter Künneth, leader of the Inner Mission's Central Institute for Apologetics in Berlin, [Walter] Künneth, [Pfarrer] Wilm, [Lehrer] Schemm [M. d. R.], *Was haben wir als evangelische Christen zum Rufe des Nationalsozialismus zu sagen?* (Dresden 1931) pp 6–17, and professor Hermann Strathmann of Erlangen, *Nationalsozialistische Weltanschauung?* (Nuremberg 1931).

Others, however, drew different conclusions from what they saw as the 'complexio oppositorum'[27] in national socialism. Was it not right for Christians to recognise what was good in the movement and work to improve it? Did not its very success without the support of the church suggest that the church had not paid enough attention to the values of nationality and race? Should the church therefore not be self-critical rather than critical? And the occupational headache of academics, was it right for them to sneer from their armchairs? Should they not use their intelligence for the good of the movement?[28] The fear was often expressed that the church might repeat its experience with socialism in the nineteenth century, when it had turned its back on the ideology and consequently, it was held, lost the working class from its membership.[29]

Considerations such as these could lead even those who felt the same about the primacy of the gospel as Schreiner to adopt a sympathetic stance. Johannes Hempel for instance argued that the development of the Nazi party to a mass party had altered the religious composition of its membership. Wide circles within it now attached great importance to being committed Christians. This 'will to Christianity' created an obligation for the church to respond. Secondly, both in its success in converting the propertied and upper classes to social reform and in the looseness of its religious concepts, national socialism showed up the failures of the church and was a judgement on it. This was particularly true of the church's failure to promote a Christian concept of nation and race. As a result the church might be forced into conflict with the 'total' state of national socialism which would try to impose its own concepts, for instance in education. The church would have to defend the principle of freedom of conscience even on behalf of those with

[27] The phrase comes from the apologia of the unrepentant German Christian Walter Birnbaum, *Zeuge meiner Zeit. Aussagen zu 1912 bis 1972* (Göttingen 1973) p 124.

[28] See, for instance, the views expressed by the right-wing political theorist Wilhelm Stapel, *Sechs Kapitel über Christentum und Nationalsozialismus* (Hamburg 1931) p 6. There is an excellent study of Stapel by Heinrich Keßler, *Wilhelm Stapel als politischer Publizist. Ein Beitrag zur Geschichte des konservativen Nationalismus zwischen den beiden Weltkriegen* (Nuremberg 1967).

[29] See, for instance, Karl Eger (former professor of practical theology at Halle) in *Kirche und das dritte Reich*, ed Klotz, 1, p 22. For the conflict between the church leadership and the Christian-Social movement among the clergy in the eighteen nineties see Klaus Erich Pollmann, *Landesherrliches Kirchenregiment und soziale Frage. Der evangelische Oberkirchenrat der altpreußischen Landeskirche und die sozialpolitische Bewegung der Geistlichen nach 1890. Veröffentlichungen der Historischen Kommission zu Berlin*, 44 (Berlin 1973).

whom it disagreed. Otherwise it would appear to be directed by the state, instead of being bound to God's word and will. However, Hempel saw this judgement on the church also as its opportunity. By performing its one duty, to preach the gospel, the church could make a decisive contribution to the movement, giving its socialism a religious base and purifying its nationalism by placing it under the will of God. Given the size and importance of the national-socialist movement the whole fate of Germany depended on the church being successful in this task.[30]

Those protestants who, like Hempel, thought that they should try to influence national socialism not condemn it could look for support from within the party to Hans Schemm, a protestant schoolteacher from Bayreuth, member of the reichstag, gauleiter of Franconia and leader of the national socialist teachers' union. In a speech to a conference of the Inner Mission, published with other contributions under the title *What have we as Protestant Christians to say to the call of National Socialism?* he told how the national socialists in Bayreuth had organised a demonstration against the leader of the social democrats whom he described as 'anti-Christian', Dr Kurt Löwenstein. Ten thousand from the population of thirty-six thousand had attended singing *Ein feste Burg ist unser Gott*. Christianity, he claimed was at the centre of their movement and the principles of blood and race were both seen as part of God's will. He adopted the slogan 'Our politics are Germany and our religion Christ'. He admitted that the movement had been guilty of mistakes and stupidity. They were no theologians. But he welcomed criticism from the church and said he wished the movement had had the benefit of it earlier.[31]

This appeal, which Schreiner noted as a 'gratifying exception' to the

---

[30] *Kirche und das dritte Reich*, ed Klotz, 1, pp 44–52. Hempel was professor for old testament studies at Göttingen. Similar arguments were advanced by Althaus, *Deutsche Stunde* and in the Württemberg *Landeskirche* by Dr Kurt Hutten, *Nationalsozialismus und Christentum* (Stuttgart 1932). (I should like to thank Richard Gutteridge for the loan of this and other pamphlets and for his advice on aspects of this paper.)

[31] Künneth, Wilm, Schemm, *Was haben wir als evangelische Christen zum Rufe des Nationalsozialismus zu sagen?*, pp 18–24. The effectiveness of this speech is admitted by the later Confessing Church leader in Saxony, Hugo Hahn, in his memoirs 'In my heart I was still inclined to Schemm's point of view even if a lot of things put me off.' [*Kämpfer wider Willen. Erinnerungen des Landesbischofs von Sachsen D. Hugo] Hahn [aus dem Kirchenkampf 1933–1945]*, ed [Georg] Prater (Metzingen 1969) p 18. For Schemm's style of campaigning see Geoffrey Pridham, *Hitler's rise to power. The Nazi movement in Bavaria 1923–33* (London 1973) pp 106–8, 150.

dictatorial Führer principle,[32] found its most far-reaching response from that small group of pastors who had joined the Nazi party.[33] One of the first to offer his services was Friedrich Wieneke, pastor at the cathedral in Soldin (Neumark) and from 1929 a Nazi municipal councillor. He wrote articles both in the protestant and Nazi press arguing, along the same lines as Schemm, that 'Christianity and National Socialism belong together'.[34] In 1931 he started a national socialist pastors' union which worked with Schemm's teachers' union, although it was a private association not an official party organisation. From this group sprang in 1932 the *Glaubensbewegung Deutschen Christen* (Faith movement of German Christians) a specifically pro-Nazi protestant church party to contest the parish elections in the *Landeskirche* of the Old Prussian Union in November 1932.[35]

The foundation of the German Christians introduced a new dimension into the protestant debate about the nature of Nazism. Were they the instruments of the Nazi party to subvert the independence of the church and make it a religious prop of the Third Reich? Or, were they the church's answer to the challenge of the hour, the instrument for preaching the gospel to the Nazi masses? Might they not provide the link between the political revolution and a religious revival?

A correspondence which has only recently come to light between Wilhelm Kube, gauleiter of the Ostmark, and Gregor Strasser, the head of the party's organisation, in 1931 enables us to trace the origins of the German Christians in more detail than previously.[36] The group of Nazi

---

[32] Schreiner, *Nationalsozialismus* p 56.

[33] It is not yet possible to say how many pastors had become party members before 1933. There are over ten million files of party members in the Berlin document centre arranged alphabetically—perhaps a social science team with a computer might be interested in classifying them? Contemporary party statistics do not record clergy as a separate category with one exception which gives a figure of 120 up to December 1930; Tyrell, *Führer befiehl* pp 379–80. It may safely be assumed that the great majority of these were protestant but it represents only a tiny minority of the 15,000 protestant clergy (Paul Troschke, 'Kirchliche Statistik.' *KJ* 58 (1931) p 184). No doubt many more joined in 1931 and 1932 but there is no evidence of a mass movement. It should be remembered that the party was itself chary of an official recruiting drive among clergy for fear of compromising its religious neutrality. For further details, see [Jonathan R. C.] Wright, '*Über den Parteien*'. [*Die politische Haltung der evangelischen Kirchenführer 1918–1933,*] AGK series B, 2 (1977) p 140.

[34] See, for instance, 'Der Geist des Christentums in der nationalsozialistischen Bewegung' *Der Märkische Adler* (the party newspaper for the Gau Ostmark) (Berlin 15 August 1930). For further details see Wright, '*Above Parties*' pp 85–6.

[35] [Kurt] Meier, *Die Deutschen Christen* (Göttingen 1964) pp 10–13.

[36] Wright, '*Über den Parteien*' pp 148–51.

clergymen started by Wieneke wanted to be allowed to organise a pro-Nazi church party to contest the parish elections. Kube who was himself a parish councillor and had been angered by the policy of cautious accommodation with the Weimar republic adopted by the Prussian church leadership, supported them. He wrote to Strasser recommending that their wish 'by themselves without any reference to the party to conquer the power of the church' should be granted.[37] Kube and Strasser were keenly aware of the dangers of becoming involved in church politics and thereby compromising the party's principle of non-intervention. Indeed Kube was accused at one stage by a protestant extreme racialist group, the *Bund für deutsche Kirche* (the association for a German church) of having committed the party to the rival and more moderate Christian-German movement, an accusation he hotly denied.[38] The German Christians (who saw themselves as less pagan than the association for a German church and more radical than the Christian Germans) were as far as the Nazi party was concerned officially a spontaneous movement of church members who were simply allowed by the party to represent Nazi views within the church.[39] Unofficially they were given the assistance of the party organisations in mobilizing the vote of Nazi party members for the church elections.[40]

It is clear that the Nazi leaders concerned did regard the German Christians as an instrument for the *Gleichschaltung* of the protestant church while refusing openly to commit the party to them. This is no reason however to doubt the sincerity of the German Christians in thinking that they would be able thereby to win influence within the party for the church. The fact that Kube and Strasser were prepared to give them encouragement was seen as evidence that some Nazi leaders at least accepted that the church had a part to play in the Third Reich. Exactly where Hitler stood was uncertain. When pastor Hossenfelder, the newly appointed Reich leader of the German Christians in June 1932 asked Strasser about this, Strasser said, 'Where Hitler is lurking at present I can't tell you, but I can tell you that in my opinion our party too requires metaphysics.'[41] Contact had been

[37] Kube to Strasser, 9 December 1931, Bundesarchiv [Koblenz] NS 22, vol 348.
[38] Kube to Strasser, 27 October 1931, *ibid* vol 376.
[39] Strasser to Kube, 17 December 1931, *ibid* NS 26 vol 1240.
[40] Two copies of official gau instructions for the church elections are known, for Silesia published in *CW* 46, no 7 (1932) cols 331–3 (Wright, *'Above Parties'* pp 93–4) and for the Ostmark in Bundesarchiv Sammlung Schumacher vol 205.
[41] Hossenfelder to [Professor] Scholder and [Dr] Nicolaisen July 1970; AEAkZ.

established with Hitler, however, through the military chaplain in Königsberg, Ludwig Müller, who became the East Prussian leader of the German Christians in 1932. He had met Hitler probably in 1929 and in 1931–2 assisted the party by acting as a mediator between the military authorities and the provincial S.A.[42] It seems very probable that at this time Müller persuaded Hitler of the advantages of a pro-Nazi Reich protestant church. Later, Hitler acknowledged, 'Müller showed himself loyal in the whole period before the change of fortunes and already at that time he always advocated the idea of a Reichskirche'.[43] Müller told Hossenfelder that Hitler had said he longed to have a religious home again.[44] Wieneke recorded that Hitler objected to the title 'Protestant Nationalsocialists' which had first been suggested for the new church party because 'politics as such cannot create religion but only be made fruitful by religion'.[45] Presumably Hitler felt that the title would have endangered the principle of religious neutrality. As a result the name 'German Christians' was adopted and this apparently satisfied Hitler.

The hopes nurtured by these contacts seemed to be fulfilled when as Reich chancellor in 1933 Hitler not only declared that the government considered the Christian churches 'most important factors for the preservation of our nationality' and promised to respect their rights, but also appointed Müller his personal representative for protestant affairs with special responsibility for the preparation of a Reich church, and encouraged Müller and the German Christians in their efforts to take control of the new church organisation.[46] There is no reason to suppose that Hitler had any other motive than political expediency for this policy. To consolidate his power in 1933 he wanted the support of both Christian churches. The concordat of July 1933 was intended to silence catholic opposition. Where the protestant church was concerned he seems to have believed, under the influence of Müller, that what he later called 'a church which identifies itself with the state, as in England', could be created.[47] He made no secret of the political advantage this would bring. For instance, he told president Kapler in April

[42] Wright, '*Über den Parteien*' pp 152–3.
[43] [Carsten] Nicolaisen, *Dokumente [zur Kirchenpolitik des Dritten Reiches]*, 2, [*1934–35*] (Munich 1975) p 81.
[44] Interview [of the author with Hossenfelder], 16 January 1968.
[45] *Kirche und das dritte Reich*, ed Klotz, 2, p 129.
[46] Nicolaisen, *Dokumente*, 1 [*Das Jahr 1933*] pp 42–3; Wright, '*Above Parties*' pp 117–42.
[47] H. R. Trevor-Roper, *Hitler's Table Talk 1941–1944* (2 ed London 1973) p 143.

1933 that he had 'as a statesman the greatest interest in a united protestant bloc if only as a counterweight to catholicism'.[48]

Nevertheless the development of party policy towards the protestant church in 1932–3 from neutrality to positive interest was naturally seen by the German Christians as evidence that it was moving towards the church and away from the anti-clerical racialism of Alfred Rosenberg and his followers. Wieneke claimed that the fact that the party recommended the German Christian programme to protestant party members showed that 'the many, often so objectionable and spiteful misrepresentations (Woden worship, idolisation of race, Romishness etc.) are without foundation'.[49] Rosenberg was fully aware of the competition from the German Christians. In August 1933 he argued in the Völkischer Beobachter that the Nazi party could not lend its political support to either the German Christians or their opponents.[50] In November 1933 the Berlin Gau leader of the German Christians, Dr Reinhold Krause, expressed views borrowed from The Myth of the 20th Century calling for amongst other things 'liberation from the Old Testament with its Jewish wage morality, from the stories of cattle merchants and souteneurs'. Under pressure from Martin Niemöller's pastors' emergency league Müller (by this time Reich bishop) felt forced to dissociate himself from the German Christians and condemn Krause. Rosenberg at once declared his intention of leaving the protestant church to which he still nominally belonged. In his letter of explanation he sided with Krause whose views he said 'are represented today to the greatest extent in the nation in the conviction that they express the further development of the German Reformation'. Many had hoped that renewal would come from within the church. This hope had been destroyed by Müller's declaration of heresy against the new movement. Rosenberg wrote tartly to Müller that his resignation from the church would no doubt be welcome to Müller, 'since for a long time German Christian preachers have considered it necessary to attack me in public in different towns'.[51]

[48] Kübel, Erinnerungen p 90. For Nazi religious policy in this period see the recent study by Leonore Siegele-Wenschkewitz, Nationalsozialismus und Kirchen. Religionspolitik von Partei und Staat bis 1935, Tübinger Schriften zur Sozial- und Zeitgeschichte, 5 (Düsseldorf 1974) pp 65–123.
[49] Kirche und das dritte Reich, ed Klotz, 2 p 129.
[50] Nicolaisen, Dokumente, 1 pp 124–5; Robert Cecil, The myth of the master race. Alfred Rosenberg and Nazi ideology (London 1972) pp 112–13.
[51] Nicolaisen, Dokumente, 1 pp 170–2. For a German Christian refutation of Rosenberg see Walter Grundmann, Gott und Nation. Ein evangelisches Wort zum Wollen des Nationalsozialismus und zu Rosenbergs Sinndeutung (Berlin, nd (1933)).

Hossenfelder suspected that Krause had been put up to his speech by Rosenberg deliberately to cause a split in the German Christians, which it did.[52] There is no confirmation for this, however, in Rosenberg's diary where the incident is simply referred to together with disparaging comments about Müller.[53]

The German Christians saw themselves as fighting on two fronts, for the party within the church and for the church within the party. They were confirmed in this view when they were attacked both by the embryonic Confessing Church and by Rosenberg. The fact that their position was disputed in both camps gave them a streak of independence and idealism which would not have been possible had they been an official party organisation. Despite the inhumanity of their programme and despite their obvious personal ambition to take over the church leadership it is important to recognise that their movement also had some of the attributes of a crusade, albeit a piratical one. There was some truth in the retrospective and no doubt romanticised judgement of Hossenfelder that 'Coming almost all from the German *Wandervogel* [the pre-1914 youth movement], almost all having been soldiers at the front' they were 'wanderers between two worlds, in their knapsack was the Greek new testament, Faust and perhaps also Horace . . . It did not suit the church reactionaries that we spoke a core German, it did not suit the National Socialist party that we preached an eastern gospel'.[54]

The German Christians exploited their dual role to overcome the resistance of sceptical parishioners. Their goal was that the 'newly awoken nation' should find 'a living relationship with the church of its fathers' and that the church should 'reach the nation truly inwardly with its witness and its life'.[55] In the words of Hitler to president Kapler, 'Both churches, the protestant and the catholic, stood in danger of losing contact with the nation and spoke a language which the nation did not understand; the German Christians wanted to re-establish contact with the nation'.[56] To achieve this aim they adopted a programme of anti-democratic and racialist demands combined with

[52] Interview 16 January 1968.

[53] Hans-Günther Seraphim, *Das politische Tagebuch Alfred Rosenbergs 1934–35 und 1939–40* (Munich 1964) p 43.

[54] Hossenfelder to Scholder and Nicolaisen July 1970; AEAkZ.

[55] Friedrich Peter, 'Kirche und Volk', *Volk und Kirche, Die amtlichen Berichte der ersten Reichstagung 1933 der Glaubensbewegung "Deutschen Christen"*, ed Joachim Hossenfelder (Berlin 1933) p 6.

[56] Kübel, *Erinnerungen* p 90.

'a racially innate belief in Christ, appropriate to the German spirit of Luther and a heroic piety'. Race, people and nation were declared to be 'orders of life given and entrusted by God, the care for the preservation of which is for us God's law'. What this might mean in practice was indicated by references to the dangers of church social work since the nation should be protected from 'the incapable and the inferior' and the condemnation of the mission to the Jews 'the entrance gate of foreign blood into our national body'.[57]

In pamphlets and sermons, the German Christians proclaimed the religious significance of the experience of national revival. Germany's defeat, humiliation and recovery enabled them to understand once again what the apostle meant by 'the fulness of time' declared Hossenfelder in the Easter of 1933.[58] The story of the passion contained the secret of Germany's revolution. They had endured unexampled suffering. After four years of superhuman struggle there had come the fearful collapse. There were those who doubted that recovery would be possible. The best saw that it was not a question of politics, economics or even bare survival but of the soul of the German nation, of belief and unbelief, Christ and anti-Christ. If this had not been so, where would the freedom fighters have found hope? Their belief that Christ and his gospel would win led them to victory over godlessness and bolshevism.[59] A less crude parallel was drawn by Franz Tügel (the German Christian leader in Hamburg and bishop there from 1939–45) between the experience of the nation finding itself again and the return of the prodigal son. 'A nation went out to revel in freedom ... it broke away from the ultimates which bind nations and men, God Himself and his holy orders, nation and fatherland, marriage and child, loyalty and faith, discipline and morality . . . But this life-sin dragged it into the depths of a colossal crisis . . . In the depths came the awakening . . . We want to go home to nation and fatherland!'. This parable had the advantage that those members of the congregation who refused to recognise the religious revival could be cast in the role of the elder

---

[57] [Kurt Dietrich] Schmidt, [Die] Bekenntnisse [und grundsätzlichen Außerungen zur Kirchenfrage des Jahres] 1933 (2 ed Göttingen 1937) pp 135–6.

[58] 'Deutschland und der Leidensweg des Heilandes', Evangelische Reden im Dritten Reich, ed Martin Thom (Berlin 1933) pp 5–9.

[59] The success of the communist free-thinker movement in urban areas was a central concern of several pastors who worked among the unemployed and joined the German Christians; Karl Themel, Lenin anti Christus. Eine Einführung in die Lehre und Methode der Gottlosen für jedermann (Berlin 1931), Walter Birnbaum, Wider die Front des Gottlosentums. Abwehr oder Verkündigung? (Potsdam 1931).

brother. ' "We are the church people!" boast many who have always held to the church, as the great nation now knocks once again at the old doors. And they stamp the ground with defiant feet and hanker after supposed injustices . . . He who has found his way home is both joyful and silent. He who knows nothing of returning home is noisy and strives to be a killjoy'.[60]

One of the clearest statements on behalf of the German Christians was given by Emanuel Hirsch, the most distinguished theologian to join their ranks.[61] In reply to Karl Barth, Hirsch argued that in addition to being the community of servants of the gospel, the church had a duty 'for the sake of the effective preaching of the gospel to carry out a preparatory service of ethical and religious training and education'. This latter represented its duty as a national church [*Volkskirche*]. Jesus was the lord of the church in both activities. He spoke not only through the bible but also through 'the leading of our lives, which we experience, if we try to find our way in faith through the reality which surrounds us'. The form the service of the church as a *Volkskirche* took changed with history. Barth (a Swiss) could not feel as deeply about the national revival as Germans. 'We tremble with the responsibility that our nation should not ruin this its hour . . . We all thought that we would have to bear . . . that the great mass of our nation would perish in godlessness and immorality, separated from Christian witness as by a wall. Now that we have been given new hope, shall our hearts not burn that the protestant church says yes to this hour . . .?' Barth represented a narcissistic church without love which had forgotten that Christ left the pious and God-fearing and went out among publicans and whores. The German Christians recognised, however, that their first service was only a preparatory one. 'One and decisive for us too is this, that the pure, simple gospel will be preached in our church'. But it would not be possible to clarify the national revival with the doctrine of justification by faith if 'we are unable to show in the preparatory service of the church a fusion of the protestant and National Socialist . . . way of life'.

What this involved was indicated by Hirsch's uncritical acceptance of racialist theory. All human achievement was dependent on its natural basis, he argued. 'If the blood is ruined, the spirit runs aground . . .' Had things been allowed to go on as they were 'bearers of good, old pure

[60] 'Die grosse Heimkehr', *Mit Gott wollen wir Taten tun. Predigten und Ansprachen 'Deutscher Christen'*, ed Wilhelm Rehm (Heilbronn 1934) pp 65–8.
[61] Emanuel Hirsch, *Das kirchliche Wollen der Deutschen Christen* (2 ed Berlin 1933) pp 5–17.

German blood' in top positions would have become a minority. The church which could have drawn attention to the danger from the doctrine of creation had done nothing. The change had come about without its help. Although the concern shown by the nation for the fate of innocent individuals did it credit, the church should look beyond this to what was 'healthy, according to God's will in the change'. It should support the state and introduce similar measures into its own organisation or it might be swamped by half-Germans excluded from state service. No-one was suggesting that there could not be communion with Jewish Christians. Should the church not recognise that 'in a German protestant church, German-ness and Christianity must find each other in a very inward way' then the sects for a new German religion would capture national socialism. The German Christians were nowhere more hated than by these sects, which knew that Barthian theology played into their hands but that a national church would easily get the better of them. Elsewhere, Hirsch asked those who spoke of the freedom of the gospel whether they meant freedom to disapprove of the national revolution. If so, they should not appeal to the gospel. If, however, they meant freedom to preach obedience to the gospel to national socialists then they should know this freedom was not in danger.[62]

How was this mixture of nationalist feeling, racialist theory and missionary enthusiasm received within the church? Given that most church members were, as we have seen, natural supporters of the Third Reich it would not have been surprising if the German Christians had enjoyed a landslide. Indeed, on one interpretation of the evidence this is what happened. In the parish elections of the Old Prussian Union in November 1932, they won on average about a third of the seats. In the elections in all *Landeskirchen* in July 1933, they won on average about seventy per cent. The explanation of these results, however, is fraught with difficulty and deserves a separate study.[63] The success of the Nazi party organisation either in directly

---

[62] 'Freiheit der Kirche, Reinheit des Evangeliums', *ibid* p 28. In explaining Hirsch's extreme racialism, it may be relevant to note that Hirsch was a Jewish name. Certainly this was suggested to me as an explanation by a senior member of the Hanover *Landeskirche* who had been a student of Hirsch's at Göttingen.

[63] For the 1932 elections see Wright, '*Above Parties*' pp 91–8. For the 1933 elections in different parts of the Reich see [Gerhard] Schäfer, *Dokumentation [zum Kirchenkampf. Die Evangelische Landeskirche in Württemberg und der Nationalsozialismus]*, 2, [*Um eine deutsche Reichskirche 1933*] (Stuttgart 1972) pp 294–345, Eberhard Klügel, *Die lutherische Landeskirche Hannovers und ihr Bischof 1933–1945* (Berlin/Hamburg 1964) pp 60–6, Helmut Baier, *Die Deutschen Christen Bayerns im Rahmen des bayerischen Kirchenkampfes*

delivering a vote of party members who were not regular church-goers, or in threatening to do so and thereby persuading the other church parties to agree to their demands in advance so that a single list containing a German Christian majority was returned without an election, has to be considered. Conversely, the ability of church authorities to have parish councillors or synod delegates whom they could trust included on the German Christian quota, where the movement did not have enough candidates of its own, has also to be allowed for. Thirdly, the existence of important groups of 'moderate' German Christians who were prepared to support the established church leadership against 'radical' German Christians meant that the German Christian victory was in some *Landeskirchen* more apparent than real. In November 1933, in the crisis caused by Krause's speech, many of the leading 'moderates' like professor Fezer of Tübingen left the German Christians; some joined Martin Niemöller's pastors' emergency league. Their resignation was followed by numerous desertions, sometimes of whole provincial groups.[64] Overlapping with the moderates was probably a further group of parishioners who voted German Christian in July 1933 in order to express their loyalty to the Third Reich—especially after Hitler had broadcast in their favour—without necessarily approving either their racialism or their desire to wrest control of the church organisation from the established leadership. There was also throughout the Third Reich a large group of church members who remained uncommitted to either the German Christians or the Confessing Church.

Nevertheless, most observers agree that from whatever motive the German Christians did enjoy substantial support within the church in the summer of 1933. Even after the movement had broken up the surviving groups claimed eight hundred and fifty thousand members.[65] There are no membership figures for 1933 but the success of the German Christians in appealing to church members of very different

(Nuremberg 1968) pp 51–6; also Jürgen Schmidt, *Martin Niemöller im Kirchenkampf, Hamburger Beiträge zur Zeitgeschichte,* 8 (Hamburg 1971) pp 103–8 and for vivid glimpses at grass roots level Reinhold von Thadden, *Auf verlorenem Posten? Ein Laie erlebt den evangelischen Kirchenkampf in Hitlerdeutschland* (Tübingen 1948) pp 73–4 (about Pomerania), *Hahn,* ed Prater pp 25–7, [Franz] Tügel, *Mein Weg [1888–1946. Erinnerungen eines Hamburger Bischofs],* ed Carsten Nicolaisen (Hamburg 1972) pp 245–6. For Nazi party and state intervention during the elections see Nicolaisen, *Dokumente,* I pp 110–22.
[64] Schäfer, *Dokumentation* 2 pp 850–78, Meier, *Die Deutschen Christen* pp 44–50.
[65] Meier, *ibid* p xii.

backgrounds is widely attested. Barth commented with characteristic force on the 'staggering lack of resistance' to the German Christians among clergy, laymen, church leaders, theology professors and students (including some of his own), educated and uneducated, old and young, liberals and orthodox, pietists, Lutherans and Calvinists who 'have succumbed in droves to the rush of this movement, succumbed as one succumbs to a genuine, proper psychosis'.[66]

At the same time the German Christians also encountered from the beginning a degree of resistance within the church which has been largely overlooked by *Kirchenkampf* historians in the Barthian tradition.[67] Tügel was kinder about his sceptical parishioners in his memoirs (composed during the second world war) than he had been in his sermon on the prodigal son in 1933, reflecting his own changed position in the interim. He wrote that he had suffered in 1932 very much from their lack of understanding of his good intentions. He believed that he had made it clear that his position 'to the crucified and resurrected Lord' had not changed. Yet many left his congregation, 'Not only individual, delicate souls, for whom any breath from the street was too sharp a draught, but whole families, whom I had looked after for years and who must really have known me . . .'. The numbers at church services held up but that was because of his political activities, 'It could not conceal from me that many of the most genuine people withdrew'.[68]

Why did such people withdraw? In the words of Hugo Hahn, leader of the Confessing Church in Saxony, 'As much as I sympathised with National Socialism, I felt that the bringing of politics into the sphere of the church was wrong'.[69] This was the characteristic expression of the resistance to the German Christians at all levels within the church in 1932-33. A resolute early example was provided by a Dr Schlickum, Nazi party member in Gau Düsseldorf, who in September 1932 rebelled against the underhand way the party was bringing politics into the church; he denounced Hossenfelder in an open letter and refused a summons to the local Gau leadership, saying that he did not accept party discipline in matters of faith. He published a critique of the German Christian programme saying that race and blood had

---

[66] Barth, *Theologische Existenz heute!* p 26.
[67] For instance, Ernst Wolf, *Barmen. Kirche zwischen Versuchung und Gnade* (2 ed Munich 1970) pp 14–61.
[68] Tügel, *Mein Weg* p 228.
[69] *Hahn*, ed Prater p 17.

nothing to do with the biblical Christ.[70] The old church parties in 1932 formed a united list under the title 'Gospel and Nation' against the German Christians demanding freedom of the church from interference by the state or political parties, although they recorded in the same breath their belief in 'the German type in nationality, society, law and state' and echoed the standard complaints against the 'immorality' of Jewish newspapers, theatre, cinema and literature which they termed 'cultural bolshevism'.[71] The church leadership in the Old Prussian Union added its warning in the form of instructions that the elections were non-political and that only candidates who could be guaranteed to promote the spiritual, moral and social welfare of the parish on the basis of the gospel should be elected.[72]

It is easy to find fault with the anti-German Christian argument that the church must be kept free of politics. As the Gospel and Nation programme made clear and as the German Christians pointed out, politics were already in the church: the church leadership was simply conservative or national liberal not national socialist. But to accept this criticism is to miss the point. What the early opposition to the German Christians was reacting against was the introduction of a new style of 'total' politics into the church (the concept totalitarian was not yet current in Germany). It was not enough for the German Christians to be represented; 'to bring our spirit to bear not just by the way but with National Socialist force and activity in the protestant church as well goes without saying' wrote pfarrer Eckert in his instructions to the Gau Ostmark for the elections of November 1932.[73] Compulsory voting by party members whether or not they were church-goers, the declaration of obedience to the leadership demanded of German Christian candidates, the ruthless use of majorities to silence the opposition, and in 1933–4 the willingness to attempt coercion by the state: these were the signs of the new politics to which the opposition objected. The demagogic style of campaigning with slogans like 'conquer your church', heckling of opponents as 'unpatriotic', public attacks on individual church leaders made possible by breaches of confidence by their own clergy—methods which the church had pre-

[70] Schlickum to Hossenfelder 5 September 1932, correspondence between Schlickum and Gau Düsseldorf 13–23 September and a copy of his brochure for the elections 28 September; A[rchiv der] E[vangelischen] K[irche der] U[nion West Berlin,] Gen[eralia] III, 51/I Beiheft [Propaganda für die kirchlichen Gemeindewahlen].
[71] *Die Reformation*, no 17 (Berlin 4 September 1932).
[72] Wright, '*Above Parties*' p 95.
[73] Eckert circular 1 September 1931; Bundesarchiv, Sammlung Schumacher, vol 205.

viously looked on as 'bolshevik'—were further examples.[74] Pointing at the heart of the movement, some critics also raised the question of whether an intolerant racialism had not superseded the gospel. Agnes von Zahn-Harnack (the daughter of Adolf von Harnack) condemned the 'shocking' anti-semitism of the German Christian propaganda chief, pfarrer Kessel, after attending one of his meetings.[75] The district synod of Elberfeld issued a public declaration against falsification of the gospel and declared 'There is no Germanic Christ'.[76] Pastor Hossenfelder's own *Generalsuperintendent* (the equivalent of a bishop), Emil Karow, recorded after a conversation with him in July 1932

... the admission of the uniqueness of the gospel is not easy for him. Even more difficult the perception of the universality of Christianity. Racial differences set limits to the thinking in this respect.—Here slogans play an important part in the thinking of these theologians. The theological ideas are also coloured by political intentions.[77]

The German Christians and the Nazi party understood their vulnerability to the charge that they were using the church as a political instrument. The first instructions for the Gau Silesia in February 1932 explained that they should reply (in the way Strasser had suggested) that they were not acting as a party but as protestants 'who have heard a call from God in our national movement'.[78] Hitler, despite his support for Müller, tried to maintain the fiction that he did not interfere in church affairs.[79] Müller, likewise, promised that he would not 'deliver the church up to the state' if he were elected Reich bishop.[80] After it had appointed August Jäger state commissioner for the protestant church in June 1933, the Prussian *Kultusministerium* felt it necessary to explain that it was only concerned with church organisa-

[74] It is interesting to see that Barth shared the view that their violent political method were the most distinctive feature of the German Christians even if this was because he felt their theological errors were so common; *Theologische Existenz heute!* pp 25–6.
[75] 'Von den deutschen Christen', *Vossische Zeitung* (Berlin 25 October 1932); AEKU Gen III, 51/I Beiheft.
[76] Schmidt, *Bekenntnisse 1933* p 17.
[77] Karow to Kapler 16 July 1932 enclosing his report of 14 July; AEKU Präsidialia II 46/IV Sekretakten.
[78] See above p 404, n 40.
[79] Nicolaisen, *Dokumente*, 1 pp 91, 95.
[80] Reported by bishop Hans Meiser of Bavaria to a meeting of leaders of the Lutheran *Landeskirchen* 26 May 1933; Landeskirchliches Archiv Nuremberg, Repositorium 101 (Personen), No XXXVI Nachlaß Landesbischof Meiser, vol 96 Verfassung der Reichskirche.

tion and its relationship to the state, which did not affect the individuality of the church or of its belief or the creed, '. . . a so-called state church is totally rejected'.[81]

The German Christian denials were never very convincing and during 1933 were increasingly belied by their willingness to resort to force to cow the opposition. Anticipating the dangers, president Kapler embarked in April 1933 on a policy of strengthening the central church organisation to make it better able to protect church interests in a centralised Reich and to take the wind out of the sails of the German Christians. To preserve the 'individuality of the church' he tried to secure the election of Friedrich von Bodelschwingh (the director of the Inner Mission) not Müller as the new Reich bishop. In May 1933 Kapler predicted that the election of Müller would result in a schism with the withdrawal of good church members to the free churches.[82] Kapler was supported by a new movement, the Young Reformers, organised in opposition to the German Christians to support church reform 'solely and exclusively from the intrinsic character of the church'. This included 'opposition in principle to the exclusion of non-Aryans from the church'.[83] The policy failed. It was undermined by the opposition of a minority of church leaders who believed that Kapler's fears of the German Christians were exaggerated (although experience was soon to make them wiser) and by the German Christian victory in the elections of July 1933—when the Young Reformers only secured a majority in one province, Westphalia. The potential of the opposition, however, is indicated by the rapid growth of Martin Niemöller's pastors' emergency league from its foundation in September 1933 to 3,000 members in November and to over 7,000 at its highest point in January 1934.[84]

Karl Barth criticised the church leadership and the Young Reformers for being opportunistic. What pressing requirement of the church made

---

[81] 'Warum der Kirchenkommissar eingesetzt wurde. Die Gründe des Kultusministeriums' *Tägliche Rundschau* (Berlin 28 June 1933).

[82] Note of a conversation with professor Fezer on 24 May in a memorandum by Kapler 25 May; Archiv der Evangelischen Kirche in Deutschland, West Berlin, A 4 Deutsche Evangelische Kirche 1933, vol 24 der Reichsbischof. For Kapler's policy see Wright, '*Above Parties*' pp 117–37.

[83] Schmidt, *Bekenntnisse 1933* p 145; Peter Neumann, *Die Jungreformatorische Bewegung*, AGK 25 (Göttingen 1971).

[84] The total number of active clergy in 1934 was about 18,800; the membership of the pastors' emergency league included theological students and retired clergymen, however, so that the totals are not directly comparable; Wilhelm Niemöller, *Der Pfarrernotbund. Geschichte einer kämpfenden Bruderschaft* (Hamburg 1973) pp [0], 31.

necessary a reform of its organisation and the introduction of bishops, he asked? Was it not obvious that the real motives were political not theological? For Barth, this meant that their efforts were on the same level as those of the German Christians.[85] Indeed, in his election address in July, Barth accused the Young Reformers of saying 'secretly, mutedly and cautiously what the German Christians were saying openly, loudly and emphatically'. He asked whether the real differences between them were not personal, sociological, or even political.[86] Barth's criticism (which he admitted was harsh) was understandable given the theological heterogeneity of the groups which combined in the Young Reformers' movement in defence of the independence of the church. It was also a natural reaction to the attempts made by the church leadership and the Young Reformers to maximise their support by emphasising points of agreement with the German Christians— both the goal of a centralised Reichskirche and the need for a new consideration of the place of nation, race and state in theology. Yet Barth's criticism was exaggerated. At the heart of the opposition to the German Christians had always been the principles of the independence of the church and the sovereignty of the gospel which represented the instinctive fears of many ordinary church members about the German Christians. That was why they looked increasingly to Barth for intellectual leadership since he made these principles absolute. Many non-Barthians would echo the tribute paid to him by Hugo Hahn,

> . . . his service in saying his immense "No" in the fateful development of the German protestant church remains unforgettable. His publication "Theological existence today!" which we read with rapture, appeared then. I dare to say that my own inward development was at that time independent of Karl Barth. Even without Karl Barth I would not have been led very differently. The same was also true of most of our small circle [in Saxony]. But nevertheless we are all indebted to Karl Barth for much clarification and strengthening. He forged weapons for us for our battle.[87]

[85] *Theologische Existenz heute!* pp 8–21.

[86] Karl Barth, [*Für die*] *Freiheit des Evangeliums, Theologische Existenz heute!*, 2 (Munich 1933) p 13.

[87] *Hahn*, ed Prater pp 32–3. Another obvious example of a leading member of the Confessing Church for whom opposition to the German Christians preceded contact with Barth is Martin Niemöller, see Barth's own tribute to him, 'Barmen' *Bekennende Kirche. Martin Niemöller zum 60. Geburtstag,* ed Joachim Beckmann, Herbert Mochalski (Munich 1952) pp 10–11.

The German protestant church and Nazi party

It is no disservice to the leading teacher of the Confessing Church to remember the extent to which the church was prepared to listen to him. In this sense the immediate background to the Barmen synod starts at the latest with the parish elections of November 1932.

How did the conflict with the German Christians affect the opposition's attitude to the Nazi party? In public they claimed to be equally loyal to the Third Reich, as indeed they wanted to be. Despite Hitler's support for Müller and the party's frequent though erratic support for the German Christians, the fiction that the government would respect the rights of the church gave the opposition the loophole they needed. They wanted to believe that the church would be allowed to exist as an independent entity within the 'total' state. Barth, in public, endorsed this view, 'She [the church] is not threatened by the National-Socialist state', he wrote, a position which he was still prepared to defend in 1938 as having been correct in 1933, although by 1938 he believed that the church should condemn the Third Reich.[88] Of course, the opposition (including Barth) was aware of the danger that the 'total' state would not stop short of the church; given the relationship of the German Christians to the Nazi party, how could they not have been? This was one reason why it was so important to resist the German Christians—as a warning to the Nazi party *not* to interfere—a policy which the subsequent desertion of the German Christians by the party appeared to justify. One of the leaders of the Young Reformers, Hanns Lilje (bishop of Hanover 1947–71) argued in retrospect that the German Christians did the church an enormous service because they exemplified the dangers of Nazism for the church and at the same time were theoretically unprotected by the state, and therefore exposed to attack. By refuting the German Christians, the Young Reformers hoped to educate both protestant opinion and the Nazi party.[89]

Whatever their misgivings about aspects of the seizure of power, particularly the treatment of Jews, the opposition in 1932–3 did not look either for a confrontation with the Nazi party or government on issues wider than the independence of the church.[90] Preoccupation

[88] *Freiheit des Evangeliums* pp 8–9; 'Die Kirche und die politische Frage von heute', Karl Barth, *Eine Schweizer Stimme, 1938–1945* (Zurich 1945) pp 80–3. Before *Theologische Existenz heute!* however Barth wrote a political denunciation of the Third Reich which his friends dissuaded him from publishing because it would have landed him in prison; Helmut Gollwitzer, *Reich Gottes und Sozialismus bei Karl Barth, Theologische Existenz heute!*, ed Karl Gerhard Steck, no 169 (Munich 1972) p 59. (I should like to thank Dr Haddon Willmer for this reference.)
[89] Interview with the author 2 December 1965.
[90] Wright, *'Above Parties'* pp 111–17.

417

with resisting the German Christians, a sense of futility in attempting to oppose a totalitarian state, fear of prison and the concentration camp made Hempel's prediction in 1932 that the church would have to take a stand for the principle of freedom of conscience on behalf of others seem unreal in 1933. The cardinal principle used against the German Christians of resisting political interference in the church inhibited the opposition from developing a sense of its own political responsibility. Recognition that the 'national revolution' which had been viewed with such high hopes by the great majority of protestants including Confessing Church supporters had become the racialist dictatorship irreconcilable with the gospel, foreseen by Schreiner in 1931, was also peculiarly difficult and painful.

University of Oxford
Christ Church

ABBREVIATIONS

AASRP	*Associated Archaeological Societies Reports and Papers*
AAWG	*Abhandlungen der Akademie [Gesellschaft* to 1942] *der Wissenschaften zu Göttingen,* (Göttingen 1843–)
AAWL	*Abhandlungen der Akademie der Wissenschaften und der Literatur* (Mainz 1950–)
ABAW	*Abhandlungen der Bayerischen Akademie der Wissenchaften* (Munich 1835–)
Abh	*Abhandlung*
Abt	*Abteilung*
ACO	*Acta Conciliorum Oecumenicorum,* ed E. Schwartz (Berlin/Leipzig 1914–40)
ACW	*Ancient Christian Writers,* ed J. Quasten and J. C. Plumpe (Westminster, Maryland/London 1946–)
ADAW	*Abhandlungen der Deutschen* [till 1944 *Preussischen*] *Akademie der Wissenschaften zu Berlin* (Berlin 1815–)
AF	*Analecta Franciscana,* 10 vols (Quaracchi 1885–1941)
AFH	*Archivum Franciscanum Historicum* (Quaracchi/Rome 1908–)
AFP	*Archivum Fratrum Praedicatorum* (Rome 1931–)
AHP	*Archivum historiae pontificae* (Rome 1963–)
AHR	*American Historical Review* (New York 1895–)
AKG	*Archiv für Kulturgeschichte* (Leipzig/Münster/Cologne 1903–)
ALKG	H. Denifle and F. Ehrle, *Archiv für Literatur- und Kirchengeschichte des Mittelalters,* 7 vols (Berlin/Freiburg 1885–1900)
Altaner	B. Altaner, *Patrologie: Leben, Schriften und Lehre der Kirchenväter* (5 ed Freiburg 1958)
AM	L. Wadding, *Annales Minorum,* 8 vols (Rome 1625–54); 2 ed, 25 vols (Rome 1731–1886); 3 ed, vol 1– , (Quaracchi 1931–)
An Bol	*Analecta Bollandiana* (Brussels 1882–)
Annales	*Annales: Economies, Sociétés, Civilisations* (Paris 1946–)
Ant	*Antonianum* (Rome 1926–)
APC	*Proceedings and Ordinances of the Privy Council 1386–1542,* ed Sir Harris Nicolas, 7 vols (London 1834–7)
—	*Acts of the Privy Council of England 1542–1629,* 44 vols (London 1890–1958)
—	*Acts of the Privy Council of England, Colonial Series (1613–1783)* 5 vols (London 1908–12)
AR	*Archivum Romanicum* (Geneva/Florence 1917–41)
ARG	*Archiv für Reformationsgeschichte* (Berlin/Leipzig/Gütersloh 1903–)
ASAW	*Abhandlungen der Sächsischen Akademie [Gesellschaft* to 1920] *der Wissenschaften zu Leipzig* (Leipzig 1850–)
ASB	*Acta Sanctorum Bollandiana* (Brussels etc 1643–)
ASC	*Anglo Saxon Chronicle*
ASI	*Archivio storico Italiano* (Florence 1842–)

ABBREVIATIONS

ASL   *Archivio storico Lombardo*, 1–62 (Milan 1874–1935); ns 1–10 (Milan 1936–47)

ASOC   *Analecta Sacri Ordinis Cisterciensis* [*Analecta Cisterciensia* since 1965] (Rome 1945–   )

ASOSB   *Acta Sanctorum Ordinis Sancti Benedicti*, ed L' D'Achery and J. Mabillon (Paris 1668–1701)

ASP   *Archivio della Società* [*Deputazione* from 1935] *Romana di Storia Patria* (Rome 1878–1934, 1935–   )

ASR   *Archives de Sociologie des Religions* (Paris 1956–   )

AV   Authorised Version

AV   *Archivio Veneto* (Venice 1871–): [1891–1921, *Nuovo Archivio Veneto*; 1922–6, *Archivio Veneto-Tridentino*]

B   *Byzantion* (Paris/Boston/Brussels 1924–   )

Bale, *Catalogus*   John Bale, *Scriptorum Illustrium Maioris Brytanniae Catalogus*, 2 parts (Basel 1557, 1559)

Bale, *Index*   John Bale, *Index Britanniae Scriptorum*, ed R. L. Poole and M. Bateson (Oxford 1902) *Anecdota Oxoniensia*, medieval and modern series 9

Bale, *Summarium*   John Bale, *Illustrium Maioris Britanniae Scriptorum Summarium* (Ipswich 1548, reissued Wesel 1549)

BEC   *Bibliothèque de l'Ecole des Chartes* (Paris 1839–   )

Beck   H-G Beck, *Kirche und theologische Literatur im byzantinischen Reich* (Munich 1959)

BEHE   *Bibliothèque de l'Ecole des Hautes Etudes: Sciences Philologiques et Historiques* (Paris 1869–   )

Bernard   E. Bernard, *Catalogi Librorum Manuscriptorum Angliae et Hiberniae* (Oxford 1697)

BF   *Byzantinische Forschungen* (Amsterdam 1966–   )

BHG   *Bibliotheca Hagiographica Graeca*, ed F. Halkin, 3 vols+1 (3 ed Brussels 1957, 1969)

BHI   *Bibliotheca historica Italica*, ed A. Ceruti, 4 vols (Milan 1876–85), 2 series, 3 vols (Milan 1901–33)

BHL   *Bibliotheca Hagiographica Latina*, 2 vols+1 (Brussels 1898–1901, 1911)

BHR   *Bibliothèque d'Humanisme et Renaissance* (Paris/Geneva 1941–   )

Bibl Ref   *Bibliography of the Reform 1450–1648, relating to the United Kingdom and Ireland*, ed Derek Baker for 1955–70 (Oxford 1975)

BIHR   *Bulletin of the Institute of Historical Research* (London 1923–   )

BISIMEAM   *Bullettino dell'istituto storico italiano per il medio evo e archivio muratoriano* (Rome 1878–   )

BJRL   *Bulletin of the John Rylands Library* (Manchester 1903–   )

BL   British Library, London

BM   British Museum, London

BN   Bibliothèque Nationale, Paris

Bouquet   M. Bouquet, *Recueil des historiens des Gaules et de la France. Rerum gallicarum et francicarum scriptores*, 24 vols (Paris 1738–1904); new ed L. Delisle, 1–19 (Paris 1868–80)

BQR   *British Quarterly Review* (London 1845–86)

Broadmead Records   *The Records of a Church of Christ, meeting in Broadmead, Bristol 1640–87*, HKS (London 1848)

BS   *Byzantinoslavica* (Prague 1929–   )

Bucer, *Deutsche Schriften*   *Martin Bucers Deutsche Schriften*, ed R. Stupperich et al (Gütersloh/Paris 1960–   )

420

ABBREVIATIONS

Bucer, *Opera Latina*	*Martini Buceri Opera Latina*, ed F. Wendel et al (Paris/Gütersloh 1955–)
Bull Franc	*Bullarium Franciscanum*, vols 1–4 ed J. H. Sbaralea (Rome 1759–68) vols 5–7 ed C. Eubel (Rome 1898–1904), new series vols 1–3 ed U. Hüntemann and J. M. Pou y Marti (Quaracchi 1929–49)
BZ	*Byzantinische Zeitschrift* (Leipzig 1892–)
CA	*Cahiers Archéologiques. Fin de L'Antiquité et Moyen-âge* (Paris 1945–)
CAH	*Cambridge Ancient History* (Cambridge 1923–39)
CalRev	Calumy Revised, ed A. G. Mathews (Oxford 1934)
CalLP	*Calendar of the Letters and Papers (Foreign and Domestic) of the Reign of Henry VIII*, 21 vols in 35 parts (London 1864–1932)
CalSPD	*Calendar of State Papers: Domestic* (London 1856–)
CalSPF	*Calendar of State Papers: Foreign*, 28 vols (London 1861–1950)
Calvin, *Opera*	*Ioannis Calvini Opera Quae Supersunt Omnia*, ed G. Baum et al, *Corpus Reformatorum*, 59 vols (Brunswick/Berlin 1863–1900)
Cardwell, *Documentary Annals*	*Documentary Annals of the Reformed Church of England*, ed E. Cardwell, 2 vols (Oxford 1839)
Cardwell, *Synodalia*	*Synodalia*, ed E. Cardwell, 2 vols (Oxford 1842)
CC	*Corpus Christianorum* (Turnholt 1952–)
CF	*Classical Folia*, [*Folia* 1946–59] (New York 1960–)
CH	*Church History* (New York/Chicago 1932–)
CHB	*Cambridge History of the Bible*
CHistS	*Church History Society* (London 1886–92)
CHJ	*Cambridge Historical Journal* (Cambridge 1925–57)
CIG	*Corpus Inscriptionum Graecarum*, ed A. Boeckh, J. Franz, E. Curtius, A. Kirchhoff, 4 vols (Berlin 1825–77)
CMH	*Cambridge Medieval History*
CModH	*Cambridge Modern History*
COCR	*Collectanea Ordinis Cisterciensium Reformatorum* (Rome/Westmalle 1934–)
COD	*Conciliorum oecumenicorum decreta* (3 ed Bologna 1973)
Coll Franc	*Collectanea Franciscana* (Assisi/Rome 1931–)
CR	*Corpus Reformatorum*, ed C. G. Bretschneider et al (Halle etc. 1834–)
CS	*Cartularium Saxonicum*, ed W. de G. Birch, 3 vols (London 1885–93)
CSCO	*Corpus Scriptorum Christianorum Orientalium* (Paris 1903–)
CSEL	*Corpus Scriptorum Ecclesiasticorum Latinorum* (Vienna 1866–)
CSer	*Camden Series* (London 1838–)
CSHByz	*Corpus Scriptorum Historiae Byzantinae* (Bonn 1828–97)
CYS	*Canterbury and York Society* (London 1907–)
DA	*Deutsches Archiv für* [*Geschichte*, –Weimar 1937–43] *die Erforschung des Mittelalters* (Cologne/Graz 1950–)
DACL	*Dictionnaire d'Archéologie chrétienne et de Liturgie*, ed. F. Cabrol and H. Leclercq (Paris 1924–)
DDC	*Dictionnaire de Droit Canonique*, ed R. Naz (Paris 1935–)
DHGE	*Dictionnaire d'Histoire et de Géographie ecclésiastiques*, ed. A. Baudrillart et al (Paris 1912–)
DNB	*Dictionary of National Biography* (London 1885–)
DOP	*Dumbarton Oaks Papers* (Cambridge, Mass., 1941–)

ABBREVIATIONS

DR   F. Dölger, *Regesten der Kaiserurkunden des oströmischen Reiches
            (Corpus der griechischen Urkunden des Mittelalters und der neueren
            Zeit*, Reihe A, Abt I), 5 vols: 1 (565–1025); 2 (1025–1204); 3 (1204–
            1282); 4 (1282–1341); 5 (1341–1453) (Munich-Berlin 1924–65)
DSAM   *Dictionnaire de Spiritualité, Ascétique et Mystique*, ed M. Viller
            (Paris 1932–   )
DTC   *Dictionnaire de Théologie Catholique*, ed A. Vacant, E. Mangenot,
            E. Amann, 15 vols (Paris 1903–50)
EcHR   *Economic History Review* (London 1927–   )
EEBS   Ἐπετηρὶς Ἑταιρείας Βυζαντινῶν Σπουδῶν (Athens 1924–   )
EETS   *Early English Text Society*
EF   *Etudes Franciscaines* (Paris 1899–1938, ns 1950–   )
EHD   *English Historical Documents* (London 1953–   )
EHR   *English Historical Review* (London 1886–   )
Ehrhard   A. Ehrhard, *Überlieferung und Bestand der hagiographischen und
            homiletischen Literatur der griechischen Kirche von den Anfängen
            bis zum Ende des 16. Jh*, 3 vols in 4, *TU* 50–2 (=4 series 5–7)
            11 parts (Leipzig 1936–52)
Emden (O)   A. B. Emden, *A Biographical Register of the University of Oxford to
            1500*, 3 vols (London 1957–9); *1500–40* (1974)
Emden (C)   A. B. Emden, *A Biographical Register of the University of
            Cambridge to 1500* (London 1963)
EO   *Echos d'Orient* (Constantinople/Paris 1897–1942)
ET   English translation
EYC   *Early Yorkshire Charters*, ed W. Farrer and C. T. Clay, 12 vols
            (Edinburgh/Wakefield 1914–65)
FGH   *Die Fragmente der griechischen Historiker*, ed F. Jacoby
            (Berlin 1926–30)
FM   *Historie de l'église depuis les origines jusqu'à nos jours*,
            ed. A. Fliche and V. Martin (Paris 1935–   )
Foedera   *Foedera, conventiones, litterae et cuiuscunque generis acta publica inter
            reges Angliae et alios quovis imperatores, reges*, 20 vols (London
            1704–35), re-ed 7 vols (London 1816–69)
Franc Stud *Franciscan Studies* (St Bonaventure, New York 1924–, ns 1941–   )
Fredericq   P. Fredericq, *Corpus documentorum inquisitionis haereticae pravitatis
            Neerlandicae*, 3 vols (Ghent 1889–93)
FStn   *Franziskanische Studien* (Münster/Werl 1914–   )
Gal C   *Gallia Christiana*, 16 vols (Paris 1715–1865)
Gangraena   T. Edwards, *Gangraena*, 3 parts (London 1646)
GCS   *Die griechischen christlichen Schriftsteller der erste drei Jahrhunderte*
            (Leipzig 1897–   )
Gee and   *Documents illustrative of English Church History*
    Hardy   ed. H. Gee and W. J. Hardy (London 1896)
GEEB   R. Janin, *La géographie ecclèsiastique de l'empire byzantin*; 1, *Le siége
            de Constantinople et le patriarcat oecumenique*, pt 3 *Les églises et les
            monastères* (Paris 1953); 2, *Les églises et les monastères des grands
            centres byzantins* (Paris 1975)
Golubovich Girolamo Golubovich, *Biblioteca bio-bibliografica della Terra
            Santa e dell' oriente francescano*:
                series 1, *Annali*, 5 vols (Quaracchi 1906–23)
                series 2, *Documenti* 14 vols (Quaracchi 1921–33)
                series 3, *Documenti* (Quaracchi 1928–   )
                series 4, *Studi*, ed M. Roncaglia (Cairo 1954–   )

Grumel, Regestes	V. Grumel, *Les Regestes des Actes du Patriarcat de Constantinople,* I: *Les Actes des Patriarches,* I: 381–715; II: 715–1043; III: 1043–1206 (Socii Assumptionistae Chalcedonenses, 1931, 1936, 1947)
Grundmann	H. Grundmann, *Religiöse Bewegungen im Mittelalter* (Berlin 1935, 2 ed Darmstadt 1970)
HBS	*Henry Bradshaw Society* (London/Canterbury 1891–)
HE	*Historia Ecclesiastica*
HistSt	*Historical Studies* (Melbourne 1940–)
HJ	*Historical Journal* (Cambridge 1958–)
HJch	*Historisches Jarhbuch der Görres Gesellschaft* (Cologne 1880—, Munich 1950–)
HKS	*Hanserd Knollys Society* (London 1847–)
HL	C. J. Hefele and H. Leclercq, *Histore des Conciles,* 10 vols (Paris 1907–35)
HMC	*Historical Manuscripts Commission*
Holzapfel, Handbuch	H. Holzapfel, *Handbuch der Geschichte des Franziskanerordens* (Freiburg 1908)
Hooker, *Works*	*The Works of . . . Mr. Richard Hooker,* ed J. Keble, 7 ed rev R. W. Church and F. Paget, 3 vols (Oxford 1888)
Houedene	*Chronica Magistri Rogeri de Houedene,* ed W. Stubbs, 4 vols, *RS* 51 (London 1868–71)
HRH	*The Heads of Religious Houses, England and Wales, 940–1216,* ed D. Knowles, C. N. L. Brooke, V. C. M. London (Cambridge 1972)
HS	*Hispania sacra* (Madrid 1948–)
HTR	*Harvard Theological Review* (New York/Cambridge, Mass., 1908–)
HZ	*Historische Zeitschrift* (Munich 1859–)
IER	*Irish Ecclesiastical Record* (Dublin 1864–)
IR	*Innes Review* (Glasgow 1950–)
JAC	*Jahrbuch für Antike und Christentum* (Münster-im-Westfalen 1958–)
Jaffé	*Regesta Pontificum Romanorum ab condita ecclesia ad a. 1198,* 2 ed S. Lowenfeld, F. Kaltenbrunner, P. Ewald, 2 vols (Berlin 1885–8, repr Graz 1958)
JBS	*Journal of British Studies* (Hartford, Conn., 1961–)
JEH	*Journal of Ecclesiastical History* (London 1950–)
JFHS	*Journal of the Friends Historical Society* (London/Philadelphia 1903–)
JHI	*Journal of the History of Ideas* (London 1940–)
JHSChW	*Journal of the Historical Society of the Church in Wales* (Cardiff 1947–)
JIntH	*Journal of Interdisciplinary History* (Cambridge, Mass., 1970–)
JLW	*Jahrbuch für Liturgiewissenschaft* (Münster-im-Westfalen 1921–41)
JMH	*Journal of Modern History* (Chicago 1929–)
JMedH	*Journal of Medieval History* (Amsterdam 1975–)
JRA	*Journal of Religion in Africa* (Leiden 1967–)
JRH	*Journal of Religious History* (Sydney 1960–)
JRS	*Journal of Roman Studies* (London 1910–)
JRSAI	*Journal of the Royal Society of Antiquaries of Ireland* (Dublin 1871–)
JSArch	*Journal of the Society of Archivists* (London 1955–)

JTS   *Journal of Theological Studies* (London 1899–   )
Knowles, MO   David Knowles, *The Monastic Order in England, 943–1216*
               (2 ed Cambridge 1963)
Knowles, RO   , *The Religious Orders in England*, 3 vols
               (Cambridge 1948–59)
Knox, *Works* *The Works of John Knox*, ed D. Laing, Bannatyne Club/Wodrow
               Society, 6 vols (Edinburgh 1846–64)
Laurent,   V. Laurent. *Les Registes des Actes du Patriarcat de Constantinople,*
   Regestes 1: *Les Actes des Patriarches,* IV: *Les Regestes de 1208 à 1309*
               (Paris 1971)
Le Neve   John Le Neve, *Fasti Ecclesiae Anglicanae 1066–1300,* rev and exp
               Diana E. Greenway, 1 St Pauls (London 1968); 2, Monastic
               Cathedrals (1971)
               Fasti Ecclesiae Anglicanae 1300–1541 rev and exp H. P. F. King,
               J. M. Horn, B. Jones, 12 vols (London 1962–7)
               Fasti Ecclesiae Anglicanae 1541–1857 rev and exp J. M. Horn,
               D. M. Smith, 1, St Pauls (1969); 2, Chichester (1971);
               3, Canterbury, Rochester, Winchester (1974); 4, York
               (1975)
Lloyd,   *Formularies of Faith Put Forth by Authority during the Reign of*
   Formularies *Henry VIII*, ed C. Lloyd (Oxford 1825)
   of faith
LRS   *Lincoln Record Society*
LQR   *Law Quarterly Review* (London 1885–   )
LThK   *Lexikon für Theologie und Kirche,* ed J. Höfer and K. Rahnes
               (2 ed Freiburg-im-Breisgau 1957–   )
LW   *Luther's Works,* ed J. Pelikan and H. T. Lehman,
               American edition (St Louis/Philadelphia, 1955–   )
MA   *Monasticon Anglicanum,* ed R. Dodsworth and W. Dugdale,
               3 vols (London 1655–73); new ed J. Caley, H. Ellis, B. Bandinel,
               6 vols in 8 (London 1817–30)
Mansi   J. D. Mansi, *Sacrorum conciliorum nova et amplissima collectio,* 31 vols
               (Florence/Venice 1757–98); new impression and continuation,
               ed L. Petit and J. B. Martin, 60 vols (Paris 1899–1927)
Martène and   E. Martène and U. Durand, *Veterum Scriptorum et Monumentorum*
   Durand,   *Historicorum, Dogmaticorum, Moralium Amplissima Collectio,*
   Collectio 9 vols (Paris 1729)
   Thesaurus *Thesaurus Novus Anecdotorum,* 5 vols (Paris 1717)
   Voyage   *Voyage Litteraire de Deux Religieux Benedictins de la Congregation*
               de Saint Maur, 2 vols (Paris 1717, 1724)
MedA   *Medium Aevum* (Oxford 1932–   )
Mendola   *Atti della Settimana di Studio,* 1959–   (Milan 1962–   )
MF   *Miscellanea Francescana* (Foligno/Rome 1886–   )
MGH   *Monumenta Germaniae Historica inde ab a.c. 500 usque ad a. 1500,*
               ed G. H. Pertz etc (Berlin, Hanover 1826–   )
   AA   *Auctores Antiquissimi*
   Ant   *Antiquitates*
   Briefe   *Epistolae* 2: *Die Briefe der Deutschen Kaiserzeit*
   Cap   *Leges* 2: *Leges in Quart* 2: *Capitularia regum Francorum*
   CM   *Chronica Minora* 1–3 (=*AA* 9, 11, 13) ed Th. Mommsen
               (1892, 1894, 1898 repr 1961)
   Conc   *Leges* 2: *Leges in Quart* 3: *Concilia*   [*regum*
   Const   4: *Constitutiones et acta publica imperatorum et*

ABBREVIATIONS

DC	*Deutsche Chroniken*
Dip	*Diplomata in folio*
Epp	*Epistolae 1 in Quart*
Epp Sel	*4: Epistolae Selectae*
FIG	*Leges 3: Fontes Iuris Germanici Antique,* new series
FIGUS	*4: , in usum scholarum*
Form	*2: Leges in Quart 5: Formulae Merovingici et Karolini Aevi*
GPR	*Gesta Pontificum Romanorum*
Leges	*Leges in folio*
Lib	*Libelli de lite*
LM	*Ant 3: Libri Memoriales*
LNG	*Leges 2: Leges in Quart 1: Leges nationum Germanicarum*
Necr	*Ant 2: Necrologia Germaniae*
Poet	*1: Poetae Latini Medii Aevi*
Quellen	*Quellen zur Geistesgeschichte des Mittelalters*
Schriften	*Schriften der Monumenta Germaniae Historica*
SRG	*Scriptores rerum germanicarum in usum scholarum*
SRG ns	,new series
SRL	*Scriptores rerum langobardicarum et italicarum*
SRM	*Scriptores rerum merovingicarum*
SS	*Scriptores*
SSM	*Staatschriften des späteren Mittelalters*
MIOG	*Mitteilungen des Instituts für österreichische Geschichtsforschung* (Graz/Cologne 1880–)
MM	F. Miklosich and J. Müller, *Acta et Diplomata Graeca medii aevi sacra et profana,* 6 vols (Vienna 1860–90)
Moorman, History	J. R. H. Moorman, *A History of the Franciscan Order from its Origins to the year 1517* (Oxford 1968)
More, *Works*	*The Complete Works of St Thomas More,* ed R. S. Sylvester et al, Yale edition (New Haven/London 1963–)
Moyen Age	*Le moyen âge. Revue d'histoire et de philologie* (Paris 1888–)
MRHEW	David Knowles and R. N. Hadcock, *Medieval Religious Houses, England and Wales* (2 ed London 1971)
MRHI	A. Gwynn and R. N. Hadcock, *Medieval Religious Houses, Ireland* (London 1970)
MRHS	Ian B. Cowan and David E. Easson, *Medieval Religious Houses, Scotland* (2 ed London 1976)
MS	Manuscript
MStn	*Mittelalterliche Studien* (Stuttgart 1966–)
Muratori	L. A. Muratori, *Rerum italicarum scriptores,* 25 vols (Milan 1723–51); new ed G. Carducci and V. Fiorini, 34 vols in 109 fasc (Città di Castello/Bologna 1900–)
NCE	*New Catholic Encyclopedia,* 15 vols (New York 1967)
NCModH	*New Cambridge Modern History,* 14 vols (Cambridge 1957–70)
nd	no date
NEB	*New English Bible*
NF	Neue Folge
NH	*Northern History* (Leeds 1966–)
ns	new series
NS	New Style
Numen	*Numen: International Review for the History of Religions* (Leiden 1954–)
OCP	*Orientalia Christiana Periodica* (Rome 1935–)

ABBREVIATIONS

ODCC	*Oxford Dictionary of the Christian Church,* ed F. L. Cross (Oxford 1957), 2 ed with E. A. Livingstone (1974)
OED	*Oxford English Dictionary*
OS	Old Style
OHS	*Oxford Historical Society*
PBA	*Proceedings of the British Academy*
PG	*Patrologia Graeca,* ed J. P. Migne, 161 vols (Paris 1857–66)
PhK	Philosophisch-historische Klasse
PL	*Patrologia Latina,* ed J. P. Migne, 217+4 index vols (Paris 1841–64)
Plummer, Bede	*Venerabilis Baedae Opera Historica,* ed C. Plummer (Oxford 1896)
PO	*Patrologia Orientalis,* ed J. Graffin and F. Nau (Paris 1903–)
Potthast	*Regesta Pontificum Romanorum inde ab a. post Christum natum 1198 ad a. 1304,* ed A. Potthast, 2 vols (1874–5 repr Graz 1957)
PP	*Past and Present* (London 1952–)
PPTS	*Palestine Pilgrims' Text Society,* 13 vols and index (London 1896–1907)
PRIA	*Proceedings of the Royal Irish Academy* (Dublin 1836–)
PRO	Public Record Office
PS	Parker Society (Cambridge 1841–55)
PW	*Paulys Realencyklopädie der klassischen Altertumswissenschaft,* new ed G. Wissowa and W. Kroll (Stuttgart 1893–)
QFIAB	*Quellen & Forschungen aus italienischen Archiven und Bibliotheken* (Rome 1897–)
RAC	*Reallexikon für Antike und Christentum,* ed T. Klauser (Stuttgart 1941–)
RB	*Revue Bénédictine* (Maredsous 1884–)
RE	*Realencyclopädie für protestantische Theologie,* ed A. Hauck, 24 vols (3 ed Leipzig, 1896–1913)
REB	*Revue des Etudes Byzantines* (Bucharest/Paris 1946–)
RecS	Record Series
RGG	*Die Religion in Geschichte und Gegenwart,* 6 vols (Tübingen 1927–32)
RH	*Revue historique* (Paris 1876–)
RHC,	*Recueil des Historiens des Croisades,* ed Académie des Inscriptions et Belles-Lettres (Paris 1841–1906)
Arm	*Historiens Arméniens,* 2 vols (1869–1906)
Grecs	*Historiens Grecs,* 2 vols (1875–81)
Lois	*Lois. Les Assises de Jérusalem,* 2 vols (1841–3)
Occ	*Historiens Occidentaux,* 5 vols (1844–95)
Or	*Historiens Orientaux,* 5 vols (1872–1906)
RHD	*Revue d'histoire du droit* (Haarlem, Gronigen 1923–)
RHDFE	*Revue historique du droit français et étranger* (Paris 1922–)
RHE	*Revue d'Histoire Ecclésiastique* (Louvain 1900–)
RHEF	*Revue d'Histoire de l'Eglise de France* (Paris 1910–)
RHR	*Revue de l'Histoire des Religions* (Paris 1880–)
RR	*Regesta Regum Anglo-Normannorum,* ed H. W. C. Davis, H. A. Cronne, Charles Johnson, R. H. C. Davis, 4 vols (Oxford 1913–69)
RS	*Rerum Brittanicarum Medii Aevi Scriptores,* 99 vols (London 1858–1911). *Rolls Series*
RSR	*Revue des sciences religieuses* (Strasbourg 1921–)
RTAM	*Recherches de théologie ancienne et médiévale* (Louvain 1929–)
RSCI	*Rivista di storia della chiesa in Italia* (Rome 1947–)

ABBREVIATIONS

RStI	*Rivista storica italiana* (Naples 1884–)
RV	Revised Version
Sitz	*Sitzungsberichte*
SA	*Studia Anselmiana* (Roma 1933–)
sa	*sub anno*
SBAW	*Sitzungsberichte der bayerischen Akademie der Wissenschaften*, PhK (Munich 1871–)
SCH	*Studies in Church History* (London 1964–)
ScHR	*Scottish Historical Review* (Edinburgh/Glasgow 1904–)
SCR	*Sources chrétiennes*, ed H. de Lubac and J. Daniélou (Paris 1941–)
SF	*Studi Francescani* (Florence 1914–)
SGre	*Studi Gregoriani*, ed G. Borino, 7 vols (Rome 1947–61)
SGra	*Studia Gratiana*, ed J. Forchielli and A. M. Stickler (Bologna 1953–)
SMon	*Studia Monastica* (Montserrat, Barcelona 1959–)
Speculum	*Speculum, A Journal of Medieval Studies* (Cambridge, Mass 1926–)
SpicFr	*Spicilegium Friburgense* (Freiburg 1957–)
SS	*Surtees Society* (Durham 1835–)
SSSpoleto	*Settimane di Studio sull'alto medioevo*, 1952– , Centro Italiano di studi sull'alto medioevo, Spoleto (Spoleto 1954–)
STC	*A Short-Title Catalogue of Books Printed in England, Scotland and Ireland and of English Books Printed Abroad 1475–1640*, ed A. W. Pollard and G. R. Redgrave (London 1926, repr 1946, 1950)
Strype, *Annals*	John Strype, *Annals of the Reformation and Establishment of Religion . . . during Queen Elizabeth's Happy Reign*, 4 vols in 7 (Oxford 1824)
Strype, *Cranmer*	John Strype, *Memorials of . . . Thomas Cranmer*, 2 vols (Oxford 1840)
Strype, *Grindal*	John Strype, *The History of the Life and Acts of . . . Edmund Grindal* (Oxford 1821)
Strype, *Memorials*	John Strype, *Ecclesiastical Memorials, Relating Chiefly to Religion, and the Reformation of it . . . under King Henry VIII, King Edward VI and Queen Mary I*, 3 vols in 6 (Oxford 1822)
Strype, *Parker*	John Strype, *The Life and Acts of Matthew Parker*, 3 vols (Oxford 1821)
Strype, *Whitgift*	John Strype, *The Life and Acts of John Whitgift*, 3 vols (Oxford 1822)
sub hag	*subsidia hagiographica*
sv	*sub voce*
SVRG	*Schriften des Vereins für Reformationsgeschichte* (Halle/Leipzig/Gütersloh 1883–)
TCBiblS	*Transactions of the Cambridge Bibliographical Society* (Cambridge 1949–)
THSCym	*Transactions of the Historical Society of Cymmrodorion* (London 1822–)
TRHS	*Transactions of the Royal Historical Society* (London 1871–)
TU	*Texte und Untersuchungen zur Geschichte der altchristlichen Literatur* (Leipzig/Berlin 1882–)
VCH	*Victoria County History* (London 1900–)
VHM	G. Tiraboschi, *Vetera Humiliatorum Monumenta*, 3 vols (Milan 1766–8)

ABBREVIATIONS

Vivarium	*Vivarium: An International Journal for the Philosophy and Intellectual Life of the Middle Ages and Renaissance* (Assen 1963–)
VV	*Vizantijskij Vremennik* 1–25 (St Petersburg 1894–1927), ns 1 (26) (Leningrad 1947–)
WA	*D. Martin Luthers Werke*, ed J. C. F. Knaake (Weimar 1883–) [*Weimarer Ausgabe*]
WA Br	*Briefwechsel*
WA DB	*Deutsche Bibel*
WA TR	*Tischreden*
WelHR	*Welsh History Review* (Cardiff 1960–)
Wharton	H. Wharton, *Anglia Sacra*, 2 parts (London 1691)
Wilkins	*Concilia Magnae Britanniae et Hiberniae A.D. 446–1717*, 4 vols, ed D. Wilkins (London 1737)
YAJ	*Yorkshire Archaeological Journal* (London/Leeds 1870–)
Zanoni	L. Zanoni, *Gli Umiliati nei loro rapporti con l'eresia, l'industria della lana ed i communi nei secoli xii e xiii, Biblioteca Historica Italica*, 2 series, 2 (Milan 1911)
ZKG	*Zeitschrift für Kirchengeschichte* (Gotha/Stuttgart 1878–)
ZOG	*Zeitschrift für osteuropäische Geschichte* (Berlin 1911–35)=*Kyrios* (Berlin 1936–)
ZRG	*Zeitschrift der Savigny-Stiftung für Rechtsgeschichte* (Weimar)
GAbt	*Germanistische Abteilung* (1863–)
KAbt	*Kanonistische Abteilung* (1911–)
RAbt	*Romanistische Abteilung* (1880–)
ZRGG	*Zeitschrift für Religions- und Geistesgeschichte* (Marburg 1948–)
Zwingli, *Werke*	*Huldreich Zwinglis Sämmtliche Werke*, ed E. Egli et al, *CR* (Berlin/Leipzig/Zurich 1905–)

DATE DUE
